Global Perspectives on Wealth and Distribution

Series Editor
Shirley Johnson-Lans, Vassar College, Poughkeepsie, USA

This book series features edited volumes and research monographs that address the multifaceted problem of poverty and inequality by integrating global and interdisciplinary perspectives to examine the systemic drivers and consequences of socioeconomic disparity. It invites scholars to explore the economic, social, and institutional dimensions of wealth and income distribution, while also engaging with broader indicators of well-being—such as disparities in health, education, labor markets, and legal systems. Contributions may focus on wage and earnings differentials, gender- and race-based inequality, intra-household resource allocation, and the socioeconomic impacts of technological change and globalization. The series encourages critical engagement with the effects of economic policy on vulnerable populations and highlights opportunities for governments and institutions worldwide to reduce inequality and promote human well-being.

All proposals submitted to the series undergo documented single-blind peer review by subject-matter experts (SME). In addition, all manuscripts are reviewed by SME prior to acceptance through a documented single-blind process.

John E. Schneider

The Economics of Pain

Regulation, Product Liability, and the Opioid Crisis

palgrave
macmillan

John E. Schneider
Avalon Health Economics
Miami, FL, USA

ISSN 2662-382X ISSN 2662-3838 (electronic)
Global Perspectives on Wealth and Distribution
ISBN 978-3-032-20354-0 ISBN 978-3-032-20355-7 (eBook)
https://doi.org/10.1007/978-3-032-20355-7

This Palgrave Macmillan imprint is published by the registered company Springer Nature Switzerland AG.
The registered company address is: Gewerbestrasse 11, 6330 Cham, Switzerland

In memory of my brother, the historian and environmental scientist Charles B. Schneider Jr., who taught me that the devil is in the details, and the journey through those details is everything. And to our parents, Charles and Inge, for equipping us for all the journeys, near and far

Preface

The primary goal of this book is to use the experiences of the opioid crisis and opioid product liability litigation in the United States as examples of how we can improve our understanding of complex healthcare issues and problems, including the thorough assessment of causal factors and a more precise estimation of the impact of harms and externalities. The identification of causal factors is critical to preventing similar problems in the future, and greater precision in the estimation of attributable costs and abatement costs is essential to product liability litigation. The secondary objective of the book is to use the experiences and data from the opioid crisis to explore remedies to similar, seemingly intractable problems. In addition to targeted abatement programs, there is a need to sort through the costs and benefits of alternative forms of governance for higher-risk prescription drugs, which inevitably will require reforming regulatory procedures and exploiting the costs and benefits of court ordering for those circumstances where regulation fails.

One of the largest and most heavily regulated industries in the U.S. has been the backdrop of a drug abuse crisis that has claimed lives and generated substantial costs over the past two decades. Among the most important goals of public health policy is to hunt down the root causes of problems, so that effective solutions can be designed and implemented. Blame for the opioid crisis has mainly been aimed at easy targets, such as manufacturers, distributors, and pharmacies. But this focus has resulted in a deflection of attention away from the multidimensional root causes of the crisis. One of the foundational origins of the crisis was the emergence in the 1990s of an entire health industry designed, incentivized, and determined to aggressively treat pain, overseen by a regulatory apparatus that struggled to effectively govern the approval, distribution, and utilization of pain medications. Despite their known potential for serious adverse events, the health industry and its regulators continued to allow and, in some cases, champion the use of opioids, even years after the risks of use and misuse came to light. At that same time, demand for pain management was expanding rapidly, fueled mainly by an expanding volume of outpatient surgeries and soaring rates of obesity and depression. How could a crisis like this occur in one of the most heavily regulated sectors of the economy?

The drive to treat pain aggressively was a byproduct of several factors, the origins of which were rooted in a 1990s shift in the U.S. healthcare system toward "patient centered" care, which encompassed what has also been referred to as the "palliative care movement," with each movement sharing the common theme of greater emphasis on the patient experience, a large part of which is comprised of improved management of pain symptoms. These movements complement other related endeavors aimed at improving the quality of care and the value of the patient experience, broadly referred to as "patient satisfaction." This confluence of developments in the U.S. health industry resulted in pain assessment being considered the "fifth vital sign," added to the pantheon of blood pressure, temperature, heart rate, and respiratory rate. As pain assessment rapidly gained prominence, so too did the expectations that pain should be treated not just effectively, but aggressively and applied across a wide swath of medical conditions and diseases.

Complicating matters, certain diseases and conditions known to be associated with pain or affect the experience of pain, like obesity and mental health problems, have been on the rise, and the rapid increase in prevalence of these conditions further buttressed the overall medical need for pain assessment and treatment. Moreover, the trend toward the migration of care to outpatient settings occurred more or less at the same time as these other trends; for example, the proportion of surgeries performed in ambulatory surgery centers grew tenfold from 1980 to 2005. In outpatient settings, patients return home the same day after undergoing surgeries and other procedures, which in turn exacerbates the need for pain management as tool to facilitate the shifting of recovery time to the home. Substance abuse is also associated with economic hardship, and the areas hit hardest by globalization and economic change where the first to witness increases in opioid utilization and opioid use disorder.

The timing of all of these factors impacting demand—changes in pain guidelines, increased prevalence of diseases and conditions featuring pain, and increased need for post-operative pain management—coincided with the approval of long-acting opioids by the U.S. Food and Drug Administration ("FDA") in the late 1990s. Factors affecting the demand for pain management began acting synergistically, exerting a powerful "demand pull" in the market for pain treatment, one expeditiously served by the emerging opioid treatments hitting the market in the late 1990s Around that time, opioids, which had been used in various forms for decades, were considered among the most effective treatments for pain, especially moderate to severe pain. The confluence of elevated demand and the approval of new long-acting opioids resulted in a rapid increase in the supply and utilization of prescription opioids, with most of the reinvigorated growth occurring in the decade from 2000 to 2010.

As prescription opioid utilization grew, so too did the abuse of illicit forms of the drug (fentanyl and heroin), and the net result was an alarming increase in rates of serious adverse events, including misuse, dependency, and overdose. However, as the opioid crisis emerged and momentum behind litigation mounted, stakeholders appeared beset with a collective amnesia regarding the entire context and environment from which the crisis initially began to grow. Claimants in the opioid litigation focused narrowly on a small number of supply chain components responsible for bringing opioids to consumers (manufacturers, distributors, and pharmacies), ignoring the complexities of the ecosystem that set the gears in motion decades prior. The result was a crisis that continued unabated for years after the earliest warning bells were rung, largely because the determination of root causes was deemphasized, even by those with professional training that emphasized the criticality of establishing causal pathways in the amelioration of health issues.

Lack of a clear understanding of root causes has not been the only problem hampering solutions to the opioid crisis. Impacted parties, mainly states and counties, put forward inflated abatement cost estimates that, when extrapolated to the national level, sum to more than the entire gross domestic product of many countries and seem, at face value, to be extraordinarily exaggerated. For example, just two counties in Ohio, with a combined population of a little more than 430,000, estimated their total future opioid-related abatement costs to be about

$3.3 billion. Representing only 0.13% of the nation's population, a simple population-based extrapolation of the estimated abatement costs from these two counties suggests that the total abatement costs to all U.S. counties would be about $254 billion. However, a "cost ceiling" model based on meta-analyses of peer-reviewed cost estimates of opioid abatement programs and opioid attributable costs and abatement costs, with appropriate adjustments for state and local responsibility, results in a range of total state and local costs between $10.5 billion and $16.3 billion. In other words, extrapolating from the two Ohio counties to the national level results in a national abatement cost estimate more than fifteen times greater than the high end of the literature-based cost ceiling estimates. And again, despite the multifactorial causation pathways leading to the increase in opioid supply, responsibility for abatement costs has fallen to only a small subset of entities along the pharmaceutical supply chain.

None of this may seem very consequential at first glance. Some might have argued that missing some of the causal factors initially, followed by vastly overstating abatement costs, are problems that the courts will sort out as they might in any other product liability matter. In other words, as long as states and counties can show evidence of opioid-attributable harms, the question of who pays and by how much is a technical matter that can be given disproportionately less consideration. However, the question of who pays, and how much, is increasingly important if, from a societal perspective, we increasingly abdicate to the courts to sort out these complex problems, ones that are in many cases supposed to be handled by legislatures and regulatory agencies. Allocating abatement costs in ways that are not fair and reasonable with regard to potentially responsible parties and not accurate in terms of costs can result in inefficient outcomes, such as stifled innovation, increased costs to consumers, decreased access to treatments, and, perhaps most importantly, an increased likelihood of the same problems emerging in the future. Large variations in cost estimates also undermine trust in the methods used to calculate them, and erosion of trust can affect the efficiency of outcomes and settlements and potentially complicate the implementation of abatement programs.

As the pace of the opioid litigation decelerates, feelings of accomplishment in effectively addressing the crisis are likely to compete with unsettling feelings that the lessons of the crisis could be lost in the fog of litigation that seemed to focus too much on the finish line and not enough on the nuances, such as causal factors and regulatory failures. Nevertheless, there is now an opportunity for a postmortem of sorts to gain a better understanding of what went wrong and what worked. The focus of this book is to take a fresh look at the data and evidence surrounding the causes and consequences of the opioid crisis. Several questions are addressed. How could a crisis like this occur in one of the most heavily regulated sectors of the economy? Will any of the lessons learned from the litigation prevent similar crises from happening again? The answer to the second question is not an optimistic one, unless stakeholders and policy makers take the time to understand what really happened, critically assess the credibility of damages and abatement cost estimates, and identify the causal factors primarily responsible for the generation of attributable harm and costs. Such assessments also require an accounting of regulatory shortcomings and whether the courts were up to the challenge of picking up where regulators left off. In light of this approach, and the questions sought to be addressed, the intended audience of this book is anyone interested in or involved in product liability, economics, health economics, public health, or public policy.

Acknowledgements Over my professional career, I have received invaluable encouragement and guidance from many, but I want to give special recognition to some of the individuals who helped shape the thinking behind this book. My academic career started as a graduate student at the University of California Berkeley, where I worked primarily with Professors James Robinson in the School of Public Health, Theodore Keeler in the Department of Economics, and Oliver Williamson in the Department of Economics and the Haas School of Business. They helped me learn how to think critically and to become a better researcher and encouraged me to always dig deeper to understand the complexities of the economics of firms, organizations, and institutions. The late Oliver Williamson, who would go on to win the Nobel Prize in Economics shortly after my time at Berkeley, was especially influential because he exposed me to the world of institutional economics, which aligned with my desire to understand the "micro-analytics" underlying the economic and organizational phenomena observable in the real world, especially the health industry. After Berkeley, at the University of Iowa, I teamed up with Professor Robert Ohsfeldt, currently at Texas A&M, and ever since Bob has been a valued friend and colleague.

After the book began to take shape, I am grateful for the very helpful early comments from the writer, journalist, and screenwriter David Orange, who has a knack for telling stories that need to be told. In addition, a very helpful early review of the complete manuscript was provided by attorney David M. Fuqua, who generously provided his thoughts from a legal perspective. Very helpful early reviews were also provided by Bronwyn Geyer, the Economics Editor at Palgrave Macmillan Editor, and two anonymous peer reviewers. Finally, there have been many at Avalon Health Economics who have either been helpful, supportive, or patient, or a combination of all three, especially Cara Scheibling, Maggie Do Valle, Ryan Bresnahan, Donna Pulgarin, Lauren Clarke, Anna Whelan, Clarissa Overmyer, Jacie Cooper, Kim Texeira, Kimmy Blau, and Alexandra Peraza. I am also indebted to my family for their support and encouragement, especially my mother, Inge Schneider, and Ivette Pradera Schneider, Audrey Schneider, Lena Schneider, and Havana Schneider. All errors and omissions are, of course, entirely my own, and are most likely things that would have been easily caught by Jamie Robinson had I dared to let him review early drafts.

Competing Interests The author has no competing interests to declare that are relevant to the content of this manuscript.

Contents

CHAPTER 1

Introduction

Soon after regulatory approval of a new generation of opioid-based analgesics for pain management, from 1999 to 2021, close to 645,000 individuals died from overdoses involving opioids, including prescription and illicit opioids, which equated to a rate of 32.4 per 100,000 population in 2021 and an average of about 28,000 deaths per year over the 23-year period.[1] In 2023, there were 81,083 deaths in the U.S. that were attributable to opioids, and of those 92% were attributable to fentanyl, an illicit synthetic opioid.[2] In addition to the humanistic burden of opioid misuse, abuse, dependency, and overdose, the economic burden on communities and systems, including healthcare, criminal justice, and social welfare, has been estimated in some studies to be more than $50 billion per year, not including costs associated with productivity losses and other indirect costs, which have been estimated in some studies to be as much as another

[1] Refer to CDC, "Understanding the Opioid Overdose Epidemic," (Washington, D.C.: U.S. Centers for Disease Control and Prevention, 2023); M. R. Spencer, A. M. Miniño, and M. Warner, "Drug Overdose Deaths in the United States, 2001–2021 (Data Brief No. 457)," in *NCHS Data Brief* (Washington, D.C.: National Center for Health Statistics, U.S. Centers for Disease Control and Prevention, 2022).

[2] CDC, "U.S. Overdose Deaths Decrease in 2023, First Time Since 2018," (Washington, D.C.: U.S. Centers for Disease Control and Prevention, National Center for Health Statistics, 2024b).

J. E. Schneider, *The Economics of Pain*, Global Perspectives on Wealth and Distribution,
https://doi.org/10.1007/978-3-032-20355-7_1

$50 billion per year.[3] The alleged harms associated with opioid misuse resulted in a large number of product liability lawsuits filed by a variety of claimants, mainly states and counties, against various members of the prescription opioid supply chain, leading to the consolidation of cases into the opioid multi-district litigation (MDL) in 2017. As of 2025, the number of cases consolidated in the MDL had grown to more than 3000.

Litigation involving product liability has been increasing in the U.S. in recent years, with some sources reporting 20% growth from 2021 to 2024.[4] The total number of individual cases is considerably higher than these data convey, as many of these cases are mass tort, MDL, or class action type cases, involving multiple plaintiffs and defendants over relatively long timeframes.[5] Moreover, the total value of damages awarded in these types of cases has also been rising rapidly.[6] Product liability cases, especially ones involving medical products and devices, are also becoming more complex, relying on newly available datasets (e.g., electronic medical records), advanced statistical and epidemiological techniques to attribute costs, identify causal pathways, and assign liability, and involving organizations and networks that feature a wider array of differentiated supply chain components.[7] Multiple responsible parties, more complex epidemiological and causal pathways, and nuanced supply chains can also bring challenges in assigning liability and responsibility. For those tasked with assessing damages and abatement costs in these types of cases, including attorneys, economists, forensic accountants, and judges, the evolving product liability landscape has made the work substantially more complex.

[3] C. Florence, F. Luo, and K. Rice, "The economic burden of opioid use disorder and fatal opioid overdose in the United States, 2017," *Drug Alcohol Depend* 218 (2021).

[4] Lex Machina, "Lex Machina 2025 Torts Litigation Report," (LexisNexis, 2025).

[5] E. Tyler and R. Combs, "2023 Litigation Statistics Series: Multidistrict Litigation," (New York, NY: Bloomberg Law, 2023).

[6] See generally Insurance Information Institute, "Facts + Statistics: Product Liability," (New York, NY: Insurance Information Institute, 2023); C. Silverman and C. E. Appel, "Nuclear Verdicts: Trends, Causes, and Solutions," (Washington, D.C.: U.S. Chamber of Commerce, Institute for Legal Reform, 2022).

[7] See for example Z. R. Paterick et al., "Medical liability in the electronic medical records era," *Proc (Bayl Univ Med Cent)* 31, no. 4 (2018); T. Varney, "Product Liability and Recall Claims Challenge Global Supply Chains," *Supply and Demand Chain Executive*, no. April 19 (2017).

1.1 Medical Products Liability

The opioid litigation is, of course, not the first prominent medical products liability case. Medical products are unique in that they are normally associated with known adverse events; in other words, they are products marketed and sold with known and ostensibly tolerable "defects." As described later in this book, one of the primary goals of drug regulators globally is to determine the optimal balance between clinical benefit and risk, with clinical benefit defined as proven safety and efficacy based on randomized clinical trials ("RCTs") and risk typically defined by rates of serious adverse events ("SAEs"), which are usually based on data from RCTs, observational clinical studies, and post-market monitoring and surveillance. Medical products liability cases can arise when not all SAEs are known *ex ante*, and additional adverse events surface *ex post*, sometimes long after the product is approved for marketing and sales. In many cases, SAEs, especially unexpected ones, require regulators to issue additional warnings, but unanticipated SAEs can also initiate lawsuits. For cases that transition to litigation, the focus may shift to how and when manufacturers became aware of real-world SAE prevalence and patterns, and the extent to which such patterns differed from those studied and reported in clinical trials. The ways and means through which post-market concerns were communicated to other members of the supply chain, mainly providers and consumers, is also important in medical products liability matters. There are numerous examples of medical product lawsuits wherein the risks, determined *ex post*, were believed to exceed the benefits, and manufacturers were alleged to have insufficiently communicated that information to the medical community and consumers; for example, thalidomide to treat pregnancy-induced nausea,[8] diethylstilbestrol ("DES") to prevent miscarriages,[9] "fen-phen" drugs

[8] See generally J. H. Kim and A. R. Scialli, "Thalidomide: the tragedy of birth defects and the effective treatment of disease," *Toxicol Sci* 122, no. 1 (2011).

[9] See generally J. L. Conlon, "Diethylstilbestrol: Potential health risks for women exposed in utero and their offspring," *Jaapa* 30, no. 2 (2017); L. Hilakivi-Clarke, "Maternal exposure to diethylstilbestrol during pregnancy and increased breast cancer risk in daughters," *Breast Cancer Res* 16, no. 2 (2014); M. A. La Merrill et al., "Consensus on the key characteristics of endocrine-disrupting chemicals as a basis for hazard identification," *Nat Rev Endocrinol* 16, no. 1 (2020); P. D. Rheingold, "Litigation involving DES," *Women Health* 1, no. 5 (1976); S. Robotti, "The heritable legacy of diethylstilbestrol: a bellwether for endocrine disruption in humans," *Biol Reprod* 105, no. 3 (2021).

for weight loss,[10] silicone breast implants,[11] Vioxx (rofecoxib) to treat pain,[12] and implantable polypropylene mesh to treat hernias and pelvic organ prolapse.[13] In each of these examples, the drugs and devices were approved by U.S. regulators based on available data from clinical studies, but post-market data showed that adverse event rates were different from those expected.

Another group of health-related product liability cases focuses on the health effects associated with the use of non-medical products. A prominent and relatively recent example is the tobacco product liability litigation from the late 1990s.[14] During that time, a mounting body of evidence enumerated the various health risks associated with tobacco use, including lung cancer and cardiovascular disease.[15] According to the U.S. Centers for Disease Control and Surveillance ("CDC"), approximately 480,000 deaths per year are attributable to tobacco use.[16] For perspective, the tobacco mortality rate is more than sixteen times higher than the average annual mortality rate associated with opioid use disorder and more than six times higher than the opioid mortality rate in 2023, which included a high proportion of deaths attributable to illicit opioids. In those cases, tobacco manufacturers were alleged to have possessed some knowledge of potential health risks and were alleged to have insufficiently warned consumers of those risks. Though the pathway to settlement was somewhat complicated,[17] in the end the claimants, which were

[10] See generally S. Garber, "Economic Effects of Product Liability and Other Litigation Involving the Safety and Effectiveness of Pharmaceuticals," (Santa Monica, CA: RAND Institute for Civil Justice, RAND Corporation, 2013).

[11] See generally M. A. Shiffman, "Silicone breast implant litigation (Part 1)," *Med Law* 13, no. 7–8 (1994).

[12] See generally Garber, "Economic Effects of Product Liability and Other Litigation Involving the Safety and Effectiveness of Pharmaceuticals."

[13] See generally L. G. Kahan and J. A. Blatnik, "Critical Under-Reporting of Hernia Mesh Properties and Development of a Novel Package Label," *J Am Coll Surg* 226, no. 2 (2018); O. A. Olavarria et al., "Lack of Regulations and Conflict of Interest Transparency of New Hernia Surgery Technologies," *J Surg Res* 247 (2020).

[14] See, for example, S. Zhou et al., "Litigation in tobacco control: past, present and future," *Tob Control* 31, no. 2 (2022).

[15] See, for example, S. P. Saha et al., "Cigarette smoke and adverse health effects: An overview of research trends and future needs," *Int J Angiol* 16, no. 3 (2007).

[16] CDC, "Current Cigarette Smoking Among Adults in the United States," (Washington, D.C.: U.S. Centers for Disease Control and Prevention, 2023).

[17] W. K. Viscusi and J. Hersch, "Tobacco Regulation through Litigation," in *Regulation versus Litigation: Perspectives from Economics and Law*, ed. D. P. Kessler (Chicago, IL:

mostly state attorneys general, signed a Master Settlement Agreement ("MSA") with 44 tobacco manufacturers. Damages in the tobacco case did not involve a lump sum or structured settlement; rather, the financial mechanism was by way of an additional excise tax on tobacco products, the proceeds of which were to accrue to the states involved in the MSA.[18] Distributors and sellers of tobacco products were not identified as defendants; instead, the focus was solely on the manufacturers, mainly their roles in marketing tobacco products and failing to sufficiently warn consumers of potential health risks. Presently, tobacco products continue to be marketed and sold in the U.S. and abroad, with very few restrictions apart from additional health warnings included on containers and packaging, messaging that is known to be largely ineffective at reducing tobacco usage.[19]

Another example of a large-scale non-medical product liability legal action focused on health outcomes is the long-running asbestos litigation. The focus of asbestos litigation has been the health effects of a mineral fiber material used in manufacturing, heavy industry, and construction materials. The causal pathway involving asbestos generally involves exposure to airborne asbestos fibers, which can become airborne during the manufacturing process or during the handling and installation of products that contain asbestos fibers. Apart from the production of asbestos materials themselves, one of the main sources of exposure was in the use of products across a wide variety of industrial applications, including manufacturing, ship building, and construction. Once airborne, asbestos fibers can become embedded in lung tissue, which can in some cases result in thickening and scarring of the tissue and the pleura surrounding the lungs.[20] In some cases, this can lead to mesothelioma, which is a cancer of the lining of the chest, the primary cause of which has been shown to be exposure to asbestos.[21] The manufactures of

National Bureau of Economic Research & The University of Chicago Press, 2011); N.F. Engstrom and R.L. Rabin, "Pursuing Public Health Through Litigation: Lessons from Tobacco and Opioids," *Stanford Law Review* 73, no. 285 (2021).

[18] Viscusi and Hersch, "Tobacco Regulation through Litigation."

[19] See, for example, W. G. Shadel et al., "Do graphic health warning labels on cigarette packages deter purchases at point-of-sale? An experiment with adult smokers," *Health Educ Res* 34, no. 3 (2019).

[20] J. C. Barrett, "Cellular and molecular mechanisms of asbestos carcinogenicity: Implications for biopersistence," *Environ Health Perspect* 102 Suppl 5, no. Suppl 5 (1994).

[21] See, for example, J. C. Barrett, P. W. Lamb, and R. W. Wiseman, "Multiple mechanisms for the carcinogenic effects of asbestos and other mineral fibers," ibid. 81 (1989); X. Xiong

asbestos were found liable in 1973 for the harmful health effects of the material, but cases continue to be tried more than 50 years later, making the litigation the longest-running product liability litigation in the U.S.[22]

Given their unique characteristics and relatively limited scope of harms, at least at the onset of litigation, it is unlikely that the medical and non-medical product liability landscapes of the past will serve as useful templates for health-related mass tort cases going forward. It is even less likely that lessons from those cases can be directly applied to settings featuring growing complexity in supply chain organization, nuanced causal pathways, and an increasingly multifaceted epidemiology of attributable health-related harms. Supply chain complexity alone can substantially change the product liability landscape. As supply chains become more complex, and production processes evolve from traditional factory "production lines" to more fragmented, logistically complex multistage supply and distribution systems blanketed with multi-level regulatory and compliance mechanisms and third-party funding and financing,[23] the process of identifying causal factors and causal entities can become considerably more challenging. This creates an added hurdle in product liability cases, as the identification of responsible parties and the allocation of responsibility among those parties is not necessarily straightforward, and in many cases, there may be good arguments for the allocation to not simply default to what is expeditious or convenient. The U.S. health care system is one such industry that has over the past two decades experienced rapid growth in complexity and technological change, especially in supply chains and distribution channels, organizational structures and information systems, product and process innovations, artificial intelligence,

et al., "An umbrella review of the evidence associating occupational carcinogens and cancer risk at 19 anatomical sites," *Environ Pollut* 345 (2024); P. Bou-Samra et al., "Epidemiological, therapeutic, and survival trends in malignant pleural mesothelioma: A review of the National Cancer Database," *Cancer Med* 12, no. 11 (2023).

[22] S. J. Carroll et al., "Asbestos Litigation," (Santa Monica, CA: RAND Corportation | RAND Insititute for Civil Justice 2005).

[23] See generally KFF, "Follow The Pill: Understanding the U.S. Commercial Pharmaceutical Supply Chain," (Menlo Park, CA: Kaiser Family Foundation, 2005). These trends are evident across many industries; for example, the automobile industry has radically changed its supply chain approach over the past two decades. See generally A. Iyer, S. Seshadri, and R. Vasher, *Toyota Supply Chain Management: A Strategic Approach to Toyota's Renowned System* (McGraw-Hill Companies, 2009).

genomic science, payment mechanisms, and regulatory mechanisms and policies.[24]

In future product liability cases, it is also likely that the epidemiology of health-related harms will become progressively more complex, mostly due to significant advances in clinical research, biostatistics, and data availability, such as electronic medical records and more detailed third-party claims data, but also in part due to creative leveraging of a rapidly growing body of medical research that can be quarried to, in some instances, redefine and expand scopes of harm.[25] One indicator of this trend is that the total number of publications and citations regarding medical negligence has grown exponentially over the past three decades.[26] For example, regarding tobacco products, whereas the initial focus was on the effects of smoking on lung cancer, ongoing research has uncovered a broader spectrum of alleged harms, including effects on cardiovascular disease, wound healing, metabolic disorders, and other cancers.[27] In addition, the roles of second-hand smoke have been further explored; for example, there is some evidence of harmful effects of second-hand smoke on asthma and attention

[24] For general discussions see P. W. Abramowitz, D. F. Chen, and D. J. Cobaugh, "Multihospital health systems: Growing complexity of pharmacy enterprise brings opportunities and challenges," *Am J Health Syst Pharm* 75, no. 7 (2018); T. G. Kannampallil et al., "Considering complexity in healthcare systems," *J Biomed Inform* 44, no. 6 (2011); R. Singh, "Why Healthcare Market Complexity Is A Reason To Innovate, Not A Reason Not To," *Forbes* Sept 27 (2021); P. Zweifel, "Innovation in health care through information technology (IT): The role of incentives," *Social Science & Medicine* 289 (2021); S. Ellerbeck, "5 innovations that are revolutionizing global healthcare," (Geneva, Switzerland: World Economic Forum, 2023).

[25] For a general discussion, refer to S. Grosso, "What is Reasonable and What Can Be Proved as Reasonable: Reflections on the Role of Evidence-Based Medicine and Clinical Practice Guidelines in Medical Negligence Claims," *Annals of Health Law* 27, no. 1 (2018); J. Kitzen et al., "The Role of Medical Literature, Clinical Trials and Experimental Research in Drug Product-Injury Litigation: A Primer with Two Examples," *Pharmacology & Pharmacy* 9 (2018). Also see Y. Zhao et al., "New Advances in Biostatistics," *Journal of Probability and Statistics* 2019, no. 1 (2019).

[26] S. Dahlawi et al., "Medical negligence in healthcare organizations and its impact on patient safety and public health: a bibliometric study," *F1000Res* 10 (2021).

[27] See generally M. Del Riccio et al., "The clinical impact of continued smoking in patients with breast and other hormone-dependent cancer: A systematic literature review," *Crit Rev Oncol Hematol* 184 (2023); C. Hajat et al., "The health impact of smokeless tobacco products: a systematic review," *Harm Reduct J* 18, no. 1 (2021); M. P. Parmar et al., "A Systematic Review of the Effects of Smoking on the Cardiovascular System and General Health," *Cureus* 15, no. 4 (2023).

deficit and hyperactivity disorders in children.[28] There has also been a growing body of research on the environmental impact of tobacco production and consumption.[29] Similarly, the epidemiology of asbestos-related harms has evolved over time. Initially, the majority of cases were related to mesothelioma, but in recent years most new cases have been filed on behalf of individuals claiming to have asbestosis, which is relatively difficult to diagnose and can include individuals who may be asymptomatic and minimally impaired.[30] Consequently, the causation arguments surrounding asbestosis are more complicated compared to mesothelioma, and these more ambiguous causal pathways have been leveraged to support the filing of additional cases. Asbestosis claims are examples of another growing type of product litigation, wherein lawsuits are based on an alleged change in risk attributable to a product, even if that elevated risk has yet to result in measurable harm. Other examples include chemical spills, accidental releases of chemicals and contaminants, and radiation leaks.[31] Claimants in these types of cases often argue that those exposed to potential harms, even in the absence of symptoms or other biomarkers confirmatory of exposure, require ongoing monitoring and surveillance to detect the emergence of attributable disease or disease progression.[32]

[28] P. Chen et al., "Secondhand Smoke Exposure and the Risk of Chronic Obstructive Pulmonary Disease: A Systematic Review and Meta-Analysis," *Int J Chron Obstruct Pulmon Dis* 18 (2023); Z. He et al., "The association between secondhand smoke and childhood asthma: A systematic review and meta-analysis," *Pediatr Pulmonol* 55, no. 10 (2020); A. Huang et al., "Association between postnatal second-hand smoke exposure and ADHD in children: a systematic review and meta-analysis," *Environ Sci Pollut Res Int* 28, no. 2 (2021); M. C. Malevolti et al., "Second-hand smoke exposure and cervical cancer: a systematic review and meta-analysis," *J Cancer Res Clin Oncol* (2023).

[29] See generally J. Lam et al., "Modelling the global economic costs of tobacco product waste," *Bull World Health Organ* 100, no. 10 (2022); T. E. Novotny and F. Zhao, "Consumption and production waste: another externality of tobacco use," *Tob Control* 8, no. 1 (1999); J. E. Schneider et al., "Tobacco litter costs and public policy: a framework and methodology for considering the use of fees to offset abatement costs," ibid.20 Suppl 1 (2011); J. E. Schneider et al., "Online Simulation Model to Estimate the Total Costs of Tobacco Product Waste in Large U.S. Cities," *Int J Environ Res Public Health* 17, no. 13 (2020).

[30] Carroll et al., "Asbestos Litigation."

[31] See, for example, P. M. Drucker, "'Accidental Release Reporting Rule' Requires Owners, Operators to Disclose Chemical Accidents to Chemical Safety Board," *The National Law Review* 15, no. 332 (2023).

[32] See, for example, E. A. Gonzalez and R. W. Valori, "Medical Monitoring Claims Are Viable in Florida," *Florida Bar Journal* 75, no. 1 (2001).

1.2 Opioid Crisis

Following the regulatory approval of long-acting opioids in the mid-1990s, utilization of the pain medications grew rapidly.[33] The drugs immediately found a place in a U.S. health industry hungry for tools and solutions to meet the growing need for pain management amidst a nationwide movement to treat pain more aggressively and to define pain as the "fifth vital sign," imbuing pain assessment with a clinical stature alongside the pantheon of body temperature, pulse rate, respiration rate, and blood pressure. Opioids were a relatively low-cost and clinically effective means of meeting these new demands. But along with amplified opioid utilization came increased rates of adverse events associated with their use, with rates of misuse, dependency and overdose increasing substantially in the two decades from the time of approval to 2021.[34] The problems evolved in three waves, with a fist wave consisting of increases in the utilization of prescription opioids, followed by a second wave marked by growth in illicit opioid markets and increases in the use of heroin, and a third wave associated with escalated use of illicit synthetic opioids, like fentanyl.[35] The relationships among the three waves have been the focus of some debate, with claimants in the opioid litigation generally asserting a linear causality across the three waves, and other more nuanced explanations arguing that a confluence of a large number of contributing factors set each of the waves in motion independently. This topic is important and will be revisited later in the book.

The global opioid crisis may share some of the traits of past product liability matters, but it is also very different in at least two very important ways. First, the current opioid crisis features many of the contemporary dynamic factors described above, including complex supply chains, novel data and methods, multifactorial causal pathways, prominent roles for regulators, and complex epidemiological factors associated with harms. There are few, if any, prior large-scale medical product liability cases that feature all

[33] G. P. Guy, Jr. et al., "Vital Signs: Changes in Opioid Prescribing in the United States, 2006–2015," *MMWR Morb Mortal Wkly Rep* 66, no. 26 (2017).

[34] CDC, "Understanding the Opioid Overdose Epidemic," (Washington, D.C.: U.S. Centers for Disease Control and Prevention, 2022); Spencer, Miniño, and Warner, "Drug Overdose Deaths in the United States, 2001–2021 (Data Brief No. 457)."

[35] D. Ciccarone, "The triple wave epidemic: Supply and demand drivers of the US opioid overdose crisis," *International Journal of Drug Policy* 71 (2019); Spencer, Miniño, and Warner, "Drug Overdose Deaths in the United States, 2001–2021 (Data Brief No. 457)."

of these factors simultaneously. Second, one of the most interesting points of departure from past large-scale product liability cases is that the entire opioid crisis has taken place under the "watchful eye" of numerous regulatory agencies, professional medical societies, healthcare delivery systems, public payers, private health insurance companies, and one very influential accreditation agency. Not a single prescription drug can reach the market and stay on the market in the U.S. without the coordinated approval and sustained endorsement of any and all of these myriad agencies and organizations. Positioned at the end of the supply chain, as a final backstop, a patient cannot obtain a prescription drug without a legal prescription issued by a licensed physician, who is also subject to oversight by the U.S. Drug Enforcement Administration ("DEA") and who is governed by rigorous professional self-regulation. Ultimately, to conform with the duties and responsibilities associated with licensure, physicians are expected to base the need for opioid prescriptions on observable measures of clinical need.[36] Again, at any point in time throughout the opioid crisis, several agencies and entities possessed the authority and ability to slow, pause or completely halt the sale and utilization of prescription opioids. Despite these layers of checks and balances and regulatory oversight, which combined far exceed those of most other consumer product markets,[37] the utilization of prescription opioids continued to rise unabated for decades, long after warning signs emerged. To put this in perspective, the opioid crisis invites comparisons to a magician performing a magic trick in front of an audience of fellow magicians, the majority of whom understand the nuances and inner machinations of the craft but are nonetheless bewildered by the outcome.

1.3 Harms and Externalities

In the U.S., the alleged "oversupply" of prescription opioids formed the basis of a widespread MDL involving several states, counties, and other stakeholders aligned against an array of disparate defendants. In these proceedings defendants are alleged to have contributed (through various pathways) to an irregular increase in the supply of prescription opioids,

[36] L. R. Webster and M. Grabois, "Current Regulations Related to Opioid Prescribing," *Pm r* 7, no. 11 Suppl (2015).

[37] P. McLaughlin and O. Sherouse, "The McLaughlin-Sherouse List: The 10 Most-Regulated Industries of 2014," (Arlington, VA: Mercatus Center, George Mason University, 2016).

one that was claimed to be inconsistent or unaligned with medical need. In turn, this oversupply of opioids was alleged to have contributed to harms associated with opioid utilization, mainly the "public nuisance" aspect of opioid use disorder ("OUD" and its primary and secondary impacts, such as undue burdens on public health services, the criminal justice system, and social and family assistance programs. In the language of economics, the alleged public nuisance aspects of OUD can be thought of as "negative externalities" associated with the "production" of pain control. Economists use the term "externalities" to refer to effects that are secondary to the transaction in question; for example, water pollution in some cases might be considered a negative externality associated with the use of pesticides on nearby farms. Externalities are defined by economists in various ways; for example, the International Monetary Fund ("IMF") describes externalities as follows: "Consumption, production, and investment decisions of individuals, households, and firms often affect people not directly involved in the transactions. Sometimes these indirect effects are tiny. But when they are large, they can become problematic—what economists call externalities,"[38] adding that "Externalities are among the main reasons governments intervene in the economic sphere."[39] We might also think of externalities as being similar to "unintended consequences," though not all externalities are unintended, and certainly some are expected given prevailing transactional and institutional features. The concept of externalities is commonly studied in economics, especially in health and environmental applications of economics.

In the MDL, the externalities in question are the SAEs associated with opioid misuse, mainly OUD, and its impact on the utilization of healthcare services, the criminal justice system, and social and family welfare systems. While SAEs are present with many prescription drugs, a unique feature of the opioid cases is the working hypothesis on the part of claimants that it is not simply the existence of SAEs, but the knowledge of them coupled with a purposeful increase in supply. In the case of opioids, it can be argued that OUD and its negative effects are external to the prescribing of opioids, with a relatively small proportion of cases progressing to OUD, but the majority used appropriately and providing clinical value, without progression to OUD or without the incurring of

[38] Helbling. T., "What Are Externalities?," *Finance & Development* 47, no. 4 (2010).

[39] Ibid.

added costs.[40] In other words, the opioid MDL is a product liability case wherein the majority of the products are used properly, perform as promised, and continue to be relied upon by the medical community. In terms of the alleged opioid-attributable harms identified in the cases, there are some important features that will be discussed throughout the book, including the following: (1) the vast majority of opioids are used as directed and result in no harms or externalities whatsoever, and continue to be viewed by healthcare providers as among the most effective treatments for moderate to severe pain; (2) cases have been predominantly focused on only three components of the prescription drug supply chain (manufacturers, distributors, and pharmacies), while deemphasizing the role of many other entities that possessed the power or legal authority to halt the flow of prescription opioids at any time; and (3) whereas it is widely known that a large and growing proportion of opioid-attributable harms is caused by *illicit* opioids, which are not sourced from the healthcare system, claimants have generally argued that the illicit markets were caused by the increase in supply of prescription opioids (i.e., the claimant's "gateway" hypothesis).

1.4 Objectives

The primary goal of this book is to use the experiences of the opioid crisis and opioid product liability litigation in the United States as examples of how we can improve our understanding of complex healthcare issues and problems, including the thorough assessment of causal factors and a more precise estimation of the impact of harms and externalities. The identification of causal factors is critical to preventing similar problems in the future, and greater precision in the estimation of attributable costs and abatement costs is essential to product liability litigation. The secondary objective of the book is to use the experiences and data from the opioid crisis to explore remedies to similar, seemingly intractable problems. In addition to targeted abatement programs, there is a need to sort through the costs and benefits of alternative forms of governance for higher-risk prescription drugs, which inevitably will require reforming regulatory procedures and exploiting the costs and benefits of court ordering for those circumstances where regulation fails.

[40] This will be explored in greater detail in Chap. 3.

The conventional wisdom regarding the opioid crisis is that manufacturers and distributors aggressively marketed the drugs to passive, unsuspecting, and largely uninformed physicians, who in turn carelessly prescribed them to their patients, some of whom demonstrated legitimate medical need, but others of whom showed obvious signs of drug-seeking behavior, substance use disorders, and mental health problems. This is of course an extensive oversimplification of what actually happened. But nevertheless, some version of this argument has essentially become the conventional wisdom, as described in popular narrative accounts like *Dreamland* by Sam Quinones, *Dopesick* by Beth Macy, *Empire of Pain* by Patrick Radden Keefe, *American Cartel* by Scott Higham and Sari Horwitz, and *Pain Killer* by Barry Meier.[41] These accounts have provided some valuable reporting on the origins of the crisis and the machinations of the key players as the crisis unfolded and persisted. In addition, narrative accounts like *Dreamland* have been essential to understanding the humanistic side of the crisis. However, the focus of each of these works is relatively siloed, with the emphasis largely focused on the role of manufacturers, the compliant bureaucrats who did their bidding, and a U.S. health system rife with misaligned incentives and fragmented care. While these factors were indeed very important, the risk of this approach is that it deflects attention away from the complex, multifaceted and intertwined root causes of the crisis, a crisis fueled by a health industry designed, incentivized, and determined to aggressively treat pain, enabled by the same regulators and institutions nominally charged with its oversight.

The backdrop to the opioid crisis is the question regarding remedies, a critical part of which is whether regulatory governance of prescription drugs can be improved, or even reformed, such that the role for prescription drug regulation can be relegated to narrower corridors where its comparative advantages can be leveraged, but its inefficiencies can be contained. Given the risks and uncertainty associated with some prescription drugs, and the importance of some sort of *ex ante* approval and

[41] S. Higham and S. Horwitz, *American Cartel: Inside the Battle to Bring Down the Opioid Industry* (New York, NY: Twelve / Hachette Book Group, 2022); B. Macy, *Dopesick* (New York, NY: Little, Brown and Company, 2018); P. R. Keefe, *Empire of Pain* (New York, NY: Doubleday, a division of Penguin Random House LLC, 2021); B. Meier, *Pain Killer* (New York, NY: Random House, 2018); S. Quinones, *Dreamland* (New York, NY: Bloomsbury Press, 2015).

monitoring function, the reform of current regulatory processes is perhaps the most important remedy.[42] Regardless of what regulators did or failed to do in response to the increasing opioid supply and growing body of research regarding adverse events, the fact is that the mechanisms employed by regulators—ones that directly control opioid approval, marketing, and the volume of distribution—proved to be entirely insufficient in governing opioid supply and utilization. This oversight vacuum, combined with a "perfect storm" of factors impacting demand, created a fertile environment for opioid misuse and subsequent litigation. Thrusting the opioid crisis into the litigation world largely ceded control to the courts, which have incentives to settle cases expeditiously.[43] Settlements, while potentially desirable to both sides, can risk obfuscating the causal pathways that led to the crisis, and can also result in only a subgroup of potentially responsible parties bearing the burden of abatement responsibility. Consequently, the broader goal of this work is to develop a better understanding of how the crisis evolved, and the impacts that it has had and continues to have on society. The conventional wisdom around the causes and impacts of the opioid crisis is, at best, incomplete, and, at worst, inaccurate. Incomplete and inaccurate analyses will invariably lead to some version of history repeating itself.

To address these gaps, this book reviews much of the relevant studies and knowledge to date and provides a clearer understanding of the complexities of the costs, causes, and liability associated with negative externalities and harms stemming from opioid misuse. The main sources of information and data relied upon for this analysis are publicly available

[42] The regulatory failures featured throughout the opioid crisis were arguably avoidable had the regulatory institutions functioned more effectively, or at least if they operated as they were intended to function; see generally K. Humphreys et al., "Responding to the opioid crisis in North America and beyond: recommendations of the Stanford-Lancet Commission," *Lancet* 399, no. 10,324 (2022). More generally, there is a long-running "regulation versus litigation" argument that (in part) views regulatory failures as creating a void increasingly filled by litigation. See, for example, T. Buchholz et al., "Regulation Through Litigation: Assessing the Role of Bounty Hunters and Bureaucrats in the American Regulatory Regime," in *Conference Series (No. 2)* (New York NY: Manhattan Institute, 2000); Engstrom and Rabin, "Pursuing Public Health Through Litigation: Lessons from Tobacco and Opioids." Also see A. Shleifer, "Efficient Regulation," in *Regulation vs. Litigation: Perspectives from Economics and Law*, ed. D. P. Kessler (Chicago, IL: University of Chicago Press, 2010).

[43] See, for example, S. R. Bough and A. E. Case-Halferty, "A Judicial Perspective on Approaches to MDL Settlement," *UMKC Law Review* 89, no. 4 (2021).

data, reports, and peer-reviewed literature, all of which are cited in the notes throughout the book and summarized in the chapter bibliographies. The materials relied upon are sourced from peer-reviewed literature from journals indexed on reputable health-related search engines, such as PubMed, as well as peer-reviewed books and book sections. Non-peer-reviewed sources, such as reports from federal and state governmental agencies, newspapers, and periodicals, were considered if the materials were produced by reputable sources of information on issues pertaining to economics, healthcare, and public policy. The goal, again, is to use the opioid crisis as an example, and perhaps a cautionary story, of how *not* to assess the costs and liability of a health crisis, and how we might leverage the opioid lessons to prevent another one like it. Within this overarching goal, there are some specific and primary themes of this book, focused on specific research questions.

1.5 Research Questions

Contemporary product liability cases like the opioid MDL present some new challenges to policy makers, courts, researchers, economists, and other stakeholders tasked with assessing attributable harms and damages, disentangling complex liability allocation problems, and funding abatement programs to mitigate alleged harms. Specifically, in the wake of the height of the crisis, four key research questions arise, each of which carries potentially important implications for the handling of future mass tort cases involving complex transactions, harms, and externalities: (1) What was the true scale of the opioid crisis, in terms of epidemiology and costs, and how should such questions of scale and scope be addressed in the future? (2) What were the main root-cause factors that contributed to the opioid crisis, so that similar crises can be more readily detected and avoided in the future? (3) How can responsibility for the crisis be reasonably and fairly allocated across the myriad contributing factors, such that new problems are not created? And (4) Given that the opioid crisis played out in one of the country's most regulated industries, why did regulatory systems fail, and how could such failures have been prevented? Also, what are the implications for the future interplay between regulators and litigators?

The first line of inquiry gets at the true scale of the crisis. There is little debate as to the importance of the opioid crisis in terms of its overall impact on individuals, the healthcare system, the judicial system, and social assistance programs. However, there is some debate as to the utilization and sources of opioids and the relevant measures of prevalence. Questions regarding scale and scope tie in with the accurate measurement of costs, which consist of attributable costs (that is, what would normally be considered "damages") and abatement costs (that is, the costs necessary to reduce the problem to acceptable or normal levels). A related issue concerns the extent to which abatement costs estimated by claimants compare to peer-reviewed estimates of attributable costs found in published literature and reports. The second line of inquiry focuses on the true *root causes* of the rapid increase in opioid supply following FDA approval. Many of the researchers and public health officials leading efforts to examine the opioid crisis have been epidemiologists, and the genesis of the field of epidemiology is based largely on the identification of root causes of public health problems. Questions regarding root causes tie in with legal inquiries regarding liability, which then tie in with the third line of inquiry regarding responsibility. In light of the multifactorial nature of the opioid crisis, how can its root causes be identified (and liability be assigned fairly and equitably) across the array of opioid supply chain components, recognizing that a multitude of entities must fully engage before a single prescription drug reaches the market? Once root cause and liability assessments are undertaken, the question then becomes how to allocate abatement costs to potentially responsible parties in a fair and equitable manner. Finally, the fourth line of inquiry focuses on remedies. Whereas regulatory failure was clearly an important factor in the genesis of the opioid crisis and its continuation over more than two decades, why exactly did regulatory institutions fail, and what, if any, were the merits of product liability litigation in filling gaps attributable to apparent regulatory shortcomings. These types of inquiries connect with broader "lessons learned" types of questions. These are questions we might ask in any product liability matter but given the scope, magnitude, and public interest regarding the opioid crisis, these questions are of paramount importance. The answers to these questions likely have implications for future mass torts, and an in-depth "postmortem" on the opioid crisis, which this book endeavors to undertake, provides an opportunity to better anticipate and prevent such crises in the future, and to mitigate them more quickly should they arise. In the event matters progress, presumably it is in the best interest of society to litigate them more efficiently and fairly. The following sections approach each of these questions in slightly greater depth.

1.5.1 Scale and Scope

The first question concerns the true scale, scope, and costs associated with harms attributable to the increase in supply of prescription opioids. This question has an epidemiological component and an economic component. Starting with the epidemiological component, if only popular news accounts are considered, one might infer that the prevalence of OUD and other opioid-attributable problems impacts large swaths of society, with alarmingly high and increasing prevalence.[44] While there is little debate as to whether opioid-related harms are a serious public health concern, the prevalence of OUD remains far below the prevalence of several other substance use disorders. For perspective, alcohol abuse and tobacco use, both of which involve substances that continue to be widely available and are minimally regulated, also result in significant harms; as mentioned above, 480,000 deaths per year are attributable to tobacco use, and another 180,000 deaths per year are associated with alcohol abuse.[45] Together, the total annual deaths from tobacco and alcohol represent more than *eight* times the total annual deaths attributable to opioids, which were about 81,000 in 2023.[46] It is also worth noting that deaths attributed to tobacco and alcohol are largely the result of legal use of those substances, whereas more than 90% of opioid deaths in 2023 were attributed to the illegal use of illicit fentanyl.[47] Again, these comparisons are only for the purposes of perspective and are not intended to diminish the importance of opioid misuse or any other substance use disorder.

In addition to epidemiology, the other principal component of scale and scope is economics. While several rigorous studies have calculated various components of the attributable costs of opioids (reviewed in detail later in Chap. 6), such as the attributable costs associated with healthcare, the criminal justice system, and social support programs, other reports have served more to sensationalize the costs, typically by casting an

[44] For a discussion of media sensationalizing various aspects of the opioid crisis, see C.D. Clark, "How sensationalism compounds the opioid crisis," *Washington Post*, no. July 5 (2017).

[45] M. B. Esser et al., "Deaths from Excessive Alcohol Use—United States, 2016–2021," *MMWR Morb Mortal Wkly Rep* 73, no. 8 (2024).

[46] CDC, "Provisional Drug Overdose Death Counts," in *National Vital Statistics System* (Washington, D.C.: National Center for Health Statistics, Centers for Disease Control and Prevention, 2024a).

[47] Ibid.

exceptionally wide net and including a diverse array of indirect costs. In addition to the attributable costs of healthcare, criminal justice, and social programs, some studies also include the indirect costs associated with lost productivity, mortality, the statistical value of lives lost, and reduced quality of life. The U.S. Joint Economic Committee ("JEC"), for example, estimated the total direct and indirect costs of the opioid crisis in the U.S. to be an astonishing $1.5 trillion in 2020,[48] an amount that in the same year would have exceeded the entire Gross Domestic Product ("GDP") of 94% of the IMF member countries, including Australia.[49] Interestingly, the $1.5 trillion estimated by the JEC was a staggering 35% of total U.S. healthcare expenditures in 2021, and about the same value as the entire U.S. automobile industry. The state of Colorado estimated its total opioid attributable costs to be $21 billion, or about $3,600 per capita.[50] That is nearly 10% of average per capita income in the state and about 6% of state GDP. Considering the costs of other substance use disorders, particularly those more prevalent then OUD,[51] one might get the impression that the state of Colorado is spending 20% or more of its GDP and as much as half of its per capita income on substance use disorders alone. Something seems amiss with some of the broad and frequently quoted opioid attributable cost estimates, even when considering the variation in scope of direct and indirect effects included in many of the calculations. The same can be said for estimates of abatement and mitigation costs, many of which appear to ignore the role of existing programs and infrastructure. For example, after receiving in 2019 a large settlement payment based on estimated abatement costs, the state of Oklahoma allocated only about 20% of those funds to the development and operations of abatement programs.[52]

[48] JEC, "The Economic Toll of the Opioid Crisis Reached Nearly $1.5 Trillion in 2020," in *Issue Brief* (Washington, D.C.: U.S. Joint Economic Committee, 2022).

[49] IMF, "GDP, current prices (Billions of U.S. dollars)," (Washington, D.C.: International Monetary Fund, 2021).

[50] J. Esquibel, "Opioid crisis has cost Colorado's economy at least $21 billion," (Aurora, CO: Colorado Consortium for Prescription Drug Abuse Prevention, 2020).

[51] See, for example W. Brangham and D. Hastings, "Alcohol-related deaths surge in Colorado with a higher mortality rate than opioids," (Washington, D.C.: Public Broadcasting System (PBS), "News Hour", 2024).

[52] K. McClung, "Most of the money Oklahoma secured from opioid companies has gone unspent," *The Frontier*, no. July 28 (2021).

Although it is likely too late to inform the opioid litigation, there is a need to sort through the relatively large literature on attributable costs and abatement costs and, perhaps more importantly, determine how these data can be appropriately adjusted to align with the kinds of compensation sought by claimants. It is particularly important to understand the nuances of abatement costs, which are the foremost concern of the states and counties contending with opioid-related problems. There are different ways of calculating the attributable costs of a harm or externality. The most common method is a standard attributable cost approach, the objectives of which are to measure the added or "excess" costs that can be reasonably and accurately attributed to the harm or externality, holding constant the effects of other likely factors. Another common approach is to measure the expected costs of abatement, which focuses mainly on the direct costs of efforts to *mitigate* the problem and the probability of future harm. Attributable costs are what we usually think about when we think about economic *damages*, and abatement costs are what we usually think of when we think of how to mitigate or alleviate a problem. In this book, both methods are applied to determine a range of costs attributable to the problem.

1.5.2 *Causation*

Perhaps the most challenging step in any analysis of harms in product liability matters is the determination of costs attributable to potentially responsible parties and the costs of abatement to mitigate harms, which is often the ultimate public policy goal. For example, if a polluted water supply is alleged to have caused cancer, the task of attributing contaminant supply and exposure to specific cancers, and the costs associated with those cancers, is a necessary but computationally complex task. The standard externality story of a polluting factory does not exactly fit easily within the parameters of modern-day industry, especially the healthcare industry and even more so the pharmaceutical industry and is unlikely to fit well with any similar health or environmental crisis of the future. In the production of automobiles, for example, each vehicle that is produced can be associated with some fraction of the pollution emitted by the factory in which the vehicle was assembled. Of course, this holds true only if the automobile is produced entirely in a single factory, which is increasingly not the case.

In contrast, the supply of opioids is the result of a multifaceted supply chain, and in some small fraction of users opioid use and misuse can generate "excess" costs and harms but in most instances it does not. In fact, most produced and consumed prescription opioids cause no harm at all and continue to be regularly and legally prescribed by physicians to address legitimate medical needs, more than two decades after warning signs emerged.[53] Given its national scope, the opioid crisis has been heavily studied, with experts and stakeholders in academia and consulting generating detailed accounts and estimates of total excess attributable costs associated with OUD. It is therefore possible, and even likely, that the abatement cost estimates put forward by individual states and counties and other claimants nationally may together sum to totals far more than these peer-reviewed published national estimates; that is, the "sum of the parts" may far exceed the plausible size of the whole. Such discrepancies in proportionality pose problems of verification, where there is a need to determine the reasons for the discrepancies, and in particular the determination of which estimates—the whole or the parts—are more aligned with the true costs. Overestimating or underestimating costs is not a harmless outcome, because it can undermine public trust and result in inefficient allocation of resources.

Consequently, an important objective of the book is to conduct an in-depth analysis of the *root causes* of the opioid crisis and apply this analysis to the identification of contributing factors and groups of entities associated with the initial causation and growth of opioid supply. As discussed above, understanding the liability landscape is essential to fairly attributing costs to potentially responsible parties, which is a task that is typically part of any solution to most externality problems. The opioid crisis has been described by experts as "multifactorial," and there is a relatively lengthy list of entities that had a hand in marshalling prescription opioids through the supply chain, from production to consumption. The idea that the opioid crisis was caused by multiple factors is neither novel nor controversial. Many experts and stakeholders begin their writings on the opioid crisis

[53] As discussed in later chapters, OUD occurs in about 2–5% of individuals consuming prescription opioids, depending on the population of focus. Also see Humphreys et al., "Responding to the opioid crisis in North America and beyond: recommendations of the Stanford-Lancet Commission."; NASEM, *Pain Management and the Opioid Epidemic: Balancing Societal and Indidivual Benefits and Risks of Prescription Opioid Use*, ed. R. J. Bonnie, M. A. Ford, and J. K. Phillips, Consensus Study Report of National Academies of Sciences, Engineering and Medicine (NASEM) (Washington, D.C.: National Academies Press, 2017).

with declarations of there being "enough blame to go around."[54] The issue is not whether there are multiple potentially responsible parties, it is that blame does not appear to be actually "going around;" it is instead migrating to a small handful of deeper-pocketed entities while ignoring some of the most obvious causal agents. If litigation is to be *de facto* relied upon to augment or even replace government regulation as the ultimate arbiter of public health and safety, which in the post-deregulation era appears to be the trend,[55] it is imperative to identify, through the process of litigation, all meaningful root causes so that legal remedies can align with public health remedies by mitigating the impact of causal factors. However, if legal remedies are based on flawed data and incomplete understandings of critical institutional details, it is unlikely that the courts will offer a more effective organizational alternative to regulation.

1.5.3 Responsibility

Assuming that estimates of attributable costs and abatement costs can be accurately estimated, the next key question is how, and to whom, to assign liability for those costs. Referring again to the traditional factory analogy, it may be a relatively straightforward exercise to determine which factories emit contaminants, and how much is emitted. In contrast, the U.S. health care system is heavily regulated and excessively fragmented and complex, characterized by complicated supply chains and layered regulatory structures. The pathway of a drug from development to consumption is anything but straightforward, as not a single prescription drug can reach a consumer without the explicit consent, approval, and actions on the part of numerous entities, including several governmental regulatory agencies and a handful of self-regulating private institutions. Prescription opioids start with extensive research and development and testing, then move to government regulators, who must verify that safety and efficacy profiles fall within an acceptable range.

[54] This is a commonly expressed sentiment; see, for example, R. Baum, "Interview with Richard Baum, Acting Director of U.S. National Drug Control Policy," in *FPC Briefing* (Washington, D.C.: US. Department of State, 2017).

[55] See, for example, R. A. Posner, "Regulation (Agencies) versus Litigation (Courts)," in *Regulation versus Litigation: Perspectives from Economics and Law*, ed. D. P. Kessler (Chicago, IL: The University of Chicago Press, 2011); Engstrom and Rabin, "Pursuing Public Health Through Litigation: Lessons from Tobacco and Opioids."; Buchholz et al., "Regulation Through Litigation: Assessing the Role of Bounty Hunters and Bureaucrats in the American Regulatory Regime."; Shleifer, "Efficient Regulation."

Based on the results of such testing, regulators then must either approve or deny permission to begin marketing and sales operations in the U.S., and (in the case of certain scheduled drugs, like opioids) regulators also establish production and distribution quotas. Upon approval, manufacturers (who may or may not have been the original developers) produce and market the opioids. But then the opioids, like any prescription drug, get passed along to distributors, prescribed by physicians, paid for by public and private insurers, dispensed by retail pharmacies, and consumed and stored by patients. Along the way, regulators continue to monitor the process, and accreditation agencies assure that those handling the drugs are doing so in a proper, guideline-compliant, and lawful manner.

It seems to make sense that, in considering liability, one would have to assess the role of each of these entities, because the decisions, actions, inactions, and failures of any link in the chain have the potential to either cause or contribute to the externality. Put differently, if all these components and processes are necessary to bring a drug to market and keep it there, it seems reasonable to evaluate the role of each entity when considering liability associated with bringing the drug to market and keeping it there. Indeed, as we will discuss at length in subsequent chapters, most analyses of the root causes of the opioid crisis clearly point to multiple factors and causes across numerous levels of the supply chain. However, perhaps in the name of judicial and analytical convenience, a relatively narrow view of the drug supply chain has prevailed in the opioid legal proceedings. The challenge lies in the concept of "fair and equitable," which is one of the guardrails of liability proceedings aimed at assuring that, among other things, no single defendant or small group of defendants is left shouldering responsibility for the actions of other potentially responsible parties.[56] Put differently, in cases with multiple defendants or multiple causative agents, the standards of liability applied to one defendant should generally be applied to all potentially responsible parties who engaged in actions (or inactions) alleged to have caused or contributed to the same negative externality. In some cases, some proportion of responsibility may also fall upon the claimants.

Questions regarding liability are intertwined with the challenge of fair and equitable allocation of liability among potentially responsible parties. In matters concerning liability, economists have generally turned to environmental economics and public health for solutions to these types of problems. For example, in the U.S., in certain environmental contamination matters,

[56] See generally H. Mann, "Is Fair and Equitable Fair, Equitable, Just, or Under Law?," *Proceedings of the Annual Meeting (American Society of International Law)* 100 (2006).

abatement costs are often allocated volumetrically, with current and former users of the site generally responsible for the proportional volume of products they produced on the site. But clearly that approach cannot easily be deployed in the case of opioids. We might know how much of total product volume (Q) was produced by manufacturer x (q_x), but it could be prohibitively challenging to then determine the proportion of harm attributable specifically to q_x. And it is also the case that q_x will flow from manufacturer to distributor to pharmacy, awaiting dispensing based on a legal prescription from a licensed provider. Practical difficulties intensify when considering the potential role of entities that are critical but indirect components of the supply chain, such as regulators, accreditation agencies, public and private payers, pharmacy benefit managers, and health systems. These entities play a critical role in putting drugs in the hands of consumers, but do not necessarily directly handle the products.

After issues regarding root causes and liability are sorted out, the typical externality problem shifts to determining "optimal" means of *allocating* attributable costs or abatement costs to potentially responsible parties, especially in the absence of an option to allocate based on a simple volumetric approach. Given the U.S. health industry's fragmented and complex organizational structure and supply chains, allocation is not at all straightforward, but the task itself is inescapable. Volumetric approaches to allocation, based on opioid sales, may only work for entities that are selling, handling, and dispensing specific and quantifiable volumes of opioids. However, this leaves out several important elements of the supply chain that influenced the supply and utilization of opioids without directly handling a specific volume of opioids, mainly policy makers, regulators, medical societies, third-party payers, and accreditation agencies. In other words, before a single prescription opioid can get into the hands of a patient, there are several organizations and institutions who must either approve or otherwise "sign off" on the transaction. Consider the U.S. Food and Drug Administration ("FDA,") which approved several different opioid-based medications and continued to allow their sale unabated for more than a decade after warning signs emerged.[57] Similarly, the federal Medicare program, state Medicaid programs, private insurance companies,

[57] The FDA shares post-market regulation of drugs with the Drug Enforcement Administration ("DEA"); however, the FDA itself employs a variety of post-market enforcement tools, including requiring post-market studies and additional clinical trials, imposing labeling requirements and restrictions on distribution, regulating manufacturing processes, requiring recalls, and revoking approvals. See generally FDA, "Postmarketing Requirements and Commitments: Introduction," (Washington, D.C.: U.S. Food and Drug Administration, 2024).

and self-insured employers continued paying for opioid-based treatment after warning signs emerged. Given the relatively low cost of opioids, in most cases third-party payers subsidized all or most of the cost of opioids, and preferred opioids to more resource-intensive approaches to pain, such as steroidal injections and cognitive behavior therapy.

Among the most direct influence and control on prescription opioids throughout the crisis has been administered by physicians themselves. State medical boards, which serve a "self-regulation" function on behalf of the medical profession, as well as numerous medical specialty societies, embraced opioids as a means of meeting the demands of the burgeoning palliative care movement, the shift to "patient-centered" care, and the rise in prominence of "pain as the fifth vital sign." Moreover, these groups saw no problem in providing direct financial incentives to providers to score better on performance measures, most of which include the effectiveness of pain control and overall patient satisfaction as key components of composite performance measures.[58] It is also the case that patient satisfaction is particularly sensitive to the effectiveness of pain control. Like the FDA and third-party payers, the medical establishment continued to embrace opioids, even after warning signs emerged. In sum, it is incontrovertible that the diffusion of opioids was fueled by a vast array of interconnected forces, each exerting upward pressure on demand and supply. These interconnected forces were not necessarily nefarious in their intent. Instead, they mostly reflected the thinking of the times and were aligned with the overall gravitation pull toward more aggressive management of pain. Moreover, the effects of any one of these forces may very well have been innocuous, but the confluence of the "perfect storm" of effects proved to be more than the system could realistically handle.

1.5.4 Remedies

The last question focuses on remedies and is perhaps the most important. Despite its unique features, the opioid crisis provides a glimpse into what could potentially become the future of mass tort product liability in the U.S. and abroad, especially for medical products.[59] Although there are

[58] This topic will be discussed in greater detail in other parts of the book. See generally M. A. Erdek, "Pay-for-Performance Reimbursement for Clinicians: Common Sense or a Wolf in Sheep's Clothing?," *Pain Med* 19, no. 11 (2018).

[59] See, for example, E. Aliferov, "The Role of Direct-Injury Government-Entity Lawsuits in the Opioid Litigation," *Fordham Law Review* 87 (2018).

some policies and procedures in place that may limit an exact replay of the opioid crisis, there are more than enough structural characteristics of the U.S. health industry, and perhaps the global health industry as well, that have the potential to breed similar medical product mass tort cases in the future. Thus, from the perspectives of policymakers, regulators, litigators, experts, clinicians, and health care leaders, there is a need not just to conduct a "root cause" forensic analysis of what happened, but to also understand how best to approach such issues should similar circumstances emerge in the future.

One important part of the debates over remedies is the "regulation versus litigation" question, wherein regulation and litigation can be viewed as alternative forms of governance to address complex healthcare transactions and externalities. In addition to emphasizing the value of root cause analyses conducted early and often, the opioid crisis underscores the gaps in knowledge and limitations of the courts in calculating accurate attributable costs and abatement costs and allocating those costs to potentially responsible parties. An important feature of the opioid crisis is its link to the failure of multiple regulatory institutions. One could argue that the regulatory failures were unavoidable given the complexities and uncertainties surrounding the probability of serious adverse events associated with using prescription opioids. If that is the case, then it brings up the question of (1) whether regulatory agencies should be reformed, and if so how, and (2) whether there may be some medical products for which the true risk profile is unknowable due to excessively high levels of uncertainty and information costs. In other words, in terms of remedies, the best solution may be to reform the regulatory system as much as possible and leave the rest to products liability litigation. However, if that path is chosen, there are some lessons to be learned that have implications for both regulatory reform and products liability litigation.

1.6 Approach

The general approach of the analyses presented in this book is grounded in economics; specifically, the areas of economics focused on externalities, public policy, and the intersection of law and economics. The economics subfield of "Law and Economics" is where economic theory intersects with issues pertaining to public policy, regulation, contracts, environmental policy, health and safety policy, and related fields in which the specifics of laws and statutes have implications for economic analyses, empirical analyses, and policy analysis.[60] As briefly discussed earlier in this chapter, in some instances the production or consumption of a product or service results in what economists term an externality.[61] The use of the term externality refers to effects that are external to the transaction.[62] Generally, this refers to secondary effects that occur after the initial transaction or incident to the initial transaction. A commonly used example in economics is pollution emitted in the manufacturing process. In this context, pollution is said to be "external" to the transaction associated with the product. Similarly, in public health, a common example is the polluting of a potable water source by chemical compounds associated with nearby (or upstream) manufacturing, farming, or service.[63] Consequently, economists typically calculate the costs of the externality, but also necessarily must address liability and responsibility in most economic analyses of externalities.[64] These applications are common in

[60] The American Economic Association ("AEA") defines and classifies economics subfields. The subfield "Law and Economics" ("K") contains the following categories: K1 (Basic Areas of Law), K2 (Regulation and Business Law), K3 (Other Substantive Areas of Law). Key relevant sub-areas include, but are not limited to, the following: K13 (Tort Law and Product Liability; Forensic Economics), K23 (Regulated Industries and Administrative Law), K32 (Energy, Environmental, Health, and Safety Law). For a general discussion of the topics covered in the subfield, see generally R. D. Cooter and T. Ulen, *Law and Economics (6th Edition)* (Pearson, 2011); W. K. Viscusi, J. M. Vernon, and J. E. Harrington, *Economics of Regulation and Antitrust (Second Edition)* (Cambridge (MA): The MIT Press, 1995).

[61] This is discussed in greater detail throughout the book. For additional background, see generally R. Cornes and T. Sandler, *The Theory of Externalities, Public Goods, and Club Goods* (Cambridge, UK: Cambridge University Press, 1986); W. Nicholson and C. Snyder, *Microeconomic Theory: Basic Principles and Extensions, 12th Edition* (Cengage Learning, 2016); A. A. Papandreou, *Externality and Institutions* (Oxford, UK: Clarendon Press, 1994).

[62] This is discussed in greater detail later in the book. For additional background, see generally Cornes and Sandler, *The Theory of Externalities, Public Goods, and Club Goods*; Lam et al., "Modelling the global economic costs of tobacco product waste."

[63] See for example M. S. Díaz-Cruz and D. Barceló, "Trace organic chemicals contamination in ground water recharge," *Chemosphere* 72, no. 3 (2008).

[64] This area is broadly considered part of the sub-field within economics referred to as Law and Economics. In addition to the economic analyses of externalities, this includes other areas of law and economics broadly related to contracts, property, and torts. For a more detailed discussion of how economists assess and utilize concepts related to liability, refer to R. D. Cooter, "Economic Theories of Legal Liability," *Journal of Economic Perspectives* 5, no. 3 (1991). For a more in-depth treatment, refer to S. K. Jain, *Economic Analysis of Liability Rules* (New York, NY: Springer, 2015).

economic analyses in public health and environmental health. In the context of opioids, OUD can be considered a "negative externality," incidental to the "production" of pain management in a select subset of consumers. The opioid matter is of course more nuanced than this, and we will explore those nuances in subsequent chapters.

The study of harms and externalities from an economics and public policy perspective implicitly requires the consideration of causal factors and liability.[65] For example, to undertake an analysis of the effect of a negative externality like pollution, it is necessary to develop a complete understanding of the sources of the pollution, and (by extension) the specific entities responsible for those sources. Thus, economists are generally accustomed to considering aspects of liability for the purposes of assigning responsibility in issues regarding externalities and inefficiencies, and further applying those concepts to the design of mechanisms to regulate and mitigate harms, including attributable costs and abatement costs.[66] However, as alluded to above, the genesis of the opioid problem in the U.S. is widely believed to be multifactorial and multifaceted, involving many interrelated factors and entities along the prescription drug supply chain and in the overall production of pain management. Recognition of pharmaceutical supply chain complexity and the multifactorial underpinnings of the opioid crisis have, however, been limitedly applied in the ongoing opioid litigation, with liability judgements largely failing to recognize these important industry features.

Accordingly, rather than focusing myopically on liability issues concerning only a limited number of factors or components, the approach presented herein considers all or at least most relevant factors and considers specific components and entities from a fair and equitable perspective. The rationale for this approach is twofold. First, the factors and entities associated with opioid supply in the U.S. are inextricably connected and intertwined. Healthcare supply chains are complex, and their

[65] See generally B. M. Frischmann and G. B. Ramello, "Externalities, scarcity, and abundance," *Front Res Metr Anal* 7 (2022).

[66] For a more detailed account of how economists approach liability, see generally Cooter, "Economic Theories of Legal Liability."; K. N. Hylton, "The Law and Economics of Products Liability," *Notre Dame Law Review* 88, no. 5 (2013); Jain, *Economic Analysis of Liability Rules*; Zhou et al., "Litigation in tobacco control: past, present and future."; D. P. Baron, "Chap. 24 Design of regulatory mechanisms and institutions," in *Handbook of Industrial Organization* (Elsevier, 1989).

diverse components do not operate independently of one another. Consequently, it would be incorrect to assume that any single component operates in a vacuum or is otherwise independent of other factors and entities. Second, the "law and economics" approach to the study of externalities generally seeks to identify all or most of the sources, causes, and responsible entities, such that "fair and reasonable" liability rules can be applied and, in some cases, mitigation and abatement mechanisms can be effectively employed. This is consistent with the field of public health, especially its subfields epidemiology and biostatistics, both of which were developed mainly as tools to determine causation.[67]

It is important to clarify the differences between "attributable costs" and "abatement costs," as issues of externalities typically feature both concepts. Attributable costs are those costs that can be assigned, usually statistically, to a specific action, intervention, behavior, or process. Attributable costs are inherently retrospective, because the information used for these types of calculations are usually in the form of "real world" observational data. Attributable costs generally align with the litigation concept of economic damages. Abatement costs, on the other hand, are the accounting costs associated with remedying problems associated with (or attributable to) an externality. For example, the attributable costs of smoking might include some proportion of the costs of treating lung cancer (i.e., the specific proportion attributable to tobacco use), but the costs of lung cancer *abatement* might include things like the costs of public health campaigns to reduce smoking rates, or the subsidizing of diagnostic centers to improve access to care. Abatement costs can be retrospective or prospective. Abatement costs that are retrospective might be similar in magnitude to attributable costs, but this does not have to be the case. Prospective abatement costs are estimates of the costs associated with mitigation of an externality, so the calculation of such costs usually requires a projection of how the magnitude of the externality will change over time. Normally, such projections assume that mitigation and abatement activities reduce the impact of the externality each year post-implementation. Some product liability cases are focused mainly on

[67] For example, refer to G. McGwin, Jr., "Causation in epidemiology," *Am J Ophthalmol* 150, no. 5 (2010); M. Parascandola and D. L. Weed, "Causation in epidemiology," *J Epidemiol Community Health* 55, no. 12 (2001); K. J. Rothman, S. Greenland, and T. L. Lash, *Modern Epidemiology (Third Edition)* (Philadelphia, PA: Wolters Kluer; Lippincot WIlliams & Wilkins, 2008).

attributable costs and economic damages, and others are focused on abatement costs.[68]

1.7 Audience

In light of this approach, the intended audience of this book is anyone interested in or involved in product liability, economics, health economics, public health, or public policy. For economists, the book presents a fully worked example of externalities and how economists typically approach externalities. The material is aligned with principles of microeconomics, but with minimal reliance on formal theory and methods so that the material can appeal to a broader audience. Also, economists working in litigation settings, either as consulting or testifying experts, may be interested in the application of basic economic concepts to a contemporary public health problem associated with harms and costs. From a public health perspective, the book puts forth a comprehensive and interdisciplinary approach to developing a deeper understanding of causation, which is critical from a prevention perspective. Similarly, those working in public policy or interested in matters related to public policy will appreciate the discussions of the role of health policy and political institutions in influencing the precursors to the opioid crisis, and the role of public policy in shaping the response to the crisis. From a legal perspective, litigators and legal scholars are likely to take interest in the applied nature of the analysis, particularly the focus on the accurate assessment of harms and causation. Finally, those who have expressed interests in the opioid crisis more generally, either from news stories or more developed accounts reported in books like *Dopesick* and its accompanying television series, will find that this book helps fill some of the gaps left by those accounts, with a focus on the industry structure and incentives that led to the opioid crisis and the landscape of product liability law into which the crisis was pushed.

[68] It is worth noting that, while economists do not necessarily design, create or implement programs to abate public health issues, economists do routinely address abatement in three important ways: (1) the *identification* of programs, services and interventions nominally intended to mitigate or abate a public health issue or medical condition; (2) the *measurement* and analysis of the costs of implementing or operating such programs, services and interventions; and (3) the *apportionment* of those implementation and operational costs to relevant causes or responsible parties.

1.8 Impetus

As a final introductory note, I want to briefly discuss my reasons for writing this book. And I should begin that discussion with the disclosure that my specific knowledge of the opioid crisis comes primarily from a two-year period where I served as an expert witness in the proceedings, working on behalf of a group of retail pharmacies. Importantly, this book does not disclose or discuss any information or data specifically related to that engagement, and in no way is intended to represent or reflect the views and opinions of the retail pharmacies with which I was engaged.[69] Perhaps more importantly, the book is not written from the perspective of retail pharmacies nor from the perspective of any particular entity directly or indirectly associated with opioid supply and demand. Instead, my perspective is based on my immersion in the field for an extended period, during which time I reviewed and scrutinized a relatively large and continually growing body of literature on virtually all aspects of opioids from a multitude of perspectives, including pharmacology, regulation, epidemiology, clinical medicine, economics, health economics, health management, product liability, and public health policy. Past interdisciplinary training in health economics was well-suited for such an endeavor given its broad focus on the intersections of statistics, economics, institutional economics, public health, epidemiology, biostatistics, and policy analysis.

The second reason for writing this book is rooted in my academic interests and past professional engagements. Exposure to the kinds of economic issues discussed in this book started while I was a doctoral student at the University of California, Berkeley, where I was able to study under some of the most prominent names in public health, economics, and business. During that time, I focused on the important role of organizations and institutions in shaping the economic contours of the U.S. health industry—an interest shared by my primary advisor, James C. Robinson. An important part of my studies included an in-depth analysis of regulation and deregulation, and

[69] All the material discussed and referenced in this book is publicly available, and none of the material is in any way related to confidential work products (e.g., other expert reports; deposition transcripts) associated with my engagement as an expert in the opioid MDL. In addition, the opinions expressed in this report are not in any way related to my engagement in the opioid MDL, and do not in any way reflect the positions and opinions of those who engaged me in the MDL. Finally, the research and writing of this book was not in any way supported by my clients in the MDL, nor did I (or my employer, Avalon Health Economics LLC) receive any financial support for researching and writing this book.

how regulatory institutions and resulting effects compared across three disparate industries: hospitals, telecommunications, and airlines.[70] Through a lens of institutional economics provided by Oliver Williamson, who served on my dissertation committee and would later win a Nobel Prize for his contributions to the field,[71] my studies focused on healthcare transactions, and how the organization of those transactions could be optimized within competitive markets, horizontally and vertically integrated systems, regulatory structures, or courts. Through these studies, which also included working closely with Berkeley regulatory economists Theodore Keeler and Kenneth Train, I was also able to conduct more in-depth studies of the nuances of the effects of regulation, factors leading to "regulatory failure," and the process of regulatory reform across multiple industries.

Some of the professional work that I have done throughout my career has focused on the economics of externalities and attributable abatement costs. Examples of these include studies of the externalities associated with tobacco outlet density and its impact on smoking prevalence, studies of the environmental externalities associated with tobacco production and use,[72] studies of the attributable costs of tobacco use, the attributable cost of calorically sweetened beverages ("CSBs"), the attributable costs of alcohol misuse, and causal factors associated with obesity.[73] In addition,

[70] Part of this work was published in J. E. Schneider, "Changes in the Effects of Mandatory Rate Regulation On Growth in Hospital Operating Costs, 1980–1996," *Review of Industrial Organization* 22, no. 4 (2003). Parts were also published as part of a book: R. L. Ohsfeldt and J. E. Schneider, *The Business of Health: The Role of Competition, Markets, and Regulation* (Washington, D.C.: The AEI Press, 2006).

[71] P. E. Earl and J. Potts, "A Nobel Prize for Governance and Institutions: Oliver Williamson and Elinor Ostrom," *Review of Political Economy* 23, no. 1 (2011).

[72] The environmental impact of tobacco has been a field of study of mine for over a decade. The work began with an engagement with the City of San Francisco, where I developed a model to estimate the costs of tobacco product waste ("TPW") in the City. This work led to San Francisco imposing a fee on tobacco sales intended to fund abatement costs attributable to TPW. Since then, I have published some articles on the topic and have been engaged in a variety of projects related to tobacco's environmental impact. These have included, for example, assisting the World Health Organization ("WHO") with their public relations activities surrounding World No Tobacco Day 2022, and participating in a large multi-year project with the State of California to develop tools to estimate environmental abatement costs. A recent example of this work is in Lam et al., "Modelling the global economic costs of tobacco product waste."

[73] Regarding causal factors associated with obesity, see generally K. Dick et al., "Mendelian randomization: estimation of inpatient hospital costs attributable to obesity," *Health Econ Rev* 11, no. 1 (2021).

over more than 35 years as a health economist, I have provided expert testimony in a wide variety of cases involving the calculation of attributable economic damages, including the use of statistical methods to determine costs attributable to various health and environmental factors. For most of these engagements, it was critical to gain an in-depth understanding of how state and local governments manage externalities associated with pollution, tobacco use, substance abuse, and poor diet (i.e., the attributable costs and abatement costs associated with the externalities) and identify the parties responsible for the externalities. Moreover, I was able to bring to these endeavors, and my current work on economic issues regarding opioids, a perspective based on my past studies in institutional economics, which is generally concerned with aligning organizational attributes with transaction attributes, and how organizations function internally and interact externally with each other and with governmental entities.

Finally, my reasons for writing this book are to offer an alternative to the way that we think about the economics of product liability and externalities in the context of the rapidly evolving way that business is conducted in the U.S. and globally, especially healthcare business. As mentioned above, the simple externality and abatement constructs from the past do not appear to work as well as they once may have, resulting in misconceptions, incomplete analyses, and inflated damages awards against a subset of easy targets. Insofar as governance and public policy leans increasingly more on the judicial system and courts to help correct instances where markets and regulatory systems fail,[74] then it is imperative to approach problems like the opioid crisis with all the tools that we have in our possession to develop a complete understanding of root causes, contributing factors, liability, and abatement. If we continue to miss opportunities to "get it right," we risk creating precedent that could in the future restrict or retard innovation, restrict access to health care,

[74] See generally T. D. Lytton, "Using litigation to make public health policy: theoretical and empirical challenges in assessing product liability, tobacco, and gun litigation," *J Law Med Ethics* 32, no. 4 (2004); J. S. Vernick et al., "Role of litigation in preventing product-related injuries," *Epidemiol Rev* 25 (2003); J. S. Vernick et al., "How litigation can promote product safety," *J Law Med Ethics* 32, no. 4 (2004); P. J. Cook, J. Ludwig, and A. Samaha, "Gun Control after Heller: Litigating against Regulation," in ***Regulation versus Litigation: Perspectives from Economics and Law***, ed. D. P. Kessler (Chicago, IL: National Bureau of Economic Research | The University of Chicago Press, 2011); Viscusi and Hersch, "Tobacco Regulation through Litigation."

increase costs, reduce productivity and efficiency, and, perhaps most importantly, mask the root causes of public health problems and other societal ills, thereby making the problems much harder to define, more difficult to fix, and slower to mitigate.[75] Put differently, to prevent another opioid crisis, we need to conduct due diligence to understand why it happened, who was responsible, how to fix it, and how to design institutional features and mechanisms to prevent it from happening again.

While it is tempting to think that outsized settlement payments by potentially responsible parties will serve as sufficient deterrence going forward, there are good reasons to disagree with this thinking. There were many entities involved either directly or indirectly in supplying the U.S. and the world with opioids, but only a small handful of them have been found accountable, and accountable for damages amounts that may or may not have any grounding in actual attributable costs or abatement costs. As the opioid litigation expanded, the list of responsible parties remained mired in decades-old thinking regarding the pharmaceutical supply chain, coupled with inaccurate assessments of abatement costs. This myopic thinking, it can be argued, can lead to a "suboptimal" use of the judicial system to improve public welfare, as many of the causal factors escape scrutiny and remain largely unchanged. Large abatement awards levied on a small number of convenient targets risk squandering many of the incentive features regarding deterrence. Hence, an added rationale for writing this book is to put forth an alternative approach to the analysis of public health harms and externalities, one that recognizes the complexities of today's health industry, and one that results in fewer unintended negative consequences, such as inhibiting future innovation, restricting access to health care, increasing costs, and obfuscating the importance of root causes.

1.9 Outline

The book is organized into nine chapters. The first set of chapters provides the necessary background regarding product liability research and analysis, the epidemiology of behaviors and harms potentially related to liability, and the economics of externalities. Following this introductory chapter, Chap. 2 ("Product Liability") defines and reviews the basic elements of

[75] See generally D. P. Kessler, "The Economic Effects of the Liability System," (Palo Alto, CA: Hoover Institution, 1999).

product liability from a law and economics perspective, including the usual methods economists utilize to study product liability, analysis of liability, and calculations of damages and abatement costs. The basic parameters of the U.S. opioid MDL are discussed. A brief overview of the pharmaceutical supply chain is also provided, given its importance in the opioid MDL. It is important to emphasize that the discussion of product liability put forth in Chap. 2 is from an economic perspective and is intended solely as background rather than as a complete recitation of the current status and interpretation of product liability laws. Chapter 3 ("Epidemiology") discusses the important role of epidemiology in product liability matters and presents some of the basic epidemiologic concepts and data relevant to product liability generally and to the opioid MDL specifically. Topics include prevalence estimates and the specific identification of harms, or "externalities." Chapter 4 ("Causation") focuses more in-depth on the causal factors linked to the growth in opioid supply and the emergence of the opioid crisis. Chapter 5 ("Responsibility") extends the discussion of causation into issues of responsibility and the allocation of liability to responsible parties. The analysis of responsibility and liability differs from the analysis of contributing factors in that it identifies potentially responsible parties associated with the increase in opioid utilization.

Chapters 6 and 7 address attributable costs and abatement costs, respectively. Attributable costs are what the legal profession typically refers to as economic damages, whereas abatement costs typically refer to the costs of mitigating the harms and externalities, or bringing them to an acceptable level. In each chapter, a "cost ceiling" model is developed based on published data, reports, and studies. The issues of potential remedies is taken up in Chap. 8 ("Remedies"), which provides an exploration of potential structural and organizational remedies to the challenge of high-risk medical products, in the context of the "regulation versus litigation" framework common to similar inquiries across other regulated industries. Finally, Chap. 9 ("Conclusions & Recommendations") summarizes the findings, discusses some important legal, economic, and policy implications, and provides some additional concluding remarks. The final chapter also offers some thoughts on how large healthcare mass torts might be more productively addressed in the future, given the lessons learned from the opioid crisis and the ensuing litigation.

References

Abramowitz, P. W., Chen, D. F., & Cobaugh, D. J. (2018, April 1). Multihospital health systems: Growing complexity of pharmacy enterprise brings opportunities and challenges. *Am J Health Syst Pharm*, *75*(7), 417–418.

Aliferov, E. (2018). The role of direct-injury government-entity lawsuits in the opioid litigation. *Fordham Law Review*, *87*.

Baron, D. P. (1989). Chapter 24 design of regulatory mechanisms and institutions. In *Handbook of Industrial Organization* (pp. 1347–447). Elsevier.

Barrett, J. C. (1994, October) Cellular and molecular mechanisms of asbestos carcinogenicity: Implications for biopersistence. *Environ Health Perspect 102* (Suppl 5), 19–23.

Barrett, J. C., Lamb, P. W., & Wiseman, R. W. (1989, May). Multiple mechanisms for the carcinogenic effects of asbestos and other mineral fibers. *Environ Health Perspect*, *81*, 81–9.

Baum, R. (2017). Interview with Richard Baum, acting director of U.S. National Drug Control Policy. In *FPC Briefing*. US. Department of State.

Bou-Samra, P., Chang, A., Azari, F., Kennedy, G., Segil, A., Guo, E., Marmarelis, M., Langer, C., & Singhal, S. (2023, June). Epidemiological, therapeutic, and survival trends in malignant pleural mesothelioma: A review of the National Cancer Database. *Cancer Med*, *12*(11), 12208–12220.

Bough, S.R., & Case-Halferty, A.E. (2021). A judicial perspective on approaches to MDL settlement. *UMKC Law Review*, *89*(4).

Brangham, W., & Hastings, D. (2024). "*Alcohol-related deaths surge in colorado with a higher mortality rate than opioids.* Public Broadcasting System (PBS), "News Hour".

Buchholz, T., Calabresi, G., Kessler, D., Viscusi, W.K., & Warren, E. (2000). Regulation through litigation: Assessing the role of bounty hunters and bureaucrats in the American regulatory regime. In *Conference Series* (No.2). Manhattan Institute.

Carroll, S.J., Hensler, D., Gross, J., Sloss, E.M., Schonlau, M., Abrahamse, A., & Ashwood, J.S. (2005). *Asbestos Litigation.* RAND Corportation | RAND Insititute for Civil Justice.

CDC. (2022). *Understanding the opioid overdose epidemic.* U.S. Centers for Disease Control and Prevention.

CDC. (2023). *Current cigarette smoking among adults in the United States.* U.S. Centers for Disease Control and Prevention.

CDC. (2024a). *Provisional drug overdose death counts.* In National Vital Statistics System. National Center for Health Statistics, Centers for Disease Control and Prevention.

CDC. (2024b). *U.S. overdose deaths decrease in 2023, first time since 2018.* U.S. Centers for Disease Control and Prevention, National Center for Health Statistics.

CDC. (2024c). *Understanding the opioid overdose epidemic.* U.S. Centers for Disease Control and Prevention.

Chen, P., Li, Y., Wu, D., Liu, F., & Cao, C. (2023). Secondhand smoke exposure and the risk of chronic obstructive pulmonary disease: A systematic review and meta-analysis. *Int J Chron Obstruct Pulmon Dis, 18*, 1067–1076.

Ciccarone, D. (2019, September 01). The triple wave epidemic: Supply and demand drivers of the US opioid overdose crisis. *International Journal of Drug Policy, 71*, 183–188.

Clark, C.D. (2017, July 5). How sensationalism compounds the opioid crisis. *Washington Post.*

Conlon, J. L. (2017, Febraury). Diethylstilbestrol: Potential health risks for women exposed in utero and their offspring. *Jaapa, 30*(2), 49–52.

Cook, P.J., Ludwig, J., & Samaha, A. (2011). Gun control after heller: Litigating against regulation. Edited by D. P. Kessler, In *Regulation versus litigation: Perspectives from economics and law.* National Bureau of Economic Research | The University of Chicago Press.

Cooter, R.D. (1991). Economic theories of legal liability. *Journal of Economic Perspectives 5*(3), 11–30.

Cooter, R.D., & Ulen, T. (2011). *Law and economics (6th Edition).* Pearson.

Cornes, R., & Sandler, T. (1986). *The theory of externalities, public goods, and club goods.* Cambridge University Press.

Dahlawi, S., Menezes, R. G., Khan, M. A., Waris A., Saifullah, & Naseer, M. M. (2021). Medical negligence in healthcare organizations and its impact on patient safety and public health: A bibliometric study. *F1000Res, 10*, 174.

Del Riccio, M., Vettori, V., Raimondi, S., Lorini, C., Masala, G., Cattaruzza, M. S., Mazzarella, L., et al. (2023, April). The clinical impact of continued smoking in patients with breast and other hormone-dependent cancer: A systematic literature review. *Crit Rev Oncol Hematol, 184*, 103951.

Díaz-Cruz, M. S., & Barceló, D. (2008, June). Trace organic chemicals contamination in ground water recharge. *Chemosphere, 72*(3), 333–342.

Dick, K., Schneider, J. E., Briggs, A., Lecomte, P., Regnier, S. A., & Lean, M. (2021, May 14). Mendelian randomization: Estimation of inpatient hospital costs attributable to obesity. *Health Econ Rev, 11*(1), 16.

Drucker, P.M. (2023). 'Accidental release reporting rule' requires owners, operators to disclose chemical accidents to chemical safety board. *The National Law Review, 15*(332).

Earl, P.E., & Potts, J. (2011, January 1). A nobel prize for governance and institutions: Oliver Williamson and Elinor Ostrom. *Review of Political Economy, 23*(1), 1–24.

Ellerbeck, S. (2023). *5 innovations that are revolutionizing global healthcare.* World Economic Forum.

Engstrom, N.F., & Rabin, R.L. (2021). Pursuing public health through litigation: Lessons from tobacco and opioids. *Stanford Law Review 73*(285).

Erdek, M. A. (2018, November 1). Pay-for-performance reimbursement for clinicians: Common sense or a Wolf in Sheep's clothing? *Pain Med, 19*(11), 2106–2108.

Esquibel, J. (2020). *Opioid crisis has cost Colorado's economy at least $21 billion.* Colorado Consortium for Prescription Drug Abuse Prevention.

Esser, M. B., Sherk, A., Liu, Y., & Naimi, T. S. (2024, Febraury 29). Deaths from excessive alcohol use—United States, 2016-2021. *MMWR Morb Mortal Wkly Rep, 73*(8), 154–61.

FDA. (2024). *Postmarketing requirements and commitments: Introduction.* U.S. Food and Drug Administration.

Florence, C., Luo, F., & Rice, K. (2021, January 1). The economic burden of opioid use disorder and fatal opioid overdose in the United States, 2017. *Drug Alcohol Depend, 218*, 108350.

Frischmann, B. M., & Ramello, G. B. (2022). Externalities, scarcity, and abundance. *Front Res Metr Anal, 7*, 1111446.

Garber, S. (2013). *Economic effects of product liability and other litigation involving the safety and effectiveness of pharmaceuticals.* RAND Institute for Civil Justice, RAND Corporation.

Gonzalez, E.A., & Valori, R.W. (2001). Medical monitoring claims are viable in Florida. *Florida Bar Journal, 75*(1).

Grosso, S. (2018). What is reasonable and what can be proved as reasonable: reflections on the role of evidence-based medicine and clinical practice guidelines in medical negligence claims. *Annals of Health Law 27*(1).

Guy, G. P., Jr., Zhang, K., Bohm, M. K., Losby, J., Lewis, B., Young, R., Murphy, L. B., & Dowell, D. (2017, July 7). Vital signs: Changes in opioid prescribing in the United States, 2006–2015. *MMWR Morb Mortal Wkly Rep, 66*(26), 697–704.

Hajat, C., Stein, E., Ramstrom, L., Shantikumar, S., & Polosa, R. (2021, December 4). The health impact of smokeless tobacco products: A systematic review. *Harm Reduct J, 18*(1), 123.

He, Z., Wu, H., Zhang, S., Lin, Y., Li, R., Xie, L., & Li, Z., et al. (2020, October). The association between secondhand smoke and childhood asthma: A systematic review and meta-analysis. *Pediatr Pulmonol, 55*(10), 2518–2531.

Helbling, T. (2010). What Are Externalities?. *Finance & Development 47*(4).

Higham, S., & Horwitz, S. (2022). *American Cartel: Inside the battle to bring down the opioid industry.* Twelve/Hachette Book Group.

Hilakivi-Clarke, L. (2014). Maternal exposure to diethylstilbestrol during pregnancy and increased breast cancer risk in daughters. *Breast Cancer Res 16*(2), 208.

Huang, A., Wu, K., Cai, Z., Lin, Y., Zhang, X., & Huang, Y. (2021, January). Association between postnatal second-hand smoke exposure and ADHD in children: A systematic review and meta-analysis. *Environ Sci Pollut Res Int, 28* (2), 1370–1380.

Humphreys, K., C. L. Shover, C. M. Andrews, A. S. B. Bohnert, M. L. Brandeau, J. P. Caulkins, J. H. Chen, et al. (2022, Febraury 5). Responding to the opioid crisis in North America and beyond: Recommendations of the Stanford-Lancet Commission. *Lancet 399*(10324), 555–604.

Hylton, K.N. (2013). The law and economics of products liability. *Notre Dame Law Review, 88*(5).

IMF. (2021). *GDP, current prices (Billions of U.S. Dollars).* International Monetary Fund.

Insurance Information Institute. (2023). *Facts + Statistics: Product Liability.* Insurance Information Institute.

Iyer, A., Seshadri, S., & Vasher, R. (2009). *Toyota supply chain management: A strategic approach to toyota's renowned system.* McGraw-Hill Companies.

Jain, S.K. (2015). *Economic analysis of liability rules.* Springer.

JEC. (2022). The economic toll of the opioid crisis reached nearly $1.5 trillion in 2020. In *Issue Brief.* U.S. Joint Economic Committee.

Kahan, L. G., & Blatnik, J. A. (2018, Febraury) Critical under-reporting of Hernia Mesh properties and development of a novel package label. *J Am Coll Surg, 226* (2), 117–1125.

Kannampallil, T. G., Schauer, G. F., Cohen, T., & Patel, V. L. (2011, December). Considering complexity in healthcare systems. *J Biomed Inform, 44*(6), 943–947.

Keefe, P.R. (2021). Empire of pain. Doubleday, *A division of penguin random house LLC.*

Kessler, D. P. (1999). *The economic effects of the liability system.* Hoover Institution.

KFF. (2005). *Follow the pill: Understanding the U.S. commercial pharmaceutical supply chain.* Kaiser Family Foundation.

Kim, J. H., & Scialli, A. R. (2011, July). Thalidomide: The tragedy of birth defects and the effective treatment of disease. *Toxicol Sci, 122*(1), 1–6.

Kitzen, J., J., Pergolizzi Jr., R. Taylor Jr., & Raffa, R. (2018). The role of medical literature, clinical trials and experimental research in drug product-injury litigation: A primer with two examples. *Pharmacology & Pharmacy 9*, 208–227.

La Merrill, M. A., Vandenberg, L. N., Smith, M. T., Goodson, W., Browne, P., Patisaul, H. B., & Guyton, K. Z., et al. (2020, January). Consensus on the key characteristics of endocrine-disrupting chemicals as a basis for hazard identification. *Nat Rev Endocrinol*, *16*(1), 45–57.

Lam, J., Schneider, J., Shadbegian, R., Pega, F., St. Claire, S., & Novotny, T. E. (2022, October 1). Modelling the global economic costs of tobacco product waste. *Bull World Health Organ*, *100*(10), 620–627.

Lex Machina. (2025). Lex Machina 2025 Torts Litigation Report. LexisNexis.

Lytton, T. D. (2004). Using litigation to make public health policy: Theoretical and empirical challenges in assessing product liability, tobacco, and gun litigation. *J Law Med Ethics*, *32*(4, Winter), 556–564.

Macy, B. (2018). *Dopesick*. Little, Brown and Company.

Malevolti, M. C., Maci, C., Lugo, A., Possenti, I., Gallus, S., Gorini, G., & Carreras, G. (2023, July 30). Second-hand smoke exposure and cervical cancer: A systematic review and meta-analysis. *J Cancer Res Clin Oncol*.

Mann, H. (2006). Is Fair and Equitable Fair, Equitable, Just, or Under Law?. *Proceedings of the Annual Meeting (American Society of International Law)*, *100*, 74–77.

McClung, K. (2021, July 28) Most of the money Oklahoma secured from opioid companies has gone unspent. *The Frontier*.

McGwin, G., Jr. (2010, November). Causation in epidemiology. *Am J Ophthalmol*, *150*(5), 599–601.

McLaughlin, P., & Sherouse, O. (2016). *The McLaughlin-Sherouse List: The 10 Most-Regulated Industries of 2014*. Mercatus Center, George Mason University.

Meier, B. (2018). *Pain Killer*. Random House.

NASEM. (2017). *Pain Management and the Opioid Epidemic: Balancing Societal and Indidivual Benefits and Risks of Prescription Opioid Use*. Edited by Bonnie, M. A. Ford and J. K. Phillips, in Consensus Study Report of National Academies of Sciences, Engineering and Medicine (NASEM). National Academies Press.

Nicholson, W., & Snyder, C. (2016). *Microeconomic Theory: Basic Principles and Extensions, 12th Edition*. Cengage Learning.

Novotny, T. E., & Zhao, F. (1999). Consumption and production waste: Another externality of tobacco use. *Tob Control*, *8*(1 Spring), 75–80.

Ohsfeldt, R.L., & Schneider, J.E. (2006). *The Business of Health: The Role of Competition, Markets, and Regulation*. The AEI Press.

Olavarria, O. A., Shah, P., Bernardi, K., Lyons, N. B., Holihan, J. L., Ko, T. C., Kao, L. S., & Liang, M. K. (2020, March). Lack of Regulations and Conflict of Interest Transparency of New Hernia Surgery Technologies. *J Surg Res*, *247*, 445–452.

Papandreou, A. A. (1994). *Externality and Institutions*. Clarendon Press.

Parascandola, M., & Weed, D. L. (2001, December). Causation in epidemiology. *J Epidemiol Community Health*, *55*(12), 905–12.

Parmar, M. P., Kaur, M., Bhavanam, S., Mulaka, G. S. R., Ishfaq, L., Vempati, R., M. F. C, et al. (2023, April). A Systematic Review of the Effects of Smoking on the Cardiovascular System and General Health. *Cureus, 15*(4), e38073.

Paterick, Z. R., Patel, N. J., Ngo, E., Chandrasekaran, K., Jamil Tajik, A., & Paterick, T. E. (2018, October). Medical liability in the electronic medical records era. *Proc (Bayl Univ Med Cent), 31*(4), 558–561.

Posner, R. A. (2011). Regulation (Agencies) versus Litigation (Courts). Edited by D. P. Kessler, in *Regulation Versus Litigation: Perspectives From Economics and Law*. The University of Chicago Press.

Quinones, S. (2015). *Dreamland*. Bloomsbury Press.

Rheingold, P. D. (1976, September–October). Litigation involving DES. *Women Health, 1*(5), 26–27.

Robotti, S. (2021, September 14). The heritable legacy of diethylstilbestrol: A bellwether for endocrine disruption in humans. *Biol Reprod, 105*(3), 687–689.

Rothman, K.J., Greenland, S., & Lash, T.L. (2008). *Modern Epidemiology* (Third Edition). Wolters Kluer; Lippincot WIlliams & Wilkins.

Saha, S. P., Bhalla, D. K., Whayne, T. F., Jr., & Gairola, C. (2007). Cigarette smoke and adverse health effects: An overview of research trends and future needs. *Int J Angiol, 16*(3 Fall), 77–83.

Schneider, J. E., Peterson, N. A., Kiss, N., Ebeid, O., & Doyle, A. S. (2011, May). Tobacco litter costs and public policy: A framework and methodology for considering the use of fees to offset abatement costs. *Tob Control, 20* (Suppl 1), i36–i41.

Schneider, J. E., Scheibling, C. M., Peterson, N. A., Granados, P. S., Fulton, L., & Novotny, T. E. (2020, June 30). Online Simulation Model to Estimate the Total Costs of Tobacco Product Waste in Large U.S. Cities. *Int J Environ Res Public Health, 17*(13).

Schneider, J.E. (2003, June 1). Changes in the Effects of Mandatory Rate Regulation On Growth in Hospital Operating Costs, 1980–1996. *Review of Industrial Organization, 22*(4), 297–312.

Shadel, W. G., Martino, S. C., Setodji, C. M., Dunbar, M., Scharf, D., & Creswell, K. G. (2019, June 1). Do graphic health warning labels on cigarette packages deter purchases at point-of-sale? An experiment with adult smokers. *Health Educ Res, 34*(3), 321–331.

Shiffman, M. A. (1994). Silicone breast implant litigation (Part 1). *Med Law 13* (7-8), 681–716.

Shleifer, A. (2010). Efficient Regulation. Edited by D. P. Kessler, in *Regulation Vs. Litigation: Perspectives From Economics and Law*. University of Chicago Press.

Silverman, C., & Appel, C.E. (2022). *Nuclear Verdicts: Trends, Causes, and Solutions*. U.S. Chamber of Commerce, Institute for Legal Reform.

Singh, R. (2021, September 27). Why Healthcare Market Complexity Is A Reason To Innovate, Not A Reason Not To. *Forbes.*

Spencer, M.R., Miniño, A.M., & Warner, M. (2022). Drug Overdose Deaths in the United States, 2001–2021 (Data Brief No. 457). In *NCHS Data Brief.* National Center for Health Statistics, U.S. Centers for Disease Control and Prevention.

Tyler, E., & Combs, R. (2023). 2023 Litigation Statistics Series: Multidistrict Litigation. Bloomberg Law.

Varney, T. (2017, April 19). Product Liability and Recall Claims Challenge Global Supply Chains. *Supply and Demand Chain Executive.*

Vernick, J. S., Mair, J. S., Teret, S. P., & Sapsin, J. W. (2003). Role of litigation in preventing product-related injuries. *Epidemiol Rev 25*, 90–98.

Vernick, J. S., Sapsin, J. W., Teret, S. P., & Mair, J. S. (2004). How litigation can promote product safety. *J Law Med Ethics*, *32*(4 Winter), 551–555.

Viscusi, W.K., & Hersch, J. (2011). Tobacco Regulation through Litigation. Edited by D. P. Kessler, in *Regulation Versus Litigation: Perspectives From Economics and Law.* National Bureau of Economic Research & The University of Chicago Press.

Viscusi, W.K., Vernon, J.M., & Harrington, J.E. (1995). *Economics of Regulation and Antitrust (Second Edition).* The MIT Press.

Webster, L. R., & Grabois, M. (2015, November). Current Regulations Related to Opioid Prescribing. *Pm R*, *7*(11 Suppl), S236–S247.

Xiong, X., Zhang, S., Liao, X., Du, J., Zheng, W., Hu, S., Wei, Q., & Yang, L. (2024, March 15). An umbrella review of the evidence associating occupational carcinogens and cancer risk at 19 anatomical sites. *Environ Pollut*, *345*, 123531.

Zhao, Y., Abebe, A., Qi, L., Zhang, M., & Zhang, X. (2019). New Advances in Biostatistics. *Journal of Probability and Statistics 2019*(1), 1352310.

Zhou, S., Ricafort, E., Bressler, D., & Devotsu, R. K. (2022, March). Litigation in tobacco control: Past, present and future. *Tob Control*, *31*(2), 291–295.

Zweifel, P. (2021, November 1). Innovation in health care through information technology (IT): The role of incentives. *Social Science & Medicine 289*, 114441.

CHAPTER 2

Product Liability

The chapter begins with a brief overview of the area of law known as product liability, which serves as the general legal framework within which the opioid litigation has taken place and serves as useful background information for the chapters that follow. In the U.S., generally, the issue of ensuring product safety is addressed through a mix of *ex ante* market incentives, *ex ante* regulation, and *ex post* liability. Markets generally provide incentives for firms to produce products that are safe and of reasonably good quality, and typically penalize firms that do not.[1] In some cases, particularly those in which consumers are at an information disadvantage or firms and consumers are unusually susceptible to uncertainty and opportunistic behavior, *ex ante* government regulation may result in more desirable outcomes than markets, or may be crafted in such a way as to enhance existing market incentives.[2] However, government regulation is far from perfect, and can also fail to result in desirable outcomes, and in some cases, it can make matters worse.[3] In such cases,

[1] W. K. Viscusi, "Market Incentives for Safety," *Harvard Business Review* 63 (1985).

[2] See generally A. E. Kahn, *The Economics of Regulation: Principles and Institutions* (Cambridge, MA: The MIT Press, 1988).

[3] For general discussions, refer to S. Breyer, *Regulation and Its Reform* (Cambridge, MA: Harvard University Press, 1982); S. Peltzman, "The Effects of Automobile Safety Regulation," in *Chicago Studies in Political Economy*, ed. G. J. Stigler (Chicago, IL: The

J. E. Schneider, *The Economics of Pain*, Global Perspectives on Wealth and Distribution,
https://doi.org/10.1007/978-3-032-20355-7_2

court ordering and *ex post* liability rules, such as those aimed at product liability, may complement inadequate market incentives or ineffective regulation in assuring sufficient levels of product safety and quality.[4] The opioid matter has some of the usual features of mass product liability torts, but also has some important differences. This chapter covers three topics, beginning with a brief overview of product liability generally. Product liability is a large and growing area of law, so the overarching goal of the chapter is to provide a broad overview of some of the main tenets rather than a complete recitation of all elements. More detailed descriptions of product liability law can be found elsewhere.[5] Second, the chapter then provides an overview of opioid litigation in the U.S., again providing a relatively brief sketch of the landscape due to the substantial scale and scope of the litigation. The final section reviews the pharmaceutical supply chain in the U.S., given its growing importance in product liability cases generally and its critical role in the U.S. opioid litigation.

2.1 Product Liability

Product liability is the area of law focused on the liability of one or more members of a supply chain for the production, distribution, and sale of products associated with alleged attributable harms or attributable excess costs.[6] More specifically, product liability "is concerned with the liability of manufacturers, retailers, distributors, importers, and others for the damage or loss caused by products which are defective, or which fail to meet the standards legitimately to be expected of them."[7] In this context,

University of Chicago Press, 1988b); "Toward a More General Theory of Regulation."; G. J. Stigler, "The Theory of Economic Regulation," ibid.

[4] R. A. Posner, "Regulation (Agencies) versus Litigation (Courts)," in *Regulation versus Litigation: Perspectives from Economics and Law*, ed. D. P. Kessler (Chicago, IL: The University of Chicago Press, 2011); R. W. Ide, "The Role of the Justice System in the Product Liability Debate," in *Product Liability and Innovation: Managing Risk in an Uncertain Environment*, ed. J. R. Hunziker and T. O. Jones (Washington, D.C.: National Academy Press, 1994).

[5] For example, refer to C. J. Miller and R. S. Goldberg, *Product Liability (Second Edition)* (New York, NY: Oxford University Press, 2004).

[6] For background, refer to Legal Information Institute, "Products Liability," (Ithica, NY: Cornell School of Law, 2023). Also refer to Miller and Goldberg, *Product Liability (Second Edition)*.

[7] *Product Liability (Second Edition)*., p. v.

"products" can have a broad interpretation, including manufactured consumer products like automobiles and medicinal products, but also "intermediate" products, such as raw materials, parts, land, building materials, software, and so on. In some cases, product liability can be extended to certain types of services.[8] Note that in healthcare applications, product liability is distinct from medical malpractice, as the latter is typically based on whether (or the degree to which) a provider followed applicable professional standards of care, such as the standards put forth in prevailing clinical practice guidelines applicable to the service provided.

Product liability claims generally can be grouped into four categories:[9] (1) products with inherent defects in design; that is, the product is manufactured as intended, but is later found to be associated with certain risks and harms; (2) products wherein transient defects are introduced in the manufacturing process, either by an unintentional manufacturing error (i.e., a discrete event or series of events) or manufacturer negligence (i.e., a flawed process); (3) products wherein manufacturers or suppliers allegedly misrepresented product efficacy or safety *ex ante*; and (4) products wherein manufacturers or suppliers allegedly failed to sufficiently inform or warn consumers and components of the supply chain of known risks associated with product use or exposure *ex post* (i.e., "failure to warn"). Product defects do not necessarily imply harm to consumers. For example, defects detected by manufacturers and suppliers may result in product recalls, and depending on circumstances and timing, such recalls may or may not prevent or otherwise precede harm or costs to customers.[10] Recalls may also result in contract disputes among various levels of the

[8] F. S. Baldwin, "Products Liability as it Applies to Service Transactions," *Journal of Air Law and Commerce* 43, no. 2 (1977).

[9] For definitional purposes, in the context of the objectives of this chapter, "products" is defined generally to include products or services (hereafter referred to generally as products), and can include specific or individual products (e.g., a defective product within a batch of otherwise non-defective products), batches of products (e.g., an entire batch of defective products, due to a manufacturing problem), or entire types of products or "product lines" (e.g., based on a design or configuration associated with potential harms, which can encompass multiple manufacturers).

[10] See, for example NHTSA, "Vehicle Safety Recall Completion Rates Report," in *Report to Congress* (Washington, D.C.: U.S. Department of Transportation, 2018). Also see S. Thirumalai and K.K. Sinha, "Product Recalls in the Medical Device Industry: An Empirical Exploration of the Sources and Financial Consequences," *Management Science* 57, no. 2 (2011).

supply chain, featuring a mix of product liability and contract law. In addition, some product liability and negligence litigation involves exposure to products (or components of products) known to cause harm (e.g., materials and food ingredients classified as potential carcinogens), regardless of whether such harm has occurred.[11] In some cases, exposures and harms associated with defective products and failures to warn may be considered as causal of a harm or public nuisance, examples of which include the litigation surrounding asbestos and tobacco.[12]

Failure to warn is often featured in product liability matters, but in some cases may overlap with various aspects of negligence litigation.[13] The failure to warn aspect of product liability cases can be featured in cases with or without inherent design defects.[14] In the case of the tobacco litigation, it was alleged that manufacturers understood the health hazards of smoking but failed to disclose this information in their marketing activities, advertising, and promotional materials.[15] Some analogous allegations have been featured in the opioid MDL, albeit with some important caveats which will be discussed later. In addition, product liability cases can involve large numbers of plaintiffs across multiple jurisdictions, in the form of class-action and MDL-type case consolidations, as featured in the asbestos, tobacco, and opioid matters. Other examples include "toxic torts," prominent examples of which include pesticides and dioxins.[16] Likewise, product liability cases can involve multiple defendants, due either to there being multiple producers of the same product or due to complex supply chains,

[11] See, for example, R. Balwierz et al., "Potential Carcinogens in Makeup Cosmetics," *Int J Environ Res Public Health* 20, no. 6 (2023).

[12] See generally L. Kendrick, "The Perils and Promise of Public Nuisance," *Yale Law Journal* 132, no. 3 (2023).

[13] See generally K. N. Hylton, "The Law and Economics of Products Liability," *Notre Dame Law Review* 88, no. 5 (2013).

[14] See generally M. S. Madden, "The Enduring Paradox of Products Liability Law Relating to Prescription Pharmaceuticals," *Pace Law Review* 21, no. 2 (2001).

[15] See generally R. A. Daynard, C. Bates, and N. Francey, "Tobacco litigation worldwide," *Bmj* 320, no. 7227 (2000); R. D. Hurt and C. R. Robertson, "Prying open the door to the tobacco industry's secrets about nicotine: the Minnesota Tobacco Trial," *Jama* 280, no. 13 (1998); J. L. Pauly et al., "Cigarettes with defective filters marketed for 40 years: what Philip Morris never told smokers," *Tob Control* 11 Suppl 1, no. Suppl 1 (2002); S. Zhou et al., "Litigation in tobacco control: past, present and future," ibid.31, no. 2 (2022).

[16] See generally T. W. Henderson, "Toxic tort litigation: medical and scientific principles in causation," *Am J Epidemiol* 132, no. 1 Suppl (1990).

with multiple upstream and downstream components. The asbestos matter, for example, cumulatively has involved thousands of defendants, including firms operating at various levels of myriad product supply chains. Similarly, in the case of opioids, there are numerous defendants, but the litigation has largely focused on a relatively narrow subset of potentially responsible parties. In cases where the supply chain is complex, the assigning of liability, which is a critical element of product liability litigation, may be equally complex.[17]

2.2 Information

All four types of product liability scenarios typically assume some level of information asymmetry between manufacturers and consumers, where members of the supply chain are presumed to possess comparatively more or better information regarding product safety relative to consumers.[18] Manufacturers and other supply chain entities may also possess comparatively more or better information processing capabilities.[19] The same information advantage may also accrue to regulators, who in most cases have access to more complete or more in-depth information than consumers and possess more advanced information processing capabilities. Consumers are assumed to possess some rudimentary ability to discern observable product quality and safety attributes, but with limitations; that is, they are generally assumed to behave in a "boundedly rational" manner, due to imperfect knowledge, asymmetrically distributed information, and bounded cognitive abilities.[20] Asymmetrically distributed information and processing capability give rise to several issues related to product liability. Manufacturers may, in some instances, behave opportunistically by reducing product quality and safety by decrements undetectable by boundedly rational consumers. This lowers production costs while potentially allowing manufacturers to maintain

[17] See generally K. Ross, "Technology Developments and the Risk of Product Liability," *In Compliance*, no. October 31 (2019).

[18] See generally Hylton, "The Law and Economics of Products Liability."

[19] K. J. Arrow, "The economics of information: An exposition," *Empirica* 23, no. 2 (1996).

[20] For a general discussion of bounded rationality, refer to O. E. Williamson, *The Mechanisms of Governance* (New York, NY: Oxford Univeristy Press, 1996). For a more in-depth discussion, see H. A. Simon, "Bounded Rationality," in *Utility and Probability*, ed. J. Eatwell, M. Milgate, and P. Newman (London: Palgrave Macmillan UK, 1990).

higher prices normally associated with higher levels of quality and safety. Consequently, in transactions with high information asymmetry, consumers may purchase products with quality and safety attributes that are not fully observable at the time of purchase and may in some cases pay prices associated with levels of quality and safety that are not aligned with product attributes. Information asymmetry can in some cases lead to opportunistic behavior on the part of manufacturers and distributors, who may view an information advantage as an opportunity to purposefully obfuscate product or service quality. Misrepresenting product attributes has the potential to exacerbate existing information asymmetries, putting consumers at a further disadvantage. Information asymmetry is generally elevated in healthcare transactions, given the gap in knowledge between treating physicians and patients, high search costs, and the relatively high level of uncertainty associated with diagnosis and treatment.[21]

2.3 Moral Hazard

In addition to information asymmetry, product liability matters often feature elements of "moral hazard." Broadly, moral hazard is described as a "lack of incentive to guard against risk where one is protected from its consequences."[22] In economics, moral hazard typically refers to organizations and consumers behaving opportunistically when insulated from the costs of those actions.[23] Moral hazard is particularly relevant in insurance

[21] See generally A. Blomqvist, "The doctor as double agent: Information asymmetry, health insurance, and medical care," *Journal of Health Economics* 10, no. 4 (1991); G. Bloom, H. Standing, and R. Lloyd, "Markets, information asymmetry and health care: towards new social contracts," *Soc Sci Med* 66, no. 10 (2008); O.A. Mascarenhas, R. Kesavan, and M.D. Bernacchi, "On Reducing Information Asymmetry in U.S. Health Care," *Health Marketing Quarterly* 30, no. 4 (2013); A. Y. Odisho and J. L. Gore, "Patient-centered approaches to creating understandable health information," *Urol Oncol* 35, no. 9 (2017); K. J. Arrow, "Uncertianty and the Welfare Economics of Medical Care," *The American Economic Review* 53, no. 5 (1963); "The economics of information: An exposition."; D. Haas-Wilson, "Arrow and the Information Market Failure in Health Care: The Changing Content and Sources of Health Information," in *Uncertain Times: Kenneth Arrow and the Changing Economics of Health Care*, ed. P. J. Hammer, D. Haas-Wilson, and W. M. Sage (Durham, NC: Duke University Press, 2003).

[22] Oxford Languages, "Definition of "Moral Hazard"," (Oxford, UK: Oxford University Press, Oxford, UK, 2023).

[23] For general background, refer to C. Parsons, "Moral Hazard in Liability Insurance," *The Geneva Papers on Risk and Insurance* 28, no. 3 (2003).

markets, and more generally in transactions and contracts wherein third-party payers are featured. For example, individuals with comprehensive automobile insurance may engage in riskier driving compared to those with no insurance. In the context of product liability, moral hazard may arise if consumers fail to use products as directed by the manufacturer or purchase insurance that lowers the costs associated with misuse.[24] In cases of third-party payment and insurance, moral hazard may be featured in circumstances where consumers "over-consume" products or services due to lower net prices and transaction costs or due to lower *ex post* costs of misuse. Likewise, another facet of moral hazard is that the purchase of liability insurance may in some cases result in the underprovision of product and service quality and safety.[25] In healthcare markets, some degree of moral hazard is typically present among those with public or private health insurance. Health insurance lowers costs to consumers at the transaction level, and lower transaction prices can lead to higher consumption (and in some cases, over-consumption) of medical care.[26] Also, insurance may lead to consumers engaging in higher levels of riskier or unhealthy behaviors, as health insurance and third-party payers may lower the costs associated with such behaviors.[27] Product risks may in some cases vary according to proper versus improper use by consumers; if the product is not found to be defective when used properly (i.e., "as directed"), manufacturer liability may be reduced. Moral hazard can also intensify in settings where consumers recognize that manufacturers can be found liable for consumer misuse, which may discourage consumers from exercising the levels of caution in product use that they might have otherwise exercised.[28]

[24] Refer to E. A. Helland and A. Tabarrok, "Product Liability and Moral Hazard: Evidence from General Aviation," *The Journal of Law and Economics* 55, no. 3 (2012).

[25] See generally Parsons, "Moral Hazard in Liability Insurance."

[26] See generally L. Einav and A. Finkelstein, "Moral Hazard in Health Insurance: What We Know and How We Know It," *J Eur Econ Assoc* 16, no. 4 (2018).

[27] For example, there is some evidence of behavior effects in obesity; see generally J. Bhattacharya and N. Sood, "Health insurance and the obesity externality," *Adv Health Econ Health Serv Res* 17 (2007); I. R. Kelly and S. Markowitz, "Incentives in obesity and health insurance," *Inquiry* 46, no. 4 (2009).

[28] Parsons, "Moral Hazard in Liability Insurance."

2.4 Uncertainty

Cases concerning alleged defects in design typically face an explicit or implicit "risk-benefit" type of analysis to determine whether the benefit of the product, as designed, outweighs the risks associated with product use. This type of risk-benefit assessment is common in regulation and litigation involving healthcare products, such as medical devices and pharmaceuticals. Pharmaceuticals, for example, typically have known utility and known risks, both of which are assessed pre-market in the form of multiphase clinical trials and other clinical studies. Data pertaining to utility and risks are also assessed post-market through monitoring and surveillance, with explicit mechanisms to track post-market product safety and performance.[29] Clinical data regarding risks and adverse events are associated with some degree of uncertainty, which is addressed at least in part by confidence intervals around point estimates, measures of statistical significance, and sensitivity analyses.[30] The presence of uncertainty and known risks is not *per se* an indicator of product defects but can instead be viewed as the result of an informed risk-benefit tradeoff. For example, for all prescription drugs, the FDA requires that drug labeling incorporate relatively detailed information regarding known side effects, potential adverse events, and other known risks. That is, the drug is essentially approved alongside a list of acceptable and relatively well-described product "defects." Accordingly, FDA labeling is a regulatory approach to ameliorating information asymmetry between manufacturers and consumers, via the clinical prescriber as intermediary.[31] There are myriad

[29] For example, for pharmaceuticals with expected higher risks, the FDA may require a post-market "Risk Evaluation and Mitigation Strategy" or "REMS," to "help ensure the benefits of the medication outweigh its risks." See generally FDA, "Risk Evaluation and Mitigation Strategies | REMS," (Washington, D.C.: U.S. Food and Drug Administration, 2023b)."

[30] See generally B. Djulbegovic, "Articulating and responding to uncertainties in clinical research," *J Med Philos* 32, no. 2 (2007); P. K. Han, "Conceptual, methodological, and ethical problems in communicating uncertainty in clinical evidence," *Med Care Res Rev* 70, no. 1 Suppl (2013); R. J. Levine, "Uncertainty in Clinical Research," *Law, Medicine and Health Care* 16, no. 3–4 (1988); A. Schnarr and M. Mertz, "States of Uncertainty, Risk-Benefit Assessment and Early Clinical Research: A Conceptual Investigation," *Sci Eng Ethics* 28, no. 6 (2022).

[31] In its drug vetting and approval process, the FDA is in a sense signaling to consumers (usually via prescriber intermediaries) that a drug is safe to use; thus, product liability cases involving assessments of divergence between "consumer expectations" of quality and safety

examples of approved prescription drugs that are associated with significant clinical benefit ***and*** significant side effects and adverse events,[32] and the post-approval presumption is generally that physicians serve as the final arbiter of the risk-benefit tradeoff facing a particular patient.[33] This issue is important and will be revisited in other parts of the book.

In addition, in such cases, it is not only important to consider risks and benefits to consumers, but from a policy perspective it may also be important to consider the impact of product liability on other factors, such as innovation, access, efficiency, productivity, and costs. Innovation has the potential to be restrained by excessive liability exposure.[34] As manufacturers observe higher levels of post-market uncertainty regarding liability combined with substantial damages awards, the risk-benefit dynamics change, and the decision to invest in R&D and bring innovative products to market can be meaningfully impacted, especially for products with inherent risks, such as pharmaceuticals and medical devices.[35] Access can also be affected by liability, as preemptive actions and court decisions can lead to loss of access, in some cases, including loss of access in product markets unaffected by the dispute.[36] For example, in the case of opioids, restrictions in supply in recent years have been a concern among clinicians

and the manufacturers provision of a community standard level of quality and safety would necessarily involve an assessment of the effectiveness of the FDA approval process for the drug in question. For a general discussion of consumer expectations, refer to Hylton, "The Law and Economics of Products Liability."

[32] For an overview refer to J. J. Coleman and S. K. Pontefract, "Adverse drug reactions," *Clin Med (Lond)* 16, no. 5 (2016).

[33] BMJ, "Risk:benefit analysis of drugs in practice," *Drug and Therapeutics Bulletin* 33, no. 5 (1995).

[34] See generally J. R. Hunziker and T. O. Jones, eds., *Product Liability and Innovation: Managing Risk in an Uncertain Environment* (Washington, D.C.: National Academy Press, 1994); W. K. Viscusi and M. J. Moore, "Product liability, research and development, and innovation," *Journal of Political Economy* 101, no. 1 (1993); A. Galasso and H. Luo, "Product Liability Litigation and Innovation: Evidence from Medical Devices," in *NBER Working Paper No. 32,215* (Cambridge, MA: National Bureau of Economic Research, 2024).

[35] P. Citron, "Medical Devices, Component Materials, and Product Liability," in *Product Liability and Innovation: Managing Risk in an Uncertain Environment*, ed. J. R. Hunziker and T. O. Jones (Washington, D.C.: National Academy Press, 1994).

[36] W. M. Sage, "Drug Product Liability and Health Care Delivery Systems," *Stanford Law Review* 40, no. 4 (1988).

treating patients who would clearly benefit from opioid-based treatment.[37] Undue liability has also been shown to increase costs and prices. For example, Manning found that as much as 50% of the differences in drug prices between the U.S. and Canada can be attributable to differences in product liability regimes.[38] This effect, which seems particularly large, is likely associated with differences in the probability of lawsuits being filed in each country, as well as the associated monetary size of those claims. One researcher observed, for example, that Canadians are "less aggressive in their use of the civil justice system in seeking redress for personal injury."[39] Finally, excessive liability can decrease productivity and efficiency in the associated industries. For example, Kessler and others found that "States that adopt liability-decreasing reforms experience approximately 1–2% greater aggregate productivity growth than states that do not, measured in terms of gross state product per worker."[40]

2.5 Responsibility

Product cases require some means of assigning responsibility and apportioning alleged harms to defendants, a process often considered one of the most challenging aspects of tort law.[41] Liability can be assigned using an

[37] See, for example, A. C. Enzinger et al., "Racial and Ethnic Disparities in Opioid Access and Urine Drug Screening Among Older Patients With Poor-Prognosis Cancer Near the End of Life," *J Clin Oncol* 41, no. 14 (2023); R. Sinatra, "Causes and consequences of inadequate management of acute pain," *Pain Med* 11, no. 12 (2010); J. Arthur et al., "Healthcare provider perceptions and reported practices regarding opioid prescription for patients with chronic pain," *Res Sq* (2023); R. N. Jamison et al., "Beliefs and attitudes about opioid prescribing and chronic pain management: survey of primary care providers," *J Opioid Manag* 10, no. 6 (2014); Z. Razouki et al., "Attributes, Attitudes, and Practices of Clinicians Concerned with Opioid Prescribing," *Pain Med* 20, no. 10 (2019); J. C. Hackworth et al., "The burden of acute pain in the U.S. in the wake of the opioid crisis," *Frontiers in Pain Research* Volume 6–2025 (2025).

[38] R. L. Manning, "Products Liability and Prescription Drug Prices in Canada and the United States," *The Journal of Law & Economics* 40, no. 1 (1997).

[39] B. A. Thomas, "A Canadian View of the Product Liability Aspects of Innovation," *Canada-U.S. Law Journal (Case Western Reserve)* 93 (1989).

[40] D. P. Kessler, "The Economic Effects of the Liability System," (Palo Alto, CA: Hoover Institution, 1999).

[41] See generally S. K. Jain, *Economic Analysis of Liability Rules* (New York, NY: Springer, 2015).

"all or nothing" approach, or liability can be apportioned between defendants and claimants. In some cases, liability can be further apportioned among multiple claimants or among multiple defendants. Using simple shorthand, we can think of liability "λ" where $0 \leq \lambda \leq 1$; that is, if a defendant is assigned full liability, then $\lambda = 1$, and if they are found not liable, then $\lambda = 0$. A finding of "strict liability" implies that the defendant is liable regardless of the circumstances associated with the cause of a defective or harmful product (i.e., $\lambda = 1$). Generally, "according to prevailing academic usage, strict liability is liability without wrongdoing. A defendant subject to strict liability must pay damages irrespective of whether she has met, or failed to meet, an applicable standard of conduct. Action that causes harm is all that is required."[42] In other words, in the product liability context, strict liability operates on the supposition that the fact "that some defective products slip past the best quality control is no excuse."[43]

In cases where strict liability is not applicable, liability is typically based on the degree of negligence, such that $0 \leq \lambda \leq 1$.[44] Negligence is often expressed generally as failing to take some "cost-justified" precaution, with liability apportioned λ to responsible parties and $1\text{-}\lambda$ to claimants.[45] For example, a court may determine that a manufacturer is 60% responsible for harm alleged to have been caused by one of their products, but that the consumer is reasonably responsible for the other 40% due to alleged improper use. In the case of multiple responsible parties, an additional liability rule is required, whereby each responsible party is apportioned a share of responsibility (ϕ) such that $\Sigma\phi \leq 1$ across all responsible parties.[46] Accordingly, in the preceding example where manufacturers bore 60% of

[42] J. C. Goldberg and B. C. Zipursky, "The Strict Liability in Fault and the Fault in Strict Liability," *Fordham Law Review* 85, no. 2 (2016). (p. 745).

[43] R. D. Cooter, "Economic Theories of Legal Liability," *Journal of Economic Perspectives* 5, no. 3 (1991).

[44] Jain, *Economic Analysis of Liability Rules.* (p. 35).

[45] For example, as Jain (2015) describes it, "whether a party is adjudged to be negligent or not depends on whether the opposite party is able to show the existence of some cost-justified precaution which could have been taken but was not taken" and that "a part id deemed to be negligent if [and only if] it can be shown that the party could have averted some harm by taking care which would have cost less than the loss due to harm." Ibid. (p. 79).

[46] Note that there are cases where some proportion of liability can also be assigned and apportioned to "absent" defendants. This will be discussed in greater detail in Chap. 8.

the liability, if there were three manufacturer defendants determined to be proportionally responsible for the harm (i.e., $\phi = 0.33$), each would have liability equal to about 20% of the attributable harm [i.e., $\lambda(\phi) = 0.60 \times 0.33 = 0.198$].

Product liability and negligence cases may also feature considerations as to whether an alleged harm is "remote" or "speculative." A harm may be considered "too remote" if it can be shown that some intermediate factor or set of factors creates a disconnect between the actions of the manufacturer and any resulting harm. Examples include products disproportionately subject to resale, repackaging, repurposing, or having a higher probability of consumer misuse. Another example may be a possible causal agent associated with a disease that develops over a relatively long period of time and has multiple contributing factors, where "the injured party may have been exposed to a variety of potentially harmful substances, likely as the result of actions by a variety of different actors."[47] For example, the attribution of severe obesity to a single type of food product would likely be difficult given at least three factors: (1) the wide variety of foods featured in the standard diet, (2) the varying impact of different foods on metabolic health, and (3) the role of other factors associated with weight gain, such as exercise and sleep.[48] Similarly, a harm may be considered "too speculative" if the available facts, data, and statistical tools cannot reliably or accurately attribute causation of harm to the product and associated defendants.[49] Another litmus test of whether a causal link is "too speculative" is whether the harm would have occurred in the absence of the actions of a potentially responsible party. This is typically referred to as a "but for" test, which asks the question "but for the existence of X,

[47] HLR, "Causation in Environmental Law: Lessons from Toxic Torts," *Harvard Law Review* 128, no. 8 (2015).

[48] See generally B. Masood and M. Moorthy, "Causes of obesity: a review," *Clinical Medicine* 23, no. 4 (2023).

[49] See generally Cooter, "Economic Theories of Legal Liability." Also note that the attribution challenge grows with the complexity of the causal pathway. For example, in the case of medicinal products, there may exist multiple causal factors for the same health condition (e.g., a particular type of cancer), and the ability to disentangle causal factors is heavily dependent on data availability, data time frames (e.g., whether "long-term follow-up" data are available), and the uncertainty of data analyses (e.g., standard errors of regression coefficients and other assessments of the sensitivity of results to small changes in parameter estimates and model assumptions).

would Y have occurred?"[50] The "but for" test with respect to the opioid crisis might be something like "but for the increase in prescription opioids, would the U.S. opioid crisis have occurred?" The answer to this question is of course very complicated, because the increase in the supply of prescription opioids was attributable to numerous factors, and another complicating factor is the existence of large and growing markets for illicit opioids. This issue will be revisited in Chap. 4 in the context of contributing factors.

2.6 Opioid Litigation

The national opioid litigation and the opioid MDL have been briefly discussed above, but it warrants some additional description given the unique attributes and features of the cases. To begin, the genesis of the litigation dates to the early 2000s, when states and counties began filing lawsuits against opioid manufacturers following reports of allegedly deceptive advertising and failing to warn the medical community and consumers of the potential addictive nature of opioids.[51] The legal frameworks for the initial wave of cases varied considerably by state and by defendant, but typically included claims of alleged negligence, product liability, breach of warranty, violation of state consumer protection laws, negligent marketing, and fraud.[52] Alleged failure to warn was an increasingly important factor in these cases, as some evidence surfaced that suggested that some manufacturers may have been aware of higher than expected opioid risks but continued actively marketing the products and failed to sufficiently share and disseminate that information to physicians and consumers and other entities along the pharmaceutical supply chain.[53]

As the volume of such cases grew, in 2017 the cases were consolidated into the MDL in the Northern District of Ohio Eastern Division, presided over by Judge Dan Polster. The cases were to be tried first in a series of 11

[50] HLR, "Rethinking Actual Causation in Tort Law," *Harvard Law Review* 130, no. 8 (2017).

[51] R. L. Haffajee and M. M. Mello, "Drug Companies' Liability for the Opioid Epidemic," *N Engl J Med* 377, no. 24 (2017).

[52] R. C. Ausness, "Opioid Lawsuits: Is There Any End in Sight?," *Health Matrix: The Journal of Law Medicine* 33, no. 1 (2023).

[53] This is discussed in greater detail in Chap. 4. See generally Haffajee and Mello, "Drug Companies' Liability for the Opioid Epidemic."

"bellwether" counties. A recent abatement order from the court summarized the structure as follows: "The chosen [bellwether] cases all include as defendants various types of participants in the opioid drug industry, including manufacturers (who make the opioids); distributors (who convey the opioids down the supply chain); and pharmacies (who dispense the opioids to end-user patients)."[54] In summarizing the main thrust of the complaints, the Court further stated "In each bellwether case, the plaintiffs are local governmental entities [. . .] which assert, among other claims, that the defendants' actions and non-actions led to a *severe oversupply* of prescription opioids, which ultimately created a *public nuisance*" (emphasis added). As of 2023, there were more than 3,300 cases consolidated in the opioid MDL, with plaintiffs consisting mainly of a mix of city and county governments and individuals.[55] Primary defendants in the MDL have included manufacturers (e.g., Purdue Pharma, Johnson & Johnson, Janssen Pharmaceuticals, Teva, and others), large independent pharmaceutical distributors (e.g., Cardinal Health, AmerisourceBergen, and McKesson), and large retail pharmacy chains (e.g., Rite Aid, Walmart, Walgreens, and CVS).[56] Other defendants include a variety of related healthcare businesses, such as pharmacy benefit managers and supermarket-based pharmacies. As of 2023, several settlements had been reached with manufacturers, distributors, and large retail pharmacies, totaling more than $55 billion, with additional settlements expected.[57]

The legal framework within which the MDL cases have been tried has been mainly based on opioids and opioid-attributable harms as a public nuisance.[58] That is, claimants have argued that the opioid crisis is not due

[54] Opioid MDL, "MDL 2804 Case No. 1:17-md-2804 Judge Dan Aaron Polster: Abatement Order," in *Re: National Opioid Litigation* (Ohio: United States District Court Northern District of Ohio, Eastern Division, 2022).

[55] E. Tyler and R. Combs, "2023 Litigation Statistics Series: Multidistrict Litigation," (New York, NY: Bloomberg Law, 2023).

[56] See generally J. Mackie, "Prescription Opioid Lawsuit Guide (2023)," *Forbes*, no. June 2 (2023).

[57] D. Ovalle, "Governments get nearly $19 billion more in opioid lawsuit settlements," *Washington Post*, no. June 9 (2023); KFF, "Payback: Tracking the Opioid Settlement Cash," in *Health News* (Menlo Park, CA: Kaiser Family Foundation, 2025).

[58] CRS, "Overview of the Opioid Litigation and Related Settlements and Settlement Proposals," in *Legal Sidebar* (U.S. Congressional Research Service, 2019); M. J. Purcell, "Settling High: A Common Law Public Nuisance Response to the Opioid Epidemic," *Columbia Journal of Law and Social Problems* 52, no. 1 (2018).

to any inherent or transient product defects; rather, it is based on the assertion that the misuse of a non-defective product has resulted in a public nuisance and the existence of a negative externality.[59] Claimants have further argued that some proportion of misuse is at least partly attributable to the increase in supply of prescription opioids. Public nuisance is broadly defined as an "unreasonable interference with a right common to the general public."[60] In the opioid MDL, "[plaintiffs] claim that the opioid products made or distributed by the defendants are a public nuisance under relevant state law—that is, that they constitute an unreasonable interference with a right held by the general public, in this case by jeopardizing public health and welfare."[61] Public nuisance can, in some cases, generally align with the economic concept of externalities;[62] for example, in a case involving manufacturers of products used illegally to produce illicit methamphetamine, the Arkansas Supreme Court defined a public nuisance as the "conduct by one landowner which unreasonably interferes [with] the use and enjoyment of the lands of another."[63] Whereas an externality represents a cost external to a transaction (e.g., air pollution incident to the production of automobiles), a public nuisance is more broadly defined as any attributable interference with a public right. In the case of pollution, it can be considered both an externality, incident to production, as well as a public nuisance, present in the environment due to actions or inactions on behalf of potentially responsible parties.

In the discussion and analyses that follow, the economic framework of externalities is applied to opioids, leaving the legal applicability of the

[59] The term "non-defective" is used here because, as discussed in the next chapter, most opioid products have (and continue to have) evidence-based clinical utility in several therapeutic areas; that is, the products are not *per se* defective. That said, some opioid products were considered, even after FDA approval, to be less safe than others. For a discussion, refer to A. M. Drewes et al., "Differences between opioids: pharmacological, experimental, clinical and economical perspectives," *Br J Clin Pharmacol* 75, no. 1 (2013). In product liability generally, "a drug is defectively designed if no reasonable health care provider with knowledge of all relevant facts would prescribe the drug for any class of patients." Miller and Goldberg, *Product Liability (Second Edition)*. (p. 313).

[60] Kendrick, "The Perils and Promise of Public Nuisance."

[61] Ibid.

[62] K. N. Hylton, "The Economics of Public Nuisance Law and the New Enforcement Actions," in *Searle Center Public Nuisance Roundtable Working Paper* (Chicago, IL: Northwestern University Searle Center Research Roundtable on Public Nuisance, 2010).

[63] Ausness, "Opioid Lawsuits: Is There Any End in Sight?."

public nuisance approach for legal scholars and experts to debate.[64] It should be noted, however, that the courts have ruled against the applicability of the public nuisance framework in a number of recent decisions. Most notably, in the wake of the Ohio retail pharmacy trial, the U.S. Court of Appeals for the Sixth Circuit requested that the Ohio Supreme Court rule on the extent to which the Ohio Product Liability Act ("OPLA") restricted the right to file public nuisance claims against product makers and sellers.[65] The Ohio Supreme Court subsequently ruled that OPLA "eliminated all forms of common law public nuisance cases for the sale of products and that the OPLA governs any public nuisance claim."[66] Legal scholars have similarly argued the limitations of public nuisance approaches to product liability; for example, Citera and Steiner characterized the problem of applying public nuisance law to the opioid crisis as being "unprincipled, impractical, and unworkable," adding that the claims "contravene the established products liability and regulatory regimes to which the opioid supply chain is answerable" and that "the judicial forum is ineffective for the crisis."[67]

Defense arguments in the opioid cases, including cases that predate the MDL formation, have evolved alongside the claimant shift from a product liability framework to a public nuisance framework. Apart from a direct challenge of the appropriateness of a public nuisance framework, these arguments have generally been along the lines of contending that the causal pathway between prescription opioid supply and opioid harms is "too speculative" and "too remote," and that supply and utilization of legal prescription opioids do not *per se* constitute a public nuisance or negative externality.[68] The "too speculative" argument by defendants has mainly been

[64] There is a relatively large volume of legal discourse on this topic. See, for example, Kendrick, "The Perils and Promise of Public Nuisance." Also see F.A. Citera and J. Steiner, "Prescription for Failure: Public Nuisance Claims Against the Opioid Industry," *U. Mia. L. Rev.* 79, no. 2 (2025).

[65] See generally D. Trevas, "Public Nuisance Lawsuits Cannot Be Pursued Against Pharmacies Selling Prescription Opioids," *Court News Ohio* Dec. 10 (2024).

[66] Ibid.

[67] Citera and Steiner, "Prescription for Failure: Public Nuisance Claims Against the Opioid Industry."

[68] See, for example, the ruling of U.S. District Judge David A. Faber of the Southern District of West Virginia who argued that public nuisance was an inappropriate framework for assessing opioid externalities, for many of the same reasons argued by defendants. For

applied to extrapolations of future abatement costs, which, they have argued, cannot be accurately attributed to the past supply of legally prescribed opioids, even if defendants were found to be responsible for past levels of supply.[69] The "too remote" argument follows along similar attribution lines, with defendants arguing, variously, that there is no reliable means of attributing harms associated with OUD to specific actions of the defendants related to marketing, distribution, and dispensing, even if some of those actions were found to be associated with an increased supply of legally prescribed opioids.[70] In addition, defendants have submitted that they possess relatively little control over the misuse of opioids; in other words, once the opioid supply leaves the hands of the manufacturers and distributors, and after a legal opioid prescription is issued to a patient, the healthcare system has little or no ability to control the use or misuse of the drug, including the prevention of diversion, misuse, and progression to OUD. Along the same lines, defendants have argued that even if the volume of opioids sourced from the healthcare system were to shrink dramatically, the opioid crisis would persist due to the rising prevalence of polysubstance abuse and the increasing availability of illicit opioids.[71] This last argument has some empirical basis; since 2013, the supply of prescription opioids has been in steady decline, but the supply of illicit opioids, mainly fentanyl, has been rising;[72] thus, with each passing year, whatever harms that could reasonably be attributable to prescription opioids, if any, would be expected to diminish rapidly. However, claimants have argued that the growth in illicit opioids is largely due to the role of past prescription opioid supply in creating illicit markets by fueling demand. Defendants in turn have countered by

a brief overview, see D. Fisher, "Latest opioid ruling puts MDL judge further out of step on public nuisance," *West Virginia Record* July 6 (2022).

[69] Opioid MDL, "MDL 2804 Case No. 1:17-md-2804 Judge Dan Aaron Polster: Abatement Order."

[70] Ibid.

[71] See generally Ausness, "Opioid Lawsuits: Is There Any End in Sight?."

[72] See generally G. C. Alexander et al., "Effect of reductions in opioid prescribing on opioid use disorder and fatal overdose in the United States: a dynamic Markov model," *Addiction* 117, no. 4 (2022); D. Ciccarone, "The rise of illicit fentanyls, stimulants and the fourth wave of the opioid overdose crisis," *Curr Opin Psychiatry* 34, no. 4 (2021); S. S. Shin et al., ""It wasn't here, and now it is. It's everywhere": fentanyl's rising presence in Oregon's drug supply," *Harm Reduct J* 19, no. 1 (2022); C. L. Shover et al., "Longitudinal changes in co-involved drugs, comorbidities, and demographics of methamphetamine-related deaths in Los Angeles County," *J Subst Use Addict Treat* 151 (2023).

arguing that illicit opioid markets have been in existence for decades and were not created by an oversupply of prescription opioids.[73] Put differently, another complicating factor in any "but for" analysis of the opioid crisis is the critical role of illicit opioids, which long predates the opioid crisis. Indeed, even in the absence of prescription opioids, illicit opioid markets in the U.S. constituted its own crisis based on the movement of large drug cartels into U.S. illicit opioid markets in the 1980s (from Southeast Asia) and 1990s (from Colombia and Mexico).[74] These arguments will be revisited later in the book.

2.7 Institutional Dynamics

The concept of the "pharmaceutical supply chain" has been a central feature of the opioid crisis and the MDL. Supply-side dynamics and industry institutional features play a critical role in the economics of externalities and in product liability litigation. For example, the long-running asbestos mass tort litigation began with a handful of large producers and users of asbestos materials, such as ship builders and makers of construction materials, but decades later the litigation has evolved to include more than 8,000 defendants across roughly 80 different types of industries, including a mix of intermediate suppliers and end-users.[75] As alluded to above, the pharmaceutical supply chain is complex and will be referenced throughout the remainder of this book, and some of the specific features will be revisited later and discussed in greater depth. Most importantly, the pharmaceutical supply chain is more complex than most product supply chains.[76] In addition to its core supply channel oriented around biotechnology firms, manufacturers, and distributors, it is regulated by multiple government agencies and myriad

[73] See generally A. Sajan, T. Corneil, and S. Grzybowski, "The street value of prescription drugs," *Cmaj* 159, no. 2 (1998); T. Wainwright, *Narconomics: How to Run a Drug Cartel* (New York, NY: PublicAffairs / Perseus, 2016).

[74] See, for example, J. T. Donahoe and A. Soliman, "What fueled the illicit opioid epidemic? New evidence from a takeover of white powder heroin markets," in *CEP Discussion Papers dp2073* (London, UK: Centre for Economic Performance, London School of Economics, 2025).

[75] See generally S. J. Carroll et al., "Asbestos Litigation," (Santa Monica, CA: RAND Corporation | RAND Insititute for Civil Justice, 2005).

[76] See generally F. M. Scherer, "The Pharmaceutical Industry," in *Handbook of Health Economics (Volume 1)*, ed. A. J. Culyer and J. P. Newhouse (New York, NY: Elsevier Science B.V., 2000).

governing bodies that heavily impact the volume and distribution of drugs as they move through the core supply channels and into the hands of patients. This process is depicted schematically in Fig. 2.1.

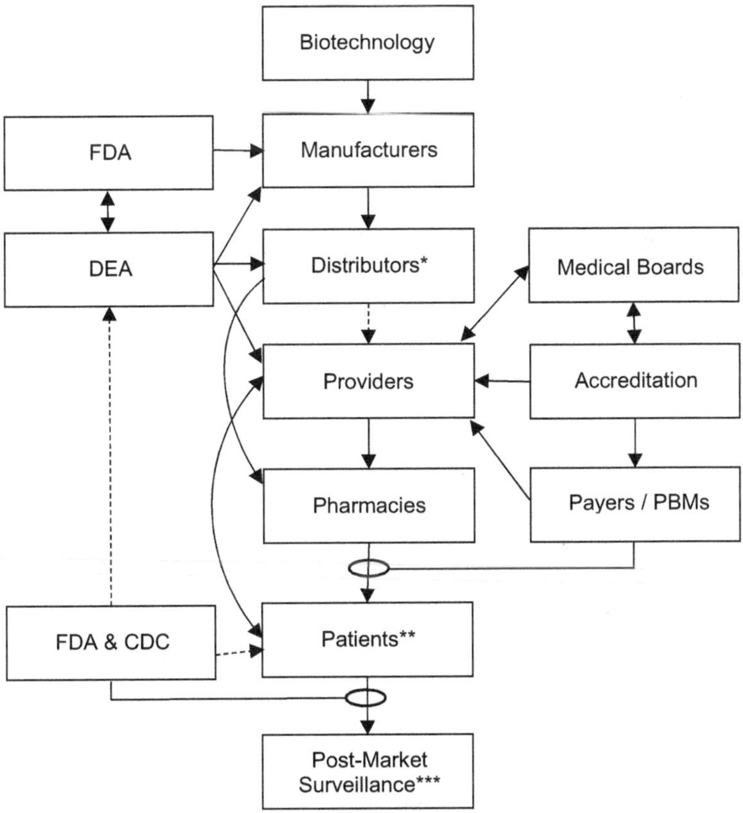

Fig. 2.1 Key Elements of the U.S. Pharmaceutical Supply Chain. *Notes* FDA = U.S. Food & Drug Administration; DEA = U.S. Drug Enforcement Administration; CDC = U.S. Centers for Disease Control & Prevention; PBM = Pharmacy Benefit Manager; *The terms "distributors" and "wholesalers" are used interchangeably; **The terms "patients" and "consumers" are used interchangeably, and in the case of third-party payers, these terms are used interchangeably with "enrollees" or "beneficiaries;" ***Post-market surveillance is typically a shared responsibility between manufacturers & regulators

The pharmaceutical supply chain normally begins with research and development ("R&D"), which consists of bench science and clinical research, conducted mainly by manufacturers but also increasingly within the emergent and mostly independent biotechnology industry, which is expected to continue to grow at double-digit compounded annual growth rates.[77] The R&D process typically involves extensive modelling and testing, and is the initial stage of the vetting of experimental biopharmaceutical compounds. Following the early stages of R&D, manufacturers typically work with the FDA, and in some cases, their biotechnology development partners, in the design and execution of rigorous clinical trials to prove product safety and efficacy.[78] These clinical studies are typically conducted with relatively high levels of transparency, with the requirement that the clinical studies be formally registered with the FDA.[79] Following the completion of clinical trials, the FDA approves (or rejects) the drug for sales and marketing in the U.S. The approval process results in the FDA establishing boundaries on claims regarding product attributes that can legally be put forward by manufacturers, and in some cases may also require additional warnings added to the drug label, such as special "black box" warnings for drugs with disproportionately higher risk of serious adverse events, such as cardiovascular events.[80] Data and decision-making associated with the FDA vetting and approval process is not generally oriented toward

[77] For background, refer to O. Gassmann, G. Reepmeyer, and M. von Zedtwitz, *Leading Pharmaceutical Innovation (Second Edition)* (Berlin, Germany: Springer-Verlag, 2008); S. S. Mehta, *Commercializing Successful Biomedical Technologies* (New York, NY: Cambridge University Press, 2008). Regarding growth rates in biotechnology, see for example Bloomberg, "Biotechnology Market Size Worth $2.44 Trillion By 2028 | CAGR 15.83%," (New York, NY: Bloomberg Business, 2021).

[78] The FDA maintains strict and extensive protocols and guidance on the design and conduct of clinical trials. See generally FDA, "Clinical Trials Guidance Documents," (Washington, D.C.: U.S. Fod & Drug Administration, 2023a).

[79] See generally J. Hewett, "ClinicalTrials.gov: Definitions, Laws, and Regulations," (Washington, D.C.: Office of Scientific Investigations, Center for Drug Evaluation and Research, U.S. Food and Drug Administration, 2018).

[80] See generally D. Bose et al., "An Audit of Black Box Warnings (BBWs) in the United States Food and Drug Administration (US-FDA) Database—A Five-Year Analysis," *Curr Drug Saf* 17, no. 1 (2022); M. T. Solotke et al., "New and incremental FDA black box warnings from 2008 to 2015," *Expert Opin Drug Saf* 17, no. 2 (2018); A. Wahab and A. Iqbal, "Black-Box Warnings of Antiseizure Medications: What is Inside the Box?," *Pharmaceut Med* 37, no. 3 (2023).

a consumer audience, and is instead aimed primarily at manufacturers, distributors, physicians, medical societies, insurers, and other regulators, as these entities are the primary "users" of FDA information. Approved drugs are subject to further oversight by the DEA, mostly in accordance with the Controlled Substances Act ("CSA") regarding drugs deemed to have disproportionate potential for diversion, misuse, dependency, or abuse. However, DEA responsibilities also extend to general oversight of prescription drug markets, including oversight and monitoring of drug storage and oversight of prescribers (i.e., prescribing patterns and prescription drug provision by physicians, clinics, and health systems), distributors, and pharmacies.[81]

Following the initial phase of regulatory involvement, manufacturers typically sell their products through distributors, which are subject to DEA regulation. In some cases, distributors purchase and store products from manufacturers prior to distribution to healthcare delivery systems and pharmacies. Distributors and wholesalers supply retail pharmacies with prescription drugs, but the drugs cannot be dispensed without a valid prescription from a licensed provider. Three large independent distributors control about 80–90% of the pharmaceutical distribution market.[82] Independent distributors typically do more than distribute pharmaceuticals, also engaging in activities such as administering pharmacy services, establishing group purchasing organizations ("GPOs"), brokering drug discounts with manufacturers and payers, drug repackaging, administering buy-back programs, inventory management, and the provision of information technology and data management.[83] Some pharmacies, such as supermarket-based pharmacies, maintain their own internal distribution networks and processes, and do not rely on the large independent distributors.

[81] DEA, "DEA Mission Statement," (Washington, D.C.: U.S. Drug Enforcement Agency, U.S. Department of Justice, 2018).

[82] KFF, "Follow The Pill: Understanding the U.S. Commercial Pharmaceutical Supply Chain," (Menlo Park, CA: Kaiser Family Foundation, 2005); Commonwealth Fund, "The Impact of Pharmaceutical Wholesalers on U.S. Drug Spending," in *Issue Briefs* (Washington, D.C.: The Commonwealth Fund, 2022).

[83] See generally "The Impact of Pharmaceutical Wholesalers on U.S. Drug Spending."

Medical boards and accreditation agencies oversee providers and establish clinical practice guidelines and other practice norms and standards, including standards of care related to drug treatment and pain management. Physician advocacy groups and specialty societies often summarize drug approval data on behalf of their constituents and devise clinical practice guidelines and protocols for emerging pharmaceutical treatments.[84] These guidelines have been shown to influence physician prescribing patterns.[85] The promulgation of clinical practice guidelines, protocols, and other communications regarding professional standards of practice from the basis for the "learned intermediary doctrine," which will be revisited in Chap. 7. Physicians are governed primarily by self-regulation, directly controlling the entry requirements into the profession as well as the standards of conduct to remain licensed. Some oversight of providers is also conducted directly by the DEA, mainly regarding improper or illegal dispensing.

With a valid and legal prescription, patients obtain prescription drugs at a retail pharmacy or a pharmacy located within a clinic, hospital, or health system. Those drugs are increasingly paid for (at least in part) by third-party payers and pharmacy benefit managers ("PBMs"), who establish payment mechanisms, reimbursement rates, and drug placement on formularies. Third-party payers that provide prescription drug coverage increasingly employ financial incentives governing prescription drug transactions, such as tiered copayments to encourage the use of lower-priced drugs. In addition, like other forms of health insurance wherein moral hazard is featured, coverage can lead to increased utilization, and PBMs came into existence largely to manage prescription drug utilization. The role of PBMs has grown substantially over the past decade and is expected to grow another 50% by 2030.[86] Similar to independent distributors, a small number of companies dominate the PBM industry, controlling about 80% of the market, with the remaining 20% supplied by

[84] For example, see D. R. Bennett, "American Medical Association Drug Evaluations," in *Medical Technology Assessment Directory: A Pilot Reference To Organizations, Assessments, and Information Resources.*, ed. C. Goodman (Washington, D.C.: Institute of Medicine (IOM), Council on Health Care Technology; National Academies Press (US), 1988).

[85] See generally G. T. Schumock et al., "Factors that influence prescribing decisions," *Ann Pharmacother* 38, no. 4 (2004).

[86] D. Myshko and P. Wehrwein, "Beyond the Big Three PBMs," *Managed Healthcare Executive* 32, no. 12 (2022).

smaller emerging PBMs, which are expected to continue to gain market share.[87] Finally, to close the loop, the FDA and drug manufacturers are responsible for post-market surveillance designed to assure that adverse event rates are consistent with the rates expected given product profiles and clinical trial outcomes, and to detect the emergence of unanticipated adverse events. The CDC is also involved in post-market surveillance of adverse events from drugs and vaccines, particularly in instances where adverse event rates raise population health concerns.[88]

Overall, spending on prescription drugs in the U.S. has grown substantially over the past two decades, increasing more than threefold from $122 billion in 2000 to $450 billion in 2023.[89] The main drivers of growth have been innovation in novel treatments, increased utilization, increased unit prices, and the increasing role of third-party coverage.[90] The flow of funds through the pharmaceutical supply chain varies mainly by whether a drug is branded (i.e., still under patent) versus generic, which can have significant differences in prices and margins. In general, according to a study by the University of Southern California, for every $100 spent at retail pharmacies, about $17 is attributable to direct production costs, $41 accrues to the manufacturer, and the residual $41 is allocated among the remaining pharmaceutical supply chain intermediaries, mainly distributors, pharmacies, PBMs, and payers.[91] That is, the majority of the

[87] Ibid.

[88] See, for example, D. S. Budnitz et al., "Emergency hospitalizations for adverse drug events in older Americans," *N Engl J Med* 365, no. 21 (2011); D. S. Budnitz et al., "National surveillance of emergency department visits for outpatient adverse drug events," *Jama* 296, no. 15 (2006); T. T. Shimabukuro et al., "Safety monitoring in the Vaccine Adverse Event Reporting System (VAERS)," *Vaccine* 33, no. 36 (2015).

[89] CMS, "National Health Expenditures by Type of Service and Source of Funds: Calendar Years 1960 to 2023," (Washington, D.C.: Centers for Medicare & Medicaid Services, Office of the Actuary, National Health Statistics Group., 2024).Also see ASPE, "Trends in Prescription Drug Spending, 2016–2021," in *Issue Brief* (Washington, D.C.: U.S. Office of Science and Data Policy, U.S. Assistant Secretary for Planning and Evaluation (ASPE), 2022).

[90] See generally E.R. Berndt, "The U.S. Pharmaceutical Industry: Why Major Growth In Times Of Cost Containment?," *Health Affairs* 20, no. 2 (2001); AAA, "Prescription Drug Spending in the U.S. Health Care System: An Actuarial Perspective," in *Issue Brief* (Washington, D.C.: American Academy of Actuaries, 2018).

[91] N. Sood et al., "Flow of Money Through the Pharmaceutical Distribution System," in *White Paper Series* (Los Angeles, CA: University of Southern California, Leonard D. Schaeffer Center for Health Policy & Economics, 2017).

resources in the pharmaceutical supply chain flow back to manufacturers, with moderate shares accruing to insurers and pharmacies and smaller shares accruing to the other components of the supply chain, such as wholesalers and PBMs. Regardless of flow of funds and resources, each of these entities, in addition to the myriad government regulators and industry accreditors overseeing the supply chain, are critical to making prescription drugs accessible to consumers.

2.8 Chapter Summary

Though the primary intent of this chapter is to provide general background, there are some important implications that flow from the discussion. First, the opioid MDL is not a "product defect" liability case in the traditional sense, in part because opioids continue to be prescribed for clinical use, in some cases featuring the exact same formulations and packaging as the products alleged to have contributed to the current crisis. Likewise, medical societies initially supported the use of opioids, and throughout the crisis maintained the ability to either caution their constituents on opioid utilization or recommend the removal of opioids from the market. Another reason that prescription opioids are not considered defective is that they were explicitly approved by regulators *ex ante*, in the exact same formulations found in past and current supplies. Instead, the opioid MDL fits into the broader product liability realm of failure to warn, combined with some opportunistic behavior on the part of some parties in efforts to exploit information asymmetries existing in all levels of the supply chain.

Opioids flowed through a supply chain and healthcare system featuring a rapidly growing reliance on pharmaceutical-based treatment and influenced by the classic institutional features of any healthcare market, including information asymmetries, uncertainty, and moral hazard. Second, the opioid MDL, at least during the apex of the bellwether cases in recent years, was based on public nuisance theory, which does not require strict liability and implies that liable parties can share responsibility among each other and, in some cases, with plaintiffs. Third, the opioid crisis is an unusual product liability application in that it has played out in one of the most heavily regulated industries in the U.S., under the watchful eye of not just one government regulator but three. Finally, the opioid crisis is multifactorial, an issue explored in greater detail in later chapters. In the context of the MDL, this is a very important fact. As shown in Fig. 2.1, in addition to the six primary members of the opioid supply chain, the supply chain is overseen by three federal regulators (FDA, DEA, and CDC) and another three independent entities (state medical boards, accreditation agencies, and payers/PBMs) employing a variety of mechanisms and controls. In the absence of some form of explicit or implicit consent and cooperation from all 12 of these groups of entities, not a single opioid would be able to reach the U.S. market or stay on the market.

References

American Academy of Actuaries. (2018). *Prescription drug spending in the U.S. health care system: An actuarial perspective*. In Issue brief. Washington, DC.

Alexander, G. C., Ballreich, J., Mansour, O., & Dowdy, D. W. (2022, April). Effect of reductions in opioid prescribing on opioid use disorder and fatal overdose in the United States: A dynamic Markov model. *Addiction*, *117*(4), 969–976.

Arrow, K. J. (1996, June 1). The economics of information: An exposition. *Empirica*, *23*(2), 119–128.

Arrow, K. J. (1963). Uncertianty and the Welfare Economics of Medical Care. *The American Economic Review*, *53*(5).

Arthur, J., Edwards, T., Lu, Z., Amoateng, D. M., Koom-Dadzie, K., Zhu, H., Long, J., Do, K. A., & Bruera, E. (2023, September 27). Healthcare provider perceptions and reported practices regarding opioid prescription for patients with chronic pain. *Research Square*.

ASPE. (2022). Trends in Prescription Drug Spending, 2016–2021. In *Issue Brief.* U.S. Office of Science and Data Policy, U.S. Assistant Secretary for Planning and Evaluation (ASPE).

Ausness, R. C. (2023). Opioid lawsuits: Is there any end in sight?. *Health Matrix: The Journal of Law Medicine*, *33*(1).

Baldwin, F. S. (1977). Products liability as it applies to service transactions. *Journal of Air Law and Commerce*, *43*(2).

Balwierz, R., Biernat, P., Jasińska-Balwierz, A., Siodłak, D., Kusakiewicz-Dawid, A., Kurek-Górecka, A., Olczyk, P., & Ochędzan-Siodłak, W. (2023, March 8). Potential Carcinogens in Makeup Cosmetics. *International Journal of Environmental Research and Public Health*, *20*(6).

Bennett, D. R. (1988). American Medical Association Drug Evaluations. In *Medical Technology Assessment Directory: A Pilot Reference to Organizations, Assessments, and Information Resources.*, edited by C. Goodman. Institute of Medicine (IOM), Council on Health Care Technology; National Academies Press (US).

Berndt, E. R. (2001). The U.S. pharmaceutical industry: Why major growth in times of cost containment?. *Health Affairs*, *20*(2), 100–114.

Bhattacharya, J., & Sood, N. (2007). Health insurance and the obesity externality. *Advances in Health Economics and Health Services Research*, *17*, 279–318.

Blomqvist, A. (1991, January 1). The doctor as double agent: Information asymmetry, health insurance, and medical care. *Journal of Health Economics*, *10*(4), 411–432.

Bloom, G., Standing, H., & Lloyd, R. (2008, May). Markets, information asymmetry and health care: Towards new social contracts. *Social Science and Medicine*, *66*(10), 2076–2087.

Bloomberg. (2021). *Biotechnology Market Size Worth $2.44 Trillion By 2028 | CAGR 15.83%*. Bloomberg Business.

BMJ. (1995). Risk: Benefit analysis of drugs in practice. *Drug and Therapeutics Bulletin*, *33*(5), 33–35.

Bose, D., Gogtay, N., Goel, T., & Konwar, M. (2022). An audit of black box warnings (BBWs) in the United States Food and Drug Administration (US-FDA) database - A five-year analysis. *Current Drug Safety*, *17*(1), 54–58.

Breyer, S. *Regulation and Its Reform*. Harvard University Press, 1982.

Budnitz, D. S., Lovegrove, M. C., Shehab, N., & Richards, C. L. (2011, November 24). Emergency hospitalizations for adverse drug events in older Americans. *New England Journal of Medicine*, *365*(21), 2002–2012.

Budnitz, D. S., Pollock, D. A., Weidenbach, K. N., Mendelsohn, A. B., Schroeder, T. J., & Annest, J. L. (2006, October 18). National surveillance of emergency department visits for outpatient adverse drug events. *Jama*, *296*(15), 1858–1866.

Carroll, S. J., Hensler, D., Gross, J., Sloss, E. M., Schonlau, M., Abrahamse, A., & Ashwood, J. S. (2005). *Asbestos Litigation*. RAND Corportation | RAND Insititute for Civil Justice.

Ciccarone, D. (2021, July 1). The rise of illicit fentanyls, stimulants and the fourth wave of the opioid overdose crisis. *Current Opinion in Psychiatry*, *34*(4), 344–350.

Citera, F. A., & Steiner, J. (2025). Prescription for Failure: Public Nuisance Claims Against the Opioid Industry. *University of Miami Law Review*, *79*(2), 317.

Citron, P. (1994). Medical devices, component materials, and product liability. In J. R. Hunziker & T. O. Jones (Eds.), *Product liability and innovation: Managing risk in an uncertain environment*, National Academy Press.

CMS. (2024). *National health expenditures by type of service and source of funds: Calendar years 1960 to 2023*. Centers for Medicare & Medicaid Services, Office of the Actuary, National Health Statistics Group.

Coleman, J. J., & Pontefract, S. K. (2016, October). Adverse drug reactions. *Clinical Medicine (London)*, *16*(5), 481–485.

Commonwealth Fund. (2022). The Impact of Pharmaceutical Wholesalers on U.S. Drug Spending. In *Issue Briefs*.

Cooter, R. D. (1991). Economic Theories of Legal Liability. *Journal of Economic Perspectives*, *5*(3), 11–30.

CRS. (2019). Overview of the Opioid Litigation and Related Settlements and Settlement Proposals. In *Legal Sidebar*: U.S. Congressional Research Service.

Daynard, R. A., Bates, C., & Francey, N. (2000, January 8). Tobacco litigation worldwide. *BMJ*, *320*(7227), 111–113.

DEA. (2018). *DEA Mission Statement.* U.S. Drug Enforcement Agency, U.S. Department of Justice.

Djulbegovic, B. (2007, March–April). Articulating and responding to uncertainties in clinical research. *Journal of Medicine and Philosophy*, *32*(2), 79–98.

Donahoe, J. T., & Soliman, A. (2025). What fueled the illicit opioid epidemic? New evidence from a takeover of white powder heroin markets. In *CEP Discussion Papers Dp2073.* Centre for Economic Performance, London School of Economics.

Drewes, A. M., Jensen, R. D., Nielsen, L. M., Droney, J., Christrup, L. L., Arendt-Nielsen, L., Riley, J., & Dahan, A. (2013, January). Differences between opioids: Pharmacological, experimental, clinical and economical perspectives. *British Journal of Clinical Pharmacology*, *75*(1), 60–78.

Einav, L., & Finkelstein, A. (2018, August). Moral Hazard in Health Insurance: What We Know and How We Know It. *Journal of the European Economic Association*, *16*(4), 957–982.

Enzinger, A. C., Ghosh, K., Keating, N. L., Cutler, D. M., Clark, C. R., Florez, N., Landrum, M. B., & Wright, A. A. (2023, May 10). Racial and ethnic disparities in opioid access and urine drug screening among older patients with poor-prognosis cancer near the end of life. *Journal of Clinical Oncology*, *41*(14), 2511–2522.

FDA. (2023a). *Clinical trials guidance documents.* U.S. Fod & Drug Administration.

FDA. (2023b). *Risk evaluation and mitigation strategies | REMS.* U.S. Food and Drug Administration.

Fisher, D. (2022, July 6). Latest opioid ruling puts MDL judge further out of step on public nuisance. *West Virginia Record.*

Galasso, A., & Luo, H. (2024). Product Liability Litigation and Innovation: Evidence from Medical Devices. In *NBER Working Paper*, *No. 32215.* National Bureau of Economic Research.

Gassmann, O., Reepmeyer, G., & von Zedtwitz, M. (2008). *Leading Pharmaceutical Innovation* (2nd ed.). Springer-Verlag.

Goldberg, J. C., & Zipursky, B. C. (2016). The strict liability in fault and the fault in strict liability. *Fordham Law Review*, *85*(2).

Haas-Wilson, D. (2003). Arrow and the information market failure in health care: The changing content and sources of health information. In P. J. Hammer, D. Haas-Wilson, & W. M. Sage (Eds.), *Uncertain times: Kenneth Arrow and the changing economics of health care.* Duke University Press.

Hackworth, J. C., Schneider, J. E., Valle, M. D., Fam, D., Argoff, C., Offidani, E., & Potenziano, J. (2025, October 7). The burden of acute pain in the U.S. in the wake of the opioid crisis. *Frontiers in Pain Research*, *6*.

Haffajee, R. L., & Mello, M. M. (2017, December 14). Drug companies' liability for the opioid epidemic. *New England Journal of Medicine*, *377* (24), 2301–2305.

Han, P. K. (2013, February). Conceptual, methodological, and ethical problems in communicating uncertainty in clinical evidence. *Medical Care Research and Review*, *70*(1, Suppl), 14s–36s.

Helland, E. A., & Tabarrok, A. (2012). Product liability and moral hazard: Evidence from general aviation. *The Journal of Law & Economics*, *55*(3), 593–630.

Henderson, T. W. (1990, July). Toxic tort litigation: Medical and scientific principles in causation. *American Journal of Epidemiology* *132*(1, Suppl), S69–78.

Hewett, J. (2018). *ClinicalTrials.gov: Definitions, laws, and regulations.* Office of Scientific Investigations, Center for Drug Evaluation and Research, U.S. Food and Drug Administration.

HLR. (2015). Causation in environmental law: Lessons from toxic torts. *Harvard Law Review*, *128*(8), 2256–2277.

HLR. (2017). Rethinking actual causation in tort law. *Harvard Law Review*, *130*(8).

Hunziker, J. R., & Jones, T. O., (Eds.). (1994). *Product liability and innovation: Managing risk in an uncertain environment.* National Academy Press.

Hurt, R. D., & Robertson, C. R. (1998, October 7). Prying open the door to the tobacco industry's secrets about nicotine: The Minnesota Tobacco Trial. *JAMA*, *280*(13), 1173–1181.

Hylton, K. N. (2010). The economics of public nuisance law and the new enforcement actions. In *Searle Center Public Nuisance Roundtable Working Paper.* Northwestern University Searle Center Research Roundtable on Public Nuisance.

Hylton, K. N. (2013). The law and economics of products liability. *Notre Dame Law Review*, *88*(5).

Ide, R. W. (1994).The role of the justice system in the product liability debate. In J. R. Hunziker & T. O. Jones (Eds.), *Product liability and innovation: Managing risk in an uncertain environment.* National Academy Press.

Jain, S. K. (2015). *Economic analysis of liability rules.* Springer.

Jamison, R. N., Sheehan, K. A., Scanlan, E., Matthews, M., & Ross, E. L. (2014, November–December). Beliefs and attitudes about opioid prescribing and chronic pain management: Survey of primary care providers. *Journal of Opioid Management*, *10*(6), 375–382.

Kahn, A. E. (1988). *The economics of regulation: Principles and institutions.* The MIT Press.

Kelly, I. R., & Markowitz, S. (2009, Winter). Incentives in obesity and health insurance. *Inquiry*, *46*(4), 418–432.

Kendrick, L. (2023).The perils and promise of public nuisance. *Yale Law Journal*, *132*(3).

Kessler, D. P. (1999). *The economic effects of the liability system*. Hoover Institution.

KFF. (2005). *Follow the pill: Understanding the U.S. commercial pharmaceutical supply chain*. Kaiser Family Foundation.

KFF. (2025). Payback: Tracking the opioid settlement cash. In *Health News*. Kaiser Family Foundation.

Legal Information Institute. (2023). *Products Liability*. Cornell School of Law.

Levine, R. J. (1988). Uncertainty in clinical research. *Law, Medicine and Health Care*, *16*(3–4), 174–182.

Mackie, J. (2023, June 2). Prescription opioid lawsuit guide. *Forbes*.

Madden, M. S. (2001). The enduring paradox of products liability law relating to prescription pharmaceuticals. *Pace Law Review*, *21*(2).

Manning, R. L. (1997). Products liability and prescription drug prices in Canada and the United States. *The Journal of Law & Economics*, *40*(1), 203–244.

Mascarenhas, O. A., Kesavan, R., & Bernacchi, M. D. (2013). On reducing information asymmetry in U.S. health care. *Health Marketing Quarterly*, *30*(4), 379–398.

Masood, B., & Moorthy, M. (2023). Causes of obesity: A review. *Clinical Medicine*, *23*(4), 284–291.

Mehta, S. S. (2008). *Commercializing successful biomedical technologies*. Cambridge University Press.

Miller, C. J., & Goldberg, R. S. (2004). *Product Liability* (2nd ed.). Oxford University Press.

Myshko, D., & Wehrwein, P. (2022). Beyond the big three PBMs. *Managed Healthcare Executive*, *32*(12).

NHTSA. (2018). Vehicle safety recall completion rates report. In *Report to Congress*. U.S. Department of Transportation, National Highway Traffic Safety Administration.

Odisho, A. Y., & Gore, J. L. (2017, September). Patient-centered approaches to creating understandable health information. *Urologic Oncology*, *35*(9), 559–563.

Opioid MDL. (2022). "MDL 2804 Case No. 1:17-md-2804 Judge Dan Aaron Polster: Abatement Order." In *Re: National Opioid Litigation*. United States District Court Northern District of Ohio, Eastern Division.

Ovalle, D. (2023, June 9). Governments get nearly $19 billion more in opioid lawsuit settlements. *Washington Post*.

Oxford, UK: Oxford University Press, 2023.

Parsons, C. (2003). Moral hazard in liability insurance. *The Geneva Papers on Risk and Insurance*, *28*(3), 448–471.

Pauly, J. L., Mepani, A. B., Lesses, J. D., Cummings, K. M., & Streck, R. J. (2002, March). Cigarettes with defective filters marketed for 40 years: What Philip Morris never told smokers. *Tobacco Control, 1*(Suppl 1), I51–61.
Peltzman, S. (1988a). The effects of automobile safety regulation. In G. J. Stigler (Ed.), *Chicago studies in political economy*. The University of Chicago Press.
Peltzman, S. (1988b). Toward a more general theory of regulation. In G. J. Stigler (Ed.), *Chicago studies in political economy*. The University of Chicago Press
Posner, R. A. (2011). Regulation (Agencies) versus litigation (Courts). In D. P. Kessler (Ed.), *Regulation versus litigation: Perspectives from economics and law*. The University of Chicago Press.
Purcell, M. J. (2018). Settling high: A common law public nuisance response to the opioid epidemic. *Columbia Journal of Law and Social Problems, 52*(1), 135–177.
Razouki, Z., Khokhar, B. A., Philpot, L. M., & Ebbert, J. O. (2019, October 1). Attributes, attitudes, and practices of clinicians concerned with opioid prescribing. *Pain Medicine, 20*(10), 1934–1941.
Ross, K. (2019, October 31). Technology developments and the risk ofproduct liability.*Compliance*.
Sage, W. M. (1988). Drug product liability and health care delivery systems. *Stanford Law Review, 40*(4), 989–1026.
Sajan, A., Corneil, T., & Grzybowski, S. (1998, July 28). The street value of prescription drugs. *CMAJ, 159*(2), 139–142.
Scherer, F. M. (2000). The pharmaceutical industry. In A. J. Culyer & J. P. Newhouse (Eds.), *Handbook of health economics* (Vol. 1). Elsevier Science B.V.
Schnarr, A., & Mertz, M. (2022, December 13). States of uncertainty, risk-benefit assessment and early clinical research: A conceptual investigation. *Science and Engineering Ethics, 28*(6), 68.
Schumock, G. T., Walton, S. M., Park, H. Y., Nutescu, E. A., Blackburn, J. C., Finley, J. M., & Lewis, R. K. (2004, April). Factors that influence prescribing decisions. *Annals of Pharmacotherapy, 38*(4), 557–562.
Shimabukuro, T. T., Nguyen, M., Martin, D., & DeStefano, F. (2015, August 26). Safety monitoring in the Vaccine Adverse Event Reporting System (VAERS). *Vaccine, 33*(36), 4398–4405.
Shin, S. S., LaForge, K., Stack, E., Pope, J., Leichtling, G., Larsen, J. E., Leahy, J. M., & Korthuis, P. T. (2022, July 11). "It wasn't here, and now it is. It's everywhere": Fentanyl's rising presence in Oregon's drug supply." *Harm Reduction Journal, 19*(1), 76.
Shover, C. L., Friedman, J. R., Romero, R., Buhr, R., Chu, B., Tang, A., Medina, J. A., & Goodman-Meza, D. (2023, August). Longitudinal changes in co-involved drugs, comorbidities, and demographics of methamphetamine-related

deaths in Los Angeles County. *Journal of Substance Use and Addiction Treatment, 151*, 209101.

Simon, H. A. (1990). Bounded Rationality. In J. Eatwell, M. Milgate, & P. Newman (Eds.), *Utility and Probability*, 15–18. Palgrave Macmillan UK.

Sinatra, R. (2010, December).Causes and consequences of inadequate management of acute pain. *Pain Medicine, 11*(12), 1859–1871.

Solotke, M. T., Dhruva, S. S., Downing, N. S., Shah, N. D., & Ross, J. S. (2018, February). New and incremental FDA black box warnings from 2008 to 2015. *Expert Opinion on Drug Safety, 17*(2), 117–123.

Sood, N., Tiffany Shih, K. V. N., & Goldman, D. (2017). Flow of Money Through the Pharmaceutical Distribution System. In *White Paper Series*. University of Southern California, Leonard D. Schaeffer Center for Health Policy & Economics.

Stigler, G. J. (1988). The theory of economic regulation. In G. J. Stigler (Ed.), *Chicago Studies in Political Economy*. The University of Chicago Press.

Thirumalai, S., & Sinha, K. K. (2011). Product recalls in the medical device industry: An empirical exploration of the sources and financial consequences. *Management Science, 57*(2), 376–392.

Thomas, B. A. (1989). A Canadian view of the product liability aspects of innovation. *Canada-U.S. Law Journal (Case Western Reserve), 93*.

Trevas, D. (2024, December 10). Public nuisance lawsuits cannot be pursued against pharmacies selling prescription opioids. *Court News Ohio*.

Tyler, E., & Combs, R. (2023). *2023 Litigation statistics series: Multidistrict litigation*. Bloomberg Law.

Viscusi, W. K. (1985). Market incentives for safety. *Harvard Business Review, 63*, 133.

Viscusi, W. K., & Moore, M. J. (1993). Product liability, research and development, and innovation. *Journal of Political Economy 101*(1), 161–184.

Wahab, A., & Iqbal, A. (2023, May). Black-box warnings of antiseizure medications: What is inside the box? *Pharmaceutical Medicine 37*(3), 233–250.

Wainwright, T. (2016). *Narconomics: How to run a drug cartel*. PublicAffairs/ Perseus.

Williamson, O. E. (1996). *The mechanisms of governance*. Oxford Univeristy Press.

Zhou, S., Ricafort, E., Bressler, D., & Devotsu, R. K. (2022, March). Litigation in tobacco control: Past, present and future. *Tobacco Control 31*(2), 291–295.

CHAPTER 3

Epidemiology

In matters regarding economic externalities and product liability it is often the case that a product or service is alleged to have caused health-related problems or harms, which can take the form of either acute events of relatively short duration, such as injuries, or chronic diseases and conditions, such as cancer, which normally are associated with longer term disease progression and ongoing need for monitoring and treatment. Both instances have implications for epidemiological analyses, which can be useful to define the harm, identify the primary causes of the harm, determine the scale of the harm (i.e., incidence and prevalence), assess the attributable health and safety effects of the harm, and determine the factors associated with the severity of the harm.[1] This chapter addresses these issues in the context of the opioid crisis in the U.S. In addition, relevant related topics are reviewed, including a brief overview of the complexities of pain, the clinical and economic burden of pain, the treatment and management of pain, and the adverse events associated with pain treatment. In some cases, opioid use is associated with serious adverse events, and such cases carry a probability of harms and costs. Economists typically refer to unintended effects, or harms, in the context of externalities; this relationship will also be explored in this chapter. The chapter

[1] For an overview, refer to R. Goldberg, "Epidemiological Uncertainty, Causation, and Drug Product Liability," *McGill Law Journal* 59, no. 4 (2014).

J. E. Schneider, *The Economics of Pain*, Global Perspectives on Wealth and Distribution,
https://doi.org/10.1007/978-3-032-20355-7_3

concludes with a discussion of causation, which is a central component of epidemiological analysis. While the goal of the chapter is primarily to establish some important background context and information regarding pain and pain management, especially the underlying epidemiology, another important goal is to emphasize that some of the salient features of pain and pain management were themselves contributors to the opioid crisis.

3.1 Complexity of Pain

The concept of pain, which plays a central role in the opioid crisis and in this book, is an extraordinarily complex medical phenomenon, and one that has evolved markedly over centuries.[2] As far back as historical records have been kept, pain and suffering were generally understood through a religious lens, with pain accepted as "a necessary part of the moral order of things."[3] As society became less secular, and religious leaders began to share the stage with social and political philosophers, the understanding of pain evolved into more of a social issue, whereby humans could enhance their level of fulfillment and improve their quality of life by reducing pain and suffering, rather than accepting it as unavoidable.[4] The conceptualization of pain then transitioned into a third phase as it entered the realm of modern medicine and its myopic focus on treatment of identifiable diseases and conditions.[5] Initially, clinical motivation for controlling pain was driven mostly by advances in surgery and surgical technique, whereby the clinical benefits of surgery could be more fully realized with more effective intraoperative anesthesia and post-operative pain control.[6] However, as the field of modern medicine continued to evolve, pain was regarded

[2] See generally J. J. Bonica, "History of pain concepts and pain therapy," *Mt Sinai J Med* 58, no. 3 (1991); R. Sabatowski et al., "Pain treatment: a historical overview," *Curr Pharm Des* 10, no. 7 (2004).

[3] A thorough discussion of the history of pain is provided in M.D. Sullivan and J.C. Ballantyne, *The Right to Pain Relief and Other Deep Roots of the Opioid Epidemic* (New York, NY: Oxford University Press, 2023).

[4] See generally S. Coninx, "Pain Philosophy: Recent Debates and Future Challenges," *Philosophy Compass* 19, no. 4 (2024).

[5] See generally M. Bliss, *The Making of Modern Medicine: Turning Points in the Treatment of Disease* (Chicago, IL: Univeristy of Chicago Press, 2011).

[6] R. Collier, "A short history of pain management," *Cmaj* 190, no. 1 (2018).

increasingly as a condition, not fundamentally different from a disease, that could potentially be mitigated, minimized, and intervened by way of medical science and treatment.

One of the more salient characteristics of pain, especially with respect to its clinical complexity and the current opioid crisis, is that its experience is largely subjective and cannot accurately and reliably be assessed by those who are not experiencing it directly.[7] Not only is pain difficult to assess by others, but patients themselves face high levels of uncertainty in the assessment of their own pain.[8] Following surgery, for example, there is wide variation in patient reported pain, even for patients undergoing the same types of procedures.[9] The implication of this is that, given the subjectivity of the experience of pain and the difficulties objectively measuring pain levels, there is also high variability in how physicians treat pain, with the default approach generally consisting of some level of trust on the part of the provider that the patient is accurately depicting their pain, or otherwise in good faith conveying a need for treatment.[10] However, in the course of the recent opioid crisis, there have been widespread reports of patients engaging in "opioid seeking" behavior[11] and large variation in

[7] See generally T. H. Wideman et al., "The Multimodal Assessment Model of Pain: A Novel Framework for Further Integrating the Subjective Pain Experience Within Research and Practice," *Clin J Pain* 35, no. 3 (2019).

[8] See, for example, B. L. Boring et al., "How and Why Patient Concerns Influence Pain Reporting: A Qualitative Analysis of Personal Accounts and Perceptions of Others' Use of Numerical Pain Scales," *Front Psychol* 12 (2021). Boring et al. describe variation in self-reported pain as follows: "while many people endeavor to report their pain as accurately as possible, there are nuanced reasons why people may modulate their pain ratings (i.e., over- or under-report their own pain). The primary reason people over-report their pain is to be taken seriously and ensure adequate attention is given to their pain." (p.11).

[9] For example, see D. C. Rosenberger and E. M. Pogatzki-Zahn, "Chronic post-surgical pain—update on incidence, risk factors and preventive treatment options," *BJA Educ* 22, no. 5 (2022); R. Zaslansky, W. Meissner, and C. R. Chapman, "Pain after orthopaedic surgery: differences in patient reported outcomes in the United States vs internationally. An observational study from the PAIN OUT dataset," *Br J Anaesth* 120, no. 4 (2018).

[10] M. S. Matthias and M. J. Bair, "The patient-provider relationship in chronic pain management: where do we go from here?," *Pain Med* 11, no. 12 (2010).

[11] See generally C. A. Grover et al., "How Frequently are "Classic" Drug-Seeking Behaviors Used by Drug-Seeking Patients in the Emergency Department?," *West J Emerg Med* 13, no. 5 (2012); L. P. Longo et al., "Addiction: part II. Identification and management of the drug-seeking patient," *Am Fam Physician* 61, no. 8 (2000); R. W. Pretorius and

physician prescribing of opioids,[12] together suggesting that the subjectivity of pain has itself been a causal agent in the crisis, obfuscating the clinical pathways that normally associate medical need and treatment utilization. Indeed, the experience of pain varies with many of the same variables associated with substance use disorders, such as comorbid health conditions, economic distress, and education.[13] Pain management expert Abdul-Ghaaliq Lalkhen described it this way in his book *An Anatomy of Pain*: "Pain as an experience is influenced by beliefs and expectations as well as psychological factors such as mood and resilience. An individual's culture, genetics, and innate ability to cope with adversity will impact their experience of pain."[14] Lalkhen further notes that "a higher level of catastrophizing, and consequently feeling a lower sense of control, is an important predictor that a patient will experience severe acute pain or develop chronic pain, when pain persists beyond what would be medically expected."[15] As noted in the preceding chapter, problems stemming from information asymmetry can lead to opportunistic behavior. In the case of opioids, the information limits regarding the objective assessment of pain allowed for opportunistic behavior on the part of various elements in the prescription drug supply chain, including manufacturers, physicians, and patients.

3.2 Burden of Pain

One of the central themes of this book is that the increase in the supply of opioids starting in the late 1990s and early 2000s was in part precipitated and fueled by concerted efforts on the part of the medical community and

G. M. Zurick, "A systematic approach to identifying drug-seeking patients," *Fam Pract Manag* 15, no. 4 (2008).

[12] See generally B. Kim et al., "Inappropriate opioid prescribing practices: A narrative review," *Am J Health Syst Pharm* 76, no. 16 (2019); D. C. McDonald, K. Carlson, and D. Izrael, "Geographic variation in opioid prescribing in the U.S," *J Pain* 13, no. 10 (2012).

[13] See generally D. A. Glei and M. Weinstein, "Economic distress, obesity, and the rise in pain," *Soc Sci Med* 339 (2023); M. Tegethoff et al., "Comorbidity of Mental Disorders and Chronic Pain: Chronology of Onset in Adolescents of a National Representative Cohort," *J Pain* 16, no. 10 (2015); A. Zajacova et al., "The Relationship Between Education and Pain Among Adults Aged 30–49 in the United States," ibid.21, no. 11–12 (2020).

[14] A. Lalkhen, *An Anatomy of Pain* (New York, NY: Scribner, 2021). (p. 16).

[15] Ibid. (p.18).

public policy advocates to increase awareness of unmet medical need regarding pain management, and to improve access to treatments, such as opioids, capable of addressing those gaps. In the next chapter it will be shown that these efforts were an influential driver of the increase in prescription opioid supply in the U.S. Through the fog of the opioid crisis, however, some have also argued that the medical community has lost its momentum in trying to meet the needs of patients experiencing acute and chronic pain, and that many of the pain treatment gaps addressed more than two decades ago continue to exist, and in some cases have worsened as organizations and providers have begun exercising an abundance of caution in prescribing opioids.[16] However, in addition to highly publicized adverse events, such as dependence, addiction, and OUD, opioids also have substantial clinical utility, and continue to address some areas of unmet need in pain management. Indeed, the tension between opioid effectiveness and opioid harms has been important to the debates surrounding opioid litigation. This section briefly summarizes the burden of pain and some of the key (and ongoing) challenges of pain management. This discussion is followed in the next section by a summary of the clinical utility of opioids.

The burden of pain in the U.S. and globally has been substantial and persistent. Blyth et al. note that despite the identification of musculoskeletal pain (and the burden of its associated disability) as a global area of unmet need by the Global Burden of Disease Study ("GBD"), little progress has been made in the form of policy initiatives.[17] For example, Payne and Foley observed more than four decades ago that cancer pain was associated with a high degree of unmet need,[18] but unmet need in the

[16] See generally NASEM, *Pain Management and the Opioid Epidemic: Balancing Societal and Indidivual Benefits and Risks of Prescription Opioid Use*, ed. R.J. Bonnie, M.A. Ford, and J.K. Phillips, Consensus Study Report of National Academies of Sciences, Engineering and Medicine (NASEM) (Washington, D.C.: National Academies Press, 2017); M. J. Vranken et al., "The perception of barriers concerning opioid medicines: A survey examining differences between policy makers, healthcare professionals and other stakeholders," *Palliat Med* 34, no. 4 (2020); J.C. Hackworth et al., "The burden of acute pain in the U.S. in the wake of the opioid crisis," *Frontiers in Pain Research* Volume 6–2025 (2025).

[17] F. M. Blyth et al., "The Global Burden of Musculoskeletal Pain-Where to From Here?," *Am J Public Health* 109, no. 1 (2019).

[18] R. Payne and K. M. Foley, "Advances in the management of cancer pain," *Cancer Treat Rep* 68, no. 1 (1984).

treatment of cancer pain continues to be an important concern.[19] Similar observations have been made regarding palliative care, with the Human Rights Watch remarking that "Although the World Health Organization ("WHO") considers palliative care an integral component of cancer care and has urged countries to improve its availability, too often palliative care continues to be the neglected child of the health care family."[20] The burden of pain clearly continues to be associated with unmet needs in acute pain and chronic pain.

The burden of acute and chronic pain falls disproportionately on certain segments of the population. For example, in 2009, the IOM report on pain found that the prevalence of low back pain is 28% higher among individuals with no high school diploma compared to those with some college or more, and 23% higher for those living outside of metropolitan statistical areas ("MSAs") compared to those living within MSAs.[21] Some of the largest differences are observed by income; in 2009, compared to the highest income groups, individuals in the lowest income group reported rates of pain prevalence 38% to 76% more than their higher income counterparts, with the largest differentials observed in headache (76%), shoulder pain (64%), hip pain (61%), neck pain (59%), and low back pain (48%).[22] The income effect on health is well described in the literature on the social determinants of health, which consistently shows the substantial effects of income, socioeconomic status, and demographics on access to health services, health literacy, and health behaviors.[23]

[19] D. S. Zhukovsky et al., "Unmet analgesic needs in cancer patients," *J Pain Symptom Manage* 10, no. 2 (1995).

[20] HRW, "Global State of Pain Treatment: Access to Palliative Care as a Human Right," (New York, NY: Human Rights Watch, 2011).

[21] IOM, "Relieving Pain in America: A Blueprint for Transforming Prevention, Care, Education, and Research," (U.S. National Institutes for Health, Institute of Medicine (IOM), 2011).

[22] Ibid.

[23] See generally J. Bor, G. H. Cohen, and S. Galea, "Population health in an era of rising income inequality: USA, 1980–2015," *Lancet* 389, no. 10077 (2017); P. L. Owens et al., "Social Determinants of Health and County Population Rates of Opioid-Related Inpatient Stays and Emergency Department Visits, 2016," in *Healthcare Cost and Utilization Project (HCUP) Statistical Briefs* (Rockville (MD): Agency for Healthcare Research and Quality (US), 2006); Z. L. Yap et al., "The role of the social determinants of health in outcomes of surgery for low back pain: a systematic review and narrative synthesis," *Spine J* 22, no. 5

3.3 Acute Pain

Acute pain is defined generally as pain that is "provoked by a specific disease or injury, serves a useful biologic purpose, is associated with skeletal muscle spasm and sympathetic nervous system activation, and is self-limited."[24] Examples of acute pain include pain associated with surgery, musculoskeletal injuries (e.g., broken bones, sprains, and strains), dental procedures, soft tissue injuries (e.g., cuts, puncture wounds, burns), blunt force trauma, labor and childbirth, and headaches. Substantial gaps exist in the treatment of acute pain.[25] For example, in a study of patients treated in the emergency department ("ED") of a tertiary care hospital, about 50% of patients reported that their pain had not been relieved upon discharge.[26] Another study found that only 60% of ED patients received pain medications, and 74% continued to report moderate to severe pain upon discharge.[27] Similarly, a large national survey found that more than 80% of patients experienced post-surgical pain within two weeks of discharge, and most of those patients indicated that their pain was moderate to severe.[28] Post-operative pain is frequently reported, with estimates ranging from 30% to 80%.[29]

(2022); M. Marmot and R.G. Wilkinson, *Social Determinants of Health (Second Edition)* (Oxford, UK: Oxford University Press, 2006).

[24] K. P. Grichnik and F. M. Ferrante, "The difference between acute and chronic pain," *Mt Sinai J Med* 58, no. 3 (1991). Also see generally S. E. E. Mills, K. P. Nicolson, and B. H. Smith, "Chronic pain: a review of its epidemiology and associated factors in population-based studies," *Br J Anaesth* 123, no. 2 (2019); S. M. Rikard et al., "Chronic Pain Among Adults—United States, 2019–2021," *MMWR Morb Mortal Wkly Rep* 72, no. 15 (2023).

[25] R. Sinatra, "Causes and consequences of inadequate management of acute pain," *Pain Med* 11, no. 12 (2010).

[26] V. Guru and I. Dubinsky, "The patient vs. caregiver perception of acute pain in the emergency department," *J Emerg Med* 18, no. 1 (2000).

[27] K. H. Todd et al., "Pain in the emergency department: results of the pain and emergency medicine initiative (PEMI) multicenter study," *J Pain* 8, no. 6 (2007).

[28] J. L. Apfelbaum et al., "Postoperative pain experience: results from a national survey suggest postoperative pain continues to be undermanaged," *Anesth Analg* 97, no. 2 (2003).

[29] See generally W. Meissner and R. Zaslansky, "A survey of postoperative pain treatments and unmet needs," *Best Pract Res Clin Anaesthesiol* 33, no. 3 (2019); M. Solca, "Acute pain management: unmet needs and new advances in pain management," *Eur J Anaesthesiol Suppl* 25 (2002).

One contributing factor associated with gaps in acute pain management has been lack of consistency on the part of providers in following acute pain clinical practice guidelines ("CPGs"). For example, a recent systematic review identified 20 pain management quality measures, but only three of which focused specifically on postoperative pain management, leading the authors to conclude that there was a scarcity of measures to guide and promote optimal postoperative pain management.[30] Other contributing factors include lack of adequate physician training, overly cautious use of opioids, misunderstandings on behalf of providers and patients regarding the appropriate use of opioids, and concerns over the side effects and serious adverse events associated with opioid use.[31] An important consequence of insufficient treatment of acute pain is progression of pain, particularly the progression of poorly treated acute pain to chronic pain, sometimes referred to the "chronification" of acute pain.[32] Though the mechanisms underlying progression from acute to chronic pain are not fully understood, initial acute pain can evolve into pain with neuropathic characteristics, which may then become resistant to treatment over time.[33] Again, there is substantial evidence of insufficient treatment of acute pain, wherein pain levels remain unchanged after substantial periods of time. For example, in addition to the previously discussed studies, Buvanendran et al. found that 66% of patients experienced moderate to extreme pain post-surgery, and 59% continued to report similar pain levels in the first two weeks after discharge.[34]

[30] J. M. Joseph et al., "Gaps in standardized postoperative pain management quality measures: A systematic review," *Surgery* 171, no. 2 (2022).

[31] See generally D. B. Carr et al., "The impact of technology on the analgesic gap and quality of acute pain management," *Reg Anesth Pain Med* 30, no. 3 (2005); D. B. Gordon et al., "Research Gaps in Practice Guidelines for Acute Postoperative Pain Management in Adults: Findings From a Review of the Evidence for an American Pain Society Clinical Practice Guideline," *J Pain* 17, no. 2 (2016); NASEM, *Pain Management and the Opioid Epidemic: Balancing Societal and Indidivual Benefits and Risks of Prescription Opioid Use*; Hackworth et al., "Burden of Acute Pain."

[32] B. Morlion et al., "Pain chronification: what should a non-pain medicine specialist know?," *Curr Med Res Opin* 34, no. 7 (2018).

[33] P. Glare, K.R. Aubrey, and P.S. Myles, "Transition from acute to chronic pain after surgery," *The Lancet* 393, no. 10180 (2019).

[34] M. Kent et al., "The ACTTION-American Pain Society-American Academy of Pain Medicine Pain Taxonomy (AAAPT): A Multidimensional Approach to Classifying Acute Pain Conditions," *The Journal of Pain* 18, no. 5 (2017).

3.4 Chronic Pain

Chronic pain is typically differentiated from acute pain in that it "may be considered a disease state" and typically "outlasts the normal time of healing, if associated with a disease or injury [and] may arise from psychological states, serves no biologic purpose, and has no recognizable end-point."[35] These distinctions are potentially important with regard to the opioid crisis, as opioids have been shown to perform differently in acute versus chronic settings. The most common origins of chronic pain include pain associated with tissue damage (i.e., nociceptive pain), such as joint injuries, repetitive stress injuries, degenerative disc disease, and osteoarthritis. Another prevalent form of chronic pain is neuropathic pain, which stems from damage to the nervous system, a common example of which includes peripheral neuropathy associated with diabetes. Other forms of chronic pain include migraine headaches, some autoimmune disorders (such as fibromyalgia), some types of cancer pain, and poorly managed acute pain (i.e., the chronification of acute pain).

According to the CDC, in 2021 about 21% of U.S. adults suffered from chronic pain, and about 7% experienced "high-impact" chronic pain, characterized by "substantial restriction to daily activities."[36] Close to the peak of opioid sales, the IOM reported that in 2009 the age-adjusted rates of U.S. adults reporting pain in the past three months ranged from 7.1% (hip pain) to 28.1% (low back pain), and that the prevalence of virtually all types of pain were increasing at that time.[37] Osteoarthritis ("OA") and rheumatoid arthritis ("RA") are among the primary causes of chronic pain. In 2015, about 11% of the U.S. noninstitutionalized population reported having OA, and these individuals were significantly more likely to report moderate or severe "pain interference with activities" ("PIA").[38] Prevalence of pain in RA is also comparatively high. For example, a 6-year study by Aaronson et al. reported that pain prevalence ranged from 10% to 23%, depending on the

[35] Grichnik and Ferrante, "The difference between acute and chronic pain."

[36] Rikard et al., "Chronic Pain Among Adults—United States, 2019–2021."

[37] IOM, "Relieving Pain in America: A Blueprint for Transforming Prevention, Care, Education, and Research."

[38] X. Zhao et al., "Clinical, humanistic, and economic burden of osteoarthritis among noninstitutionalized adults in the United States," *Osteoarthritis Cartilage* 27, no. 11 (2019).

effectiveness of pain management.[39] Other studies have found considerably higher rates of severe pain in RA; for example, Eberhard observed that even *managed* RA was associated with a prevalence of severe pain as high as 34%, and that individuals were likely to plateau over time and fail to show continued improvement.[40] Pain is also highly prevalent among individuals with cancer, with a recent meta-analysis finding that the overall prevalence of pain among cancer patients of 44.5%, with nearly a third (30.6%) of patients experiencing moderate to severe pain.[41]

3.5 Pain Management

There are numerous treatments and approaches aimed at the management of acute and chronic pain. These approaches generally fall into two categories: pharmacologic treatments and non-pharmacologic treatments. Pharmacologic treatments can be further partitioned into opioid versus non-opioid drugs. Opioid-based treatments, which are featured in acute and chronic pain management, will be discussed separately below. First-line non-opioid treatments for acute pain include over the counter ("OTC") drugs such as acetaminophen (e.g., Tylenol®) and OTC nonsteroidal anti-inflammatory drugs ("NSAIDs"), such as aspirin, ibuprofen (e.g., Advil® and Motrin®), and naproxen (e.g., Aleve®).[42] Second-line treatments often include prescription NSAIDs, which include, for example, acetic acids (e.g., diclofenac and indomethacin) and selective COX-2 inhibitors (e.g., celecoxib, or Celebrex®).[43]

Management of chronic pain typically includes many of the same treatments aimed at acute pain, but also can include antidepressants, anticonvulsants (e.g., gabapentin), capsaicin, sodium channel blockers, alpha-2

[39] M. Aronsson et al., "Comparison of chronic widespread pain prevalence with different criteria in two cohorts of rheumatoid arthritis," *Clin Rheumatol* 41, no. 4 (2022).

[40] A. Eberhard et al., "Predictors of unacceptable pain with and without low inflammation over 5 years in early rheumatoid arthritis-an inception cohort study," *Arthritis Res Ther* 23, no. 1 (2021).

[41] R. A. H. Snijders et al., "Update on Prevalence of Pain in Patients with Cancer 2022: A Systematic Literature Review and Meta-Analysis," *Cancers (Basel)* 15, no. 3 (2023).

[42] O. Amaechi, M. M. Huffman, and K. Featherstone, "Pharmacologic Therapy for Acute Pain," *Am Fam Physician* 104, no. 1 (2021).

[43] Ibid.

adrenoreceptor agonists (e.g., clonidine), and cannabinoids.[44] Among the non-opioid pharmacologic options for chronic pain, NSAIDs are the most commonly used, mostly due to their efficacy and relatively low cost.[45] For more advanced acute and chronic pain, clinicians also have available several interventional pain therapies, such as epidural steroid injections, radiofrequency ablation ("RFA") and spinal cord stimulators.[46] In some cases, non-pharmacologic treatments, such as manual therapies (e.g., physical therapy and chiropractic manipulation), acupuncture, and cognitive behavioral therapy, can also effectively manage pain.[47]

3.6 Aggregate Costs of Pain

The costs of pain treatment vary considerably depending on type of treatment, intensity of treatment, and the success of treatment. Gaskin and Richard estimated the total costs of pain in the U.S. using data from the Medical Expenditure Panel Survey ("MEPS"), finding that the attributable "excess" healthcare costs of pain summed to nearly $436 billion (in 2024 dollars).[48] The impact of pain on work productivity, as measured by absenteeism, presenteeism, and depressed wages, added another $487 billion, bringing the total cost of pain to $923 billion (in 2024 dollars).[49] These costs, which are based on 2010 data, are most likely an underestimate of total

[44] NASEM, *Pain Management and the Opioid Epidemic: Balancing Societal and Indidivual Benefits and Risks of Prescription Opioid Use.*

[45] See generally A. Shetty et al., "A systematic review and network meta-analysis of pharmaceutical interventions used to manage chronic pain," *Sci Rep* 14, no. 1 (2024).

[46] See, for example, E. Biel et al., "The Application of Radiofrequency Ablation in Acute and Chronic Pain Management," *Aana j* 92, no. 3 (2024); N. Strand et al., "Advances in Pain Medicine: a Review of New Technologies," *Curr Pain Headache Rep* 26, no. 8 (2022); O. Viswanath et al., "Evolving Spinal Cord Stimulation Technologies and Clinical Implications in Chronic Pain Management," ibid.23, no. 6 (2019).

[47] AC Skelly et al., "Noninvasive Nonpharmacological Treatment for Chronic Pain: A Systematic Review Update," in *Comparative Effectiveness Review, No. 227* (Rockville, MD: Agency for Healthcare Research and Quality (AHRQ), 2020); NASEM, *Pain Management and the Opioid Epidemic: Balancing Societal and Indidivual Benefits and Risks of Prescription Opioid Use.*

[48] D. J. Gaskin and P. Richard, "The economic costs of pain in the United States," *J Pain* 13, no. 8 (2012). Data reported by authors in 2010 dollars, trended forward to 2024 using the U.S. Consumer Price Index ("CPI").

[49] Ibid. Author's 2010 data trended forward to 2024 using CPI.

attributable pain costs, for three reasons. First, there has been considerable growth in the use of novel interventional pain techniques, such as epidural steroid injections, RFAs, spinal cord stimulators, and surgeries. For example, a study of Medicare beneficiaries from 2000 to 2013 found that the utilization of interventional pain treatments grew more than two-fold over the time period.[50] Second, these estimates are likely to exclude the costs of "chronification" of acute pain and other costs associated with the undertreatment of pain.[51] Third, these costs most likely underestimate the costs of SAEs associated with pain treatments, particularly opioids and NSAIDs.[52]

3.7 Opioid-Based Treatment

Opiates refer generally to a class of chemical compounds that are obtained from natural plant matter, specifically poppy plants, and opioids are chemical compounds that are synthesized in a laboratory to mimic plant-based biochemistry.[53] In humans, opioids activate nerve cells in the brain and body called "opioid receptors" which interfere with pain signaling between the body and brain. Opioid medications refer generally to a class of prescription drugs that include pain relievers such as oxycodone (e.g., OxyContin®; Percocet®), hydrocodone (e.g., Vicodin®), oxymorphone (e.g., Opana®), morphine (e.g., Kadian®, Avinza®), codeine, and fentanyl, all of which have been approved by the FDA.[54] In addition to opioids available legally by prescription, there are also illegal "street" versions of opioids, such as heroin and synthetic fentanyl.[55] Hereafter, the term

[50] L. Manchikanti et al., "An updated assessment of utilization of interventional pain management techniques in the Medicare population: 2000–2013," *Pain Physician* 18, no. 2 (2015).

[51] See generally A. Althaus et al., "Postoperative Pain Trajectories and Pain Chronification-an Empirical Typology of Pain Patients," *Pain Med* 19, no. 12 (2018); D. Borsook et al., "When pain gets stuck: the evolution of pain chronification and treatment resistance," *Pain* 159, no. 12 (2018); D. J. Pak et al., "Chronification of Pain: Mechanisms, Current Understanding, and Clinical Implications," *Curr Pain Headache Rep* 22, no. 2 (2018).

[52] The attributable costs of opioid SAEs will be explored in detail in Chap. 6.

[53] ADPC, "Opiates or Opioids—What's the difference?," (Salem, OR: State of Oregon, Alcohol and Drug Policy Commission (ADPC), 2023).

[54] FDA, "Timeline of Selected FDA Activities and Significant Events Addressing Opioid Misuse and Abuse," (U.S. Food and Drug Administration, 2021).

[55] According to the National Institute on Drug Abuse ("NIDA"), heroin is defined as "an opioid drug made from morphine, a natural substance taken from the seed pod of the various

"opioids" is used to refer generally to this class of prescription drugs. When the terms "opioid supply," "opioid demand," and "opioid misuse," are used, the terms are referring generally to prescription *and* illicit opioids. However, in some cases it is necessary to further differentiate by using the term "prescription opioid" to refer generally to opioids sourced from the healthcare system by way of a legal and valid prescription, "non-prescription opioid" to refer generally to opioids that were initially sourced by the healthcare system but then subsequently diverted to non-medical use, and "illicit opioids" to refer generally to opioids sourced exclusively through illegal channels, such as drug trafficking. In the latter group, it is assumed generally that illicit opioids consist mainly of heroin (an opiate) and synthetic fentanyl, though in some instances illicit opioids can include illicitly obtained prescription opioids (e.g., stolen shipments and those distributed unlawfully by prescription drug sellers and drug dealers), and counterfeit opioid pills, which can contain a mix of opioid and non-opioid ingredients. The specific composition of illicit opioids has evolved over time and has varied geographically, but in recent years illicit opioids have consisted predominantly of synthetic fentanyl.

Although prescription opioids have been alleged to have contributed to the opioid crisis in the U.S., opioids continue to be prescribed by physicians for the treatment of pain in instances where the drugs continue to demonstrate clinical benefit. The Stanford-Lancet Commission on opioids emphasized the "dual nature" of opioids, acknowledging that "opioids are both essential to modern medical practice and at the same time potentially dangerous."[56] Earlier, the IOM report on pain referred to the "opioid conundrum," stating that "the committee recognizes the serious problem with diversion and abuse of opioid drugs, as well as questions about their long-term usefulness. However, the committee believes that when opioids are used as prescribed and appropriately monitored, they can be safe and effective, especially for acute, postoperative, and procedural pain, as well as for patients near the end of life who

opium poppy plants grown in Southeast and Southwest Asia, Mexico, and Colombia. Heroin can be a white or brown powder, or a black sticky substance known as black tar heroin." See NIDA, "Heroin Drug Facts," (Washington, D.C.: National Institute on Drug Abuse | U.S. National Institutes for Health, 2021).

[56] K. Humphreys et al., "Responding to the opioid crisis in North America and beyond: recommendations of the Stanford-Lancet Commission," *Lancet* 399, no. 10324 (2022). (p.24).

desire more pain relief."[57] Accordingly, a recurring theme in this book is that opioids are unique in that, though misuse of opioids can in some cases lead to adverse events and harms, opioids were and continue to be clinically effective pain medications, approved by the FDA following rigorous clinical studies and utilized in practice with most users not experiencing any side effects and some others experiencing minimal and tolerable side effects or adverse events.[58] According to a consensus study conducted jointly by the National Academies of Sciences, Engineering and Medicine ("NASEM," "The prescription of medication represents a rapid method of addressing a pain complaint, certainly accomplished more easily than providing a course of physical therapy, psychological counseling, spinal injection, or many other available approaches to the treatment of pain. For that reason, analgesics, including powerful opioid pain relievers, are an appealing option."[59]

Evidence of the clinical efficacy of opioid-based pharmacological treatments has been established for patients with specific characteristics in a variety of clinical settings, including the treatment of pain associated with critical care, acute injuries, procedural pain, some chronic conditions, and palliative care. In intensive care and critical care settings, one of the advantages of opioids is their potency and reliability of effects, which is particularly valuable in patients who are less able to clearly express pain levels.[60] In general, opioids have been shown to be clinically effective in critical care and intensive care settings, including pain management in post-surgical recovery and patients on mechanical ventilators.[61] These

[57] IOM, "Relieving Pain in America: A Blueprint for Transforming Prevention, Care, Education, and Research." (p.22).

[58] For an overview of the opioid clinical utility, refer to NASEM, *Pain Management and the Opioid Epidemic: Balancing Societal and Indidivual Benefits and Risks of Prescription Opioid Use*. This study is at times alternatively referred to as the "Consensus Study" by the National Academy of Sciences.

[59] Ibid., p.64.

[60] V. Pota et al., "Pain in Intensive Care: A Narrative Review," *Pain Ther* 11, no. 2 (2022).

[61] See, for example, Y. Aoki et al., "Effects of fentanyl administration in mechanically ventilated patients in the intensive care unit: a systematic review and meta-analysis," *BMC Anesthesiol* 22, no. 1 (2022); L. Q. Rong et al., "High-dose versus low-dose opioid anesthesia in adult cardiac surgery: A meta-analysis," *J Clin Anesth* 57 (2019); J. A. J. Martyn, J. Mao, and E. A. Bittner, "Opioid Tolerance in Critical Illness," *N Engl J Med* 380, no. 4 (2019); NASEM, *Pain Management and the Opioid Epidemic: Balancing Societal and Indidivual Benefits and Risks of Prescription Opioid Use*.

benefits also extend to palliative care settings, including cases with breakthrough cancer pain, advanced stages of cancer,[62] and end-stage renal disease.[63] Consistent with the critical care findings, opioids have also been shown to be effective in the short-term treatment of acute pain.[64] In contrast, the evidence supporting opioid use in chronic non-cancer pain is mixed, due primarily to the tradeoffs associated with effectiveness of pain relief versus adverse events, especially SAEs associated with longer-term use, such as dependence and OUD. For example, a systematic review by Avouac et al. found that opioids significantly decreased pain levels and improved functioning in patients with osteoarthritis.[65] However, several other systematic reviews of opioid use for chronic pain found either very small or insignificant pain control effects but significant adverse events associated with longer-term opioid-based treatment.[66] Nevertheless, in certain clinical scenarios, such as poor tolerance of NSAIDs, opioid-based treatment may be considered the optimal treatment for acute pain

[62] See, for example, B. LeBon, G. Zeppetella, and I. J. Higginson, "Effectiveness of topical administration of opioids in palliative care: a systematic review," *J Pain Symptom Manage* 37, no. 5 (2009); F. A. Bailey et al., "Palliative care intervention for choice and use of opioids in the last hours of life," *J Gerontol A Biol Sci Med Sci* 63, no. 9 (2008); M. Fallon, G. Hanks, and N. Cherny, "Principles of control of cancer pain," *Bmj* 332, no. 7548 (2006); J. A. Paice et al., "Use of Opioids for Adults With Pain From Cancer or Cancer Treatment: ASCO Guideline," *J Clin Oncol* 41, no. 4 (2023).

[63] See, for example, A. Wyne et al., "Opioid and benzodiazepine use in end-stage renal disease: a systematic review," *Clin J Am Soc Nephrol* 6, no. 2 (2011).

[64] See, for example, R. Daoust et al., "Efficacy of prescribed opioids for acute pain after being discharged from the emergency department: A systematic review and meta-analysis," *Acad Emerg Med* 30, no. 12 (2023).

[65] J. Avouac, L. Gossec, and M. Dougados, "Efficacy and safety of opioids for osteoarthritis: a meta-analysis of randomized controlled trials," *Osteoarthritis Cartilage* 15, no. 8 (2007).

[66] See, for example, M. C. Osani, L. S. Lohmander, and R. R. Bannuru, "Is There Any Role for Opioids in the Management of Knee and Hip Osteoarthritis? A Systematic Review and Meta-Analysis," *Arthritis Care Res (Hoboken)* 73, no. 10 (2021); P. Welsch et al., "Opioids for chronic osteoarthritis pain: An updated systematic review and meta-analysis of efficacy, tolerability and safety in randomized placebo-controlled studies of at least 4 weeks double-blind duration," *Eur J Pain* 24, no. 4 (2020); R. Chou et al., "Research gaps on use of opioids for chronic noncancer pain: findings from a review of the evidence for an American Pain Society and American Academy of Pain Medicine clinical practice guideline," *J Pain* 10, no. 2 (2009); R. Chou et al., "The effectiveness and risks of long-term opioid therapy for chronic pain: a systematic review for a National Institutes of Health Pathways to Prevention Workshop," *Ann Intern Med* 162, no. 4 (2015).

and some types of chronic pain, if managed properly.[67] In recent years, even after significant changes in opioid prescribing guidelines, the clinical use of opioids has continued in therapeutic areas in which clinical utility is well established and the risk-benefit profile supports continued use.[68] Opioid-based treatments have also generally been considered good "value for money," typically resulting in favorable cost-effectiveness attributes, due in part to their relatively low per-unit costs.[69]

3.8 Opioid Utilization

As perceptions of pain evolved, so too did the role of opioids. Though the forms of opioids fueling the current crisis are a relatively recent phenomenon, the use of opioids to treat pain and its associated maladies has a much deeper history.[70] Some of the more recent history will be discussed later in the context of root causes and contributing factors related to contemporary issues, but issues regarding opioid utilization have a complex history that pre-dates recent events. Medical and non-medical use of opioids globally is believed to date as far back as the sixteenth century.[71]

[67] See generally J. L. Goodwin, J. J. Kraemer, and Z. H. Bajwa, "The use of opioids in the treatment of osteoarthritis: when, why, and how?," *Curr Rheumatol Rep* 11, no. 1 (2009); R. Payne, "Limitations of NSAIDs for pain management: toxicity or lack of efficacy?," *J Pain* 1, no. 3 Suppl (2000).

[68] See generally D. Dowell et al., "Prescribing Opioids for Pain—The New CDC Clinical Practice Guideline," *N Engl J Med* 387, no. 22 (2022).

[69] For example, refer to I. Backhaus, A. Mannocci, and G. La Torre, "A Systematic Review of Economic Evaluation Studies of Drug-Based Non-Malignant Chronic Pain Treatment," *Curr Pharm Biotechnol* 20, no. 11 (2019); B. Hass et al., "Cost-effectiveness of strong opioids focussing on the long-term effects of opioid-related fractures: a model approach," *Eur J Health Econ* 10, no. 3 (2009); J. Marsden et al., "Superiority and cost-effectiveness of monthly extended-release buprenorphine versus daily standard of care medication: a pragmatic, parallel-group, open-label, multicentre, randomised, controlled, phase 3 trial," *EClinicalMedicine* 66 (2023); J. Shi et al., "Cost Effectiveness of Pharmacological Management for Osteoarthritis: A Systematic Review," *Appl Health Econ Health Policy* 20, no. 3 (2022).

[70] See generally H. Joseph, S. Stancliff, and J. Langrod, "Methadone maintenance treatment (MMT): a review of historical and clinical issues," *Mt Sinai J Med* 67, no. 5–6 (2000); R. G. Lande, "American Civil War medical practice, the post-bellum opium crisis and modern comparisons," *Hist Psychiatry* 31, no. 4 (2020).

[71] A. Moosavyzadeh et al., "The medieval Persian manuscript of Afyunieh: the first individual treatise on the opium and addiction in history," *J Integr Med* 16, no. 2 (2018).

According to one historian, "Starting in the sixteenth century, manuscripts can be found describing drug abuse and tolerance in Turkey, Egypt, Germany, and England. Nowhere was the problem of addiction greater than in China where the practice of smoking opium began in the mid-seventeenth century after tobacco smoking was banned."[72] Morphine was first synthesized in Germany in 1804, and its heroin derivative was later synthesized in 1874.[73] In the intervening decades, a combination of economic cycles, conflicts, wars, and other factors have resulted in periods of fluctuation in the use and misuse of opioids throughout many different parts of the world, including the U.S.[74]

In the U.S., the most recent change in opioid use and misuse began roughly 30 years ago, in the early 1990s, following the FDA approval of the first long-acting (12-hour) opioid-based pain relievers MS Contin (1987) and OxyContin (1995),[75] and a parallel shift in the healthcare sector toward patient-centered care and palliative care combined with an embracing of patient-reported pain as the "fifth vital sign." This "perfect storm" of supply and demand effects led to relatively rapid growth in opioid utilization from the late 1990s and through the first decade of the 2000s. According to data collected in the National Survey on Drug Use and Health ("NSDUH"), the prevalence of individuals using *any* opioid in the past year was 27.0% in 2021.[76] The NSDUH is based on a sample of the U.S. population ages 18 and older,[77] and is broadly

[72] M. J. Brownstein, "A brief history of opiates, opioid peptides, and opioid receptors," *Proc Natl Acad Sci U S A* 90, no. 12 (1993).

[73] Lalkhen, *An Anatomy of Pain*.

[74] A. Case and A. Deaton, *Deaths of Despair and the Future of Capitalism* (Princeton, NJ: Princeton University Press, 2020).

[75] FDA, "Timeline of Selected FDA Activities and Significant Events Addressing Opioid Misuse and Abuse."

[76] Refer to NSDUH Table 1.61B "Any Use of Opioids in Past Year: Among People Aged 12 or Older; by Age Group and Demographic Characteristics, Percentages, 2021." Also note that these NDUH questions pertain only past-year users of *any* prescription drug.

[77] According to the Substance Abuse and Mental Health Services Administration ("SAMHSA"), "NSDUH is an annual multimode survey sponsored by the Substance Abuse and Mental Health Services Administration within the U.S. Department of Health and Human Services. NSDUH covers residents of households and people in noninstitutional group settings (e.g., shelters, boarding houses, college dormitories, migratory workers' camps, halfway houses). The survey excludes people with no fixed address (e.g., people who are homeless and not in shelters), military personnel on active duty, and residents of

considered a reliable[78] and commonly cited[79] source of data on drug use patterns in the U.S., including data on drug misuse and substance use disorder ("SUD").[80]

The genesis of the recent opioid crisis is frequently offhandedly attributed to a single letter written to the editors of one of the most prominent medical journals in the world. As Jones et al. describes it, "The misrepresentation of one study largely laid the groundwork for the marketing practices that spawned the opioid epidemic in the United States. In 1980, the *New England Journal of Medicine* published a letter from a Boston University Medical Center physician, Dr. Hershel Jick, who studied more than 11,000 patients receiving opioids in the inpatient setting. Jick concluded that 'despite widespread use of narcotic drugs in hospitals, the development of addiction is rare in medical patients with no

institutional group settings, such as jails, nursing homes, mental health institutions, and long-term care hospitals." Sample sizes are approximately 70,000–80,000 each year. See generally SAMHSA, "National Survey on Drug Use and Health (NSDUH), 2021 Data," (Washington, D.C.: U.S. Department of Health and Human Services, Substance Abuse and Mental Health Services Administration (SAMHSA), Center for Behavioral Health Statistics and Quality, 2022).

[78] See generally "Reliability of Key Measures in the National Survey on Drug Use and Health," in *Methodology Series M-8, HHS Publication No. SMA 09–4425* (Rockville (MD): U.S. Department of Health and Human Services, Substance Abuse and Mental Health Services Administration, Office of Applied Studies, 2010).

[79] NSDUH is widely cited as a source of epidemiologic data on opioid use and misuse; for some examples, see variously S. Davenport, A. Weaver, and M. Caverly, "Economic Impact of Non-Medical Opioid Use in the United States: Annual Estimates and Projections for 2015 through 2019," (Schaumburg, IL: Society of Actuaries, 2019); C. Florence, F. Luo, and K. Rice, "The economic burden of opioid use disorder and fatal opioid overdose in the United States, 2017," *Drug Alcohol Depend* 218 (2021); F. Luo, M. Li, and C. Florence, "State-Level Economic Costs of Opioid Use Disorder and Fatal Opioid Overdose—United States, 2017," *MMWR Morb Mortal Wkly Rep* 70, no. 15 (2021); A. Aslam and P. Y. Kwo, "Epidemiology and Disease Burden of Alcohol Associated Liver Disease," *J Clin Exp Hepatol* 13, no. 1 (2023); N. Chelikam et al., "Epidemiology, Burden, and Association of Substance Abuse Amongst Patients With Cardiovascular Disorders: National Cross-Sectional Survey Study," *Cureus* 14, no. 7 (2022); K. H. Yang et al., "Trends in major depressive episodes and mental health treatment among older adults in the United States, 2010–2019," *J Affect Disord* 318 (2022).

[80] The NSDUH defines "misuse" as "use in any way not directed by a doctor, including use without a prescription of one's own; use in greater amounts, more often, or longer than told; or use in any other way not directed by a doctor."

history of addiction.'"[81] Though Jick's non-peer-reviewed letter appeared more than a decade before FDA approval of long-acting opioids like OxyContin, the letter continued to be cited by physicians, manufacturers, and other stakeholders as an authoritative source on the addictive properties of opioids.[82] This conventional wisdom, based on a letter that was neither peer-reviewed nor based on any sort of case-controlled study, essentially provided cover for manufacturers, distributors, and thousands of physician prescribers putting opioids in the hands of patients, allowing them to publicly state, and in some cases believe, that opioids were not associated with unusual or concerning addictive properties or serious adverse events. While the letter is anecdotally credited with helping fuel the initial proliferation of prescription opioids, it was of course not the sole source of the problem; in fact, as it turned out, it was neither the spark nor the fan for the flames. The main precipitating factors will be discussed in greater detail in Chap. 4, which provides a more in-depth exploration of the myriad root causes and contributing factors that led to the current opioid crisis.

3.9 Opioid Misuse

As alluded to in the introduction, with regard to opioid misuse it is important to differentiate between opioids that are prescribed and used as directed, versus those that are either (1) prescribed and subsequently used improperly, or (2) obtained illegally. Both of these scenarios constitute "non-medical" use or misuse. The concept of non-medical use typically refers to an instance of prescription drug use that is inconsistent with how the medication was prescribed by a medical care provider.[83] The non-medical use of opioids is broadly defined, including prescription drug "non-adherence" (for example, taking medications at intervals different

[81] G. H. Jones et al., "The opioid epidemic in the United States-Overview, origins, and potential solutions," *Cancer* 124, no. 22 (2018).

[82] P.T.M. Leung et al., "A 1980 Letter on the Risk of Opioid Addiction," *New England Journal of Medicine* 376, no. 22 (2017).

[83] J. M. Tetrault and J. L. Butner, "Non-Medical Prescription Opioid Use and Prescription Opioid Use Disorder: A Review," *Yale J Biol Med* 88, no. 3 (2015); E. Ulker and E. Del Fabbro, "Best Practices in the Management of Nonmedical Opioid Use in Patients with Cancer-Related Pain," *Oncologist* 25, no. 3 (2020).

than prescribed),[84] but also including behaviors that could be considered misuse, such as taking more pills than prescribed, continuing to take the medication after pain subsides, or taking medication for means other than pain control. The National Academies of Science *Consensus Study* on opioids observed that "Any prescription medication that produces pleasurable effects or potential functional benefits poses an inherent risk or misuse."[85] According to NSDUH data, the prevalence of individuals misusing any opioid in 2021 was 3.4%.[86] This is broadly consistent with studies that use alternative sources of data. For example, Saha et al. reported an opioid misuse rate of 4.1% based on data from the 2012–2013 National Epidemiologic Survey on Alcohol and Related Conditions-III ("NESARC-III").[87] The period studied by Saha et al. coincides with the peak period of prescription opioid supply in the U.S. (i.e., around 2012), which may explain why its findings are slightly higher than the current NSDUH prevalence of misuse. These data suggest that approximately 96–97% of prescription opioids are used medically "as directed." These data are consistent with anecdotal evidence from medical professionals and other experts, who generally agree that "the vast majority of the people prescribed opioids do not misuse them."[88]

Misuse is a subset of what is often referred to as "new persistent opioid use" ("NPOU"), which is defined as use of prescription opioids significantly longer than initially prescribed. Definitions vary considerably, but most define NPOU as opioid use more than 2–3 months following the initial "index" prescription (e.g., at time of discharge following surgery).[89] Though the use of opioids more than 2–3 months beyond the index

[84] For background refer to R. Nieuwlaat et al., "Interventions for enhancing medication adherence," *Cochrane Database Syst Rev* 2014, no. 11 (2014).

[85] NASEM, *Pain Management and the Opioid Epidemic: Balancing Societal and Indidivual Benefits and Risks of Prescription Opioid Use.*

[86] Refer to NSDUH Table 1.19B "Any Use of Opioids in Past Year and Misuse of Opioids in Past Year and Past Month: Among People Aged 12 or Older; by Detailed Age Category, Percentages, 2021."

[87] T. D. Saha et al., "Nonmedical Prescription Opioid Use and DSM-5 Nonmedical Prescription Opioid Use Disorder in the United States," *J Clin Psychiatry* 77, no. 6 (2016).

[88] NASEM, *Pain Management and the Opioid Epidemic: Balancing Societal and Indidivual Benefits and Risks of Prescription Opioid Use.*

[89] L. D. Delaney and J. F. Waljee, "New persistent opioid use: definitions and opportunities," *Reg Anesth Pain Med* 46, no. 2 (2021).

prescription may raise concerns, it may or may not be indicative of opioid misuse. In other words, persistent use could be caused by at least five factors: (1) failure of the index dosage to adequately control pain; (2) complications following the initial procedure; (3) variation in patient pain tolerance or patient preferences; (4) variation in physician preferences and usual approach regarding pain management; and (5) drug-seeking behavior by patients, indicating misuse.[90] It is important to note that only the last of these—drug-seeking behavior by patients—would *per se* constitute misuse, whereas the other four explanations reflect patients taking opioids lawfully prescribed by physicians based on a physician's clinical perception of medical need. That is, the presence of NPOU does not necessarily imply misuse. Epidemiological data generally support misuse being a subset of NPOU, with observed NPOU rates usually higher than average misuse rates, in the 4–10% range, depending on type of initial procedure, sample size, and study design.[91]

The term "opioid use disorder" ("OUD," which is listed in the American Psychiatric Association DSM-5, generally refers to repeated or consistent misuse of opioids, and includes more clinically serious forms of abuse or addiction.[92] Misuse is a subset of non-medical use, and OUD is a subset of misuse. The NSDUH also assesses the prevalence of a subset of individuals with SUD specifically pertaining to opioids, commonly termed opioid use disorder.[93] The 2021 survey found an annual "any opioid"

[90] See generally R. Bologheanu et al., "New Persistent Opioid Use After Surgery," *JAMA Netw Open* 8, no. 2 (2025); R. Howard et al., "Evidence-Based Opioid Prescribing Guidelines and New Persistent Opioid Use After Surgery," *Ann Surg* 278, no. 2 (2023); A. O. Luby et al., "Trends in Opioid Prescribing and New Persistent Opioid Use After Surgery in the United States," ibid.281, no. 3 (2025); K. B. Santosa et al., "Long-term Health Outcomes of New Persistent Opioid Use After Surgery Among Medicare Beneficiaries," ibid.278 (2023).

[91] For example, see K. Hessami et al., "Perioperative opioid dispensing and persistent use after benign hysterectomy: a systematic review and meta-analysis," *Am J Obstet Gynecol* 229, no. 1 (2023); O. D. Lawal et al., "Rate and Risk Factors Associated With Prolonged Opioid Use After Surgery: A Systematic Review and Meta-analysis," *JAMA Netw Open* 3, no. 6 (2020); K. Nasser et al., "New persistent opioid use after bariatric surgery: a systematic review and pooled proportion meta-analysis," *Surg Endosc* 37, no. 1 (2023); C. Ung et al., "Persistent Opioid Use after Ophthalmic Surgery in Opioid-Naive Patients and Associated Risk Factors," *Ophthalmology* 128, no. 9 (2021).

[92] See generally A. M. Dydyk, N. K. Jain, and M. Gupta, "Opioid Use Disorder," in *StatPearls* (Treasure Island (FL): StatPearls Publishing LLC., 2021).

[93] The NSDUH adopts a standard definition of OUD, which they report as follows: "Respondents were classified as having an [OUD] if they met criteria in the *Diagnostic and*

OUD prevalence of 2.1% among individuals aged 18 or older.[94] There is some reported variance in rates of OUD in various population subgroups. Studies of Medicaid populations, for example, which disproportionately cover lower income individuals (who are at higher risk for SUDs[95]), reflect a somewhat wider range of OUD prevalence. A study of West Virginia Medicaid enrollees found an annual OUD prevalence of 5.5%,[96] and a study of Oregon Medicaid enrollees found OUD rates ranging from 2.5 to 5.0%.[97] It should be noted that some researchers believe that the NSDUH methodology undercounts OUD because it is a population-based survey, and drug users are more likely to be incarcerated, homeless, or hospitalized. Some studies have shown that using what are sometimes referred to as "capture re-capture" statistical estimation methods, population OUD prevalence estimates can be as high as 4–5%, which is consistent with rates observed in Medicaid populations and approximately double the NSDUH estimate. However, the origins of capture re-capture techniques are in animal tracking and management, where the probabilities of

Statistical Manual of Mental Disorders, 5th edition (DSM-5)." The survey uses two measures of OUD: (1) opioid use disorder due to any use of opioids; and (2) opioid use disorder due to the misuse of opioids. OUD due to any use was defined as "having a heroin use disorder or a pain reliever use disorder. Respondents who reported *any* use of prescription pain relievers in the past year and met DSM-5 criteria for pain reliever use disorder were classified as having a pain reliever use disorder." Disorder due to misuse was defined as "having a heroin use disorder or a pain reliever use disorder among past year misusers of prescription pain relievers. Respondents who reported the misuse of prescription pain relievers in the past year and met DSM-5 criteria for pain reliever use disorder were classified as having a pain reliever use disorder due to misuse." NSDUH further notes that "Respondents were not counted as having an opioid use disorder if they did not meet the full substance use disorder criteria for heroin or prescription pain relievers individually."

94 Refer to NSDUH Table 5.1B: "Substance Use Disorder for Specific Substances in Past Year: Among People Aged 12 or Older; by Age Group, Percentages, 2021."

95 This is discussed in greater detail later in the book. For a brief overview of higher SUD rates in the Medicaid population, see generally H. Saunders and R. Rudowitz, "Demographics and Health Insurance Coverage of Nonelderly Adults With Mental Illness and Substance Use Disorders in 2020," (San Francisco, CA: Kaiser Family Foundation (KFF), 2022).

96 B. Saloner et al., "The Affordable Care Act In The Heart Of The Opioid Crisis: Evidence From West Virginia," *Health Aff (Millwood)* 38, no. 4 (2019).

97 R. Springer et al., "Prescription opioid use patterns, use disorder diagnoses and addiction treatment receipt after the 2014 Medicaid expansion in Oregon," *Addiction* 114, no. 10 (2019).

occurrence in different rounds of "capture" (or in different locations) are generally statistically independent.[98] This is less likely to be the case in the real world, where confounding factors like socioeconomic conditions in a geographic area may result in the correlation of rates based on different sources from the same area. In addition, the results of the approach are more likely to be biased if the probability of capture differs among population subgroups. Consequently, estimates from capture-recapture studies are associated with relatively wide confidence intervals (1.6–4.1%), intervals that encompass the NSDUH estimate of 2.1%.[99]

In addition to OUD, use of opioids during pregnancy can in some cases be associated with neonatal abstinence syndrome ("NAS")[100] and neonatal opioid withdrawal syndrome ("NOWS"). The term NAS typically refers to a condition present in some infants born to mothers who engaged in some form of drug use or polysubstance abuse during pregnancy. It is typically described as a "temporary phenomenon that may or may not require treatment," and that "available data do not suggest an association between NAS in particular and long-term adverse developmental outcomes, regardless of whether NAS was severe enough to require treatment."[101] The incidence of NAS is relatively low, estimated to be 0.73% in the U.S. in 2017.[102] NOWS is considered a subset of NAS, and refers generally to NAS that is attributable specifically to opioid misuse.[103] In both

[98] K. Tilling, "Capture-recapture methods—useful or misleading?," *International Journal of Epidemiology* 30, no. 1 (2001).

[99] K. M. Keyes et al., "What is the prevalence of and trend in opioid use disorder in the United States from 2010 to 2019? Using multiplier approaches to estimate prevalence for an unknown population size," *Drug Alcohol Depend Rep* 3 (2022).

[100] Although NAS is often attributed to opioids, the definition of NAS refers generally to substance abuse during pregnancy, and attribution to a specific abused substance, such as opioids, is often difficult. See generally P. Kocherlakota, "Neonatal abstinence syndrome," *Pediatrics* 134, no. 2 (2014).

[101] NASEM, *Pain Management and the Opioid Epidemic: Balancing Societal and Indidivual Benefits and Risks of Prescription Opioid Use.*

[102] A. H. Hirai et al., "Neonatal Abstinence Syndrome and Maternal Opioid-Related Diagnoses in the US, 2010–2017," *Jama* 325, no. 2 (2021).

[103] A. E. Weller et al., "Neonatal Opioid Withdrawal Syndrome (NOWS): A Transgenerational Echo of the Opioid Crisis," *Cold Spring Harb Perspect Med* 11, no. 3 (2021).

cases, even if NAS cases can be linked specifically to opioid use, it is difficult to quantitively disentangle effects attributable to medical use versus non-medical use of opioids.[104]

At some level of abstraction, OUD can also be thought of in the context of a drug adverse event. Most prescription medications are associated with some level of risk of adverse events, and the FDA's regulatory responsibility is mainly to balance the tradeoffs associated with treatment effectiveness and treatment-related adverse events.[105] This balancing typically results in average post-approval and post-market rates of prescription drug SAEs ranging from 2.5% to 6.7%, depending on therapeutic application, patient characteristics, and treatment settings.[106] Implicit in the regulatory approval process is that adverse event rates for approved drugs represent the outcome of an analysis of the "costs" (adverse events) and "benefits" (clinical utility) of a novel drug; that is, the rates are the regulatory outcome of an assessment of the tradeoff between clinical efficacy and clinical risk.[107] Following approval, adverse event rates that are consistent with those observed in pre-approval clinical studies

[104] NASEM, *Pain Management and the Opioid Epidemic: Balancing Societal and Indidivual Benefits and Risks of Prescription Opioid Use.*

[105] An example of this is the management of adverse bleeding events in use of anti-thrombotic therapy. See generally K. Sugano, "How do we manage serious gastrointestinal adverse events associated with anti-thrombotic therapy?," *Expert Rev Gastroenterol Hepatol* 9, no. 1 (2015). Cardiovascular adverse events are also relatively prevalent; see for example D. M. Rackham et al., "Evidence behind FDA alerts for drugs with adverse cardiovascular effects: implications for clinical practice," *Pharmacotherapy* 34, no. 4 (2014).

[106] See generally S. V. Taché, A. Sönnichsen, and D. M. Ashcroft, "Prevalence of adverse drug events in ambulatory care: a systematic review," *Ann Pharmacother* 45, no. 7–8 (2011); D. S. Budnitz et al., "US Emergency Department Visits Attributed to Medication Harms, 2017–2019," *Jama* 326, no. 13 (2021); J. J. Coleman and S. K. Pontefract, "Adverse drug reactions," *Clin Med (Lond)* 16, no. 5 (2016); M. Pirmohamed et al., "Adverse drug reactions as cause of admission to hospital: prospective analysis of 18 820 patients," *Bmj* 329, no. 7456 (2004); R. Raschetti et al., "Suspected adverse drug events requiring emergency department visits or hospital admissions," *Eur J Clin Pharmacol* 54, no. 12 (1999); J. Sultana, P. Cutroneo, and G. Trifirò, "Clinical and economic burden of adverse drug reactions," *J Pharmacol Pharmacother* 4, no. Suppl 1 (2013); GAO, "Adverse Drug Events: The Magnitude of Health Risk is Uncertain Because of Limited Incidence Data," (Washington D.C.: U.S. General Accounting Office, 2000). Also see generally N. Rafter et al., "Adverse events in healthcare: learning from mistakes," *Qjm* 108, no. 4 (2015).

[107] Some insight as to how the FDA balances such risks is described in FDA, "Benefit-Risk Assessment for New Drug and Biological Products: Guidance for Industry," (Washington, D.C.: U.S. Food & Drug Administration, 2021).

represent rates that would generally be considered "actuarially expected" by the regulatory, clinical, payer, and provider communities. Rates of SAEs among specific FDA approved drugs vary considerably, but for some drugs rates can be relatively high, in the range of 3–10%, depending on the drug and its therapeutic application.[108] As discussed above, average rates of SAEs in opioid utilization range from 2 to 5%, depending on clinical application and population subgroup.[109] Accordingly, the 2.1% prevalence of OUD can be considered an SAE occurring in some instances following sustained misuse, and occurring at rates somewhat similar to SAE rates associated with various other approved drugs.

3.10 Polysubstance Use

Individuals who misuse opioids are also highly likely to abuse other drugs, engaging in what is often termed "polysubstance use" ("PSU"), which is generally defined as the misuse of more than one drug at the same time or over a relatively short period.[110] In 2019, among all deaths attributable to some form of drug overdose, nearly 50% involved observable PSU.[111] Even among the more prevalent SUDs, such as alcohol abuse, PSU has

[108] See generally S. Chenchula, S. Atal, and C. R. S. Uppugunduri, "A review of real-world evidence on preemptive pharmacogenomic testing for preventing adverse drug reactions: a reality for future health care," *Pharmacogenomics J* 24, no. 2 (2024); K. P. Collins et al., "Landscape analysis of adverse events and dose intensity for FDA approved oncology small molecules," *Cancer Chemother Pharmacol* 95, no. 1 (2025); S.S. Lynch, "Adverse Drug Reactions (Adverse Drug Effects, Medication Side Effects)," in *Merck Manual* (Rahway, N. J.: 2025); K. B. Sonawane, N. Cheng, and R. A. Hansen, "Serious Adverse Drug Events Reported to the FDA: Analysis of the FDA Adverse Event Reporting System 2006–2014 Database," *J Manag Care Spec Pharm* 24, no. 7 (2018).

[109] See, for example, C. Els et al., "Adverse events associated with medium- and long-term use of opioids for chronic non-cancer pain: an overview of Cochrane Reviews," *Cochrane Database Syst Rev* 10, no. 10 (2017); S. J. Herzig et al., "Opioid utilization and opioid-related adverse events in nonsurgical patients in US hospitals," *J Hosp Med* 9, no. 2 (2014); D. L. Murphy et al., "Comparative Rates of Mortality and Serious Adverse Effects Among Commonly Prescribed Opioid Analgesics," *Drug Saf* 41, no. 8 (2018); S. Shafi et al., "Association of Opioid-Related Adverse Drug Events With Clinical and Cost Outcomes Among Surgical Patients in a Large Integrated Health Care Delivery System," *JAMA Surg* 153, no. 8 (2018).

[110] CDC, "Polysubstance Use Facts," (Washington, D.C.: U.S. Centers for Disease Control and Prevention, 2022a).

[111] Ibid.

been observed in relatively high prevalence. For example, one study found that 11.3% of individuals diagnosed with a SUD had concurrent alcohol and illicit drug use disorders.[112] Similarly, Liu et al. found that the prevalence of simultaneous alcohol use among cocaine users was 77% and the estimated prevalence of simultaneous cannabis use among cocaine users was 64%.[113] As one might expect, these same relationships have been observed among individuals who misuse opioids. Morley et al., for example, analyzed data from the Global Drug Survey.[114] Controlling for country of residence and various sociodemographic factors, misuse of illicit drugs was associated with a *four-fold* greater likelihood of opioid misuse compared to those who did not misuse illicit drugs. It is also the case that, in recent years, as the supply of diverted prescription opioids and illicit opioids has become more restricted, individuals engaging in PSU have expanded their menu to include new high-toxicity drugs, such as Xylazine, an adrenergic receptor agonist approved for use only in animals.[115] In addition, there has been reversion back to the use of drugs like cocaine and methylamphetamine, leading some public health experts to describe the current period of drug abuse in the U.S. as an "addiction crisis" rather than an opioid crisis.[116]

3.11 Sources of Opioids

Whereas incidence and prevalence of adverse outcomes are typically the focus of epidemiological studies, it is also important to identify the "vector" of harm; that is, the specific avenue through which the suspected causal agent reaches the affected individual. The most widespread usage of

[112] E. A. Crummy et al., "One Is Not Enough: Understanding and Modeling Polysubstance Use," *Front Neurosci* 14 (2020).

[113] Y. Liu et al., "The importance of considering polysubstance use: lessons from cocaine research," *Drug Alcohol Depend* 192 (2018).

[114] K. I. Morley et al., "Polysubstance use and misuse or abuse of prescription opioid analgesics: a multi-level analysis of international data," *Pain* 158, no. 6 (2017).

[115] J. Pergolizzi, Jr. et al., "The New Stealth Drug on the Street: A Narrative Review of Xylazine as a Street Drug," *Cureus* 15, no. 6 (2023). Also see K. Ruiz-Colón et al., "Xylazine intoxication in humans and its importance as an emerging adulterant in abused drugs: A comprehensive review of the literature," *Forensic Sci Int* 240 (2014).

[116] See, for example, J. Hoffman, "'A Monster': Super Meth and Other Drugs Push Crisis Beyond Opioids," *The New York Times*, no. Nov. 13 (2023).

the term *vector* is with regard to organisms, such as insects and rodents, as vectors transmitting pathogens to humans and other animals that subsequently result in bacterial or viral infections;[117] for example, mosquitos transmitting viruses to humans and causing malaria. Some have likened the opioid crisis to the concept of vectors, describing the opioid as the potentially harmful agent that is transmitted by way of a variety of vectors to humans, some of whom subsequently experience serious adverse events.[118] In the case of opioids, primary vectors include three source domains: (1) prescription opioids sourced via the healthcare system, through legal prescriptions written by licensed providers and dispensed by licensed providers and pharmacies; (2) non-prescription opioids obtained unlawfully from family and friends, by way of "diversion;" and (3) non-prescription illicit opioids sourced illegally from dealers and strangers. Again, given that the majority of opioids are not misused, and do not result in harms, the focus of these vectors is on sourcing that results in misuse or harm.

Several studies have sought to identify the various sources of misused opioids. One of the most comprehensive of these studies is by Park and Wu (2020), who analyzed data from the NSDUH (from 2015 to 2016), which was described above as a commonly referenced study on sources of opioids.[119] Across all age and sex categories, the authors found that 36.6% of individuals who reported opioid misuse during the past year obtained the opioids directly from the healthcare system. The majority (40.3%) obtained opioids unlawfully from friends and family members,[120] and another 23.1% obtained them unlawfully from a variety of other sources, including drug dealers.[121] These results are broadly consistent with other

[117] For background, see generally A. J. Wilson et al., "What is a vector?," *Philos Trans R Soc Lond B Biol Sci* 372, no. 1719 (2017).

[118] W. M. Compton and C. M. Jones, "Epidemiology of the U.S. opioid crisis: the importance of the vector," *Ann N Y Acad Sci* 1451, no. 1 (2019).

[119] J. Y. Park and L. T. Wu, "Sources of Misused Prescription Opioids and Their Association with Prescription Opioid Use Disorder in the United States: Sex and Age Differences," *Subst Use Misuse* 55, no. 6 (2020).

[120] Typically obtained for free from these sources.

[121] Includes the following sources: (1) bought from friend or relative, (2) took from friend or relative without asking, (3) bought from drug dealer or other stranger, and (4) "other" (including stolen from doctor office, clinic, hospital, or pharmacy, or obtained some other way).

studies. For example, Schepis et al., in two different studies, found very consistent results within similar age groups.[122] Data on opioid sourcing appears to be broadly consistent with the diversion of prescription medications more generally. For example, a systematic review and meta-analysis conducted by Hulme et al. reviewed 54 studies on the diversion of prescription medications and (compared to the findings of Park and Wu) found higher average rates of sourcing from friends and family (57% vs. 40.3%) and lower average rates associated with sourcing directly from the healthcare system (29% vs. 36.6%).[123]

3.11.1 Prescription Opioids

Although the opioid crisis was due in large part to the rapid proliferation of illicit opioids, opioid litigation has been focused on prescription opioids. This has been of course a matter of necessity; regardless of the causal role of illicit opioids, drug dealers and cartels do not constitute good targets for product liability litigation. Accordingly, given that the objectives of this book focus on the product liability aspects of the opioid crisis, the focus is on the supply of prescription opioids. According to the studies discussed above, among individuals who misuse opioids, about 30–37% of the opioids are sourced from the healthcare system by way of a legal prescription. The focus of the MDL on the supply of prescription opioids is largely because claimants have typically alleged that the supply of prescription opioids are in some way related to the prevalence of OUD overall, regardless of the specific source of the opioids causing the OUD.[124] This connection is of course an over-simplification, but it nevertheless has formed the basis for many of the ongoing opioid cases. Due to

[122] T. S. Schepis, S. E. McCabe, and C. J. Teter, "Sources of opioid medication for misuse in older adults: results from a nationally representative survey," *Pain* 159, no. 8 (2018); T. S. Schepis, T. E. Wilens, and S. E. McCabe, "Prescription Drug Misuse: Sources of Controlled Medications in Adolescents," *J Am Acad Child Adolesc Psychiatry* 58, no. 7 (2019).

[123] S. Hulme, D. Bright, and S. Nielsen, "The source and diversion of pharmaceutical drugs for non-medical use: A systematic review and meta-analysis," *Drug Alcohol Depend* 186 (2018).

[124] For a review, see CRS, "Overview of the Opioid Litigation and Related Settlements and Settlement Proposals," in *Legal Sidebar* (U.S. Congressional Research Service, 2019); E. Weeks and P. Sanford, "Financial Impact of the Opioid Crisis on Local Government: Quantifying Costs for Litigation and Policymaking," *Kansas Law Review* 67 (2019).

this unusual feature of the MDL, the role of prescription opioids and illicit opioids are inextricably intertwined, regardless of the veracity of the assertion that the presence of prescription opioids precipitated the crisis. As discussed early, illicit opioid markets long predated the FDA approval of long acting opioids in the early 1990s. Moreover, while it is in some cases observable to first-responders and clinicians, it has been and remains a challenge to accurately differentiate OUD-attributable harms with regard to the source of opioids (this will be revisited in subsequent chapters).[125]

There are two common ways of measuring prescription opioids: the number of prescriptions dispensed (e.g., one prescription consisting of 30 pills), or morphine milligram equivalents ("MME"), which accounts for variation in dosage. Both measures are commonly featured in opioid studies, with many studies reporting outcomes based on both. In this book, the focus is on the number of prescriptions rather than MMEs, for three reasons. First, the "transaction" at issue in cases involving prescription opioids is the legal dispensing of dosage-specific prescriptions written by licensed providers; for example, a retail pharmacy is dispensing a *prescription*, not a multiple of MMEs. Second, for clinical studies of the exact relationship between dosage and clinical outcome, MMEs may serve as a more appropriate measure. However, for studies of liability, costs, and policy, the legal unit of transaction (i.e., prescriptions) seems more relevant. Third, several studies have shown that the two measures do not vary temporally (i.e., the levels move more or less in sync over time) and generally can substitute for one another in studies of prescribing patterns.[126]

From the late 1990s until around 2012, opioid prescription rates in the U.S. increased,[127] and the increases over that time period is alleged to have

[125] See generally J. S. Potter et al., "A method to diagnose opioid dependence resulting from heroin versus prescription opioids using the Composite International Diagnostic Interview," *Contemp Clin Trials* 31, no. 2 (2010).

[126] For example, see M. V. Kiang et al., "Opioid prescribing patterns among medical providers in the United States, 2003–17: retrospective, observational study," *Bmj* 368 (2020); B. R. Meisenberg et al., "Assessment of Opioid Prescribing Practices Before and After Implementation of a Health System Intervention to Reduce Opioid Overprescribing," *JAMA Netw Open* 1, no. 5 (2018).

[127] CDC, "Opioid Precribing Data, 2006–2020," (Based on IQVIA Xponent data, 2006–2020; reported by U.S. Centers for Disease Control and Prevention 2022b).

contributed to the harm central to the current opioid litigation. However, it is important to note that, beginning in 2012, the total number of opioid prescriptions nationwide began to steadily fall, and continued to fall through 2020, when the MDL cases were well under way (Fig. 3.1). The red dashed line in Fig. 3.1 shows a plot of a two-year moving average. Generally, when stakeholders and researchers refer to the harms associated with the "oversupply" of prescription opioids, they are referring to the growth in prescription opioid supply during the period beginning with FDA approval and continuing to the inflection point in 2012 when prescription opioid rates began to fall. Allowing about five years post approval for baseline market penetration,[128] this period would be roughly

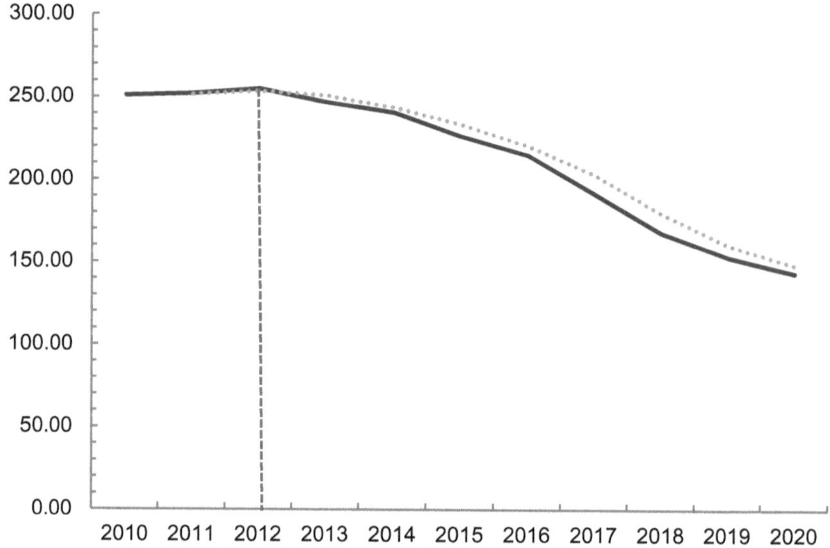

Fig. 3.1 Total U.S. Opioid Prescriptions, 2010–2020 (millions)

[128] Estimate based on the average amount of time expected for a typical pharmaceutical drug to "plateau" in terms of sales. See generally F. J. Garjón et al., "Adoption of new drugs by physicians: a survival analysis," *BMC Health Serv Res* 12 (2012); Á Lublóy, "Factors affecting the uptake of new medicines: a systematic literature review," ibid.14 (2014).

the 10-year period from 2003 to 2012. In the opioid MDL, claimants have argued generally that the growth in supply during this period lead to an "oversupply" of opioids as well as an increase in the supply of illicit opioids. The term "oversupply" has economic implications and will be revisited in subsequent chapters.

The decline in opioid prescriptions was precipitated by several factors, all of which were generally due to greater awareness of the problem and a growing urgency to address the issues on the part of policy makers and key stakeholders. The most commonly cited mitigating factors have been the following: (1) response to changes in pain-related and opioid-specific clinical practice guidelines ("CPGs") and provider education on the part of physicians, health systems, state medical societies, specialty medical societies, and the Centers for Disease Control and Prevention ("CDCP"), which (after considerable delay) issued guidelines that cautioned providers as to the clinical tradeoffs associated with opioid use and emphasized discretion in the prescribing of opioids;[129] (2) increased state and federal government oversight and monitoring of opioid prescriptions (e.g., due to increased use of prescription drug monitoring programs, or "PDMPs"[130]

[129] There were many such guidelines issued by various medical societies, health systems, and interest groups, and utilization guidelines issued by the Centers for Disease Control and Prevention ("CDC") essentially summarized emerging clinical guidelines. See generally A. S. B. Bohnert, G. P. Guy, Jr., and J. L. Losby, "Opioid Prescribing in the United States Before and After the Centers for Disease Control and Prevention's 2016 Opioid Guideline," *Ann Intern Med* 169, no. 6 (2018); J. E. Goldstick et al., "Changes in Initial Opioid Prescribing Practices After the 2016 Release of the CDC Guideline for Prescribing Opioids for Chronic Pain," *JAMA Netw Open* 4, no. 7 (2021); L. Gumidyala et al., "Effect of CDC Opioid-Prescribing Guidelines in a Community Hospital Emergency Department," *J Public Health Manag Pract* 27, no. Suppl 3 (2021); J. F. Scherrer et al., "Comparison of Opioids Prescribed for Patients at Risk for Opioid Misuse Before and After Publication of the Centers for Disease Control and Prevention's Opioid Prescribing Guidelines," *JAMA Netw Open* 3, no. 12 (2020); A. L. O'Brien et al., "Impact of Opioid Restriction Legislation on Prescribing Practices for Outpatient Plastic and Reconstructive Surgery," *Plast Reconstr Surg* 150, no. 1 (2022); F. Sandbrink et al., "Opioid Prescribing and Opioid Risk Mitigation Strategies in the Veterans Health Administration," *J Gen Intern Med* 35, no. Suppl 3 (2020).

[130] For example, refer to R. S. D'Souza, M. Lang, and J. S. Eldrige, "Prescription Drug Monitoring Program," in *StatPearls* (Treasure Island (FL): StatPearls Publishing LLC, 2022); C. S. Davis, M. Pierce, and N. Dasgupta, "Evolution and convergence of state laws governing controlled substance prescription monitoring programs, 1998–2011," *Am J Public Health* 104, no. 8 (2014); H. Y. Chang et al., "Impact of prescription drug monitoring programs and pill mill laws on high-risk opioid prescribers: A comparative

(3) an overall increase in laws and regulations governing the prescribing of opioids;[131] and (4) a variety of other factors, such as public awareness campaigns to educate patients on proper use of analgesics,[132] and legal actions against high-volume prescribers.[133] These factors generally led to higher levels of overall awareness and vigilance among clinicians and patients, which in turn resulted in markedly and consistently declining prescription opioid utilization over the past decade. However, it is interesting to note that some research has shown that the decrease in prescription opioid supply was also due in part to the evolving channels and forms of illicit opioids. For example, Donohoe and Soliman found that organizational changes in the Mexican and Colombian drug cartels and the switch from "black tar" heroin to white powdered heroin around 2012 contributed to an increase in misuse of illicit opioids.[134]

3.11.2 Diverted Opioids

An important issue in the opioid crisis is the "diversion" of prescription opioids to non-medical uses. Diversion is generally defined as "the diversion of licit drugs for illicit purposes [and] involves the diversion of drugs from legal and medically necessary uses towards uses that are illegal and typically not medically authorized or

interrupted time series analysis," *Drug Alcohol Depend* 165 (2016); L. Rutkow et al., "Effect of Florida's Prescription Drug Monitoring Program and Pill Mill Laws on Opioid Prescribing and Use," *JAMA Intern Med* 175, no. 10 (2015).

[131] C. S. Davis and A. J. Lieberman, "Laws limiting prescribing and dispensing of opioids in the United States, 1989–2019," *Addiction* 116, no. 7 (2021).

[132] See for example D. Wood et al., "Impact of a prescriber and patient educational intervention on discharge analgesia prescribing and hospital readmission rates following elective unilateral total hip and knee arthroplasty," *BMJ Open Qual* 11, no. 3 (2022); M. V. Hill et al., "An Educational Intervention Decreases Opioid Prescribing After General Surgical Operations," *Ann Surg* 267, no. 3 (2018).

[133] See generally H. Kim et al., "The Concentration of Opioid Prescriptions by Providers and Among Patients in the Oregon Medicaid Program," *Psychiatr Serv* 67, no. 4 (2016); T. Lyapustina et al., "Effect of a "pill mill" law on opioid prescribing and utilization: The case of Texas," *Drug Alcohol Depend* 159 (2016).

[134] J.T. Donahoe and A. Soliman, "What fueled the illicit opioid epidemic? New evidence from a takeover of white powder heroin markets," in *CEP Discussion Papers dp2073* (London, UK: Centre for Economic Performance, London School of Economics, 2025).

necessary."[135] More generally, it refers to any act that diverts or redirects a prescription drug from medical use to non-medical use.[136] Diversion can occur at least four different ways: (1) by patients who initially legally obtain the prescription but subsequently divert the prescription to misuse either unknowingly (e.g., by failing to secure the prescription) or knowingly by giving or selling unused drugs to others, including family and friends; (2) by individuals who fraudulently obtain the prescription, either directly from health care providers or other sources, such as family and friends; (3) by individuals via criminal theft from health care providers or households; and (4) by healthcare workers who have direct access to controlled substances.[137] Patients and other individuals are generally more likely to be materially involved in opioid diversion relative to other types of drug diversion, including stockpiling unused medications and storing them insecurely, intentionally seeking prescriptions from doctors and hospital emergency departments for non-medical use, or improperly obtaining opioids from family and friends.[138]

The most common type of diversion is the first category described above, where individuals legally obtain an opioid prescription, based on their physician's perception of medical need, and subsequent diversion occurs as a result of unsafe storage or purposeful redirecting of unused pills. An estimated 50–75% of prescription opioids are unused by patients.[139]

[135] Refer to CMS, "Drug Diversion in the Medicaid Program: State Strategies for Reducing Prescription Drug Diversion in Medicaid," (Baltimore, MD: U.S. Department of Health and Human Services, Centers for Medicare and Medicaid Services, 2012).

[136] LAPPA, "Drug Diversion in Health Care," in *Fact Sheet* (Washington, D.C.: Legislative Analysis and Public Policy Association, 2023).

[137] See generally K. H. Berge et al., "Diversion of drugs within health care facilities, a multiple-victim crime: patterns of diversion, scope, consequences, detection, and prevention," *Mayo Clin Proc* 87, no. 7 (2012); M. E. Buttram et al., "Increasing rates of buprenorphine diversion in the United States, 2002 to 2019," *Pharmacoepidemiol Drug Saf* 30, no. 11 (2021); J. A. Inciardi et al., "Mechanisms of prescription drug diversion among drug-involved club- and street-based populations," *Pain Med* 8, no. 2 (2007); E. D. Porter et al., "Surgery Prescription Opioid Misuse and Diversion in US Adults and Associated Risk Factors," *J Surg Res* 275 (2022); K. Sundararajan et al., "The potential for diversion of prescribed opioids among orthopaedic patients: Results of an anonymous patient survey," *PLoS One* 16, no. 8 (2021).

[138] J. A. Inciardi et al., "The Diversion of Prescription Opioid Analgesics," *Law Enforc Exec Forum* 7, no. 7 (2007).

[139] See generally M. C. Bicket et al., "Prescription Opioid Analgesics Commonly Unused After Surgery: A Systematic Review," *JAMA Surg* 152, no. 11 (2017); K. Kumar et al., "Unused Opioid Pills After Outpatient Shoulder Surgeries Given Current Perioperative

Among patients with unused medications, most accumulate the unused drugs and only a relatively small percent (5–10%) undertake efforts to secure accumulated drugs appropriately in a locked container or otherwise dispose of them properly.[140] Unused opioids are either subsequently misused by the original recipient, after taking the prescribed dose or after symptoms have subsided or are diverted to others. About a third of patients admit that they have actively engaged in the sharing or diverting of their unused opioids to others.[141] Recall that, according to studies cited earlier, among those who misuse opioids about 40–60% obtain opioids from family and friends. Another more purposeful means of accumulating prescription opioids is by way of "doctor shopping," where individuals visit more than one doctor and seek redundant opioid prescriptions from each of them. A review of the literature of the definition of "doctor shopping" found that the most commonly used thresholds for the identification of doctor shopping behavior are individuals seeking opioid prescriptions from four or more prescribers.[142] Claims data from health insurers can also be used to identify doctor shopping. For example, using commercial payer claims data from 2012, Esposito et al. found that 22% of plan enrollees exhibited patterns consistent with engaging in some degree of doctor shopping for opioids.[143]

Prescribing Habits," *Am J Sports Med* 45, no. 3 (2017); B. C. Maughan et al., "Unused opioid analgesics and drug disposal following outpatient dental surgery: A randomized controlled trial," *Drug Alcohol Depend* 168 (2016); S. Mercadante et al., "Opioids in advanced cancer: use, storage and disposal in the home," *BMJ Support Palliat Care* (2022); M. J. Sabatino et al., "Excess Opioid Medication and Variation in Prescribing Patterns Following Common Orthopaedic Procedures," *J Bone Joint Surg Am* 100, no. 3 (2018).

[140] See generally E. T. Lewis, M. A. Cucciare, and J. A. Trafton, "What do patients do with unused opioid medications?," *Clin J Pain* 30, no. 8 (2014); A. Reddy et al., "Patterns of storage, use, and disposal of opioids among cancer outpatients," *Oncologist* 19, no. 7 (2014); GAO, "Prescription Opioids: Patient Options for Safe and Effective Disposal of Unused Opioids," (Washington, D.C.: U.S. Government Accountability Office, 2019).

[141] See, for example, Lewis, Cucciare, and Trafton, "What do patients do with unused opioid medications?."; Porter et al., "Surgery Prescription Opioid Misuse and Diversion in US Adults and Associated Risk Factors."

[142] C. Delcher et al., "Defining "Doctor Shopping" with Dispensing Data: A Scoping Review," *Pain Med* 23, no. 7 (2022).

[143] D. B. Esposito et al., "Medical record-based ascertainment of behaviors suggestive of opioid misuse, diversion, abuse, and/or addiction among individuals showing evidence of doctor/pharmacy shopping," *J Pain Res* 12 (2019).

Some drug seeking and doctor shopping behavior is conducted in a more determined and organized fashion, essentially crossing over into what would be considered drug dealer behavior. Rigg et al. offers a narrative account of this type of behavior.[144] The authors studied a sample of 50 drug dealers self-described as "prescription drug sellers" in the 2008–2010 period, administering a confidential survey on the ways in which dealers typically engaged in drug seeking and doctor shopping behavior. Dealers typically targeted physician and pain clinics that were known to be more likely to issue opioid prescriptions, and they would visit these clinics armed with chronicles of persistent pain, and in some cases also equipped with fraudulent imaging reports, such as doctored magnetic resonance imaging ("MRI") reports suggestive of a clinical source of pain. According to Rigg et al., one dealer described it this way: "I'd go to like 10 pain clinics [per] month and I'd bring the same MRI to everyone. It was the same thing ... I was getting 240 pills from like 10 different doctors. I'd sell them for 10 dollars apiece." Survey results showed that to fill the prescriptions, dealers would typically target smaller family-owned pharmacies and pain clinics with in-house pharmacies. As the "book of business" of these criminal prescription drug sellers expanded, it was common for them to recruit others to help obtain a larger total supply to meet increasing demand. This was typically accomplished by recruiting "sponsors" to engage in similar fraudulent drug seeking behavior, in exchange for payment, or by enlisting actual patients willing to sell all or most of their prescription opioids in exchange for payment.[145]

3.11.3 Illicit Opioids

Illicit drugs and the black markets that distribute them are not new and existed long before the current opioid crisis.[146] Throughout history,

[144] K. K. Rigg, S. P. Kurtz, and H. L. Surratt, "Patterns of prescription medication diversion among drug dealers," *Drugs (Abingdon Engl)* 19, no. 2 (2012).

[145] Ibid.

[146] S. Grzybowski, "The black market in prescription drugs," *Lancet* 364 Suppl 1 (2004); D.R. Gerstein and L.W. Green, "Preventing Drug Abuse: What do we Know?," in *Illicit Drug Use in the United States* (Washington, D.C.: National Research Council (US) Committee on Substance Abuse Prevention Research, National Academies Press (US), 1993).

including the recent opioid crisis, there has been infiltration of illicit opioids in the U.S. and abroad. Haley et al., for example, noted that heroin-related morality rates in large U.S. cities have been mostly unchanged since the 1970s.[147] Over the past decade opioid utilization in the U.S. has involved an increasing proportion of illicit opioids. According to the studies cited earlier, among those who misuse opioids, about 23% are sourced illegally, mainly through the black market and involving drug dealers or other means, such as the types of sellers described above by Rigg et al. In the early part of the past decade, heroin seizures and heroin-related overdose mortality was rising.[148] Though heroin usage appears to have fallen slightly in recent years, it has been supplanted by the abuse of synthetic fentanyl, which has grown in terms of number of seizures and number of overdose deaths.[149]

Synthetic fentanyl is substantially more lethal than other forms of opioids, and has markedly different distribution channels, relying mainly on internet-based transactions (via the "dark web") with more than 90% of the supply originating in China-based laboratories.[150] Fentanyl comes in a variety of forms, but it is also likely to be mixed and laced with other abused drugs, like cocaine, with some users unaware of its presence.

[147] S.J. Haley, J.A. Johnson, and L.J. Frazier, *Opioids and Population Health: A Primer* (Burlington, MA: Jones & Bartlett Learning, 2022).

[148] See generally D. Rosen et al., "Characteristics and consequences of heroin use among older adults in the United States: a review of the literature, treatment implications, and recommendations for further research," *Addict Behav* 36, no. 4 (2011); C. J. Ruhm, "Geographic Variation in Opioid and Heroin Involved Drug Poisoning Mortality Rates," *Am J Prev Med* 53, no. 6 (2017); CBO, "The Opioid Crisis and Recent Federal Policy Responses," (Washington, DC: U.S. Congressional Budget Office, 2022).

[149] See generally D. Ciccarone, "The rise of illicit fentanyls, stimulants and the fourth wave of the opioid overdose crisis," *Curr Opin Psychiatry* 34, no. 4 (2021); L. C. Dismukes, "How Did We Get Here? Heroin and Fentanyl Trafficking Trends: A Law Enforcement Perspective," *N C Med J* 79, no. 3 (2018); Y. Han et al., "The rising crisis of illicit fentanyl use, overdose, and potential therapeutic strategies," *Transl Psychiatry* 9, no. 1 (2019); J. O'Donnell et al., "Trends in and Characteristics of Drug Overdose Deaths Involving Illicitly Manufactured Fentanyls—United States, 2019–2020," *MMWR Morb Mortal Wkly Rep* 70, no. 50 (2021); J. J. Palamar et al., "Trends in seizures of powders and pills containing illicit fentanyl in the United States, 2018 through 2021," *Drug Alcohol Depend* 234 (2022).

[150] B. Westhoff, *Fentanyl, Inc.* (New York, NY: Grove Press, 2019).

Fentanyl has also surfaced in counterfeit oxycodone pills.[151] Part of the appeal of fentanyl to drug traffickers and dealers is that because it is inexpensive and more potent, it can be used as a "filler" to create more overall volume of shipments without diluting potency.[152] The shift away from abuse of prescription opioids is evident in studies of OUD-attributable deaths. For example, Walley et al. found that, in a study of about 3,000 OUD decedents with complete toxicology reports over the period from 2013 to 2015 (i.e., after rates of prescription opioids had started its steep decline), 61.4% had heroin detected and 45.3% had fentanyl detected in postmortem toxicology analyses.[153] However, among the 16.8% decedents with one or more active opioid prescription at time of death, prescribed opioids were "rarely" detected in the toxicology reports. More recent data show approximately the same proportions. For example, a CDC study of 38 states and the District of Columbia, based on data from 2018 to 2019, found that prescription-sourced opioids were found in only 2% of OUD-attributable deaths.[154] This is consistent with the findings of Donohoe and Soliman, who found that organizational changes and product changes in illicit markets increased the availability and demand for heroin.[155]

3.12 Gateway Hypotheses

Differentiation between prescription opioids and illicit opioids is critical to the accurate assessment of causation of the opioid crisis and the implementation of effective abatement programs. This is especially important

[151] G. E. Hartmann and R. Sethi, "The Role of Non-Pharmaceutical Fentanyl-Contaminated Counterfeit Oxycodone in Increasing Opioid Overdoses: A Commentary Review," *Prim Care Companion CNS Disord* 25, no. 6 (2023).

[152] NASEM, *Pain Management and the Opioid Epidemic: Balancing Societal and Indidivual Benefits and Risks of Prescription Opioid Use.*

[153] A. Y. Walley et al., "The Contribution of Prescribed and Illicit Opioids to Fatal Overdoses in Massachusetts, 2013–2015," *Public Health Rep* 134, no. 6 (2019).

[154] J. O'Donnell et al., "Using death scene and toxicology evidence to define involvement of heroin, pharmaceutical morphine, illicitly manufactured fentanyl and pharmaceutical fentanyl in opioid overdose deaths, 38 states and the District of Columbia, January 2018-December 2019," *Addiction* 117, no. 5 (2022).

[155] Donahoe and Soliman, "What fueled the illicit opioid epidemic? New evidence from a takeover of white powder heroin markets."

because, given the incursion of illicit opioids in the latest waves of the opioid crisis, especially synthetic opioids like fentanyl, it is increasingly difficult to disentangle harms attributable to prescription opioids versus those attributable to illicit opioids. It follows that it is increasingly difficult to disentangle the abatement costs attributable to prescription opioids versus the abatement costs attributable to illicit opioids. The Court admitted this point in the Ohio proceedings regarding retail chain pharmacies: "... the Court has no basis upon which to determine the proportion of harm arising from people who did not use prescription opioids but nevertheless became addicted to illicit opioids because of the *presence* of an oversupply of prescription opioids in the communities. This lack of evidence undermines Plaintiffs' critique that [the Defense] approach underestimates the OUD population attributable to the oversupply and diversion of prescription opioids."[156] (emphasis added). What the court is alluding to—that the "presence" of *prescription* opioids in a community may in some way be related to *illicit* opioid use—is a hypothesis that has been espoused by some researchers and employed by some claimants in the opioid MDL. The hypothesis is that, for many illicit drug users and persons with OUD attributed to illicit drug use, prescription opioids at some time in the past served as a "gateway" to illicit opioid use. The nominal basis for this "gateway hypothesis" is that some studies have shown an association between illicit opioid use and prior misuse of prescription opioids.[157]

The gateway hypothesis must contend with three important facts. First, illicit markets for opioids long predate the approval of prescription opioids by the FDA. As the NASEM report on opioids stated, "Prescription opioids did not create the black markets for illicit opioids. The illicit opioid markets already had a long history in the United States."[158] Some of this

[156] Opioid MDL, "MDL 2804 Case No. 1:17-md-2804 Judge Dan Aaron Polster: Abatement Order," in *Re: National Opioid Litigation* (Ohio: United States District Court Northern District of Ohio, Eastern Division, 2022). (p.50).

[157] See, for example, S. E. Lankenau et al., "Misuse of prescription and illicit drugs among high-risk young adults in Los Angeles and New York," *J Public Health Res* 1, no. 1 (2012); P. Mateu-Gelabert et al., "Injection and sexual HIV/HCV risk behaviors associated with nonmedical use of prescription opioids among young adults in New York City," *J Subst Abuse Treat* 48, no. 1 (2015); R. A. Pollini et al., "Problematic use of prescription-type opioids prior to heroin use among young heroin injectors," *Subst Abuse Rehabil* 2, no. 1 (2011).

[158] NASEM, *Pain Management and the Opioid Epidemic: Balancing Societal and Indidivual Benefits and Risks of Prescription Opioid Use.*

history has been discussed earlier. Second, the gateway hypothesis has been explored generally (for example, in adolescents progressing from alcohol or marijuana), but the supporting evidence of the importance of so-called gateway substances in predicting or explaining subsequent substance abuse has been mixed.[159] There are at least two reasons for the inconsistency in findings, one related to the difficulty in statistical attribution (e.g., controlling for confounding factors) and the other being the "too remote" types of concerns discussed in Chap. 2. Third, empirical investigations of the gateway hypothesis in illicit drug use have, perhaps necessarily, been based on "convenience" surveys of illicit drug users; specifically, survey respondents identified either by observed behaviors regarding drug misuse and abuse or voluntary response to surveys conducted among populations known for high prevalence of illicit drug use. Consequently, this empirical approach generally results in substantial potential for bias.[160] The identification of drug users by way of convenience sampling is highly likely to disproportionately select "heavy" drug users, and (as discussed above) those heavy drug users are highly likely to currently engage in PSU, and to have engaged in PSU in the past, including abuse of a variety of prescription drugs and other illicit drugs. For example, in a study of 696 individuals in Los Angeles and San Francisco who inject illicit drugs, in the past 30 days 43% had also abused crack cocaine, 22% had misused methamphetamine, and 23% had misused tranquilizers.[161] Not surprisingly, 23% of these heavy users had also misused prescription opioids. Other studies have found similar patterns.[162]

In these types of studies, sampling is likely biasing results by disproportionately selecting regular and heavy drug users, and such users are highly likely to have in the past abused a wide range of other illicit drugs. Past use of methamphetamine, tranquilizers, and prescription opioids in these studies occurred in relatively equal proportions, which also raises the

[159] See generally M. L. Miller and Y. L. Hurd, "Testing the Gateway Hypothesis," *Neuropsychopharmacology* 42, no. 5 (2017).

[160] For a discussion of these issues, see for example T. Lines et al., "Nature and extent of selection bias resulting from convenience sampling in the emergency department," *Emerg Med J* 39, no. 4 (2022).

[161] S. Arreola et al., "Characteristics of people who initiate injection drug use later in life," *Drug Alcohol Depend* 138 (2014).

[162] See, for example, R. N. Bluthenthal et al., "Factors associated with initiating someone into illicit drug injection," ibid.144.

question of which of the drugs, if any, served as the so-called "gateway." Regular users of illicit drugs are much more likely to engage in the abuse of a variety of drugs and are also more likely to have engaged in the abuse of a variety of drugs in the past, a concept sometimes referred to as "shared vulnerability."[163] This is due in part to regular drug users sharing similar socioeconomic characteristics and sharing similar pre-existing conditions, such as SUDs and mental illnesses.[164] Thus, the evidence supporting a causal link between prescription opioid abuse and illicit opioid abuse is fairly weak, and is based primarily on associations rather than statistical analyses of causation. Nevertheless, MDL claimants' hypotheses regarding the links between prescription opioid use and subsequent illicit opioid use have resulted in a comingling of the causal effects of these sources, and a comingling of the harms associated with OUD attributable to prescription opioids versus illicit opioids.

3.13 Externalities

The term "externalities" has already been introduced, but it is a broad concept that warrants some additional discussion. The term is one that is largely attributed to the economics profession, and the context in which the term is typically used is that "externalities occur because economic agents have effects on third parties that are not reflected in market transactions."[165] Externalities can result in positive effects (i.e., benefits or savings) or negative effects (i.e., harms or costs) on third parties; positive effects are referred to as "positive externalities" and negative effects are referred to as "negative externalities." The economics sub-fields of environmental economics, law and economics, and health economics offer commonly cited examples of such externalities, usually regarding the economic, legal, and regulatory implications of pollution, contamination, potentially harmful products, and other threats to public health and safety. There is a formal "economics of externalities" that has been developed, but the use of the concepts in this book are mainly as a means of developing

[163] M. T. Tsuang et al., "Co-occurrence of abuse of different drugs in men: the role of drug-specific and shared vulnerabilities," *Arch Gen Psychiatry* 55, no. 11 (1998).

[164] A. T. McLellan, "Substance Misuse and Substance use Disorders: Why do they Matter in Healthcare?," *Trans Am Clin Climatol Assoc* 128 (2017).

[165] W. Nicholson and C. Snyder, *Microeconomic Theory: Basic Principles and Extensions, 12th Edition* (Cengage Learning, 2016).

a conceptual framework within which to better understand the opioid crisis, including its causes, consequences, and potential solutions. Accordingly, more detailed discussions of the economics of externalities are left for others.[166]

In public health, a common example of a positive externality is "herd immunity" associated with vaccinations and immunizations, where the benefits of preventive vaccines indirectly accrue to the unvaccinated and increase the overall utility and value of immunization. An example of a negative externality in public health is industrial contamination of clean air or potable water. In environmental economics, a classic example of a positive externality is a farmer who grows apple trees that, by way of pollination, benefit the needs of bees from a nearby beekeeper. The usual example of an environmental negative externality is pollution (e.g., soil, water, or air) resulting from some type of economic activity, like the manufacturing of automobiles or the mining of raw materials. Negative externalities are caused by "factors of production" (e.g., factories, transportation, distribution, etc.) that negatively affect private parties or "public goods" or otherwise impose some harm or cost on a group of firms or individuals.[167] In general, the cost of a negative externality refers to a cost incurred by entities that are not party to the transaction that is contributing to a cost or harm. The most common example is pollution. If the production of a product or service produces pollution, some proportion of the costs of that pollution may not be incurred solely by the parties to the transaction (e.g., a steel producer selling steel to a construction company), but is instead released into the air, soil, or water, resulting in costs incurred by a larger group.[168] Environmental externalities overlap considerably

[166] See, for example, Jean-Paul Chavas, "Economics of Externalities: An Overview," in *Handbook of Production Economics*, ed. Subhash C. Ray, Robert G. Chambers, and Subal C. Kumbhakar (Singapore: Springer Nature Singapore, 2022); J. Hurley and E. Mentzakis, "Health-related externalities: evidence from a choice experiment," *J Health Econ* 32, no. 4 (2013).

[167] "Public goods" refers to goods that are "non-rivalrous" (i.e., consumption by one person does not leave less for another person) and "non-excludable" (i.e., it would be cost-prohibitive to exclude non-paying beneficiaries). Shared environmental resources, such as air, soil, and water, are commonly cited examples of public goods.

[168] See generally A.A. Papandreou, *Externality and Institutions* (Oxford, UK: Clarendon Press, 1994); R. Cornes and T. Sandler, *The Theory of Externalities, Public Goods, and Club Goods* (Cambridge, UK: Cambridge University Press, 1986); R.H. Coase, "The Problem of Social Cost," *Journal of Law and Economics* 3 (1960).

with public health externalities, especially in the contamination of shared resources, such as water, soil, and air, particularly those instances that have the potential to impact population health.[169]

Negative externalities in a public health context can also include effects attributable to substance use and abuse, such as drug abuse, alcohol abuse and tobacco use.[170] For example, alcohol misuse has been shown to result in negative externalities associated with a variety of costs extending beyond those directly linked to consumption, such as increased risk of chronic disease, domestic issues, assaults, motor vehicle accidents, financial distress, decreased work productivity, and property damage.[171] Externalities associated with alcohol have often been described as "the burdens that fall upon others rather than the individuals choosing to drink."[172] According to

[169] There are many examples of cross over between environmental science, public health, and externalities. An overview of the relationship between environmental pollution and healthcare is featured in J.J. Pierce, R.F. Weiner, and P.A. Vesilind, *Environmental Pollution and Control (Fourth Edition)* (Boston, MA: Butterworth-Heinemann; Elsevier, 1998). For additional specific examples, see variously O. M. Faroon et al., "Effects of polychlorinated biphenyls on development and reproduction," *Toxicol Ind Health* 17, no. 3 (2001); M. Fay et al., "ATSDR evaluation of health effects of chemicals. V. Xylenes: health effects, toxicokinetics, human exposure, and environmental fate," ibid.14, no. 5 (1998); H. E. Hicks and C. T. De Rosa, "Great lakes research–important human health findings and their impact on ATSDR's Superfund research program," *Int J Hyg Environ Health* 205, no. 1–2 (2002).

[170] See, for example, T. K. Greenfield et al., "Externalities from alcohol consumption in the 2005 US National Alcohol Survey: implications for policy," *Int J Environ Res Public Health* 6, no. 12 (2009); V. U. Ekpu and A. K. Brown, "The Economic Impact of Smoking and of Reducing Smoking Prevalence: Review of Evidence," *Tob Use Insights* 8 (2015); Y. H. Hendlin and S. A. Bialous, "The environmental externalities of tobacco manufacturing: A review of tobacco industry reporting," *Ambio* 49, no. 1 (2020); J. Lam et al., "Modelling the global economic costs of tobacco product waste," *Bull World Health Organ* 100, no. 10 (2022).

[171] See generally Greenfield et al., "Externalities from alcohol consumption in the 2005 US National Alcohol Survey: implications for policy."; R. A. Dunn and N. W. Tefft, "Drinking-and-driving in the United States from 1983–2017: comparing survey and model-based estimates of prevalence," *Anal Methods Accid Res* 31 (2021); T. K. Greenfield et al., "The Relationship Between the U.S. State Alcohol Policy Environment and Individuals' Experience of Secondhand Effects: Alcohol Harms Due to Others' Drinking," *Alcohol Clin Exp Res* 43, no. 6 (2019); P.J. Cook and M.J. Moore, "Alcohol," in *Handbook of Health Economics*, ed. A.J. Culyer and J.P. Newhouse (New York, N.Y.: Elsevier Science B.V., 2000).

[172] Greenfield et al., "Externalities from alcohol consumption in the 2005 US National Alcohol Survey: implications for policy."

a study by Greenfield et al., on a lifetime basis, 60% of surveyed individuals reported suffering from an alcohol-related externality imposed by another party, including intoxicated drivers, physical violence, marital and family problems, and property damage.[173] Another common public health example of a negative externality is the production and consumption of tobacco.[174] Tobacco production has been shown to result in negative externalities associated with soil and water contamination, and tobacco consumption has been shown to result in significant negative health effects. Tobacco consumption has also been shown to result in significant externalities associated with litter and waste.[175] Generally, from an economics perspective, OUD can be considered a negative externality associated with production of pain management wherein some proportion of usage can be considered misuse, on the part of either those legally prescribed opioids or those misusing diverted prescription opioids. These issues are explored in greater detail throughout the remainder of book.

In practice, the economic approach to externalities can be thought of as a four-step process.[176] The first step is to identify and define the externality, including the sources and the pathways through which the externality generates measurable harms or costs.[177] The second step is to calculate the costs associated with the externality, including attributable costs, which aligns with the usual concept of economic damages, but in some cases also

[173] Ibid.

[174] P. DeCicca, D. Kenkel, and M. F. Lovenheim, "The Economics of Tobacco Regulation: A Comprehensive Review," *J Econ Lit* 60, no. 3 (2022).

[175] Lam et al., "Modelling the global economic costs of tobacco product waste."; T. E. Novotny and F. Zhao, "Consumption and production waste: another externality of tobacco use," *Tob Control* 8, no. 1 (1999).

[176] For further reading, see generally R.D. Cooter and T. Ulen, *Law and Economics (6th Edition)* (Pearson, 2011); Papandreou, *Externality and Institutions*; D.J. Phaneuf and T. Requate, *A Course in Environmental Economics: Theory, Policy, and Practice* (Cambridge, UK: Cambridge University Press, 2017); Cornes and Sandler, *The Theory of Externalities, Public Goods, and Club Goods.*

[177] While there is important debate as to the *extent* of opioid-attributable costs, and considerable discussion as to which entities have incurred such costs, OUD-attributable costs are generally believed to exist. See, for example, Davenport, Weaver, and Caverly, "Economic Impact of Non-Medical Opioid Use in the United States: Annual Estimates and Projections for 2015 through 2019."; Florence, Luo, and Rice, "The economic burden of opioid use disorder and fatal opioid overdose in the United States, 2017." The topic of attributable costs and abatement costs will be discussed in greater detail in Chap. 4.

including the costs associated with mitigation or abatement of the externality. The third step is the identification of parties responsible for the "production" of the negative externality.[178] Finally, the fourth step is the identification of a mechanism by which to allocate liability and associated attributable costs or abatement costs among potentially responsible parties, typically by way of some combination of private ordering, bargaining, taxes, licensure, regulation, or courts.[179] The remainder of this book focuses on various aspects of each of these steps. The remainder of this chapter is focused on the first of these—identifying and defining the externality.

3.14 Opioid Externalities

Identifying and defining an externality is not always as straightforward as it may seem. Economists Cornes and Sandler, who wrote extensively on externalities, aptly described it this way: "There is a strong temptation to avoid an explicit definition of an externality, since even this first step has been a fertile source of controversy ..."[180] Comparisons of OUD with other known public health externalities, like those resulting from substance abuse and environmental harms, should be made with an understanding of some important caveats. First, as alluded to earlier, prescription opioids can be thought of as a factor of production in the production of pain management, and OUD can be considered a negative externality (or "public nuisance") attributable in part to the misuse of *one* of the factors of production. It is important to further note that OUD is attributable in part to the use of opioids from three sources, discussed in the previous chapter: (1) prescribed opioids, sourced from the healthcare system and misused by the same patients to which the drugs were prescribed; (2) diverted opioids, sourced from family or friends or others and misused by the recipient; and (3) illicit opioids, sourced from diverters, dealers and other black market sources. Thus, OUD is a negative

[178] For example, in the case of carbon dioxide, it is not caused by a single factory but multiple factories, and not a single vehicle but multiple vehicles, etc.

[179] For further reading, see generally Cooter and Ulen, *Law and Economics (6th Edition)*; Cornes and Sandler, *The Theory of Externalities, Public Goods, and Club Goods*; Papandreou, *Externality and Institutions*; O Shy, *Industrial Organization* (Cambridge, MA: The MIT Press, 1995).

[180] Cornes and Sandler, *The Theory of Externalities, Public Goods, and Club Goods.* (p.29).

externality associated with three distinct source pathways, sources that in many cases cannot be reliably differentiated *ex post*.

Second, the pathways linking prescription opioids with the externality are considerably more complex than the standard externality example. To begin, prescription opioids have established clinical efficacy, and most prescribed opioids are used as directed and without consequence. In contrast, if the production of a chemical results in pollution, then some fraction of each unit of that chemical can be associated with a proportional fraction of the attributable cost of the pollution, however small. In the case of OUD, the externality is not directly associated with the production of pain control, the manufacturing of opioids, or even the consumption of opioids. Moreover, whereas OUD is a result of opioid *misuse*, it is not necessarily a result of *prescription* opioid misuse. And again, as alluded to earlier, in cases where OUD can be attributed to prescription opioids, the causes of the increased supply of prescription opioids are attributable to multiple factors and agents, which will be described in detail later. The issues of clinical utility and medical need also have implications for use of the term "oversupply." Economists typically define an oversupply of a product or service as mostly a temporal phenomenon; that is, one that market forces will correct in the long run by either lowering prices or reducing production. The idea that market supply and market demand could remain unaligned for an extended period, thereby creating chronic oversupply or undersupply, is not typically considered. However, claimants in the opioid MDL cases make this argument directly, suggesting that the negative externality is due largely to the 2003–2012 "oversupply" of prescription opioids. The argument depends substantially on the issue of how much of the change in supply was associated with medical need versus other factors. The opioid MDL claimants generally argue that there was no connection between the increase in opioid supply and any concomitant increase in demand, as approximated by medical need. This issue is revisited later in the book, as it is critical to the understanding of exactly how the negative externality is defined in practice.

Third, unlike externalities associated with alcohol and tobacco, which are minimally regulated products,[181] prescription drugs in the U.S. are

[181] See generally M. B. Esser and D. H. Jernigan, "Policy Approaches for Regulating Alcohol Marketing in a Global Context: A Public Health Perspective," *Annu Rev Public Health* 39 (2018); S. Gottlieb, "Supreme court rules that FDA cannot regulate tobacco industry," *Bmj* 320, no. 7239 (2000).

heavily regulated.[182] The healthcare regulatory apparatus is extensive, including: (1) an extensive approval and post-market surveillance process conducted by the FDA; (2) production, distribution, and utilization oversight by the DEA; (3) controls on incursion of diverted and illicit drugs by the DEA, the Department of Justice ("DOJ"), and state and local law enforcement; (4) monitoring of population health and drug adverse events by the CDC; (5) extensive state laws governing the practice of medicine and the licensing of all healthcare professionals, including oversight of any provider initiating prescriptions for medications and also including rules governing the corporate practice of medicine;[183] and (6) accreditation by private governing bodies, which act as *de facto* regulators in that they dictate industry standards.[184] In short, it is impossible for a prescription drug to enter the market and stay on the market without the explicit and ongoing consent of multiple regulators and agencies. As a result, any list of factors contributing to increased opioid supply must include the regulatory agencies and other institutions directly charged with overseeing opioid approval, supply, and utilization. Moreover, opioid "oversupply" generated a negative externality within a heavily regulated market, implying that regulators essentially failed to address the problems that initially warranted regulatory organization. Insofar as OUD can be considered a negative public health externality, it is one that has been driven by multifactorial sources and one that has been contributed to by the same governmental organizations directly tasked with overseeing and regulating its sources and uses. In addition, state-level policymakers who explicitly supported aggressive pain management programs, rewarded providers financially for complying with pain management guidelines and directly funded opioid prescriptions via their Medicaid programs are now plaintiffs in the opioid MDL, meaning that plaintiffs in the MDL include institutions who at one time actively promoted and funded the products in question. Again, there is little precedent for these dynamics in the externality literature, and even less in the product liability literature.

[182] See generally R. I. Field, "Why is health care regulation so complex?," *P t* 33, no. 10 (2008).

[183] J.M. Zhu, H. Rooke-Ley, and E. Fuse Brown, "A Doctrine in Name Only—Strengthening Prohibitions against the Corporate Practice of Medicine," *New England Journal of Medicine* 389, no. 11 (2023).

[184] See generally Field, "Why is health care regulation so complex?."

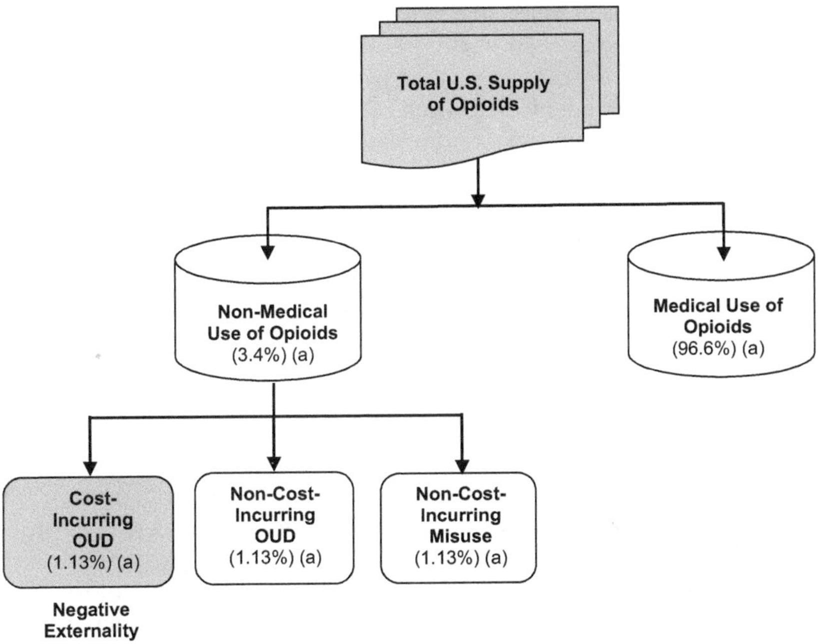

Fig. 3.2 Association of Opioid Supply with OUD Harms and Externalities. *Notes* OUD = opioid use disorder (see text, This chapter); (a) population prevalence based on NSDUH survey data (see text, This chapter)

These facts are important and will be revisited in later chapters in the context of contributing factors and liability.

Figure 3.2 Maps the relationships between opioid supply and cost-incurring OUD, which is the opioid-related externality. Note that the "total opioid supply" depicted at the top of the diagram refers to prescription opioids and illicit opioids combined. Again, in the opioid MDL, no meaningful distinctions were made between these two sources, as they were alleged to be comingled by way of the "gateway" hypothesis. Considering the clinical utility of opioids, the first branch of the figure distinguishes between opioid supply that is used "as directed," in response to clinician perception of medical need, versus *non-medical* use of opioids, which includes various forms of misuse. The non-medical use bucket would also include all illicit forms of opioids. This distinction is important for two reasons. First, again it emphasizes that most prescription opioids are used as directed and do not result in negative externalities, harms, or attributable costs. Opioids prescribed by a licensed prescriber pursuant to a legitimate perceived medical need, and used as directed by patients, represent lawful and proper consumption of medications, and do not *per se* result in meaningful negative externalities, external attributable costs, or abatement costs. The second reason that this distinction is important is that, unlike most other negative externalities, the production of the supply is *not* the direct cause of the negative externality. Returning to the factory example, discharge from the factory resulted in a negative externality, the costs of which were, in the absence of remedies, absorbed by the farmer. In general, the more the factory produces, the higher the externality costs. This is not the case with opioid supply, as the production of opioid supply and the "production of pain relief" are not *de facto* directly contributing to any externalities or harms that may be attributable to production, such as attributable costs and abatement costs. As the figure depicts, there are two additional pathways between production and potential externality-attributable costs. Put differently, it is not clear that more supply would have resulted in a higher prevalence of the cost-incurring externality, because there are three other buckets into which the added supply can flow: medical use of opioids, non-cost incurring OUD, and non-cost incurring misuse.

Note that "proper medical use" in this context does not necessarily require, in the case of prescription opioids, that prescribed treatments are "medically necessary," based on objective measures of medical need assessed by prescribing physicians *ex ante* or *ex post*. In other words, a prescription drug can be used properly and as directed even if the prescribing of that drug by a physician, based on perceived medical necessity, could *ex post* be deemed to have been medically unnecessary or medically inappropriate. In fact, generally, physicians themselves believe that at least 20% of prescription medications are clinically unnecessary.[185] Rates of unnecessary and inappropriate prescribing are even higher among antibiotic medications.[186] Uncertainty in diagnosis can itself drive higher

[185] For example, see H. Lyu et al., "Overtreatment in the United States," *PLoS One* 12, no. 9 (2017).

[186] For example, see K. P. Chua, M. A. Fischer, and J. A. Linder, "Appropriateness of outpatient antibiotic prescribing among privately insured US patients: ICD-10-CM based cross sectional study," *Bmj* 364 (2019).

utilization rates, a topic that will be explored more in the next chapter. Finally, it is also possible to assign some approximate population-level epidemiologic data to Fig. 3.2, for illustrative purposes. Starting with the first branch, recall from the earlier discussion that the prevalence of individuals misusing opioids was 3.4%, based on NSDUH data. It can be inferred from that estimate that the remaining 96.6% of the population is *not* misusing prescribed opioids.

The second branch of Fig. 3.2 further disaggregates the misuse group, depicting the relationship between non-medical use of opioids and the negative externality in question (i.e., OUD with potential attributable costs). Non-medical use, which includes all illicit opioids, can lead to three possible outcomes: (1) "non-cost-incurring" misuse; (2) "non-cost-incurring" OUD; and (3) "cost-incurring" OUD. An example of "non-cost-incurring misuse" would be taking more than the prescribed amount of the drug; for example, taking four or five pills per day instead of the prescribed three pills per day.[187] An example of "non-cost incurring OUD" would be an individual who experiences a transient or delimited episode of OUD but does not seek medical attention during the episode, whose activities of daily living ("ADLs") and employment are not meaningfully impacted by the OUD episode, and for whom there may have been some degree of clinical uncertainty regarding diagnosis.[188] An example of cost-incurring OUD would be an episode of OUD incurring healthcare costs, criminal justice system costs, social and family assistance costs, or other attributable harms.[189]

[187] See generally Tetrault and Butner, "Non-Medical Prescription Opioid Use and Prescription Opioid Use Disorder: A Review."

[188] See generally general discussions of these issues in P. J. Freda, J. H. Moore, and H. R. Kranzler, "The phenomics and genetics of addictive and affective comorbidity in opioid use disorder," *Drug Alcohol Depend* 221 (2021); J. Strang et al., "Opioid use disorder," *Nat Rev Dis Primers* 6, no. 1 (2020); F. Vorspan et al., "Biomarkers to predict staging and treatment response in opioid dependence: A narrative review," *Drug Dev Res* 82, no. 5 (2021). Also, there are reported difficulties in diagnosing substance use disorder concurrent with psychiatric disorders, which are common among those who misuse opioids. See generally T. R. Kosten and H. D. Kleber, "Differential diagnosis of psychiatric comorbidity in substance abusers," *J Subst Abuse Treat* 5, no. 4 (1988).

[189] Studies on costs will be discussed in greater detail in Chap. 4. For a general overview of costs associated with OUD, refer to Davenport, Weaver, and Caverly, "Economic Impact of Non-Medical Opioid Use in the United States: Annual Estimates and Projections for 2015 through 2019."; Florence, Luo, and Rice, "The economic burden of opioid use disorder and

At a sufficient level of abstraction, these categories can be thought of as aligning with the three standard categories of SUD severity—mild, moderate, and severe.[190] According to the 2021 NSDUH data, the prevalence of any SUD resulting from the misuse of prescription pain relievers is approximately evenly distributed among the mild, moderate, and severe categories.[191] Accordingly, a reasonable assumption would be that OUD cases are similarly evenly distributed among these three possible outcomes shown in Fig. 3.2, resulting in an estimated 1.13% prevalence assigned to each category (i.e., the 3.4% misuse prevalence divided by 3). This results in an estimated OUD prevalence of about 2.26% (i.e., the sum of the prevalence of "cost-incurring OUD" and "non-cost-incurring OUD"), which is aligned with the estimated OUD prevalence discussed earlier in the chapter. The three categories also align with attributable costs, with non-cost-incurring misuse expected to result in negligible costs, non-cost-incurring OUD expected to result in very low attributable costs, and cost-incurring OUD expected to have some measurable level of attributable costs. It would also be reasonable to assume that abatement efforts would be targeted at the cost-incurring OUD group, where such efforts would be expected to have the largest marginal benefit. Accordingly, only the latter category, cost-incurring OUD, would be expected to be associated in some way with an externality constituting a harm or a public nuisance.

3.15 Causation

In addition to matters of incidence, prevalence, and source vectors, epidemiology is also concerned with *causation*, and the issue of causation is central to the economic assessment of negative externalities, particularly in the case of externalities associated with impacts on health and safety. McGwin described the importance of causation in epidemiology this way: "Epidemiology has a vested interest in causation as, despite its numerous and often vague definitions, it is a discipline with the goal of identifying causes of disease (both modifiable and nonmodifiable) so that

fatal opioid overdose in the United States, 2017."; Luo, Li, and Florence, "State-Level Economic Costs of Opioid Use Disorder and Fatal Opioid Overdose—United States, 2017."

[190] Refer to J. McNeely and A. Adam, Substance Use Screening and Risk Assessment in Adults, (Baltimore (MD): Johns Hopkins University, 2020).

[191] Refer to NSDUH Table 5.3B—"Substance Use Disorder Severity Level for Specific Substances in Past Year: Among People Aged 12 or Older; Percentages, 2021."

the disease or its consequences might be prevented."[192] A classic epidemiology causation story is physician John Snow's use of mapping to help determine the cause of a localized cholera outbreak in London, ultimately discovering that cholera had been transmitted by a single publicly shared water pump.[193] In a collection of essays, epidemiologist Kenneth Rothman cautioned that, while Snow's discovery undoubtedly represents a valuable step in the development of the epidemiology field and the understanding of causation, "it presumes that only one cause exists for a disease, and if that is known, then to seek other causes is futile."[194] Rothman goes on to say that "However, by way of counterexample, epidemiologists can show that many organisms can cause pneumonia, [...] the identification of proximal causes does not rule out causes further upstream ... "[195] Further emphasizing the importance of investigating all causes, Rothman further noted that "Every disease has several causes, in two senses: first, many causal pathways can exist that end in the disease, starting with distal antecedents and progressing towards proximal causes; and second, each causal pathway has multiple components that act in concert to produce the effect through that mechanism."[196] The issue of the causation of the increase in opioid supply will be discussed in greater depth in the following chapter.

3.16 Chapter Summary

The epidemiology of opioid misuse and OUD has several important implications for product liability. First, opioids had, and continue to have, established clinical utility. This is quite different from most other products subject to product liability claims and litigation, where defective or excessively high-risk products are removed from the market. Second, the prevalence of NPOU (4–10%), opioid misuse (3–4%), and OUD (2–3%), while concerning from a public health

[192] G. McGwin, Jr., "Causation in epidemiology," *Am J Ophthalmol* 150, no. 5 (2010).

[193] M. B. Ruths, "The lesson of John Snow and the broad street pump," *AMA Journal of Ethics: Virtual Mentor* 11, no. 6 (2009).

[194] P. Fine et al., "John Snow's legacy: epidemiology without borders," *Lancet* 381, no. 9874 (2013).

[195] Ibid.

[196] Ibid. Also refer to K.J. Rothman, S. Greenland, and T.L. Lash, *Modern Epidemiology (Third Edition)* (Philadelphia, PA: Wolters Kluer; Lippincot WIlliams & Wilkins, 2008).

perspective, are largely aligned with adverse event rates for many prescription drugs. While these rates have remained relatively stable in recent years, the rates of prescription opioid utilization have fallen precipitously, suggesting that OUD rates have been buoyed by the incursion of illicit opioids, including heroin and fentanyl. Rapidly declining rates of prescription opioid utilization over the past decade are due mainly to changes in clinical practice guidelines, increased oversight on the parts of state and federal regulators (who had largely failed in their oversight role in the years leading up to the crisis), and other programs, such as public awareness campaigns and drug take-back programs. The economics of externalities provides a useful conceptual lens through which to view the harms identified by epidemiologists. From the externality perspective, claimants are essentially arguing that defendants increased the supply of opioids, which in turn increased the prevalence of OUD. However, OUD is a negative externality associated with three distinct source pathways, sources that in many cases cannot be reliably differentiated *ex post*. Perhaps more importantly, OUD is comprised of three sub-components, only one of which is associated with measurable harms.

Through the lens of a traditional epidemiology causation model, the opioid crisis is multifactorial and layered in ways that are substantially different from the usual causal models. A contaminated water supply, for example, may cause a breakout of water-borne illnesses, but once the sources of the contamination are identified, the causal pathway from source (contamination) to externality (illness) can be further investigated. Opioids have clinical utility and continue to be utilized in clinical settings, in response to legitimate medical need. In some cases, some individuals develop OUD, but most opioid users do not. Individuals at greater risk for OUD include those with pre-existing conditions related to substance use disorders and mental health conditions. The causal pathway from opioid supply to public nuisance-causing OUD is considerably more complex than the standard epidemiological causal model. First, for an opioid to get into the hands of a consumer, it travels through a labyrinth of regulatory oversight by federal and state governing bodies and accreditation agencies, followed by organizational control by payers, health systems, and physicians, who establish clinical norms and standards regarding medical appropriateness of treatment. As such, medical products are among the most heavily controlled and monitored products in the U.S. To say that one segment of the supply chain failed is to say that all or most pieces of the system failed, as each segment is intertwined in multiple ways with each other. Second, as discussed in Chap. 2 and again at the end of this chapter, there are at least 20 different causal variables that contributed to the increase in opioid supply from approximately 1995 to 2012.

References

ADPC. (2023). *Opiates or Opioids—What's the difference?* Salem, OR: State of Oregon Alcohol and Drug Policy Commission.

Alhaj-Suliman, S. O., Milavetz, G., & Salem, A. K. (2020). Model-based meta-analysis to compare primary efficacy-endpoint, efficacy-time course, safety, and tolerability of opioids used in the management of osteoarthritic pain in humans. *Current Drug Metabolism*, *21*(5), 390–399.

Althaus, A., Arránz Becker, O., Moser, K. H., Lux, E. A., Weber, F., Neugebauer, E., & Simanski, C. (2018, December 1). Postoperative pain trajectories and pain chronification-an empirical typology of pain patients. *Pain Medicine*, *19* (12), 2536–2545.

Amaechi, O., Huffman, M. M., & Featherstone, K. (2021). Pharmacologic therapy for acute pain. *Am Fam Physician*, *104*(1), 63–72.

Aoki, Y., Kato, H., Fujimura, N., Suzuki, Y., Sakuraya, M., & Doi, M. (2022). Effects of fentanyl administration in mechanically ventilated patients in the intensive care unit: A systematic review and meta-analysis. *BMC Anesthesiology*, *22*(1), 323.

Apfelbaum, J. L., Chen, C., Mehta, S. S., & Gan, T. J. (2003). Postoperative pain experience: Results from a national survey suggest postoperative pain continues to be undermanaged. *Anesthesia Analgesia*, *97*(2), 534–540.

Aronsson, M., Bergman, S., Lindqvist, E., & Andersson, M. L. E. (2022). Comparison of chronic widespread pain prevalence with different criteria in two cohorts of rheumatoid arthritis. *Clin Rheumatol* *41*(4), 1023–1032.

Arreola, S., Bluthenthal, R. N., Wenger, L., Chu, D., Thing, J., & Kral, A. H. (2014). Characteristics of people who initiate injection drug use later in life. *Drug and Alcohol Dependence*, *138*, 244–250.

Aslam, A., & Kwo, P. Y. (2023). Epidemiology and disease burden of alcohol associated liver disease. *Journal of Clinical and Experimental Hepatology*, *13* (1), 88–102.

Avouac, J., Gossec, L., & Dougados, M. (2007). Efficacy and safety of opioids for osteoarthritis: A meta-analysis of randomized controlled trials. *Osteoarthritis and Cartilage*, *15*(8), 957–65.

Backhaus, I., Mannocci, A., & La Torre, G. (2019). A systematic review of economic evaluation studies of drug-based non-malignant chronic pain treatment. *Current Pharmaceutical Biotechnology*, 20(11), 910–919.

Bailey, F. A., Ferguson, L., Williams, B. R., Woodby, L. L., Redden, D. T., Durham, R. M., Goode, P. S., & Burgio, K. L. (2008). Palliative care intervention for choice and use of opioids in the last hours of life. *Journals of Gerontology: Series A Biological Sciences and Medical Sciences, 63*(9), 974–978.

Berge, K. H., Dillon, K. R., Sikkink, K. M., Taylor, T. K., & Lanier, W. L. (2012). Diversion of drugs within health care facilities, a multiple-victim crime: Patterns of diversion, scope, consequences, detection, and prevention. *Mayo Clinic Proceedings, 87* (7), 674–682.

Bicket, M. C., Long, J. J., Pronovost, P. J., Alexander, G. C., & Wu, C. L. (2017). Prescription opioid analgesics commonly unused after surgery: A systematic review. *JAMA Surgery, 152*(11), 1066–1071.

Biel, E., Pivarunas, A., Prentice, T., Rowe, N., & Zhang, S. J. (2024). The application of radiofrequency ablation in acute and chronic pain management. *The AANA Journal, 92*(3), 220–231.

Bliss, M. (2011). *The making of modern medicine: Turning points in the treatment of disease*. Univeristy of Chicago Press.

Bluthenthal, R. N., Wenger, L., Chu, D., Quinn, B., Thing, J., & Kral, A. H. (2014) Factors associated with initiating someone into illicit drug injection. *Drug and Alcohol Dependence, 144*, 186–192.

Blyth, F. M., Briggs, A. M., Schneider, C. H., Hoy, D. G., & March, L. M. (2019). The global burden of musculoskeletal pain-where to from here? *American Journal of Public Health, 109* (1), 35–40.

Bohnert, A. S. B., Guy, G. P., Jr., & Losby, J. L. (2018). Opioid prescribing in the United States before and after the centers for disease control and prevention's 2016 opioid guideline. *Annals of Internal Medicine, 169* (6), 367–375.

Bologheanu, R., Bilir, A., Kapral, L., Gruber, F., & Kimberger, O. (2025). New persistent opioid use after surgery. *JAMA Network Open, 8*(2), e2460794.

Bonica, J. J. (1991). History of pain concepts and pain therapy. *Mount Sinai Journal of Medicine, 58*(3), 191–202.

Bor, J., Cohen, G. H., & Galea, S. (2017). Population health in an era of rising income inequality: USA, 1980–2015. *Lancet, 389*(10077), 1475–1490.

Boring, B. L., Walsh, K. T., Nanavaty, N., Ng, B. W., & Mathur, V. A. (2021). How and why patient concerns influence pain reporting: A qualitative analysis of personal accounts and perceptions of others' use of numerical pain scales. *Frontiers in Psychology, 12*, 663890.

Borsook, D., Youssef, A. M., Simons, L., Elman, I., & Eccleston, C. (2018). When pain gets stuck: The evolution of pain chronification and treatment resistance. *Pain, 159*(12), 2421–2436.

Brownstein, M. J. (1993). A brief history of opiates, opioid peptides, and opioid receptors. *The Proceedings of the National Academy of Sciences of the United States of America, 90* (12), 5391–5393.

Budnitz, D. S., Shehab, N., Lovegrove, M. C., Geller, A. I., Lind, J. N., & Pollock, D. A. (2021, October 5). US emergency department visits attributed to medication harms, 2017–2019. *Jama, 326*(13), 1299–1309.

Buttram, M. E., Kurtz, S. P., Margolin, Z. R., & Severtson, S. G. (2021). Increasing rates of buprenorphine diversion in the United States, 2002 to 2019. *Pharmacoepidemiology and Drug Safety, 30*(11), 1514–1519.

Carr, D. B., Reines, H. D., Schaffer, J., Polomano, R. C., & Lande, S. (2005). The impact of technology on the analgesic gap and quality of acute pain management. *Regional Anesthesia and Pain Medicine, 30*(3), 286–291.

Case, A., & Deaton, A. (2020). *Deaths of despair and the future of capitalism.* Princeton University Press.

CBO. (2022). *The opioid crisis and recent federal policy responses.* U.S. Congressional Budget Office.

CDC. (2022a). *Opioid precribing data, 2006–2020. Based on IQVIA Xponent data.* U.S. Centers for Disease Control and Prevention.

CDC. (2022b). *Polysubstance use facts.* U.S. Centers for Disease Control and Prevention.

Chang, H. Y., Lyapustina, T., Rutkow, L., Daubresse, M., Richey, M., Faul, M., Stuart, E. A., & Alexander, G. C. (2016). Impact of prescription drug monitoring programs and pill mill laws on high-risk opioid prescribers: A comparative interrupted time series analysis. *Drug Alcohol Depend, 165*, 1–8.

Chavas, J.- P. (2022). Economics of externalities: An overview. In S. C. Ray, R. G. Chambers & S. C. Kumbhakar (Eds.), *Handbook of production economics* (pp. 925–949). Springer Nature Singapore.

Chelikam, N., Vyas, V., Dondapati, L., Iskander, B., Patel, G., Jain, S., Singla, T., et al. (2022). Epidemiology, burden, and association of substance abuse amongst patients with cardiovascular disorders: National cross-sectional survey study. *Cureus, 14*(7), e27016.

Chenchula, S., Atal, S., & Uppugunduri, C. R. S. (2024). A review of real-world evidence on preemptive pharmacogenomic testing for preventing adverse drug reactions: A reality for future health care. The Pharmacogenomics Journal, *24* (2), 9.

Chou, R., Ballantyne, J. C., Fanciullo, G. J., Fine, P. G., & Miaskowski, C. (2009). Research gaps on use of opioids for chronic noncancer pain: Findings from a review of the evidence for an American Pain Society and American Academy of Pain Medicine clinical practice guideline. *The Journal of Pain, 10*(2), 147–159.

Chou, R., Turner, J. A., Devine, E. B., Hansen, R. N., Sullivan, S. D., Blazina, I., Dana, T., Bougatsos, C., & Deyo, R. A. (2015). The effectiveness and risks of long-term opioid therapy for chronic pain: A systematic review for a National Institutes of Health Pathways to Prevention Workshop. *Annals of Internal Medicine, 162*(4), 276–286.

Chua, K. P., Fischer, M. A., & Linder, J. A. (2019). Appropriateness of outpatient antibiotic prescribing among privately insured US patients: ICD-10-CM based cross sectional study. *BMJ 364*, k5092.

Ciccarone, D. (2021). The rise of illicit fentanyls, stimulants and the fourth wave of the opioid overdose crisis. *Current Opinion in Psychiatry, 34*(4), 344–350.

CMS. (2012). *Drug diversion in the medicaid program: State strategies for reducing prescription drug diversion in medicaid.* U.S. Department of Health and Human Services, Centers for Medicare and Medicaid Services.

Coase, R. H. (1960). The Problem of Social Cost. *Journal of Law and Economics, 3* (1960), 1–44.

Coleman, J. J., & Pontefract, S. K. (2016, October 5). Adverse drug reactions. *Clinical Medicine (Lond)*, 16, 481–485.

Collier, R. (2018). A short history of pain management. *Cmaj, 190*(1), E26–E27.

Collins, K. P., Yin, D., Pithavala, Y. K., & Mittapalli, R. K. (2025). Landscape analysis of adverse events and dose intensity for FDA approved oncology small molecules. *Cancer Chemother Pharmacol, 95*(1), 17.

Compton, W. M., & Jones, C. M. (2019). Epidemiology of the U.S. opioid crisis: The importance of the vector. *Annals of the New York Academy of Sciences*, 1451 (1), 130–143.

Coninx, S. (2024). Pain philosophy: Recent debates and future challenges. *Philosophy Compass, 19*(4), e12981.

Cook, P. J., & Moore, M. J. (2000). Alcohol. In A. J. Culyer & J. P. Newhouse (Eds.), *Handbook of health economics.* Elsevier Science.

Cooter, R. D., & Ulen, T. (1986). *Law and economics* (6th Edn.). Pearson.

Cornes, R., & Sandler, T. (1986). *The theory of externalities, public goods, and club goods.* Cambridge University Press.

CRS. (2019). Overview of the opioid litigation and related settlements and settlement proposals. U.S. Congressional Research Service.

Crummy, E. A., O'Neal, T. J., Baskin, B. M., & Ferguson, S. M. (2020). One is not enough: Understanding and modeling polysubstance use. *Frontiers in Neuroscience, 14*, 569.

D'Souza, R. S., Lang, M., & J. S. Eldrige (2022). Prescription drug monitoring program. In *StatPearls.* StatPearls Publishing LLC.

Daoust, R., Paquet, J., Marquis, M., Williamson, D., Fontaine, G., Chauny, J. M., & Frégeau, A., et al. (2023). Efficacy of prescribed opioids for acute pain after being discharged from the emergency department: A systematic review and meta-analysis. *Academic Emergency Medicine, 30*(12), 1253–1263.

Davenport, S., Weaver, A., & Caverly, M. (2019). *Economic impact of non-medical opioid use in the United States: Annual estimates and projections for 2015 through 2019.* Society of Actuaries.

Davis, C. S., & Lieberman, A. J. (2021). Laws limiting prescribing and dispensing of opioids in the United States, 1989–2019. *Addiction 116*(7), 1817–1827.

Davis, C. S., Pierce, M., & Dasgupta, N. (2014). Evolution and convergence of state laws governing controlled substance prescription monitoring programs, 1998–2011. *American Journal of Public Health, 104*(8), 1389–95.

DeCicca, P., Kenkel, D., & Lovenheim, M. F. (2022). The economics of tobacco regulation: A comprehensive review. *Journal of Economic Literature, 60*(3), 883–970.

Delaney, L. D., & Waljee, J. F. (2021). New persistent opioid use: Definitions and opportunities. *Regional Anesthesia & Pain Medicine, 46*(2), 97–98.

Delcher, C., Bae, J., Wang, Y., Doung, M., Fink, D. S., & Young, H. W. (2022). Defining "Doctor shopping" with dispensing data: A scoping review. *Pain Medicine 23*(7), 1323–32.

Dismukes, L. C. (2018). How did we get here? Heroin and fentanyl trafficking trends: A law enforcement perspective. *North Carolina Medical Journal, 79*(3), 181–184.

Donahoe, J. T., & Soliman, A. (2025). What fueled the illicit opioid epidemic? New evidence from a takeover of white powder heroin markets. In *CEP Discussion Papers (dp2073)*. Centre for Economic Performance, London School of Economics.

Dowell, D., Ragan, K. R., Jones, C. M., Baldwin, G. T., & Chou, R. (2022). Prescribing opioids for pain—The new CDC clinical practice guideline. *The New England Journal of Medicine, 387*, (22), 2011–13.

Dunn, R. A., & Tefft, N. W. (2021). Drinking-and-driving in the United States from 1983–2017: Comparing survey and model-based estimates of prevalence. *Analytic Methods in Accident Research, 31.*

Dydyk, A. M., Jain, N. K., & Gupta, M. (2021). Opioid use disorder. In *StatPearls*. StatPearls Publishing LLC.

Eberhard, A., Bergman, S., Mandl, T., Olofsson, T., Rydholm, M., Jacobsson, L., & Turesson, C. (2021). Predictors of unacceptable pain with and without low inflammation over 5 years in early rheumatoid arthritis—an inception cohort study. *Arthritis Research and Therapy*, 23(1), 169.

Ekpu, V. U., & Brown, A. K. (2015). The economic impact of smoking and of reducing smoking prevalence: Review of evidence. *Tob Use Insights, 8*, 1–35.

Els, C., Jackson, T. D., Kunyk, D., Lappi, V. G., Sonnenberg, B., Hagtvedt, R., Sharma, S., Kolahdooz, F., & Straube, S. (2017). Adverse events associated with medium- and long-term use of opioids for chronic non-cancer pain: An overview of Cochrane Reviews. *The Cochrane Database of Systematic Reviews, 10*(10), CD012509.

Esposito, D. B., Cepeda, M. S., Lyons, J. G., Yin, R., & Lanes, S. (2019). Medical record-based ascertainment of behaviors suggestive of opioid misuse, diversion, abuse, and/or addiction among individuals showing evidence of doctor/pharmacy shopping. *Journal of Pain Research, 12*, 2291–2303.

Esser, M. B., & Jernigan, D. H. (2018). Policy approaches for regulating alcohol marketing in a global context: A public health perspective. *Annual Review of Public Health*, *39*, 385–401.

Fallon, M., Hanks, G., & Cherny, N. (2006). Principles of control of cancer pain. *BMJ*, *332*, (7548), 1022–1024.

Faroon, O. M., Keith, S., Jones, D., & de Rosa, C. (2001). Effects of polychlorinated biphenyls on development and reproduction. *Toxicology and Industrial Health*, *17*(3), 63–93.

Fay, M., Eisenmann, C., Diwan, S., & de Rosa, C. (1998). ATSDR evaluation of health effects of chemicals. V. Xylenes: Health effects, toxicokinetics, human exposure, and environmental fate. *Toxicology and Industrial Health*, (*14*) (5), 571–781.

FDA. (2021). *Benefit-risk assessment for new drug and biological products: Guidance for industry.* U.S. Food & Drug Administration.

FDA. (2021). Timeline of Selected FDA Activities and Significant Events Addressing Opioid Misuse and Abuse. *U.S. Food and Drug Administration.*

Field, R. I. (2008). "Why is health care regulation so complex?". *P&T*, *33*(10), 607–608.

Fine, P., Victora, C. G., Rothman, K. J., Moore, P. S., Chang, Y., Curtis, V., Heymann, D. L., et al. (2013, April 13). John Snow's legacy: Epidemiology without borders. *Lancet*, 381(9874), 1302–11.

Florence, C., Luo, F., & Rice, K. (2017). The economic burden of opioid use disorder and fatal opioid overdose in the United States. *Drug Alcohol Dependence*, *218*, 108350.

Freda, P. J., Moore, J. H., & Kranzler, H. R. (2021). The phenomics and genetics of addictive and affective comorbidity in opioid use disorder. *Drug Alcohol Depend*, *221*, 108602.

GAO. (2000). *Adverse drug events: The magnitude of health risk is uncertain because of limited incidence data.* U.S. General Accounting Office.

GAO. (2019). Prescription opioids: Patient options for safe and effective disposal of unused opioids. U.S. Government Accountability Office.

Garjón, F. J., Azparren, A., Vergara, I., Azaola, B., & Loayssa, J. R. (2012). Adoption of new drugs by physicians: A survival analysis. *BMC Health Services Research*, *12*.

Gaskin, D. J., & Richard, P. (2012). The economic costs of pain in the United States. *The Journal of Pain*, *13* (8), 715–724.

Gerstein, D. R., & Green, L. W. (1993). Preventing drug abuse: What do we know? In *Illicit drug use in the United States.* National Research Council (US) Committee on Substance Abuse Prevention Research, National Academies Press (US).

Glare, P., Aubrey, K. R., & Myles, P. S. (2019). Transition from acute to chronic pain after surgery. *The Lancet* *393*(10180), 1537–1546.

Glei, D. A., & Weinstein, M. (2023). Economic distress, obesity, and the rise in pain. *Social Science & Medicine, 339*, 116399.

Goldberg, R. (2014). Epidemiological uncertainty, causation, and drug product liability. *McGill Law Journal, 59* (4).

Goldstick, J. E., G. P. Guy, J. L. Losby, G. Baldwin, Myers, M., & A. S. B., Bohnert (2021). Changes in initial opioid prescribing practices after the 2016 release of the CDC guideline for prescribing opioids for chronic pain. *JAMA Network Open, 4*(7), e2116860.

Goodwin, J. L., Kraemer, J. J., & Bajwa, Z. H. (2009). "The use of opioids in the treatment of osteoarthritis: When, why, and how?". *Current Rheumatology Reports, 11*(1), 5–14.

Gordon, D. B., de Leon-Casasola, O. A., Wu, C. L., Sluka, K. A., Brennan, T. J., & Chou, R. (2016). Research gaps in practice guidelines for acute postoperative pain management in adults: Findings from a review of the evidence for an american pain society clinical practice guideline. *The Journal of Pain, 17*, 2 (Feb 2016), 158–166.

Gottlieb, S. (2000). Supreme court rules that FDA cannot regulate tobacco industry. *Bmj 320.* (7239), 894.

Greenfield, T. K., Cook, W. K., Karriker-Jaffe, K. J., Patterson, D., Kerr, W. C., Xuan, Z., & Naimi, T. S. (2019). The relationship between the U.S. state alcohol policy environment and individuals' experience of secondhand effects: Alcohol harms due to others' drinking. *Alcohol, Clinical and Experimental Research, 43* (6), 1234–1243.

Greenfield, T. K., Ye, Y., Kerr, W., Bond, J., Rehm, J., & Giesbrecht, N. (2009). Externalities from alcohol consumption in the 2005 US National Alcohol Survey: Implications for policy. *International Journal of Environmental Research and Public Health 6* (12), 3205–3224.

Grichnik, K. P., & F. M. Ferrante (1991). The difference between acute and chronic pain. *Mount Sinai Journal of Medicine, 58*(3), 217–220.

Grover, C. A., Elder, J. W., Close, R. J., & Curry, S. M. (2012). "How frequently are "Classic" Drug-seeking behaviors used by drug-seeking patients in the emergency department?". *World Journal of Emergency Medicine, 13*, (5), 416–421.

Grzybowski, S. (2004). The black market in prescription drugs. *Lancet, 364*(1), S28–29.

Gumidyala, L., Savul, S. A., Shofer, F. S., & Green-McKenzie, J. (2021). Effect of CDC opioid-prescribing guidelines in a community hospital emergency department. *Journal of Public Health Management and Practice, 27* (Suppl 3), S186–s90.

Guru, V., & Dubinsky, I. (2000). The patient versus caregiver perception of acute pain in the emergency department. *The Journal of Emergency Medicine, 18*(1), 7–12.

Hackworth, J. C., Schneider, J. E., Do Valle, M., Fam, D., Argoff, C., Offidani, E., and Potenziano, J. (2025). The burden of acute pain in the U.S. in the wake of the opioid crisis. *Frontiers in Pain Research, 6.*

Haley, S. J., Johnson, J. A., & Frazier, L. J. (2022). *Opioids and Population Health: A Primer.* Jones & Bartlett Learning.

Han, Y., Yan, W., Zheng, Y., Khan, M. Z., Yuan, K., & Lu, L. (2019). The rising crisis of illicit fentanyl use, overdose, and potential therapeutic strategies. *Transl Psychiatry, 9*(1), 282.

Hartmann, G. E., & R. Sethi (2023). The role of non-pharmaceutical fentanyl-contaminated counterfeit oxycodone in increasing opioid overdoses: A commentary review. *The Primary Care Companion for CNS Disorders, 25* (6).

Hass, B., Lungershausen, J., Hertel, N., Poulsen Nautrup, B., Kotowa, W., & Liedgens, H. (2009). Cost-effectiveness of strong opioids focussing on the long-term effects of opioid-related fractures: A model approach. *The European Journal of Health Economics, 10*(3), 309–321.

Hendlin, Y. H., & Bialous, S. A. (2020). The environmental externalities of tobacco manufacturing: A review of tobacco industry reporting. *Ambio 49*(1), 17–34.

Herzig, S. J., Rothberg, M. B., Cheung, M., Ngo, L. H., & Marcantonio, E. R. (2014). Opioid utilization and opioid-related adverse events in nonsurgical patients in US hospitals. *Journal of Hospital Medicine, 9*(2), 73–81.

Hessami, K., Welch, J., Frost, A., AlAshqar, A., Arian, S. E., Gough, E., & Borahay, M. A. (2023). Perioperative opioid dispensing and persistent use after benign hysterectomy: A systematic review and meta-analysis. *American Journal of Obstetrics and Gynecology, 229* (1), 23–32.

Hicks, H. E., & De Rosa, C. T. (2002). Great lakes research–important human health findings and their impact on ATSDR's Superfund research program. *International Journal of Hygiene and Environmental Health, 205* (1–2), 49–61.

Hill, M. V., Stucke, R. S., McMahon, M. L., Beeman, J. L., & Barth, R. J., Jr (2018). An educational intervention decreases opioid prescribing after general surgical operations. *Annals of Surgery 267*(3), 468–472.

Hirai, A. H., Ko, J. Y., Owens, P. L., Stocks, C., & Patrick, S. W. (2021). Neonatal abstinence syndrome and maternal opioid-related diagnoses in the US, 2010-2017. *JAMA, 325*(2), 146–155.

Hoffman, J. (2023, November 13). 'A Monster': Super meth and other drugs push crisis beyond opioids. *The New York Times.*

Howard, R., Ryan, A., Hu, H. M., Brown, C. S., Waljee, J., Bicket, M. C., Englesbe, M., & Brummett, C. M. (2023). Evidence-based opioid prescribing guidelines and new persistent opioid use after surgery. *Annals of Surgery, 278* (2), 216–221.

HRW. (2011). *Global state of pain treatment: Access to palliative care as a human right*. Human Rights Watch.

Hulme, S., Bright, D., & Nielsen, S. (2018). The source and diversion of pharmaceutical drugs for non-medical use: A systematic review and meta-analysis. *Drug Alcohol Depend*, 186, 242–256.

Humphreys, K., Shover, C. L., Andrews, C. M., Bohnert, A. S. B., Brandeau, M. L., Caulkins, J. P., Chen, J. H., et al. (2022). Responding to the opioid crisis in North America and beyond: Recommendations of the Stanford-Lancet Commission. *Lancet*, 399(10324), 555–604.

Hurley, J., & Mentzakis, E. (2013). Health-related externalities: Evidence from a choice experiment. *Journal of Health Economics*, *32* (4), 671–681.

Inciardi, J. A., Surratt, H. L., Kurtz, S. P., & Cicero, T. J. (2007). Mechanisms of prescription drug diversion among drug-involved club- and street-based populations. *Pain Medicine*, *8*(2), 171–183.

Inciardi, J. A., H. L. Surratt, Lugo, Y., & Cicero, T. J. (2007). The diversion of prescription opioid analgesics. *Law Enforcement Executive Forum*, *7*(7), 127–241.

IOM. (2011). *Relieving pain in America: A blueprint for transforming prevention, care, education, and research*. U.S. National Institutes for Health, Institute of Medicine.

Jones, G. H., Bruera, E., Abdi, S., & Kantarjian, H. M. (2018). The opioid epidemic in the United States-Overview, origins, and potential solutions. *Cancer*, *124*(22), 4279–4286.

Joseph, H., Stancliff, S., & Langrod, J. (2000). Methadone maintenance treatment (MMT): A review of historical and clinical issues. *Mount Sinai Journal of Medicine*, *67*(5–6), 347–364.

Joseph, J. M., Gori, D., Curtin, C., Hah, J., Ho, V. T., Asch, S. M., & Hernandez-Boussard, T. (2000, February 2022). Gaps in standardized postoperative pain management quality measures: A systematic review. *Surgery*, *171*, 453–458.

Kent, M., Tighe, P., Belfer, I., Brennan, T. J., Bruehl, S., Brummett, C., & Buckenmaier, C. III, et al. (2017). The ACTTION-American Pain Society-American Academy of pain medicine pain taxonomy (AAAPT): A multidimensional approach to classifying acute pain conditions. *The Journal of Pain*, *18*(5), 479.

Keyes, K. M., Rutherford, C., Hamilton, A., Barocas, J. A., Gelberg, K. H., Mueller, P. P., Feaster, D. J., El-Bassel, N., & Cerdá, M. (2022). What is the prevalence of and trend in opioid use disorder in the United States from 2010 to 2019? Using multiplier approaches to estimate prevalence for an unknown population size. *Drug and Alcohol Dependence Reports*, *3*.

Kiang, M. V., Humphreys, K., Cullen, M. R., & Basu, S. (2020). Opioid prescribing patterns among medical providers in the United States, 2003–17: Retrospective, observational study. *BMJ* 368, l6968.

Kim, B., Nolan, S., Beaulieu, T., Shalansky, S., & Ti, L. (2019). Inappropriate opioid prescribing practices: A narrative review. *American Journal of Health-System Pharmacy*, *76*(16), 1231–1237.

Kim, H., Hartung, D. M., Jacob, R. L., McCarty, D., & McConnell, K. J. (2016, April 1). The concentration of opioid prescriptions by providers and among patients in the oregon medicaid program. *Psychiatric Services 67*(4), 397–404.

Kocherlakota, P. (2014) Neonatal abstinence syndrome. *Pediatrics*, *134*(2), e547–561.

Kosten, T. R., & H. D. Kleber. (1988). Differential diagnosis of psychiatric comorbidity in substance abusers. *Journal of Substance Abuse Treatment*, *5* (4), 201–206.

Kumar, K., Gulotta, L. V., Dines, J. S., Allen, A. A., Cheng, J., Fields, K. G., YaDeau, J. T., & Wu, C. L. (2017). Unused opioid pills after outpatient shoulder surgeries given current perioperative prescribing habits. *The American Journal of Sports Medicine*, *45*(3), 636–641.

Lalkhen, A. (2021). *An Anatomy of Pain*. Scribner.

Lam, J., Schneider, J., Shadbegian, R., Pega, F., St Claire, S., & Novotny, T. E. (2022). Modelling the global economic costs of tobacco product waste. *Bulletin of the World Health Organization*, *100*(10), 620–627.

Lande, R. G. (2020). American Civil War medical practice, the post-bellum opium crisis and modern comparisons. *History of Psychiatry*, *31*(4), 483–494.

Lankenau, S. E., Schrager, S. M., Silva, K., Kecojevic, A., Bloom, J. J., Wong, C., & Iverson, E. (2012, February 14). Misuse of prescription and illicit drugs among high-risk young adults in Los Angeles and New York. *Journal of Public Health Research*, *1*(1), 22–30.

LAPPA. (2023). Drug diversion in health care. In *Fact Sheet*. Legislative Analysis and Public Policy Association.

Lawal, O. D., Gold, J., Murthy, A., Ruchi, R., Bavry, E., Hume, A. L., Lewkowitz, A. K., Brothers, T., & Wen, X. (2020). Rate and risk factors associated with prolonged opioid use after surgery: A systematic review and meta-analysis. *JAMA Network Open*, *3*(6), e207367.

LeBon, B., Zeppetella, G., & Higginson, I. J. (2009). Effectiveness of topical administration of opioids in palliative care: A systematic review. *Journal of Pain and Symptom Management*, *37*(5), 913–917.

Leung, P. T. M., Macdonald, E. M., Stanbrook, M. B., Dhalla, I. A., & Juurlink, D. N. (2017). A 1980 letter on the risk of opioid addiction. *New England Journal of Medicine*, *376*(22), 2194–2195.

Lewis, E. T., Cucciare, M. A., & Trafton, J. A. (2014). What do patients do with unused opioid medications?. *The Clinical Journal of Pain*, *30*(8), 654–662.

Lines, T., Burdick, C., Dewez, X., Aldridge, E., Neal-Williams, T., Walker, K., Akhlaghi, H., Paul, B., & Taylor, D. M. (2022). Nature and extent of selection bias resulting from convenience sampling in the emergency department. *Emergency Medicine Journal*, *39*(4), 325–330.

Liu, Y., Guazzelli Williamson, V., Setlow, B., Cottler, L. B., & Knackstedt, L. A. (2018). The importance of considering polysubstance use: Lessons from cocaine research. *Drug Alcohol Depend*, *192*, 16–28.

Longo, L. P., Parran, T., Jr., Johnson, B., & Kinsey, W. (2000). Addiction: Part II. Identification and management of the drug-seeking patient. *American Family Physician*, *61*(8), 2401–2408.

Lublóy, Á (2014). Factors affecting the uptake of new medicines: A systematic literature review. *BMC Health Services Research*, *14*, 469.

Luby, A. O., Alessio-Bilowus, D., Hu, H. M., Brummett, C. M., Waljee, J. F., & Bicket, M. C. (2014). Trends in opioid prescribing and new persistent opioid use after surgery in the United States. *Annals of Surgery*, *281*(3), 347–352.

Luo, F., Li, M., & Florence, C. (2021). State-level economic costs of opioid use disorder and fatal opioid overdose—United States, 2017. *MMWR Morbidity and Mortality Weekly Report*, *70*(15), 541–446.

Lyapustina, T., Rutkow, L., Chang, H. Y., Daubresse, M., Ramji, A. F., Faul, M., Stuart, E. A., & Alexander, G. C. (2016). Effect of a "pill mill" law on opioid prescribing and utilization: The case of Texas. *Drug Alcohol Depend*, *159* (Feb 1 2016): 190–197.

Lynch, S.S. (2025). Adverse drug reactions (Adverse drug effects, medication side effects). In *Merck Manual.*

Lytton, T. D. (2004). Using litigation to make public health policy: Theoretical and empirical challenges in assessing product liability, tobacco, and gun litigation. *Journal of Law, Medicine and Ethics*, *32*(4), 556–564.

Lyu, H., Xu, T., Brotman, D., Mayer-Blackwell, B., Cooper, M., Daniel, M., Wick, E. C., et al. (2017). Overtreatment in the United States. *PLoS One*, *12*(9) (2017), e0181970.

Manchikanti, L., Pampati, V., Falco, F. J., & Hirsch, J. A. (2015). An updated assessment of utilization of interventional pain management techniques in the Medicare population: 2000–2013. *Pain Physician*, 18(2), E115–127.

Marmot, M., & Wilkinson, R. G. (2006). *Social determinants of health* (2nd Edn.). Oxford University Press.

Marsden, J., Kelleher, M., Gilvarry, E., Mitcheson, L., Bisla, J., Cape, A., Cowden, F., et al. (2023). Superiority and cost-effectiveness of monthly extended-release buprenorphine versus daily standard of care medication: A pragmatic, parallel-group, open-label, multicentre, randomised, controlled, phase 3 trial. *EClinicalMedicine*, *66*, 102311.

Martyn, J. A. J., Mao, J., & Bittner, E. A. (2019). Opioid tolerance in critical illness. *New England Journal of Medicine*, *380*(4), 365–378.

Mateu-Gelabert, P., Guarino, H., Jessell, L., & Teper, A. (2015). Injection and sexual HIV/HCV risk behaviors associated with nonmedical use of prescription opioids among young adults in New York City. *Journal of Substance Abuse Treatment*, *48*(1), 13–20.

Matthias, M. S., & Bair, M. J. (2010). The patient-provider relationship in chronic pain management: Where do we go from here?. *Pain Medicine*, *11*(12), 1747–1749.

Maughan, B. C., Hersh, E. V., Shofer, F. S., Wanner, K. J., Archer, E., Carrasco, L. R., & Rhodes, K. V. (2016). Unused opioid analgesics and drug disposal following outpatient dental surgery: A randomized controlled trial. *Drug Alcohol Depend*, *168*, 328–334.

McDonald, D. C., Carlson, K., & Izrael, D. (2012). Geographic variation in opioid prescribing in the U.S. *Journal of Pain*, *13*(10), 988–996.

McGwin, G., Jr (2010). Causation in epidemiology. *American Journal of Ophthalmology*, *150*(5), 599–601.

McLellan, A. T. (2017). Substance misuse and substance use disorders: Why do they matter in healthcare?. *Transactions of the American Clinical and Climatological Association*, *128* (2017), 112–130.

McNeely, J., & Adam, A. (2020). *Substance use screening and risk assessment in adults*. Johns Hopkins University.

Meisenberg, B. R., Grover, J., Campbell, C., & Korpon, D. (2018). Assessment of opioid prescribing practices before and after implementation of a health system intervention to reduce opioid overprescribing. *JAMA Network Open*, *1*(5), e182908.

Meissner, W., & Zaslansky, R. (2019). A survey of postoperative pain treatments and unmet needs. *Best Practice & Research Clinical Anaesthesiology*, 33(3), 269–286.

Mercadante, S., Adamoli, L., Bellavia, G., Castellana, L., Favara, T., Insalaco, L., Mauceri, M., et al. (2022). Opioids in advanced cancer: Use, storage and disposal in the home. *BMJ Support Palliat Care*.

Miller, M. L., & Hurd, Y. L. (2017). Testing the gateway hypothesis. *Neuropsychopharmacology*, *42*(5), 985–986.

Mills, S. E. E., Nicolson, K. P., & Smith, B. H. (2019). Chronic pain: A review of its epidemiology and associated factors in population-based studies. *British Journal Anaesth*, *123* (2), e273–e283.

Moosavyzadeh, A., Ghaffari, F., Mosavat, S. H., Zargaran, A., Mokri, A., Faghihzadeh, S., & Naseri, M. (2018). The medieval Persian manuscript of Afyunieh: The first individual treatise on the opium and addiction in history. *Journal of Integrative Medicine*, *16*(2), 77–83.

Morley, K. I., Ferris, J. A., Winstock, A. R., & Lynskey, M. T. (2017). Polysubstance use and misuse or abuse of prescription opioid analgesics: A multi-level analysis of international data. *Pain*, *158*(6), 1138–1144.

Morlion, B., Coluzzi, F., Aldington, D., Kocot-Kepska, M., Pergolizzi, J., Mangas, A. C., Ahlbeck, K., & Kalso, E. (2018) Pain chronification: What should a non-pain medicine specialist know? *Current Medical Research and Opinion*, *34*(7), 1169–1178.

Murphy, D. L., Lebin, J. A., Severtson, S. G., Olsen, H. A., Dasgupta, N., & Dart, R. C. (2018). Comparative rates of mortality and serious adverse effects among commonly prescribed opioid analgesics. *Drug Safety*, *41*(8), 787–795.

NASEM. (2017). Consensus Study Report of National Academies of Sciences, Engineering and Medicine (NASEM). In R. J. Bonnie, M. A. Ford & J. K. Phillips (Eds.), *Pain management and the opioid epidemic: Balancing societal and indidivual benefits and risks of prescription opioid use*. National Academies Press.

Nasser, K., Verhoeff, K., Mocanu, V., Kung, J. Y., Purich, K., Switzer, N. J., Birch, D. W., & Karmali, S. (2023). New persistent opioid use after bariatric surgery: A systematic review and pooled proportion meta-analysis. *Surgical Endoscopy*, *37*(1), 703–714.

Nicholson, W., & Snyder, C. (2016). *Microeconomic theory: Basic principles and extensions* (12th Edn.). Cengage Learning.

NIDA. (2021). *Heroin drug facts*. National Institute on Drug Abuse | U.S. National Institutes for Health.

Nieuwlaat, R., Wilczynski, N., Navarro, T., Hobson, N., Jeffery, R., Keepanasseril, A., & Agoritsas, T., et al. (2014). Interventions for enhancing medication adherence. *Cochrane Database of Systematic Reviews*, 2014(11), Cd000011.

Novotny, T. E., & Zhao, F. (1999). Consumption and production waste: Another externality of tobacco use. *Tob Control*, *8*(1), 75–80.

O'Brien, A. L., Krasniak, P. J., Schroeder, M. J., Desai, M. N., Diaz, A., & Chetta, M. D. (2022). Impact of opioid restriction legislation on prescribing practices for outpatient plastic and reconstructive surgery. *Plastic and Reconstructive Surgery*, *150*(1), 213–221.

O'Donnell, J., Gladden, R. M. , Kariisa, M., & Mattson, C. L. (2022). Using death scene and toxicology evidence to define involvement of heroin, pharmaceutical morphine, illicitly manufactured fentanyl and pharmaceutical fentanyl in opioid overdose deaths, 38 states and the District of Columbia, January 2018-December 2019. *Addiction*, *117*(5), 1483–1490.

O'Donnell, J., Tanz, L. J., Gladden, R. M., Davis, N. L., & Bitting, J. (2021). Trends in and characteristics of drug overdose deaths involving illicitly manufactured fentanyls—United States, 2019–2020. *MMWR Morbidity and Mortality Weekly Report*, *70*(50), 1740–1746.

Opioid MDL. (2022). MDL 2804 Case No. 1:17-md-2804 judge dan aaron polster: Abatement order. In *Re: National opioid litigation*. United States District Court Northern District of Ohio.

Osani, M. C., Lohmander, L. S., & Bannuru, R. R. (2021). Is there any role for opioids in the management of knee and hip osteoarthritis? A systematic review and meta-analysis. *Arthritis Care and Research (Hoboken)*, *73*(10), 1413–1424.

Owens, P. L., Weiss, A. J., Barrett, M. L., & Reid, L. D. (2006). Social determinants of health and county population rates of opioid-related inpatient stays and emergency department visits, 2016. In *Healthcare cost and utilization project (HCUP) statistical briefs*. Agency for Healthcare Research and Quality (US).

Paice, J. A., Bohlke, K., Barton, D., Craig, D. S., El-Jawahri, A., Hershman, D. L., Kong, L. R., et al. (2023, February 1). Use of opioids for adults with pain from cancer or cancer treatment: ASCO guideline. *Journal of Clinical Oncology*, *41* (4), 914–930.

Pak, D. J., Yong, R. J., Kaye, A. D., & Urman, R. D. (2018). Chronification of pain: Mechanisms, current understanding, and clinical implications. *Current Pain and Headache Reports* *22*(2), 9.

Palamar, J. J., Ciccarone, D., Rutherford, C., Keyes, K. M., Carr, T. H., & Cottler, L. B. (2022). Trends in seizures of powders and pills containing illicit fentanyl in the United States, 2018 through 2021. *Drug Alcohol Depend*, *234*, 109398.

Papandreou, A. A. (1994). *Externality and institutions*. Clarendon Press.

Park, J. Y., & Wu, L. T. (2020). Sources of misused prescription opioids and their association with prescription opioid use disorder in the United States: Sex and age differences. *Substance Use and Misuse*, *55*(6) (2020), 928–936.

Payne, R. (2000). Limitations of NSAIDs for pain management: Toxicity or lack of efficacy?. *Journal of Pain*, *1*(3 Suppl), 14–18.

Payne, R., & Foley, K. M. (1984). Advances in the management of cancer pain. *Cancer Research and Treatment*, *68*(1), 173–183.

Pergolizzi, J., Jr., LeQuang, J. A. K., Magnusson, P., Miller, T. L., Breve, F., & Varrassi, G. (2023). The new stealth drug on the street: A narrative review of xylazine as a street drug. *Cureus*, *15*(6), e40983.

Phaneuf, D. J., & Requate, T. (2017). *A course in environmental economics: Theory, policy, and practice*. Cambridge University Press.

Pierce, J. J., Weiner, R. F., & Vesilind, P. A. (1998). *Environmental pollution and control* (4th Edn.). Butterworth-Heinemann; Elsevier.

Pirmohamed, M., James, S., Meakin, S., Green, C., Scott, A. K., Walley, T. J., Farrar, K., Park, B. K., & Breckenridge, A. M. (2004). Adverse drug reactions as cause of admission to hospital: prospective analysis of 18,820 patients. *BMJ* 329(7456), 15–19.

Pollini, R. A., Banta-Green, C. J., Cuevas-Mota, J., Metzner, M., Teshale, E., & Garfein, R. S. (2011). Problematic use of prescription-type opioids prior to heroin use among young heroin injectors. *Substance Abuse and Rehabilitation*, *2*(1), 173–180.

Porter, E. D., Sacks, O. A., Ramkumar, N., & Barth, R. J., Jr. (2022). Surgery prescription opioid misuse and diversion in US adults and associated risk factors. *Journal of Surgical Research, 275*, 208–217.

Pota, V., Coppolino, F., Barbarisi, A., Passavanti, M. B., Aurilio, C., Sansone, P., & Pace, M. C. (2022). Pain in intensive care: A narrative review. *Pain and Therapy, 11*(2), 359–367.

Potter, J. S., Prather, K., Kropp, F., Byrne, M., Sullivan, C. R., Mohamedi, N., Copersino, M. L., & Weiss, R. D. (2010). A method to diagnose opioid dependence resulting from heroin versus prescription opioids using the Composite International Diagnostic Interview. *Contemporary Clinical Trials, 31*(2), 185–188.

Pretorius, R. W., & Zurick, G. M. (2008). A systematic approach to identifying drug-seeking patients. *Family Practice Management, 15*(4), A3–A5.

Rackham, D. M., Herink, C. M., Stevens, I. G., Cardoza, N. M., & Singh, H. (2014). Evidence behind FDA alerts for drugs with adverse cardiovascular effects: Implications for clinical practice. *Pharmacotherapy, 34*(4), 358–372.

Rafter, N., Hickey, A., Condell, S., Conroy, R., O'Connor, P., Vaughan, D., & Williams, D. (2015). Adverse events in healthcare: Learning from mistakes. *Qjm, 108*(4), 273–277.

Raschetti, R., Morgutti, M., Menniti-Ippolito, F., Belisari, A., Rossignoli, A., Longhini, P., & La Guidara, C. (1999). Suspected adverse drug events requiring emergency department visits or hospital admissions. *European Journal of Clinical Pharmacology, 54*(12), 959–963.

Reddy, A., de la Cruz, M., Rodriguez, E. M., Thames, J., Wu, J., Chisholm, G., Liu, D., et al. (2014). Patterns of storage, use, and disposal of opioids among cancer outpatients. *Oncologist, 19*(7), 780–785.

Rigg, K. K., Kurtz, S. P., & Surratt, H. L. (2012). Patterns of prescription medication diversion among drug dealers. *Drugs (Abingdon Engl), 19*(2) (2012), 144–155.

Rikard, S. M., Strahan, A. E., Schmit, K. M., & Guy, G. P., Jr. (2023). Chronic Pain Among Adults—United States, 2019–2021. *MMWR Morbidity and Mortality Weekly Report, 72*(15), 379–385.

Rong, L. Q., Kamel, M. K., Rahouma, M., Naik, A., Mehta, K., Abouarab, A. A., Di Franco, A., et al. (2019). High-dose versus low-dose opioid anesthesia in adult cardiac surgery: A meta-analysis. *Journal of Clinical Anesthesia, 57*, 57–62.

Rosen, D., Hunsaker, A, Albert, S. M., Cornelius, J. R., & Reynolds, C. F. (2011). Characteristics and consequences of heroin use among older adults in the United States: A review of the literature, treatment implications, and recommendations for further research. *Addictive Behaviors, 36*(4), 279–285.

Rosenberger, D. C., & Pogatzki-Zahn, E. M. (2022). Chronic post-surgical pain —update on incidence, risk factors and preventive treatment options. *BJA Education*, *22*(5), 190–196.

Rothman, K. J., Greenland, S., & Lash, T. L. (2008). *Modern epidemiology* (3rd Edn.). Wolters Kluer; Lippincot WIlliams & Wilkins.

Ruhm, C. J. (2017) . Geographic variation in opioid and heroin involved drug poisoning mortality rates. *American Journal of Preventive Medicine*, *53*(6), 745–753.

Ruiz-Colón, K., Chavez-Arias, C., Díaz-Alcalá, J. E., & Martínez, M. A. (2014). Xylazine intoxication in humans and its importance as an emerging adulterant in abused drugs: A comprehensive review of the literature. *Forensic Science International*, *240*, 1–8.

Ruths, M. B. (2009). The lesson of John Snow and the broad street pump. *AMA Journal of Ethics: Virtual Mentor*, *11*(6), 470–472.

Rutkow, L., Chang, H. Y., Daubresse, M., Webster, D. W., Stuart, E. A., & Alexander, G. C. (2015). Effect of Florida's prescription drug monitoring program and pill mill laws on opioid prescribing and use. JAMA Internal Medicine, *175*(10), 1642–1649.

Sabatino, M. J., Kunkel, S. T., Ramkumar, D. B., Keeney, B. J., & Jevsevar, D. S. (2018). Excess opioid medication and variation in prescribing patterns following common orthopaedic procedures. *Journal of Bone and Joint Surgery*, *100*(3), 180–188.

Sabatowski, R., Schäfer, D., Kasper, S. M., Brunsch, H., & Radbruch, L. (2004). Pain treatment: A historical overview. *Current Pharmaceutical Design*, *10*(7), 701–716.

Saha, T. D., Kerridge, B. T., Goldstein, R. B., Chou, S. P., Zhang, H., Jung, J., & Pickering, R. P., et al. (2016). Nonmedical prescription opioid use and DSM-5 nonmedical prescription opioid use disorder in the United States. *Journal of Clinical Psychiatry*, *77*(6), 772–780.

Saloner, B., Landis, R., Stein, B. D., & Barry, C. L. (2019). The affordable care act in the heart of the opioid crisis: Evidence From West Virginia. *Health Aff, (Millwood)*, 38(4), 633–642.

SAMHSA. (2022). *National survey on drug use and health (NSDUH), 2021 data.* U.S. Department of Health and Human Services, Substance Abuse and Mental Health Services Administration (SAMHSA), Center for Behavioral Health Statistics and Quality.

SAMHSA. (2010). Reliability of key measures in the national survey on drug use and health. In (*Methodology series M-8, HHS publication No. SMA 09-4425*). U.S. Department of Health and Human Services, Substance Abuse and Mental Health Services Administration, Office of Applied Studies.

Sandbrink, F., Oliva, E. M., McMullen, T. L., Aylor, A. R., Harvey, M. A., Christopher, M. L., & Cunningham, F., et al. (2020) . Opioid Prescribing and Opioid Risk Mitigation Strategies in the Veterans Health Administration. *Journal of General Internal Medicine, 35*(Suppl 3), 927–934.

Santosa, K. B., Priest, C. R., Oliver, C. R., Kenney, B., Bicket, M. C., Brummett, C. M., & Waljee, J. F. (2023). Long-term health outcomes of new persistent opioid use after surgery among medicare beneficiaries. *Annals of Surgery, 278*, e491–e95.

Saunders, H., & Rudowitz, R. (2022). *Demographics and health insurance coverage of nonelderly adults with mental illness and substance use disorders in 2020.* Kaiser Family Foundation (KFF).

Schepis, T. S., McCabe, S. E., & Teter, C. J. (2018). Sources of opioid medication for misuse in older adults: Results from a nationally representative survey. *Pain 159*(8), 1543–1549.

Schepis, T. S., Wilens, T. E., & McCabe, S. E. (2019). Prescription drug misuse: Sources of controlled medications in adolescents. *Journal of the American Academy of Child and Adolescent Psychiatry, 58*(7), 670–680.

Scherrer, J. F., Tucker, J., Salas, J., Zhang, Z., & Grucza, R. (2020). Comparison of opioids prescribed for patients at risk for opioid misuse before and after publication of the centers for disease control and prevention's opioid prescribing guidelines. *JAMA Network Open, 3*(12), e2027481.

Shafi, S., Collinsworth, A. W., Copeland, L. A., Ogola, G. O., Qiu, T., Kouznetsova, & M., Liao, I. C., et al. (2018). Association of opioid-related adverse drug events with clinical and cost outcomes among surgical patients in a large integrated health care delivery system. *JAMA Surgery, 153*(8), 757–763.

Shetty, A., Delanerolle, G., Cavalini, H., Deng, C., Yang, X., Boyd, A., Fernandez, T., et al. (2024). A systematic review and network meta-analysis of pharmaceutical interventions used to manage chronic pain. *Scientific Reports, 14*(1), 1621.

Shi, J., Fan, K., Yan, L., Fan, Z., Li, F., Wang, G., Liu, H., et al. (2022). Cost effectiveness of pharmacological management for osteoarthritis: A systematic review. *Applied Health Economics and Health Policy, 20*, (3), 351–370.

Shy, O. (1995). *Industrial organization*. The MIT Press.

Sinatra, R. (2010). Causes and consequences of inadequate management of acute pain. *Pain Medication, 11*(12), 1859–1871.

Skelly, A. C., Chou, R., Dettori, J. R., Turner, J. A., Friedly, J. L., Rundell, S. D., Fu, R., et al. (2020). Noninvasive nonpharmacological treatment for chronic pain: A systematic review update. In *Comparative effectiveness review (227)*. Agency for Healthcare Research and Quality (AHRQ).

Snijders, R. A. H., Brom, L., Theunissen, M., & van den Beuken-van Everdingen, M. H. J. (2023). Update on prevalence of pain in patients with cancer 2022: A systematic literature review and meta-analysis. *Cancers (Basel), 15*(3).

Solca, M. (2002). Acute pain management: Unmet needs and new advances in pain management. *European Journal of Anaesthesiology, 25*, 3–10.

Sonawane, K. B., Cheng, N., & Hansen, R. A. (2018). Serious adverse drug events reported to the FDA: Analysis of the FDA adverse event reporting system 2006–2014 database. *Journal of Managed Care and Specialty Pharmacy, 24* (7), 682–690.

Springer, R., Marino, M., Bailey, S. R., Angier, H., O'Malley, J. P., Hoopes, M., Lindner, S., DeVoe, J. E., & Huguet, N. (2019). Prescription opioid use patterns, use disorder diagnoses and addiction treatment receipt after the 2014 Medicaid expansion in Oregon. *Addiction, 114*(10), 1775–1784.

Strand, N., J, M., Tieppo Francio, V., M, M., Turkiewicz, M., El Helou, A., M, M., et al. (2022). Advances in pain medicine: A review of new technologies. *Current Pain and Headache Reports, 26*, (8), 605–616.

Strang, J., Volkow, N. D., Degenhardt, L., Hickman, M., Johnson, K., Koob, G. F., Marshall, B. D. L., Tyndall, M., & Walsh, S. L. (2020). Opioid use disorder. *Nature Reviews Disease Primers, 6*(1), 3.

Sugano, K. (2015). How do we manage serious gastrointestinal adverse events associated with anti-thrombotic therapy?. *Expert Review of Gastroenterology and Hepatology, 9*(1), 5–8.

Sullivan, M. D., & Ballantyne, J. C. (2023). *The right to pain relief and other deep roots of the opioid epidemic.* Oxford University Press.

Sultana, J., Cutroneo, P., & Trifirò, G. (2013). Clinical and economic burden of adverse drug reactions. *J Pharmacol Pharmacother, 4*(Suppl 1), S73–77.

Sundararajan, K., Ajrawat, P., Canizares, M., Power, J. D., Perruccio, A. V., Sarro, A., Montoya, L., & Rampersaud, Y. R. (2021). The potential for diversion of prescribed opioids among orthopaedic patients: Results of an anonymous patient survey. *PLoS One, 16*(8), e0256741.

Taché, S. V., Sönnichsen, A., & Ashcroft, D. M. (2011). Prevalence of adverse drug events in ambulatory care: A systematic review. *Annals of Pharmacotherapy, 45*(7–8), 977–989.

Tegethoff, M., Belardi, A., Stalujanis, E., & Meinlschmidt, G. (2015). Comorbidity of mental disorders and chronic pain: Chronology of onset in adolescents of a national representative cohort. *Journal of Pain, 16*(10), 1054–1064.

Tetrault, J. M., & Butner, J. L. (2015). Non-medical prescription opioid use and prescription opioid use disorder: A review. *Yale Journal of Biology and Medicine, 88*(3), 227–233.

Tilling, K. (2001). Capture-recapture methods—Useful or misleading?. *International Journal of Epidemiology, 30*(1), 12–14.

Todd, K. H., Ducharme, J., Choiniere, M., Crandall, C. S., Fosnocht, D. E., Homel, P., & Tanabe, P. (2007). Pain in the emergency department: Results of the pain and emergency medicine initiative (PEMI) multicenter study. *Journal of Pain, 8*(6), 460–466.

Tsuang, M. T., Lyons, M. J., Meyer, J. M., Doyle, T., Eisen, S. A., Goldberg, J., & True, W., et al. (1998). Co-occurrence of abuse of different drugs in men: The role of drug-specific and shared vulnerabilities. *Archives of General Psychiatry, 55*(11), 967–972.

Ulker, E., & Del Fabbro, E. (2020). Best practices in the management of non-medical opioid use in patients with cancer-related pain. *Oncologist 25*(3), 189–196.

Ung, C., Yonekawa, Y., Waljee, J. F., Gunaseelan, V., Lai, Y. L., & Woodward, M. A. (2021). Persistent opioid use after ophthalmic surgery in opioid-naive patients and associated risk factors. *Ophthalmology, 128*(9), 1266–1273.

Vernick, J. S., Mair, J. S., Teret, S. P., & Sapsin, J. W. (2003). Role of litigation in preventing product-related injuries. *Epidemiologic Reviews 25* (2003), 90–98.

Vernick, J. S., Sapsin, J. W., Teret, S. P., & Mair, J. S. (2004). How litigation can promote product safety. *Journal of Law, Medicine and Ethics, 32*(4), 551–555.

Viswanath, O., Urits, I., Bouley, E., Peck, J. M., Thompson, W., & Kaye, A. D. (2019). Evolving spinal cord stimulation technologies and clinical implications in chronic pain management. *Current Pain and Headache Reports, 23* (6), 39.

Vorspan, F., Marie-Claire, C., Bellivier, F., & Bloch, V. (2021). Biomarkers to predict staging and treatment response in opioid dependence: A narrative review. *Drug Development Journals, 82*(5), 668–677.

Vranken, M. J., Linge-Dahl, L., Mantel-Teeuwisse, A. K., Radbruch, L., Schutjens, M. D., Scholten, W., Payne, S., & Jünger, S. (2020). The perception of barriers concerning opioid medicines: A survey examining differences between policy makers, healthcare professionals and other stakeholders. *Palliative Medicine, 34*(4), 493–503.

Walley, A. Y., Bernson, D., Larochelle, M. R., Green, T. C., Young, L., & Land, T. (2019). The contribution of prescribed and illicit opioids to fatal overdoses in massachusetts, 2013–2015. *Public Health Reports, 134*(6), 667–674.

Weeks, E., & Sanford, P. (2019). Financial impact of the opioid crisis on local government: Quantifying costs for litigation and policymaking. *Kansas Law Review, 67.*

Weller, A. E., Crist, R. C., Reiner, B. C., Doyle, G. A., & Berrettini, W. H. (2021). Neonatal opioid withdrawal syndrome (NOWS): A Transgenerational echo of the opioid crisis. *Cold Spring Harb Perspect Med, 11*(3).

Welsch, P., Petzke, F., Klose, P., & Häuser, W. (2020). Opioids for chronic osteoarthritis pain: An updated systematic review and meta-analysis of efficacy, tolerability and safety in randomized placebo-controlled studies of at least 4 weeks double-blind duration. *European Journal of Pain, 24*(4), 685–703.

Westhoff, B. (2019) *Fentanyl, Inc.* Grove Press.

Wideman, T. H., Edwards, R. R., Walton, D. M., Martel, M. O., Hudon, A., & Seminowicz, D. A. (2017). The multimodal assessment model of pain: A novel

framework for further integrating the subjective pain experience within research and practice. *The Clinical Journal of Pain*, *35*(3), 212–221.
Wilson, A. J., Morgan, E. R., Booth, M., Norman, R., Perkins, S. E., Hauffe, H. C., Mideo, N., et al. (2017). "What is a vector?". *Philosophical Transactions of the Royal Society of London. Series B, Biological Sciences*, *372*(1719).
Wood, D., Moy, S. F., Zhang, S., & Lightfoot, N. (2022). Impact of a prescriber and patient educational intervention on discharge analgesia prescribing and hospital readmission rates following elective unilateral total hip and knee arthroplasty.. *BMJ Open Quality*, *11*(3.
Wyne, A., Rai, R., Cuerden, M., Clark, W. F., & Suri, R. S. (2011). Opioid and benzodiazepine use in end-stage renal disease: A systematic review. *Clinical Journal of the American Society of Nephrology*, *6*(2), 326–333.
Yang, K. H., Han, B. H., Moore, A. A., & Palamar, J. J. (2022). Trends in major depressive episodes and mental health treatment among older adults in the United States, 2010–2019. *Journal of Affective Disorders*, *318*, 299–303.
Yap, Z. L., Summers, S. J., Grant, A. R., Moseley, G. L., & Karran, E. L. (2022). The role of the social determinants of health in outcomes of surgery for low back pain: A systematic review and narrative synthesis. *Spine Journal*, *22*(5), 793–809.
Zajacova, A., Rogers, R. G., Grodsky, E., & Grol-Prokopczyk, H. (2020). The relationship between education and pain among adults aged 30–49 in the United States. *Journal of Pain*, *21*(11–12), 1270–1280.
Zaslansky, R., Meissner, W., & Chapman, C. R. (2018). Pain after orthopaedic surgery: Differences in patient reported outcomes in the United States vs internationally. An observational study from the PAIN OUT dataset. *British Journal of Anaesthesia*, *120*(4), 790–797.
Zhao, X., Shah, D., Gandhi, K., Wei, W., Dwibedi, N., Webster, L. , & Sambamoorthi, U. (2019). Clinical, humanistic, and economic burden of osteoarthritis among noninstitutionalized adults in the United States. *Osteoarthritis Cartilage*, *27*(11), 1618–1626.
Zhu, J. M., Rooke-Ley, H., & Fuse Brown, E. (2023). A doctrine in name only—Strengthening prohibitions against the corporate practice of medicine. *New England Journal of Medicine*, *389*(11) (2023), 965–968.
Zhukovsky, D. S., Gorowski, E., Hausdorff, J., Napolitano, B., & Lesser, M. (1995). Unmet analgesic needs in cancer patients. *Journal of Pain and Symptom Management* *10*(2), 113–119.

CHAPTER 4

Causation

Claimants in the opioid MDL have focused mainly on compensation of expected future abatement costs as a pathway to mitigating opioid-attributable harms. However, a careful analysis of causation could potentially be of even greater value in terms of mitigation. Correcting problems at the source is more likely to result in sustained improvement. The goal of this chapter is to conduct an analysis of root causes and contributing factors associated with the increase in prescription opioid supply following FDA approval through to about 2012, when the rate of prescription opioid utilization began its precipitous decline. The basis for the analysis is a comprehensive review of the literature to date, focusing on published studies and reports that assess causal factors related to the opioid crisis. The discussion here is not limited to the factors commonly associated with opioids in the ongoing opioid litigation, which has been relatively narrowly focused on the roles of manufacturers, distributors, and pharmacies. Instead, the goal here is to cast a reasonably wider net, focusing on the main drivers identified consistently in the large and growing body of research on the contributing factors underlying the present-day opioid crisis, consistent with the emphasis in the field of epidemiology on the criticality of the identification of root causes. The aim of the following chapter (Chap. 5 "Responsibility") is to continue the discussion of causation and contributing factors, but instead in the context of identifiable potentially responsible groups and parties.

J. E. Schneider, *The Economics of Pain*, Global Perspectives on Wealth and Distribution,
https://doi.org/10.1007/978-3-032-20355-7_4

Continuing some of the themes from the preceding chapter, the focus in this chapter is on factors that contributed to an increase in opioid supply. The rationale for this focus in that claimants in the opioid MDL have argued generally that an increase in the supply of prescription opioids has led to an increase in the prevalence of OUD, which constitutes the harm, public nuisance, or negative externality. Causal hypotheses pertaining to the increase in opioid supply, while variable across studies, generally take one of two general forms: (1) manufacturers "aggressively" marketed opioids to physicians and health systems, which (by way of the issuance of prescriptions) increased the supply of opioids beyond levels necessary to meet medical need (which in turn increased OUD prevalence); or (2) several factors, of which manufacturer marketing is one, contributed to an increase in opioid supply, which increased the supply of opioids beyond levels necessary to meet medical need (which in turn increased OUD prevalence). The latter hypothesis has taken several forms, mainly in the number of causal factors identified; for example, in most cases, observers have recognized the additional critical roles of regulators and accreditation agencies. The first hypothesis is overly narrow, and at odds with the preponderance of evidence on the topic. The second hypothesis is more aligned with real-world evidence, but most attempts at exploring and testing the multifactorial causal framework have not been sufficiently exhaustive, leaving out numerous key factors. For example, a more plausible pathway leading up to the growth in opioid supply might be something like this: (1) several interrelated contributing factors led to increased opioid demand and supply of opioids; (2) failure on the part of drug regulators rendered the normal access controls, surveillance of adverse events, and monitoring of drug supply largely ineffective; (3) increased supply of prescription opioids led to increased *diversion* of prescription opioids to illicit uses; (4) insufficient drug control policies and weak law enforcement led to an increased supply of *illicit* opioids; (5) increased supply of diverted *and* illicit opioids led to increased prevalence of opioid *misuse*; (6) increased prevalence of opioid misuse led to increased prevalence of OUD; and (7) increased prevalence of OUD led to increased prevalence of cost-incurring OUD (i.e., OUD associated with some level of measurable harm, or public nuisance, as discussed in the preceding chapter). This hypothesized causal framework will be revisited throughout this chapter and the next, along with evidence supporting each component.

The preponderance of evidence suggests that the causation of the increase in the supply of opioids in the U.S. from the late 1990s until about 2012 was multifactorial, driven by a mix of interrelated factors, including public and private initiatives to increase the demand for pain control coinciding with important organizational changes in the health care sector, increased medical need, and failure on the part of regulators to prevent the crisis from worsening.[1] For example, a 2022 report from the U.S. Congressional Budget Office ("CBO") described it this way: "Several factors have contributed to the opioid crisis: an increase in the prescribing of opioids, changes in illegal opioid markets, and greater demand for opioids among people in some demographic groups that have experienced declines in real wages and social cohesion. Those factors have reinforced each other."[2] The CBO also held that the increase in opioid supply was the "result of aggressive promotion efforts by pharmaceutical companies. Clinical norms also began to emphasize assessing patients' pain and treating it with prescription opioids. In addition, oversight and reimbursement incentives in the health care system encouraged opioid prescribing."[3] Emphasizing the broad-ranging multifactorial causal aspects of the opioid crisis, the Stanford-Lancet Commission on opioids also submitted that "the origins of the current crisis reflect dramatic failures within the corporate sector, regulatory and legislative bodies, the medical profession, and

[1] See generally S. A. Bernard et al., "Management of Pain in the United States-A Brief History and Implications for the Opioid Epidemic," *Health Serv Insights* 11 (2018); D. J. Clark and M. A. Schumacher, "America's Opioid Epidemic: Supply and Demand Considerations," *Anesth Analg* 125, no. 5 (2017); S. R. Friedman et al., "The Opioid/Overdose Crisis as a Dialectics of Pain, Despair, and One-Sided Struggle," *Front Public Health* 8 (2020); L. Manchikanti et al., "Opioid epidemic in the United States," *Pain Physician* 15, no. 3 Suppl (2012); W. M. Compton and C. M. Jones, "Epidemiology of the U.S. opioid crisis: the importance of the vector," *Ann N Y Acad Sci* 1451, no. 1 (2019); L. Manchikanti et al., "Reframing the Prevention Strategies of the Opioid Crisis: Focusing on Prescription Opioids, Fentanyl, and Heroin Epidemic," *Pain Physician* 21, no. 4 (2018); M. D. Sullivan and J.C. Ballantyne, *The Right to Pain Relief and Other Deep Roots of the Opioid Epidemic* (New York, NY: Oxford University Press, 2023); CBO, "The Opioid Crisis and Recent Federal Policy Responses," (Washington, DC: U.S. Congressional Budget Office, 2022); N. B. King et al., "Determinants of increased opioid-related mortality in the United States and Canada, 1990–2013: a systematic review," *Am J Public Health* 104, no. 8 (2014); D. Blumenthal and S. Seervai, "To Combat the Opioid Epidemic, We Must Be Honest About All Its Causes," *Harvard BusinessReview*, no. Oct 26 (2017).

[2] CBO, "The Opioid Crisis and Recent Federal Policy Responses."

[3] Ibid.

the health care system."[4] In addition, Sullivan and Ballantyne, in their book *The Right to Pain Relief*, emphasized that the role of manufacturer marketing had to be understood in the context of the changes in the medical profession toward the embracing of palliative care and patient-centered care, including the role of quality metrics explicitly designed to grade healthcare providers on their ability to manage patients' pain, and medical societies championing more aggressive approaches to pain.[5] The authors concluded that "No doubt all these factors contributed to the vast increase in the prescribing of opioids for pain ..." For the most part, the multifactorial root causes of the crisis make sense to those who have followed the evolution of the U.S. health care system during the past few decades. This is in contrast to the generally narrower view taken by claimants and the courts in opioid litigation, which for the most part aligns with the premise that the crisis is largely the result of the actions by a small proportion of the prescription drug supply chain. As this chapter will clearly show, this narrow view has the effect of downplaying the roles of some of the most consequential drivers of the increase in opioid supply and distracts from the critical process of identifying root causes.

4.1 Multifactor Causation

Causation can be modelled conceptually and statistically within the framework of multivariable regression analysis. Consider an outcome "y" that is hypothesized to be a function of two factors, "x" and "z" such that $y = f(x, z)$. Generally, causation has two parts. The first part is conceptual. To infer causation, there must be a logical *possibility* that x causes y, with the concept of "possibility" defined by the facts and circumstances concerning the institutional, structural, biological, and clinical details of the relationship between x and y. That is, to explore whether x causes y, we would first need to develop a thorough conceptual framework or theory that supports the identification of specific hypotheses describing the probable causal pathway.[6] Having done

[4] K. Humphreys et al., "Responding to the opioid crisis in North America and beyond: recommendations of the Stanford-Lancet Commission," *Lancet* 399, no. 10324 (2022).

[5] Sullivan and Ballantyne, *The Right to Pain Relief and Other Deep Roots of the Opioid Epidemic.*

[6] See generally R. S. Zawadzki, J. D. Grill, and D. L. Gillen, "Frameworks for estimating causal effects in observational settings: comparing confounder adjustment and instrumental variables," *BMC Med Res Methodol* 23, no. 1 (2023).

that, the second part of causal inference is normally some sort of statistical test for causation to determine the direction and magnitude of the causal effect, should such an effect exist. Addressing the statistical element of causation, to explore whether x *causes* y, a researcher may begin by assessing the correlation between x and y; if, for example, x and y are highly correlated (e.g., ≥ 70%) one can infer that there is a *correlation* and an *association* between x and y.[7] Correlation can help support or bring into question the inferences from a conceptual framework. To further explore causation, a researcher may then estimate a simple multivariable regression model using real-world data. Such a regression would result in a coefficient associated with x that provides information about the magnitude and direction of the effect of x on y, holding constant the effects of confounding variables, like z.

However, even controlling for the confounding effects of z, regression results do not necessarily provide strong evidence of causation. To get closer to an assessment of causation, we may further specify a "dynamic" version of the regression model, where we make some assumptions regarding the temporal sequence of causation; for example, "x must occur first, which will then result in y." To accommodate temporal effects, a dynamic model might take the form of $y_t = f(x_{(t-1)}, z_{(t-1)})$, where now we are interested in the effect of an earlier (or lagged) value of x on a current value of y, where period "*t*" is the current period and *t*-1 refers to an earlier period. A variety of forms of this model can be specified to account for such a dynamic process. In this model, a statistically significant coefficient on the lagged x variable would provide a step closer to being able to infer causation, because we are in essence giving x more time to impact y. However, this alone might be necessary but not sufficient to infer a causal relationship between x and y. Additional steps to inferring causation would normally need to include the following:[8] (1) the confounding z variables are also important; thus, we would need to assure that all or most potentially important confounding

[7] See generally P. Schober, C. Boer, and L. A. Schwarte, "Correlation Coefficients: Appropriate Use and Interpretation," *Anesth Analg* 126, no. 5 (2018).

[8] For a more in-depth treatment of statistical inference of causation, see generally P. Kennedy, *A Guide to Econometrics (Fourth Edition)* (Cambridge, MA: MIT Press, 1998); K.J. Rothman, S. Greenland, and T.L. Lash, *Modern Epidemiology (Third Edition)* (Philadelphia, PA: Wolters Kluer; Lippincot WIlliams & Wilkins, 2008); E. Vittinghoff et al., *Regression Methods in Biostatistics (Second Edition)*, ed. M. Gail and et al., Statistics for Biology and Health (New York, NY: Springer Science and Business Media, 2012); Zawadzki, Grill, and Gillen, "Frameworks for estimating causal effects in observational settings: comparing confounder adjustment and instrumental variables."

variables are included in the model, as the absence of confounding variables can result in biased coefficients for the included variables (typically referred to as "omitted variable bias"); and (2) we would need to assure that the independent variables are not endogenous (i.e., co-determined with the dependent variable), as endogeneity can also result in biased coefficients. There are statistical tools that can be used to address each of these. For example, to address endogeneity, two-stage least squares regression requires the use of an "instrumental variable" ("IV") that is unconfounded with the outcome measure but highly correlated with the independent variable in question.[9] The use of the "instrument," rather than the original variable of interest, reduces the bias associated with endogeneity.

The main focus of this chapter is the identification of factors that were likely causally related to the increase in opioid supply. In other words, the focus is on the "right hand side" explanatory variables discussed above. In popular discourse over the opioid crisis, and in the opioid MDL more specifically, the causation question has been somewhat muddled and underdeveloped. Most of the MDL cases have adopted a relatively simplistic public nuisance framework, arguing that OUD is the source of the negative externality (i.e., the nuisance), and that prescription opioid supply (which the courts have argued is predominantly determined by manufacturers, distributors, and retail pharmacists) is ultimately the cause of the nuisance, via the harms associated with OUD. By the standards of causal inference in epidemiology, this generalized depiction of how drugs come to market and how adverse events result in harms in U.S. prescription drug markets is overly simplistic as a causal model or framework. Let us start with the root causes of OUD, which again in the MDL cases is argued to be the primary factor associated with the public nuisance. Working backwards, we know that OUD is one consequence of the misuse of opioids. In most cases, misuse of opioids does not result in OUD, which is a topic that has been addressed. The fact that misuse does not *per se* result in OUD suggests that there are other factors that either interact with misuse or have an independent effect on OUD. In this regard, opioid misuse can be thought of as a "necessary but not sufficient" cause of OUD.[10]

[9] See generally Kennedy, *A Guide to Econometrics (Fourth Edition)*. Also see T. J. Iwashyna and E. H. Kennedy, "Instrumental variable analyses. Exploiting natural randomness to understand causal mechanisms," *Ann Am Thorac Soc* 10, no. 3 (2013).

[10] Refer to G. McGwin, Jr., "Causation in epidemiology," *Am J Ophthalmol* 150, no. 5 (2010).

If we know that the OUD causal pathway is primarily through misuse, then we need to identify the specific factors that encourage or cause misuse of opioids. As briefly discussed above and will be revisited again in later chapters, drug misuse is driven by a wide range of factors, including prior history of drug abuse, pre-existing SUDs, pre-existing mental health conditions, socioeconomic status, macroeconomic conditions, and access to opioids.[11] The latter factor, access, is the conceptual link to prescription opioids, in that access is in part a function of the supply of prescription opioids, the supply of diverted opioids, the supply of illicit opioids, drug prices, and transaction costs, which in this case would be things like transportation and time costs. Access is also a function of the usual factors that drive demand for health care, such as income and insurance coverage.[12] The supply of prescription opioids, which again is the focus of the opioid MDL, is a function of demand (i.e., medical need), physician practice patterns, regulatory policy (e.g., FDA labels; DEA production quotas), and market dynamics, including prices and transaction costs. Supply is also a function of clinical practice norms, such as those propagated and promoted by state medical boards and specialty medical societies.[13] Physician practice patterns are also a function of accreditation standards and insurer payment mechanisms. Linking all these functional relationships together results in OUD being a function of at least 20 distinct variables, all of which are part of what a recent RAND Corporation report referred to as an opioid "ecosystem" driven by the interconnectedness among medical need, access, mental health, substance abuse, demographics, and

[11] For a review of factors associated with opioid misuse, see generally K. M. Burcher, A. Suprun, and A. Smith, "Risk Factors for Opioid Use Disorders in Adult Postsurgical Patients," *Cureus* 10, no. 5 (2018); A. Cragg et al., "Risk Factors for Misuse of Prescribed Opioids: A Systematic Review and Meta-Analysis," *Ann Emerg Med* 74, no. 5 (2019); T. J. Ives et al., "Predictors of opioid misuse in patients with chronic pain: a prospective cohort study," *BMC Health Serv Res* 6 (2006); F. A. Montiel Ishino et al., "A comprehensive multivariate model of biopsychosocial factors associated with opioid misuse and use disorder in a 2017–2018 United States national survey," *BMC Public Health* 20, no. 1 (2020).

[12] For background, refer to C.E. Phelps, *Health Economics (Third Edition)* (Boston, MA: Addison Wesley, 2003). (pp. 100–171).

[13] See generally E. A. Nutescu et al., "Factors that influence prescribing within a therapeutic drug class," *J Eval Clin Pract* 11, no. 4 (2005); G. T. Schumock et al., "Factors that influence prescribing decisions," *Ann Pharmacother* 38, no. 4 (2004).

socioeconomic factors.[14] Despite this complex web of associations, causal pathways, and relationships, opioid cases have focused narrowly on an alleged direct causal relationship between the supply of prescription opioids and OUD, including mainly only three (or about 23%) of the thirteen critical supply components discussed earlier. As the preceding discussion implies, it would be difficult to argue that the actions of these three groups of entities were primarily responsible for the increase in opioid supply, given the host of numerous other critical factors underlying opioid supply and progression to OUD.

From an economic perspective, this array of contributing factors were ones that increased the supply of opioids, increased the demand for opioids, or increased both supply and demand, the net result of which was an overall increase in the supply of opioids. When both supply and demand increase, the market equilibrium output level increases. The mix of "supply push" and "demand-pull" factors in opioid markets can also be thought of as "enabling" or causative factors, the influence of which combined in synergistic and additive ways to increase the total volume of opioids on the market. Specifically, the following seven factors have been often identified as enabling or causative drivers of increases in the supply and demand for *prescription* opioids (Fig. 4.1): (1) regulation and regulatory failure; (2) demand for pain treatment and medical need; (3) public policies aimed at raising awareness and promoting improved pain management; (4) advocacy on the part of medical societies aimed at raising awareness and promoting improved pain management; (5) provider ratings rewarding providers for improved pain management; (6) marketing; and (7) drug trafficking and the incursion of illicit drugs.

As discussed earlier, although the focus of this book is mainly on the supply of prescription opioids, the overall supply of opioids in the U.S. has also been driven by an increase in illegally trafficked *illicit* opioids, primarily produced abroad, smuggled into the U.S., and distributed by drug traffickers operating in regional networks.[15] Whereas this book is focused

[14] For example, see B.D. Stein et al., "America's Opioid Ecosystem," (Santa Monica, CA: RAND Corporation, 2023).

[15] See generally J. O'Donnell et al., "Trends in and Characteristics of Drug Overdose Deaths Involving Illicitly Manufactured Fentanyls—United States, 2019–2020," *MMWR Morb Mortal Wkly Rep* 70, no. 50 (2021); J. J. Palamar et al., "Trends in seizures of powders and pills containing illicit fentanyl in the United States, 2018 through 2021," *Drug Alcohol Depend* 234 (2022).

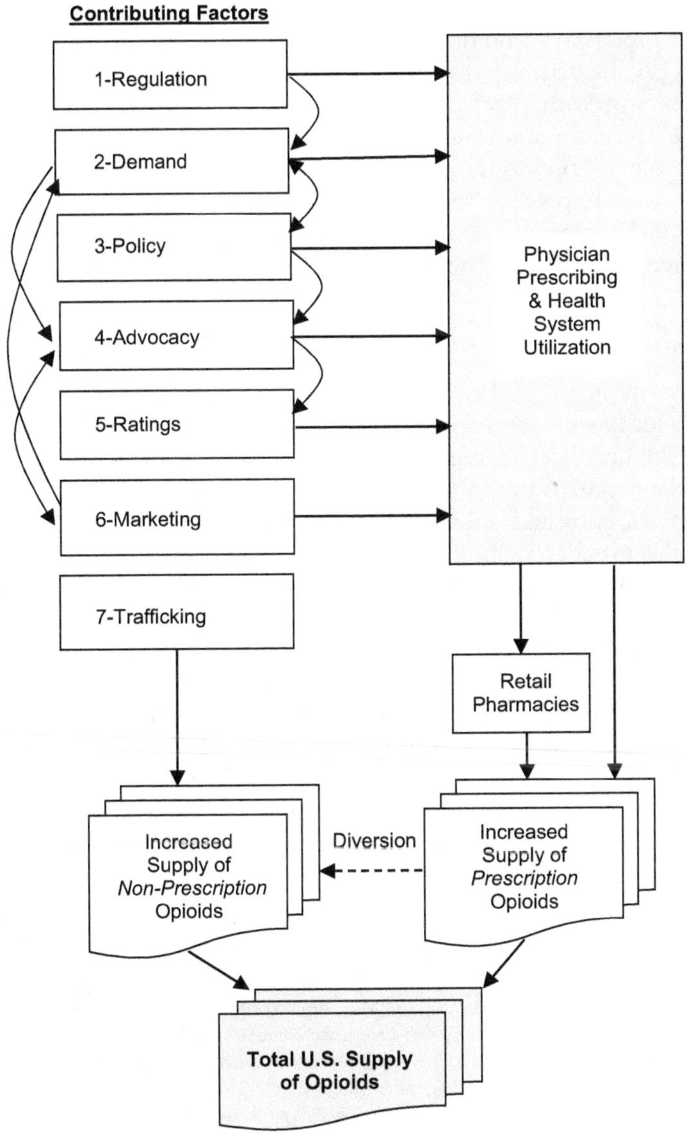

Fig. 4.1 Contributing factors associated with prescription opioid supply, Non-prescription opioid supply, and total opioid supply

primarily on the role of opioids sourced through the healthcare system (that is, prescription opioids), the sources of the harms associated with opioids can be attributed to increases in both prescription opioids *and* illicit opioids, with the latter playing an increasingly prominent role in OUD in recent years. Given that it is difficult to disaggregate OUD attributable to prescription opioids versus OUD attributable to illicit opioids, it is important to consider the roles of both sources.[16] Thus, drug trafficking is identified in Fig. 4.1 as the seventh contributing factor. A detailed discussion of the seven contributing factors follows the figure.

4.2 Regulation

Many components of the U.S. economy, especially healthcare, are regulated by local, state, and federal government agencies. Drug regulation is part of the healthcare regulatory apparatus but has many unique features that make it one of the most stringent areas of regulation across the U.S. economy. Controlled substances, like opioids, are the most regulated within the broader scope of prescription drug regulation. The National Academy of Sciences Consensus Study report on opioids described it this way: "Once the FDA has approved an opioid formulation (or other controlled substance) for therapeutic use, federal and state agencies have the authority to control the amount, storage, and distribution of the drug at *every stage in the course of commerce.* One key purpose of these restrictions is to limit access to and use of the drug to the amounts and indications for which it was lawfully prescribed and to curtail its distribution outside of lawful channels of commerce" (emphasis added).[17] This includes, if necessary, placing legal restrictions on "precursor and essential

[16] See generally J. F. Peppin and J. J. Coleman, "CDC's Efforts to Quantify Prescription Opioid Overdose Deaths Fall Short," *Pain Ther* 10, no. 1 (2021); J. F. Peppin et al., "What Your Death Certificate Says About You May Be Wrong: A Narrative Review on CDC's Efforts to Quantify Prescription Opioid Overdose Deaths," *Cureus* 13, no. 9 (2021); R. M. Gladden et al., "Changes in Opioid-Involved Overdose Deaths by Opioid Type and Presence of Benzodiazepines, Cocaine, and Methamphetamine—25 States, July-December 2017 to January-June 2018," *MMWR Morb Mortal Wkly Rep* 68, no. 34 (2019).

[17] NASEM, *Pain Management and the Opioid Epidemic: Balancing Societal and Indidivual Benefits and Risks of Prescription Opioid Use*, ed. R.J. Bonnie, M.A. Ford, and J.K. Phillips, Consensus Study Report of National Academies of Sciences, Engineering and Medicine (NASEM) (Washington, D.C.: National Academies Press, 2017).

chemicals" necessary for the production of scheduled drugs.[18] It is challenging to think of any other industry in the global economy that is subject to this level of regulatory oversight.

In the U.S., drug regulation is carried out primarily by the FDA, through its approval and post-market monitoring and surveillance responsibilities. Regarding medical care, the FDA describes its mission as "protecting the public health by ensuring the safety, efficacy, and security of human and veterinary drugs, biological products, and medical devices."[19] Regulation of drugs is also carried out by the U.S. Drug Enforcement Administration ("DEA"), which is responsible for establishing production and distribution quotas for all Schedule I or II controlled substances[20] and controlling the incursion of illicit drugs, including illicit opioids. Regarding prescription drugs, the DEA's main responsibilities include preventing and monitoring drug diversion, particularly regarding controlled substances. The agency describes its role in this regard as follows: "to prevent, detect, and investigate the diversion of controlled pharmaceuticals and listed chemicals from legitimate sources while ensuring an adequate and uninterrupted supply for legitimate medical, commercial, and scientific needs," and specifically regarding controlled substances, "Enforcement of the provisions of the Controlled Substances Act as they pertain to the manufacture, distribution, and dispensing of legally produced controlled substances."[21]

While it is the nominal intent of regulatory policy to maintain or improve social welfare,[22] it is also the case that regulators, and the

[18] Ibid.

[19] FDA, "FDA Mission," in *What We Do* (Washington, D.C.: U.S. Food and Drug Administration, 2023).

[20] According to the DEA, Schedule I refers to "drugs with no current medical use with high potential for abuse and/or addiction," and Schedule II refers to "drugs with some medically acceptable uses, but with high potential for abuse and/or addiction." See generally DEA, "Drug Scheduling," (Washington, D.C.: U.S. Department of Justice, U.S. Drug Enforcement Administration, 2023).

[21] Refer to "Diversion Control Division: Program Description," (Washington, DC: U.S. Department of Justice, U.S. Drug Enforcement Administration, Diversion Control Division, 2023).

[22] The *Oxford Reference* defines "social welfare" as follows: "The well-being of society or the community at large. In economic terms, social welfare is an aggregation of the welfare or utility of the individual members of the society." For discussions of welfare aspects of regulation, see generally P.L. Joskow and R.C. Noll, "Regulation in Theory and Practice:

regulatory statutes they are charged with enforcing, can be ineffective or even harmful, in some cases leading to what economists and policy analysts have broadly termed "regulatory failure."[23] Failure can be the result of poorly designed regulatory mechanisms, ineffective enforcement, or undue influence on the part of the regulated industry, via political influence, lobbying and other influence tactics.[24] Anthony Ogus described regulatory failure and deregulation this way: "The [regulatory] systems either did not succeed in achieving their ostensible aim (normally the correction of market failure) or did so inefficiently ..."[25] Vietor further described three types of regulatory failure: (1) retention of regulations "beyond their time;" (2) faulty design of regulatory mechanisms; and (3) bureaucratic inertia and inefficiencies within regulatory agencies, including disproportionate influence by politicians and lobbyists representing the regulated industry.[26] Failure on the part of U.S. government drug

An Overview," in *Studies in Public Regulation*, ed. G. Fromm (Cambridge, MA: The MIT Press, 1981); K.E. Train, *Optimal Regulation* (Cambridge, MA: The MIT Press, 1991); A. Ogus, *Regulation: Legal Form and Economic Theory*, Clarendon Law Series (New York, NY: Oxford Univeristy Press, 1994); OECD, "Regulatory Policy and the Road to Sustainable Growth," (Paris, France: Organization for Economic Cooperation and Development, 2010).

[23] For a general discussion of these issues, see generally S. Breyer, *Regulation and Its Reform* (Cambridge, MA: Harvard University Press, 1982); P.J. Quirk, *Industry Influence in Federal Regulatory Agencies* (Princeton, NJ: Princeton University Press, 1981); J.G. Sidak and D.F. Spulber, *Deregulatory Takings and the Regulatory Contract* (New York, NY: Cambridge University Press, 1997); J.E. Schneider, "Changes in the Effects of Mandatory Rate Regulation On Growth in Hospital Operating Costs, 1980–1996," *Review of Industrial Organization* 22, no. 4 (2003); G.M. Grossman and E. Helpman, *Special Interest Politics* (Cambridge, MA: The MIT Press, 2001); J-J. Laffont and J. Tirole, *A Theory of Incentives in Procurement and Regulation* (Cambridge (MA): The MIT Press, 1993); C. Menard and M. M. Shirley, eds., *Handbook of the New Institutional Economics* (Berlin: Springer, 2008); W.K. Viscusi, J.M. Vernon, and J.E. Harrington, *Economics of Regulation and Antitrust (Second Edition)* (Cambridge (MA): The MIT Press, 1995). These issues are revisited in Chap. 8 as part of an analysis of "regulation versus litigation" as alternative means of addressing complex transactions and externalities.

[24] Breyer, *Regulation and Its Reform*; Grossman and Helpman, *Special Interest Politics*; S. Peltzman, "Toward a More General Theory of Regulation," in *Chicago Studies in Political Economy*, ed. G.J. Stigler (Chicago, IL: The University of Chicago Press, 1988); Ogus, *Regulation: Legal Form and Economic Theory.*

[25] *Regulation: Legal Form and Economic Theory.* (p.56)

[26] R.H.K. Vietor, *Contrived Competition: Regulation and Deregulation in America* (Cambridge, MA: The Belknap Press of Harvard University Press, 1994).

regulators, mainly in Vietor's second and third domains, was the primary factor contributing to the increase in opioid supply according to a recent report from the Stanford-Lancet Commission on opioids, with the Commission concluding that "the initial wave of the opioid crisis arose from weak laws and regulations as well as poor implementation of these laws and regulations."[27]

4.2.1 *Food & Drug Administration*

Approval by regulators of prescription drugs in the U.S. is not only legally required before prescription drugs can be sold, but the "stamp of approval" conferred by FDA approval is interpreted by clinicians, payers, and consumers as a signal of product safety and quality.[28] In the U.S., prescription drugs must undergo rigorous clinical testing prior to entering the market. Clinical studies generally occur in three phases, and the investigational drug or device must successfully complete each phase. FDA review is intendedly thorough; only about 10% of investigational drugs survive from initial trial phases to final FDA approval.[29] The average cost of advancing a pharmaceutical compound through this process, ending in FDA approval, is close to $1 billion per compound.[30] Clinical studies are typically carried out by manufacturers or their biotechnology partners, but it is the FDA that evaluates the design and outcomes of these clinical studies as part of the regulatory approval process. Once a manufacturer submits its dossier of clinical

[27] Humphreys et al., "Responding to the opioid crisis in North America and beyond: recommendations of the Stanford-Lancet Commission."

[28] See generally S.S. Mehta, *Commercializing Successful Biomedical Technologies: Basic Principles for the Development of Drugs, Diagnostics and Devices* (Cambridge, UK: Cambridge University Press, 2008); P.M. Danzon and S. Nicholson, eds., *The Economics of the Biopharmaceutical Industry*, Oxford Handbook (New York, NY: Oxford University Press, 2012).

[29] O. J. Wouters, M. McKee, and J. Luyten, "Estimated Research and Development Investment Needed to Bring a New Medicine to Market, 2009–2018," *Jama* 323, no. 9 (2020).

[30] See generally J. A. DiMasi, H. G. Grabowski, and R. W. Hansen, "Innovation in the pharmaceutical industry: New estimates of R&D costs," *J Health Econ* 47 (2016); Wouters, McKee, and Luyten, "Estimated Research and Development Investment Needed to Bring a New Medicine to Market, 2009–2018."

evidence, the FDA conducts a rigorous assessment of the data, which typically takes about 12–18 months.[31]

FDA approval is necessary before any prescription drug can be marketed or sold, and at launch newly approved drugs typically have a period of market exclusivity, depending on the age of associated patents. Thus, the combination of FDA approval and market exclusivity create financial incentives for drug manufacturers to maximize sales in the window immediately following approval and prior to patent expiry or significant market entry from competitors.[32] During this window, and in some cases beyond this period, the FDA and the manufacturer are also responsible for post-market surveillance and monitoring to assure that adverse event rates occur at rates similar to those found in clinical studies, and to assess the risks associated with any new adverse events that may surface.[33] In addition to reducing post-market safety issues and assuring product effectiveness, the rigorous safety standards established by the FDA for pharmaceutical drugs are also considered a means of reducing the need for post-market product liability litigation.[34]

It is also worthwhile noting that the biopharmaceutical industry is substantially dependent on the FDA for "signaling" the safety, efficacy, and commercial viability of reviewed drugs. In addition to public interest, such signals are valuable to manufacturers in numerous ways, including product and enterprise valuation and added quality

[31] See generally M. K. Keng, C. M. Wenzell, and M. A. Sekeres, "A drug's life: the pathway to drug approval," *Clin Adv Hematol Oncol* 11, no. 10 (2013); S. W. Moore, "An overview of drug development in the United States and current challenges," *South Med J* 96, no. 12 (2003).

[32] See generally A. Dabrowska and S. Thaul, "How FDA Approves Drugs and Regulates Their Safety and Effectiveness," (Washington, D.C.: Congressional Research Service, 2018); H. Grabowski et al., "Continuing trends in U.S. brand-name and generic drug competition," *J Med Econ* 24, no. 1 (2021); A. S. Kesselheim, J. Avorn, and A. Sarpatwari, "The High Cost of Prescription Drugs in the United States: Origins and Prospects for Reform," *Jama* 316, no. 8 (2016).

[33] P. J. Pitts et al., "twenty-first century pharmacovigilance: efforts, roles, and responsibilities," *Lancet Oncol* 17, no. 11 (2016).

[34] For a more in-depth of this issue, refer to T.J. Philipson, E. Sun, and D. Goldman, "The Effects of Product Liability Exemption in the Presence of the FDA," in *Regulation versus Litigation: Perspectives from Economics and Law*, ed. D.P. Kessler (Chicago, IL: National Bureau of Economic Research | The University of Chicago Press, 2011).

control.[35] Manufacturers typically outsource clinical research to contract research organizations ("CROs") and academic-based provider groups. Given the highly technical nature of clinical research, the relationship between researchers and manufacturers is likely to exhibit some non-trivial degree of information symmetry, and perhaps at times some degree of opportunistic behavior on the part of contracted researchers seeking to fulfill contract obligations and obtain future work. The more egregious examples of this include falsifying data and other types of fraud.[36] In this capacity, the FDA to some extent serves as an external monitor of research design and study protocols and provides valuable feedback to manufacturers regarding the accuracy and integrity of outsourced research. In some cases, it may be difficult for manufacturers to independently assess the quality of work by CROs. At the same time, however, information asymmetry between the FDA and manufacturers adds complexity and uncertainty to manufacturers' assessment of the performance of the FDA in this monitoring capacity.

Following the same type of rigorous clinical testing described above, the FDA approved the first long-acting opioid-based pain relievers MS Contin in 1987 and OxyContin in 1995,[37] and approved fentanyl ("Actiq") in 1998. It was not until 2001 (i.e., 14 years after the first opioid was approved and six years after OxyContin approval) that the FDA began holding meetings regarding possible harms related to prescription opioids.[38] Interestingly, a change in product labeling that resulted from the 2001 meetings *increased* opioid use because the label indicated approved uses that included a larger number of clinical indications.[39]

[35] Regarding signaling pertaining to enterprise value and commercialization, see for example J. Williamson and A. J. Spicer, "Review of the impact of the FDA's Fast Track Designation on biotechnology companies' share prices," *Drug Discov Today* 28, no. 11 (2023b); "Evaluating the impact of the FDA's orphan drug designation on share prices of biotechnology companies," *Drug Discov Today* 28, no. 12 (2023a).

[36] See, for example, E. Gunasekera and R. Brooker, "Phantom Participants with Real-World Ramifications: Clinical Drug Trial Data Falsification," *The National Law Review* Volume XV, no. Number 282 (2022).

[37] FDA, "Timeline of Selected FDA Activities and Significant Events Addressing Opioid Misuse and Abuse," (U.S. Food and Drug Administration, 2021).

[38] Ibid.

[39] B. Whittaker, "Did the FDA ignite the opioid epidemic?," *CBS 60 Minutes*, no. February 24 (2019).

Apart from changes in labeling, the first significant action taken by the FDA was a warning letter issued to a single opioid manufacturer in 2003, after long-acting opioids had been on the market for 16 years. The Stanford-Lancet Commission on opioids would later describe the OxyContin outcome as "approved for wide use by the FDA under the fraudulent premise that it was less addictive than other opioids, a mistake that stained the FDA's reputation."[40] Some researchers and observers have argued that the FDA was negligent in both the initial approval process, which included the approval of numerous opioid-based products, and in post-market surveillance, arguing that opioid licenses could have been withdrawn and stricter distribution controls could have been imposed at any time.[41] For example, post-approval, the FDA could have required the implementation of strict risk evaluation and mitigation strategies ("REMS"), an authority it has had since 2007. The FDA could have also devoted more resources to vetting and approving non-opioid pain medications, which some have argued received little attention due to the embracing of opioids by the medical community, even after the surfacing of concerns over opioid use.[42] In addition, the FDA largely failed to act on early indications that manufacturer marketing tactics were becoming increasingly unaligned with the rules and laws governing such practices.[43] According to a recent article published in the *Journal of the American Medical Association*, entitled "How FDA Failures Contributed to the Opioid Crisis," "... despite this mounting criticism, FDA policies for approving and labeling opioids remain largely unchanged. The FDA has not undertaken a root cause analysis of its regulatory errors [and] to the contrary, the agency has adopted a defensive posture and sought to shift blame."[44] The article's author, Dr. Andrew Kolodny, elsewhere referred to

[40] Humphreys et al., "Responding to the opioid crisis in North America and beyond: recommendations of the Stanford-Lancet Commission."

[41] A detailed description of the regulatory "missed opportunities" on the part of the FDA is provided by L. Noah, "Federal Regulatory Responses to the Prescription Opioid Crisis: Too Little, Too Late?," *Utah Law Review* 2019, no. 4 (2019).

[42] C.L. Hooper, "How the FDA Helped Fuel the Opioid Epidemic," *Wall Street Journal*, no. May 2 (2023).

[43] A. Kolodny, "How FDA Failures Contributed to the Opioid Crisis," *AMA J Ethics* 22, no. 1 (2020).

[44] Ibid.

the FDA's role in the opioid crisis as "the worst medical regulatory failure in U.S. history."[45]

4.2.2 *Drug Enforcement Administration*

The DEA has been similarly faulted for its failure to control opioid supply. For prescription drugs, the DEA is responsible for establishing annual production quotas ("APQs") for certain scheduled prescription drugs, including opioid products, and is responsible for basing production quotas on statistical models of medical need.[46] However, the DEA is widely viewed as having failed at this task. As the Stanford-Lancet Commission described it, "... the FDA was not the only pliant regulator. Between 1994 and 2015, the quota of oxycodone that the [DEA] permitted to be legally manufactured was raised over 20 times from 3.85 million grams in 1994 to a high of 153.75 million grams in 2013."[47] In addition, a report by the U.S. Office of the Inspector General ("OIG) published in 2019 was very critical of the DEA's actions regarding opioids. The function of the OIG is "to prevent and detect fraud, waste, abuse, misconduct, and mismanagement in the government, and to promote economy, efficiency, and effectiveness in our agency's operations and programs."[48] The OIG report on the DEA concluded that the agency "was slow to respond to the significant increase in the use and diversion of opioids since 2000" and

[45] G. Posner, "FDA's Janet Woodcock failed to stop the opioid epidemic," *USA Today*, no. February 3 (2021).

[46] The U.S. DEA Administrator is "required to set individual quotas for each registered manufacturer seeking to produce such substances and to limit or reduce individual quotas as necessary to prevent oversupply." See CRS, "The Controlled Substances Act (CSA): A Legal Overview for the 117th Congress," (Washington, D.C.: United States Congressional Research Service, 2021a). (p.15); also see generally DEA, "DEA reduces amount of opioid controlled substances to be manufactured in 2017," (United States Drug Enforcement Administration, 2016). The GAO found the DEA deficient in effectively carrying out its role in monitoring prescription drugs generally and opioids specifically; see generally GAO, "Drug Shortages: Better Management of the Quota Process for Controlled Substances Needed; Coordination between DEA and FDA Should Be Improved," in *GAO-15-202* (Washington, D.C.: U.S. Government Accountability Office 2015).

[47] Humphreys et al., "Responding to the opioid crisis in North America and beyond: recommendations of the Stanford-Lancet Commission."

[48] FTC, "What you need to know about the Office of Inspector General," (Washington, D. C.: U.S. Federal Trade Commission; Office of the Inspector General, 2023).

"did not use its available resources, including its data systems and strongest administrative enforcement tools, to detect and regulate diversion effectively."[49] The OIG report also found that "DEA policies and regulations did not adequately hold registrants accountable or prevent the diversion of pharmaceutical opioids." Moreover, the DEA, in establishing APQs, is responsible for taking into consideration diversion. Investigations have shown that the DEA largely failed at both tasks. For example, like the OIG report, a West Virginia Attorney General ("AG report directly faulted the DEA in contributing to increased opioid sales, finding that the DEA "routinely increased production quotas of opioids by substantial amounts" from 2010 to 2016, and "broadly accepted manufacturers' [demand] projections ..."[50]

The accounts of the West Virginia AG mirror similar critical reports nationally. For example, in May of 2023 news outlets reported that the DEA "has allowed one of the nation's largest wholesale drug distributors to keep shipping highly addictive painkillers for nearly four years after a judge recommended it be stripped of its license for its 'cavalier disregard' of thousands of suspicious orders fueling the opioid crisis," adding that the reason for the delay appears to have been the "revolving door" between industry and DEA leadership.[51] The failure of the DEA to effectively control opioid shipments is the primary focus of the narrative account provided in the book *American Cartel*, which describes how the DEA proved to be ineffective at controlling opioid supply largely because it was heavily influenced by special interests, despite initially confronting distributors over suspicious orders.[52] One of the challenges faced by the agency was that their work was complicated by having to balance the potential for diversion and misuse with the recognized clinical utility of opioids and the

[49] OIG, "Review of the Drug Enforcement Administration's Regulatory and Enforcement Efforts to Control the Diversion of Opioids," in *Evaluation and Inspections Division 19–05* (Washington, D.C.: United States Department of Justice; Office of the Inspector General 2019).

[50] Attorney General of West Virginia, "DEA's Failure to Combat Diversion Cost Lives: Results from the West Virginia Attorney General's Investigation into the DEA's Catastrophic Failure to Manage the National Drug Quota System from 2010–2016," (Office of the Attorney General, State of West Virginia, 2020).

[51] J. Mustian and J. Goodman, "DEA's failure to punish drug distributor blamed in opioid crisis raises revolving door questions," (PBS / Associated Press, 2023).

[52] S. Higham and S. Horwitz, *American Cartel: Inside the Battle to Bring Down the Opioid Industry* (New York, NY: Twelve / Hachette Book Group, 2022).

growing medical need for pain management, but some observers have argued that they could have been more effective in determining levels of legitimate medical need.[53] The DEA has also been faulted in its failure to control the influx of illicit opioids, which has resulted in an abundant supply of relatively low-cost illicit opioids.[54] The relatively low cost of illicit opioids increased access to the drugs, which in turn increased OUD-related harms.[55] In sum, like the FDA, the DEA largely failed in its role as regulator and monitor of prescription opioid supply and diversion and illicit opioid intrusion.

4.2.3 *Centers for Disease Control & Prevention*

While it is the FDA's purpose to approve and monitor prescription drugs, and it is the DEA's duty to control the distribution of scheduled prescription drugs and incursion of illicit drugs, it is the CDC's duty to prevent, control, and manage outbreaks, epidemics, and pandemics, describing their mission as: "... to protect America from health, safety, and security threats [...]."[56] Some observers and public health authorities, including the CDC, have viewed opioid misuse as an "epidemic."[57] It has been and continues to be the responsibility of the CDC to monitor and mitigate developing public health problems, especially epidemics and developing patterns suggestive of epidemics. For example, the CDC conducts surveillance and monitoring of emerging diseases and conditions through the National Notifiable Diseases Surveillance System ("NNDSS"), which aggregates data from more than 3,000 state and local public health agencies across the U.S. to detect and monitor diseases, outbreaks,

[53] S. Horwitz and S. Higham, "Could the DEA have stopped the opioid epidemic by cutting off the supply?," *Washington Post*, no. December 28 (2019).

[54] N. Miroff et al., "Cause of death: Washington faltered as fentanyl gripped America," (Washington, D.C.: The Washington Post, 2022).

[55] See generally CEA, "The Role of Opioid Prices in the Evolving Opioid Crisis," (Washington, D.C.: U.S. Council of Economic Advisers, 2019).

[56] CDC, "Mission, Role and Pledge," (Washington, D.C.: U.S. Centers for Disease Control and Prevention, 2023).

[57] In this book I have referred to the increasing prevalence of OUD as the "opioid crisis," and have not used the term epidemic. However, several observers, including the CDC (after some delay) and the plaintiffs in opioid matters typically refer to the increase in OUD as an "epidemic."

epidemics, and pandemics like Covid-19.[58] Although the CDC is not normally considered a regulator or regulatory agency in the same capacity as the FDA and DEA, it has a public duty and is relied upon as a public health "watchdog," responsible for detecting, monitoring, and interceding in disease outbreaks and epidemics as resource to the public health community, the medical community, and individuals. Like other regulatory agencies, the CDC has a set of legal and regulatory tools that it can employ to undertake its mission, including a scope of enforcement authority included in Section 361 of the Public Health Service Act ("PHSA").[59]

It is not unusual for the CDC to be criticized when it is believed to be falling short of its mission to monitor population health and safety. For example, recently the CDC was faulted for their slow and poorly coordinated response to the Covid-19 pandemic, prompting its director to declare that "... in our big moment, our performance did not reliably meet expectations."[60] In the case of the increase in opioid volume and rising rates of OUD, the CDC has been similarly faulted for its slow and poorly coordinated response. The CDC first reported on opioid-related overdose deaths in two different reports issued in 2009—one on national trends[61] and one on opioid-related overdose in the state of Washington.[62] Neither report referred to the escalating rates of opioid-related overdose in the context of an "epidemic," a term the CDC appears to have first used in 2011, referring specifically to an "epidemic of overdoses" in the discussion section of a data report.[63] A year later, in 2012, the CDC more clearly referred to rising rates of OUD as an epidemic in a Grand Rounds report entitled "Prescription

[58] For example, see S. Rowan et al., "From Tick to Test: A Comprehensive Review of Tick-Borne Disease Diagnostics and Surveillance Methods in the United States," *Life (Basel)* 13, no. 10 (2023).

[59] Refer to CRS, "Scope of CDC Authority Under Section 361 of the Public Health Service Act (PHSA)," (Washington, D.C.: Congressional Research Service, 2021b).

[60] K. Mahr, "CDC director orders agency overhaul, admitting flawed Covid-19 response," *Politico* August 17 (2022). Also see BMJ, "US CDC announces major changes after criticism of its responses to Covid-19 and monkeypox," *BMJ* 378, no. August 23 (2022).

[61] M. Warner, L. H. Chen, and D. M. Makuc, "Increase in fatal poisonings involving opioid analgesics in the United States, 1999–2006," *NCHS Data Brief*, no. 22 (2009).

[62] CDC, "Overdose deaths involving prescription opioids among Medicaid enrollees—Washington, 2004–2007," *MMWR Morb Mortal Wkly Rep* 58, no. 42 (2009).

[63] "Vital signs: overdoses of prescription opioid pain relievers—United States, 1999–2008," *MMWR Morb Mortal Wkly Rep* 60, no. 43 (2011).

Drug Overdoses: a U.S. Epidemic."[64] While the CDC offered some recommendations regarding how the epidemic could be alleviated, it took the agency another five years to become more actively involved. It was not until 2016 that the CDC issued guidelines on opioid prescribing, well over a decade after OUD rates began to rise and four years *after* the precipitous decline in opioid prescriptions had already begun.[65] And perhaps more importantly, four years after its own application of the term "epidemic" in reference to rising OUD rates. In addition for being faulted for its slow response, after the release of the opioid prescribing guidelines the CDC was criticized for lack of transparency in the guideline drafting process, inadequate and unclear content of the guidelines, and poor implementation of the guidelines, facing criticism from the American Medical Association ("AMA"),[66] physicians,[67] and others, with one observer referring to the guidelines as "disastrous."[68] In addition, the CDC has been faulted for delays in differentiating the sources (i.e., the "vectors," in epidemiology terms) of OUD, a process critical to the understanding of any unexpected rise in a disease or condition, especially one described as an epidemic by the CDC itself.[69] As discussed earlier, gaining a thorough understanding of root causes of health conditions, diseases, outbreaks, and epidemics is fundamental to

[64] "CDC grand rounds: prescription drug overdoses—a U.S. epidemic," *MMWR Morb Mortal Wkly Rep* 61, no. 1 (2012).

[65] See generally D. Dowell, T. M. Haegerich, and R. Chou, "CDC Guideline for Prescribing Opioids for Chronic Pain–United States, 2016," *Jama* 315, no. 15 (2016); J. E. Goldstick et al., "Changes in Initial Opioid Prescribing Practices After the 2016 Release of the CDC Guideline for Prescribing Opioids for Chronic Pain," *JAMA Netw Open* 4, no. 7 (2021); L. Gumidyala et al., "Effect of CDC Opioid-Prescribing Guidelines in a Community Hospital Emergency Department," *J Public Health Manag Pract* 27, no. Suppl 3 (2021); J. V. Pergolizzi, Jr., M. Rosenblatt, and J. A. LeQuang, "Three Years Down the Road: The Aftermath of the CDC Guideline for Prescribing Opioids for Chronic Pain," *Adv Ther* 36, no. 6 (2019).

[66] AMA, "AMA urges CDC to revise opioid prescribing guideline," in *Press Release* (Chicago, IL: American Medical Association, 2020).

[67] See, for example, M. E. Schatman and S. J. Ziegler, "Pain management, prescription opioid mortality, and the CDC: is the devil in the data?," *J Pain Res* 10 (2017).

[68] M.A. Rothstein and J. Irzyk, "The CDC should rescind, not 'update,' its 2016 opioid guideline," *The Hill* February 18 (2022).

[69] See, for example, Peppin and Coleman, "CDC's Efforts to Quantify Prescription Opioid Overdose Deaths Fall Short."; Peppin et al., "What Your Death Certificate Says About You May Be Wrong: A Narrative Review on CDC's Efforts to Quantify Prescription Opioid Overdose Deaths."

the fields of public health and epidemiology, and failure to do so risks allowing the problem to worsen.[70]

4.3 Demand

As discussed in the preceding chapters, it is important to note that the primary role of prescription opioids, and the basis for FDA approval of opioids, has been and continues to be clinical utility; specifically, the clinical need to effectively manage pain. Clinical utility is normally expected to align with demand for treatments; that is, individuals with certain clinical indications become candidates for applicable treatments for those indications. In the case of opioids, the confluence of seven important factors created an important added dimension that magnified the medical need and demand for pain management and, specifically, opioid-based treatments (Fig. 4.2). These were: (1) increases in life expectancy and

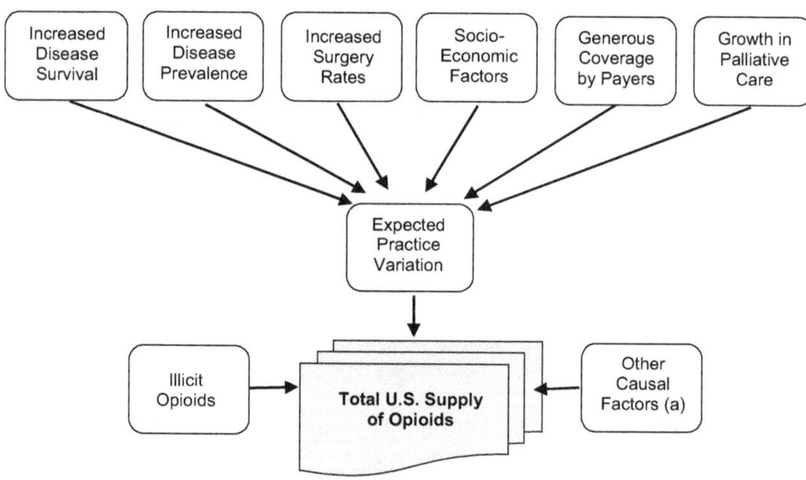

Fig. 4.2 Factors affecting demand & medical need for opioids. *Notes* (a) "other factors" includes all factors not classified as medical need; "other factors" are shown in Fig. 4. 1 and described in text

[70] See generally T. A. Glass et al., "Causal inference in public health," *Annu Rev Public Health* 34 (Glass et al., 2013).

improvement in disease-specific survival rates; (2) increasing prevalence of specific diseases and conditions associated with increased the demand for pain management; (3) increased rates of surgery and migration of care from inpatient settings to outpatient settings; (4) increase in prevalence of socioeconomic factors associated with mental health, substance abuse, and pain tolerance; (5) the rise to prominence in the medical community of the palliative care and patient-centered care movements; (6) generous coverage of opioids by public and private payers, which lowered transaction costs and in turn enhanced access to opioids; and (7) normal geographic variation in physician practice patterns and perceptions of medical need, heightened by the diagnostic uncertainty regarding pain symptoms (i.e., in the case of pain management, clinical uncertainty is expected to increase utilization).

4.3.1 Disease Survival

The proportion of the U.S. population that is aged 65 and over has grown steadily over the past several decades, and is expected to more than double by 2040.[71] Increased aging of the population, increased life expectancy, and improved survival rates from cancer and other chronic diseases has added further demands on the health system to develop more effective means of controlling acute and chronic pain for a growing number of individuals who are living longer with acute and chronic health problems.[72] The CDC has reported that population-based estimates of chronic pain among U.S. adults range from 11% to 40%.[73] Increased survival from disease further contributes to the ongoing aging of the population, and the aging population has increasingly become the focus

[71] Urban Institute, "The US Population Is Aging," (Washington, D.C.: The Urban Institute, 2010).

[72] See generally V. Jairam et al., "National Patterns in Prescription Opioid Use and Misuse Among Cancer Survivors in the United States," *JAMA Network Open* 3, no. 8 (Jairam et al., 2020); A. Zajacova, H. Grol-Prokopczyk, and Z. Zimmer, "Pain Trends Among American Adults, 2002–2018: Patterns, Disparities, and Correlates," *Demography* 58, no. 2 (Zajacova et al., 2021).

[73] J. Dahlhamer et al., "Prevalence of Chronic Pain and High-Impact Chronic Pain Among Adults—United States, 2016," *MMWR Morb Mortal Wkly Rep* 67, no. 36 (Dahlhamer et al., 2018).

of the palliative care movement,[74] which will be discussed in greater below. Kaye et al. described this way: "As patients age, the incidence and prevalence of certain pain syndromes increase [and] some elderly patients incorrectly believe that pain is a normal process of aging."[75] In addition, longer average life expectancies result in the lengthening of the time individuals live with chronic disease. Many chronic diseases and associated risk factors are associated with pain,[76] and opioid-based treatments offered an expedient means by which to treat such pain. Moreover, older patients experience pain differently, and excess burden of pain is associated with increased risk of dementia, thereby increasing the importance of treatment for this segment of the population.[77]

4.3.2 *Disease Prevalence*

Another important factor related to medical need is the increasing prevalence of specific chronic diseases and conditions, particularly those associated with increased demand for pain management. Two chronic conditions are notable due to their sharp increase in prevalence over the past two decades: (1) mental illness; and (2) metabolic disorders, such as obesity and diabetes. Research has consistently shown that individuals with mental illness are significantly more likely to also have a substance use disorder, including opioid misuse.[78] Two systematic literature reviews and meta-analyses conducted at the height of opioid supply (2012–2013) found strong associations between non-medical prescription opioid use ("NMPOU") and the prevalence of substance use disorders ("SUD").

[74] F. M. Knaul et al., "Alleviating the access abyss in palliative care and pain relief-an imperative of universal health coverage: the Lancet Commission report," *Lancet* 391, no. 10,128 (Knaul et al., 2018).

[75] A. D. Kaye, A. Baluch, and J. T. Scott, "Pain management in the elderly population: a review," *Ochsner J* 10, no. 3 (Kaye et al., 2010).

[76] H. E. Foley et al., "Association of chronic pain with comorbidities and health care utilization: a retrospective cohort study using health administrative data," *Pain* 162, no. 11 (Foley et al., 2021).

[77] A. P. A. Dagnino and M. M. Campos, "Chronic Pain in the Elderly: Mechanisms and Perspectives," *Front Hum Neurosci* 16 (Dagnino & Campos, 2022).

[78] See generally J. O. Adeola and R. D. Urman, "Psychiatric Comorbidities Associated with Persistent Postoperative Opioid Use," *Curr Pain Headache Rep* 26, no. 9 (Adeola & Urman, 2022).

Fischer et al. found that the pooled prevalence of "any mental health symptoms" among individuals reporting NMPOU was 32%.[79] The pooled prevalence of reported pain in the same population was 48%. A meta-analysis by Goldner et al. reached remarkably similar estimates, finding a pooled prevalence of mental health problems of 43% among those reporting NMPOU.[80] These studies show a consistent association between mental illness and SUD, generally, and individuals who misuse opioids are highly likely to also have mental health problems. The prevalence of mental health disorders among at-risk opioid abusers (e.g., those who have already had a hospitalization or incident involving law enforcement) is nearly 60%.[81] In addition, according to a recent systematic review and meta-analysis, among individuals diagnosed with OUD, the prevalence of current depression was 36.1%.[82]

Similarly, rising rates of obesity have contributed to increased demand for pain management. The obesity epidemic is a global phenomenon but particularly concerning in the U.S., where rates have increased substantially in recent years. According to a Commonwealth Fund study, "Buried in recent headlines is the sobering fact that obesity is still on the rise in the United States. The latest federal data show that nearly 40% of American adults were obese in 2015–16, up from 34% in 2007–08. The prevalence of severe obesity also went up during the same period, from 5.7% to 7.7%. In 1985, no state had an obesity rate higher than 15%. In 2016, five states had rates over 35%."[83] Overall, from 2000 to 2018, obesity prevalence increased an unprecedented 39%, and rates of severe obesity increased an

[79] B. Fischer et al., "The prevalence of mental health and pain symptoms in general population samples reporting nonmedical use of prescription opioids: a systematic review and meta-analysis," *J Pain* 13, no. 11 (Fischer et al., 2012).

[80] E. M. Goldner et al., "Prevalence of Axis-1 psychiatric (with focus on depression and anxiety) disorder and symptomatology among non-medical prescription opioid users in substance use treatment: systematic review and meta-analyses," *Addict Behav* 39, no. 3 (Goldner et al., 2014).

[81] C. Bakos-Block et al., "Prevalence of Mental Health Disorders among Individuals Enrolled in an Emergency Response Program for Treatment of Opioid Use Disorder," *Subst Abuse* 14 (Bakos-Block et al., 2020).

[82] T. Santo, Jr. et al., "Prevalence of mental disorders among people with opioid use disorder: A systematic review and meta-analysis," *Drug Alcohol Depend* 238 (Song et al., 2022).

[83] D. Blumenthal and S. Seervai, "Rising Obesity in the United States Is a Public Health Crisis," (Washington, D.C.: The Commonwealth Fund, Blumenthal & Seervai, 2018).

alarming 96% over the same time period.[84] The connection between obesity and pain is both direct and indirect. The direct effect has been observed in studies of reported pain by individuals with varying degrees of obesity. For example, Hitt et al. found that, based on a study of 3637 individuals, those classified as Class I obese (i.e., those with body mass index, or "BMI," of 30 to 34.9) were 1.8 times more likely to report severe pain relative to normal weight participants, Class II obese respondents (i.e., those with BMI of 35 to 39.9) were 1.9 times more likely to report severe pain, and Class III obese individuals were 2.3 times more likely to report severe pain.[85] The second pathway between obesity and demand for pain treatment is indirect, as obesity is causative of a variety of serious health conditions that increase the need for medical care services and pain management. Generally, these conditions include, but are not limited to, coronary artery disease, heart failure, cardiac arrhythmia, stroke, insulin resistance, glucose intolerance, diabetes mellitus, hypertension, dyslipidemia, sleep apnea, arthritis, hyperuricemia, gall bladder disease, musculoskeletal conditions, menstrual irregularities, and certain types of cancer.[86]

4.3.3 Surgery Rates

FDA approval of opioids coincided with two important trends in surgery, which in turn increased the demand for the treatment of post-surgical pain. First, apart from a slight dip during the Covid-19 pandemic, rates of surgeries in the U.S. have been steadily increasing for

[84] C.M. Hales et al., "Prevalence of obesity and severe obesity among adults: United States, 2017–2018 (NCHS Data Brief, no 360)," in *NCHS Data Brief* (Hyattsville, MD: National Center for Health Statistics, Hales et al., 2020).

[85] H. C. Hitt et al., "Comorbidity of obesity and pain in a general population: results from the Southern Pain Prevalence Study," *J Pain* 8, no. 5 (Hitt et al., 2007).

[86] There is a large and growing body of literature on the health risks associated with obesity. See generally A. Afshin et al., "Health Effects of Overweight and Obesity in 195 Countries over 25 Years," *N Engl J Med* 377, no. 1 (Afshin et al., 2017); F. X. Pi-Sunyer, "Comorbidities of overweight and obesity: current evidence and research issues," *Med Sci Sports Exerc* 31, no. 11 Suppl (1999); T. D. Rea et al., "Body mass index and the risk of recurrent coronary events following acute myocardial infarction," *Am J Cardiol* 88, no. 5 (Rea et al., 2001); H. Sung et al., "Global patterns in excess body weight and the associated cancer burden," *CA Cancer J Clin* 69, no. 2 (Sung et al., 2019); M. Abdelaal, C. W. le Roux, and N. G. Docherty, "Morbidity and mortality associated with obesity," *Ann Transl Med* 5, no. 7 (Abdelaal et al., 2017).

decades.[87] While use rates of some surgeries, such as hysterectomies, have decreased, the rates of increasingly more prevalent musculoskeletal surgeries, such as hip and knee arthroplasties and spinal procedures, have increased sharply over the past decade.[88] In the two-decade period from 2000 to 2019, the estimated annual volume of total hip arthroplasty ("THA") and total knee arthroplasty ("TKA") increased by 177% and 156%, respectively.[89] Second, the diffusion of opioids coincided with a substantial migration of care from inpatient hospital settings to outpatient and ambulatory surgery settings, especially for less invasive surgical procedures.[90] The movement of care from the inpatient to outpatient setting was driven by several factors, including lower overhead costs, advances in surgical techniques, reductions in time needed to perform surgeries, and advances in the creation of sterile environments outside of the inpatient hospital. The trend started in the 1990s and has continued; for example, from 2015 to 2019, rates of shoulder arthroplasty performed in outpatient settings increased fourfold.[91] More broadly, in the Medicare population, the proportion of surgeries performed on an outpatient basis increased from 68.9% in 2011 to 85.4% in 2018.[92] More recently, the Covid-19 pandemic further accelerated the migration of surgeries and services to

[87] A. S. Mattingly et al., "Trends in US Surgical Procedures and Health Care System Response to Policies Curtailing Elective Surgical Operations During the COVID-19 Pandemic," *JAMA Netw Open* 4, no. 12 (Mattingly et al., 2021).

[88] K.R. Fingar et al., "Most Frequent Operating Room Procedures Performed in U.S. Hospitals, 2003–2012. HCUP Statistical Brief #186," in *HCUP Statistical Brief* (Rockville, MD: U.S. Agency for Healthcare Research and Quality, Fingar et al., 2014). Also see D. Shukla et al., "Retrospective analysis of trends in surgery volumes between 2016 and 2019 and impact of the insurance deductible: Cross-sectional study," *Ann Med Surg (Lond)* 63 (Shukla et al., 2021); H. Maradit Kremers et al., "Prevalence of Total Hip and Knee Replacement in the United States," *J Bone Joint Surg Am* 97, no. 17 (Maradit Kremers et al., 2015).

[89] I. Shichman et al., "Projections and Epidemiology of Primary Hip and Knee Arthroplasty in Medicare Patients to 2040–2060," *JB JS Open Access* 8, no. 1 (Shichman et al., 2023).

[90] See, for example, N. Mehta et al., "Trends in outpatient versus inpatient total shoulder arthroplasty over time," *JSES International* 6, no. 1 (Mehta et al., 2022).

[91] J. Almand et al., "The successful migration of total joint arthroplasty from the hospital inpatient to outpatient ASC setting," *Knee* 34 (Almand et al., 2022).

[92] L. G. Burke et al., "Trends in performance of hospital outpatient procedures and associated 30-day costs among medicare beneficiaries from 2011 to 2018," *Healthc (Amst)* 11, no. 4 (Burke et al., 2023).

outpatient settings, mainly due to the scarcity of available inpatient beds during the height of the pandemic.[93] Outpatient settings require the release of patients within 24 hours and typically before pain levels begin to subside, thereby increasing the need for the provision of post-operative prescription analgesics.[94] To alleviate the need for patients to return soon after surgery, due to complaints of pain, clinicians erred on the side of prescribing more than enough supply.[95] This contributed to excess supply, which in turn increased the probability of diversion of unused supply to non-medical use.[96] In addition, studies have generally shown increased rates of opioid use and dependency following outpatient surgery.[97] Opioid-based pain management helped meet this rising demand, at times without consistent regard to the clinical necessity and volume of pain treatment needed at discharge.[98]

4.3.4 Socioeconomic Factors

Substantial evidence supports the premise that socioeconomic and macroeconomic factors played a prominent role in the increase in opioid

[93] See generally A. S. Piple et al., "The Persistent Effects of the COVID-19 Pandemic on Total Joint Arthroplasty Changes in Practice Patterns in the United States From 2020 to 2021," *J Arthroplasty* 38, no. 8 (Piple et al., 2023); O. A. Shariq et al., "Performance of General Surgical Procedures in Outpatient Settings Before and After Onset of the COVID-19 Pandemic," *JAMA Netw Open* 6, no. 3 (Shariq et al., 2023).

[94] See generally K. Rajput and N. Vadivelu, "Acute Pain Management of Chronic Pain Patients in Ambulatory Surgery Centers," *Curr Pain Headache Rep* 25, no. 1 (Rajput & Vadivelu, 2021); N. Rawal, "Postoperative pain treatment for ambulatory surgery," *Best Pract Res Clin Anaesthesiol* 21, no. 1 (Rawal, 2007); S. A. Schug and C. Chong, "Pain management after ambulatory surgery," *Curr Opin Anaesthesiol* 22, no. 6 (Schug & Chong, 2009); C. L. Chen et al., "Long-Term Trends in Postoperative Opioid Prescribing, 1994 to 2014," *J Am Acad Orthop Surg Glob Res Rev* 4, no. 1 (Chen et al., 2020). Note that in many cases post-operative pain medications are prescribed and dispensed in anticipation of future pain as opposed to treatment for existing pain.

[95] See generally M. D. Neuman, B. T. Bateman, and H. Wunsch, "Inappropriate opioid prescription after surgery," *Lancet* 393, no. 10180 (Neuman et al., 2019).

[96] See generally J. A. Inciardi et al., "Mechanisms of prescription drug diversion among drug-involved club—and street-based populations," *Pain Med* 8, no. 2 (Inciardi et al., 2007).

[97] E. C. Sun et al., "Incidence of and Risk Factors for Chronic Opioid Use Among Opioid-Naive Patients in the Postoperative Period," *JAMA Intern Med* 176, no. 9 (E. C. Sun et al., 2016).

[98] Neuman, Bateman, and Wunsch, "Inappropriate opioid prescription after surgery."

utilization and OUD, particularly in the U.S. As economists Case and Deaton contend in their book *Deaths of Despair and the Future of Capitalism*, referring to mortality associated with substance use disorder, "deaths of despair are prevalent among those who have been left behind."[99] Throughout the U.S., during the past several decades there have been significant shifts in the structure of the economy, characterized predominantly by a decline in economic activity related to industrial manufacturing, agriculture, energy, and mining.[100] The decline in heavy industry and manufacturing has occurred alongside rapid growth in high-technology and service industries, such as semi-conductors, telecommunications, information systems, and healthcare. This evolution, however, has taken place heterogeneously across the country. Large metropolitan regions and areas with highly educated workforces have been home to new high-technology industries and services, whereas regions formerly dependent on manufacturing and industry have for the most part found it more difficult to adapt. Consequently, while high-growth regions flourish, inflation adjusted household incomes have risen at the lowest pace in decades, contributing to higher levels of disparities in income and wealth.[101] Moreover, the geographic distribution of these opposing economic trends was largely uneven over this period, as some regions of the U.S. "gained" (e.g., those with large urban areas and technology corridors with highly trained labor forces) and other regions "lost" (e.g., those heavily dependent on manufacturing, mining, and agriculture).[102] Areas with lower per-capita incomes are generally associated with lower levels of educational attainment and diminished educational outcomes, which can

[99] A. Case and A. Deaton, *Deaths of Despair and the Future of Capitalism* (Princeton, NJ: Princeton University Press, Case & Deaton, 2020). Also see N. Dasgupta, L. Beletsky, and D. Ciccarone, "Opioid Crisis: No Easy Fix to Its Social and Economic Determinants," *Am J Public Health* 108, no. 2 (Dasgupta et al., 2018).

[100] These industries are typically thought to have been most impacted (negatively) by "globalization," which is the migration of certain industries and jobs to countries with lower wages and benefits. See generally J. Stiglitz, *Globalization and its Discontents* (New York, NY: W.W. Norton & Co., Stiglitz, 2002).

[101] See generally R.J. Gordon, *The Rise and Fall of American Growth: The U.S. Standard of Living Since the Civil War* (Princeton, NJ: Princeton University Press, Gordon, 2016).

[102] See generally R. Florida, "America's Worsening Geographic Inequality," (Bloomberg News, Florida, 2018).

in turn exacerbate problems of adaptation to economic change, and create a cycle of economic decline that becomes increasingly difficult to attenuate.[103]

In general, economic hardship and lower socioeconomic status have been shown to be important and significant drivers of worse overall health and higher rates of mental illness, substance abuse, and SUD.[104] For example, using NSDUH data, one study found that "among persons who reported ever using illicit drugs, persons with an income less than $20,000 were 36% more likely to report having substance abuse problems compared to those with an income above $75,000."[105] Similarly, numerous other studies have shown a relationship between poverty status and rates of mental illness, substance abuse, and SUDs.[106] Consequently, the regions of the U.S. that suffered disproportionately from the economic shifts have been shown to have increasing rates of

[103] D. Coady and A. Dizioli, "Income Inequality and Education Revisited: Persistence, Endogeneity, and Heterogeneity," in *IMF Working Paper* (Washington, DC: International Monetary Fund (IMF), Fiscal Affairs Department, Coady & Dizioli, 2017). Also see, for example, L. Lobao et al., "Socioeconomic Transition in the Appalachia Coal Region," (Columbus, OH: World Bank Group | Ohio State University, Lobao et al., 2021).

[104] There is a well-developed literature on the economic and social determinants of health, including SUD. For example, see K. Baptiste-Roberts and M. Hossain, "Socioeconomic Disparities and Self-reported Substance Abuse-related Problems," *Addict Health* 10, no. 2 (Baptiste-Roberts & Hossain, 2018); P. Pratap et al., "Public Health Impacts of Underemployment and Unemployment in the United States: Exploring Perceptions, Gaps and Opportunities," *Int J Environ Res Public Health* 18, no. 19 (Pratap et al., 2021); M. Bartley, J. Ferrie, and S.M. Montgomery, "Health and Labour Market Disadvantage: Unemployment, Non-Employment, and Job Insecurity," in *Social Determinants of Health (Second Edition)*, ed. M. Marmot and R.G. Wilkinson (New York, NY: Oxford University Press, Bartley et al., 2006); W.C. Cockerham, *Social Causes of Health and Disease (Second Edition)* (Malden, MA: Polity Press, Cockerham, 2013). For an in-depth narrative on this topic, also see Case and Deaton, *Deaths of Despair and the Future of Capitalism*.

[105] Baptiste-Roberts and Hossain, "Socioeconomic Disparities and Self-reported Substance Abuse-related Problems."

[106] See, for example, R. Ghertner and L. Groves, "The Opioid Crisis and Economic Opportunity: Geographic and Economic Trends," in *ASPE Research Brief* (Washington, D.C.: Office of the Assistant Secretary for Planning and Evaluation, U.S. Department of Health and Human Services, Ghertner & Groves, 2018). Also see Case and Deaton, *Deaths of Despair and the Future of Capitalism*.

depression, substance abuse, and SUD.[107] Thus, it is not surprising that early indicators of opioid misuse first became apparent in regions of the country that were least able to adapt their labor forces to growth industries and were, consequently, experiencing rising rates of depression and substance abuse.[108]

Opioid misuse generally followed a pattern of diffusion analogous to other forms of substance abuse, with a timeline and geographic dispersion that aligned with shifts in the economic base.[109] For example, according to the 2021 data from NSDUH, the prevalence of opioid misuse was 2.8% in geographic areas with mean per capita incomes ≥ 200% of the poverty level, but more than double (5.7%) in areas ≤ 100% of the poverty level.[110] The Consensus Study Report of the U.S. National Academies of Science, entitled *Pain Management and the Opioid Epidemic*, described the link between socioeconomic factors and opioid misuse this way: "The pain-relieving and other effects of opioids (e.g., the feelings of pleasure, relaxation, and contentment that opioids can induce) may give rise to use of the drugs to manage stress, depression, anxiety, or other acute psychological states or chronic mental health disorders, which may be caused or worsened by social conditions (such as poverty, unemployment, lack of opportunity, and hopelessness). In these instances of misuse, the intended medical indications of opioids to alleviate physical pain may be coopted by treatment of these mental or social conditions."[111] It is also the case that declining economic conditions can increase demand and utilization of

[107] See generally J. Sareen et al., "Relationship Between Household Income and Mental Disorders: Findings From a Population-Based Longitudinal Study," *Archives of General Psychiatry* 68, no. 4 (Sareen et al., 2011).

[108] P. S. Sullivan et al., "The Geography of Opioid Use Disorder: A Data Triangulation Approach," *Infect Dis Clin North Am* 34, no. 3 (Sullivan et al., 2020).

[109] Refer to A. Hollingsworth, C. J. Ruhm, and K. Simon, "Macroeconomic conditions and opioid abuse," *J Health Econ* 56 (Hollingsworth et al., 2017); Compton and Jones, "Epidemiology of the U.S. opioid crisis: the importance of the vector."; D. Judd, C. R. King, and C. Galke, "The Opioid Epidemic: A Review of the Contributing Factors, Negative Consequences, and Best Practices," *Cureus* 15, no. 7 (Judd et al., 2023).

[110] Refer to NSDUH Table 1.99B "Misuse of Opioids in Past Year: Among People Aged 12 or Older; by Age Group and Geographic and Socioeconomic Characteristics, Percentages, 2021."

[111] NASEM, *Pain Management and the Opioid Epidemic: Balancing Societal and Indidivual Benefits and Risks of Prescription Opioid Use.* (In-text citations removed from quote)

illicit drugs.[112] In sum, socioeconomic factors increased SUD rates, which in turn increased demand for prescription opioids *and* illicit opioids. These factors played a very important role in increasing opioid supply, certainly one that exacerbated the impact and actions of other contributing factors.

4.3.5 Payer Coverage

Following FDA approval, prescription opioids were reimbursed by most public and private payers as part of even the most basic coverage plans. According to a study by Lin et al., Medicare and state Medicaid plans covered an average of 19 different opioid medications as of 2018, and private commercial payers covered an average of 18 different opioids, all of which were classified as "Tier 1," meaning they were associated with the lowest copayment (usually about $10 per prescription fill) and the easiest access.[113] Coverage by state Medicaid programs were of particular importance because of the comparatively higher rates of SUD and mental illness among enrollees in these types of programs,[114] conditions which are important risk factors for opioid misuse. In 1991, state Medicaid programs paid for only 2.1 million prescription opioids, but by 2015 the count had risen to 41.6 million opioid prescriptions.[115] From 1991 to 2019, state Medicaid programs, including those in many of the states that are currently plaintiffs in the opioid MDL, directly paid for nearly $20 billion worth

[112] See generally E. Brown and G. L. Wehby, "Economic Conditions and Drug and Opioid Overdose Deaths," *Med Care Res Rev* 76, no. 4 (Brown & Wehby, 2019); C. S. Carpenter, C. B. McClellan, and D. I. Rees, "Economic conditions, illicit drug use, and substance use disorders in the United States," *J Health Econ* 52 (Carpenter et al., 2017).

[113] D. H. Lin et al., "Prescription Drug Coverage for Treatment of Low Back Pain Among US Medicaid, Medicare Advantage, and Commercial Insurers," *JAMA Netw Open* 1, no. 2 (D. H. Lin et al., 2018).

[114] See generally R. E. Clark, M. Samnaliev, and M. P. McGovern, "Treatment for co-occurring mental and substance use disorders in five state Medicaid programs," *Psychiatr Serv* 58, no. 7 (Clark et al., 2007); H. Saunders and R. Rudowitz, "Demographics and Health Insurance Coverage of Nonelderly Adults With Mental Illness and Substance Use Disorders in 2020," (San Francisco, CA: Kaiser Family Foundation (KFF), Saunders & Rudowitz, 2022).

[115] M. M. Alsultan and J. J. Guo, "Utilization, Spending, and Price of Opioid Medications in the US Medicaid Programs Between 1991 and 2019," *Am Health Drug Benefits* 15, no. 1 (Alsultan & Guo, 2022).

of opioids.[116] The Medicare Part D program, the federal program that provides drug benefits for those age 65 and over, also funded a large volume of opioid prescriptions. According to an OIG report, more than a third of Medicare Part D enrollees was prescribed at least one prescription opioid in 2016.[117] The same OIG report found that in many cases, opioids prescribed to Medicare beneficiaries, and paid for by the Medicare program, far exceeded daily dosages recommended by manufacturers.

Apart from the inconvenient optics of states continuing to pay for opioids while claiming damages attributable to the same opioids, any payment or subsidy of medical care is likely to result in higher utilization. Reimbursing medical services through insurance coverage is a form of subsidy, which in turn reduces net prices faced by enrollees at the "point of sale." This is form of moral hazard, which was described in Chap. 2. Several studies have shown that the more comprehensive the coverage is, the more medical services consumed by covered enrollees. The most notable study of the effect of insurance on utilization was the RAND Health Insurance Experiment, which found that individuals with comprehensive coverage accrued expenditures that were about 45% higher than those with less comprehensive coverage,[118] due to higher rates of utilization. Certain subgroups of services exhibited an even larger effect; for example, expenditures on outpatient services were 68% higher in the group with comprehensive insurance. Thus, it is highly likely that the extensive coverage of opioid-based pain medications to some extent contributed to higher utilization and higher overall demand. A 2019 report by the U.S. Council of Economic Advisers ("CEA") directly explored this hypothesis. The report notes that public subsidies (via Medicare and Medicaid coverage) for opioid prescriptions increased from 17% in 2001 to 63% in 2015, further finding that "the number of potency-adjusted opioids per capita subsidized by Medicare increased 2400% between 2001 and 2010, the largest increase among all third-party payers."[119] The CEA report concluded that rates of prescription opioids could have been as

[116] Ibid.

[117] OIG, "Opioids in Medicare Part D: Concerns about Extreme Use and Questionable Prescribing," in *HHS OIG Data Brief (OEI-02-17-00250)* (Washington, D.C.: U.S. Office of the Inspector General, OIG., 2017).

[118] J. P. Newhouse, *Free for All? Lessons from the RAND Health Insurance Experiment* (Cambrindge, MA: Harvard University Press, Newhouse, 1993).

[119] CEA, "The Role of Opioid Prices in the Evolving Opioid Crisis."

much as 50% lower if such extensive third-party payer coverage had not markedly reduced out-of-pocket costs to consumers. It is worth noting that opioid utilization attributable to third-party coverage does not necessarily imply that those opioids were medically unnecessary; that is, reducing financial barriers to healthcare services has been shown to increase the volume of utilization but not necessarily alter the proportion of care considered medical unnecessary.[120]

4.3.6 Palliative Care

The increase in demand for pain management associated with disease survival, increases in prevalence of diseases associated with pain, and increased surgery rates occurred alongside what has subsequently been termed the "palliative care movement," wherein the medical community began focusing attention on the importance of symptom control, especially toward the end of life, a main feature of which was the concept of the "right to pain control" as a fundamental human right.[121] A working definition of palliative care is "interdisciplinary care (medicine, nursing, social work, chaplaincy, and other specialties when appropriate) that focuses on improving quality of life for persons of any age who are living with any serious illness and for their families."[122] The emergence of the palliative care movement and the concept of a "right to pain control" played out in some 1990s court cases involving the ethics and legality of withholding of treatment for terminally ill patients, including the more controversial topic of physician-assisted suicide. For example, in deliberations concerning limits on physician-assisted suicide, two Supreme Court rulings affirmed a right to palliative care and pain control, requiring states

[120] Newhouse, *Free for All? Lessons from the RAND Health Insurance Experiment.*

[121] For an in-depth discussion of the rise of the palliative care movement and the emergence of a legal right to pain control, see M. D. Sullivan and J. C. Ballantyne, "The Right to Pain Relief: Its Origins in End-of-life Care and Extension to Chronic Pain Care," *Clin J Pain* 38, no. 1 (M. D. Sullivan & Ballantyne, 2021); Sullivan and Ballantyne, *The Right to Pain Relief and Other Deep Roots of the Opioid Epidemic*; D. J. Wilkie and M. O. Ezenwa, "Pain and symptom management in palliative care and at end of life," *Nurs Outlook* 60, no. 6 (Wilkie & Ezenwa, 2012).

[122] A. S. Kelley and R. S. Morrison, "Palliative Care for the Seriously Ill," *N Engl J Med* 373, no. 8 (Kelley & Morrison, 2015). (p.747)

to not obstruct the provision of adequate pain control.[123] The movement included a shift throughout the medical community to "patient centered care," which, consistent with the palliative care movement, was focused on treating specific patient needs, rather than solely treating specific underlying diseases and conditions.[124]

Between 2000 and 2003, the number of U.S. hospitals with palliative care programs nearly doubled, from 632 hospitals, or about 15%, to 1027 hospitals, or more than 25% of hospitals.[125] By 2013, the peak of opioid prescribing, more than 67% of U.S. hospitals operated palliative care programs, and by 2016 the proportion reached 75%.[126] Control of pain symptoms is one of the primary goals of palliative care, as pain is one of the most consistently reported symptoms of long-term illnesses, such as cancer, advanced heart disease, chronic kidney disease, chronic obstructive pulmonary disease ("COPD"), and multiple sclerosis.[127] In palliative care settings, as many as 50% of patients report the presence of chronic pain.[128] As medical advocacy groups began championing palliative approaches to treating patients with long-term illnesses, prescription opioids were viewed by physicians as a means of helping more actively engage in the palliative care movement and help meet its objectives.[129]

[123] See generally R. A. Burt, "The Supreme Court speaks–not assisted suicide but a constitutional right to palliative care," ibid.337, no. 17 (Burt, 1997).

[124] See, for example, M. L. Millenson, "New roles and rules for patient-centered care," *J Gen Intern Med* 29, no. 7 (Millenson, 2014).

[125] T. Dumanovsky et al., "The Growth of Palliative Care in U.S. Hospitals: A Status Report," *J Palliat Med* 19, no. 1 (Dumanovsky et al., 2016).

[126] CAPC, "The Case for Hospital Palliative Care," (New York, NY: Center to Advance Palliative Care, CAPC, 2018).

[127] D. G. Harris, "Management of pain in advanced disease," *Br Med Bull* 110, no. 1 (Harris, 2014).

[128] See generally L. Kernick et al., "Prevalence and management of chronic nonmalignant pain in palliative care populations: A systematic review," *Palliat Support Care* (Kernick et al., 2023); R. A. H. Snijders et al., "Update on Prevalence of Pain in Patients with Cancer 2022: A Systematic Literature Review and Meta-Analysis," *Cancers (Basel)* 15, no. 3 (Snijders et al., 2023).

[129] See generally Sullivan and Ballantyne, "The Right to Pain Relief: Its Origins in End-of-life Care and Extension to Chronic Pain Care."; Sullivan and Ballantyne, *The Right to Pain Relief and Other Deep Roots of the Opioid Epidemic.*

4.3.7 *Practice Variation*

As discussed in Chap. 3, medical need for pain management, regardless of the causes and nature of the pain, is largely based on qualitative judgment by treating physicians. Such clinical judgement is likely to be heavily influenced by the complexity and subjectivity of pain, with creates significant information asymmetry in diagnosis and treatment decisions. Consequently, high levels of clinical uncertainty are likely to result in correspondingly high levels of baseline variation in physician practice patterns; that is, some physicians are more likely to recommend treatment "a" over treatment "b" (or in some cases deciding whether any treatment is necessary) for the same patient with the same clinical presentation and similar clinical data.[130] In the case of opioids, it is reasonable to assume that clinical uncertainly had the effect of increasing utilization, as physicians are more likely to err on the side of treatment in instances with high diagnostic uncertainty.[131]

Physicians not only have differing practice patterns, but they often have differing perceptions of medical need.[132] The contributory role of physicians in opioid supply is discussed again in later chapters, but in the context of medical need it is first important to consider the concept of "normal" practice variation. An argument made by some observers in the opioid crisis is that demand factors alone do not explain variation in opioid supply and utilization. That may be at least partly true, but as the discussion above puts forth, there were some very important demand factors associated with the increase in prevalence and intensity of pain treatment. Layered atop the underlying demand factors was *geographic variation* in treatment patterns, variation exacerbated by the information asymmetries between patients and providers in the pain management arena.

The phenomenon of geographic variation in physician practice patterns and medical care utilization is consistently observed in virtually all U.S. geographic areas for a wide cross section of medical care services, and for

[130] See generally B. Patel et al., "Navigating Uncertainty in Clinical Practice: A Structured Approach," *J Gen Intern Med* 39, no. 5 (Patel et al., 2024).

[131] For example, see D. Wang et al., "Does diagnostic uncertainty increase antibiotic prescribing in primary care?," *NPJ Prim Care Respir Med* 31, no. 1 (Wang et al., 2021).

[132] For general discussions, refer to J. Skinner, "Causes and Consequences of Regional Variations in Health Care," in *Handbook of Health Economics (Volume 2)*, ed. M.V. Pauly, T. G. McGuire, and P.P. Barros (New York, NY: Elsevier B.V., Skinner, 2012).

decades health economists and health services researchers have studied persistent "unexplained" geographic variations in healthcare utilization rates.[133] Surgery rates differ substantially from one geographic area to another, without regard to patient characteristics or other observable indicators of medical need.[134] For example, Kauh et al. conducted a study of more than one million individuals with cataracts enrolled in a nationwide managed-care network, finding that the highest age-standardized cataract surgery rate (37.3% in Lake Charles, Louisiana) was nearly five-fold higher than the lowest rate (7.5% in Honolulu, Hawaii).[135] Similarly, Song et al. analyzed variation across five large U.S. metropolitan areas for several common medical procedures among quintiles of utilization.[136] For patients with knee or hip osteoarthritis the authors found that "2.1% to 3.4% received arthroscopy in the first quintile of orthopedic surgeons, whereas 25.5% to 30.7% did in the fifth quintile."

The "unexplained" component of geographic variation has generally been attributed to regional and local differences in physician practice patterns, which include local institutional standards, informal rules, and professional and social norms,[137] but may also include variation in

[133] For example, see CBO, "Geographic Variation in Health Care Spending," (Washington, D.C.: Congress of the United States, Congressional Budget Office, CBO., 2005); J. D. Lurie, J. E. Bell, and J. Weinstein, "What rate of utilization is appropriate in musculoskeletal care?," *Clin Orthop Relat Res* 467, no. 10 (Lurie et al., 2009).

[134] See, for example, T. D. Azad et al., "Geographic variation in the surgical management of lumbar spondylolisthesis: characterizing practice patterns and outcomes," *Spine J* 18, no. 12 (Azad et al., 2018); R. D. Becher et al., "Geographic Variation in the Utilization of and Mortality After Emergency General Surgery Operations in the Northeastern and Southeastern United States," *Ann Surg* 275, no. 2 (Becher et al., 2022); S. B. Floyd et al., "Geographic variation in the treatment of proximal humerus fracture: an update on surgery rates and treatment consensus," *J Orthop Surg Res* 14, no. 1 (Floyd et al., 2019); C. Y. Kauh et al., "Geographic Variation in the Rate and Timing of Cataract Surgery Among US Communities," *JAMA Ophthalmol* 134, no. 3 (Kauh et al., 2016).

[135] "Geographic Variation in the Rate and Timing of Cataract Surgery Among US Communities."

[136] Z. Song et al., "Physician Practice Pattern Variations in Common Clinical Scenarios Within 5 US Metropolitan Areas," *JAMA Health Forum* 3, no. 1 (Song et al., 2022).

[137] For a broad discussion if the institutional economics of standards and norms, refer to E. Posner, "Standards, Rules, and Social Norms," *Harvard Journal of Law and Public Policy* 21 (E. Posner, 1997); H.P. Young, "The Evolution of Social Norms," *Annual Review of Economics* 7, no. 1 (Young, 2015); D. Dequech, "Institutions and Norms in Institutional Economics and Sociology," *Journal of Economic Issues* 40, no. 2 (Dequech, 2006).

individual physician training, capabilities and prefs.[138] For example, a recent report from the National Bureau of Economic Research ("NBER") found that about 33% of regional variation is due to variation in physician treatment intensity, and that "... physicians are roughly three times as important as non-physician supply side factors in driving regional variation."[139] It is also likely that uncertainty plays an important role in practice variation, with variation in uncertainty driven primarily by patient characteristics and the information processing capabilities of clinicians and their organizations.[140] Evidence of uncertainty on the part of clinicians is in part reflected in relatively high rates of inappropriate use, with some studies showing rates of inappropriate use in the range of 17–35%.[141] Similar rates of inappropriate use have been observed in the prescribing of medication.[142] The implication of geographic variation in practice patterns is that if we observe two prescription opioid rates, one in area

[138] See generally M. R. Chassin, "Explaining geographic variations. The enthusiasm hypothesis," *Med Care* 31, no. 5 Suppl (Chassin, 1993); A. J. Epstein and S. Nicholson, "The formation and evolution of physician treatment styles: an application to cesarean sections," *J Health Econ* 28, no. 6 (Epstein & Nicholson, 2009); S. Folland and M. Stano, "Sources of small area variations in the use of medical care," ibid.8, no. 1 (Folland & Stano, 1989); J. Skinner, "Causes and Consequences of Regional Variations in Health Care," in *Handbook of Health Economics: Volume 2*, ed. M.V. Pauly, T. McGuire, and P. P. Barros (Elsevier, Skinner, 2011); A. E. Carroll, "The High Costs of Unnecessary Care," *Jama* 318, no. 18 (Carroll, 2017); H. Lyu et al., "Overtreatment in the United States," *PLoS One* 12, no. 9 (Lyu et al., 2017).

[139] The study also concluded that "... around [60%] of the physicians' role comes from differences across regions in physician practice intensity within the same specialty, while the other [40%] reflects differences across regions in physician specialty mix ..." Refer to I. Badinski et al., "Geographic Variation in Healthcare Utilization: The Role of Physicians," (National Bureau of Economic Research (NBER), Badinski et al., 2023).

[140] See, for example, V. Bhise et al., "Defining and Measuring Diagnostic Uncertainty in Medicine: A Systematic Review," *J Gen Intern Med* 33, no. 1 (Bhise et al., 2018).

[141] See generally M. R. Chassin et al., "Does inappropriate use explain geographic variations in the use of health care services? A study of three procedures," *Jama* 258, no. 18 (Chassin et al., 1987); A. L. Siu et al., "Inappropriate use of hospitals in a randomized trial of health insurance plans," *N Engl J Med* 315, no. 20 (Siu et al., 1986); C. M. Winslow et al., "The appropriateness of performing coronary artery bypass surgery," *Jama* 260, no. 4 (Winslow et al., 1988); Carroll, "The High Costs of Unnecessary Care."; Lyu et al., "Overtreatment in the United States."

[142] For example, see M. D. Buck et al., "Potentially inappropriate medication prescribing in outpatient practices: prevalence and patient characteristics based on electronic health records," *Am J Geriatr Pharmacother* 7, no. 2 (Buck et al., 2009).

"a" and one in area "b," and the rate for "a" is 50% higher, it is highly likely that some proportion of the 50% differential is attributable solely to "normal" physician practice variation, including variation in physician practice patterns and the varying effects of uncertainty. Based on the NBER study, the proportion of variation attributable to normal practice variation could be as much as 33%.

High levels of geographic variation have been observed in opioid prescribing, and studies have shown that at least one third of this variation can be explained by variables measuring medical need and sociodemographic factors.[143] For example, McDonald et al. analyzed pharmacy records for 135 million opioid prescriptions, and specified a county-level regression model with an array of variables representing medical need and demand for medical care, including population characteristics such as education, poverty status, percent uninsured, and the availability of prescribers.[144] The results of the regression were as expected given the preceding discussion; in general, a more educated, higher-income population was associated with less opioid utilization, and poverty status and higher rates of uninsurance were associated with higher levels of opioid utilization. The availability of prescribing physicians was included as a proxy for access and was also associated with higher opioid utilization. The model had an R-squared of 0.33, suggesting that the variables included in the model explained about 33% of the observed variation in opioid prescribing.[145] In sum, there is undoubtedly some non-trivial proportion

[143] See, for example, D. C. McDonald, K. Carlson, and D. Izrael, "Geographic variation in opioid prescribing in the U.S," *J Pain* 13, no. 10 (McDonald et al., 2012); J. H. Lee et al., "Geographic variation in the use of triptans and opioids for the acute treatment of migraine attacks," *Headache* 61, no. 10 (Lee et al., 2021); J. T. Painter, L. J. Crofford, and J. Talbert, "Geographic variation of chronic opioid use in fibromyalgia," *Clin Ther* 35, no. 3 (Painter et al., 2013).

[144] McDonald, Carlson, and Izrael, "Geographic variation in opioid prescribing in the U.S."

[145] The findings from McDonald et al. are likely an underestimate in terms of the amount of variation in opioid utilization explained by these types of models. For example, estimating similar exploratory models using publicly available state-level data can result in R^2 measures of between 50% and 60%. These estimates were derived from some exploratory analyses of variations on the basic model structure of $OPR_{it} = f\ (X_{it})$, where OPR_{it} is the opioid prescription rate per 100 population in state i in year t, and X_{it} is a vector of variables serving as proxies for medical need for pain treatment, including population characteristics, prevalence of comorbid disease (obesity; mental illness), and socioeconomic measures, including education, unemployment, uninsurance, and income.

of opioid prescribing that is based on medical need and changes in medical need. Statistical analyses of variation in physician practice patterns show that one third of variation is based solely on differences in physician practice patterns. In the case of opioids, studies have shown that another third of observed variation in utilization can be explained by population characteristics, disease prevalence, and socioeconomic factors.

4.4 Policy

Beginning in the late 1990s, there began a widespread effort throughout the U.S. public and private health care system to improve "patient centered" care generally and pain management specifically.[146] The movement overlapped with the palliative care and patient-centered care movements, but was considerably broader, advocating for better pain management for everyone, not just those with long-term chronic diseases. Federal and state governments played a prominent and vocal role in the promotion of more aggressive pain management as part of patient-centered care and, more generally, as part of overall efforts aimed at "quality improvement."[147] For example, in 2000, the U.S. Congress declared the beginning of a "Decade of Pain Control and Research."[148] A year later, the U.S. Institute of Medicine ("IOM") released its landmark study entitled *Crossing the Quality Chasm: A New Health System for the twenty-first Century*, in which the authors identified patient-centered care as one of the six primary domains of health care quality, defining it as "providing care that is respectful of and responsive to individual patient preferences, needs, and values and ensuring that patient values guide all clinical decisions."[149] A decade later the IOM released a pain-focused report, entitled *Relieving Pain in America: A Blueprint for Transforming Prevention, Care, Education, and Research*, with its 364 pages devoted entirely to pain

[146] See generally A.D. Sinaiko et al., "Delivery of Patient Centered Care in the U.S. Health Care System: What is standing in its way?," (Washington, D.C.: Robert Wood Johnson Foundation & Academy Health, Sinaiko et al., 2019).

[147] See generally S. Imhof and B. Kaskie, "How can we make the pain go away? Public policies to manage pain at the end of life," *Gerontologist* 48, no. 4 (Imhof & Kaskie, 2008).

[148] Refer to F. Brennan, "The US Congressional "Decade on Pain Control and Research" 2001–2011: A Review," *J Pain Palliat Care Pharmacother* 29, no. 3 (Brennan, 2015).

[149] IOM, *Crossing the Quality Chasm: A New Health System for the twenty-first Century* (Washington, D.C.: Institute of Medicine (IOM), National Academy Press, IOM, 2001).

control as a means of addressing patient preferences and values and as a means of attaining some of the main goals of patient-centered care.[150] The report reached a number of findings and recommendations, including but not limited to redefining pain as a public health problem, calling for consensus on a population-based strategy for reducing pain, improving pain assessment and management programs, tailoring pain care to each patient's experience, reducing barriers to adequate pain care, and reducing regulatory barriers to the provision of care, including ones that "inhibit the medically appropriate use of opioids."[151] One of the central themes of the IOM study was the need for improvement in access to pain control: "Not all Americans have the same access to pain care [and] significant numbers are at risk of undertreatment . . . "[152]

One of the principal recommendations of the IOM pain report was for the U.S. Department of Health and Human Services ("DHHS") to develop "a comprehensive population health-level strategy for pain, prevention, treatment, management, and research."[153] Beginning in 2010, the DHHS and National Institutes of Health ("NIH") engaged with numerous government health agencies to "develop recommendations to increase the recognition of pain as a significant public health problem," which led to the creation of the "National Pain Strategy" ("NPS").[154] In addition, during this time, several focused policy campaigns explicitly advocated for improvement in pain control, regularly referring to pain as the "the fifth vital sign" and pain as a critical part of patient-centered care and any effort to improve healthcare quality.[155] There were concerns, for example, that access to pain control was not sufficient, especially for

[150] "Relieving Pain in America: A Blueprint for Transforming Prevention, Care, Education, and Research," (U.S. National Institutes for Health, Institute of Medicine (IOM), Infeld et al., 2011).

[151] Ibid.

[152] Ibid.

[153] Ibid.

[154] J. Gross and D. B. Gordon, "The Strengths and Weaknesses of Current US Policy to Address Pain," *Am J Public Health* 109, no. 1 (Gross & Gordon, 2019).

[155] See generally N. Levy, J. Sturgess, and P. Mills, ""Pain as the fifth vital sign" and dependence on the "numerical pain scale" is being abandoned in the US: Why?," *Br J Anaesth* 120, no. 3 (Levy et al., 2018); N. E. Morone and D. K. Weiner, "Pain as the fifth vital sign: exposing the vital need for pain education," *Clin Ther* 35, no. 11 (Morone & Weiner, 2013).

underrepresented minorities and lower income individuals.[156] This type of messaging was delivered frequently and consistently from virtually all government-based health care agencies associated with research, coverage, and reimbursement, including public payers like state Medicaid programs and the Veterans Health Administration.[157]

4.5 Advocacy

Physicians not only regularly prescribed opioids following FDA approval, but through their professional associations and societies they actively promoted and advocated for the use of opioid-based pain treatment. In response to these large-scale health policy initiatives on the part of federal and state governments and in response to the emergence of the palliative care and patient-centered care movements, beginning in the 1990s medical societies and medical research organizations began drafting policies, clinical pathways, and CPGs outlining processes and "best practices" focused on improvement in diagnosis and treatment of various forms of acute and chronic pain. Examples of these activities are numerous and widespread.[158] A large and diverse number of medical societies actively promoted aggressive pain management and opioid utilization, including the U.S. Pain Foundation, the American Academy of Pain Medicine, the Academy of Integrated Pain Management, the American Pain Society, the National Pain Foundation, the American Chronic Pain Association,

[156] S. H. Meghani et al., "Advancing a national agenda to eliminate disparities in pain care: directions for health policy, education, practice, and research," *Pain Med* 13, no. 1 (Meghani et al., 2012).

[157] See generally Imhof and Kaskie, "How can we make the pain go away? Public policies to manage pain at the end of life."; Gross and Gordon, "The Strengths and Weaknesses of Current US Policy to Address Pain."; Bernard et al., "Management of Pain in the United States-A Brief History and Implications for the Opioid Epidemic."

[158] See generally APSQCC, "Quality improvement guidelines for the treatment of acute pain and cancer pain. American Pain Society Quality of Care Committee," *Jama* 274, no. 23 (APSQCC, 1995); D. V. Ernstzen, Q. A. Louw, and S. L. Hillier, "Clinical practice guidelines for the management of chronic musculoskeletal pain in primary healthcare: a systematic review," *Implement Sci* 12, no. 1 (Ernstzen et al., 2017); K. L. Schmidt, M. A. Alpen, and B. A. Rakel, "Implementation of the Agency for Health Care Policy and Research Pain Guidelines," *AACN Clin Issues* 7, no. 3 (Schmidt et al., 1996). For a list of medical societies prominently involved in the promotion of aggressive pain management, also see Manchikanti et al., "Reframing the Prevention Strategies of the Opioid Crisis: Focusing on Prescription Opioids, Fentanyl, and Heroin Epidemic."

the American Society of Pain Management Nursing, the American Society of Pain Educators, the American Pain Foundation, the Federation of State Medical Boards, the American Geriatric Society, and others.[159]

While there was general awareness among provider groups and within the medical community more generally of the risks of opioids around the early 2000s,[160] the initial wave of clinical pain guidelines focused more on the "right to pain relief," the importance of patient-centered care, and the clinical effectiveness of pain control rather than on the risks and clinical tradeoffs associated with opioid-based pain medications.[161] For example, in 2010 the International Association for the Study of Pain ("IASP"), self-described as "the leading global organization supporting the study and practice of pain and pain relief,"[162] declared that providing relief from pain was the "moral duty of physicians and that access to adequate pain relief is a fundamental human right."[163]

It is also important to note that many of the medical societies encouraging the use of prescription opioids for pain management also received funding from opioid manufacturers.[164] It is unclear the extent to which such funding may have influenced medical society policies, as it is generally not unusual for drug manufacturers to support medical societies and disease-specific organizations. Examples include patient assistance programs ("PAPs"), creation of registries to support ongoing research, and patient and provider education efforts.[165] However, some experts believe

[159] See, for example, Manchikanti et al.

[160] For example, based on a PubMed search with key words "opioid" and "misuse," between 1990 and 2000 there were between 400 and 500 publications per year containing both search terms. This is discussed later in more detail.

[161] Sullivan and Ballantyne, *The Right to Pain Relief and Other Deep Roots of the Opioid Epidemic.*

[162] Refer to the IASP website (https://www.iasp-pain.org/about/).

[163] A. Lalkhen, *An Anatomy of Pain* (New York, NY: Scribner, Lalkhen, 2021). (p.77)

[164] See generally HSGAC, "Fueling an Epidemic: Exposing the Financial Ties Between Opioid Manufacturers and Third Party Advocacy Groups," (Washington, D.C.: U.S. Senate Homeland Security and Governmental Affairs Committee, Ranking Members Office, HSGAC, 2018); M. S. McCoy et al., "Conflicts of Interest for Patient-Advocacy Organizations," *N Engl J Med* 376, no. 9 (McCoy et al., 2017).

[165] See, for example, S. Stein et al., "Principles for interactions with biopharmaceutical companies: the development of guidelines for patient advocacy organizations in the field of rare diseases," *Orphanet J Rare Dis* 13, no. 1 (S. Stein et al., 2018).

that medical policies regarding opioid use were at least to some extent impacted by financial support from manufacturers.[166] For example, the U. S. Federation of Medical Boards ("FMB"), which represents state medical boards, used funding from opioid manufacturer Purdue Pharmaceuticals to draft opioid prescribing guidelines.[167] The FMB was not alone, as a multitude of medical specialty societies, many of which received funding from opioid manufacturers, echoed the narrative of the need to treat pain more aggressively, and specifically endorsing the value of opioids in pain management. To be sure, as the preceding section discussed, the support of a greater focus on pain and its treatment was not at all out of step with Perhaps not surprisingly, of the approximately 14 different medical societies promoting aggressive pain control over the past two decades, only half of them remain in existence today, and those that have survived have substantially modified their messaging regarding aggressive pain management and the use of opioids.[168]

4.6 Ratings

Third-party payers, both public and private, have been alleged to have contributed to the increase in opioid supply in several ways, including: (1) by providing coverage for opioid-based pain treatments, which in turn increased access to opioids for individuals with third-party coverage (discussed earlier, as a demand factor); (2) by employing payment mechanisms that encouraged more aggressive pain control, shorter hospital stays, and imposed penalties for hospital readmissions; and (3) by insufficiently leveraging and employing their comprehensive patient-level administrative

[166] See generally HSGAC, "Fueling an Epidemic: Exposing the Financial Ties Between Opioid Manufacturers and Third Party Advocacy Groups."; McCoy et al., "Conflicts of Interest for Patient-Advocacy Organizations."; L. Manchikanti, "National drug control policy and prescription drug abuse: facts and fallacies," *Pain Physician* 10, no. 3 (Manchikanti, 2007); Manchikanti et al., "Reframing the Prevention Strategies of the Opioid Crisis: Focusing on Prescription Opioids, Fentanyl, and Heroin Epidemic."

[167] Humphreys et al., "Responding to the opioid crisis in North America and beyond: recommendations of the Stanford-Lancet Commission."

[168] Using the list provided by Manchikanti et al. (Figure 7 in the article), the following societies appear to be no longer in existence (with month and year of ceased operations in parentheses): Academy of Integrative Pain Management (January 2019), American Pain Society (June 2019), American Pain Foundation (May 2012), American Society of Pain Educators (merged with another organization), and The National Pain Foundation (2010).

databases to identify at-risk claims and patients. Having addressed the first of these earlier, this section focuses on the latter two factors.

An important avenue through which third-party payers affected growth in opioid utilization was through innovations in organizational forms and payment mechanisms. Throughout most of the history of health insurance, public and private payers acted more like other indemnity insurers, where claims were paid on a "fee for service" ("FFS") basis and the insurers main role was the application of actuarial science to calculate expected costs.[169] During the "Decade of Pain Control," but not necessarily directly a result of it, this relatively passive role of public and private payers gave way to a more active role, fueled in part by rapidly rising health care expenditures but also driven by a growing demand on the part of healthcare purchasers, such as government payers and employers, for a greater attention to "value," and specifically "value for money."[170] The shift in emphasis to value started on the demand side, with the advent of "managed care" and its employer-driven focus on gatekeeping, utilization review, and use of payment mechanisms designed to incentivize efficiency. Among private commercial insurers, especially managed care organizations ("MCOs"), per-enrollee, per-diem, and per-episode "capitated" payment mechanisms directly incentivized physicians to actively engage in utilization management, including efforts to reduce overutilization of medical care resources.[171] Given that patients with poorly controlled pain have more physician office visits and higher costs,[172] capitated payment mechanisms provided additional financial

[169] For a general discussion of evolution in payment mechanisms, see generally J. C. Robinson, "Payment mechanisms, nonprice incentives, and organizational innovation in health care," *Inquiry* 30, no. 3 (Robinson, 1993); "Theory and practice in the design of physician payment incentives," *Milbank Q* 79, no. 2 (Robinson, 2001).

[170] See generally M.E. Porter and T.H. Lee, "The Strategy That Will Fix Health Care," *Harvard Business Review*, no. October (Porter & Lee, 2013); E. Teisberg, S. Wallace, and S. O'Hara, "Defining and Implementing Value-Based Health Care: A Strategic Framework," *Acad Med* 95, no. 5 (Teisberg et al., 2020).

[171] See, for example, Y. Ding and C. Liu, "Alternative payment models and physician treatment decisions: Evidence from lower back pain," *J Health Econ* 80 (Ding & Liu, 2021); B.C. James and G.P. Poulsen, "The Case for Capitation," *Harvard Business Review*, no. July–August (James & Poulsen, 2016).

[172] See generally M. Gore et al., "The burden of chronic low back pain: clinical comorbidities, treatment patterns, and health care costs in usual care settings," *Spine (Phila Pa 1976)* 37, no. 11 (Gore et al., 2012); J. Hong et al., "Costs associated with treatment of chronic low back pain: an analysis of the UK General Practice Research Database," ibid. 38, no. 1

incentives to aggressively manage pain, as lower utilization (e.g., through the prevention of office visits) typically results in higher net payments to providers. The structuring of coverage and reimbursement policies also favored pharmacological treatment over non-pharmacological treatment, as pharmacological treatment is generally less expensive than more resource intensive non-pharmacological treatment.[173] In addition, MCO and other third-party payer use of tiered pharmacy benefits, often administered independently by contracted PBMs, resulted in opioids being assigned to lower-cost tiers associated with the lowest copayment and the least restrictive access.[174]

An added hallmark of the managed care era and the shift to "value-driven" care was the advent of "value-based reimbursement" ("VBR") payment mechanisms. Payment mechanisms based on VBR were generally structured to financially reward health plans and providers for achieving higher scores on a variety of standardized assessments of quality of care (also referred to as "pay-for-performance").[175] Versions of such programs were widely enacted by federal payers (e.g., Medicare and Veterans Health Administration), state payers (e.g., all state Medicaid programs), private payers, and self-insured employers.[176] Similar programs have been implemented by large health systems and prominently featured in contracts with

(J. Hong et al., 2013); C. E. Whitten, C. M. Evans, and K. Cristobal, "Pain Management Doesn't have to be a Pain: Working and Communicating Effectively with Patients who have Chronic Pain," *Perm J* 9, no. 2 (Whitten et al., 2005).

[173] Refer to, for example, J. Heyward et al., "Coverage of Nonpharmacologic Treatments for Low Back Pain Among US Public and Private Insurers," *JAMA Netw Open* 1, no. 6 (Heyward et al., 2018); Lin et al., "Prescription Drug Coverage for Treatment of Low Back Pain Among US Medicaid, Medicare Advantage, and Commercial Insurers."; M. E. Schatman and L. R. Webster, "The health insurance industry: perpetuating the opioid crisis through policies of cost-containment and profitability," *J Pain Res* 8 (Schatman & Webster, 2015).

[174] The alleged increased access and utilization associated with lower out-of-pocket costs (by way of tier placement) is in part the nominal basis for opioid lawsuits filed against PBMs; for example, see N. Tong, "Arkansas files opioid epidemic lawsuit against PBMs Optum, Express Scripts," (Fierce Healthcare, 2024).

[175] See generally T. T. Chee et al., "Current State of Value-Based Purchasing Programs," *Circulation* 133, no. 22 (Chee et al., 2016).

[176] See generally MACPAC, "Medicaid and CHIP Payment and Access Commission's (MACPAC's) June 2011 Report to the Congress: The Evolution of Managed Care in Medicaid," (Washington, D.C.: Department of Health and Human Services; Medicaid and CHIP Payment and Access Commission, 2011); Y. Marjoua and K. J. Bozic, "Brief history of quality movement in US healthcare," *Curr Rev Musculoskelet Med* 5, no. 4 (Marjoua & Bozic, 2012).

providers.[177] According to the IOM, by 2005, toward the beginning of the increase in opioid supply, more than 100 pay-for-performance and incentive programs had been implemented by U.S. commercial payers.[178] Examples of such quality measures upon which VBR systems are based are the Healthcare Effectiveness Data and Information Set ("HEDIS"), Hospital Consumer Assessment of Healthcare Providers and Systems ("HCAHPS"), Merit-Based Incentive Payments ("MIPS"), and the Physician Quality Reporting System ("PQRS Aligned with the general shift in emphasis to patient-centered care and palliative care, quality assessment tools typically include one or more metrics directly and explicitly related to the utilization and effectiveness of pain management.[179] Scores from these assessment tools fed into value-based payment mechanisms and overall quality assessment efforts, where providers had the opportunity to be paid more for higher assessment scores. The scores also fed into the existing accreditation process and were used by accreditation agencies as part of their overall assessment of health care providers.

It is likely that the use of these value-based mechanisms encouraged the prescribing of opioids as a means of helping to achieve broader performance goals. There is some empirical evidence supporting this relationship. For example, in a survey of 1,404 physicians practicing in Colorado, Carrico et al. found that physicians who reported that VBR mechanisms influenced their opioid prescribing were three times more likely to prescribe opioids compared to physicians who were not incentivized by VBR mechanisms.[180] Similarly, a survey of physicians by Schneider et al. found that more than half of respondents believed that patient satisfaction scores

[177] See generally C.L. Damberg et al., "An Evaluation of the Use of Performance Measures in Health Care," (Arlington, VA: National Quality Forum & RAND Corporation, Damberg et al., 2011).

[178] IOM, *Rewarding Provider Peformance: Aligning Incentives in Medicare*, Pathways to Quality Health Care: Committee on Redesigning Health Insurance Peformance Measures, Payment, and Performance Improvement Programs (Washington, DC: U.S. Institute of Medicine; National Academies Press, 2007).

[179] "Relieving Pain in America: A Blueprint for Transforming Prevention, Care, Education, and Research."

[180] J. A. Carrico et al., "The Association of Patient Satisfaction-Based Incentives with Primary Care Physician Opioid Prescribing," *J Am Board Fam Med* 31, no. 6 (Carrico et al., 2018).

would decline if they prescribed fewer opioids.[181] This relationship is also reflected in broader indicators of VBR; for example, Webster et al., in a study of workers compensation claims, found that every one point increase in a "cost containment score" was associated with a 13% increase in early (post-surgery) opioid prescribing, where the cost containment score was defined as a "composite score representing the relative level of workers compensation managed care and cost containment initiatives."[182]

A third link between third-party payers and the increase in opioid utilization was through their delay in deploying their administrative data to identify and monitor enrollee utilization patterns suggestive of opioid misuse. Interestingly, around the time that the CDC first labeled the rise in opioid overdoses an epidemic (which was around 2011), the CDC's recommendations for mitigating the problem focused mainly on health care providers and payers: "Insurers and prescription drug monitoring programs can identify and take action to reduce both inappropriate and illegal prescribing. Third-party payers can limit reimbursement in ways that reduce inappropriate prescribing, discourage efforts to obtain [opioid-based pain medications] from multiple health-care providers, and improve clinical care."[183] Other studies have generally supported the CDC's contention that payers were well positioned to use their administrative data to control access to opioids through mechanisms such as prior authorization and utilization review.[184]

Administrative and claims data form the backbone of payer operations. As one of the main conduits through which healthcare expenditures flow,

[181] B. J. Schneider et al., "The effect of patient satisfaction scores on physician clinical decision making: A possible factor driving utilization of opioid prescriptions, magnetic resonance imaging, and interventional spine procedures," *Interv Pain Med* 1, no. 1 (Schneider et al., 2022).

[182] B. S. Webster et al., "Geographic variation in opioid prescribing for acute, work-related, low back pain and associated factors: a multilevel analysis," *Am J Ind Med* 52, no. 2 (Webster et al., 2009).

[183] CDC, "Vital signs: overdoses of prescription opioid pain relievers—United States, 1999–2008."

[184] See generally M. S. Andersen et al., "Association of opioid utilization management with prescribing and overdose," *Am J Manag Care* 28, no. 2 (Andersen et al., 2022). Also see S.T. Parente, "Exploring Ex Ante Regulatory Mechanisms for Detecting Prescription Drug Misuse," in *Regulation versus Litigation: Perspectives from Economics and Law*, ed. D.P. Kessler (Chicago, IL: National Bureau of Economic Research | The University of Chicago Press, 2011).

public and private insurers have strong incentives to use their administrative data to regularly conduct utilization review ("UR") and employ other tools to broadly manage and control expenditures.[185] Such uses can readily be targeted to specific purposes, including the detection and monitoring of utilization patterns. As one health economist described it, "insurance claims data provide an electronic trace of the entire set of transactions that could demonstrate misuse *ex post*."[186] Consistent with their early recommendation that payers play a more active role in opioid-related monitoring, the CDC even funded a study in 2005 focused on how payer administrative data could be used for disease surveillance.[187] Payer administrative data track most or all interactions that enrollees have with the healthcare system, mainly for the purposes of UR and utilization management (such as "prior authorization") and claims processing and payment, but also for the purposes of operating disease management programs.[188] Claims data typically include information regarding patient characteristics, primary and secondary diagnosis codes (which identify current and past diagnoses), physician visits, emergency department visits, hospitalizations, and prescription drug orders, including the presence of National Drug Codes, or "NDCs"[189] prescriber information, and pharmacy identifiers. These data are often used to identify a variety of utilization patterns and adverse events, due mainly to their detail and their ability to link together

[185] See generally H. L. Bailit and C. Sennett, "Utilization management as a cost-containment strategy," *Health Care Financ Rev* 1991, no. Suppl (Bailit & Sennett, 1992); S. M. Cadarette and L. Wong, "An Introduction to Health Care Administrative Data," *Can J Hosp Pharm* 68, no. 3 (Cadarette & Wong, 2015); P. T. Tyree, B. K. Lind, and W. E. Lafferty, "Challenges of using medical insurance claims data for utilization analysis," *Am J Med Qual* 21, no. 4 (Tyree et al., 2006).

[186] Parente, "Exploring Ex Ante Regulatory Mechanisms for Detecting Prescription Drug Misuse."

[187] B. Rudolph and R. Davis, "Administrative Data and Disease Surveillance: An Integration Toolkit," in *NAHDO-CDC Cooperative Agreement Project; CDC Assessment Initiative* (Washington, D.C.: The National Association of Health Data Organizations (NAHDO), Rudolph & Davis, 2005).

[188] See generally ibid.

[189] NDCs are the industry standard means of identifying prescription drugs and consist of a unique 10-digit or 11-digit code with 3 segments: the labeler, the product, and the commercial package size.

services provided by multiple providers in multiple settings.[190] These data also support analyses of past medical usage and usage patterns. It is likely that payer administrative data could have initially been used more effectively to identify patients engaging in behavior consistent with misuse and cost-incurring OUD, as several subsequent studies have conducted these types of analyses using payer administrative data.[191] Some have argued that the implementation of *ex ante* regulatory mechanisms utilizing payer administrative data could have been used as a more efficient and effective means of identifying and mitigating improper use patterns, especially when combined with other initiatives such as PDMPs.[192] Further supporting these points is evidence that more recent efforts by payers to monitor and control opioid utilization have been shown to be effective.[193]

[190] See, for example, R. Baron, G. Mick, and M. Serpell, "The relevance of real-world data for the evaluation of neuropathic pain treatments," *Pain Manag* 12, no. 7 (Baron et al., 2022); S. S. Dhruva et al., "Attribution of Adverse Events Following Coronary Stent Placement Identified Using Administrative Claims Data," *J Am Heart Assoc* 9, no. 4 (Dhruva et al., 2020); Y. L. Huang, J. Moon, and J. B. Segal, "A comparison of active adverse event surveillance systems worldwide," *Drug Saf* 37, no. 8 (Huang et al., 2014); M. Kalinich et al., "Prediction of severe immune-related adverse events requiring hospital admission in patients on immune checkpoint inhibitors: study of a population level insurance claims database from the USA," *J Immunother Cancer* 9, no. 3 (Kalinich et al., 2021).

[191] For example, see S. E. Heins et al., "Claims-based measures of prescription opioid utilization: A practical guide for researchers," *Drug Alcohol Depend* 228 (Heins et al., 2021); J. Jayawardhana, A. J. Abraham, and M. Perri, "Opioid Analgesics in Georgia Medicaid: Trends in Potential Inappropriate Prescribing Practices by Demographic Characteristics, 2009–2014," *J Manag Care Spec Pharm* 24, no. 9 (Jayawardhana et al., 2018); Y. Liu et al., "Potential misuse and inappropriate prescription practices involving opioid analgesics," *Am J Manag Care* 19, no. 8 (Liu et al., 2013); J. Logan et al., "Opioid prescribing in emergency departments: the prevalence of potentially inappropriate prescribing and misuse," *Med Care* 51, no. 8 (Logan et al., 2013). Indeed, in recent years there have been specific algorithms developed for this purpose. For example, see K. Rough et al., "Using prescription claims to detect aberrant behaviors with opioids: comparison and validation of 5 algorithms," *Pharmacoepidemiol Drug Saf* 28, no. 1 (Rough et al., 2019); J. W. Sun et al., "Predicting overdose among individuals prescribed opioids using routinely collected healthcare utilization data," *PLoS One* 15, no. 10 (J. W. Sun et al., 2020).

[192] See generally Parente, "Exploring Ex Ante Regulatory Mechanisms for Detecting Prescription Drug Misuse."

[193] For example, see M. C. García et al., "Declines in Opioid Prescribing After a Private Insurer Policy Change—Massachusetts, 2011–2015," *MMWR Morb Mortal Wkly Rep* 65, no. 41 (García et al., 2016); T. Molfenter et al., "The payer's role in addressing the opioid epidemic: It's more than money," *J Subst Abuse Treat* 101 (Molfenter et al., 2019); S. Shen et al., "The implementation of opioid prescribing report cards in Medicaid managed care: a community quality collaborative," *Am J Manag Care* 27, no. 12 (Shen et al., 2021).

The role of third-party payers is inextricably linked to the role of provider accreditation agencies, as accreditation is typically a prerequisite for payer reimbursement. Highly influential healthcare accreditation agencies joined the call for improvement in pain management by tying pain management to accreditation. Accreditation is *per se* voluntary, but in U.S. healthcare markets it is a prerequisite to obtaining reimbursement from payers, including large public payers and commercial payers, and is therefore *de facto* mandatory and considered part of the core healthcare regulatory infrastructure. In 2001, the leading healthcare provider accreditation group "The Joint Commission" (formerly "The Joint Commission on the Accreditation of Healthcare Organizations," or "JCAHO") drafted guidelines and standards for organizations to improve pain management, "as part of a national effort to address the widespread problem of under-assessment and undertreatment of pain."[194] The Joint Commission also began incorporating pain management metrics (based on the same quality assessment scales described above) into its accreditation requirements, which again created additional financial and performance incentives for providers to approach pain treatment aggressively.

Because of the importance of these accreditation requirements, some experts believe that the Joint Commission bears a significant share of responsibility for the over-prescribing of opioids.[195] For example, in a letter to the editors at the *Journal of the American Medical Association* ("JAMA"), Chhabra et al., regarding the role of the Joint Commission, stated "there was no clamor within the health care community for such a regulatory-based approach to pain management," and further emphasized the problems posed by conflicts of interest between the Joint Commission and opioid manufacturers: "Purdue Pharma, the manufacturer of OxyContin, was 1 of 2 drug companies that provided funding for The Joint Commission's pain management educational programs. Purdue also distributed videos and monographs about pain management on The Joint

[194] D.W. Baker, "The Joint Commission's Pain Standards: Origins and Evolution," (Oakbrook Terrace, IL: The Joint Commission, 2017).

[195] See generally D. W. Baker, "History of The Joint Commission's Pain Standards: Lessons for Today's Prescription Opioid Epidemic," *Jama* 317, no. 11 (D.W. Baker, 2017); N. Chhabra and J. B. Leikin, "The Joint Commission and the Opioid Epidemic," ibid. 318, no. 1; R. Hirsch, "The Opioid Epidemic: It's Time to Place Blame Where It Belongs," *Mo Med* 114, no. 2 (Chhabra & Leikin, 2017).

Commission's website."[196] The letter further stated that "We believe that accrediting organizations should not partner with private pharmaceutical companies on issues that appear to be a conflict of interest." Chhabra et al. also point out that "once the opioid epidemic was recognized, The Joint Commission did not take steps to address this problem in a timely manner, as the epidemic has progressed for more than 18 years."[197] This conflict-of-interest problem involving the Joint Commission was also flagged by the Stanford-Lancet Commission on opioids in their report.[198]

4.7 Marketing

The confluence of increased medical need, heightened emphasis on pain management, and the rise of quality assessment significantly increased the demand for pain management treatments, including prescription analgesics like opioids.[199] The impetus for drug manufacturers to not only promptly respond to increases in demand, but to also continually adjust supply based on demand forecasts, is based on normal business practices[200] but also in part on concerns over the potential negative impact of drug shortages; for example, one study noted that "[shortages] not only have large costs to clinicians, hospitals, supply chain participants, patients, and families, but also have an immense impact on patients' lives and quality of life."[201] Sensitivity to supply disruptions and shortages would have been expected to be heightened amidst the pain advocacy efforts in the late 1990s and early 2000s. Thus, given the unequivocal rise in demand for

[196] Chhabra and Leikin, "The Joint Commission and the Opioid Epidemic."

[197] Ibid.

[198] Humphreys et al., "Responding to the opioid crisis in North America and beyond: recommendations of the Stanford-Lancet Commission."

[199] See generally M. Daubresse et al., "Ambulatory diagnosis and treatment of nonmalignant pain in the United States, 2000–2010," *Med Care* 51, no. 10 (Daubresse et al., 2013); A. Stokes et al., "Trends in Prescription Analgesic Use Among Adults With Musculoskeletal Conditions in the United States, 1999–2016," *JAMA Netw Open* 2, no. 12 (Stokes et al., 2019).

[200] See, for example, J. Wechsler, "Rising Demand Drives Drug Shortages," *Pharmaceutical Technology*, no. Dec 8 (Wechsler, 2022). Also see Mehta, *Commercializing Successful Biomedical Technologies: Basic Principles for the Development of Drugs, Diagnostics and Devices.*

[201] M. P. Socal and J. M. Sharfstein, "Drug Shortages-A Study in Complexity," *JAMA Netw Open* 7, no. 4 (Socal & Sharfstein, 2024).

pain management, some proportion of the increase in the supply of prescription opioids was driven by these core fundamentals of demand and supply. In addition to organic increases in demand, for FDA-approved drugs manufacturers are permitted to engage in marketing and promotion of their products, and there is broad evidence that consumers and providers generally respond to such marketing and influence.[202]

In the case of opioids, however, in addition to the expected supply response to rising demand, there were some allegations of opportunistic behavior, with some arguing that manufacturers of opioids saw an opportunity in the rapidly increasing demand for effective and inexpensive pharmacologic treatments for pain, and began aggressively marketing the products to physicians and promoting them to medical societies.[203] Marketing and promotion fed into a provider community eager to adopt novel means by which to manage and control patient pain, bolstered by pain management guidelines and accreditation criteria calling for better pain control and incentive-based payment mechanisms financially rewarding more effective pain management and higher patient satisfaction.[204] This type of "supplier induced demand" aligned with the preponderance of messaging from government agencies, public and private payers, accreditation agencies, and medical societies, all of which were

[202] See generally L. Agha and D. Zeltzer, "Drug Diffusion Through Peer Networks: The Influence of Industry Payments," in *NBER Working Paper No. 26338* (National Bureau of Economic Research, Agha & Zeltzer, 2020); D. Kenkel and A. Mathios, "Promotion to Physicians and Consumers," in *The Economics of the Biopharmaceutical Industry*, ed. P.M. Danzon and S. Nicholson (Oxford, UK: Oxford University Press, Kenkel & Mathios, 2012).

[203] See generally S. E. Hadland, M. S. Krieger, and B. D. L. Marshall, "Industry Payments to Physicians for Opioid Products, 2013–2015," *Am J Public Health* 107, no. 9 (Hadland et al., 2017); S. E. Hadland et al., "Association of Pharmaceutical Industry Marketing of Opioid Products With Mortality From Opioid-Related Overdoses," *JAMA Netw Open* 2, no. 1 (Hadland et al., 2019); A. Alpert et al., "Origins of the Opioid Crisis and its Enduring Impacts," in *NBER Working Paper No. 26500* (National Bureau of Economic Research, Alpert et al., 2019); J. H. Marks, "Lessons from Corporate Influence in the Opioid Epidemic: Toward a Norm of Separation," *J Bioeth Inq* 17, no. 2 (Marks, 2020). Also see S. Spithoff et al., "Drivers of the opioid crisis: An appraisal of financial conflicts of interest in clinical practice guideline panels at the peak of opioid prescribing," *PLoS One* 15, no. 1 (Spithoff et al., 2020). For detailed narrative on this topic, also refer to B. Macy, *Dopesick* (New York, NY: Little, Brown and Company, Macy, 2018).

[204] According to M.D. Sullivan and Ballantyne (2023), "The Sackler's technique was to support the voices that were already out there in pursuit of the goals of the company" (p.50); see Sullivan and Ballantyne, *The Right to Pain Relief and Other Deep Roots of the Opioid Epidemic.*

synergistically fueling the demand side of the market. The confluence of these factors further increased overall demand for opioids and helped shift prescribing patterns from non-pharmacological approaches to pharmacologic approaches to pain management, and from non-opioid to opioid-based treatments.[205] Manufacturers increased production and kept prices relatively low to meet the rising demand, while at the same time actively marketing opioids to physicians and hospitals. The Stanford-Lancet Commission described manufacturer marketing of opioids as the "the most lavishly funded promotion campaign in the history of medicine."[206]

In the product liability cases filed against opioid manufacturers, specific alleged marketing tactics were at issue, including marketing for off-label use, deceptive information regarding the addictive features of opioids (including "misbranding with the intent to defraud or mislead"), deceptively marketing opioids as appropriate for longer-term chronic pain, and concealing information (i.e., failure to warn) of the addictive features of opioids.[207] In addition, as discussed above, some drug manufacturers were creative in the means through which they engaged in provider marketing, in many cases directly funding or subsidizing the work of key medical opinion leaders, medical societies focused on pain management, medical schools and training programs, and the development of pain management guidelines.[208] Some

[205] See generally V. Jairam et al., "Temporal Trends in Opioid Prescribing Patterns Among Oncologists in the Medicare Population," *J Natl Cancer Inst* 113, no. 3 (Jairam et al., 2021); Sullivan and Ballantyne, *The Right to Pain Relief and Other Deep Roots of the Opioid Epidemic*; K. T. Pritchard et al., "Trends in the Use of Opioids vs Nonpharmacologic Treatments in Adults With Pain, 2011–2019," *JAMA Netw Open* 5, no. 11 (Pritchard et al., 2022); Stokes et al., "Trends in Prescription Analgesic Use Among Adults With Musculoskeletal Conditions in the United States, 1999–2016."

[206] Humphreys et al., "Responding to the opioid crisis in North America and beyond: recommendations of the Stanford-Lancet Commission."

[207] See generally R.C. Ausness, "Opioid Lawsuits: Is There Any End in Sight?," *Health Matrix: The Journal of Law Medicine* 33, no. 1 (Ausness, 2023).

[208] For example, refer to HSGAC, "Fueling an Epidemic: Exposing the Financial Ties Between Opioid Manufacturers and Third Party Advocacy Groups."; M. Infeld et al., "Continuing Medical Education and the Marketing of Fentanyl for Breakthrough Pain: Marketing Messages in an Industry-Funded CME Module on Breakthrough Pain," *World Medical & Health Policy* 11, no. 1 (Infeld et al., 2019); D.H. Lin et al., "Financial Conflicts of Interest and the Centers for Disease Control and Prevention's 2016 Guideline for Prescribing Opioids for Chronic Pain," *JAMA Internal Medicine* 177, no. 3 (D.H. Lin et al., 2017); Marks, "Lessons from Corporate Influence in the Opioid Epidemic: Toward a Norm of Separation."; Ausness, "Opioid Lawsuits: Is There Any End in Sight?."

manufacturers also contributed to the political campaigns of elected officials in position to improve access to opioids.[209]

In addition to manufacturers, two related components of the pharmaceutical supply chain were alleged to have contributed to the increase in the supply of opioids: (1) large independent drug distributors, and (2) some advisors and consultants working directly with drug manufacturers. The three largest national distributors of healthcare products control about 90% of the drug distribution market.[210] Large independent wholesale distributors normally maintain relational contracts with manufacturers, and typically assume ownership and control of prescription drug inventory from manufacturers to facilitate market access and distribution nationally.[211] Large national independent distributors were generally aware of sharp increases in opioid orders but are alleged to have failed to disclose some suspicious orders to the DEA and were said to have engaged in some of the same deceptive marketing practices as the manufacturers with which they maintain contracts.[212] Several observers have considered the actions of some manufacturers and distributors as important contributing factors in the growth of opioid prescriptions and sales. In addition to distributors, a large U.S. consulting company was also identified as a defendant, alleged to have contributed to the negative externality and public nuisance via its advisory and consulting role to other potentially

[209] Higham and Horwitz, *American Cartel: Inside the Battle to Bring Down the Opioid Industry*.

[210] KFF, "Follow The Pill: Understanding the U.S. Commercial Pharmaceutical Supply Chain," (Menlo Park, CA: Kaiser Family Foundation, Kff., 2005).

[211] See generally A.W. Mulcahy and V. Kareddy, "Prescription Drug Supply Chains: An Overview of Stakeholders and Relationships," (Santa Monica, CA: RAND Corporation, Mulcahy & Kareddy, 2021); E. Seeley, "The Impact of Pharmaceutical Wholesalers on U. S. Drug Spending," in *Issue Brief* (Commonwealth Fund, Seeley, 2022).

[212] See generally R. L. Haffajee and M. M. Mello, "Drug Companies' Liability for the Opioid Epidemic," *N Engl J Med* 377, no. 24 (2017); O. Dyer, "Drug distributors and Johnson & Johnson will pay $26bn as America's biggest opioid settlement is finalised," *Bmj* 376 (Dyer, 2022); OAG, "AG Yost Announces Ohio's Historic $808 Million Settlement with Opioid Distributors," news release, 2021; J. J. Coleman, "The supply chain of medicinal controlled substances: addressing the Achilles heel of drug diversion," *J Pain Palliat Care Pharmacother* 26, no. 3 (Coleman, 2012); G. H. Jones et al., "The opioid epidemic in the United States-Overview, origins, and potential solutions," *Cancer* 124, no. 22 (Jones et al., 2018).For more information on the role of distributors and the relationships between distributors and manufacturers, refer to Seeley, "The Impact of Pharmaceutical Wholesalers on U.S. Drug Spending."

responsible businesses. In MDL, it was the management consulting firm McKinsey & Company's advising of opioid manufacturers that was alleged to have encouraged manufacturers to be more determined in the marketing and sale of opioids.[213] Based on public documents uncovered through the discovery process in the MDL, the *New York Times* reported that "McKinsey's extensive work with Purdue included advising it to focus on selling lucrative high-dose pills, the records show, even after the drugmaker pleaded guilty in 2007 to federal criminal charges that it had misled doctors and regulators about OxyContin's risks. The firm also told Purdue that it could 'band together' with other opioid makers to head off 'strict treatment' by the Food and Drug Administration."[214] McKinsey was also advising other opioid manufacturers on issues regarding opioid marketing strategies.[215]

4.8 Drug Trafficking

As briefly discussed in Chap. 2, whereas the focus of the opioid MDL and the focus of this book is on the role of *prescription* opioids in the opioid crisis, in specific instances the harms and externalities may not be accurately or precisely attributable to specific sources; mainly, either prescription sources, via the health care system, or illicit sources, via diversion and drug trafficking. Moreover, in the past several years, as deterrence and abatement programs have started taking effect, the problem has shifted to one of primarily illicit opioids, fueled predominantly by various forms of unlawful drug trafficking.[216] Drug trafficking is defined broadly as "... the illegal transporting of or transacting in controlled substances."[217] Under

[213] J. Woodruff, "How a Powerful Corporate Consulting Firm Helped Create the Opioid Epidemic: Interview with Massachusetts Attorney General Maura Healy," (Washington, D. C.: PBS News Hour, Woodruff, 2021).

[214] M. Forsythe and W. Bogdanich, "McKinsey Settles for Nearly $600 Million Over Role in Opioid Crisis," *New York Times* Nov. 5 (Forsythe & Bogdanich, 2021).

[215] C. Hamby and M. Forsythe, "Behind the Scenes, McKinsey Guided Companies at the Center of the Opioid Crisis," ibid.June 29 (Hamby & Forsythe, 2022).

[216] D.A. McGranahan and T.S. Parker, "The Opioid Epidemic: A Geography in Two Phases (Number 287)," in *Economic Research Report* (Washington, D.C.: U.S. Department of Agriculture, Economic Research Service, McGranahan & Parker, 2021).

[217] Legal Information Institute, "Drug Trafficking," (Ithaca, NY: Cornell Law School, Legal Information Institute, 2021).

federal law, Title 21 (§ 841) makes it unlawful for any person to knowingly or intentionally "manufacture, distribute, or dispense, or possess with intent to manufacture, distribute, or dispense, a controlled substance." Thus, the group "drug traffickers" includes not only criminals involved in the business of illicit drug manufacturing and distributing but can also include individuals and patients who knowingly divert controlled substances for non-medical use.

There is ample evidence that illegally trafficked illicit opioids (heroin and fentanyl) have contributed disproportionately to OUD and opioid overdoses, particularly in more recent years as the supply of prescription opioids continues to fall.[218] Recently there has been a substantial increase in the supply of illicit trafficked and smuggled opioids, sourced mainly from Mexico and Canada (via border crossing) and China (via either direct mail or via Canada or Mexico borders).[219] In the years after rates of prescription opioid utilization began to decline, the DEA estimated that Mexico's heroin production grew from 42 metric tons in 2014 to 106 metric tons in 2018, an increase of 152%,[220] as Mexican cartels diversified from cocaine to heroin due to the relatively low production costs associated with heroin, and the fact that cartels could produce it themselves rather than importing from South American countries.[221] Between 2013 and 2017, as sales of prescription opioids were falling precipitously, the volume of illicit opioids seized by law enforcement each year increased 96%,

[218] See generally V. Felbab-Brown, "Fending off fentanyl and hunting down heroin: Controlling opioid supply from Mexico," in *The Opioid Crisis in America: Domestic and International Dimensions* (Washington, D.C.: Brookings Institution, Felbab-Brown, 2020); C. Fleiz et al., "Fentanyl is used in Mexico's northern border: current challenges for drug health policies," *Addiction* 115, no. 4 (2020); N. G. Shah et al., "The influence of living along the U.S.-Mexico border on unintentional drug overdose death, New Mexico (USA), 2005–2009," *Drug Alcohol Depend* 125, no. 1–2 (Shah et al., 2012); USDOJ, "New Mexico High Intensity Drug Trafficking Area," in *Drug Market Analysis 2011* (U.S. Department of Justice, National Drug Intelligence Center, 2011); L. C. Dismukes, "How Did We Get Here? Heroin and Fentanyl Trafficking Trends: A Law Enforcement Perspective," *N C Med J* 79, no. 3 (Dismukes, 2018).

[219] GAO, "Illicit Opioids: While Greater Attention Given to Combating Synthetic Opioids, Agencies Need to Better Assess their Efforts," in *Report to Congressional Requesters* (Washington, D.C.: U.S. Government Accountability Office, GAO., 2018).

[220] USDOJ, "2019 National Drug Threat Assessment (NDTA)," (U.S. Department of Justice, Drug Enforcement Administration, 2019).

[221] For a more detailed discussion of these issues, refer to T. Wainwright, *Narconomics: How to Run a Drug Cartel* (New York, NY: PublicAffairs / Perseus, 2016).

from 579 pounds to 1135 pounds.[222] This trend has continued, with a 2025 study finding that the percentage of fentanyl seizures in pill form increased from 10.3% in 2017 to 49.0% in 2023, with a total of 115.6 million individual fentanyl pills seized in 2023.[223]

Some regions across the country, designated as High Intensity Drug Trafficking Areas ("HIDTAs),[224] have been disproportionately affected by illicit opioids and have been compelled to expand monitoring and enforcement activities.[225] For example, a 2010 DOJ report described the Atlanta HIDTA as follows: "Mexican DTOs [drug trafficking organizations] use the Atlanta HIDTA region as the leading distribution center for powder cocaine, ice methamphetamine, commercial-grade marijuana, and Mexican heroin supplied in the region and many eastern U.S. drug markets."[226] In later years, drug trafficking in the region began to focus more on heroin and synthetic opioids, like fentanyl.[227] In 2011, there were about 5,000,000 heroin seizures in the Atlanta HIDTA, but in 2019 that number had grown to more than 35,000,000.[228] Data from 2020 and 2021 show a decline in heroin seizures, but this was most likely due to rapid increases in the volume of trafficked fentanyl. Fentanyl has had particular appeal to the DTOs for some of the reasons described earlier in this report, including relying on its higher potency to increase the

[222] HSGAC, "Combating the Opioid Epidemic: The Interception of Illicit Opioids by the Border Patrol," (Washington, D.C.: United States Senate: Committee on Homeland Security & Governmental Affairs, HSGAC., 2018).

[223] J. J. Palamar et al., "National and regional trends in fentanyl seizures in the United States, 2017–2023," *Int J Drug Policy* 138 (Palamar et al., 2025).

[224] According to the DEA, "High Intensity Drug Trafficking Areas (HIDTA) program, created by Congress with the Anti-Drug Abuse Act of 1988, provides assistance to Federal, state, local, and tribal law enforcement agencies operating in areas determined to be critical drug-trafficking regions of the United States. This grant program is administered by the Office of National Drug Control Policy (ONDCP)." There are currently 33 regional HIDTAs, covering parts of all 50 states.

[225] See generally EOP, "High Intensity Drug Trafficking Areas Program: 2022 Report to Congress," (Washington, D.C.: Executive Office of the President of the United States, Office of National Drug Control Policy, EOP., 2022).

[226] USDOJ, "Atlanta High Intensity Drug Trafficking Area: Drug Market Analysis 2010," (Washington, D.C.: National Drug Intelligence Center, U.S. Department of Justice, 2010).

[227] NETI, "Atlanta—Carolinas HIDTA 2021 Summary Slides," (Washington, D.C.: The National Emerging Threats Initiative, Neti., 2022).

[228] Ibid.

volume of available product. In the Atlanta HIDTA, fentanyl seizures escalated from trivial amounts in 2015 to nearly 40,000,000 seizures in 2021.[229] The DEA, in its 2024 *National Drug Threat Assessment* report, summarized the escalating problem of illicit opioids, particularly fentanyl, this way: "Synthetic drugs have transformed not only the drug landscape in the United States, with deadly consequences to public health and safety; synthetic drugs have also transformed the criminal landscape in the United States, as the drug cartels who make these drugs reap huge profits from their sale."[230]

Like the delayed response to rising rates of opioid misuse on the part of the FDA and CDC, the DEA and other law enforcement agencies were slow to react to the increase in trafficking of illicit opioids.[231] For example, some have argued that the DEA and other law enforcement agencies were unprepared to fight the onslaught of opioids smuggled into the U.S. from China and Mexico and were slow to adapt to changes in smuggling tactics.[232] In addition, delays in testing for illicit fentanyl masked the increasing role of illicit opioids in OUD cases and OUD attributable deaths and led some observers to incorrectly assume that most cases of OUD were due to prescription opioids.[233] For example, a study of drug-related deaths conducted in Massachusetts found that "of 2,916 decedents with complete toxicology reports, 1,789 (61.4%) had heroin and 1,322 (45.3%) had fentanyl detected in postmortem toxicology reports. Of the 491 (16.8%) decedents with ≥ 1 opioid prescription active on the date of

[229] Ibid.

[230] DEA, "2024 National Drug Threat Assessment," (Washington, D.C.: U.S. Department of Justice, Drug Enforcement Administration, DEA., 2024).

[231] See generally GAO, "Illicit Opioids: While Greater Attention Given to Combating Synthetic Opioids, Agencies Need to Better Assess their Efforts." Also see OIG, "Review of the Drug Enforcement Administration's Regulatory and Enforcement Efforts to Control the Diversion of Opioids."

[232] See, for example, Felbab-Brown, "Fending off fentanyl and hunting down heroin: Controlling opioid supply from Mexico."; "Why America Is Struggling to Stop the Fentanyl Epidemic: The New Geopolitics of Synthetic Opioids," *Foreign Affairs*, no. May 15 (Felbab-Brown, 2023); GAO, "Illicit Opioids: While Greater Attention Given to Combating Synthetic Opioids, Agencies Need to Better Assess their Efforts."

[233] See generally J. O'Donnell et al., "Using death scene and toxicology evidence to define involvement of heroin, pharmaceutical morphine, illicitly manufactured fentanyl and pharmaceutical fentanyl in opioid overdose deaths, 38 states and the District of Columbia, January 2018-December 2019," *Addiction* 117, no. 5 (O'Donnell et al., 2022).

death, prescribed opioids were commonly not detected in toxicology reports."[234] Prescription opioid volume declined precipitously in the past decade, along with rates of misuse attributable to prescription opioids. However, a contemporaneous rise in the role of illicit opioids continued to result in OUD-attributable deaths, mainly due to the increased influx and lethality of illicit opioids.[235]

4.9 Physicians

As noted above, Fig. 4.1 shows all the prescription drug related "effects" of the contributing factors channeling into "physician and health system prescribing." The rationale for structuring the diagram and the argument this way is to emphasize that the only pathway to increased supply of *prescription* opioids is through the direct actions of licensed physicians. As such, physicians have played an unusually influential and prominent role in the increase in prescription opioids, and one that merits separate discussion in the context of contributing factors. In a multivariable study of factors associated with geographic variation in prescription opioid, McDonald et al. found that "The availability of active physicians in a county is by far the strongest correlate of opioid amounts prescribed."[236] Needless to say, suggesting that physicians play a major role in the prescribing of any drug is not particularly novel or controversial. As a condition of licensure, practicing physicians are professionally and legally responsible for the safety and quality of care provided to their patients. For example, in the American Medical Association's ("AMA") "Declaration of Professional Responsibility" the first obligation is to "treat the sick and injured with competence and compassion and without prejudice," and to employ their "knowledge and skills when needed, though doing so may put us at risk."[237] It follows that,

[234] A. Y. Walley et al., "The Contribution of Prescribed and Illicit Opioids to Fatal Overdoses in Massachusetts, 2013–2015," *Public Health Rep* 134, no. 6 (Walley et al., 2019).

[235] Another way to approach these contemporaneous (and potentially offsetting) effects is via data modelling; for an example of such, see T. Y. Lim et al., "Modeling the evolution of the US opioid crisis for national policy development," *Proc Natl Acad Sci U S A* 119, no. 23 (Lim et al., 2022).

[236] McDonald, Carlson, and Izrael, "Geographic variation in opioid prescribing in the U.S."

[237] https://www.ama-assn.org/delivering-care/public-health/ama-declaration-professional-responsibility

during the years when greater emphasis was placed on the importance of treating pain, physicians increased their prescribing of opioids.

The medical profession is indirectly regulated by some of the governmental agencies described above, such as the DEA, but for practical purposes physicians are largely "self-regulated." An essay in the *Ethics Journal of the American Medical Association* described this self-regulation as follows: "In return for a physician's commitment to altruistic service, a guarantee of professional competence, the demonstration of morality and integrity in their activities, and their agreement to address issues of social concern, society grants to both individual physicians and the profession considerable autonomy in practice, status in the community, financial rewards, and the privilege of self-regulation."[238] In so doing, society "delegated some of its own traditional powers to the profession, with regulation being one of the most important."[239] In the medical profession, the mechanisms of self-regulation consist mainly of accreditation of medical schools and training programs, establishing medical school and training program curriculum, managing and self-enforcing the entire licensure process, and controlling most additional medical certifications. Self-regulation implies individual responsibility: "Integral to effective self-regulation is the responsibility and obligation to ensure that these standards are met and to remediate or discipline unethical, immoral, or incompetent practices."[240] As the palliative care and patient-centered care movements grew, the professional responsibilities and ethical obligations of physicians expanded to include pain management, which was reinforced by medical society guidelines and by case law regarding the compulsory provision of palliative treatments and end-of-life care.[241] According to bioethicist Ben Rich, one of the primary goals of the palliative care movement was to "...

[238] S. R. Cruess and R. L. Cruess, "The medical profession and self-regulation: a current challenge," *Virtual Mentor* 7, no. 4 (Cruess & Cruess, 2005). (p.1)

[239] Ibid.

[240] Ibid.

[241] See generally Sullivan and Ballantyne, *The Right to Pain Relief and Other Deep Roots of the Opioid Epidemic*; M. Crowley-Matoka et al., "Problems of quality and equity in pain management: exploring the role of biomedical culture," *Pain Med* 10, no. 7 (Crowley-Matoka et al., 2009); R. Learch and J. Cumberledge, "Physicians' responsibility to understand patients' pain," *Virtual Mentor* 15, no. 5 (Learch & Cumberledge, 2013).

persuade the medical community that its duty to relieve pain and suffering is not only an ethical one but is enshrined in law."[242]

As shown in Fig 4.1, physicians and the organizations in which they practice are the sole juncture in the opioid supply chain capable of generating and adding to the supply of prescription opioids, via the issuance of legal prescriptions. It is reasonable to assume that licensed and practicing physicians, based on their "knowledge and skills," would have been at least generally knowledgeable about the clinical tradeoffs associated with opioid-based analgesics—a legal principle commonly referred to as "learned intermediary doctrine."[243] Even if some physicians were not initially aware of the risks, the medical community routinely disseminates information and communicates observations to each other via meetings, conferences, state medical boards, specialty medical societies, and published medical literature.[244] The widely used medical literature indexing database "PubMed" identifies about 400 articles published per year with keywords "opioid abuse" from 1973 to 2000, with the number increasing sharply thereafter (Fig. 4.3). In 2016 alone, when greater awareness of opioid-related problems was beginning to gain traction in the U.S., there were approximately 2,000 peer-reviewed articles indexed in PubMed containing the keywords "opioid abuse."

Given this relatively steep growth in knowledge dissemination regarding clinical attributes and risks of opioid-based treatments, during this time it would be reasonable to assume that the medical community, including provider groups, health systems, and specialty societies, were at least generally aware of the risks and tradeoffs associated with opioid use and misuse yet continued to prescribe opioids.[245] For example, in Gray et

[242] B. A. Rich, "Physicians' legal duty to relieve suffering," *West J Med* 175, no. 3 (Rich, 2001).

[243] See generally R. G. Thornton, "The learned intermediary doctrine and its effects on prescribing physicians," *Proc (Bayl Univ Med Cent)* 16, no. 3 (Thornton, 2003).

[244] For example, see Á Lublóy, "Factors affecting the uptake of new medicines: a systematic literature review," *BMC Health Serv Res* 14 (Lublóy, 2014); AHRQ, "Communication and Dissemination Strategies To Facilitate the Use of Health and Health Care Evidence (Contract No. 290–2007-10,056-I #7 from AHRQ)," (Washington, D.C.: Agency for Healthcare Research and Quality, U.S. Department of Health and Human Services, AHRQ, 2012).

[245] See generally A. N. Romman et al., "Opioid Prescribing to Medicare Part D Enrollees, 2013–2017: Shifting Responsibility to Pain Management Providers," *Pain Med* 21, no. 7 (Romman et al., 2020); B.M. Gray et al., "Clinical Knowledge and Trends in Physicians'

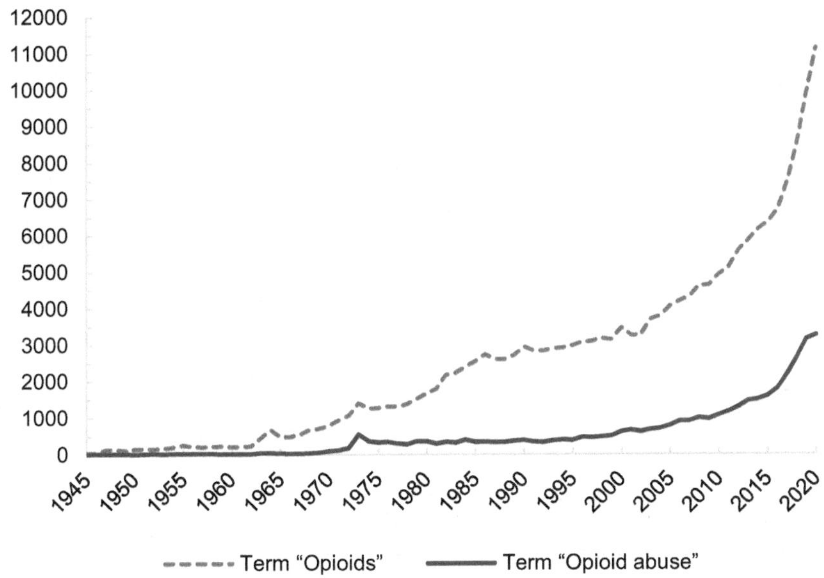

Fig. 4.3 Cumulative number of publications indexed on PubMed related to opioids and opioid abuse, 1945–2020

al., study results showed that physicians with knowledge of opioid risks had prescribing patterns similar to those with less knowledge of opioid risks, suggesting that physicians with knowledge of risk were to some extent essentially "discounting" the importance of that risk.[246] It should be noted that, throughout most of the period of opioid supply growth, a wide variety of FDA approved non-opioid treatments for pain were available, including nonsteroidal anti-inflammatory drugs ("NSAIDs"), antidepressants, anticonvulsants (e.g., gabapentin), capsaicin, sodium channel blockers, alpha-2 adrenoreceptor agonists (e.g., clonidine), and cannabinoids, suggesting that it would be difficult for physicians to have argued that they lacked suitable pharmacologic alternatives to opioids during this

Prescribing of Opioids for New Onset Back Pain, 2009–2017," *JAMA Network Open* 4, no. 7 (Gray et al., 2021).

[246] "Clinical Knowledge and Trends in Physicians' Prescribing of Opioids for New Onset Back Pain, 2009–2017."

time.[247] For more advanced pain, physicians also had available several interventional pain therapies, such as epidural steroid injections, radiofrequency ablation ("RFA") and spinal cord stimulators.[248] In some cases, non-pharmacologic treatments, such as manual therapies (e.g., chiropractic manipulation), acupuncture, and cognitive behavioral therapy, can also effectively manage pain.[249] Knowledge on the part of opioid prescribing physicians regarding risk-benefit tradeoffs was also a factor in several criminal cases filed against high volume prescribers.[250] Providing some additional counterfactual evidence of the influence of published medical literature and practice guidelines, prescribing patterns later moved away from opioid-based treatments when a growing volume of published studies and practice guidelines began incorporating additional language cautioning physicians on potential for misuse, implying that in the case of pain management physicians are generally receptive to changes in clinical practice standards.[251]

Despite the likelihood of physician exposure to information regarding the risks of opioids, physician prescribing patterns were clearly causative of the growth in opioid supply in the U.S., especially the patterns of

[247] NASEM, *Pain Management and the Opioid Epidemic: Balancing Societal and Indidivual Benefits and Risks of Prescription Opioid Use.*

[248] See, for example, E. Biel et al., "The Application of Radiofrequency Ablation in Acute and Chronic Pain Management," *Aana j* 92, no. 3 (Biel et al., 2024); N. Strand et al., "Advances in Pain Medicine: a Review of New Technologies," *Curr Pain Headache Rep* 26, no. 8 (Strand et al., 2022); O. Viswanath et al., "Evolving Spinal Cord Stimulation Technologies and Clinical Implications in Chronic Pain Management," ibid. 23, no. 6 (Viswanath et al., 2019).

[249] AC Skelly et al., "Noninvasive Nonpharmacological Treatment for Chronic Pain: A Systematic Review Update," in *Comparative Effectiveness Review, No. 227* (Rockville, MD: Agency for Healthcare Research and Quality (AHRQ), Skelly et al., 2020); NASEM, *Pain Management and the Opioid Epidemic: Balancing Societal and Indidivual Benefits and Risks of Prescription Opioid Use.*

[250] See generally J. B. Berman and G. Li, "Characteristics of criminal cases against physicians charged with opioid-related offenses reported in the US news media, 1995–2019," *Inj Epidemiol* 7, no. 1 (Berman & Li, 2020); C. S. Davis and D. H. Carr, "Self-regulating profession? Administrative discipline of "pill mill" physicians in Florida," *Subst Abus* 38, no. 3 (Davis & Carr, 2017).

[251] See generally Gray et al., "Clinical Knowledge and Trends in Physicians' Prescribing of Opioids for New Onset Back Pain, 2009–2017."; Goldstick et al., "Changes in Initial Opioid Prescribing Practices After the 2016 Release of the CDC Guideline for Prescribing Opioids for Chronic Pain."

physicians described as "high volume prescribers."[252] According to a study by Kiang et al. based on national prescribing data, "In 2017, the top 1% of providers accounted for 49% of all opioid doses and 27% of all opioid prescriptions. In absolute terms, the top 1% of providers prescribed an average of 748,000 MMEs [or] nearly 1,000 times more than the middle 1%."[253] High volume prescribers also appeared to be consistent in their practice patterns, as more than 50% of providers in the upper 1% in one year were also in the upper 1% in earlier years. Similar patterns have been observed at the state level. For example, Kim et al. found that in Oregon the upper 10% of opioid users accounted for 83% of utilization, and similarly the upper 10% of opioid prescribers accounted for 81% of the opioid dosages prescribed.[254] Physicians who are more likely to prescribe opioids improperly are more likely to be male, over age 40, non-board certified, and operating in small private practices.[255] One legal researcher described the role of physicians this way: "the medical community deserves a fair dose of the blame for what has happened. I do not mean venal operators of pill mills or other bad apples among health care professionals; instead, I have in mind the far larger number of well-intentioned physicians who have allowed themselves to get duped too easily and then found themselves far out of their depths."[256] In other words, many believed that the crisis could not be attributable solely to "bad apple" pill mills, but rather a failure of the whole orchard.

The critical role of prescribing physicians in the growth in the supply of prescription opioids also has implications for the role of manufacturers. Even if manufacturers failed to sufficiently warn of opioid adverse events, it appears that the typical practicing physician would have been exposed to

[252] W. G. LeBrett et al., "High Opioid Prescribing Profiles Among Gastroenterologists: A Nationwide Analysis," *Clin Gastroenterol Hepatol* (LeBrett et al., 2021); N. Nataraj et al., "Identifying opioid prescribing patterns for high-volume prescribers via cluster analysis," *Drug Alcohol Depend* 197 (Nataraj et al., 2019).

[253] M. V. Kiang et al., "Opioid prescribing patterns among medical providers in the United States, 2003–17: retrospective, observational study," *Bmj* 368 (Kiang et al., 2020).

[254] H. Kim et al., "The Concentration of Opioid Prescriptions by Providers and Among Patients in the Oregon Medicaid Program," *Psychiatr Serv* 67, no. 4 (Kim et al., 2016).

[255] J. M. DuBois et al., "A Mixed-Method Analysis of Reports on 100 Cases of Improper Prescribing of Controlled Substances," *J Drug Issues* 46, no. 4 (DuBois et al., 2016).

[256] Noah, "Federal Regulatory Responses to the Prescription Opioid Crisis: Too Little, Too Late?."

counterbalancing messaging regarding opioid adverse events, from the usual sources of medical information and from the continuing medical education ("CME") required to maintain licensure. This is likely among the main reasons why many physicians themselves have admitted fault in over-prescribing opioids.[257] As one physician described it, "any medical professional who claims that whatever errors he or she made was because of what these [manufacturer] representatives told them probably shouldn't be practicing medicine and certainly not prescribing medications."[258] The same physician went on to make the point that "If we accept the argument that these doctors were misled, then it must be asked how someone who spent 4 years in medical school and at least an additional 3 years in postgraduate training could be so ignorant about opioids."[259] The popular physician commentator Atul Gawande went a step further, declaring in a *Vox* interview "We as a profession have caused an epidemic [. . .]. The cause in the opioid epidemic starts with getting a prescription of opioids from physicians [. . .]. We started it."[260] In the interview, Gawande said it was not the manufacturer representatives who convinced physicians to prescribe more opioids, but rather "it was really out of the movement that said [. . .] that we did not treat pain. That we left people in terrible pain and suffering, and it was a kind of inhumanity that I thought was unacceptable."[261] In the last sentence, Gawande is clearly referring to the important role of the "pain as the fifth vital sign" and the palliative care movement in the growth in opioid prescribing, a concept explored earlier in this chapter in the context of medical need. These arguments are not

[257] See generally S. Chouinard, A. Prasad, and R. Brown, "Survey Assessing Medical Student and Physician Knowledge and Attitudes Regarding the Opioid Crisis," *Wmj* 117, no. 1 (Chouinard et al., 2018); K. Theisen et al., "The United States opioid epidemic: a review of the surgeon's contribution to it and health policy initiatives," *BJU Int* 122, no. 5 (Theisen et al., 2018); Sullivan and Ballantyne, *The Right to Pain Relief and Other Deep Roots of the Opioid Epidemic.*

[258] S.A. King, "The Opioid Epidemic: Who Is to Blame?," *Psychiatric Times* 35, no. 6 (King, 2018).

[259] Ibid.

[260] S. Kliff, ""We started it": Atul Gawande on doctors' role in the opioid epidemic," (Vox Media, Kliff, 2017).

[261] Ibid.

lost on the American public, more than a third of whom believe that physician prescribing was the main driver of the opioid crisis.[262]

4.10 Hospitals & Heath Systems

It is also important to note that physician prescribing of opioids, when combined with the incentives associated with quality ratings employed by accreditation agencies and payers, resulted in health care organizations, such as medical groups, hospitals, and health systems, directly adopting and embracing pain management guidelines and encouraging member physicians to be more aggressive in their approach to pain management, including the use of opioid-based treatments.[263] The term "health system" generally refers to providers with some degree of vertical integration (i.e., the combing of "upstream" and "downstream" inputs and services). These can be community hospitals with affiliated outpatient feeders, larger health systems with multiple hospitals and outpatient feeders, and integrated delivery networks ("IDNs") which provide the full continuum of services and are able to underwrite some degree of financial risk. In some cases, IDNs may also include entities classified as Accountable Care Organizations ("ACOs"), which are organizations designed to improve coordination and efficiency throughout the continuum of care, including prevention, diagnosis, treatment, and disease management.[264] Health systems directly dispense more than 25% of U.S. prescription drugs.[265] Though health system opioid dispensing rates have declined proportional

[262] D. Scott, "1 in 3 Americans blame doctors for national opioid epidemic, STAT-Harvard poll finds," *STAT* March 17 (Scott, 2016).

[263] See, for example, O. Mazurenko et al., "Clinical perspectives on hospitals' role in the opioid epidemic," *BMC Health Serv Res* 20, no. 1 (Mazurenko et al., 2020).

[264] See generally E. A. Blackstone and J. P. Fuhr, Jr., "The Economics of Medicare Accountable Care Organizations," *Am Health Drug Benefits* 9, no. 1 (Blackstone & Fuhr, 2016); S. M. Siddique and S. J. Mehta, "Market Evaluation: Finances, Bundled Payments, and Accountable Care Organizations," *Anesthesiol Clin* 35, no. 4 (Siddique & Mehta, 2017); M. Wilson et al., "The impacts of accountable care organizations on patient experience, health outcomes and costs: a rapid review," *J Health Serv Res Policy* 25, no. 2 (Wilson et al., 2020).

[265] E. M. Tichy et al., "National trends in prescription drug expenditures and projections for 2020," *Am J Health Syst Pharm* 77, no. 15 (2020).

to overall national rates, from 2015 to 2019 health systems in the U.S. dispensed 6.55 billion units of opioids.[266]

As discussed in the context of medical need and coverage by third-party payers, the shift to outpatient care was a change that occurred contemporaneously with changes in payment mechanism incentives intended to reduce inpatient hospital length of stay. Fixed prospectively determined payments, such as those based on diagnosis-related groups ("DRGs") and other forms of bundled payments for inpatient care, provide financial incentives for shorter lengths of stay and earlier discharge,[267] and early discharge implies that patients are more likely to be discharged before pain has subsided. The incidence of pain among patients at time of hospital discharge is reported to be nearly 50%.[268] Thus, fixed payments and shorter lengths of stay offer added incentives to provide or prescribe pain medication at discharge. Similarly, the discussions above regarding value-based reimbursement are also relevant to incentives faced by hospitals and health systems. Most VBR arrangements impose financial penalties for readmissions within a 30-day period post-discharge. However, patients with poorly controlled pain are significantly more likely to be readmitted to the hospital within that 30-day period, thereby increasing incentives for providers to assure that patients have sufficient supplies of pain medications upon discharge.[269] The combination of substantial dispensing rates and financial incentives for earlier discharge and readmission avoidance has resulted in clinicians themselves faulting hospitals and health systems for contributing to the increase in opioid supply. For example, in a survey of hospital-based clinicians, Mazurenko et al. found that "the vast majority of

[266] T. Khouja et al., "Opioid Prescribing in United States Health Systems, 2015 to 2019," *Value Health* 24, no. 9 (2021).

[267] See generally A. Cook and S. Averett, "Do hospitals respond to changing incentive structures? Evidence from Medicare's 2007 DRG restructuring," *J Health Econ* 73 (Cook & Averett, 2020); C. A. Yee, S. D. Pizer, and A. Frakt, "Medicare's Bundled Payment Initiatives for Hospital-Initiated Episodes: Evidence and Evolution," *Milbank Q* 98, no. 3 (Yee et al., 2020).

[268] L. Y. Lin, T. C. Hung, and Y. H. Lai, "Pain control and related factors in hospitalized patients," *Medicine (Baltimore)* 100, no. 30 (L. Y. Lin et al., 2021).

[269] See, for example, see T. Hernandez-Boussard et al., "The Fifth Vital Sign: Postoperative Pain Predicts 30-day Readmissions and Subsequent Emergency Department Visits," *Ann Surg* 266, no. 3 (Hernandez-Boussard et al., 2017); I. Hong et al., "Association of Pain on Hospital Discharge with the Risk of 30-Day Readmission in Patients with Total Hip and Knee Replacement," *J Arthroplasty* 35, no. 12 (I. Hong et al., 2020).

clinicians believed hospitals are contributing to the opioid epidemic."[270] Surveyed clinicians cited several reasons, including the use of opioids to facilitate earlier discharge. In addition, in some cases larger hospitals and health systems were the recipients of grants and other payments directly from manufacturers and distributors marketing opioids.[271]

4.11 Retail Pharmacies

After a physician has prescribed a medication for treatment, the prescription is typically filled by a pharmacy, usually by a retail pharmacy but in some cases by other types of pharmacies, such as in-hospital pharmacies, pharmacies located within physician clinics, or specialty pharmacies. The opioid MDL has predominantly focused on the role of retail pharmacies, mainly the large chains but also including some other types of pharmacies. The nominal rationale for the inclusion of pharmacies is complicated because retail pharmacies, by virtue of their role in the supply chain, cannot independently or directly increase or influence the supply of opioids;[272] instead, they can only dispense what has already been prescribed legally by licensed physicians. However, pharmacies are alleged in the MDL to have contributed to opioid use indirectly by way of insufficient monitoring in their presumed "gatekeeper" capacity. According to the MDL public document depository maintained by the University of California San Francisco, plaintiffs have alleged that some of the larger national retail pharmacies have, in some instances, not consistently followed DEA guidelines on drug dispensing, neglected to conduct proper screening or report suspicious prescriptions to the DEA, or neglected to "follow a plan to prevent the illegal diversion of drugs."[273]

[270] Mazurenko et al., "Clinical perspectives on hospitals' role in the opioid epidemic."

[271] See generally T. S. Anderson et al., "Financial Payments to Teaching Hospitals by Companies Marketing Opioids," *J Gen Intern Med* 35, no. 10 (Anderson et al., 2020).

[272] The economic rationale for this is that retail pharmacies have no ability to control the production or market supply of opioids, have no ability to influence physician prescribing of opioids, and have no ability to otherwise "induce" demand for opioids. The implication of this is that retail pharmacies are not and have not been "active participants" in the market supply of opioids.

[273] L. Kurtzman, "New Industry Documents Highlight Role of Pharmacies in Driving Opioid Epidemic," in *UCSF Research Summary* (San Francisco, CA: University of California San Francisco, Kurtzman, 2022).

In some cases, some smaller, independent pharmacies engaged in more egregious activities, where relationships with area physicians were leveraged to increase the number of opioid prescriptions and other drugs (i.e., commonly referred to as "pill mills").[274] Apart from the isolated "pill mill" type cases, pharmacies (and pharmacists) face a number of important challenges in mitigating the volume of prescription opioids. Unlike providers and payers, pharmacies lack patient medical record data and other forms of more detailed clinical data for established customers, and lack virtually any kind of clinical data for new customers.[275] Furthermore, while pharmacists are accustomed to questioning the authenticity of issued prescriptions, they are not generally accustomed to questioning the medical appropriateness of prescriptions, and in surveys have expressed concerns over second-guessing clinical decisions by physicians and possibly overstepping their scope of practice.[276]

4.12 Patient Misuse

Any discussion of supply-side factors in the increase of opioid supply must also address the demand-pull role of consumers; specifically, the role of patients and other individuals in actively seeking opioids with the intent of misuse. This is to be distinguished from the traditional sources of demand for medical care services, discussed earlier in the chapter. Here the term "patients" is used broadly to refer to individuals who meet any of the following criteria: (1) those prescribed opioids and subsequently misused them or knowingly diverted opioids for non-medical uses; (2) those who unlawfully obtained prescription opioids from others (i.e., via diversion or theft); and (3) those who obtained non-prescription illicit opioids from sellers, including drug traffickers or any entity involved in the sale or distribution of illicit drugs. In each of these

[274] For example, refer to K. K. Rigg, S. J. March, and J. A. Inciardi, "Prescription Drug Abuse & Diversion: Role of the Pain Clinic," *J Drug Issues* 40, no. 3 (Rigg et al., 2010); A. Kennedy-Hendricks et al., "Opioid Overdose Deaths and Florida's Crackdown on Pill Mills," *Am J Public Health* 106, no. 2 (Kennedy-Hendricks et al., 2016).

[275] See generally P. Bach and D. Hartung, "Leveraging the role of community pharmacists in the prevention, surveillance, and treatment of opioid use disorders," *Addict Sci Clin Pract* 14, no. 1 (Bach & Hartung, 2019).

[276] See generally D. M. Hartung et al., "Pharmacists' Role in Opioid Safety: A Focus Group Investigation," *Pain Med* 19, no. 9 (Hartung et al., 2018).

scenarios, individuals *de facto* become opioid misusers. Individuals who knowingly misuse opioids or facilitate misuse among others violate laws regarding proper use of prescription medications. Several federal laws apply to these types of cases, including "Obtaining Controlled Substances by Misrepresentation, Fraud, etc." [21 USC § 843(a)(3)], "Use of a Communication Facility to Facilitate Drug Felony" [21 USC § 843(b)], and "Simple Possession" [21 USC § 844]. The first two offenses are serious and come with a maximum four-year sentence. In addition, patients receiving controlled substances are often asked by provider organizations to sign contracts regarding responsible use of those prescription drugs.[277]

As discussed in Chap. 3, individuals are more likely to be materially involved in the diversion of opioids compared to other types of prescription drugs, including behaviors such as intentionally seeking prescriptions from doctors and hospital emergency departments for non-medical use, or improperly obtaining opioids from family and friends. One study showed that 34% of patients prescribed opioids actively engaged in diverting unused prescription drugs to others.[278] Related to diversion, some individuals also actively engage in "drug-seeking" behavior, whereby they seek to obtain prescriptions from multiple providers (sometimes referred to as "doctor shopping") or obtain prescriptions from the healthcare system fraudulently, based on feigned symptoms.[279] An OIG report, for example,

[277] In studies of medication adherence and proper use (and misuse) patient responsibility is often identified as a critical element. This can be seen in the literature on "opioid contracts." See generally J. Hariharan, G. C. Lamb, and J. M. Neuner, "Long-term opioid contract use for chronic pain management in primary care practice. A five year experience," *J Gen Intern Med* 22, no. 4 (Hariharan et al., 2007); J. V. Pergolizzi et al., "A multicentre evaluation of an opioid patient-provider agreement," *Postgrad Med J* 93, no. 1104 (J. V. Pergolizzi et al., 2017); L. Svirsky, "Opioid Treatment Agreements and Patient Accountability," *Hastings Cent Rep* 51, no. 4 (2021).

[278] E. T. Lewis, M. A. Cucciare, and J. A. Trafton, "What do patients do with unused opioid medications?," *Clin J Pain* 30, no. 8 (Lewis et al., 2014).

[279] See generally C. A. Grover et al., "How Frequently are "Classic" Drug-Seeking Behaviors Used by Drug-Seeking Patients in the Emergency Department?," *West J Emerg Med* 13, no. 5 (Grover et al., 2012); G. R. Hansen, "The drug-seeking patient in the emergency room," *Emerg Med Clin North Am* 23, no. 2 (Hansen, 2005); L. P. Longo et al., "Addiction: part II. Identification and management of the drug-seeking patient," *Am Fam Physician* 61, no. 8 (Longo et al., 2000); R. W. Pretorius and G. M. Zurick, "A systematic approach to identifying drug-seeking patients," *Fam Pract Manag* 15, no. 4 (Pretorius & Zurick, 2008); R. B. Vukmir, "Drug seeking behavior," *Am J Drug Alcohol*

found clear evidence of doctor shopping among Medicare Part D enrollees, identifying more than 22,000 individuals exhibiting definitive doctor shopping behavior.[280] Again, regardless of diversion method, individuals knowingly diverting prescription drugs or seeking them for non-medical use is unlawful and has contributed to the supply of opioids available for non-medical use.

4.13 Interrelated Factors

Several of these contributing factors are interrelated in important ways. The curved arrows on either side of the contributing factor column of Fig. 4.1 show important interrelatedness among contributing factors. Regulatory approval paved the way for opioid utilization. Socioeconomic factors can increase mental and physical stress and the prevalence of SUDs and can also worsen health and create demand for additional health care. At the same time, socioeconomic factors such as unemployment, job displacement, and lower per capita income can create a fertile environment for drug traffickers and other illegal behavior.[281] Changes in demand and medical need formed the nominal medical basis for some of the pain control advocacy on the part of state and federal government and medical professional societies. Medical need also formed some of the basis for public and private insurers paying for opioid prescriptions. Public policy also supported initiatives on the part of medical societies and helped support and encourage the use of quality ratings generally, and the inclusion of pain measures in quality ratings. Public policy and medical advocacy also influenced payers, encouraging them to offer generous coverage for opioids and other pain treatments as part of the palliative care movement. Medical advocacy groups also directly supported the use of pain measures as critical elements in provider quality rating scales. Marketing by

Abuse 30, no. 3 (Vukmir, 2004); F. Weiss et al., "Compulsive drug-seeking behavior and relapse. Neuroadaptation, stress, and conditioning factors," *Ann N Y Acad Sci* 937 (Weiss et al., 2001).

[280] OIG, "Opioids in Medicare Part D: Concerns about Extreme Use and Questionable Prescribing."

[281] Refer to previously cited Carpenter et al. Carpenter, McClellan, and Rees, "Economic conditions, illicit drug use, and substance use disorders in the United States." Also see J. Arkes, "Recessions and the participation of youth in the selling and use of illicit drugs," *Int J Drug Policy* 22, no. 5 (Arkes, 2011).

manufacturers likely increased demand for opioids, insofar as opioid marketing resulted in effects similar to other types of marketing.

4.14 Supply & Utilization

The lower part of Fig. 4.1 shows the relationships between the seven contributing factors and increases in the supply of prescription and non-prescription opioids, noting that the only sources of growth in *non-prescription* opioids are via drug trafficking and diversion. The period corresponding to the effects of the contributing factors on increases in opioid prescribing is approximately the late 1990s through about 2010–2011, which is the period bounded by FDA approval of opioids and the beginning of the decline in the rate of opioid prescriptions, as shown in Fig. 3.1. The lower portion of Fig. 4.1 has four important implications. First, the first six contributing factors are similar in that they each contribute to an increase in *physician prescribing*, which then in turn contributes to an increase in the supply of prescription opioids. Second, the seventh contributing factor, drug tracking, feeds exclusively into an increase in the supply of *non-prescription* illicit opioids. Third, the supply of non-prescription opioids is also contributed to via illegal diversion of prescription drugs, as discussed above in the context of patient behavior as a contributing factor. A prescription drug that is diverted becomes a non-prescription drug. Fourth, the total supply of opioids in the U.S. is the sum of prescription opioids, sourced by the healthcare system, and non-prescription illicit opioids, sourced by a mix of diversion and drug trafficking. These "feeders" into total opioid supply are very important because, in the opioid MDL, the harms and externalities are focused on OUD, without regard to OUD attributable to the healthcare system versus illicit sources.

4.15 Multivariable Analyses

As discussed earlier in this chapter, an important approach to the determination of causation is the use of multivariable regression, whereby the outcome of interest (which in this case could be opioid supply or OUD) is statistically modelled as a function of hypothesized effects; for example, the seven factors discussed in this chapter. Earlier in the chapter the concept of geographic variation was discussed in the context of demand for medical care. Models explaining geographic variation can also shed light on causation. Geographic variation in opioid prescribing rates has been found to be substantial. For example, using the CDC prescribing data based on the IQVIA Xponent database from 2006 to 2017, Scheiber et al. observed two to three-fold geographic differences in opioid prescribing rates.[282] An important empirical inquiry is to explore the extent to which this observed variation is driven by the contributing factors described in this chapter. In the absence of data constraints, one approach to this question would be to specify a regression model with opioid supply as the dependent variable and include as explanatory variables a set of measures that capture some aspect of the effects of each contributing factor. As an illustration, we could model the change in opioid supply (Δy) as a function of two hypothesized causal factors, x_1 and x_2, to determine the relative importance of each causal factor, using regression analysis to estimate the equation $\Delta y = \alpha + \beta_1 x_1 + \beta_2 x_2 + \varepsilon$, where the model coefficients (β_1 and β_2) inform the relative importance of each factor.[283] Unfortunately, in the case of opioid supply, such data does not exist in an analytically convenient or practical format. For example, the magnitude of the role of the FDA in the change in opioid supply is difficult to estimate because we would need to model a counterfactual of "no FDA approval," which is a non-existent outcome in the years that opioids have been on the market; that is, a "before and after" model would not resolve this issue, as there was no opioid-related role for the FDA until opioids were approved. Regarding the role of the DEA, the agency explicitly determined the available supply of opioids through its enforcement of production quotas, which makes it difficult to model an accurate marginal DEA effect because, at least in theory, the DEA effect would dominate all other explanatory variables in any opioid supply model. Public policy and medical advocacy are also problematic to assess because these policies did not vary meaningfully by state or county, so at best any temporal changes in these policies, to the extent that such changes can be accurately measured, would affect all states and counties in the U.S. similarly.

Though these types of data constraints may limit the empirical assessment of some of the variables described in this chapter, it is possible to

[282] L. Z. Schieber et al., "Trends and Patterns of Geographic Variation in Opioid Prescribing Practices by State, United States, 2006–2017," *JAMA Netw Open* 2, no. 3 (Schieber et al., 2019).

[283] This would require an added step consisting of some version of a "relative importance analysis" using the data from the regression analysis (for example, "standardizing" the β coefficients so that they each are measured on the same scale).

measure the impact of some of the other variables. In particular, multivariable regression models can be specified to include observable demand factors like diagnoses, demographics, and socioeconomic status, and observable supply factors, like physicians per capita. For example, in a study based on a large sample of workers compensation claims from 2002 to 2003, Webster et al. measured the percent of claimants with at least one "early" opioid prescription, defined as one or more prescriptions within the first 15 days post-surgery.[284] The authors found a remarkably high level of variation in opioid prescription rates per claimant per state, from a rate of only 5.7% in Massachusetts to 52.9% in South Carolina, with nearly 80% of the variation explained by state-level household income inequality, number of physicians per capita, and a workers compensation "cost containment effort score" which measured the extent to which workers compensation plans implemented cost-control programs and incentives, similar to VBR. Individual factors, such as pain severity, also explained a small but significant proportion of the variation. Using a different database of commercial payer claims from a later period (2017–2018), Zhao et al. was able to develop a regression model that explained a similar proportion (80%) of the variation in prescription rates, with independent variables capturing demographics, levels of chronic and acute pain, and use of adjuvant analgesics.[285] Finally, the regression model developed by McDonald et al., which was discussed briefly earlier in the chapter, analyzed county-level pharmacy records for 135 million opioid prescriptions from 2008.[286] The authors found that the volume of prescription opioids was positively associated with population, poverty status, insurance status, and the number of active physicians and surgeons in the county, with the model overall explaining 33% of the variation in opioid prescribing. In sum, studies of geographic variation in opioid prescribing in which measures of demographics, socioeconomics, and physician supply are included as independent control variables appear to be able to explain between 33% and 80% of the variation in opioid prescribing, depending on model specification and data sources. Given that Badinski et al. found that 33.3% of variation in physician practice patterns

[284] Webster et al., "Geographic variation in opioid prescribing for acute, work-related, low back pain and associated factors: a multilevel analysis."

[285] D. Zhao et al., "Geographic Variation in the Use of Gabapentinoids and Opioids for Pain in a Commercially Insured Adult Population in the United States," *J Pain Res* 15 (Zhao et al., 2022).

[286] McDonald, Carlson, and Izrael, "Geographic variation in opioid prescribing in the U.S."

is unexplained by any of the usual measurable supply and demand factors that drive variation in practice patterns,[287] it is likely that multivariable models of variation in opioid prescribing are capturing as much of the variation as can be expected from such models.

4.16 Substantive Case Study: West Virginia

The preceding discussion focuses on concepts, data, and analyses that are broadly applicable to opioid demand and supply and externalities in the U. S., with a focus on the root causes of the increase in opioid supply that began in the early 2000s. This section provides some comments regarding the applicability of the preceding discussion to a particular state, relying on a descriptive case study approach. West Virginia is selected because it is generally regarded as "ground zero" for the opioid crisis in Appalachia.[288] There is no *a priori* reason to expect that the broad concepts, data, and analyses discussed above should not generally apply to any region, state, or county in the U.S. To be sure, it is likely that some factors are more influential (or "matter more") in some regions, states, and counties relative to other factors, but there is no reason to believe that any region, state, or county would be broadly exempt from any aspect of the preceding discussion regarding causal factors. In addition, it is likely that some regions, states, and counties may be *more* affected by one or more of the contributing factors or have exhibited a disproportionate impact from one or more of the factors. In this section, the preceding discussion of contributing factors is applied to the case of West Virginia, with each contributing factor discussed in the same order in which they occur above.

4.16.1 Regulatory Failure

The failure of federal regulations on the part of the FDA, DEA and CDC affected all states, but there is compelling evidence that the DEA's failures

[287] Badinski et al., "Geographic Variation in Healthcare Utilization: The Role of Physicians."

[288] See generally J. Massey et al., "Opioid Overdose Outbreak—West Virginia, August 2016," *MMWR Morb Mortal Wkly Rep* 66, no. 37 (Massey et al., 2017); C. McGreal, "Why were millions of opioid pills sent to a West Virginia town of 3,000?," *The Guardian* Wednesday, October 2 (McGreal, 2019); R. Merino et al., "The Opioid Epidemic in West Virginia," *Health Care Manag (Frederick)* 38, no. 2 (Merino et al., 2019).

in controlling the supply of prescription opioids and its failures in limiting the incursion of illicit opioids disproportionately affected West Virginia. Specifically, the failure of the DEA in establishing quotas led to several counties in the state receiving unusually large volumes of prescription opioids. Much of this oversupply migrated to physician offices operating "pill mills," writing prescriptions at unusually high rates.[289] Many of the pill mill physicians later faced criminal charges.[290] As briefly mentioned above, a report by the West Virginia Attorney General's ("WVAG") office detailed these shortcomings, summarizing them as follows:[291] (1) the DEA received and granted requests for production increases "... based on growing sales [and] did not justify the requested increases based on more than mere assertions of consumer demand or increased sales—and critically, did not demonstrate that projected increases in demand were not tied to the well-documented diversion and abuse of opioids that were occurring at this time;" (2) the FDA provided the DEA with data and mathematical models to project opioid sales for a given year, however the projections "... did not account for diversion, but even so they were frequently lower—substantially—than the APQs that the DEA ultimately set;"[292] and (3) evidence suggests that the DEA "... appears to have broadly accepted manufacturers' projections over the FDA's [...] [and] the DEA often departed from the FDA's recommendations while frequently granting increases based on manufacturers' proffers." Further supporting the assertion that the DEA is an important factor in the context of regulatory failure, in several places in the report the WVAG concludes

[289] See generally Rigg, March, and Inciardi, "Prescription Drug Abuse & Diversion: Role of the Pain Clinic."

[290] For accounts of West Virginia "pill mills" and the role of the DEA and distributors, see generally McGreal, "Why were millions of opioid pills sent to a West Virginia town of 3,000?."; S. Quinones, "Physicians Get Addicted Too," *The Atlantic* May (Quinones, 2019); WVNews, "More doctors from Southern WV accused in fed 'pill mill' probe," *West Virginia News* September 24 (WVNews., 2019).

[291] Attorney General of West Virginia, "DEA's Failure to Combat Diversion Cost Lives: Results from the West Virginia Attorney General's Investigation into the DEA's Catastrophic Failure to Manage the National Drug Quota System from 2010–2016." Quotes are from the Executive Summary, pp. ES1-ES3

[292] APQ refers to the DEA's "annual production quotas."

that these regulatory failures were largely responsible for increased opioid volume and increased prevalence of OUD.[293]

4.16.2 Demand

In the case of West Virginia, it is plausible that a higher proportion of prescribed opioids has been attributable at least in part to demand factors and medical need, especially when compared to the rest of the nation. There are several reasons for this, including: (1) West Virginia has higher rates of cancer incidence compared to the U.S. average; (2) West Virginia has higher rates of surgery compared to the U.S. average; (3) West Virginia has a relatively high proportion of residents engaged in manual labor, some of which in heavy industry, and these occupations are generally associated with greater medical need and pain management; (4) West Virginia has higher rates of mental illness compared to the rest of the country, and there is a well-established causal pathway between mental illness and SUD;[294] (5) West Virginia has the highest rates of obesity in the nation, and obesity is associated with myriad health risks and comorbidities; (6) West Virgina's Medicaid program subsidized opioid utilization; and (7) important West Virginia socioeconomic factors are associated with higher demand for pain prevalence and pain treatment. Beginning with cancer rates, over the past two decades West Virginia has consistently ranked higher than the national average in overall crude and age-adjusted cancer incidence rates (Fig. 4.4).[295] Similarly, West Virginia consistently had a higher volume of inpatient surgeries per 1000 persons compared to the rest of the country (Fig. 4.5).[296]

A third factor potentially affecting medical need is based on the relationship between health status and physically demanding jobs, such as

[293] For example, on p. ES1, the report states "We do know, however, how many people died as a consequence of the DEA's refusal to lower the permissible amount of pain pills that could be introduced into the marketplace. The Agency's failures were deadly."

[294] See generally P. F. Buckley, "Prevalence and consequences of the dual diagnosis of substance abuse and severe mental illness," *J Clin Psychiatry* 67 Suppl 7 (Buckley, 2006); S. Ross and E. Peselow, "Co-occurring psychotic and addictive disorders: neurobiology and diagnosis," *Clin Neuropharmacol* 35, no. 5 (Ross & Peselow, 2012); K. Santucci, "Psychiatric disease and drug abuse," *Curr Opin Pediatr* 24, no. 2 (Santucci, 2012).

[295] Source: https://www.cdc.gov/cancer/uscs/.

[296] Measured as per 1,000 Medicare enrollees; Source: https://data.dartmouthatlas.org/.

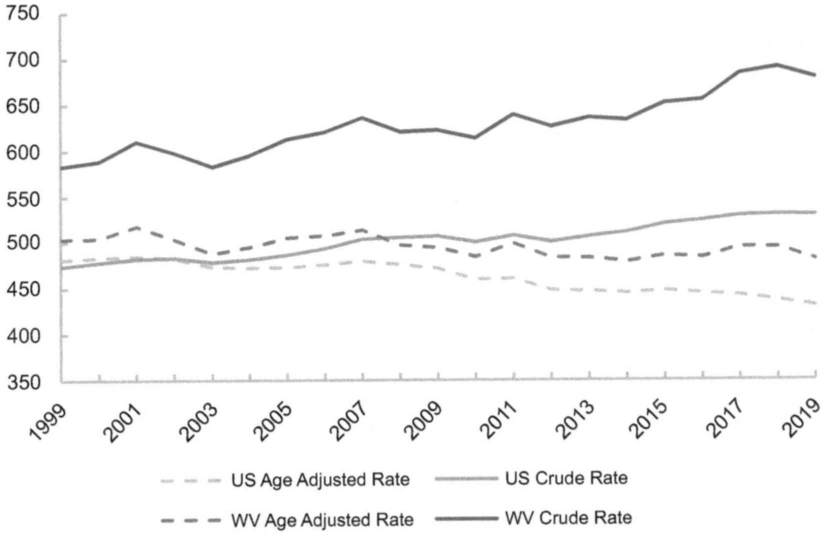

Fig. 4.4 All cancers incidence rate, 1999–2019, West Virginia and U.S

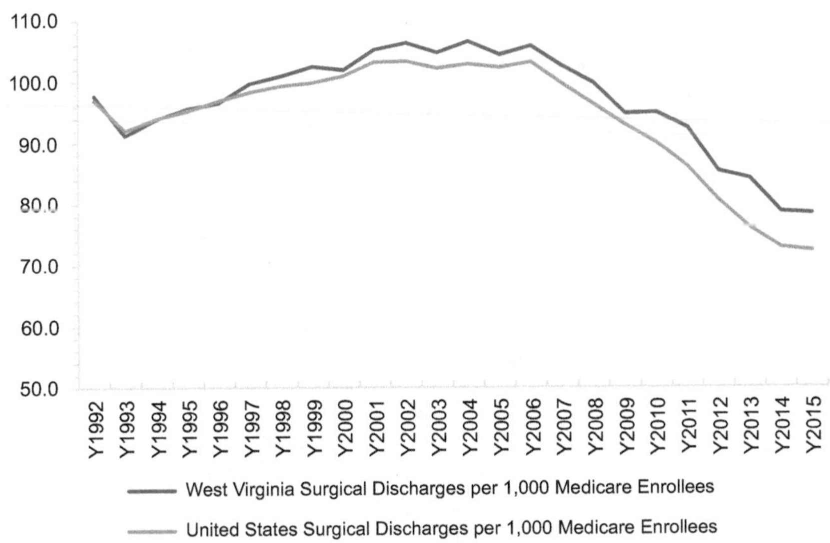

Fig. 4.5 Surgical discharges per 1000 medicare enrollees, West Virginia and U.S

those in heavy industry (e.g., natural resource extraction, such as mining and natural gas), construction, commercial transportation, manufacturing, and agriculture. In West Virginia, these types of industries constitute 33% of total statewide employment.[297] Nationally, according to the U.S. Bureau of Labor Statistics, the proportion is about 26%. Research has shown that workers in these types of industries have higher rates of health problems, including occupational exposures to chemicals and particulate matter, musculoskeletal conditions, soft tissue and musculoskeletal injuries, and other conditions, many of which require pain management.[298] The DEA, in one of its drug intelligence reports, directly acknowledged that such factors could in part explain higher medical need for opioids in West Virginia.[299]

Fourth, West Virginia has higher rates of mental illness compared to the rest of the country. According to 2021 NSDUH estimates, the prevalence of individuals reporting any type of mental illness has been higher in West Virginia compared to the U.S. for every year from 2009 to 2019, the gap growing to 5 percentage points by 2019 (Fig. 4.6).[300] Studies have consistently shown that individuals with mental illness are significantly more likely to also have a substance use disorder. As discussed earlier in the chapter, two systematic literature reviews and meta-analyses found robust associations between non-medical prescription opioid use and prevalence of SUDs, implying a strong and consistent association between mental illness and SUD, generally. Individuals who misuse opioids are highly likely to also have mental health problems.

[297] Based on 2020 data; see B. Lego, J. Deskins, and E. Bowen, "2022–2026 West Virginia Economic Outlook," (Morgantown, WV: Bureau of Business & Economic Research, John Chambers College of Business & Economics, West Virginia University, Lego et al., 2021).

[298] See generally J. Mai, G. Franklin, and D. Tauben, "Guideline for Prescribing Opioids to Treat Pain in Injured Workers," *Phys Med Rehabil Clin N Am* 26, no. 3 (Mai et al., 2015); M. P. Purdue et al., "The proportion of cancer attributable to occupational exposures," *Ann Epidemiol* 25, no. 3 (Purdue et al., 2015); W. S. Shaw, C. Roelofs, and L. Punnett, "Work Environment Factors and Prevention of Opioid-Related Deaths," *Am J Public Health* 110, no. 8 (Shaw et al., 2020); K. Torén and P. D. Blanc, "Asthma caused by occupational exposures is common—a systematic analysis of estimates of the population-attributable fraction," *BMC Pulm Med* 9 (Torén & Blanc, 2009).

[299] DEA, "The West Virginia Drug Situation," (Washington, D.C.: U.S. Drug Enforcement Administration, DEA, 2017).

[300] Refer to NSDUH data; see https://pdas.samhsa.gov/saes/state.

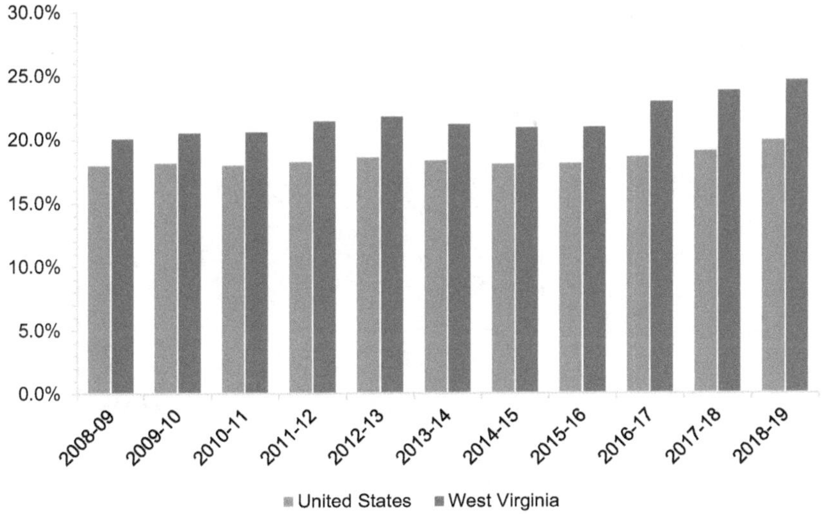

Fig. 4.6 Prevalence of any mental illness in past year, 2009–2019, West Virginia and U.S

Fifth, according to the CDC, West Virginia leads the nation in rates of obesity, with an obesity prevalence of 40.6% in 2021 (Fig. 4.7).[301] By comparison, the average obesity rate for the U.S. in the same year was 33.5%. Obesity is directly associated with higher need for pain management,[302] and it is causally related to a variety of serious health conditions that increase the need for medical care services, including pain management.

[301] CDC, "Adult Obesity Prevalence Maps," in *Overweight and Obesity, Data and Statistics* (Atlanta (GA): U.S. Centers for Disease Control and Prevention; Behavioral Risk Factor Surveillance System (BRFSS), CDC., 2022). CDC reports data from the U.S. Behavioral Risk Factor Surveillance System ("BRFSS").

[302] See generally K. M. Leyland et al., "Obesity and the Relative Risk of Knee Replacement Surgery in Patients With Knee Osteoarthritis: A Prospective Cohort Study," *Arthritis Rheumatol* 68, no. 4 (Leyland et al., 2016); C. Reyes et al., "Association Between Overweight and Obesity and Risk of Clinically Diagnosed Knee, Hip, and Hand Osteoarthritis: A Population-Based Cohort Study," ibid., no. 8; R. Shiri et al., "The association between obesity and low back pain: a meta-analysis," *Am J Epidemiol* 171, no. 2 (Shiri et al., 2010); T. T. Zhang et al., "Obesity as a Risk Factor for Low Back Pain: A Meta-Analysis," *Clin Spine Surg* 31, no. 1 (Zhang et al., 2018).

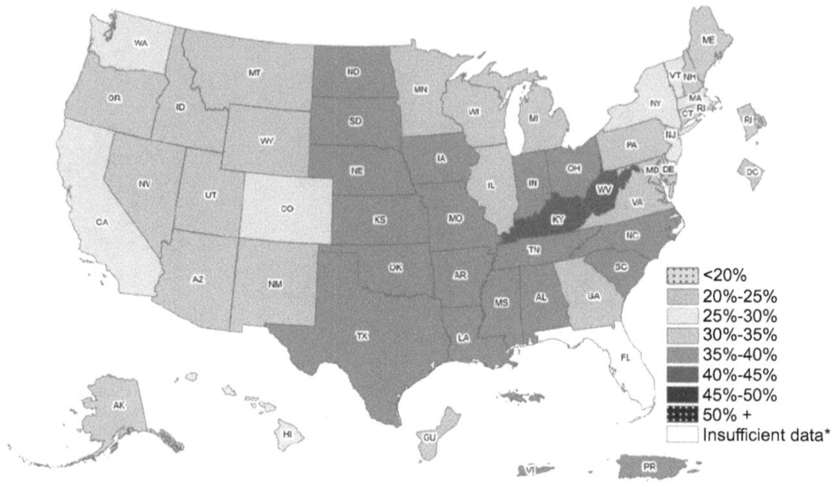

Fig. 4.7 Prevalence of self-reported obesity among U.S. adults by state and territory, BRFSS, 2021 *Source* CDC

Generally, these conditions include, but are not limited to, the following: coronary artery disease, heart failure, cardiac arrhythmia, stroke, insulin resistance, glucose intolerance, diabetes mellitus, hypertension, dyslipidemia, sleep apnea, arthritis, hyperuricemia, gall bladder disease, musculoskeletal conditions, menstrual irregularities, and certain types of cancer.[303]

Another important consideration related to medical need is that perceptions of medical necessity (and subsequent utilization of treatments based on those perceptions) vary substantially across different regions of the country. This variation has an "explained" component, based on objective measures of medical need (like the ones discussed above), and an "unexplained" component, based on other mostly unobservable factors. As discussed earlier in the chapter, the "unexplained" component of

[303] There is a substantial and growing literature on the health risks associated with obesity. See generally Afshin et al., "Health Effects of Overweight and Obesity in 195 Countries over 25 Years."; Pi-Sunyer, "Comorbidities of overweight and obesity: current evidence and research issues."; Rea et al., "Body mass index and the risk of recurrent coronary events following acute myocardial infarction."; Sung et al., "Global patterns in excess body weight and the associated cancer burden."

geographic variation in medical care utilization has generally been attributed to regional and local differences in physician practice patterns and norms.[304] For example, recall that the earlier cited NBER report found that about 33% of regional variation is due to variation in physician treatment intensity, and that "... physicians are roughly three times as important as non-physician supply side factors in driving regional variation."[305] This is consistent with accounts of physicians practicing in West Virginia at the time of the escalating opioid utilization. For example, according to one narrative of one physician's personal experience, "... For a while, [he] still suggested exercise, a balanced diet, and quitting smoking, all of which can alleviate chronic pain. But his patients, by and large, didn't want to hear any of this, and he was busy. So, he too gradually embraced pain pills. Nothing ended an appointment quicker than pulling out a prescription pad."[306] This is a good example of a clinical practice pattern influenced by local market demographics and socioeconomic factors. The critical implication of this is that any analysis of "expected versus actual" health care utilization rates must account for baseline differences in utilization patterns and practice patterns, which are driven primarily by physician practice norms and preferences rather than objective measures of medical need.

The sixth demand-side factor is that West Virginia's state Medicaid program extended comprehensive health coverage benefits to all eligible state residents throughout the period from FDA approval of opioids to present, during which time opioid analgesics were a covered benefit. According to the U.S. Center for Medicare and Medicaid Services ("CMS"), in West Virginia the state Medicaid program processed and approved more than 400,000 prescriptions for opioids in 2013 and peaking at more than 600,000 prescriptions just one year later in 2014

[304] See generally Chassin, "Explaining geographic variations. The enthusiasm hypothesis."; Epstein and Nicholson, "The formation and evolution of physician treatment styles: an application to cesarean sections."; Folland and Stano, "Sources of small area variations in the use of medical care."; Skinner, "Causes and Consequences of Regional Variations in Health Care."

[305] The study also concluded that "... around [60%] of the physicians' role comes from differences across regions in physician practice intensity within the same specialty, while the other [40%] reflects differences across regions in physician specialty mix ..." Refer to Badinski et al., "Geographic Variation in Healthcare Utilization: The Role of Physicians."

[306] Quinones, "Physicians Get Addicted Too"

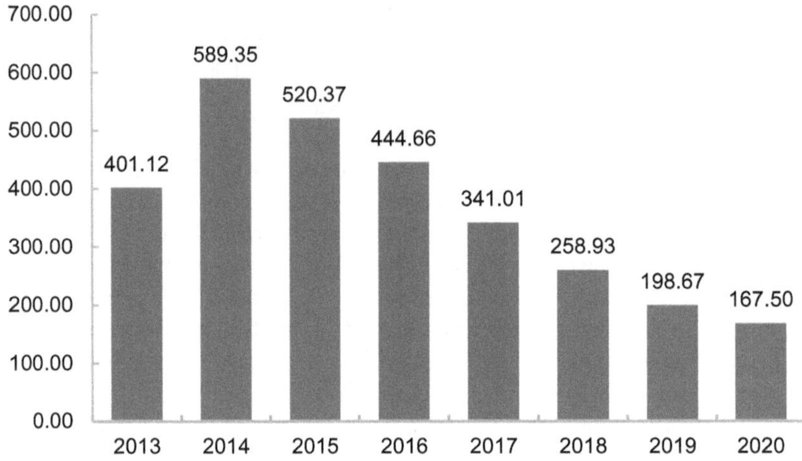

Fig. 4.8 Total Medicaid opioid prescriptions processed and paid by West Virginia Medicaid (thousands), 2013–2020

(Fig. 4.8).[307] This is broadly consistent with national trends in Medicaid opioid funding, which were discussed above. The state Medicaid program had at its disposal an arsenal of data to track the geographic dispersion of opioid utilization, prescribing patterns of specific physicians and hospitals, the characteristics of opioid-using patients, and temporal changes in prevalence of OUD and OUD-associated characteristics.[308] However, there is

[307] Refer to Center for Medicare and Medicaid Services, "Medicaid Opioid Prescribing Rates—by Geography."

[308] See, for example, L. Clemans-Cope et al., "State Variation in Medicaid Prescriptions for Opioid Use Disorder from 2011 to 2018," (Washington, D.C.: The Urban Instuitute, Clemans-Cope et al., 2019); CMS, "Drug Diversion in the Medicaid Program: State Strategies for Reducing Prescription Drug Diversion in Medicaid," (Baltimore, MD: U.S. Department of Health and Human Services, Centers for Medicare and Medicaid Services, CMS, 2012); W. Gao et al., "Predicting opioid use disorder and associated risk factors in a Medicaid managed care population," *Am J Manag Care* 27, no. 4 (Gao et al., 2021); Jayawardhana, Abraham, and Perri, "Opioid Analgesics in Georgia Medicaid: Trends in Potential Inappropriate Prescribing Practices by Demographic Characteristics, 2009–2014."; Kim et al., "The Concentration of Opioid Prescriptions by Providers and Among Patients in the Oregon Medicaid Program."; N. Kravitz-Wirtz et al., "Association of Medicaid Expansion With Opioid Overdose Mortality in the United States," *JAMA Netw Open* 3, no. 1 (Kravitz-Wirtz et

no evidence that the state Medicaid program took any specific actions to address this rapid increase, or to address the emerging geographic patterns of prescribing that would later result in criminal charges against physicians and pill mills.

Finally, other important demand-side factor are socioeconomic factors. Over the decade, the economy of West Virginia has consistently lagged behind the U.S. average economic performance, due in part to disproportionate reliance on heavy industry and manufacturing.[309] For example, West Virginia experienced a decline in population and employment from 2010 to 2020, while the U.S. averaged net gains in population and employment (Table 4.1). Growth in real gross domestic product ("GDP," a general measure of economic growth) was 1.6% over the period in the U.S., whereas West Virginia experienced 0% growth over the decade. Though there are no large differences in average annual unemployment rates between West Virginia and the U.S., West Virginia has consistently had higher rates of unemployment over the past two decades, with relatively large gaps throughout the 1990s and early 2000s, corresponding to increasing opioid supply.[310] Finally, real per capita income grew by 2.3% in the U.S. from 2010 to 2020, but only 1.9% in West Virginia over the period. In sum, it is plausible that at least some proportion of the demand and medical need for opioids in West Virginia can be attributable to these economic conditions, consistent

al., 2020); W. H. Lo-Ciganic et al., "Integrating human services and criminal justice data with claims data to predict risk of opioid overdose among Medicaid beneficiaries: A machine-learning approach," *PLoS One* 16, no. 3 (Lo-Ciganic et al., 2021); C. McAdam-Marx et al., "Costs of opioid abuse and misuse determined from a Medicaid database," *J Pain Palliat Care Pharmacother* 24, no. 1 (McAdam-Marx et al., 2010); L. Peterson et al., "Health care use and spending for Medicaid patients diagnosed with opioid use disorder receiving primary care in Federally Qualified Health Centers and other primary care settings," *PLoS One* 17, no. 10 (Peterson et al., 2022); C. L. Roland, J. Lake, and G. M. Oderda, "Prevalence of Prescription Opioid Misuse/Abuse as Determined by International Classification of Diseases Codes: A Systematic Review," *J Pain Palliat Care Pharmacother* 30, no. 4 (Roland et al., 2016); Rough et al., "Using prescription claims to detect aberrant behaviors with opioids: comparison and validation of 5 algorithms."; R. Springer et al., "Prescription opioid use patterns, use disorder diagnoses and addiction treatment receipt after the 2014 Medicaid expansion in Oregon," *Addiction* 114, no. 10 (Springer et al., 2019).

[309] Lego, Deskins, and Bowen, "2022–2026 West Virginia Economic Outlook."

[310] BLS, "Labor Force Statistics from the Current Population Survey," (Washington, D.C.: U.S. Bureau of Labor Statistics, BLS, 2024).

Table 4.1 Levels and changes in key socioeconomic measures, West Virginia, 2010–2020

Economic measure	*U.S. 2010–2020*	*West Virginia 2010–2020*	*Percentage point difference in rate (a)*	*Percent difference in rate (b)*
Population (c)	0.70%	– 0.40%	1.10%	157.14%
Employment (c)	0.90%	– 0.70%	1.60%	177.78%
Real GDP (c)	1.60%	0.00%	1.60%	NA
Unemployment rate (d)	8.10%	8.40%	– 0.30%	– 3.70%
Real per capita income (c)	2.30%	1.90%	0.40%	17.39%

Source See text. *Notes* GDP = gross domestic product; (a) difference in rates is expressed as US rate minus the West Virginia rate; (b) percent change in rates is expressed as the difference in rates divided by the US rate (i.e., resulting in the percent difference between US and WV); (c) average annual change in growth (%); (d) rate at end of period

with the general discussion put forth earlier in this chapter on the strong causal relationship between socioeconomic conditions and substance use disorder.

4.16.3 Ratings

West Virginia Medicaid utilized performance measurement tools and quality ratings in its reimbursement systems, providing financial incentives to providers to obtain higher quality ratings and performance scores. As discussed earlier in the chapter, quality ratings typically include measures of patient satisfaction, and patient satisfaction measures typically include questions regarding the adequacy of pain management. According to a 2014 report by the West Virginia Medicaid program, "The state requires plans to maintain accreditation by the National Committee for Quality Assurance and to submit data on HEDIS, CAHPS, and other performance measures, including all CMS-recommended core measures for adults and children."[311] The state program also directly supports VBR, stating that "MCOs can participate in a performance incentive program in which the

[311] CMS, "Managed Care in West Virginia," in *Medicaid.gov* (Washington, D.C.: Centers for Medicare and Medicaid Services, 2014).

state pays them up to 1.5% of the total annual capitation for improving scores on select quality measures from year to year." All of these programs would have required data collection and performance evaluation based on patient satisfaction and, either directly or indirectly via satisfaction scores, would have also assessed patient pain control.

4.16.4 Drug Trafficking

Drug trafficking has played an important role in the incursion and distribution of illicit opioids in West Virginia. Twenty out of West Virginia's 55 counties (37%) lie directly in the Appalachian HIDTA, which covers mostly the southwest part of the state. Another 16 West Virginia counties border the Appalachian HIDTA, which means that more than 65% of the state's counties are either directly in or bordering the Appalachian HIDTA. Illicit opioids in West Virginia are mainly trafficked from nearby cities and states, with a disproportionately large amount sourced from Detroit, Chicago, and Columbus.[312] Consequently, West Virginia has had one of the highest rates of death from abuse of illicit opioids.[313] In 2003, in the earlier years of the rise in opioid utilization nationally, the U.S. Department of Justice summarized West Virginia's illicit drug problem as follows: "West Virginia is an economically depressed state, with one of the lowest median household incomes ($29,673) and per capita personal incomes ($22,881) in the United States in 2001. More than 16% of West Virginians lived in poverty in 2001. According to state and local law enforcement officials, low wages and a high poverty rate have induced some residents to turn to illicit drug production, transportation, or distribution as a means of support."[314]

4.16.5 Physicians

At the peak of opioid supply nationally (roughly 2010–2013), physicians in West Virginia issued more opioid prescriptions per capita than any

[312] DEA, "The West Virginia Drug Situation."

[313] Merino et al., "The Opioid Epidemic in West Virginia."; S. Warfield et al., "Opioid-Related Outcomes in West Virginia, 2008–2016," *Am J Public Health* 109, no. 2 (Warfield et al., 2019).

[314] DOJ, "West Virginia Drug Threat Assessment," (Washington, D.C.: U.S. Department of Justice (DOJ), National Drug Intelligence Center (NDIC), DOJ., 2003).

other state. In 2012, the prescription opioid rate in the U.S. was 81.3 per 100 persons. In West Virginia, in contrast, the rate was 136.9 per 100 persons—nearly 70% higher than the national average.[315] High-volume physician prescribers played a key role in generating such high volume, and many high-volume prescribers later faced criminal charges.[316] But the problem was not limited only to "rogue" high-volume prescribers; as one investigative account from West Virginia described it, "the epidemic began because hundreds of thousands of well-meaning doctors overprescribed narcotic painkillers, thinking they were doing the right thing for suffering patients. They had been influenced by pain specialists who said it was the humane thing to do, encouraged by insurance companies that said it was the most cost-effective thing to do, and cajoled by drug companies that said it was a safe thing to do."[317]

4.16.6 *Case Study Summary*

To summarize the case study results, not only are the effects of some contributing factors clearly relevant to West Virginia, but in many ways, West Virginia can be thought of as a useful illustration of the multifactorial ways in which the increase in opioid supply and demand evolved in the U.S., involving a multitude of factors and effects. In West Virginia, it began with the economic shift away from the industries upon which the state had been reliant for decades. The resulting economic decline created a fertile environment for increases in rates of SUD and growth in markets for illicit drugs. At the same time, due to the overall poor health of its residents, especially the economically distressed ones and those who worked or once worked in physically demanding jobs in heavy industry, physicians in West Virginia developed treatment intensity patterns that featured an increased reliance on pharmacological approaches to pain management, including opioids. These factors, when added to the full set of contributing factors and potentially responsible parties acting at a

[315] Based on CDC dispensing data previously described.

[316] See, for example, S. Higham, S. Horwitz, and S. Rich, "76 billion opioid pills: Newly released federal data unmasks the epidemic," *Washington Post* July 16 (Higham et al., 2019); McGreal, "Why were millions of opioid pills sent to a West Virginia town of 3,000?."; Quinones, "Physicians Get Addicted Too."; WVNews, "More doctors from Southern WV accused in fed 'pill mill' probe".

[317] Quinones, "Physicians Get Addicted Too" (p. 3).

national level, combined to create an environment in West Virginia highly conducive to an increase in opioid prescribing and utilization.

4.17 Chapter Summary

The implications of the discussion presented in this chapter can be summarized in three points. First, the opioid crisis clearly grew out of the confluence of several important contributing factors, each contributing a part of the "perfect storm" that lead to growth in the rates of prescription opioids. Literature, reports, and commentary from experts consistently point to nine factors consisting of a mix of "supply push" and "demand-pull" factors that can also be thought of as "enabling" or "causative" factors, the influence of which combined in synergistic and additive ways to increase the volume of opioids on the market, including regulatory failure, medical need, public policy, medical advocacy, ratings and accreditation, manufacturer marketing, socioeconomic factors, and advisor advocacy. The overall supply of opioids in the U.S. has also been driven by an increase in illegally trafficked *illicit* opioids; thus, drug trafficking is identified as the tenth contributing factor. Second, regarding medical need, about a third of the differences in physician prescribing patterns is attributed to normal variation in practice patterns. Another third has been shown to vary based on a combination of medical need, patient characteristics, and socioeconomic factors. This leaves another third to distribute across the remaining contributing factors. Third, the West Virginia case study illustrates, in a descriptive and conceptual way, how these factors have been featured in a state broadly impacted by the opioid crisis.

References

Abdelaal, M., le Roux, C. W., & Docherty, N. G. (2017, April). Morbidity and mortality associated with obesity. *Annals of Translational Medicine*, *5* (7), 161.

Adeola, J. O., & Urman, R. D. (2022, September). Psychiatric comorbidities associated with persistent postoperative opioid use. *Current Pain and Headache Reports*, *26*(9), 701–708.

Afshin, A., Forouzanfar, M. H., Reitsma, M. B., Sur, P., Estep, K., Lee, A., Marczak, L., Mokdad, A. H. Moradi-Lakeh, M. Naghavi, M. Salama, J. S. Vos, T. Abate, K. H. Abbafati, C. Ahmed, M. B. Al-Aly, Z. Alkerwi, A. Al-Raddadi, R. Amare, A. T. ... Murray, C. J. L. (2017, July 6). Health effects of

overweight and obesity in 195 countries over 25 years. *New England Journal of Medicine*, *377*(1), 13–27.
Agha, L., & Zeltzer, D. (2020). Drug diffusion through peer networks: The influence of industry payments. In *NBER working paper No. 26338*. National Bureau of Economic Research.
AHRQ. (2012). *Communication and dissemination strategies to facilitate the use of health and health care evidence (Contract No. 290-2007-10056-I #7 from AHRQ)*. Agency for Healthcare Research and Quality, U.S. Department of Health and Human Services.
Almand, J., Pickering, T., Parsell, D., Stronach, B., Carlisle, R., & McIntyre, L. (2022, January). The successful migration of total joint arthroplasty from the hospital inpatient to outpatient ASC setting. *Knee*, *34*, 17–23.
Alpert, A., Evans, W. N., Lieber, E. M., & Powell, D. (2019). Origins of the opioid crisis and its enduring Impacts. In *NBER working paper No. 26500*. National Bureau of Economic Research.
Alsultan, M. M., & Guo, J. J. (2022, March). Utilization, spending, and price of opioid medications in the US medicaid programs between 1991 and 2019. *American Health & Drug Benefits*, *15*(1), 31–37.
AMA. (2020). AMA urges CDC to revise opioid prescribing guideline. In *Press Release*. American Medical Association.
Andersen, M. S., Lorenz, V., Pant, A., Bray, J. W., & Alexander, G. C. (2022, February 1). Association of opioid utilization management with prescribing and overdose. *American Journal of Managed Care*, *28*(2), 63–68.
Anderson, T. S., Krieger, M. S., Marshall, B. D. L., Cerdá, M., & Hadland, S. (2020, October). Financial payments to teaching hospitals by companies marketing opioids. *Journal of General Internal Medicine*, *35*(10), 3108–3110.
APSQCC. (1995, December 20). Quality improvement guidelines for the treatment of acute pain and cancer pain: American pain society quality of care committee. *Jama*, *274*(23), 1874–1880.
Arkes, J. (2011, September). Recessions and the participation of youth in the selling and use of illicit drugs. *International Journal of Drug Policy*, *22*(5), 335–340.
Attorney General of West Virginia. (2020). *DEA's failure to combat diversion cost lives: Results from the West Virginia attorney general's investigation into the DEA's catastrophic failure to manage the national drug quota system from 2010–2016*. Office of the attorney general, State of West Virginia.
Ausness, R. C. (2023). Opioid Lawsuits: Is there any end in sight? *Health Matrix: The Journal of Law-Medicine*, *33*(1).
Azad, T. D., Vail, D., O'Connell, C., Han, S. S., Veeravagu, A., & Ratliff, J. K. (2018, December). Geographic variation in the surgical management of lumbar spondylolisthesis: Characterizing practice patterns and outcomes. *The Spine Journal*, *18*(12), 2232–2238.

Bach, P., & Hartung, D. (2019, September 2). Leveraging the role of community pharmacists in the prevention, surveillance, and treatment of opioid use disorders. *Addiction Science & Clinical Practice 14*(1), 30.

Badinski, I., Finkelstein, A., Gentzkow, M., Hull, P., & Williams, H. (2023). *Geographic variation in healthcare utilization: The role of physicians.* National Bureau of Economic Research (NBER).

Bailit, H. L., & Sennett, C. (1992, March). Utilization management as a cost-containment strategy. *Health Care Financing Review, 1991*(Suppl), 87–93.

Baker, D. W. (2017, March 21). History of the joint commission's pain standards: Lessons for today's prescription opioid epidemic. *Jama, 317*(11), 1117–1118.

Baker, D. W. (2017). *The joint commission's pain standards: Origins and evolution.* The Joint Commission.

Bakos-Block, C., Langabeer, J. R., Yatsco, A., Cardenas-Turanzas, M., & Champagne-Langabeer, T. (2020). Prevalence of mental health disorders among individuals enrolled in an emergency response program for treatment of opioid use disorder. *Substance Abuse, 14*,1178221820981998.

Baptiste-Roberts, K., & Hossain, M. (2018, April). Socioeconomic disparities and self-reported substance abuse-related problems. *Addiction and Health, 10*(2), 112–122.

Baron, R., Mick, G., & Serpell, M. (2022, October). The relevance of real-world data for the evaluation of neuropathic pain treatments. *Pain Management, 12* (7), 845–857.

Bartley, M., Ferrie, J., & Montgomery, S. M. (2006). Health and labour market disadvantage: Unemployment, non-employment, and job insecurity. In M. Marmot & R. G. Wilkinson. (Eds.), *Social Determinants of Health* (2nd ed). Oxford University Press.

Becher, R. D., Jin, L., Warren, J. L., Gill, T. M., DeWane, M. P., Davis, K. A., & Zhang, Y. (2022, February 1). Geographic variation in the utilization of and mortality after emergency general surgery operations in the northeastern and southeastern United States. *Annals of Surgery, 275*(2), 340–347.

Berman, J. B., & Li, G. (2020, October 1). Characteristics of criminal cases against physicians charged with opioid-related offenses reported in the us news media, 1995-2019. *Injury Epidemiology, 7*(1), 50.

Bernard, S. A., Chelminski, P. R., Ives, T. J., & Ranapurwala, S. I. (2018). Management of pain in the United States-a brief history and implications for the opioid epidemic. *Health Services Insights, 11*, 1178632918819440.

Bhise, V., Rajan, S. S., Sittig, D. F., Morgan, R. O., Chaudhary, P., & Singh, H. (2018, January). Defining and measuring diagnostic uncertainty in medicine: A systematic review. *Journal of General Internal Medicine, 33*(1), 103–115.

Biel, E., Pivarunas, A., Prentice, T., Rowe, N., & Zhang, S. J. (2024, June). The application of radiofrequency ablation in acute and chronic pain management. *AANA Journal, 92*(3), 220–231.

Blackstone, E. A., & Fuhr Jr, J. P. (2016, February). The economics of medicare accountable care organizations. *American Health & Drug Benefits*, *9*(1), 11–19.

BLS. (2024). *Labor force statistics from the current population survey*. U.S. Bureau of Labor Statistics.

Blumenthal, D., & Seervai, S. (2017, October 26). To combat the opioid epidemic: We must be honest about all its causes. *Harvard Business Review*. https://hbr.org/2017/10/to-combat-the-opioid-epidemic-we-must-be-honest-about-all-its-causes

Blumenthal, D., & Seervai, S. (2018). *Rising obesity in the United States is a public health crisis*. The Commonwealth Fund.

BMJ. (2022, August 23). US CDC announces major changes after criticism of its responses to Covid-19 and monkeypox. *BMJ*, *378*.

Brennan, F. (2015, September). The US congressional "Decade on pain control and research" 2001–2011: A review. *Journal of Pain & Palliative Care Pharmacotherapy*, *29*(3), 212–227.

Breyer, S. (1982). *Regulation and its reform*. Harvard University Press.

Brown, E., & Wehby, G. L. (2019, August). Economic conditions and drug and opioid overdose deaths. *Medical Care Research and Review*, *76*(4), 462–477.

Buck, M. D., Atreja, A., Brunker, C. P., Jain, A., Suh, T. T., Palmer, R. M., Dorr, D. A., Harris, C. M., & Wilcox, A. B. (2009, April). Potentially inappropriate medication prescribing in outpatient practices: prevalence and patient characteristics based on electronic health records. *American Journal of Geriatric Pharmacotherapy*, *7*(2), 84–92.

Buckley, P. F. (2006). Prevalence and consequences of the dual diagnosis of substance abuse and severe mental illness. *Journal of Clinical Psychiatry*, *67* (7), 5–9.

Burcher, K. M., Suprun, A., & Smith, A. (2018, May 11). Risk factors for opioid use disorders in adult postsurgical patients. *Cureus*, *10*(5), 2611.

Burke, L. G., Burke, R. C., Orav, E. J., Bryan, A. F., Friend, T. H., Richardson, D. A., Jha, A. K., & Tsai, T. C. (2023, October 30). Trends in performance of hospital outpatient procedures and associated 30-day costs among medicare beneficiaries from 2011 to 2018. *Healthcare (Amsterdam)*, *11*(4), 100718.

Burt, R. A. (1997, October 23). The Supreme court speaks–not assisted suicide but a constitutional right to palliative care. *New England Journal of Medicine*, *337*(17), 1234–1236.

Cadarette, S. M., & Wong, L. (2015, May-June). An introduction to health care administrative data. *Canadian Journal of Hospital Pharmacy*, *68*(3), 232–237.

CAPC, (2018). *The case for hospital palliative care*. Center to Advance Palliative Care.

Carpenter, C. S., McClellan, C. B., & Rees, D. I. (2017. March). Economic conditions: Illicit drug use, and substance use disorders in the United States. *Journal of Health Economics*, *52*, 63–73.

Carrico, J. A., Mahoney, K., Raymond, K. M., Mims, L., Smith, P. C., Sakai, J. T., Mikulich-Gilbertson, S. K., Hopfer, C. J., & Bartels, K. (2018, November–December). The Association of patient satisfaction-based incentives with primary care physician opioid prescribing. *Journal of the American Board of Family Medicine*, *31*(6), 941–943.

Carroll, A. E. (2017, November 14). The high costs of unnecessary care. *Jama*, *318*(18), 1748–1749.

Case, A., & Deaton, A. (2020). *Deaths of despair and the future of capitalism*. Princeton University Press.

CBO. (2005). *Geographic variation in health care spending*. Congress of the United States: Congressional Budget Office.

CBO. (2022). *The opioid crisis and recent federal policy responses*. U.S. Congressional Budget Office.

CDC. (2009, October 30). Overdose deaths involving prescription opioids among medicaid enrollees - Washington, 2004-2007. *Morbidity and Mortality Weekly Report 58*(42), 1171–1175.

CDC. (2022). Adult obesity prevalence maps. In *Overweight and obesity, data and statistics*. U.S. Centers for Disease Control and Prevention; Behavioral Risk Factor Surveillance System (BRFSS).

CDC. (2023). *Mission, role and pledge*.U.S. Centers for Disease Control and Prevention.

CDC. (2011, November 4). Vital signs: Overdoses of prescription opioid pain relievers—United States, 1999–2008. *Morbidity and Mortality Weekly Report*, *60*(43), 1487–1492.

CDC. (2012, January 13). CDC grand rounds: Prescription drug overdoses - a U.S. epidemic. *Morbidity and Mortality Weekly Report*, *61*(1), 10–13.

CEA. (2019). *The role of opioid prices in the evolving opioid crisis*. U.S. Council of Economic Advisers.

Chassin, M. R. (1993, May). Explaining geographic variations. The enthusiasm hypothesis. *Medical Care*, *31*(5 Suppl), 37–44.

Chassin, M. R., Kosecoff, J., Park, R. E., Winslow, C. M., Kahn, K. L., Merrick, N. J., Keesey, J., et al. (1987, November 13). Does inappropriate use explain geographic variations in the use of health care services? A study of three procedures. *Jama*, *258*(18), 2533–2537.

Chee, T. T., Ryan, A. M., Wasfy, J. H., & Borden, W. B. (2016, May 31). Current state of value-based purchasing programs. *Circulation*, *133*(22), 2197–2205.

Chen, C. L., Jeffery, M. M., Krebs, E. E., Thiels, C. A., Schumacher, M. A., Schwartz, A. J., Thombley, R., et al. (2020, January). Long-term trends in postoperative opioid prescribing, 1994 to 2014. *Journal of the American Academy of Orthopaedic Surgeons Global Research & Reviews*, *4*(1).

Chhabra, N., & Leikin, J. B. (2017, July 4). The joint commission and the opioid epidemic. *Jama*, *318*(1), 91–92.

Chouinard, S., Prasad, A., & Brown, R. (2018, March). Survey assessing medical student and physician knowledge and attitudes regarding the opioid crisis. *Wmj*, *117*(1), 34–37.

Clark, D. J., & Schumacher, M. A. (2017, November). America's opioid epidemic: Supply and demand considerations. *Anesthesia & Analgesia*, *125*(5), 1667–1674.

Clark, R. E., Samnaliev, M., & McGovern, M. P. (2007, July). Treatment for co-occurring mental and substance use disorders in five state medicaid programs. *Psychiatric Services*, *58*(7), 942–948.

Clemans-Cope, L., Lynch, V., Winiski, E., & Epstein, M. (2014). Managed care in West Virginia. In *Medicaid.gov*. Centers for Medicare and Medicaid Services.

Clemans-Cope, L., Lynch, V., Winiski, E., & Epstein, M. (2019). *State variation in medicaid prescriptions for opioid use disorder from 2011 to 2018*. The Urban Instuitute.

CMS. (2012). *Drug diversion in the medicaid program: State strategies for reducing prescription drug diversion in medicaid*. U.S. Department of Health and Human Services, Centers for Medicare and Medicaid Services.

Coady, D., & Dizioli, A. (2017). Income inequality and education revisited: Persistence, endogeneity, and heterogeneity. In *IMF working paper*. International Monetary Fund (IMF), Fiscal Affairs Department.

Cockerham, W. C. (2013). *Social causes of health and disease* (2nd ed.). Polity Press.

Coleman, J. J. (2012, September). The supply chain of medicinal controlled substances: Addressing the achilles heel of drug diversion. *Journal of Pain & Palliative Care Pharmacotherapy* *26*(3), 233–250.

Compton, W. M., & Jones, C. M. (2019, September). Epidemiology of the U.S. opioid crisis: The importance of the vector. *Annals of the New York Academy of Sciences*, *1451*(1), 130–143.

Cook, A., & Averett, S. (2020, September). Do hospitals respond to changing incentive structures? Evidence from medicare's 2007 DRG restructuring. *Journal of Health Economics*, *73*, 102319.

Cragg, A., Hau, J. P., Woo, S. A., Kitchen, S. A., Liu, C., Doyle-Waters, M. M., & Hohl, C. M. (2019, November). Risk factors for misuse of prescribed opioids: A systematic review and meta-analysis. *Annals of Emergency Medicine*, *74*(5), 634–646.

Crowley-Matoka, M., Saha, S., Dobscha, S. K., & Burgess, D. J. (2009, October). Problems of quality and equity in pain management: Exploring the role of biomedical culture. *Pain Medicine*, *10*(7), 1312–1324.

CRS. (2021a). *The controlled substances act (CSA): A legal overview for the 117th congress.* United States Congressional Research Service.

CRS.(2021b). *Scope of CDC authority under section 361 of the public health service act (PHSA).* Congressional Research Service.

Cruess, S. R., & Cruess, R. L. (2005, April 1). The medical profession and self-regulation: A current challenge. *Virtual Mentor, 7*(4).

Dabrowska, A., & Thaul, S. (2018). How FDA approves drugs and regulates their safety and effectiveness. Congressional Research Service.

Dagnino, A. P. A., & Campos, M. M. (2022). Chronic pain in the elderly: Mechanisms and perspectives. *Frontiers in Human Neuroscience, 16*, 736688.

Dahlhamer, J., Lucas, J., Zelaya, C., Nahin, R., Mackey, S., DeBar, L., Kerns, R., et al. (2018, September 14). Prevalence of chronic pain and high-impact chronic pain among adults - United States, 2016. *Morbidity and Mortality Weekly Report, 67*(36), 1001–1006.

Damberg, C. L., Sorbero, M. E., Lovejoy, S. L., Lauderdale, K., Wertheimer, S., Smith, A., Waxman, D., & Schnyer, C. (2011). *An evaluation of the use of performance measures in health care.* National Quality Forum & RAND Corporation.

Danzon, P. M., & Nicholson, S. (eds). (2012). *The economics of the biopharmaceutical industry*: Oxford handbook. Oxford University Press.

Dasgupta, N., Beletsky, L., & Ciccarone, D. (2018, February). Opioid crisis: No easy fix to its social and economic determinants. *American Journal of Public Health, 108*(2), 182–186.

Daubresse, M., Chang, H. Y., Yu, Y., Viswanathan, S., Shah, N. D., Stafford, R. S., Kruszewski, S. P., & Alexander, G. C. (2013, October). Ambulatory diagnosis and treatment of nonmalignant pain in the United States, 2000-2010. *Medical Care. 51*(10), 870–878.

Davis, C. S., & Carr, D. H. (2017, July–September). Self-regulating profession? Administrative discipline of "pill mill" physicians in Florida. *Substance Abuse, 38* (3), 265–268.

DEA. (2017). *The West Virginia drug situation.* U.S. Drug Enforcement Administration.

DEA. (2023). *Diversion control division: Program description.* U.S. Department of Justice, U.S. Drug Enforcement Administration, Diversion Control Division.

DEA. (2016). *DEA reduces amount of opioid controlled substances to be manufactured in 2017.* United States Drug Enforcement Administration.

DEA. (2023). *Drug scheduling.* U.S. Department of Justice, U.S. Drug Enforcement Administration.

DEA. (2024). *2024 national drug threat assessment.* U.S. Department of Justice, Drug Enforcement Administration.

Dequech, D. (2006). Institutions and norms in institutional economics and sociology. *Journal of Economic Issues, 40*(2), 473–481.

Dhruva, S. S., Parzynski, C. S., Gamble, G. M., Curtis, J. P., Desai, N. R., Yeh, R. W., Masoudi, F. A., et al. (2020, February 18). Attribution of adverse events following coronary stent placement identified using administrative claims data. *Journal of the American Heart Association*, *9*(4), 013606.

DiMasi, J. A., Grabowski, H. G., & Hansen, R. W. (2016. May). Innovation in the pharmaceutical industry: New estimates of R&D costs. *Journal of Health Economics*, 47, 20–33.

Ding, Y., & Liu, C. (2021, December). Alternative payment models and physician treatment decisions: Evidence from lower back pain. *Journal of Health Economics*, *80*, 102548.

Dismukes, L. C. (2018, May–June). How did we get here? Heroin and fentanyl trafficking trends: A law enforcement perspective. *North Carolina Medical Journal*, *79*(3), 181–184.

DOJ. (2003). *West Virginia drug threat assessment*. U.S. Department of Justice (DOJ), National Drug Intelligence Center (NDIC).

Dowell, D., Haegerich, T. M., & Chou, R. (2016, April 19). CDC guideline for prescribing opioids for chronic pain–United States, 2016. *Jama*, *315*(15), 1624–1645.

DuBois, J. M., Chibnall, J. T., Anderson, E. E., Eggers, M., Baldwin, K., & Vasher, M. (2016, October). A mixed-method analysis of reports on 100 cases of improper prescribing of controlled substances. *Journal of Drug Issues*, *46*(4), 457–472.

Dumanovsky, T., Augustin, R., Rogers, M., Lettang, K., Meier, D. E., & Morrison, R. S. (2016, January). The growth of palliative care in U.S. hospitals: A status report. *Journal of Palliative Medicine*, *19*(1), 8–15.

Dyer, O. (2022, March 1). Drug distributors and Johnson & Johnson will pay $26bn as America's biggest opioid settlement is finalised. *Bmj*, 376, o529.

EOP. (2022). *High intensity drug trafficking areas program: 2022 report to congress*. Executive Office of the President of the United States, Office of National Drug Control Policy.

Epstein, A. J., & Nicholson, S. (2009, December). The formation and evolution of physician treatment styles: An application to cesarean sections. *Journal of Health Economics*, *28*(6), 1126–1140.

Ernstzen, D. V., Louw, Q. A., & Hillier, S. L. (2017, January 5). Clinical practice guidelines for the management of chronic musculoskeletal pain in primary healthcare: A systematic review. *Implementation Science*, *12*(1), 1.

FDA. (2021). *Timeline of selected FDA activities and significant events addressing opioid misuse and abuse*. U.S. Food and Drug Administration.

FDA. (2023). FDA mission. In *What We Do*. U.S. Food and Drug Administration.

Felbab-Brown, V. (2020). Fending off fentanyl and hunting down heroin: Controlling opioid supply from Mexico. In *The opioid crisis in America: Domestic and international dimensions*. Brookings Institution.

Felbab-Brown, V. (2023, May 15). *Why america is struggling to stop the fentanyl epidemic: The new geopolitics of synthetic opioids.* Foreign Affairs.

Fingar, K. R., Stocks, C., Weiss, A. J., & Steiner, C. A. (2014). Most frequent operating room procedures performed in U.S. hospitals, 2003-2012: HCUP statistical brief #186. In *HCUP statistical brief.* U.S. Agency for Healthcare Research and Quality.

Fischer, B., Lusted, A., Roerecke, M., Taylor, B., & Rehm, J. (2012, November). The prevalence of mental health and pain symptoms in general population samples reporting nonmedical use of prescription opioids: a systematic review and meta-analysis. *Journal of Pain*, 13(11), 1029–1044.

Fleiz, C., Arredondo, J., Chavez, A., Pacheco, L., Segovia, L. A., Villatoro, J. A., Cruz, S. L., Medina-Mora, M. E., & de la Fuente, J. R. (2020, April). Fentanyl is used in Mexico's northern border: Current challenges for drug health policies. *Addiction, 115*(4), 778–781.

Florida, R. (2018) *America's worsening geographic inequality.* Bloomberg News.

Floyd, S. B., Campbell, J., Chapman, C. G., Thigpen, C. A., Kissenberth, M. J., & Brooks, J. M. (2019, January 21). Geographic variation in the treatment of proximal humerus fracture: an update on surgery rates and treatment consensus. *Journal of Orthopaedic Surgery and Research, 14*(1), 22.

Foley, H. E., Knight, J. C., Ploughman, M., Asghari, S., & Audas, R. (2021, November 1). Association of chronic pain with comorbidities and health care utilization: A retrospective cohort study using health administrative data. *Pain, 162*(11), 2737–2749.

Folland, S., & Stano, M. (1989, March). Sources of small area variations in the use of medical care. *Journal of Health Economics, 8*(1), 85–107.

Forsythe, M., & Bogdanich, W. (2021, Novermber 5). McKinsey settles for nearly $600 million over role in opioid crisis. *New York Times.*

Friedman, S. R., Krawczyk, N., Perlman, D. C., Mateu-Gelabert, P., Ompad, D. C., Hamilton, L., Nikolopoulos, G., Guarino, H., & Cerdá, M. (2020). The opioid/overdose crisis as a dialectics of pain, despair, and one sided struggle. *Frontiers in Public Health, 8*, 540423.

FTC. (2023). *What you need to know about the office of inspector general.* U.S. Federal Trade Commission; Office of the Inspector General.

Gao, W., Leighton, C., Chen, Y., Jones, J., & Mistry, P. (2021, April). Predicting opioid use disorder and associated risk factors in a Medicaid managed care population. *American Journal of Managed Care, 27*(4), 148–154.

GAO. (2015). Drug shortages: Better management of the quota process for controlled substances needed; Coordination between DEA and FDA should be improved. In *GAO-15-202.* U.S. Government Accountability Office.

GAO. (2018). Illicit opioids: While greater attention given to combating synthetic opioids, agencies need to better assess their efforts. In *Report to congressional requesters.* U.S. Government Accountability Office.

García, M. C., Dodek, A. B., Kowalski, T., Fallon, J., Lee, S. H., Iademarco, M. F., Auerbach, J., & Bohm, M. K. (2016, October 21). Declines in opioid prescribing after a private insurer policy change - massachusetts, 2011–2015. *Morbidity and Mortality Weekly Report*, *65*(41), 1125–1131.

Ghertner, R., & Groves, L. (2018). The Opioid Crisis and Economic Opportunity: Geographic and Economic Trends. In *ASPE research brief: Office of the assistant secretary for planning and evaluation*. U.S. Department of Health and Human Services.

Gladden, R. M., O'Donnell, J., Mattson, C. L., & Seth, P. (2019, August 30). Changes in Opioid-Involved Overdose Deaths by Opioid Type and Presence of Benzodiazepines, Cocaine, and Methamphetamine - 25 States, July–December 2017 to January–June 2018. *Morbidity and Mortality Weekly Report*, *68*(34), 737–744.

Glass, T. A., Goodman, S. N., Hernán, M. A., & Samet, J. M. (2013). Causal inference in public health. *Annual Review of Public Health*, *34*, 61–75.

Goldner, E. M., Lusted, A., Roerecke, M., Rehm, J., & Fischer, B. (2014, March). Prevalence of Axis-1 psychiatric (with focus on depression and anxiety) disorder and symptomatology among non-medical prescription opioid users in substance use treatment: systematic review and meta-analyses. *Addictive Behaviors*, *39*(3), 520–531.

Goldstick, J. E., Guy, G. P., Losby, J. L., Baldwin, G., Myers, M., & Bohnert, A. S. B. (2021, July 1). Changes in Initial Opioid Prescribing Practices After the 2016 Release of the CDC Guideline for Prescribing Opioids for Chronic Pain. *JAMA Network Open*, *4*(7), 2116860.

Gordon, R. J. (2016). *The rise and fall of American growth: The U.S. standard of living since the Civil War*. Princeton University Press.

Gore, M., Sadosky, A., Stacey, B. R., Tai, K. S., & Leslie, D. (2012, May 15). The burden of chronic low back pain: Clinical comorbidities, treatment patterns, and health care costs in usual care settings. *Spine (Phila Pa 1976)*, *37*(11), 668–77.

Grabowski, H., Long, G., Mortimer, R., & Bilginsoy, M. (2021, January–December). Continuing trends in U.S. brand-name and generic drug competition. *Journal of Medical Economics*, *24*(1), 908–917.

Gray, B. M., Vandergrift, J. L., Weng, W., Lipner, R. S., & Barnett, M. L. (2021). Clinical knowledge and trends in physicians' prescribing of opioids for new onset back pain, 2009-2017. *JAMA Network Open*, *4*(7), 2115328–28.

Gross, J., & Gordon, D. B. (2019, January). The strengths and weaknesses of current US policy to address pain. *American Journal of Public Health*, *109*(1), 66–72.

Grossman, G. M., & Helpman, E. (2001). *Special interest politics*. The MIT Press.

Grover, C. A., Elder, J. W., Close, R. J., & Curry, S. M. (2012, November). How frequently are "classicdrug-seeking behaviors used by drug-seeking patients in the emergency department? *Western Journal of Emergency Medicine, 13*(5), 416–421.

Gumidyala, L., Savul, S. A., Shofer, F. S., & Green-mckenzie, J. (2021, May–June 01). Effect of CDC opioid-prescribing guidelines in a community hospital emergency department. *Journal of Public Health Management and Practice*, 27(Suppl 3), s186–s90.

Gunasekera, E., & Brooker, R. (2022, Number). Phantom participants with real-world ramifications: Clinical drug trial data falsification. *The National Law Review*, *XV*, 282.

Hadland, S. E., Krieger, M. S., & Marshall, B. D. L. (2017, September). Industry payments to physicians for opioid products, 2013–2015. *American Journal of Public Health, 107*(9), 1493–1495.

Hadland, S. E., Rivera-Aguirre, A., Marshall, B. D. L., & Cerdá, M. (2019, January 4). Association of pharmaceutical industry marketing of opioid products with mortality from opioid-related overdoses. *JAMA Network Open*, 2(1), 186007.

Haffajee, R. L., & Mello, M. M. (2017, December 14). Drug companies' Liability for the opioid epidemic. *New England Journal of Medicine, 377*(24), 2301–2305.

Hales, C. M., Carroll, M. D., Fryar, C. D., & Ogden, C. L. (2020). Prevalence of obesity and severe obesity among adults: United States, 2017–2018 (NCHS data brief, no 360). In *NCHS data brief.* National Center for Health Statistics.

Hamby, C., & Forsythe, M. (2022, June 29). *Behind the scenes, McKinsey guided companies at the center of the opioid crisis.* New York Times.

Hansen, G. R. (2005, May). The drug-seeking patient in the emergency room. *Emergency Medicine Clinics of North America, 23*(2), 349–365.

Hariharan, J., Lamb, G. C., & Neuner, J. M. (2007, April). Long-term opioid contract use for chronic pain management in primary care practice: A five year experience. *Journal of General Internal Medicine, 22*(4), 485–490.

Harris, D. G. (2014, June). Management of pain in advanced disease. *British Medical Bulletin, 110*(1), 117–128.

Hartung, D. M., Hall, J., Haverly, S. N., Cameron, D., Alley, L., Hildebran, C., O'Kane, N., & Cohen, D. (2018, September 1). Pharmacists' role in opioid safety: A focus group investigation. *Pain Medicine, 19*(9)1799–1806.

Heins, S. E., Buttorff, C., Armstrong, C., & Pacula, R. L. (2021, November 1). Claims-based measures of prescription opioid utilization: A practical guide for researchers. *Drug and Alcohol Dependence, 228*, 109087.

Hernandez-Boussard, T., Graham, L. A., Desai, K., Wahl, T. S., Aucoin, E., Richman, J. S., Morris, M. S., et al. (2017, September). The fifth vital sign: Postoperative pain predicts 30-day readmissions and subsequent emergency department visits. *Annals of Surgery, 266*(3), 516–524.

Heyward, J., Jones, C. M., Compton, W. M., Lin, D. H., Losby, J. L., Murimi, I. B., Baldwin, G. T., et al. (2018, October 5). Coverage of Nonpharmacologic treatments for low back pain among US public and private insurers. *JAMA Network Open*, *1*(6), 183044.
Higham, S., & Horwitz, S. (2022). *American cartel: Inside the battle to bring down the opioid industry*. Twelve/Hachette Book Group.
Higham, S., Horwitz, S., & Rich, S. (2019, July 16). *76 billion opioid pills: Newly released federal data unmasks the epidemic.*Washington Post.
Hirsch, R. (2017, March-April). The Opioid Epidemic: It's Time to Place Blame Where It Belongs. *Missouri Medicine*, *114*(2), 82–90.
Hitt, H. C., McMillen, R. C., Thornton-Neaves, T., Koch, K., & Cosby, A. G. (2007, May). Comorbidity of obesity and pain in a general population: Results from the Southern pain prevalence study. *Journal of Pain*, *8*(5), 430–436.
Hollingsworth, A., Ruhm, C. J., & Simon, K. (2017, December). Macroeconomic conditions and opioid abuse. *Journal of Health Economics*, *56*, 222–233.
Hong, I., Westra, J. R., Goodwin, J. S., Karmarkar, A., Kuo, Y. F., & Ottenbacher, K. J. (2020, December). Association of pain on hospital discharge with the risk of 30-day readmission in patients with total hip and knee replacement. *Journal of Arthroplasty*, *35*(12), 3528–3534.2.
Hong, J., Reed, C., Novick, D., & Happich, M. (2013, January 1). Costs associated with treatment of chronic low back pain: An analysis of the UK General Practice Research Database. *Spine (Phila Pa 1976)*, *38*(1), 75–82.
Hooper, C. L. (2023, May 2). How the FDA Helped Fuel the Opioid Epidemic. *Wall Street Journal*. https://www.wsj.com/health/pharma/how-the-fda-helped-fuel-the-opioid-epidemic-ketorolac-approval-toradol-5159453b
Horwitz, S., & Higham, S. (2019, December 28). *Could the DEA have stopped the opioid epidemic by cutting off the supply*? Washington Post.
HSGAC. (2018). *Fueling an epidemic: Exposing the financial ties between opioid manufacturers and third party advocacy groups*. U.S. Senate Homeland Security and Governmental Affairs Committee, Ranking Members Office.
HSGAC. (2018). Combating the opioid epidemic: The interception of illicit opioids by the border patrol. United States Senate: Committee on Homeland Security & Governmental Affairs.
Huang, Y. L., Moon, J., & Segal, J. B. (2014, August). A comparison of active adverse event surveillance systems worldwide. *Drug Safety*, *37*(8), 581–596.
Humphreys, K., Shover, C. L., Andrews, C. M., Bohnert, A. S. B., Brandeau, M. L., Caulkins, J. P., Chen, J. H., et al. (2022, February 5). Responding to the opioid crisis in North America and beyond: Recommendations of the stanford-lancet commission. *Lancet*, *399*(10324), 555–604.
Imhof, S., & Kaskie, B. (2008, August). How can we make the pain go away? Public policies to manage pain at the end of life. *Gerontologist*, *48*(4), 423–431.

Inciardi, J. A., Surratt, H. L., Kurtz, S. P., & Cicero, T. J. (2007, March). Mechanisms of prescription drug diversion among drug-involved club- and street-based populations. *Pain Medicine, 8*(2), 171–183.

Infeld, M., Bell, A., Marlin, C., Waterhouse, S., Uliassi, N., & Fugh-Berman, A. (2007). *Rewarding provider peformance: Aligning incentives in medicare.* Pathways to quality health care: Committee on redesigning health insurance peformance measures, payment, and performance improvement programs. U.S. Institute of Medicine; National Academies Press.

Infeld, M., Bell, A., Marlin, C., Waterhouse, S., Uliassi, N., & Fugh-Berman, A. (2011). *Relieving pain in America: A blueprint for transforming prevention, care, education, and research.* U.S. National Institutes for Health, Institute of Medicine (IOM).

Infeld, M., Bell, A., Marlin, C., Waterhouse, S., Uliassi, N., & Fugh-Berman, A. (2019).Continuing medical education and the marketing of fentanyl for breakthrough pain: Marketing messages in an industry-funded CME module on breakthrough pain. *World Medical & Health Policy, 11*(1) 43–58.

IOM. (2001). *Crossing the quality chasm: A new health system for the twenty-first century.* institute of medicine (IOM), National Academy Press.

Ives, T. J., Chelminski, P. R., Hammett-Stabler, C. A., Malone, R. M., Perhac, J. S., Potisek, N. M., Shilliday, B. B., DeWalt, D. A., & Pignone, M. P. (2006 April 4). Predictors of opioid misuse in patients with chronic pain: A prospective cohort study. *BMC Health Services Research, 6*, 46.

Iwashyna, T. J., & Kennedy, E. H. (2013, June). Instrumental variable analyses. Exploiting natural randomness to understand causal mechanisms. *Annals of the American Thoracic Society, 10*(3), 255–260.

Jairam, V., Yang, D. X., Pasha, S., Soulos, P. R., Gross, C. P., Yu, J. B., & Park, H. S. (2021, March 1). Temporal trends in opioid prescribing patterns among oncologists in the medicare population. *Journal of the National Cancer Institute, 113*(3), 274–281.

Jairam, V., Yang, D. X., Verma, V., Yu, J. B., & Park, H. S. (2020). National patterns in prescription opioid use and misuse among cancer survivors in the United States. *JAMA Network Open, 3*(8), 2013605–05.

James, B. C., & Poulsen, G. P. (2016, July–August). *The case for capitation.* Harvard Business Review.

Jayawardhana, J., Abraham, A. J., & Perri, M. (2018, September). Opioid analgesics in georgia medicaid: Trends in potential inappropriate prescribing practices by demographic characteristics, 2009–2014. *Journal of Managed Care & Specialty Pharmacy, 24*(9), 886–894.

Jones, G. H., Bruera, E., Abdi, S., & Kantarjian, H. M. (2018, Novermber 15). The opioid epidemic in the United States-Overview, origins, and potential solutions. *Cancer, 124*(22), 4279–4286.

Joskow, P. L., & Noll, R. C. (1981). Regulation in theory and practice: An overview. In G. Fromm (Ed.), *Studies in public regulation*. The MIT press.

Judd, D., King, C. R., & Galke, C. (2023, July). The opioid epidemic: A review of the contributing factors, negative consequences, and best practices. *Cureus*, 15(7), 41621.

Kalinich, M., Murphy, W., Wongvibulsin, S., Pahalyants, V., Yu, K. H., Lu, C., Wang, F., et al. (2021, March). Prediction of severe immune-related adverse events requiring hospital admission in patients on immune checkpoint inhibitors: study of a population level insurance claims database from the USA. *Journal for ImmunoTherapy of Cancer 9*(3).

Kauh, C. Y., Blachley, T. S., Lichter, P. R., Lee, P. P., & Stein, J. D. (2016, March). Geographic Variation in the Rate and Timing of Cataract Surgery Among US Communities. *JAMA Ophthalmology 134*(3), 267–276.

Kaye, A. D., Baluch, A., & Scott, J. T. (2010, Fall). Pain management in the elderly population: A review. *Ochsner Journal*, *10*(3), 179–187.

Kelley, A. S., & Morrison, R. S. (2015, August 20). Palliative Care for the Seriously Ill. *New England Journal of Medicine*, *373*(8), 747–755.

Keng, M. K., Wenzell, C. M., & Sekeres, M. A. (2013, October). A drug's life: The pathway to drug approval. *Clinical Advances in Hematology & Oncology*, *11*(10), 646–655.

Kenkel, D., & Mathios, A. (2012). Promotion to physicians and consumers. In (ed.), P. M. Danzon & S. Nicholson. *The Economics of the Biopharmaceutical Industry*. Oxford University Press.

Kennedy, P. (1998). *A Guide to econometrics* (4th ed). MIT Press.

Kennedy-Hendricks, A., Richey, M., McGinty, E. E., Stuart, E. A., Barry, C. L., & Webster, D. W. (2016, February). Opioid overdose deaths and florida's crackdown on pill mills. *American Journal of Public Health*, *106*(2) 291–297.

Kernick, L., Glare, P., Hosie, A., Chiu, A., & Kissane, D. W. (2023, April 11). Prevalence and management of chronic nonmalignant pain in palliative care populations: A systematic review. *Palliative & Supportive Care* 1–7.

Kesselheim, A. S., Avorn, J., & Sarpatwari, A. (2016, August 23–30). The high cost of prescription drugs in the United States: Origins and prospects for reform. *Jama*, *316*(8), 858–871.

Kff., (2005). Follow The pill: Understanding the U.S. commercial pharmaceutical supply chain. Kaiser Family Foundation.

Khouja, T., Tadrous, M., Matusiak, L., & Suda, K. (2021, September). Opioid prescribing in United States health systems, 2015 to 2019. *Value in Health*, *24*(9), 1279–1284.

Kiang, M. V., Humphreys, K., Cullen, M. R., & Basu, S. (2020, January 29). Opioid prescribing patterns among medical providers in the United States, 2003-17: Retrospective, observational study. *Bmj*, 368, l6968.

Kim, H., Hartung, D. M., Jacob, R. L., McCarty, D., & McConnell, K. J. (2016, April 1). The concentration of opioid prescriptions by providers and among patients in the oregon medicaid program. *Psychiatric Services 67*(4), 397–404.

King, N. B., Fraser, V., Boikos, C., Richardson, R., & Harper, S. (2014, August). Determinants of increased opioid-related mortality in the United States and Canada, 1990-2013: A systematic review. *American Journal of Public Health, 104*(8), 32–42.

King, S. A. (2018). The opioid epidemic: Who is to blame? *Psychiatric Times*, 35(6).

Kliff, S. (2017). *We started itAtul gawande on doctors' role in the opioid epidemic.* Vox Media.

Knaul, F. M., Farmer, P. E., Krakauer, E. L., De Lima, L., Bhadelia, A., Kwete, X. J., Arreola-Ornelas, H., et al. (2018, April 7). Alleviating the access abyss in palliative care and pain relief-an imperative of universal health coverage: the Lancet Commission report. *Lancet*, *391*(10128), 1391–1454.

Kolodny, A. (2020, August 1). How FDA failures contributed to the opioid crisis. *AMA Journal of Ethics*, *22*(1), 743–50.

Kravitz-Wirtz, N., Davis, C. S., Ponicki, W. R., Rivera-Aguirre, A., Marshall, B. D. L., Martins, S. S., & Cerdá, M. (2020, January 3). Association of medicaid expansion with opioid overdose mortality in the United States. *JAMA Network Open*, *3*(1), 1919066.

Kurtzman, L.(2022). New industry documents highlight role of pharmacies in driving opioid epidemic. In *UCSF research summary.* University of California San Francisco.

Laffont, J.J., & Tirole, J.(1993). *A theory of incentives in procurement and regulation.* The MIT Press.

Lalkhen, A.(2021). *An anatomy of pain.* Scribner.

Learch, R., & Cumberledge, J. (2013, May 1). Physicians' responsibility to understand patients' pain. *Virtual Mentor*, *15*(5), 430–433.

LeBrett, W. G., Iyengar, P. S., Lee, A. H., Chen, F. W., & Chang, L. (2021, October 16). *High opioid prescribing profiles among gastroenterologists: A nationwide analysis.* Clinical Gastroenterology and Hepatology.

Lee, J. H., Shewale, A. R., Barthold, D., & Devine, B. (2021, November). Geographic variation in the use of triptans and opioids for the acute treatment of migraine attacks. *Headache*, *61*(10), 1499–1510.

Legal Information Institute. (2021). *Drug trafficking.* Cornell Law School.

Lego, B., Deskins, J., & Bowen, E. (2021). 2022–2026 *West Virginia economic outlook.* Bureau of Business & Economic Research, John Chambers College of Business & Economics, West Virginia University.

Levy, N., Sturgess, J., & Mills, P. (March 2018). Pain as the fifth vital signand dependence on the "numerical pain scale" is being abandoned in the US: Why? *British Journal of Anaesthesia*, *120*(3), 435–438.

Lewis, E. T., Cucciare, M. A., & Trafton, J. A. (2014, August). What do patients do with unused opioid medications? *Clinical Journal of Pain*, *30*(8), 654–662.

Leyland, K. M., Judge, A., Javaid, M. K., Diez-Perez, A., Carr, A., Cooper, C., Arden, N. K., & Prieto-Alhambra, D. (2016, April). Obesity and the Relative Risk of Knee Replacement Surgery in Patients With Knee Osteoarthritis: A Prospective Cohort Study. *Arthritis & Rheumatology*, *68*(4) 817–825.

Lim, T. Y., Stringfellow, E. J., Stafford, C. A., DiGennaro, C., Homer, J. B., Wakeland, W., Eggers, S. L., et al. (2022, June 7). Modeling the evolution of the US opioid crisis for national policy development. *Proceedings of the National Academy of Sciences of the United States of America*, *119*(23), 2115714119.

Lin, D. H., Jones, C. M., Compton, W. M., Heyward, J., Losby, J. L., Murimi, I. B., Baldwin, G. T., et al. (2018, June 1). Prescription drug coverage for treatment of low back pain among US medicaid: Medicare advantage, and commercial insurers. *JAMA Network Open*, *1*(2), 180235.

Lin, D. H., Lucas, E., Murimi, I. B., Kolodny, A., & Alexander, G. C. (2017). Financial conflicts of interest and the centers for disease control and prevention's 2016 guideline for prescribing opioids for chronic pain. *JAMA Internal Medicine*, *177*(3), 427–428.

Lin, L. Y., Hung, T. C., & Lai, Y. H. (2021, July 30). Pain control and related factors in hospitalized patients. *Medicine (Baltimore)*, *100*(30), 26768.

Liu, Y., Logan, J. E., Paulozzi, L. J., Zhang, K., & Jones, C. M. (2013, August). Potential misuse and inappropriate prescription practices involving opioid analgesics. *American Journal of Managed Care*, *19*(8), 648–658.

Lobao, L., Partridge, M., Hean, O., Kelly, P., Chung, S., & Bulmer, E. R. (2021). *Socioeconomic transition in the appalachia coal region.*World Bank Group | Ohio State University.

Lo-Ciganic, W. H., Donohue, J. M., Hulsey, E. G., Barnes, S., Li, Y., Kuza, C. C., Yang, Q., et al. (2021). Integrating human services and criminal justice data with claims data to predict risk of opioid overdose among Medicaid beneficiaries: A machine-learning approach. *PLoS One 16*(3), 0248360.

Logan, J., Liu, Y., Paulozzi, L., Zhang, K., & Jones, C. (2013, August). Opioid prescribing in emergency departments: The prevalence of potentially inappropriate prescribing and misuse. *Medical Care*, *51*(8), 646–653.

Longo, L. P., Parran, T., Johnson, J. B., & Kinsey, W. (2000, April 15). Addiction: Part II. Identification and management of the drug-seeking patient. *American Family Physician, 61*(8), 2401–2408.

Lublóy, Á. (2014, October 20). Factors affecting the uptake of new medicines: A systematic literature review. *BMC Health Services Research*, *14*, 469.

Lurie, J. D., Bell, J. E., & Weinstein, J. (2009, October). What rate of utilization is appropriate in musculoskeletal care? *Clinical Orthopaedics and Related Research*, *467*(10), 2506–2511.

Lyu, H., Xu, T., Brotman, D., Mayer-Blackwell, B., Cooper, M., Daniel, M., Wick, E. C., et al. (2017). Overtreatment in the United States. *PLoS one*, *12*(9), 0181970.

MACPAC. (2011, June). *Medicaid and CHIP payment and access commission's (MACPAC's) report to the congress: The evolution of managed care in medicaid*. Department of Health and Human Services; Medicaid and CHIP Payment and Access Commission.

Macy, B. (2018). *Dopesick*. Little, Brown and Company.

Mahr, K. (2022, August 17). *CDC director orders agency overhaul, admitting flawed Covid-19 response*. Politico.

Mai, J., Franklin, G., & Tauben, D. (2015, August). Guideline for prescribing opioids to treat pain in injured workers. *Physical Medicine and Rehabilitation Clinics of North America*, *26*(3), 453–465.

Manchikanti, L. (2007, May). National drug control policy and prescription drug abuse: Facts and fallacies. *Pain Physician*, *10*(3), 399–424.

Manchikanti, L., Helm 2nd, S., Fellows, B., Janata, J. W., Pampati, V., Grider, J. S., & Boswell, M. V. (2012, July). Opioid epidemic in the United States. *Pain Physician*, *15*(3), 9–38.

Manchikanti, L., Sanapati, J., Benyamin, R. M., Atluri, S., Kaye, A. D., & Hirsch, J. A. (2018, July). Reframing the prevention strategies of the opioid crisis: Focusing on prescription opioids, fentanyl, and heroin epidemic. *Pain Physician*, *21*(4), 309–326.

Maradit Kremers, H., Larson, D. R., Crowson, C. S., Kremers, W. K., Washington, R. E., Steiner, C. A., Jiranek, W. A., & Berry, D. J. (2015, September 2). Prevalence of total hip and knee replacement in the United States. *Journal of Bone and Joint Surgery. American*, *97*(17), 1386–1397.

Marjoua, Y., & Bozic, K. J. (2012, December). Brief history of quality movement in US healthcare. *Current Reviews in Musculoskeletal Medicine*, *5*(4), 265–273.

Marks, J. H. (2020, June). Lessons from corporate influence in the opioid epidemic: Toward a norm of separation. *Journal of Bioethical Inquiry*, *17*(2), 173–189.

Massey, J., Kilkenny, M., Batdorf, S., Sanders, S. K., Ellison, D., Halpin, J., Gladden, R. M., et al. (2017, September 22). Opioid overdose outbreak—West Virginia, August 2016. *Morbidity and Mortality Weekly Report*, *66*(37), 975–980.

Mattingly, A. S., Rose, L., Eddington, H. S., Trickey, A. W., Cullen, M. R., Morris, A. M., & Wren, S. M. (2021, December 1). Trends in US surgical procedures and health care system response to policies curtailing elective surgical operations during the COVID-19 pandemic. *JAMA Network Open*, *4*(12), 2138038.

Mazurenko, O., Andraka-Christou, B. T., Bair, M. J., Kara, A. Y., & Harle, C. A. (2020, June 8). Clinical perspectives on hospitals' role in the opioid epidemic. *BMC Health Services Research*, *20*(1), 521.

McAdam-Marx, C., Roland, C. L., Cleveland, J., & Oderda, G. M. (2010, March). Costs of opioid abuse and misuse determined from a Medicaid database. *Journal of Pain & Palliative Care Pharmacotherapy*, *24*(1), 5–18.

McCoy, M. S., Carniol, M., Chockley, K., Urwin, J. W., Emanuel, E. J., & Schmidt, H. (2017, March 2). Conflicts of interest for patient-advocacy organizations. *New England Journal of Medicine*, *376*(9), 880–885.

McDonald, D. C., Carlson, K., & Izrael, D. (2012, October). Geographic variation in opioid prescribing in the U.S. *Journal of Pain*, *13*(10), 988–996.

McGranahan, D. A., & Parker, T. S. (2021). The opioid epidemic: A geography in two phases (Number 287). In *Economic research report*. U.S. Department of Agriculture, Economic Research Service.

McGreal, C. (2019, October 2). *Why were millions of opioid pills sent to a West Virginia town of 3000?* The Guardian.

McGwin Jr, G. (2010, November). Causation in epidemiology. *American Journal of Ophthalmology*, *150*(5), 599–601.

Meghani, S. H., Polomano, R. C., Tait, R. C., Vallerand, A. H., Anderson, K. O., & Gallagher, R. M. (2012, January). Advancing a national agenda to eliminate disparities in pain care: directions for health policy, education, practice, and research. *Pain Medicine*, *13*(1), 5–28.

Mehta, N., Bohl, D. D., Cohn, M. R., McCormick, J. R., Nicholson, G. P., Garrigues, G. E., & Verma, N. N. (2022, January 01). Trends in outpatient versus inpatient total shoulder arthroplasty over time.*JSES International*, *6*(1), 7–14.

Mehta, S. S. (2008). *Commercializing successful biomedical technologies: Basic principles for the development of drugs, diagnostics and devices.* Cambridge University Press.

Menard, C., & Shirley, M. M., (eds). (2008). *Handbook of the new institutional economics.* Springer.

Merino, R., Bowden, N., Katamneni, S., & Coustasse, A. (2019, April-June). The opioid epidemic in West Virginia. *Health Care Manager (Frederick)*, *38*(2), 187–195.

Millenson, M. L. (2014, July). New roles and rules for patient-centered care. *Journal of General Internal Medicine*, *29*(7), 979–980.

Miroff, N., Higham, S., Rich, S., Georges, S., & O'Connor, E. P. (2022). Cause of death: Washington faltered as fentanyl gripped America. The Washington Post.

Molfenter, T., McCarty, D., Jacobson, N., Kim, J. S., Starr, S., & Zehner, M. (2019, June). The payer's role in addressing the opioid epidemic: It's more than money. *Journal of Substance Abuse Treatment*, *101* 72–78.

Montiel Ishino, F. A., McNab, P. R., Gilreath, T., Salmeron, B., & Williams, F. (2020, November 18). A comprehensive multivariate model of biopsychosocial factors associated with opioid misuse and use disorder in a 2017–2018 United States national survey. *BMC Public Health, 20*(1), 1740.

Moore, S. W. (2003, December). An overview of drug development in the United States and current challenges. *Southern Medical Journal, 96*(12), 1244–1255 quiz 56.

Morone, N. E., & Weiner, D. K. (2013, November). Pain as the fifth vital sign: Exposing the vital need for pain education. *Clinical Therapeutics, 35*(11), 1728–1732.

Mulcahy, A. W., & Kareddy, V. (2021). Prescription drug supply chains: An overview of stakeholders and relationships. RAND Corporation.

Mustian, J., & Goodman, J. (2023). *DEA's failure to punish drug distributor blamed in opioid crisis raises revolving door questions.* PBS/Associated Press.

NASEM.(2017). Pain management and the opioid epidemic: Balancing societal and indidivual benefits and risks of prescription opioid use. In (Eds.), R. J. Bonnie, M. A. Ford, & J. K. Phillips *Consensus study report of national academies of sciences, engineering and medicine (NASEM).* National Academies Press.

Nataraj, N., Zhang, K., Guy Jr, G. P., & Losby, J. L. (2019, April 1). Identifying opioid prescribing patterns for high-volume prescribers via cluster analysis. *Drug and Alcohol Dependence, 197*, 250–254.

Neti., (2022). *Atlanta—carolinas HIDTA 2021 summary slides.* The National Emerging Threats Initiative.

Neuman, M. D., Bateman, B. T., & Wunsch, H. (2019, April 13). Inappropriate opioid prescription after surgery. *Lancet, 393*(10180), 1547–1557.

Newhouse, J. P. (1993). *Free for all? lessons from the RAND health Insurance experiment.* Harvard University Press.

Noah, L. (2019).Federal regulatory responses to the prescription opioid crisis: Too little, too late? *Utah Law Review 2019, 4.*

Nutescu, E. A., Park, H. Y., Walton, S. M., Blackburn, J. C., Finley, J. M., Lewis, R. K., & Schumock, G. T. (2005, August). Factors that influence prescribing within a therapeutic drug class. *Journal of Evaluation in Clinical Practice, 11* (4), 357–365.

O'Donnell, J., Gladden, R. M., Kariisa, M., & Mattson, C. L. (May 2022). Using death scene and toxicology evidence to define involvement of heroin, pharmaceutical morphine, illicitly manufactured fentanyl and pharmaceutical fentanyl in opioid overdose deaths, 38 states and the district of Columbia, January 2018–December 2019. *Addiction, 117*(5), 1483–1490.

O'Donnell, J., Tanz, L. J., Gladden, R. M., Davis, N. L., & Bitting, J. (2021, December 17). Trends in and characteristics of drug overdose deaths involving illicitly manufactured fentanyls - United States, 2019-2020. *Morbidity and Mortality Weekly Report*, *70*(50), 1740–1746.

Oag. (2021). *AG Yost announces Ohio's historic $808 million settlement with opioid distributors.* News Release.

OECD. (2010). *Regulatory policy and the road to sustainable growth.* Organization for Economic Cooperation and Development.

Ogus, A. (1994). *Regulation Legal form and economic theory: Clarendon law series.* Oxford Univeristy Press.

OIG. (2017). Opioids in medicare Part D: Concerns about extreme use and questionable prescribing. In *HHS OIG data brief (OEI–02–17–00250).* U.S. Office of the Inspector General.

OIG. (2019). Review of the drug enforcement administration's regulatory and enforcement efforts to control the diversion of opioids. In *Evaluation and inspections division 19–05.* United States Department of Justice; Office of the Inspector General.

Painter, J. T., Crofford, L. J., & Talbert, J. (2013, March). Geographic variation of chronic opioid use in fibromyalgia. *Clinical Therapeutics*, *35*(3), 303–311.

Palamar, J. J., Ciccarone, D., Rutherford, C., Keyes, K. M., Carr, T. H., & Cottler, L. B. (2022, May 1). Trends in seizures of powders and pills containing illicit fentanyl in the United States, 2018 through 2021. *Drug and Alcohol Dependence*, *234*, 109398.

Palamar, J. J., Fitzgerald, N., Carr, T. H., Cottler, L. B., & Ciccarone, D. (2025, April). National and regional trends in fentanyl seizures in the United States, 2017-2023. *International Journal of Drug Policy*, *138*, 104417.

Parente, S. T.(2011). Exploring ex ante regulatory mechanisms for detecting prescription drug misuse. In *Regulation versus litigation: Perspectives from economics and law*, (Ed.), D. P. Kessler. National Bureau of Economic Research | The University of Chicago Press.

Patel, B., Gheihman, G., Katz, J. T., Begin, A. S., & Solomon, S. R. (2024, April). Navigating uncertainty in clinical practice: A structured approach. *Journal of General Internal Medicine*, *39*(5), 829–836.

Peltzman, S. (1988). Toward a more general theory of regulation. In *Chicago studies in political economy*, (Ed.), G. J. Stigler. The University of Chicago Press.

Peppin, J. F., & Coleman, J. J. (2021, June). CDC's efforts to quantify prescription opioid overdose deaths fall short. *Pain and Therapy*, *10*(1), 25–38.

Peppin, J. F., Coleman, J. J., Paladini, A., & Varrassi, G. (2021, September). What your death certificate says about you may be wrong: A narrative review on CDC's efforts to quantify prescription opioid overdose deaths. *Cureus*, *13*(9), 18012.

Pergolizzi, J. V., Curro, F. A., Col, N., Ghods, M. P., Vena, D., Taylor, R., Naftolin, F., & LeQuang, J. A. (2017, October). A multicentre evaluation of an opioid patient-provider agreement. *Postgraduate Medical Journal, 93* (1104), 613–617.

Pergolizzi Jr, J. V., Rosenblatt, M., & LeQuang, J. A. (2019, June). Three years down the road: The aftermath of the CDC guideline for prescribing opioids for chronic pain. *Advances in Therapy, 36*(6), 1235–1240.

Peterson, L., Murugesan, M., Nocon, R., Hoang, H., Bolton, J., Laiteerapong, N., Pollack, H., & Marsh, J. (2022). Health care use and spending for medicaid patients diagnosed with opioid use disorder receiving primary care in federally qualified health centers and other primary care settings. *PLoS One, 17*(10), 0276066.

Phelps, C. E. (2003). *Health economics* (3rd ed). Addison Wesley.

Philipson, T. J., Sun, E., & Goldman, D. (2011). The effects of product liability exemption in the presence of the FDA. In *Regulation versus litigation: Perspectives from economics and law*, D. P. Kessler (Ed.), National Bureau of Economic Research | The University of Chicago Press.

Piple, A. S., Wang, J. C., Bouz, G. J., Chung, B. C., Mayfield, C. K., Richardson, M. K., Oakes, D. A., et al. (2023, August) The persistent effects of the COVID-19 pandemic on total joint arthroplasty changes in practice patterns in the United States from 2020 to 2021. *Journal of Arthroplasty, 38*(8) 1438–1443.

Pi-Sunyer, F. X. (1999, November) Comorbidities of overweight and obesity: Current evidence and research issues. *Medicine & Science in Sports & Exercise, 31*(11 Suppl), S602–8.

Pitts, P. J., Louet, H. L., Moride, Y., & Conti, R. M. (2016, November). Twenty-first century pharmacovigilance: Efforts, roles, and responsibilities. *The Lancet Oncology*, 17(11, 486–92.

Porter, M. E., & Lee, T. H. (2013, October). *The strategy that will fix health Care.* Harvard Business Review.

Posner, E. (1997) . Standards, rules, and social norms. *Harvard Journal of Law and Public Policy, 21.*

Posner, G. (2021, February 3). *FDA's Janet woodcock failed to stop the opioid epidemic.* USA Today.

Pratap, P., Dickson, A., Love, M., Zanoni, J., Donato, C., Flynn, M. A., & Schulte, P. A. (2021, September 23). Public health impacts of underemployment and unemployment in the United States: Exploring perceptions, gaps and opportunities. *International Journal of Environmental Research and Public Health, 18*(19).

Pretorius, R. W., & Zurick, G. M. (2008, April). A systematic approach to identifying drug-seeking patients. *Family Practice Management, 15*(4), 3–5.

Pritchard, K. T., Baillargeon, J., Lee, W. C., Raji, M. A., & Kuo, Y. F. (2022, November 1) Trends in the use of opioids vs nonpharmacologic treatments in adults with pain, 2011–2019. *JAMA Network Open, 5*(11), 2240612.

Purdue, M. P., Hutchings, S. J., Rushton, L., & Silverman, D. T. (2015, March). The proportion of cancer attributable to occupational exposures. *Annals of Epidemiology, 25*(3), 188–192.

Quinones, S. (2019, May). *Physicians get addicted too.* The Atlantic.

Quirk, P. J. (1981). *Industry influence in federal regulatory agencies.* Princeton University Press.

Rajput, K., & Vadivelu, N. (2021, January 14). Acute pain management of chronic pain patients in ambulatory surgery centers. *Current Pain and Headache Reports, 25*(1), 1.

Rawal, N. (2007, March). Postoperative pain treatment for ambulatory surgery. *Best Practice & Research Clinical Anaesthesiology, 21*(1), 129–148.

Rea, T. D., Heckbert, S. R., Kaplan, R. C., Psaty, B. M., Smith, N. L., Lemaitre, R. N., & Lin, D. (2001, September 1). Body mass index and the risk of recurrent coronary events following acute myocardial infarction. *American Journal of Cardiology, 88*(5), 467–472.

Reyes, C., Leyland, K. M., Peat, G., Cooper, C., Arden, N. K., & Prieto-Alhambra, D. (2016, August). Association between overweight and obesity and risk of clinically diagnosed knee, hip, and hand osteoarthritis: A population-based cohort study. *Arthritis & Rheumatology, 68*(8), 1869–1875.

Rich, B. A. (2001, September). Physicians' legal duty to relieve suffering. *Western Journal of Medicine, 175*(3), 151–152.

Rigg, K. K., March, S. J., & Inciardi, J. A. (2010). Prescription drug abuse & diversion: Role of the pain clinic. *Journal of Drug Issues, 40*(3), 681–702.

Robinson, J. C. (1993, Fall). Payment mechanisms, nonprice incentives, and organizational innovation in health care. *Inquiry, 30*(3), 328–333.

Robinson, J. C. (2001). Theory and practice in the design of physician payment incentives. *The Milbank Quarterly, 79*(2), 149–177.

Roland, C. L., Lake, J., & Oderda, G. M. (2016, December). Prevalence of prescription opioid misuse/abuse as determined by international classification of diseases codes: A systematic review. *Journal of Pain & Palliative Care Pharmacotherapy*, 30(4), 258–268.

Romman, A. N., Hsu, C. M., Chou, L. N., Kuo, Y. F., Przkora, R., Gupta, R. K., & Lozada, M. J. (2020, November 7). Opioid prescribing to medicare part D Enrollees, 2013-2017: Shifting responsibility to pain management providers. *Pain Medicine, 21*(7), 1400–1407.

Ross, S., & Peselow, E. (2012, September–October). Co-occurring psychotic and addictive disorders: Neurobiology and diagnosis. *Clinical Neuropharmacology, 35*(5), 235–243.

Rothman, K. J., Greenland, S., & Lash, T. L. (2008). *Modern epidemiology* (3 ed). Wolters Kluer; Lippincot WIlliams & Wilkins.

Rothstein, M. A., & Irzyk, J. (2022, February 18). *The CDC should rescind, not 'update,' its 2016 opioid guideline.* The Hill.

Rough, K., Huybrechts, K. F., Hernandez-Diaz, S., Desai, R. J., Patorno, E., & Bateman, B. T. (2019, January). Using prescription claims to detect aberrant behaviors with opioids: Comparison and validation of 5 algorithms. *Pharmacoepidemiology and Drug Safety*, *28*(1) 62–69.

Rowan, S., Mohseni, N., Chang, M., Burger, H., Peters, M., & Mir, S. (2023, October 13). From tick to test: A comprehensive review of tick-borne disease diagnostics and surveillance methods in the United States. *Life (Basel)*, *13*(10).

Rudolph, B., & Davis, R.(2005). Administrative data and disease surveillance: An integration toolkit. In *NAHDO-CDC cooperative agreement project: CDC assessment initiative*. The National Association of Health Data Organizations (NAHDO).

Santo Jr, T., Campbell, G., Gisev, N., Martino-Burke, D., Wilson, J., Colledge-Frisby, S., Clark, B., Tran, L. T., & Degenhardt, L. (2022, September 1). Prevalence of mental disorders among people with opioid use disorder: A systematic review and meta-analysis. *Drug and Alcohol Dependence*, *238*, 109551.

Santucci, K. (2012, Aprirl). Psychiatric disease and drug abuse. *Current Opinion in Pediatrics*, *24*(2), 233–237.

Sareen, J., Afifi, T. O., McMillan, K. A., & Asmundson, G. J. G. (2011). Relationship between household income and mental disorders: Findings from a population-based longitudinal study. *Archives of General Psychiatry*, *68*(4), 419–427.

Saunders, H., & Rudowitz, R. (2022). Demographics and health insurance coverage of nonelderly adults with mental illness and substance use disorders in 2020. Kaiser Family Foundation (KFF).

Schatman, M. E., & Webster, L. R. (2015). The health insurance industry: Perpetuating the opioid crisis through policies of cost-containment and profitability. *Journal of Pain Research*, *8*, 153–158.

Schatman, M. E., & Ziegler, S. J. (2017). Pain management, prescription opioid mortality, and the CDC: Is the devil in the data? *Journal of Pain Research*, *10* 2489–2495.

Schieber, L. Z., Guy, G. P., Seth, J. P., Young, R., Mattson, C. L., Mikosz, C. A., & Schieber, R. A. (2019, March 1). Trends and patterns of geographic variation in opioid prescribing practices by state, United States, 2006-2017. *JAMA Network Open*, *2*(3), 190665.

Schmidt, K. L., Alpen, M. A., & Rakel, B. A. (1996, August). Implementation of the agency for health care policy and research pain guidelines. *AACN Clinical Issues*, *7*(3), 425–435.

Schneider, B. J., Ehsanian, R., Kennedy, D. J., Schmidt, A., Huynh, L., & Maher, D. P. (2022, March). The effect of patient satisfaction scores on physician clinical decision making: A possible factor driving utilization of opioid prescriptions, magnetic resonance imaging, and interventional spine procedures. *Interventional Pain Medicine*, *1*(1), 100012.

Schneider, J. E. (2003, June 01). Changes in the effects of mandatory rate regulation on growth in hospital operating costs, 1980–1996. *Review of Industrial Organization*, *22*(4), 297–312.

Schober, P., Boer, C., & Schwarte, L. A. (2018, May). Correlation coefficients: Appropriate use and interpretation. *Anesthesia & Analgesia*, *126*(5), 1763–1768.

Schug, S. A., & Chong, C. (2009, December). Pain management after ambulatory surgery. *Current Opinion in Anaesthesiology*, *22*(6), 738–743.

Schumock, G. T., Walton, S. M., Park, H. Y., Nutescu, E. A., Blackburn, J. C., Finley, J. M., & Lewis, R. K. (2004, April). Factors that influence prescribing decisions. *Annals of Pharmacotherapy*, *38*(4), 557–562.

Scott, D. (2016, March 17). *1 in 3 Americans blame doctors for national opioid epidemic, STAT-Harvard poll finds.*STAT.

Seeley, E. (2022). The impact of pharmaceutical wholesalers on U.S. drug spending. Issue Brief: Commonwealth Fund.

Shah, N. G., Lathrop, S. L., Flores, J. E., & Landen, M. G. (2012, September 1). The influence of living along the U.S. Mexico border on unintentional drug overdose death, New Mexico (USA), 2005-2009. *Drug and Alcohol Dependence*, 125(1–32), 19–26.

Shariq, O. A., Bews, K. A., Etzioni, D. A., Kendrick, M. L., Habermann, E. B., & Thiels, C. A. (2023, March 1). Performance of general surgical procedures in outpatient settings before and after onset of the COVID-19 Pandemic. *JAMA Network Open*. *6*(3), 231198.

Shaw, W. S., Roelofs, C., & Punnett, L. (2020, August). Work environment factors and prevention of opioid-related deaths. *American Journal of Public Health*, 110(8), 1235–1241.

Shen, S., Candon, M., Fadeyibi, O., Kaplan, K., Lim, S., Mandell, D. S., Neimark, G., et al. (2021, December 1). The implementation of opioid prescribing report cards in Medicaid managed care: A community quality collaborative. *American Journal of Managed Care*, *27*(12), 429–34.

Shichman, I., Roof, M., Askew, N., Nherera, L., Rozell, J. C., Seyler, T. M., & Schwarzkopf, R. (2023, January–March). Projections and epidemiology of primary hip and knee arthroplasty in medicare patients to 2040–2060. *JBJS Open Access*, *8*(1).

Shiri, R., Karppinen, J., Leino-Arjas, P., Solovieva, S., & Viikari-Juntura, E. (2010, January 15). The association between obesity and low back pain: A meta-analysis. *American Journal of Epidemiology*, *171*(2), 135–154.

Shukla, D., Patel, S., Clack, L., Smith, T. B., & Shuler, M. S. (2021, March). Retrospective analysis of trends in surgery volumes between 2016 and 2019 and impact of the insurance deductible: Cross-sectional study. *Annals of Medicine and Surgery (London)*, *63*, 102176.

Sidak, J. G., & Spulber, D. F. (1997). *Deregulatory takings and the regulatory contract*. Cambridge University Press.

Siddique, S. M., & Mehta, S. J. (2017, December). Market evaluation: Finances, bundled payments, and accountable care organizations. *Anesthesiology Clinics*, *35*(4), 715–724.

Sinaiko, A. D., Szumigalski, K., Eastman, D., & Chien, A. T. (2019). Delivery of patient centered care in the U.S. health care system: What is standing in its way? Robert Wood Johnson Foundation & Academy Health.

Siu, A. L., Sonnenberg, F. A., Manning, W. G., Goldberg, G. A., Bloomfield, E. S., Newhouse, J. P., & Brook, R. H. (1986, November 13). Inappropriate use of hospitals in a randomized trial of health insurance plans. *New England Journal of Medicine*, *315*(20), 1259–1266.

Skelly, A. C., Chou, R., Dettori, J. R., Turner, J. A., Friedly, J. L., Rundell, S. D., Fu, R., & Ferguson, A. J. (2020). Noninvasive nonpharmacological treatment for chronic pain: A systematic review update. In *Comparative effectiveness review, no. 227*. Agency for Healthcare Research and Quality (AHRQ).

Skinner, J. (2011). Causes and Consequences of Regional Variations in Health Care. In M. V. Pauly, T. McGuire, & P. P. (Eds.), *Handbook of health economics* (vol 2) Elsevier.

Skinner, J. (2012). Causes and consequences of regional variations in health care. In M. V. Pauly, T. G. McGuire, & P. P. Barros. (Eds.), *Handbook of health economics* (Vol 2) Elsevier B.V.

Snijders, R. A. H., Brom, L., Theunissen, M., & van den Beuken-van Everdingen, M. H. J. (2023, January 18). Update on prevalence of pain in patients with cancer 2022: A systematic literature review and meta-analysis. *Cancers (Basel)*, *15*(3).

Socal, M. P., & Sharfstein, J. M. (2024, April 1). Drug shortages-a study in complexity. *JAMA Network Open*, *7*(4), 244168.

Song, Z., Kannan, S., Gambrel, R. J., Marino, M., Vaduganathan, M., Clapp, M. A., Seiglie, J. A., & Resnick, M. J. (2022, January). Physician practice pattern variations in common clinical scenarios within 5 US metropolitan areas. *JAMA Health Forum*, *3*(1), 214698.

Spithoff, S., Leece, P., Sullivan, F., Persaud, N., Belesiotis, P., & Steiner, L. (2020). Drivers of the opioid crisis: An appraisal of financial conflicts of interest in clinical practice guideline panels at the peak of opioid prescribing. *PLoS One*, *15*(1), 0227045.

Springer, R., Marino, M., Bailey, S. R., Angier, H., O'Malley, J. P., Hoopes, M., Lindner, S., DeVoe, J. E., & Huguet, N. (October 2019). Prescription opioid use patterns, use disorder diagnoses and addiction treatment receipt after the 2014 Medicaid expansion in Oregon. *Addiction*, *114*(10), 1775–1784.

Stein, B. D., Kilmer, B., Taylor, J., & Vaiana, M. E. (2023). America's opioid ecosystem. RAND Corporation.

Stein, S., Bogard, E., Boice, N., Fernandez, V., Field, T., Gilstrap, A., Kahn, S. R., Larkindale, J., & Mathieson, T. (2018, January 22). Principles for interactions with biopharmaceutical companies: The development of guidelines for patient advocacy organizations in the field of rare diseases. *Orphanet Journal of Rare Diseases*, 13(1), 18.

Stiglitz, J. (2002). *Globalization and its Discontents.* W.W. Norton & Co.

Stokes, A., Berry, K. M., Hempstead, K., Lundberg, D. J., & Neogi, T. (2019, December 2). Trends in prescription analgesic use among adults with musculoskeletal conditions in the United States, 1999-2016. *JAMA Network Open 2* (12), 1917228.

Strand, N., J, M., Tieppo Francio, V., M, M., Turkiewicz, M., El Helou, A., M, M., et al. (2022, August). Advances in pain medicine: A review of new technologies. *Current Pain and Headache Reports*, *26*(8), 605–616.

Sullivan, M. D., & Ballantyne, J. C. (2021, October 26). The right to pain relief: Its origins in end-of-life care and extension to chronic pain care. *Clinical Journal of Pain*, *38*(1), 58–63.

Sullivan, M. D., & Ballantyne, J. C. (2023). *The right to pain relief and other deep roots of the opioid epidemic.* Oxford University Press.

Sullivan, P. S., Bradley, H. M., Rio, C. D., & Rosenberg, E. S. (2020, September). The geography of opioid use disorder: A data triangulation approach. *Infectious Disease Clinics of North America*, *34*(3), 451–464.

Sun, E. C., Darnall, B. D., Baker, L. C., & Mackey, S. (2016, September 1). Incidence of and risk factors for chronic opioid use among opioid-naive patients in the postoperative period. *JAMA Internal Medicine*, *176*(9), 1286–1293.

Sun, J. W., Franklin, J. M., Rough, K., Desai, R. J., Hernández-Díaz, S., Huybrechts, K. F., & Bateman, B. T. (2020). Predicting overdose among individuals prescribed opioids using routinely collected healthcare utilization data. *PLoS One*, *15*(10), 0241083.

Sung, H., Siegel, R. L., Torre, L. A., Pearson-Stuttard, J., Islami, F., Fedewa, S. A., Sauer, A. G., & Jemal, A. (2019, March). Global patterns in excess body weight and the associated cancer burden. *CA: A Cancer Journal for Clinicians*, *69*(2), 88–112.

Svirsky, L. (2021, July). Opioid treatment agreements and patient accountability. *Hastings Center Report*, *51*(4), 46–49.

Teisberg, E., Wallace, S., & O'Hara, S. (2020, May). Defining and implementing value-based health care: A strategic framework. *Academic Medicine*, *95*(5), 682–685.

Theisen, K., Jacobs, B., Macleod, L., & Davies, B. (2018, November). The United States opioid epidemic: A review of the surgeon's contribution to it and health policy initiatives. *BJU International*, *122*(5), 754–759.

Thornton, R. G. (2003, July). The learned intermediary doctrine and its effects on prescribing physicians. *Proceedings (Baylor University Medical Center)*, *16*(3), 359–361.

Tichy, E. M., Schumock, G. T., Hoffman, J. M., Suda, K. J., Rim, M. H., Tadrous, M., Stubbings, J., et al. (2020, July 23). National trends in prescription drug expenditures and projections for 2020. *American Journal of Health-System Pharmacy*, *77*(15), 1213–1230.

Tong, N. (2024). *Arkansas files opioid epidemic lawsuit against PBMs optum, express scripts*. Fierce Healthcare.

Torén, K., & Blanc, P. D. (2009, January 29). Asthma caused by occupational exposures is common—a systematic analysis of estimates of the population-attributable fraction. *BMC Pulmonary Medicine*, *9*, 7.

Train, K. E. (1991). *Optimal Regulation*. The MIT Press.

Tyree, P. T., Lind, B. K., & Lafferty, W. E. (2006, July–August). Challenges of using medical insurance claims data for utilization analysis. *American Journal of Medical Quality*, *21*(4), 269–275.

Tyree, P. T., Lind, B. K., & Lafferty, W. E.(2010). *Atlanta high intensity drug trafficking area: Drug market analysis 2010*. National Drug Intelligence Center, U.S. Department of Justice.

Tyree, P. T., Lind, B. K., & Lafferty, W. E.(2011). New Mexico high intensity drug trafficking area. In *Drug market analysis 2011*. U.S. Department of Justice, National Drug Intelligence Center.

Urban Institute. (2010). The US population is aging. The Urban Institute.

USDOJ. (2019). *2019 national drug threat assessment (NDTA)*. U.S. Department of Justice, Drug Enforcement Administration.

Vietor, R. H. K. (1994). *Contrived competition: Regulation and deregulation in America*. The Belknap Press of Harvard University Press.

Viscusi, W. K., Vernon, J. M., & Harrington, J. E. (1995). *Economics of regulation and antitrust* (2nd ed). The MIT Press.

Viswanath, O., Urits, I., Bouley, E., Peck, J. M., Thompson, W., & Kaye, A. D. (2019, May 1). Evolving spinal cord stimulation technologies and clinical implications in chronic pain management. *Current Pain and Headache Reports*, *23*(6), 39.

Vittinghoff, E., Glidden, D. V., Shiboski, S. C., & McCulloch, C. E. (2012). Statistics for biology and health. (Ed.), M. Gail and et al. *Regression Methods in Biostatistics* (2nd ed.) Springer Science and Business Media.

Vukmir, R. B. (2004, August). Drug seeking behavior. *American Journal of Drug and Alcohol Abuse*, *30*(3), 551–575.

Wainwright, T. (2016). *Narconomics: How to run a drug cartel*. PublicAffairs/ Perseus.

Walley, A. Y., Bernson, D., Larochelle, M. R., Green, T. C., Young, L., & Land, T. (2019, November–December). The contribution of prescribed and illicit opioids to fatal overdoses in massachusetts, 2013–2015. *Public Health Reports, 134*(6), 667–674.

Wang, D., Liu, C., Zhang, X., & Liu, C. (2021, March 25). Does diagnostic uncertainty increase antibiotic prescribing in primary care? *NPJ primary care respiratory medicine, 31*(1), 17.

Warfield, S., Pollini, R., Stokes, C. M., & Bossarte, R. (2019, February). Opioid-related outcomes in West Virginia, 2008–2016. *American Journal of Public Health, 109*(2), 303–305.

Warner, M., Chen, L. H., & Makuc, D. M. (2009, September). Increase in fatal poisonings involving opioid analgesics in the United States, 1999–2006. *NCHS Data Brief, 22*, 1–8.

Webster, B. S., Cifuentes, M., Verma, S., & Pransky, G. (2009, February). Geographic variation in opioid prescribing for acute, work-related, low back pain and associated factors: a multilevel analysis. *American Journal of Industrial Medicine, 52*(2), 162–171.

Wechsler, J. (2022, December 8). *Rising demand drives drug shortages.* Pharmaceutical Technology.

Weiss, F., Ciccocioppo, R., Parsons, L. H., Katner, S., Liu, X., Zorrilla, E. P., Valdez, G. R., et al. (2001, June). Compulsive drug-seeking behavior and relapse: Neuroadaptation, stress, and conditioning factors. *Annals of the New York Academy of Sciences, 937*, 1–26.

Whittaker, B. (2019, February 24). *Did the FDA ignite the opioid epidemic?* CBS 60 Minutes.

Whitten, C. E., Evans, C. M., & Cristobal, K. (2005, Spring). Pain management doesn't have to be a pain: Working and communicating effectively with patients who have Chronic pain. *The Permanente Journal, 9*(2), 41–48.

Wilkie, D. J., & Ezenwa, M. O. (2012, November–December). Pain and symptom management in palliative care and at end of life. *Nursing Outlook, 60*(6), 357–364.

Williamson, J., & Spicer, A. J. (2023a, December). Evaluating the impact of the FDA's orphan drug designation on share prices of biotechnology companies. *Drug Discovery Today, 28*(12), 103807.

Williamson, J., & Spicer, A. J. (2023b, November). Review of the impact of the FDA's fast track designation on biotechnology companies' share prices. *Drug Discovery Today, 28*(11), 103771.

Wilson, M., Guta, A., Waddell, K., Lavis, J., Reid, R., & Evans, C. (2020, April). The impacts of accountable care organizations on patient experience, health outcomes and costs: A rapid review. *Journal of Health Services Research & Policy, 25*(2), 130–138.

Winslow, C. M., Kosecoff, J. B., Chassin, M., Kanouse, D. E., & Brook, R. H. (1988, July 22–29). The appropriateness of performing coronary artery bypass surgery. *Jama, 260*(4), 505–509.

Woodruff, J.(2021). How a powerful corporate consulting firm helped create the opioid epidemic: Interview with massachusetts attorney general maura healy. PBS News Hour.

Wouters, O. J., McKee, M., & Luyten, J. (2020, March 3). Estimated research and development investment needed to bring a new medicine to market, 2009–2018. *Jama*, *323*(9), 844–853.

WVNews. (2019, September 24). *More doctors from Southern WV accused in fed 'pill mill' probe*.West Virginia News.

Yee, C. A., Pizer, S. D., & Frakt, A. (2020, September). Medicare's bundled payment initiatives for hospital-initiated episodes: Evidence and evolution. *The Milbank Quarterly*, *98*(3), 908–974.

Young, H. P. (2015). The evolution of social norms.*Annual Review of Economics*, *7*(1), 359–387.

Zajacova, A., Grol-Prokopczyk, H., & Zimmer, Z. (2021). Pain trends among American adults, 2002–2018: Patterns, disparities, and correlates.*Demography*, *58*(2), 711–738.

Zawadzki, R. S., Grill, J. D., & Gillen, D. L. (2023, May 22). Frameworks for estimating causal effects in observational settings: Comparing confounder adjustment and instrumental variables. *BMC Medical Research Methodology*, *23*(1), 122.

Zhang, T. T., Liu, Z., Liu, Y. L., Zhao, J. J., Liu, D. W., & Tian, Q. B. (2018, February). Obesity as a risk factor for low back pain: A meta-analysis. *Clinical Spine Surgery*, *31*(1), 22–27.

Zhao, D., Baek, J., Hume, A. L., McPhillips, E. A., & Lapane, K. L.(2022). Geographic variation in the use of gabapentinoids and opioids for pain in a commercially insured adult population in the United States. *Journal of Pain Research*, *15*, 443–454.

CHAPTER 5

Responsibility

Researchers and experts working in areas of applied law and economics, particularly areas involving studies of harms and externalities, often must address issues concerning liability. This is not to say that economists are positioned to legally determine or assign liability. Instead, that is normally left for stakeholders to argue and for the courts to decide. Within the context of the economic objectives of this book, the interest here is in identifying the *types* of entities and groups of entities that are normally associated with each of the factors that contributed to growth in the supply of opioids. As discussed in the first chapter, to undertake an analysis of the effect of a harm or negative externality like air pollution, it is necessary to develop a complete understanding of the sources of the air pollution, and by extension the specific entities or groups of entities potentially responsible for those sources. This is particularly important if mitigation and abatement are the ultimate policy goals, which is often the case. Thus, economists are generally accustomed to considering aspects of liability for the purposes of understanding responsibility in issues regarding externalities and further applying those concepts to the design of mechanisms to mitigate and abate attributable harms and costs of externalities.[1] As alluded to throughout this book, the genesis of the opioid

[1] For a more detailed account of how economists approach liability, see generally R. D. Cooter, "Economic Theories of Legal Liability," *Journal of Economic Perspectives* 5,

J. E. Schneider, *The Economics of Pain*, Global Perspectives on Wealth and Distribution,
https://doi.org/10.1007/978-3-032-20355-7_5

problem in the U.S. is widely believed to be multifactorial and multifaceted, involving numerous interrelated factors and entities along the complex prescription drug supply chain. Again, the goal of this chapter is not to suggest or claim that certain entities are legally liable for the increase in opioid supply, or that some entities may be more liable than others; that determination is left for the courts and the reader to decide. Along the same lines, the goal here is not to offer any sort of legal opinion, or even a legal framework, through which liability should be apportioned to entities found liable; again, that is an exercise best left for legal experts and the courts. Instead, the focus of this chapter is to further explore, within the context of the economics of liability, general issues in product liability and to describe the groups of entities associated with the contributing factors identified in the preceding chapter.

As discussed in preceding chapter, recognition of pharmaceutical supply chain complexity and the multifactorial underpinnings of the opioid crisis have been relatively underexplored throughout the ongoing opioid litigation, with liability deliberations and subsequent judgments appearing to not fully recognize (or at least weigh) the salient features of the industry and its regulators. As discussed briefly in the first chapter, rather than focusing myopically on liability issues concerning only a limited set of entities and groups, a more comprehensive approach should consider all or at least most relevant factors in the consideration of liability. Emphasis on causation is, after all, the backbone of epidemiology. However, apart from the logical need to fully understand causation in order to devise effective remedies, there are at least two other supporting rationales for allocating responsibility. First, the factors and entities associated with opioid supply in the U.S. are inextricably connected and intertwined. Healthcare supply chains are complex, and the industry's diverse public and private components do not operate independently of one another. Consequently, it would be inappropriate to assume that any single component operates in a vacuum or operates independently of related factors and entities. Second, the law and economics approach to the study of externalities and liability seeks to identify all or most relevant sources, causes, and groups of responsible entities, such that "fair and reasonable" and "optimal" mitigation and abatement mechanisms can

no. 3 (1991); K. N. Hylton, "The Law and Economics of Products Liability," *Notre Dame Law Review* 88, no. 5 (2013); S. K. Jain, *Economic Analysis of Liability Rules* (New York, NY: Springer, 2015); W. K. Viscusi, "The Dimensions of the Product Liability Crisis," *The Journal of Legal Studies* 20, no. 1 (1991).

be employed. In analyses of negative externalities, instances of "multi-causality," where more than one entity causes or contributes to the negative externality, are relatively common.[2] One area in which economists have studied multicausal externalities is in environmental contaminants, especially those cases with conceivable public health implications, such as the pollution of shared public goods like soil, water, and air.[3] For example, in the U.S. certain polluted sites (e.g., those classified as "Superfund" sites[4]) typically require abatement of contaminated detritus, deposits, and soil, and the costs of that abatement are normally allocated among parties deemed responsible for the contamination of the site.[5]

5.1 Potentially Responsible Parties

Mass tort product liability cases and large-scale public health and environmental contamination cases typically involve the identification of "potentially responsible parties" ("PRPs") associated with the causation, enablement, or continuation of a harm or externality, where each PRP is potentially liable for their share of the estimated attributable cost or abatement cost.[6] In such cases, liability is often assigned retroactively,

[2] See, for example, Sect. 10.6 ("Multi-Causality"; pp.257–258) of D. J. Phaneuf and T. Requate, *A Course in Environmental Economics: Theory, Policy, and Practice* (Cambridge, UK: Cambridge University Press, 2017). Also see Cooter, "Economic Theories of Legal Liability."; R. D. Cooter and T. Ulen, *Law and Economics (6th Edition)* (Pearson, 2011); R.H. Coase, "The Problem of Social Cost," *Journal of Law and Economics* 3 (1960); Cooter, "Economic Theories of Legal Liability."; L. Priya, G. K. Varghese, and I. K. Shah, "Liability allocation in pollution involving multiple responsible parties," *Environ Sci Pollut Res Int* 27, no. 36 (2020).

[3] See generally Phaneuf and Requate, *A Course in Environmental Economics: Theory, Policy, and Practice.*

[4] The "Superfund Law" is the shorthand name for environmental contamination cases tried under the Comprehensive Environmental Response, Compensation and Liability Act ("CERCLA").

[5] See generally Priya, Varghese, and Shah, "Liability allocation in pollution involving multiple responsible parties."; S. Bookspan, "Potentially Responsible Party Searches: Finding the Cause of Urban Grime," *The Public Historian* 13, no. 2 (1991). Also see Sect. 10.7 ("Examples of Environmental Liability Laws" pp. 258–261) of Phaneuf and Requate, *A Course in Environmental Economics: Theory, Policy, and Practice.*

[6] The term "potentially responsible party" is used generally here but was introduced as part of the aforementioned CERCLA law. In the context of opioids, the term is used more generally than the strict CERCLA application. See generally Bookspan, "Potentially

followed by the identification of attributable abatement costs and the formation of some form of liability allocation method among the PRPs. In environmental abatement cases, the goal in theory is to identify all PRPs. According to Weber, "A single party is rarely responsible for the toxic waste pollution of a site. Usually, a toxic waste site, such as a landfill, will have numerous [PRPs]: generators; transporters; current owners and their lessees; former owners and operators and their successor corporations; individual corporate officers; and even governmental agencies."[7] Though the concept of PRPs is mainly featured in cases involving alleged environmental contamination, from an economics perspective the general framework could be applicable to a variety of circumstances featuring negative externalities attributable to multiple causal factors.

The identification of PRPs in externalities featuring multifactor causation can range from straightforward to complex. In the polluted river example offered earlier, if the contaminants can be clearly identified, then the list of PRPs starts with the identification of upstream entities potentially releasing those contaminants into the river. Another example of a relatively straightforward application of PRPs was the identification of responsible parties in the tobacco litigation, as the attention was solely on marketing tactics and alleged failure to warn on the part of tobacco manufacturers.[8] In practice, however, it may be challenging to identify an exhaustive set of PRPs, for several reasons.[9] First, in the case of aged industrial sites, the history of occupancy and activities on the site might become increasingly blurred

Responsible Party Searches: Finding the Cause of Urban Grime."; M. L. Manewitz, "Potentially Responsible Parties: Liability Issues," *Fordham Environmental Law Review* 5, no. 2 (2011); Priya, Varghese, and Shah, "Liability allocation in pollution involving multiple responsible parties."; W. Shin et al., "Evaluation of multiple PRPs' contributions to soil contamination in reclaimed sites around an abandoned smelter," *Sci Total Environ* 642 (2019).

[7] A. D. Weber, "Misery Loves Company: Spreading the Costs of CERCLA Cleanup," *Vanderbilt Law Review* 42, no. 5 (1989).

[8] In the tobacco MSA, responsible parties were identified as any participating tobacco manufacturer, and during and after the litigation were referred to collectively as "Participating Manufacturers." See generally PHLC, "The Master Settlement Agreement: An Overview," (St. Paul, Minnesota: Public Health Law Center at Mitchell Hamline School of Law, 2019).

[9] M. A. Stach, "Only "Innocent" Parties Need Apply: The Death of Private Party Cost Recovery Actions Under Superfund?," *William & Mary Environmental Law and Policy Review* 20, no. 1 (1995).

over time. In such cases, the identification of PRPs is an interdisciplinary endeavor, involving a mix of social science research, historical analysis, and scientific assessment. For example, in touting the value of historians in conducting PRP research, one study noted "In determining such environmental liability questions, the historian can often tell as much as the chemist or the geologist or the hydrographer about the contamination of the site. The historian's evidence is as convincing as laboratory analytical data or subsurface groundwater flow charts."[10] Second, in some cases extensive scientific research is required. For example, in a case involving sediment in the Hylebos Waterway in Tacoma, Washington, rigorous field research "effectively dismissed the assumption [...] that contaminated sediments from a particular source would be as likely to migrate down the Waterway as up the Waterway. As a result, major documented sources of contamination near the mouth should be expected to bear a larger share of the total cleanup compared with sources farther toward the head."[11]

A third challenge in the identification of PRPs, especially in environmental cases, has been the identification and assignment of responsibility to absent or defunct parties, where some identifiable PRPs are insolvent, no longer exist, or otherwise face impediments to being named as defendants. In such cases, absent PRPs can still be allocated some portion of responsibility, typically referred to as "orphan shares."[12] Hall et al. describe the problem this way: "The problem [of allocation] is aggravated by the presence of 'orphan' shares, which are the shares left by absent or insolvent PRPs that must be allocated among the rest of the group. Often these 'orphan' shares are substantial, including former owners and operators who had a major role in the mismanagement of the hazardous waste giving rise to the problem, but who are not available to pay for the cleanup."[13] In

[10] Bookspan, "Potentially Responsible Party Searches: Finding the Cause of Urban Grime."

[11] P. McLaren and R. P. Beveridge, "Sediment trend analysis of the Hylebos Waterway: implications for liability allocations," *Integr Environ Assess Manag* 2, no. 3 (2006).

[12] See generally K. K. Kilbert, "Neither Joint Nor Several: Orphan Shares in Private CERCLA Actions," *Environmental Law* 41, no. 4 (2011); D.R. Hansen, "CERCLA Cost Allocation and Nonparties' Responsibility: Who Bears the Orphan Shares?," *UCLA Journal of Environmental Law and Policy* 11, no. 1 (1992).

[13] R. M. Hall, R. H. Harris, and J. A. Reinsdorf, "Superfund Response Cost Allocations: The Law, The Science and The Practice," *The Business Lawyer (American Bar Association)* 49, no. 4 (1994).

environmental cases, there is also the concept of "responsible party plaintiffs," which are claimants (e.g., current property owners) bearing some responsibility for the exacerbation of the externality but are also suing defendants alleged to have contributed to contamination in the past.[14]

5.2 Supply Chain Liability

As discussed in the preceding chapter, the opioid crisis is also one with clear multi-causality, as many experts and stakeholders have argued. Accordingly, many of the public documents in the opioid MDL have also discussed or at least made mention of the multi-causal roots to the opioid crisis. For example, in the Ohio abatement order pertaining to large retail pharmacies, the Court stated that "… all three categories of actors along the *pharmaceutical supply chain*—that is, manufacturers, distributors, and dispensers of prescription opioids—contributed to the nuisance in the Counties …" (emphasis added).[15]

In the same order, the Court argued that "The numerous defendants named in these MDL proceedings fall overwhelmingly into these three categories [i.e., manufacturers, distributors, and pharmacies]. The Court finds this *natural grouping*, which corresponds to the tripartite opioid supply scheme contemplated by the Controlled Substances Act forms a rational basis to equitably apportion one-third of the responsibility for the nuisance to pharmacies for improper dispensing conduct in the Counties" (emphasis added).[16] Thus, in the MDL, the court relied on a "natural grouping" of the three pharmaceutical supply chain entities identified in the 1970 Controlled Substances Act ("CSA"). Although the Court recognized that there are multi-causal factors linked to various stages of the pharmaceutical supply chain, the court's reliance on the CSA grouping represents a relatively narrow interpretation of the pharmaceutical supply chain, and leaves out several very important components

[14] See generally Kilbert, "Neither Joint Nor Several: Orphan Shares in Private CERCLA Actions."

[15] Opioid MDL, "MDL 2804 Case No. 1:17-md-2804 Judge Dan Aaron Polster: Abatement Order," in *Re: National Opioid Litigation* (Ohio: United States District Court Northern District of Ohio, Eastern Division, 2022). (pp. 57–58).

[16] Ibid. (pp. 57–58).

that, as the preceding chapters have argued, are critical to any pharmaceutical reaching the market and remaining on the market. Figure 5.1 replicates the pharmaceutical supply chain diagram presented in Chap. 2, but with the named opioid MDL entities highlighted. Note that there is

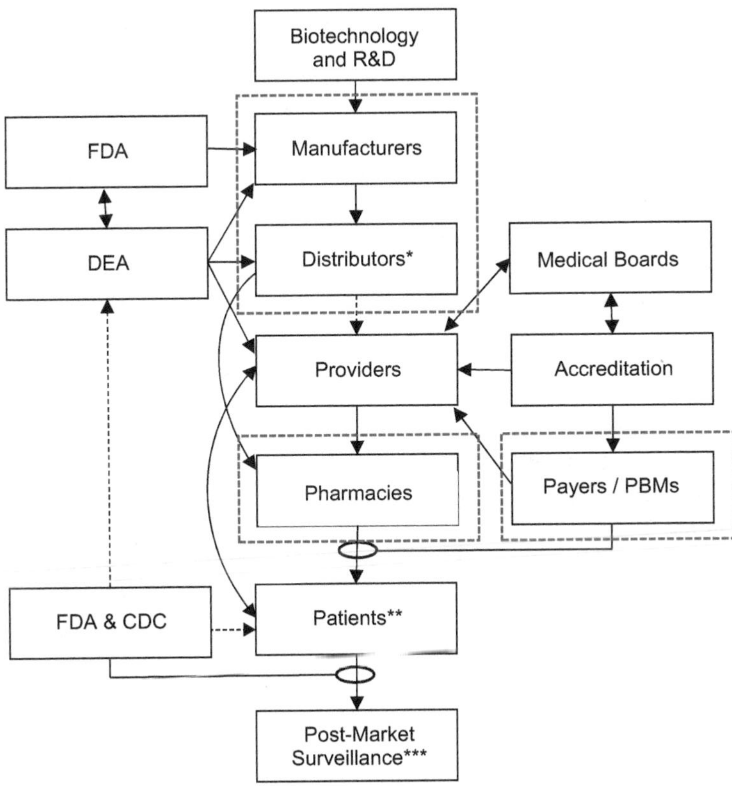

Fig. 5.1 Key Elements of the U.S. Pharmaceutical Supply Chain. Opioid MDL Defendants in Boxes with Dashed Border. *Notes* FDA = U.S. Food & Drug Administration; DEA = U.S. Drug Enforcement Administration; CDC = U.S. Centers for Disease Control & Prevention; PBM = Pharmacy Benefit Manager; MDL = opioid multidistrict litigation; *The terms "distributors" and "wholesalers" are used interchangeably; **The term "patients" is used interchangeably with "consumers," or in the case of insurance, "enrollees" or "beneficiaries;" ***Post-market surveillance is typically a shared responsibility between manufacturers & regulators

a dashed border around the box labeled "payers/PBMs," reflecting the inclusion of some PBMs as defendants in the opioid MDL.[17]

As the earlier discussions have emphasized, the approach to determining liability in the opioid litigation has been relatively narrow in terms of its perception and depiction of the pharmaceutical supply chain. Specifically, there are several reasons why it could be argued that this grouping is too narrow. First, and perhaps most importantly, basing the grouping on the CSA is potentially problematic because there have been many critical and important changes to the U.S. pharmaceutical industry since the enactment of the CSA, which was more than 50 years ago. To begin with, spending on pharmaceuticals has grown more than *ten-fold* since the CSA. In 1970, per capita spending on pharmaceuticals in the U.S. was about $100 per year, but today it averages more than $1,300 - per year.[18] The escalating utilization and expenditures associated with prescription drugs increasingly flow through public and private payers, where drug utilization is regularly managed by third-party PBMs relying on managed care payment mechanisms, such as tiered copayments (including incentives to use generics), mail order options, electronic claims filing and payment, formularies, and therapeutic interchange.[19] In addition, the volume of prescription drugs paid for by Medicare and state Medicaid programs tripled since 2010.[20] Consequently, the tripartite can be considered narrow because it ignores the financing and funding side of the market for opioids. Public and private payers continued paying for opioids through each era of the crisis, from the growth in supply following FDA approval to well after concerns over OUD rates surfaced.

Another reason that the grouping could be considered narrow is that it does not fully account for the multifaceted process required to bring a prescription drug to market and maintain sales and utilization. On the regulatory side, not a single prescription drug can be sold in the U.S. without

[17] See generally N. Tong, "Arkansas files opioid epidemic lawsuit against PBMs Optum, Express Scripts," (Fierce Healthcare, 2024).

[18] CBO, "Prescription Drugs: Spending, Use, and Prices," (Washington, D.C.: U.S. Congressional Budget Office, 2022); E. M. Tichy et al., "National trends in prescription drug expenditures and projections for 2022," *Am J Health Syst Pharm* 79, no. 14 (2022).

[19] See generally A. Lyles and F. B. Palumbo, "The effect of managed care on prescription drug costs and benefits," *Pharmacoeconomics* 15, no. 2 (1999); K. W. Schafermeyer, "The impact of managed care on pharmacy practice," *Pharm Pract Manag Q* 19, no. 4 (2000).

[20] CBO, "Prescription Drugs: Spending, Use, and Prices."

active involvement from the FDA and, in the case of scheduled drugs like opioids, also the DEA. The drug regulatory landscape also evolved markedly over the decades, with the FDA approval process becoming significantly more rigorous and scientific over time.[21] For example, currently the drug approval and monitoring activities of the FDA are carried out primarily by its Center for Drug Evaluation and Research ("CDER), which came into existence in the late 1980s, bringing together the existing but more fragmented process of drug review.[22] Similarly, the DEA sets production and distribution quotas, which implies that the agency has direct control of the supply of any scheduled drug.[23] The opioid crisis would most likely not have occurred were it not for the simultaneous failure of these two critical regulatory institutions. Similarly, the non-government regulators also failed. The narrow tripartite overlooks the critical role of independent accreditation agencies, which establish operational standards for all health care providers. As discussed in the previous chapter, these agencies, mainly the Joint Commission, dictated the standards that providers needed to achieve to obtain accreditation, and these standards explicitly included pain management targets. Like providers, accreditation agencies had ample opportunities to modify these targets as the opioid crisis mounted, but were slow to do so.

A third reason that the tripartite is incomplete is that it ignores the critical role of the medical community. As discussed in the previous chapter, physicians, health care systems, medical boards, and specialty medical societies each had ample opportunities to exercise self-regulation and take measures to slow the rise in opioid supply, especially given their proximity to the literature, science, and perhaps most importantly the patients themselves. In Figure 5.1, the medical community sits in the middle of the diagram, well positioned to influence the process in numerous ways. Earlier changes in clinical practice guidelines could have at least started to alter physician prescribing habits and would have allowed the largely self-regulated industry to identify outlier prescription rates more readily. The CDC could have encouraged these changes, particularly after

[21] C. D. Soelberg et al., "The US Opioid Crisis: Current Federal and State Legal Issues," *Anesth Analg* 125, no. 5 (2017); J. J. Darrow, J. Avorn, and A. S. Kesselheim, "FDA Approval and Regulation of Pharmaceuticals, 1983–2018," *Jama* 323, no. 2 (2020).

[22] FDA, "A Brief History of the Center for Drug Evaluation and Research," (Washington, D.C.: U.S. Food & Drug Administartion, 2018).

[23] CRS, "The Controlled Substances Act (CSA): A Legal Overview for the 117th Congress," (Washington, D.C.: United States Congressional Research Service, 2021).

it had declared the opioid crisis to be an epidemic. There is perhaps some administrative appeal, particularly in legal settings, to simplifying scientific and organizational complexities, including simplification of the nuances of the increasingly complex pharmaceutical supply chain. However, given the magnitude of the opioid crisis, in terms of attributable costs and harms, oversimplification of the supply chain could lead directly to unfair and inequitable abatement cost judgements against any subset of entities subjectively selected to represent the supply chain.

5.3 Orphan Shares

The argument to consider more responsible parties than those included in the current opioid cases is based on the primary objectives of epidemiological analysis and the economics of externalities. As discussed in Chap. 4, the actions and behavior of the entities behind each of the contributing factors potentially played either a causative or participatory role in the proliferation of prescription opioids in the U.S. For example, had the FDA denied approval of OxyContin, or approved it with added conditions and warnings, prescription opioid supply would have either not existed or grown at a much slower pace.[24] The same might be said for the DEA; had the DEA not been ineffective and "captured" by special interests, as many have argued, prescription opioid supply might have never reached concerning levels. The identification and inclusion of the full set of responsible parties is not necessarily straightforward in any industry, especially healthcare. However, based on the preceding discussion, many important parties have been left out of debates regarding opioid liability.

Many of these excluded parties could be thought of as bearing orphan shares of responsibility, not necessarily due to insolvency or non-existence, as in the typical environmental application, but instead due to some combination of organizational structure, alleged sovereign immunity of government agencies, or lack of understanding of the entity's importance in the supply chain. For example, as discussed in the previous chapter, physicians clearly bear a significant level of responsibility, as they were and continue to be the main barrier standing between the supply of prescription drugs and the consumers of prescription drugs in their role as the ultimate arbiters of

[24] This is an argument by some experts; see for example the previously cited L. Noah, "Federal Regulatory Responses to the Prescription Opioid Crisis: Too Little, Too Late?," *Utah Law Review* 2019, no. 4 (2019).

medical need. But physicians in the U.S. are not a monolithic enterprise; rather, they are organized in a mostly "atomistic" way, with some practicing as employees of large health systems, some practicing in large independent groups, some practicing in smaller independent groups, and some continuing to operate in solo practice.[25] Hospitals and health systems are more concentrated, but are similarly complex organizationally, with some patients receiving pain treatment following inpatient procedures and others visiting emergency departments, urgent care clinics, hospital outpatient clinics, and affiliated organizations for treatment of acute and chronic pain.[26] Some U.S. health systems feature vertically integrated ownership, while others operate through partnerships and joint ventures.[27] Patients are even more diffuse, not organized into groups and numbering in the tens of millions, with 131,778,501 opioids dispensed to patients in 2022.[28] For post-surgical pain management, an estimated 67,922,137 patients obtained opioid prescriptions from 2016 to 2022.[29] Even with a only a small proportion of these users expected to misuse the drugs or experience SAEs, and a similarly small proportion engaging in drug seeking behavior, the transaction costs associated with including these parties individually as defendants in the MDL, or in any mass tort setting, would likely be prohibitively high. However, it could also be argued that the organizational structure of a responsible party should not *de facto* immunize the entire group from liability.

Including governmental agencies as responsible parties is similarly challenging, as they are presumably protected by "sovereign immunity." However, there is some precedent for holding government agencies responsible for harms attributable to actions or inactions on the part of the

[25] For a general overview, refer to J.B. Rebitzer and M.E. Votruba, "Organizational Economics and Physcian Practices," in *NBER Working Paper Series (Working Paper 17,535)* (Cambridge, MA: National Bureau of Economic Research, 2011).

[26] See generally M. P. Charns, "Organization design of integrated delivery systems," *Hosp Health Serv Adm* 42, no. 3 (1997); T. S. Snail and J. C. Robinson, "Organizational diversification in the American hospital," *Annu Rev Public Health* 19 (1998).

[27] See, for example, J. Heeringa et al., "Horizontal and Vertical Integration of Health Care Providers: A Framework for Understanding Various Provider Organizational Structures," *Int J Integr Care* 20, no. 1 (2020).

[28] CDC, United States Dispensing Rate Maps.

[29] J. Zhang et al., "Opioid Prescribing by US Surgeons, 2016–2022," *JAMA Netw Open* 6, no. 12 (2023).

agencies. For example, in 2014, the Center for Food Safety filed suit against the FDA, arguing that the approval process violated the Administrative Procedure Act of 1946 because the FDA failed to "allow for meaningful public participation before the rule became final."[30] The FDA was also sued in a case regarding its alleged failure to act on evidence of harm related to menthol-flavored tobacco products, the complaint stating that "FDA's delay, inaction, and failure 'to move quickly' has been devastating, leading to millions of people initiating smoking cigarettes, and thousands of premature deaths."[31] Recently, the FDA was sued by states over restrictions on abortion drug access.[32] Similarly, the DEA has been sued for a variety of issues.[33] The CDC has also been sued, most recently in a large number of lawsuits concerning the agency's actions in response to the COVID-19 pandemic.[34] More generally, the concept of "public duty doctrine" has been applied in cases where governmental agencies are potentially liable for "breach of duty owed to the general public."[35] Additionally, some cases may meet the requirements of the Federal Tort Claims Act ("FTCA"), which can waive sovereign immunity of governmental agencies where the discretionary action of the agency is inconsistent with policy and results in harm.[36] In the case of environmental externalities, such as CERCLA cases, the federal government is in some instances considered a PRP if it can be shown that government entities contributed to site contamination; as Weber noted, "Although the PRP will not be able to obtain an affirmative recovery from the federal

[30] D. R. Winters, "Suing The Food And Drug Administration To Reform Its Oversight Of Food Additives "*Health Affairs*, no. Blog, July 7 (2017).

[31] S. A. Glantz, "ASH & AATCLC sue FDA for continuing to allow the sale of menthol tobacco products," (San Francisco, CA: University of California, San Francisco, 2020). This action later compelled the FDA to.

[32] J. E. Cutler, "Several States Sue FDA Over Abortion Drug Access Restrictions," (New York, NY: Bloomberg Law, 2023).

[33] For example, see D. B. Brushwood, "Drug enforcement administration liability for false arrest of physician," *J Pain Palliat Care Pharmacother* 23, no. 2 (2009).

[34] For a general discussion see K. Mahr, "'It's a tsunami': Legal challenges threatening public health policy," *Politico*, no. May 10 (2022).

[35] See generally J. C. McMillan, "Government Liability and the Public Duty Doctrine," *Villanova Law Review* 32, no. 2 (1987).

[36] See generally CRS, "The Federal Tort Claims Act (FTCA): A Legal Overview," (Washington, D.C.: U.S. Congressional Research Service, 2023).

government, a successful claim reduces its cleanup cost liability."[37] The same can be argued for state governments, which could be considered "responsible party plaintiffs."[38] State governments are claimants in the opioid cases, yet, as discussed in Chap. 4, they are PRPs as well, insofar as they funded and paid for prescription opioids via their Medicaid programs, even after concerns began to surface,[39] operated Medicaid programs that relied on providers accredited and incentivized by the Joint Commission, and employed VBR-type mechanisms whereby providers benefited financially from more aggressive treatment of pain. Moreover, state governments, via their extensive and detailed Medicaid program data, could most likely have played a larger role in detecting patterns and implementing utilization protocols.

There are two important points that should be emphasized regarding the application of the PRP concept to the opioid crisis. First, the PRP application is done so from the perspectives of economics and epidemiology, rather than a legal perspective. In other words, the goal here is not to assess liability from a legal perspective, nor is it the goal to suggest that CERCLA laws should be applied outside of environmental cases. That exercise is left to legal professionals and the courts. Similarly, the goal is not to suggest that all public health-oriented product liability cases should be approached in the same manner as environmental cases, even if in some cases the overlaps are considerable. Instead, the goal here is to identify groups of entities associated with contributing factors, with the ultimate goal of developing a better understanding of root causes. The PRP framework seems to be a reasonable approach to the general problem of multicausality, especially in the presence of non-standard defendants.

Second, and perhaps more importantly, the intent in applying the PRP concept to the opioid crisis is not to argue that entities within PRP groupings *should* be liable from a legal perspective. Instead, the goal is that, by identifying the key PRP groupings, one can accomplish two goals: (1) the ability to map causal factors to specific groups of entities for the purposes of addressing the negative externality and abating its impact; and (2) to conceptualize and assess the proportional contribution of each

[37] Weber, "Misery Loves Company: Spreading the Costs of CERCLA Cleanup."

[38] See generally Kilbert, "Neither Joint Nor Several: Orphan Shares in Private CERCLA Actions."

[39] Refer to L. Clemans-Cope et al., "State Variation in Medicaid Prescriptions for Opioid Use Disorder from 2011 to 2018," (Washington, D.C.: The Urban Instuitute, 2019).

element. For example, if only three PRP groupings are identified, as was the case in the opioid MDL abatement ruling on retail pharmacies in Ohio, the implication is that abatement responsibilities assigned to retail pharmacies were predicated on the existence of only three identified PRP groups, without regard to the potential contributions of the other two groups or any other group. Including other key entities and groups, even if some of those entities are not expected to legally be assigned any liability, enables a more accurate assessment of true proportion of responsibility associated with each PRP grouping.

5.4 Contributing Factors vs. PRPs

Again, PRPs are to be distinguished from the "contributing factors" discussed in the previous chapter. Contributing factors are *causal factors* and *root causes* which, according to the literature, enabled, caused, or directly contributed to the increase in supply of prescription opioids or the demand for prescription opioids. Some of these factors also contributed to the supply and demand for illicit opioids. However, in the context of the economics of externalities, it is also necessary to identify the specific *entities* and groups of entities that enabled, caused, or directly contributed to the externality; for example, in the usual externalities examples, it is usually not factories in general that are contaminating a river, but specific factories or groups of factories, and it is not farms in general harmed by the contaminants, but specific farms or groups of farms. It is also important to not only identify entities that enabled, caused, or directly contributed to the increase in the supply of prescription opioids, but to also identify entities that, by virtue of their position on the pharmaceutical supply chain, may have played a "participatory" type of role; that is, not necessarily enabling or causing the increase in opioid supply, but otherwise participating in the process.

In some cases, the discussion of contributing factors directly or indirectly implies specific PRPs. In the case of opioids, each contributing factor does not map precisely into a specific PRP or group of PRPs. For example, socioeconomic factors, while clearly important drivers of SUD, opioid utilization, and opioid misuse, do not directly constitute or imply an identifiable PRP or set of PRPs. However, socioeconomic factors exacerbated drug-seeking behavior by individuals, which in turn magnified the contributing roles of physicians and drug traffickers (refer to the discussion of Fig. 4.1). In addition, the impact of socioeconomic factors could have been more effectively mitigated by federal and state governmental agencies. In the context of externalities, PRPs should have some connection, directly or indirectly, to the enabling or causation of the externality, or some tangent participatory role. In this regard, PRPs have a link with the contributing factors discussed in Chap. 4. It is also important to note that PRPs can be identified either through their actions or inactions. Contributing factors led to an increase in physician prescribing and in turn an increase in the supply of prescription and illicit opioids (refer to Fig. 4.1). This increased supply led to an increase in the volume of diverted prescription opioids and an increase in the volume of misused prescription opioids. Some proportion of the increased volume of misused prescription opioids, combined with the continued influx of illicit opioids, led to the negative externality of cost-incurring OUD (as depicted in Fig. 3.2).

As an example, consider the contributing factor of regulatory failure presented in the previous chapter. That discussion identified the FDA, DEA, and the CDC as entities responsible for regulatory failure. In the case of the FDA, as an example, the liability pathway would be as follows: (1) the contributing factor (regulatory failure) involves the actions and inactions of the PRPs; in this case, approval by FDA based on incomplete data followed by poor execution of monitoring, post-market surveillance of SAEs (which included a role for the CDC), combined with lax supply controls by the DEA, both in terms of poorly implemented and enforced quotas and poor interdictions of illicit opioids; (2) these actions and inactions enabled or caused an increase in physician prescribing of opioids and an increase in the supply of illicit opioids (as depicted in Fig. 4.1); (3) an increase in the supply of opioids led to an increase in the volume of diverted opioids; (4) an increase in the supply of illicit opioids and diverted opioids led to an increase in incidence and prevalence of opioid misuse (Fig. 4.1); (5) an increase in incidence and prevalence of opioid misuse led to an increase incidence and prevalence of OUD; and (6) an increase in the incidence and prevalence of OUD led to an increase in the incidence and prevalence of *cost-incurring* OUD.

5.5 PRP Groupings

Factors contributing to an increase in opioid supply map intuitively to several specific PRP groupings, as shown in Fig. 5.2. The figure resembles the left-hand side of Fig. 4.1, repeating the arrows that indicate the interconnectedness between the various contributing factors, which in many cases apply similarly to the PRP groupings. The right side of Fig. 5.2 identifies a total of 15 PRP groupings: (1) FDA; (2) DEA; (3) CDC; (4) physicians; (5) hospitals and health systems; (6) patients; (7) federal government; (8) state governments; (9) accreditation agencies; (10) private commercial payers; (11) manufacturers; (12) distributors; (13) advisors and consultants; (14) retail pharmacies; and (15) drug traffickers. Again, most of these PRPs were mentioned either directly or indirectly in the preceding chapter. The objective here is not to suggest that all the entities that fit these PRP groupings have liability or potential liability for increased opioid supply in a legal sense; that is left for stakeholders to argue and for the courts to decide. Instead, within the context of the economic objectives of this book, the interest here is in identifying the *types* of entities that are normally associated with each contributing factor, having already presented the evidence associated with each contributing factor.

Contributing factors grouped under regulatory failure include the FDA, the DEA, and the CDC. Contributing factors related to medical need include physicians, hospitals, health systems, payers, pharmacies, and patients. Contributing factors associated with public policy encouraging or requiring more aggressive pain control include the federal and state governments. Contributing factors associated with more aggressive advocacy on the part of the medical community include accreditation agencies, public and private payers, hospitals and health systems, and physicians (by way of state medical boards and medical specialty societies). Contributing factors associated with marketing and promotion include manufacturers, distributors, and advisors. Contributing factors associated with advisor advocacy include large consulting companies under contract with manufacturers and distributors. Contributing factors associated with drug trafficking include drug traffickers themselves (i.e., as suppliers) and individuals actively seeking illicit or diverted opioids (i.e., as customers). Other PRPs include entities "secondary" to the contributing factors, such as retail pharmacies, which dispensed opioids based on physician judgments regarding medical need. The discussion below provides some further explanation of the links between the contributing factors and the PRPs associated with those contributing factors, summarizing some of the main points from the preceding chapter.

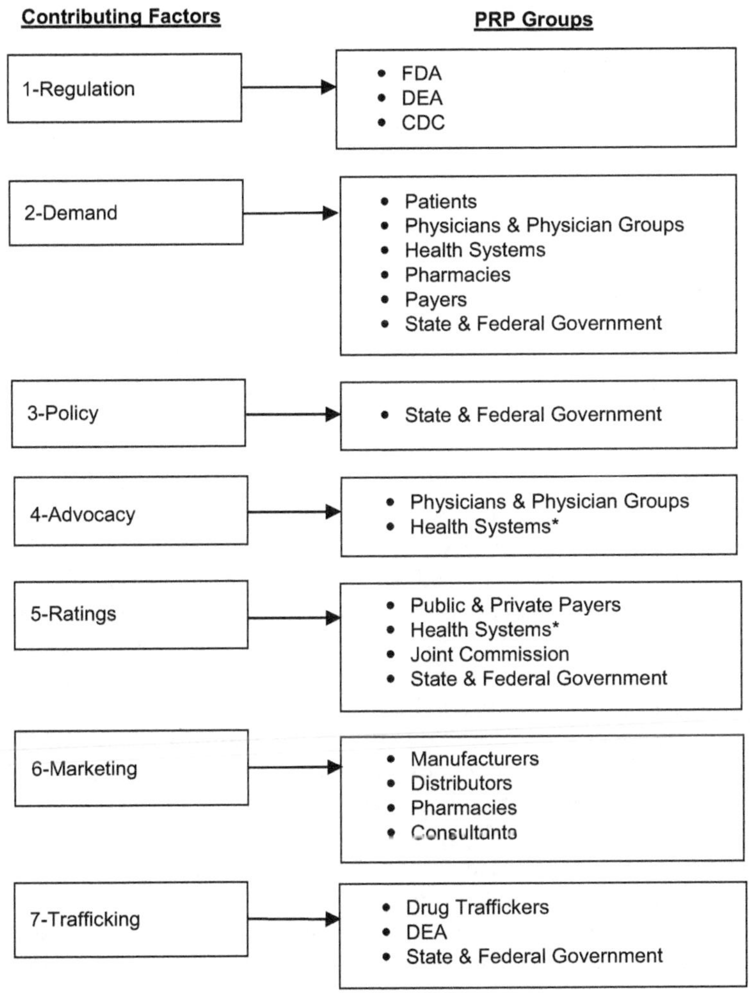

Fig. 5.2 Contributing Factors Associated with Prescription Opioid Supply, Non-Prescription Opioid Supply, and Total Opioid Supply: Mapping to Groups of Potentially Responsible Parties (PRPs); FDA = Food & Drug Administration; DEA = Drug Enforcement Administration; CDC = Centers for Disease Control & Prevention; (*) in the context of medical advocacy, this PRP grouping also includes specialty medical societies associated with pain management (see text, Chap. 4)

5.6 Discussion

Most of the rationale for the inclusion of these PRP groupings was provided in the preceding chapter, in the context of contributing factors. This section provides some additional context for the identification of PRP groups and the mapping between contributing factors and PRP groups. Starting with regulatory failure, at first glance, it may seem futile to blame regulatory agencies for the actions of specific entities or groups of entities they are charged with overseeing. However, there is considerable precedent for such discourse, as well as myriad instances in which regulatory agencies have been sued by industry and consumer interests over issues regarding alleged failure to perform their statutory duties adequately and effectively. The preceding chapter reviewed the role of the FDA in the approval and post-market monitoring of prescription opioids, and how many industry experts agree that the FDA largely failed in performing those tasks effectively. But the identification of the FDA as a PRP precedes the opioid crisis and extends to a wide range of activities that it is charged with conducting. Regarding drug-related adverse events generally, the FDA has been broadly criticized for failing to conduct sufficient review of clinical evidence and depending too heavily on manufacturers to directly provide such evidence. Downing et al. analyzed post-market safety events of novel FDA-approved drugs from 2001–2010 and found that 32% of the drugs were associated with post-market safety events, defined as emerging safety risks identified after initial regulatory approval.[40] The FDA has been faulted for conducting some regulatory reviews hastily, overseen by a leadership that has a "revolving door" with industry.[41] The FDA is also charged with regulating and overseeing the nation's food supply, and its performance on food regulation has been regarded by experts as distressing, with commentary such as "[the FDA] has repeatedly failed to take timely action on a wide range of safety and health issues the agency has been aware of for several years, including dangerous pathogens found in water used to grow produce and heavy metal contamination in baby foods. The agency has been slow to acknowledge numerous other

[40] N. S. Downing et al., "Postmarket Safety Events Among Novel Therapeutics Approved by the US Food and Drug Administration Between 2001 and 2010," *Jama* 317, no. 18 (2017).

[41] See generally F. Manjoo, "America Desperately Needs a Much Better F.D.A.," *The New York Times*, no. Sept 2 (2021).

chemicals of concern, including PFAS [per- and polyfluorinated substances], so-called forever chemicals, which can be found in the food supply and are used in food packaging."[42] As one might expect, given these types of assessments, the FDA has been the subject of numerous lawsuits regarding its mishandling of food oversight.[43]

Bureaucratic dysfunction on the part of the FDA is of course not unique among government regulatory agencies. For example, the U.S. Environmental Protection Agency ("EPA") has been regularly faulted and sued for a variety of issues, including flawed processes, undue industry influence, and slow response to threats to the environment and public health. An outside review of EPA use of scientific data, for example, was deemed flawed by an external review conducted by the U.S. National Academies of Sciences.[44] The EPA has also been accused of failing to effectively evaluate and regulate harmful chemical compounds, such as endocrine-disrupting pesticides, which were the subject of a 2022 lawsuit filed by environmental and public health groups.[45] According to a University of California report, "In the 40 years between enactment of the original Toxic Substances Control Act ("TSCA") in 1976 and its 2016 amendments, EPA regulated less than 1% of the existing chemicals on the market."[46] Likewise, the Federal Aviation Administration ("FAA"), charged with overseeing the safety of the nation's air transportation system, has been faulted for lapses in oversight, including, for example, its failures in the vetting of Boeing's 737 MAX, which was associated with two fatal accidents, and its missteps leading up to a nationwide failure in vital information systems in early 2023, which resulted in the temporary cessation of all air transport

[42] H. Bottemiller Evich, "The FDA's Food Failure," *Politico* (2022).

[43] See, for example, Winters, "Suing The Food And Drug Administration To Reform Its Oversight Of Food Additives".

[44] NASEM, "The Use of Systematic Review in EPA's Toxic Substances Control Act Evaluations," (Washington, D.C.: National Academies of Science, Engineering, and Medicine (NASEM), 2021).

[45] U.S. District Court for the Northern District of California, "Alianza Nacional de Campesinas et al. v. U.S. Environmental Protection Agency et al. (Case No. 22-cv-9030)," (San Francisco, CA 2022).

[46] PRHE, "EPA's failure to properly implement TSCA puts lives at risk," (San Francisco, CA: Program on Reproductive Health and the Environment (PRHE), University of California, San Francisco, 2022).

activity and the cancellation of thousands of flights.[47] Regulatory agencies fail not simply because of bureaucratic inertia, as is often reported, but instead due to difficulty adapting to changes within the industries they are charged with overseeing and due to reliance on those industries to address information gaps and uncertainty.[48] Nevertheless, industry and consumers rely on regulatory agencies to establish and enforce safety and quality standards, and the failure of those agencies to do so can result in negative externalities and serious harm to the public.

Apart from the specific federal agency roles of the FDA, DEA, and CDC, state and federal governments also serve important roles as policy advocates and third-party payers. Government advocates specific objectives in several ways. The most prominent means of government advocacy is by way of direct messaging by its elected representatives and administrative leaders, typically in the form of reports, press releases, and public speeches. Though normally advocacy refers to the advocacy of special interests to governmental bodies, in the form of lobbying, advocacy information flows both ways and can be employed by government representatives to further their specific policy or political objectives. A second way government can engage in advocacy is through the influence of regulatory agency operations, the commissioning of specific studies, and the publication of data.[49] Finally, another avenue of influence is by way of budget allocation, whereby program and grant funding are allocated by policy goals and biases rather than other factors.[50] In the healthcare sector, governments have further ability to influence consumer and provider behavior by way of their third-party payer functions, specifically their

[47] See generally S. Beasley, "Expert panel rips Boeing, FAA for failures in certifying 737 MAX," *Politico*, no. Oct. 11 (2019); CBS, "FAA chief grilled by lawmakers over computer outage, aviation safety," (New York, NY: CBS News, 2023).

[48] For a general discussion of these issues, refer to O.E. Williamson, "Public and Private Bureaucracies: a Transaction Cost Economics Perspectives," *The Journal of Law, Economics, and Organization* 15, no. 1 (1999).

[49] See generally J. L. Short, "The politics of regulatory enforcement and compliance: Theorizing and operationalizing political influences," *Regulation & Governance* 15, no. 3 (2021).

[50] Regarding grant funding, see, for example, W. P. Wahls, "Biases in grant proposal success rates, funding rates and award sizes affect the geographical distribution of funding for biomedical research," *PeerJ* 4 (2016).

ability to administratively establish coverage and reimbursement policies that influence, for example, provider treatment choice. Finally, federal, state, and local governments play an important indirect role in opioid supply growth by way of their level of support for economically at-risk individuals, as those individuals are known to be at greater risk for mental health problems and substance use disorders.

Demand and medical need are identified as an important contributing factor in the previous chapter due to a combination of organizational changes in the healthcare sector (e.g., the growing share of outpatient treatment) and changes in demand for pain management related to increased survival and increased prevalence of chronic disease. Another component of medical need is "normal" geographic variation in practice patterns; that is, differing views by providers regarding how to approach treatment for a given condition for a specific patient. An additional challenge related to medical need is the subjectivity of pain. Mapping these components to PRPs applies chiefly to the latter component. In other words, if opioid-based treatment is clearly medically indicated, then the provision of that treatment is not generally considered contributory to the share of supply associated with opioid-related harms. Consequently, at issue are only prescription opioids for which medical need is opportunistically misrepresented by patients, as part of opioid seeking behavior, or otherwise ambiguous to prescribing physicians, health systems, dispensing pharmacies, and insurers due to the inherent subjectivity of pain. Accordingly, for this subset of prescriptions, there is some level of responsibility on the part of the health system, mainly prescribing physicians, to conduct further due diligence regarding medical need. Physicians and health systems are perhaps in the best position to undertake such additional vetting, followed by third-party payers. Physicians and the organizations in which they practice typically have the most complete data upon which to make decisions regarding medical need, including longitudinal medical records and the physical presence of the patients themselves. Similarly, as discussed earlier, administrative data from third-party payers can also effectively be used to identify at-risk individuals, similar to their use in the management of chronic disease.[51]

[51] See generally M. C. Kapp, "Overview: disease management," *Health Care Financ Rev* 30, no. 1 (2008); S. A. Musich et al., "Overview of Disease Management Approaches," *Disease Management & Health Outcomes* 12, no. 5 (2004).

5.7 Allocation of Responsibility

The aim of this section is to apply the earlier discussion of the roles of the PRPs to create a framework for the allocation of attributable cost ceilings and abatement costs. Again, the goal here is not to offer a legal framework through which to legally assign liability; that is a task that is best left for the courts. However, as discussed variously throughout this book, it is the work of an economist to determine causal factors and entities in the quest for solutions to problems of externalities. For allocation, the working hypothesis is that, given the multifactorial nature of the causal factors in the opioid crisis, abatement costs could be shared in some manner among PRP groups. As discussed throughout this book, the notion that responsibility for opioid abatement costs should be shared is not necessarily a controversial stance and has been put forth by several observers as the optimal way to approach the problem. Again, in the environmental example, PRPs bear the burden of establishing a fair and reasonable basis for apportioning liability,[52] and ideally the liability of each PRP group would roughly equal its proportionate share of abatement and mitigation costs.[53] In this chapter the focus is on exploring some simple means of allocating reasonable attributable costs and abatement costs to PRP groups, leaving "within-PRP group" allocation of responsibility for the reader to explore or the courts to decide.

Returning to the economics of externalities, particularly the environmental economics examples, the 1986 Superfund amendments[54] stated that "Congress expressly codified this right of contribution and provided that in contribution actions 'the court may allocate response costs among liable parties using such equitable factors as the court determines are appropriate.'"[55] Most of the factors typically applied in these cases are unique to environmental issues,[56] but essentially the goal in these cases has been to: (1) allocate responsibility among existing and orphan PRPs based

[52] Refer to Hansen, "CERCLA Cost Allocation and Nonparties' Responsibility: Who Bears the Orphan Shares?."

[53] Weber, "Misery Loves Company: Spreading the Costs of CERCLA Cleanup."

[54] Typically referred to as the Superfund Amendments and Reauthorization Act ("SARA").

[55] Hall, Harris, and Reinsdorf, "Superfund Response Cost Allocations: The Law, The Science and The Practice."

[56] See generally Kilbert, "Neither Joint Nor Several: Orphan Shares in Private CERCLA Actions." In environmental applications, the so-called "Gore Factors" are often employed.

on "volumetric" contribution shares, and (2) if available data do not support a volumetric approach (i.e., contribution shares are volumetrically unknown, or known for only some PRP groups but not all), then shares should be calculated in a "fair and equitable manner." Returning to the general discussion of liability presented in Chap. 2, in the case of multiple responsible parties, each responsible party is apportioned a share of responsibility (ϕ) such that $\Sigma\phi \leq 1$ across all responsible parties. Also recall from Chap. 2 the discussion of the degree of liability or negligence, which is expressed as λ where $0 \leq \lambda \leq 1$, with liability apportioned λ to responsible parties and $1\text{-}\lambda$ to claimants. Accordingly, for defendant *i* in a case involving multiple defendants, the level of responsibility "r" can be expressed as $r_i = \lambda_i\phi_i$; that is, the level of responsibility of any defendant is a function of their degree of liability and their share of responsibility among PRPs. Both parameters can be determined by the courts, but they should be determined independently as they are distinctly different concepts.

In the case of the opioid PRP groups, a purely volumetric approach to calculating ϕ (i.e., based on volume of opioid prescriptions or MMEs) would be impractical, because it would be computationally challenging to attribute specific shares of volume to regulators, factors driving medical need, medical societies, government policy, socioeconomic factors, and so on. Consequently, reliance on a volumetric approach would be potentially unfair to the entities for which a volumetric approach is at least conceptually feasible. There is the additional challenge in the opioid litigation that most of the PRPs refer to groups of entities. Whereas federal regulators (FDA, DEA, and CDC), accreditation agencies, and manufacturers represent relatively monolithic organizations, in contrast, state governments, medical societies, physicians, health systems, distributors, pharmacies, and patients are represented by large groups, most of which are heterogeneous in composition. Moreover, for PRP groups with many members, like physicians and consumers, the transaction costs associated with a volumetric approach would render it impractical.

Given the inherent challenges of a purely volumetric approach, the alternative to calculating ϕ is to allocate based on an *ad hoc* method so long as the method is considered "fair and equitable" and considers orphan shares.[57] Indeed, this appears to be largely how the allocation

[57] Hall et. al. (*op cit.*) provides a detailed description of cases wherein recourse to "fair and equitable" allocations were featured. As expected, in many of these cases shares were assigned in an *ad hoc* fashion based on the preponderance of available evidence.

issue was approached in the Ohio retail pharmacy decision, where the presence of three defendants resulted in an even one-third apportionment to the large retail pharmacies based on the narrowly defined pharmaceutical supply chain tripartite. The court described the allocation decision this way: "Upon careful consideration of the evidence and equities in this case, the Court finds it is reasonable and fair to allocate *one-third* of the recoverable abatement costs to the Pharmacy Defendants for the harm caused by improper dispensing conduct in the Counties. This allocation considers the fact that all three categories of actors along the pharmaceutical supply chain—that is, manufacturers, distributors, and dispensers of prescription opioids—contributed to the nuisance in the Counties, and it would be inequitable to hold these Defendants liable for more than a one-third share. The numerous defendants named in these MDL proceedings fall overwhelmingly into these three categories."[58] (emphasis added) Again, as put forth in earlier chapters, it can be argued that this is a narrow portrayal of the modern-day U.S. pharmaceutical supply chain, and that arguably there are many more entities involved in bringing a drug to the market and maintaining its presence in the market.

5.8 Allocation Models

In theory, there are several allocation approaches that would satisfy the "fair and equitable" requirement. The most conceptually straightforward approach would be to simply assign each PRP group an equal share. Again, this is precisely the approach adopted by the court in the Ohio retail pharmacy abatement matter, albeit on a truncated number of PRP groups.[59] Given the 15 PRPs identified earlier, this allocation approach would result in $\phi = 6.67\%$ for each of the PRP groups. This assumes that most of the 12 PRP groups outside of the traditional tripartite are allocated "orphan" shares. One interpretation of this approach would be that, even if the 12 PRP groups assigned orphan shares are for practical and legal purposes unable to financially share responsibility for abatement costs, they should nevertheless be allocated a proportional share because it would not be fair and equitable to assign those shares solely to the non-

[58] See Opioid MDL, "MDL 2804 Case No. 1:17-md-2804 Judge Dan Aaron Polster: Abatement Order." (pp. 57–58).

[59] Recall that in the Ohio retail pharmacy abatement order the Court assigned 33.3% to retail pharmacies but did not comment on how the remaining 67.7% should be allocated.

orphan PRPs. In this example, if the level of responsibility for each PRP group was found to be 50%, the resulting overall responsibility share would be $(0.50)(0.0667) = 0.033$; thus, each defendant would bear an overall responsibility of 3.3%. Again, this aspect of allocation is ultimately a legal debate left to the courts to decide, but from an economic perspective, it accomplishes the goal of reasonably distributing responsibility for the harm or negative externality.

Alternatively, another approach to allocation would be to differentiate among PRP groups in terms of more "causative" type roles versus more "participatory" type roles, regardless of orphan status. In other words, it could be argued that some PRP groups should be assigned greater responsibility because they are known to have actively played some part in *initiating* the oversupply of opioids, via some combination of actively leveraging their position in the pharmaceutical supply chain to approve, generate, promote, or encourage the use of opioids, leading to some degree of increased prescriptions written by physicians. Such an assumption would of course have to be evidence-based and determined by the courts, but it seems plausible to assume that some sort of differentiation along these lines could be made among PRPs. Causative roles could be distinguished from PRP groups associated more with participatory-type functions, whereby some entities may have failed to observe or monitor trends in a timely manner but had limited means by which to intercede in addressing or preventing subsequent problems. In this regard, participatory PRPs could also be considered ones that possessed no independent means through which to actively increase opioid supply.

Returning to the discussion and arguments put forth in Chap. 4, some contributing factors and associated PRP groups are arguably more causative than others. Among the regulators, the FDA clearly played a causative role by way of initial approval, as did the DEA by way of its management of quotas. Physicians and health systems also played an active role, primarily through the initiation of prescriptions but also through the embracing of financial incentives to provide more pain management and through medical society leadership embracing more aggressive pain management, patient-centered care, and palliative care. State and federal governments actively embraced aggressive approaches to pain management while at the same time paying for large volumes of opioid prescriptions through their healthcare coverage programs. Accreditation agencies and private commercial payers embraced financial incentives associated with aggressive treatment of pain, while at the same time accepting funding from manufacturers (in the case of accreditation agencies) or underwriting opioid-based treatments and prescriptions (in the case of commercial payers). Like state and federal payers, commercial insurers continued funding opioid use throughout the crisis, while maintaining coverage policies that in some instances discouraged non-pharmacological approaches to pain management. Finally, manufacturers and distributors could be considered causative in their organized marketing and influence campaigns, purposefully targeting physicians, hospitals, regulators, accreditation agencies, and politicians. In addition, distributors were alleged to have in some cases failed to report suspicious orders to the DEA.

In contrast, it could reasonably be argued that the entities at the distal end of the supply chain, which include pharmacies and patients, were largely unable to meaningfully alter the trajectory of opioid prescribing and sales, given that these entities were not "generating" the upstream flow of prescriptions, nor were they well-positioned to prevent the generation of new upstream prescriptions. Put differently, they were not positioned to generate or otherwise influence "supply push" in any way comparable to most of the other, more causative PRP groups. Similarly, patients have a limited impact on "demand pull" because ultimately their receipt of an opioid prescription is dependent entirely on physicians' determination of legitimate medical need. Individuals engaged in the procurement or consumption of illicit opioids can help sustain markets for illicit opioids, and patients engaging in the misuse of prescription opioids can help sustain high-volume physician prescribers, by way of opioid-seeking behavior and doctor shopping. However, neither group could be considered able to meaningfully generate an added volume of prescription opioids. In the case of retail pharmacies, in addition to being unable to independently generate new prescriptions, they largely lacked the data and scope of practice to effectively determine the underlying medical need of each lawfully prescribed prescription. The same could be argued for the CDC, which would normally have had a more passive monitoring role, especially if the crisis had not been eventually termed an "epidemic" by their own researchers and others. Also, the role of management consultants and advisors, while important given their influential position within the health industry, would have had limited influence when compared to other more causative PRPs; for example, advisors and consultants offer advice that does not necessarily have to be followed by the leadership of manufacturers and distributors.

Accordingly, one could reasonably consider the CDC, consultants, pharmacies, and patients as lower-share PRP groups, while assigning higher shares to the other PRP groups. In this "weighted" approach, the derivation of weights could be calculated by assigning the participatory PRP groups a share equal to 50% of the proportional rate [i.e., ϕ (0.50), or $\phi_p = 50\% \times 6.67\% = 3.33\%$] and pro-rate the higher causative PRP share to $\phi_c = 7.88\%$ such that the shares for the 15 PRP groups sum to 100% (i.e., $\Sigma\phi_{p,c} = 1$). These estimated shares can then be applied to the attributable cost ceiling and the abatement cost ceiling, or some other amount determined by the courts. Again, there are a number of allocation methods that would accomplish similar goals of differentiating among causative versus less causative PRP groups; this approach offers one relatively straightforward means of doing so.

5.9 Chapter Summary

Pharmaceutical supply chains are complex systems that require explicit actions from developers, manufacturers, regulators, distributors, physicians, provider groups, accreditation agencies, payers, and pharmacies before a single drug can get into the hands of a consumer. Totaling the PRPs identified in the discussion above results in a total of 15 PRP groupings. The number of PRPs could be somewhat higher or lower depending on how entities are identified within each contributing factor, but it would be difficult to argue that the number is substantially different from this. This number is considerably larger than the tripartite identified in the 1970 CSA and the recent Ohio abatement order, which consisted only of manufacturers, distributors, and pharmacies. More importantly, there is substantial evidence supporting the identification of these groups of entities as having some role in the opioid crisis, with some of them having an arguably causative or enabling role. While it may be conceptually convenient to fall back on the three traditional members of the pharmaceutical supply chain in considering issues related to liability, the U.S. opioid crisis provides a useful example of why the three supply chain entities constitute a narrow portrayal of the modern-day pharmaceutical supply chain. As many experts have argued, it is difficult to conceive of the growth in prescription opioid supply beginning in the early 2000s as being possible without the "perfect storm" of actions and inactions on the part of several of the contributing factors and associated PRP groups.

In product liability cases with multiple causal factors and multiple defendants, it is usually necessary to develop a fair and equitable allocation model to apportion responsibility for harms (e.g., attributable costs and abatement costs) among PRP groups. In environmental cases, such allocation approaches have mainly relied on volumetric measures, such as the amount of product produced by the past users of a particular industrial site. In cases where volumetric approaches are not practical, allocation approaches have been somewhat more arbitrary, based on fair and reasonable approximations. The latter approach was taken in the opioid MDL, where the presence of three defendant PRP groups encouraged an apportionment of one-third of abatement responsibility to one of the categories (retail pharmacies) and the remaining two thirds to be distributed among the other two PRP groups. The approach to allocation was somewhat arbitrary, and at the very least non-quantitative. This suggests that other allocation methods would also work, assuming reasonable arguments can be made to support such allocation approaches. In this chapter two different approaches have been put forth: one like the Ohio decision to allocate proportionally, but applied to all PRP groups, and one with some simple adjustments for hypothesized differentials in degree of causality among PRP groups.

References

Beasley, S. (2019, October 11). Expert panel rips Boeing, FAA for failures in certifying 737 MAX. *Politico.*

Bookspan, S. (1991). Potentially responsible party searches: Finding the cause of Urban grime. *The Public Historian*, *13*(2), 25–34.

Bottemiller Evich, H. (2022). The FDA's food failure. *Politico.*

Brushwood, D. B. (2009). Drug enforcement administration liability for false arrest of physician. *Journal of Pain & Palliative Care Pharmacotherapy*, *23* (2), 156–162.

California, U.S. District Court for the Northern District of. (2022). Alianza Nacional de Campesinas Et Al. v. U.S. environmental protection agency et al. (Case No. 22-cv-9030).

CBO. (2022). *Prescription drugs: Spending, use, and prices.* U.S. Congressional Budget Office.

CBS News. (2023). *FAA chief grilled by lawmakers over computer outage, aviation safety.*

Charns, M. P. (1997). Organization design of integrated delivery systems. *Hospital & Health Services Administration*, *42*(3 Fall), 411–432.

Clemans-Cope, L., Lynch, V., Winiski, E., & Epstein, M. (2019). *State variation in medicaid prescriptions for opioid use disorder from 2011 to 2018*. The Urban Instuitute.

Coase, R. H. (1960). The problem of social cost. *Journal of Law and Economics, 3*, 1–44.

Cooter, R. D. (1991). Economic theories of legal liability. *Journal of Economic Perspectives, 5*(3), 11–30.

Cooter, R. D., & Ulen, T. (2011). *Law and economics (6th Edition)*. Pearson.

CRS. (2021). *The controlled substances act (CSA): A legal overview for the 117th congress*. United States Congressional Research Service.

CRS. (2023). *The federal tort claims act (FTCA): A legal overview*. U.S. Congressional Research Service.

Cutler, J. E. (2023). *Several states sue FDA over abortion drug access restrictions*. Bloomberg Law.

Darrow, J. J., Avorn, J., & Kesselheim, A. S. (2020, January 14). FDA approval and regulation of pharmaceuticals, 1983–2018. *JAMA, 323*(2), 164–176.

Downing, N. S., Shah, N. D., Aminawung, J. A., Pease, A. M., Zeitoun, J. D., Krumholz, H. M., & Ross, J. S. (2017, May 9). Postmarket safety events among novel therapeutics approved by the US food and drug administration between 2001 and 2010. *JAMA, 317*(18), 1854–1863.

FDA. (2018). *A brief history of the center for drug evaluation and research*. U.S. Food & Drug Administartion.

Glantz, S. A. (2020). *ASH & AATCLC Sue FDA for continuing to allow the sale of menthol Tobacco products*. University of California.

Hall, R. M., Harris, R. H., & Reinsdorf, J. A. (1994). Superfund response cost allocations: The law, the science and the practice. *The Business Lawyer (American Bar Association), 49*(4), 1489–1540.

Hansen, D. R. (1992). CERCLA cost allocation and Nonparties' responsibility: Who bears the orphan shares? *UCLA Journal of Environmental Law and Policy, 11*(1), 37–76

Heeringa, J., Mutti, A., Furukawa, M. F., Lechner, A., Maurer, K. A., & Rich, E. (2020, January 20) Horizontal and vertical integration of health care providers: A framework for understanding various provider organizational structures. *International Journal of Integrated Care, 20*(1), 2.

Hylton, K. N. (2013). The law and economics of products liability. *Notre Dame Law Review, 88*(5).

Jain, S. K. (2015). *Economic analysis of liability rules*. Springer.

Kapp, M. C. (2008) Overview: Disease management. *Health Care Financing Review, 30*(1), 1–3.

Kilbert, K. K. (2011). Neither joint nor several: Orphan shares in private CERCLA actions. *Environmental Law, 41*(4), 1045–1092.

Lyles, A., & Palumbo, F. B. (1999, February). The effect of managed care on prescription drug costs and benefits. *Pharmacoeconomics, 15*(2), 129–140.

Mahr, K. (2022, May 10) "'It's a tsunami': Legal challenges threatening public health policy." *Politico*, no.

Manewitz, M. L. (2011). Potentially responsible parties: Liability issues. *Fordham Environmental Law Review, 5*(2), Article 6.

Manjoo, F. (2021, September 2). America Desperately Needs a Much Better F.D. A. *The New York Times.*

McLaren, P., & Beveridge, R. P. (2006, July) Sediment trend analysis of the Hylebos waterway: Implications for liability allocations. *Integrated Environmental Assessment and Management, 2*(3), 262–272.

McMillan, J. C. (1987). Government liability and the public duty doctrine. *Villanova Law Review, 32*(2).

Musich, S. A., Schultz, A. B., Burton, W. N., & Edington, D. W. (2004, January 05). Overview of disease management approaches. *Disease Management & Health Outcomes, 12*(5), 299–326.

NASEM. (2021). *The use of systematic review in EPA's toxic substances control act evaluations.* National Academies of Science, Engineering, and Medicine.

Noah, L. (2019). Federal regulatory responses to the prescription opioid crisis: Too little, too late? *Utah Law Review, 2019*(4).

Opioid MDL (2022). MDL 2804 Case No. 1:17-md-2804 Judge Dan Aaron Polster: Abatement Order. *Re: National Opioid Litigation.*

Phaneuf, D. J., & Requate, T. (2017). *A course in environmental economics: Theory, policy, and practice.* Cambridge University Press.

PHLC. (2019). *The master settlement agreement: An overview*. Public Health Law Center at Mitchell Hamline School of Law.

PRHE. (2022). EPA's failure to properly implement TSCA puts lives at risk. Program on Reproductive Health and the Environment, University of California.

Priya, L., Varghese, G. K., & Shah, I. K. (2020, December). Liability allocation in pollution involving multiple responsible parties. *Environmental Science and Pollution Research, 27*(36), 45133–45147.

Rebitzer, J. B., & Votruba, M. E. (2011). *Organizational economics and physcian practices.* (NBER Working Paper No. 17535). National Bureau of Economic Research.

Schafermeyer, K. W. (2000, January). The impact of managed care on pharmacy practice. *Pharmacy Practice Management Quarterly, 19*(4), 99–116.

Shin, W., Choung, S., Han, W. S., Hwang, J., & Kang, G. (2018, November 15). Evaluation of multiple PRPs' contributions to soil contamination in reclaimed sites around an abandoned smelter. *Science of the Total Environment, 642*, 314–321.

Short, J. L. (2021). The politics of regulatory enforcement and compliance: Theorizing and operationalizing political influences. *Regulation & Governance*, *15*(3), 653–685.

Snail, T. S., & Robinson, J. C. (1998). Organizational diversification in the American hospital. *Annual Review of Public Health*, *19*, 417–453.

Soelberg, C. D., R. E. Brown Jr., D. D. V., Meyer, J. E., & Ramachandran, B. K. (2017, November). The US Opioid Crisis: Current Federal and State Legal Issues. *Anesthesia & Analgesia*, *125*(5), 1675–1681.

Stach, M. A. (1995). Only "innocent" parties need apply: The death of private party cost recovery actions under superfund? *William & Mary Environmental Law and Policy Review*, *20*(1).

Tichy, E. M., Hoffman, J. M., Suda, K. J., Rim, M. H., Tadrous, M., Cuellar, S., Clark, J. S., Ward, J., & Schumock, G. T. (2022, July 8). National trends in prescription drug expenditures and projections for 2022. *American Journal of Health-System Pharmacy*, *79*(14), 1158–1172.

Tong, N. (2024). Arkansas files opioid epidemic lawsuit against PBMs optum, Express scripts. *Fierce Healthcare*.

Viscusi, W. K. (1991). The dimensions of the product liability crisis. *The Journal of Legal Studies*, *20*(1), 147–177.

Wahls, W. P. (2016). Biases in grant proposal success rates, funding rates and award sizes affect the geographical distribution of funding for biomedical research. *PeerJ*, *4*, e1917.

Weber, A. D. (1989). Misery loves company: Spreading the costs of CERCLA cleanup. *Vanderbilt Law Review*, *42*(5).

Williamson, O. E. (1999). Public and private Bureaucracies: A transaction cost economics perspectives. *The Journal of Law, Economics, and Organization*, *15*(1), 306–342.

Winters, D. R. (2017, July 7). Suing the food and drug administration to reform its oversight of food additives. *Health Affairs*, Blog.

Zhang, J., Waljee, J. F., Nguyen, T. D., Bohnert, A. S., Brummett, C. M., Bicket, M. C., & Chua, K. P. (2023, December 1). Opioid prescribing by US Surgeons, 2016–2022. *JAMA Netw Open*, *6*(12), e2346426.

CHAPTER 6

Attributable Costs

Having discussed issues pertaining to responsibility, in the next two chapters the focus is turned to economic damages and costs. Economic damages usually consist of costs attributable to harms and costs necessary to abate the effects of harms. This chapter, which addresses attributable costs of OUD, begins by revisiting the distinctions between attributable costs and abatement costs, as economic analyses of externalities often feature both. Typically, product liability cases involve the calculation of economic damages, and such damages are usually equal to the estimated attributable costs of the harm. Thus, for the purposes of this analysis, the concepts of economic damages and attributable costs can be thought of as essentially interchangeable. Abatement costs, in contrast, are the accounting costs associated with remedying problems attributable to the externality. For example, revisiting the example provided in Chap. 1, the attributable costs of smoking might include some proportion of the costs of treating lung cancer, but the state and local costs of lung cancer *abatement* might include the costs of public health campaigns to reduce smoking rates. In some cases, economic damages may essentially be equal to abatement costs, depending on how each is defined. In this chapter, the focus is on economic damages and attributable costs, assessed by way of a review of literature and reports on the attributable costs of OUD to state and local government. Attributable cost estimates from the literature are used to develop a simple "cost ceiling" model that provides a maximum

J. E. Schneider, *The Economics of Pain*, Global Perspectives on Wealth and Distribution,
https://doi.org/10.1007/978-3-032-20355-7_6

plausible total state and local attributable costs associated with OUD and OUD-related harms.

6.1 Attributable Costs

While there is considerable debate regarding the "true" costs of the opioid crisis, there have been several rigorous studies published in which such costs have been enumerated. Cost estimates have been developed from the perspectives of the federal government, state and local governments, and society. The opioid MDL cases, however, have focused mainly on direct costs incurred by state and local governments. State and local governments have argued, generally, that they have incurred direct "excess" costs attributable to OUD across several areas of operation, including healthcare services, the criminal justice system, and various social and family assistance programs.[1] These cost groupings represent reported OUD-attributable costs that could in theory be incurred by state and local governments associated with managing and abating the opioid crisis. Accordingly, this chapter reports the results of a comprehensive review of the literature on the direct costs of the opioid crisis on the part of state and local governments. The review considers three major types of direct state and local OUD-attributable costs: healthcare ("HC") costs, criminal justice system ("CJS") costs, and social and family assistance ("SFA") costs. Using the data abstracted from the review of the literature and applying a series of adjustments to make the cost parameters comparable and consistent with the objectives of the opioid MDL claimants, an "attributable cost ceiling" model is developed, with the goal of generating estimates of the highest likely level of total opioid-attributable costs faced by state and local governments.

The approach to the comprehensive review was to retrieve and review all studies in which the primary aim was to calculate estimates of direct attributable cost associated with OUD and able to support apportionment to state and local governments. The same search strategy was executed in a broader online search to capture materials not published in the peer-reviewed medical literature (e.g., reports from specific cities and states, research organizations, and governmental agencies). Studies that did not

[1] A detailed overview, for example, is provided by E. Weeks and P. Sanford, "Financial Impact of the Opioid Crisis on Local Government: Quantifying Costs for Litigation and Policymaking," *Kansas Law Review* 67 (2019).

disaggregate federal government from state and/or local government attributable costs were excluded, unless data were available enabling such disaggregation.[2] As discussed above, the reason for these inclusion criteria is that the opioid MDL has been mainly focused on state and local government expenditures, as these are the entities nominally incurring attributable costs. Published literature reviews (e.g., systematic literature reviews and meta-analyses) were consulted as a means of identifying additional source documents but were not separately used as sources for cost estimates. The remaining studies are reviewed below in three groups: (1) studies focused on "excess" state and local HC costs nominally attributable to OUD; (2) studies focused on "excess" state and local CJS costs nominally attributable to OUD; and (3) studies focused on "excess" state and local SFA costs nominally attributable to OUD.

6.2 Healthcare Costs

Substance use disorders are associated with significant excess healthcare costs, including excess inpatient, outpatient, emergency department, and prescription drug costs.[3] Opioid-attributable healthcare costs include the costs of inpatient and outpatient treatment, plus the costs of acute management of overdose, which can also include emergency department ("ED") visits and intensive care unit ("ICU") stays.[4] The most common treatments for SUD, including OUD, include medication-assisted therapy

[2] There was considerable heterogeneity in the methods and scope of state and local OUD-attributable costs addressed by each of the studies meeting inclusion criteria. However, most covered some combination of state Medicaid covered health care costs, state and local costs associated with substance abuse programs and public welfare programs, and direct costs associated with state and local judiciary functions (i.e., courts, police, and corrections).

[3] See generally M. Li et al., "Medical Costs of Substance Use Disorders in the US Employer-Sponsored Insurance Population," *JAMA Netw Open* 6, no. 1 (2023); C. Peterson et al., "Assessment of Annual Cost of Substance Use Disorder in US Hospitals," ibid.4, no. 3 (2021); F. Qeadan et al., "Healthcare utilization trends among patients with opioid use disorder in U.S. Hospitals: an analysis of length of stay, total charges, and costs, 2005–2020," *BMC Health Serv Res* 25, no. 1 (2025).

[4] See generally J. R. Langabeer et al., "Prevalence and charges of opioid-related visits to U.S. emergency departments," *Drug Alcohol Depend* 221 (2021); A. J. Weiss et al., "Opioid-Related Inpatient Stays and Emergency Department Visits by State, 2009–2014," in *Healthcare Cost and Utilization Project (HCUP) Statistical Briefs* (Rockville (MD): Agency for Healthcare Research and Quality (US), 2006).

("MAT"), which in the case of OUD typically consists of methadone, buprenorphine, or extended-release naltrexone, also referred to as Revia® or Vivitrol®. These treatments have been shown to be clinically efficacious in the treatment of OUD and have been utilized to treat OUD for decades.[5] In emergency overdose situations, naloxone, also referred to by its trade name Narcan®, can rapidly reverse some of the effects of opioid overdoses.[6] Outpatient treatment may also include non-pharmacological therapy ("NPT"), consisting of individual or group counseling, psychotherapy, and related interventions.[7] Most studies of healthcare costs attributable to OUD have focused on state Medicaid populations. Given that Medicaid programs are partly funded by states, OUD attributable costs within the Medicaid population are generally believed to reflect OUD attributable costs incurred by state and local governments, with the caveat that on average about half of all state Medicaid expenses are funded by the federal government.

Several studies have calculated excess state and local healthcare costs nominally attributable to OUD. This excess cost approach generally involves the following steps: (1) using health care claims data (e.g., from Medicare, Medicaid, or commercial payers) to identify cases with a primary diagnosis of OUD (typically based on ICD-9/10 codes); (2) matching OUD cases with a non-OUD "control" group that has similar

[5] See generally Y. Adi et al., "Oral naltrexone as a treatment for relapse prevention in formerly opioid-dependent drug users: a systematic review and economic evaluation," *Health Technol Assess* 11, no. 6 (2007); P. A. Donaher and C. Welsh, "Managing opioid addiction with buprenorphine," *Am Fam Physician* 73, no. 9 (2006); J. B. King, A. M. Sainski-Nguyen, and B. K. Bellows, "Office-Based Buprenorphine Versus Clinic-Based Methadone: A Cost-Effectiveness Analysis," *J Pain Palliat Care Pharmacother* 30, no. 1 (2016); S. M. Murphy et al., "Cost-Effectiveness of Buprenorphine-Naloxone Versus Extended-Release Naltrexone to Prevent Opioid Relapse," *Ann Intern Med* 170, no. 2 (2019); S. E. Wakeman et al., "Comparative Effectiveness of Different Treatment Pathways for Opioid Use Disorder," *JAMA Netw Open* 3, no. 2 (2020); A. R. Zullo et al., "AHRQ Comparative Effectiveness Technical Briefs," in *Prevention, Diagnosis, and Management of Opioids, Opioid Misuse, and Opioid Use Disorder in Older Adults* (Rockville (MD): Agency for Healthcare Research and Quality (US), 2020).

[6] See generally A. Shah et al., "Healthcare utilization and costs associated with treatment for opioid dependence," *J Med Econ* 21, no. 4 (2018); M. A. Schuckit, "Treatment of Opioid-Use Disorders," *New England Journal of Medicine* 375, no. 4 (2016).

[7] See generally J. Hargett, A. Criswell, and M. Palokas, "Nonpharmacological interventions for acute pain management in patients with opioid abuse or opioid tolerance: a scoping review," *JBI Evid Synth* 20, no. 11 (2022).

characteristics (e.g., typically matched on age sex, and presence of comorbid conditions); and (3) statistically comparing the total annual costs of the two groups. In theory, if the OUD group has costs that are statistically significantly higher than the control group, the difference between the OUD and control groups is said to be attributable to OUD. This approach is generally referred to as a "matched case control" comparison ("MCC") method.[8] A common version of MCC is "propensity score matching" ("PSM"), where statistical analyses can be used to develop a "propensity score," and case-control matching can be carried out by matching cases with similar propensity scores. Table 6.1 summarizes the results from the studies in which Medicaid attributable OUD costs were estimated.

The data shown in Table 6.1 are remarkably comparable across studies, despite differences in methodology and data sources. McAdams-Marx et al. (2010) is one of the earlier examples of this approach. They conducted a case-control study of Medicaid enrollees (2002–2003) with an OUD diagnosis matched with control cases with similar characteristics but without OUD.[9] Based on data from the Medicaid Analytic eXtract ("MAX") files (which at the time included data from 17 states), a total of 50,162 Patients with an OUD diagnosis were matched to 150,486 control patients.[10] About 84% of OUD patients and 52% of controls had one or more comorbid conditions. Total costs were significantly higher for OUD patients ($14,537) compared to matched controls ($8663) ($p < 0.001$), resulting in an average OUD attributable excess cost of $5874 per case. After adjusting for baseline characteristics using a two-

[8] See generally S. Rose and M. J. van der Laan, "Why Match? Investigating Matched Case Control Study Designs with Causal Effect Estimation," *The International Journal of Biostatistics* 5 (2009).

[9] C. McAdam-Marx et al., "Costs of opioid abuse and misuse determined from a Medicaid database," *J Pain Palliat Care Pharmacother* 24, no. 1 (2010).

[10] At the time of the McAdams-Marx et al. study, MAX files contained data from 17 states, but the files have since been expanded. The MAX files are commonly used for research on Medicaid population. See generally Y. Li et al., "Internal validation of Medicaid Analytic eXtract (MAX) data capture for comprehensive managed care plan enrollees from 2007 to 2010," *Pharmacoepidemiol Drug Saf* 27, no. 10 (2018); J. K. Nguyen and P. Sanghavi, "A national assessment of legacy versus new generation Medicaid data," *Health Serv Res* 57, no. 4 (2022); M. C. Ward, C. Lally, and B. G. Druss, "Medicaid Expenditures for Fee-for-Service Enrollees with Behavioral Diagnoses: Findings from a 50 State Claims Analysis," *Community Ment Health J* 53, no. 1 (2017).

Table 6.1 Summary of studies of excess state-level healthcare costs attributable to opioid use disorder in Medicaid populations, 2021 US$

	Data source year	*Excess medicaid costs per OUD case ($2021) (*)*	*Total excess OUD medicaid costs (National) (a) ($2021) (*)*
McAdams-Marx et al., 2010 (b, c, g)	2002	$8097	$7,242,591,782
Birnbaum et al., 2011 (c, g)	2006	$10,359	$9,265,702,047
Leslie et al., 2019 (d, g)	2013	$7169	$6,412,161,226
Florence et al., 2021 (d, f)	2013	$13,771	$12,317,019,174
Davenport et al., 2019 (h)	2017	$9802	$11,183,000,000
Five-Study Average		$9840	$9,284,094,846

Notes OUD = opioid use disorder (see text, Chap. 3); (*) All cost data are adjusted to 2021 dollars using the All-Items Consumer Price Index; (b) Average of difference in matched OUD cases and controls based on a variety of methods employed by authors; (c) Based on data from Florida Medicaid; (d) Based on data from Medicaid Analytic eXtract (MAX) files (17 states); extrapolated to total U.S.; data based on 2013 data and adjusted to 2021 dollars; (e) based on the Medicaid sample from IBM MarketScan claims data; (f) cost data adapted from Florence et al. 2021 and calculated for 38 states (with no national extrapolations); (g) calculated from data reported in study; (h) Davenport et al. is the "Society of Actuaries" (SOA) report; relied on data from IMB MarketScan, Milliman's Consolidated Health Cost Guidelines, and the Centers for Medicare and Medicaid Services (CMS) 5% Sample Standard Analytical Files

stage multivariable regression, the OUD group continued to show average costs higher than the non-OUD group ($p < 0.001$). Across the various estimates reported in the study, the average excess Medicaid cost per OUD patient was $8097 (2021 dollars).

Birnbaum et al. employed two different methodologies, one where costs were estimated using a "quantity" method, wherein the number of opioid abuse patients was multiplied by the average cost per opioid abuse patient, and by an "apportionment" method, which calculated the overall costs of drug abuse and apportioned shares based on the proportional volume of prescription opioids.[11] The study relied on only one source of Medicaid data from a single state (Florida), the most recent time period for which was 2006. Like the approach employed by McAdams-Marx et al., matching relied on demographic variables (age and sex) and a comorbidity index. Data for OUD prevalence were based on the NSDUH survey data. After adjusting to 2021 dollars, the results were

[11] H. G. Birnbaum et al., "Societal costs of prescription opioid abuse, dependence, and misuse in the United States," *Pain Med* 12, no. 4 (2011).

total OUD excess costs of $9266 million. Like McAdams-Marx et al., Leslie et al. also used the 17-state Medicaid MAX files (1999 and 2013) to estimate healthcare costs associated with OUD.[12] The authors compared inpatient, outpatient, and prescription medication costs for individuals with OUD relative to a comparison group of individuals without OUD matched only by age, sex, and state. Results were extrapolated to the entire U.S. Medicaid population using population-based sample weights. The authors found total Medicaid excess costs of $6412 million, more than $2000 million less than the amount found by Birnbaum et al.

Two of the more widely cited studies have been Florence et al.[13] and Lou et al.,[14] both of which were published in 2021 by research teams from the CDC. The Florence et al. study relied on a sample of Medicaid data from IBM MarketScan data (2012–2013) and conducted an MCC based on demographic variables, health status, and a comorbidity index. Prevalence of past-year OUD was estimated using the NSDUH data. The resulting national attributable healthcare costs in the Medicaid population were $12,317 million, which was nearly double the estimate from Leslie et al. and $3000 million more than the Birnbaum et al. estimate. Lou et al. used these cost estimates to generate state-level healthcare cost estimates for 38 states and the District of Columbia. Because Lou et al. did not attempt to calculate national-level Medicaid costs, the study is excluded from the table.

One of the more comprehensive studies to date is by Davenport et al., sponsored by the Society of Actuaries ("SOA").[15] This study also used an MCC design based on data from Milliman's Consolidated Health Cost Guidelines for the years 2014–2017.[16] Thus, the data used in this study

[12] D. L. Leslie et al., "The economic burden of the opioid epidemic on states: the case of Medicaid," *Am J Manag Care* 25, no. 13 Suppl (2019).

[13] C. Florence, F. Luo, and K. Rice, "The economic burden of opioid use disorder and fatal opioid overdose in the United States, 2017," *Drug Alcohol Depend* 218 (2021).

[14] F. Luo, M. Li, and C. Florence, "State-Level Economic Costs of Opioid Use Disorder and Fatal Opioid Overdose—United States, 2017," *MMWR Morb Mortal Wkly Rep* 70, no. 15 (2021).

[15] S. Davenport, A. Weaver, and M. Caverly, "Economic Impact of Non-Medical Opioid Use in the United States: Annual Estimates and Projections for 2015 through 2019," (Schaumburg, IL: Society of Actuaries, 2019). Note that this study was peer reviewed but published independently by the Society of Actuaries.

[16] Milliman is a nationally recognized actuarial consulting firm which provides services to federal, state, and local governmental organizations, as well a wide variety of private companies (e.g., commercial health insurers; large health systems). The Milliman data is

were about four years more recent than those presented in the 2021 study by Florence et al. Like the preceding MCC studies, matching in the Davenport et al. study was based on age, sex, state, and health status, with the latter measured by risk scores. In addition to excess costs attributable to individuals with OUD, the study also included costs associated with infants born with NAS and NOWS, and for family members of those with diagnosed OUD. In 2021 dollars, excess Medicaid costs were estimated to be $9802 per OUD case, summing to $11,183 million nationally. The authors' total national estimate was comparable to that of the widely cited 2021 study by Florence et al., and the Davenport et al. results were generally higher than those of earlier studies, possibly due to the inclusion of costs associated with NAS and NOWS and individuals associated with family members of those diagnosed with OUD. The results of Davenport et al. are also very close to the five-study average in terms of per-case and total national costs.[17]

6.3 Criminal Justice System

Another main component of potentially attributable OUD costs at a state and local level is associated with the operation of the criminal justice system. These costs typically include costs associated with police, courts, and corrections. Opioid-related police costs typically include attributable costs related to interdiction, investigation, and street-level enforcement.[18] Attributable court costs include drug courts and higher court caseloads. Added corrections costs include higher demand for capacity, the costs of treatment for incarcerated individuals with OUD, and the costs of providing naloxone and related treatments upon release.[19] To determine the excess CJS costs attributable to OUD, the methods differ from the healthcare studies

considered one of the most comprehensive Medicaid datasets and contains records for approximately 6 million Medicaid enrollees nationally.

[17] The Davenport et al. estimate of OUD-attributable costs per case is also generally comparable to that of L. M. Scarpati et al., "Drivers of excess costs of opioid abuse among a commercially insured population," *Am J Manag Care* 23, no. 5 (2017).

[18] J. P. Caulkins et al., "Opioids and the Criminal Justice System: New Challenges Posed by the Modern Opioid Epidemic," *Annual Review of Criminology* 4, no. 1 (2021).

[19] See generally ibid.; C. K. Scott et al., "The impact of the opioid crisis on U.S. state prison systems," *Health Justice* 9, no. 1 (2021); T. N. A. Winkelman and R. S. Silva, "Opioid Use Disorder Treatment for People Involved in the US Criminal Justice System-Promising Advances and Critical Implementation Challenges," *JAMA Netw Open* 4, no. 9 (2021).

described above because it is generally not practical to employ a matching approach. Instead, these studies typically approach cost attribution using an "apportionment" method, whereby attributable costs are estimated based on the proportion of all CJS interactions believed to be associated with opioids or OUD. Frequently cited studies are shown in Table 6.2; note that some of these studies also calculated excess healthcare costs and were discussed above in that context. Some studies that focused on specific states were omitted from the table to maintain comparability; however, some state-specific studies are discussed separately.

Hansen et al. used data from the Bureau of Justice Statistics (2003) and the Federal Bureau of Investigation's Uniform Crime Statistics (2006).[20] The authors used an apportionment approach to allocate expenditures on drug law violations associated with opioids. This approach resulted in a national annual cost estimate of $9501 million (in 2021 dollars). Birnbaum et al. and Florence et al. used data from the Criminal Justice Expenditure and Employment Extracts ("JEEE") for 2005–2006 and 2015, respectively, and then applied an apportionment method to determine the share attributable to OUD. Though their methods and data were similar, the two studies reached very different attributable cost estimates of $5274 million and $14,879 million, respectively. Davenport et al. also relied upon JEEE data (2015) and

Table 6.2 Summary of studies of excess state and local criminal justice system costs attributable to opioid use disorder, 2021 US$

	Data source year	*Total excess judicial costs (National) ($2021) (*)*
Hansen et al., 2011 (a)	2003	$9,500,954,174
Birnbaum et al., 2011 (b)	2006	$5,274,288,698
Florence et al., 2021 (c)	2015	$14,879,350,495
Davenport et al., 2019 (c)	2019	$11,229,000,000
Four-Study Average		$10,220,898,342

Notes OUD = opioid use disorder (see text, Chap. 3); (*) All cost data are adjusted to 2021 dollars using the All-Items Consumer Price Index; (a) based on data from the Bureau of Justice Statistics (2003) and the Federal Bureau of Investigation's Uniform Crime Statistics (2006); (b) based on data from the Criminal Justice Expenditure and Employment Extracts (2005–2006); (c) excluding property loss and adjusted for state and local; based on data from the Criminal Justice Expenditure and Employment Extracts (2015)

[20] R. N. Hansen et al., "Economic costs of nonmedical use of prescription opioids," *Clin J Pain* 27, no. 3 (2011).

an apportionment approach and estimated total state and local CJS attributable to OUD of $11,229 million, an estimate in between those of Hansen et al. and Florence et al. but somewhat higher than the four-study average.

The Florence et al. study results appear to be somewhat of an outlier. In the earlier work by Florence et al., OUD-attributable CJS costs (based on 2012–2013 data) were estimated to be $7654 million in the U.S.,[21] or about half of the total attributable CJS costs found in their later work. However, examining OUD case rates reported in each of those studies, the number of OUD cases upon which their estimates are based increased only 10% between the two study periods, perhaps due in part to a decline in opioid supply in the time between the two studies. It seems unlikely that a 10% increase in OUD rates could result in a doubling of CJS costs, especially given that a large proportion of CJS costs are "fixed" in the short run and not sensitive to case volume (this important point will be discussed in greater detail later).

As an example of a state-specific study, Zajac et al. focused on CJS costs in Pennsylvania from 2007 to 2016, estimating OUD-attributable costs associated with police, courts, and corrections.[22] Similar to other studies of OUD attributable CJS costs, the authors relied on an apportionment approach based on proportions of cases in which opioids were identified as the principal source of the CJS interaction. Expected costs were compared to actual costs, with the difference attributed to OUD. The results showed that attributable police costs were essentially $0, attributable court costs were on average an additional $7.4 million per year, and attributable corrections costs averaged an additional $45 million per year over the study period. The latter was due mainly to a period of higher-than-expected costs from 2008–2013. Following that peak, from 2013 to 2016, both the actual and expected corrections costs fell precipitously, and by 2016 the attributable cost gap had narrowed to $25 million. In sum, according to Zajac et al., in the most recent year of the analysis, CJS costs attributable to OUD in Pennsylvania were about $36.6 million (adjusted to 2021 dollars).[23]

[21] C. S. Florence et al., "The Economic Burden of Prescription Opioid Overdose, Abuse, and Dependence in the United States, 2013," *Med Care* 54, no. 10 (2016).

[22] G. Zajac et al., "Estimated costs to the Pennsylvania criminal justice system resulting from the opioid crisis," *Am J Manag Care* 25, no. 13 Suppl (2019).

[23] The per-case calculation is based on the 2021 annual estimate derived from Zajac et al. divided by the number of individuals with an opioid-related arrest in Pennsylvania in 2021 (n = 2803) (based on a spreadsheet report entitled "Opioid Seizures and Arrests CY 2013—Current Quarterly County State Police")

6.4 Social and Family Assistance

Social and family assistance and other related support services include prevention programs, educational outreach to providers and consumers, child and family welfare, counselling, food and nutritional assistance, housing assistance, and income assistance. For example, in the state of Florida, the State Opioid Response ("SOR") Project "is designed to address the opioid crisis and reduce opioid-related deaths by providing a comprehensive array of evidence-based prevention, medication-assisted treatment, and recovery support services."[24] In some cases, social and family assistance programs may also include parts of programs aimed at the abatement of opioid-attributable harms, including drug takeback programs to facilitate disposal of diverted opioids, needle exchange programs, and messaging campaigns. The review identified only one study that separately calculated OUD-attributable SFA costs at a state and local level. Davenport et al. used an apportionment method to attribute SFA costs associated with OUD based on four common SFA cost categories: (1) child welfare; (2) food and nutritional assistance; (3) housing assistance; and (4) income assistance.[25] Again, these cost categories may in some cases also include prevention, outreach, communication activities, and other activities addressing social determinants of health,[26] so it is likely that the Davenport et al. estimate includes some services beyond the four that were identified. The OUD-attributable costs of these programs at the state and local level summed nationally to $8522 million (2021 dollars).

6.5 Methodological Considerations

The studies described above represent the most recent studies meeting the study inclusion criteria based on methodological rigor and comprehensive reporting of methods and results. The studies, which differ in methodology,

[24] FDCF, "Florida's State Opioid Response Project: Annual Report, 2019 (Updated January 2020)," (Tallahassee, FL: Florida Department of Children and Families (FDCF), 2020).

[25] Davenport et al. defined income assistance as the sum of Temporary Assistance for Needy Families ("TANF") and Supplemental Security Income ("SSI").

[26] See generally C. Blanco et al., "America's opioid crisis: the need for an integrated public health approach," *Transl Psychiatry* 10, no. 1 (2020); T. M. Haegerich et al., "Evidence for state, community and systems-level prevention strategies to address the opioid crisis," *Drug Alcohol Depend* 204 (2019); B. Lee et al., "Systematic Evaluation of State Policy Interventions Targeting the US Opioid Epidemic, 2007–2018," *JAMA Netw Open* 4, no. 2 (2021).

reach remarkably consistent results. Despite meeting study inclusion criteria, it is worth noting that there are some methodological issues associated with even the most comprehensive studies. In the course of the review, the following issues were observed: (1) variation in the development of "logic frameworks" regarding causal pathways, root causes of OUD and OUD-attributable costs, and the empirical testing of causal hypotheses; (2) variation in the discussion or consideration of types of biases and limitations in some MCC studies; (3) incomplete accounting of trends in key variables when extrapolating to larger populations or to future time periods; and (4) lack of clarity in the distinction between operating costs versus list prices or charges. Note that while these limitations are important to consider, they do not necessarily undermine the findings of the studies.

6.5.1 *Hypothesis Testing*

When designing empirical studies, it is important to identify *a priori* a specific set of testable hypotheses and causal pathways. For example, we might want to know the effect of x on y (x→y) or the extent to which y is a function of x and a set of other variables (z) such that $y = f(x, z)$. Most research hypotheses imply a causal pathway; for example, x caused y (or a *change* in x caused a *change* in y), or we might want to know whether there exists a multi-part causal pathway (e.g., z→x→y). Regardless of the inquiry in question, the advantage of doing the conceptual work in advance is that it helps the researcher decide how to structure the data and analysis such that the study is technically able to accomplish its objectives. The studies reviewed above are inconsistent in the application of this sort of logic framework, and no study attempted to put forth a causal pathway specifically linking prescription opioid supply to OUD. Ignoring the conceptual part of the causal pathway raises the risk of incorrectly attributing causative factors to outcomes by relying on statistical associations. For example, opioid-related costs can be apportioned to CJS expenditures, but without specifying a causal pathway and estimating a statistical model that is sufficiently robust to test causal hypotheses (as discussed in Chap. 3), it may be possible that confounding factors had more of an impact than opioids, or that opioids were serving as a proxy for other factors, such as income or other social determinants of health, which have been shown to be causally related to substance use disorders (this will be discussed more in later chapters).

6.5.2 *Study Design*

As discussed above, in determining excess costs the method relied upon most in these studies was MCC, which was in some cases employed to determine an excess OUD cost. Excess cost per case is then used to extrapolate to a larger population, such as a state Medicaid population or a broader national population. Despite its conceptual appeal, MCC methods also have some limitations that are worth noting. Some of these limitations are inherent to the methodology itself, but these problems are often exacerbated by researchers employing the methods incorrectly. For example, one study found that only 43% of MCC of studies are conducted correctly.[27] The two most common limitations of the MCC design are: (1) "confounding bias,"[28] where some unknown proportion of excess costs will be "over-attributed" to the outcome of interest because the outcome of interest is also attributable to unmeasured or unobserved variables; for example, in the case of OUD, individuals with OUD are substantially more likely to have other comorbid conditions,[29] including at baseline;[30]; and (2) "collider bias," which arises when the variable in question (in this case, OUD costs) is in part a function of the ability to accurately identify

[27] D. J. Niven et al., "Matched case-control studies: a review of reported statistical methodology," *Clin Epidemiol* 4 (2012).

[28] It is a misconception to assume that MCC minimizes confounding bias; there is no guarantee that it does. See generally E. Shahar and D. J. Shahar, "Causal diagrams and the logic of matched case-control studies," ibid.; S. Tenny, C. C. Kerndt, and M. R. Hoffman, "Case Control Studies," in *StatPearls* (Treasure Island (FL): StatPearls Publishing Copyright © 2022, StatPearls Publishing LLC., 2022); N. Pearce, "Analysis of matched case-control studies," *Bmj* 352 (2016).

[29] McAdam-Marx et al., "Costs of opioid abuse and misuse determined from a Medicaid database." In the study sample, OUD patients were much more likely to have other substance abuse conditions, psychiatric disorders, HIV/AIDS, endocarditis, skin infections, cirrhosis, hepatitis, and other conditions, with odds ratios ranging from 4.841 for any comorbidity to as much as 9.372 for other substance abuse, 5.254 for HIV/AIDS, and 8.838 for hepatitis. In sum, 84% of OUD patients compared to 52% among non-OUD controls had comorbidities. High rates of comorbidities among individuals with OUD remains evident in more recent studies as well; for example, a CDC study found that among OUD decedents, 41% had evidence of past mental health conditions and mental health treatment. See L. J. Tanz et al., "Drug Overdose Deaths Among Persons Aged 10–19 Years—United States, July 2019-December 2021," *MMWR Morb Mortal Wkly Rep* 71, no. 50 (2022).

[30] A. Shei et al., "Characteristics of High-Cost Patients Diagnosed with Opioid Abuse," *J Manag Care Spec Pharm* 21, no. 10 (2015).

patients of interest without bias;[31] that is, higher-cost OUD patients are likely to be "over-represented" in the data.[32] Put differently, for an OUD patient to be identified, it is likely that they have already incurred costs and had interactions with the health system, which in turn raises their costs. Again, several studies have reported substantially higher levels of comorbidities among OUD patients.[33] Many of these comorbidities are associated with chronic conditions (e.g., mental health disorders, hepatitis, HIV, and many others), and individuals with multiple chronic conditions have significantly more contact with the health system.[34] These identification-associated costs would not have been incurred in the control group, but are not necessarily related to OUD; for example, OUD may have been a secondary diagnosis made during an unrelated visit or hospitalization. When combined with confounding bias and the difficulties posed by unobservable confounders, this bias can be significant. Both methodological issues generally bias the results in the direction of *over-estimation* of effect sizes. Incomplete accounting of confounding factors results in the effects of the confounding variables being comingled with the effects of the variable of interest. Collider bias results in the disproportionate identification of higher cost cases, which again leads to the over-estimation of effect sizes. Finally, it is important to note that MCC methods do not address *causation*, they can only measure *correlation*.[35] Thus, with MCC study designs, it is possible that attributable cost estimates will be biased upward.

[31] See generally G. J. Griffith et al., "Collider bias undermines our understanding of COVID-19 disease risk and severity," *Nat Commun* 11, no. 1 (2020). Also for general background refer to R. Etzioni, M. Mandel, and R. Gulati, "Causal Inference," in *Statistics for Health Data Science* (Switzerland: Springer, 2020).

[32] For example, refer to W. Yuan et al., "Temporal bias in case-control design: preventing reliable predictions of the future," *Nat Commun* 12, no. 1 (2021).

[33] Some of this material is discussed above. For additional data on OUD comorbidities, refer to C. E. Grella et al., "Gender and comorbidity among individuals with opioid use disorders in the NESARC study," *Addict Behav* 34, no. 6–7 (2009); McAdam-Marx et al., "Costs of opioid abuse and misuse determined from a Medicaid database."; Y. Pan and R. Xu, "Mining comorbidities of opioid use disorder from FDA adverse event reporting system and patient electronic health records," *BMC Med Inform Decis Mak* 22, no. Suppl 2 (2022); E. C. Strain, "Assessment and treatment of comorbid psychiatric disorders in opioid-dependent patients," *Clin J Pain* 18, no. 4 Suppl (2002).

[34] For example, see S. H. van Oostrom et al., "Multimorbidity of chronic diseases and health care utilization in general practice," *BMC Fam Pract* 15 (2014).

[35] Tenny, Kerndt, and Hoffman, "Case Control Studies."

6.5.3 *Extrapolation*

Another area in which these types of studies can be limited is extrapolation. While the studies reviewed above did not extrapolate to future time periods, in the opioid MDL claimants typically employed extrapolation methods to estimate expected abatement costs in future periods, with the future period considered by claimants as the "window" in which the harm or externality could reasonably be returned to "normal" or "acceptable" levels.[36] Extrapolations typically take two forms: extrapolating "up" to a population of interest (e.g., a state Medicaid population) or extrapolating "out" to future time periods. First, consider the case of extrapolating to a larger population. Most case-control or matching methodologies are based on a sample, where all the cases with condition *x* are identified, and then each case is matched (based on, for example, demographic characteristics) with a similar case that does not have condition *x*. If matches cannot be found for some cases with condition *x*, those cases must be dropped from the analysis. In such instances, calculations of excess costs are then based only on the remaining sample. But an important question is whether the resulting sample is representative of the population. There is nothing about the MCC study design that assures that the results of an excess cost calculation will be representative of the population from which study groups and controls were drawn.[37]

Extrapolations to future periods have somewhat different limitations but can in some cases be more consequential. Three common limitations of "forward" extrapolation are: (1) the accuracy of the extrapolation depends on the extent to which the initial calculation of excess cost is accurate and unbiased and that uncertainty in the initial estimate can either be ignored or assumed to carry over in future periods; (2) the extent to which the initial excess costs and prevalence are expected to remain constant over time; that is, in the case of OUD, forward extrapolations would need to account for expected changes in OUD prevalence, changes in the ability of the healthcare system to manage OUD, and changes in the supply and utilization of prescription opioids; and (3) extrapolations

[36] See, for example, D. Rhubart et al., "Conceptualizing and Measuring Abatement from the Opioid Epidemic: A Case Study from Pennsylvania," *Milbank Q* 100, no. 4 (2022).

[37] See generally Griffith et al., "Collider bias undermines our understanding of COVID-19 disease risk and severity."

should account for exogenous factors, such as exogenous events or contemporaneous trends, that can impact the outcome directly or modify the causal pathways.

All three limitations are important to forward extrapolations of opioid attributable costs and abatement costs. It will be shown in later chapters that the attributable costs and abatement costs claimed by plaintiffs in the opioid MDL cases are likely substantially higher than actual abatement costs, and therefore any extrapolation forward would magnify this overestimation. The second limitation is also likely to be an important issue in the opioid MDL cases, which are focused on the public nuisance aspects of OUD. The volume of prescription opioids has declined precipitously since 2012, and several mitigation programs aimed at prescription drugs have already been in place for many years (e.g., prescription drug monitoring programs and naloxone distribution). The share of OUD cases attributable to prescription drugs has also fallen precipitously. Thus, any extrapolation forward would have to assume a significantly diminishing role of prescription opioids and a significantly diminishing effect of prescription opioids on OUD in later time periods. Finally, the third limitation, which is the ability to account for exogenous and contemporaneous effects, is also potentially important. In the case of opioid-related costs, this challenge is especially important to CJS and SFA costs, which are driven by state and local budgets that do not vary much from one year to the next, and where approximately 50–80% of average costs are fixed in the short run (more on this point later).[38]

To further illustrate the latter limitation, consider the results of Zajac et al., reviewed above in the CJS cost discussion, where the authors calculated differences between actual and expected corrections costs over time in Pennsylvania.[39] The authors attribute the gap between actual and expected costs to OUD-attributable costs. However, what is more interesting is the precipitous *decline* in OUD-attributed corrections costs beginning in 2013.[40] While 2013 marked the beginning of the rapid

[38] S. J. Wilson and J. Lemoine, "Methods of Calculating the Marginal Cost of Incarceration: A Scoping Review," *Criminal Justice Policy Review* (2021). This study also reported "long run" fixed costs of approximately 30%. This is discussed more in the context of plausible abatement ceilings.

[39] Zajac et al., "Estimated costs to the Pennsylvania criminal justice system resulting from the opioid crisis."

[40] BJS, "Correctional Populations in the United States, 2021—Statistical Tables," (Washington, D.C.: U.S. Bureau of Justice Statistics, 2023).

decline in the utilization of prescription opioids, the trend also appears to be very consistent with the national decline in the number of individuals housed in the U.S. corrections system coinciding with the passage of the Fair Sentencing Act ("FSA") of 2010.[41] Because the FSA applied mainly to new cases going forward, its effects were not observed until a few years later, and are likely to have explained at least part of the decline in CJS costs observed in Pennsylvania in 2013.[42] Consequently, any attempt to extrapolate corrections costs would have to account for the exogenous nationwide decline in the size of the incarcerated population, which appears to have started its decline after the passage of the FSA. In services with relatively high proportions of fixed costs, like CJS services, a decline in total volume implies that marginal costs will remain relatively low, as minimal new capacity (if any) is needed to handle higher demand potentially attributable to other needs, such as OUD.

6.5.4 *Fair Market Value*

Some studies of healthcare costs assume equivalence between prices, or charged amounts, and the reasonable fair market value of those services. However, in healthcare markets this can bias estimates upward because charged amounts do not typically reflect amounts transacted in the marketplace. This distinction is important because state and local attributable costs should only be those associated with the incurred costs of producing those services, rather than hypothetical "prices" assigned to the services. For example, the purchase of an additional police vehicle should not be assigned a cost equal to the market price or list price of the vehicle, but rather it should be assigned a cost equal to the net procurement cost, which in the case of state and local governments would normally include significant volume discounts and perhaps other incentive-related discounting, such as favorable financing terms and longer term supply agreements.[43] The discrepancy between list prices and

[41] Also note that in 2008 the Second Chance Act was signed into law in 2008. Combined with the Fair Sentencing Act, these laws most likely reversed the upward trend in incarcerations, independent of any opioid-related factors.

[42] USSC, "Report to the Congress: Impact of the Fair Sentencing Act of 2010," (Washington, D.C.: United States Sentencing Commission, 2015).

[43] See, for example, T.L. Crow, "Patrol Fleet Leasing Equals Efficient Spending," (The Bill Blackwood Law Enforcement Management Institute of Texas, 2006).

procurement costs is likely to persist across virtually all state and local government expenditures, as government is typically a large volume buyer, and normally able to exercise some degree of monopsony buying power.[44]

Healthcare costs are even more susceptible to these valuation issues. In the health industry, there is agreement among industry experts that prices, which are often referred to as "charges" in the U.S. health industry, are generally *not* reflective of fair market value.[45] Indeed, there is a long tradition in the U.S. medical care industry of health care providers submitting bills and charges for services rendered but accepting much less than those amounts in full satisfaction of those charges.[46] This widespread practice suggests that health and medical prices have, at best, a relatively loose relationship with fair market value. This is in part reflected by the exceedingly high rate of variation in prices for the exact same procedures across geographic market areas and among providers in the same markets.[47] These variations in prices also lead to extremely high levels of variation in differences between costs and charges among service providers, irrespective of the fair and reasonable value of services rendered.[48] It is unclear the degree to which the cost estimates reported in studies reviewed in this chapter represent the reasonable value or fair market value of medical expenses versus list prices and charges. Similarly, it is unclear the extent to which economic experts in the opioid MDL cases are relying on estimates of resource use that are based on fair market value versus estimates based on list price amounts. It is likely that the studies

[44] See generally OECD, "Monopsony and Buyer Power," in *Series Roundtables on Competition Policy (Competition Committee)* (Paris, France: Organization for Economic Cooperation and Development, 2008).

[45] See, for example, V. Arora, C. Moriates, and N. Shah, "The Challenge of Understanding Health Care Costs and Charges," *AMA J Ethics* 17, no. 11 (2015).

[46] See generally S.A. Finkler, *Issues in Cost Accounting for Health Care Organizations* (Gaithersburg, MD: Aspen Publishers, Inc., 1994); U.S. House of Representatives, "Pricing Practices of Hospitals," (Washington, D.C.: U.S. House of Representatives, Committee on Ways and Means, Subcommittee on Oversight, 108th Congress, 2005).

[47] See generally R. Y. Hsia, Y. Akosa Antwi, and E. Weber, "Analysis of variation in charges and prices paid for vaginal and caesarean section births: a cross-sectional study," *BMJ Open* 4, no. 1 (2014); D. A. Redelmeier et al., "Charges for medical care at different hospitals," *Arch Intern Med* 160, no. 10 (2000); W. P. Welch et al., "Geographic variation in expenditures for physicians' services in the United States," *N Engl J Med* 328, no. 9 (1993).

[48] See generally G. Bai and G. F. Anderson, "Extreme Markup: The Fifty US Hospitals With The Highest Charge-To-Cost Ratios," *Health Aff (Millwood)* 34, no. 6 (2015).

utilizing Medicaid data more or less reflect reasonable or fair market value, because Medicaid databases typically include Medicaid payments or Medicaid allowable amounts, both of which would generally be more reflective of fair market value than would a provider's list prices.[49] Overall, across studies of attributable healthcare costs, including the opioid MDL stakeholders' reliance on economic data (some of which may be based on charges rather than fair market value), this can be an important consideration.

6.6 Attributable Cost Ceiling

The remainder of this chapter is focused on the development of an "attributable cost ceiling" model based on the adjusted cost data extracted from published peer-reviewed cost studies. Most published cost estimates are best thought of as attributable or excess costs, analogous to what forensic economists would generally consider economic damages. Again, the rationale for this approach is that, given the large body of published evidence on opioid misuse and OUD-attributable costs, it is appropriate to consider this body of work in determining damages related to OUD-attributable costs. The attributable cost ceiling model described in this section utilizes the most rigorous of this evidence to allocate OUD-attributable costs to state and local governments, which in turn allows the state or county's specific share of prescription opioids to be used as a basis for allocation. In other words, the working hypothesis is "if the preponderance of evidence concludes that state and local OUD-attributable costs nationally are \$x, and plaintiffs are arguing that members of the prescription drug supply chain are responsible for \$x, then a particular state or county's share of \$x should be approximately equal to the state or county's share of the prescription opioids that allegedly contributed to \$x."

The cost ceiling approach can also be viewed as a counterfactual hypothesis: If all reported state and county attributable costs were to be summed across the nation, the total should at least be in the same "ballpark" as the

[49] Medicaid rates are generally considered "low" relative to other payers. However, after adjustments for Disproportionate Share Hospital Payments ("DSH") and other supplemental payments, the rates generally cover operating costs, and in some cases may exceed costs. See generally P. Cunningham et al., "Understanding Medicaid Hospital Payments and the Impact of Recent Policy Changes," (Washington, D.C.: Kaiser Family Foundation (KFF), 2016).

totals found by some of the leading experts on OUD-attributable costs, assuming necessary adjustments to make the estimates comparable. A key component of the model is the calculation of maximum attributable (or "excess") costs based on the literature, adjusted to accurately reflect state and local government shares of those costs. For the cost ceiling model, the study averages presented above were used as the key inputs. Consistent with how the data are reported above, the data abstraction process included the following baseline adjustments: (1) for healthcare costs, only Medicaid-related costs are selected, as a proportion of these costs are the responsibility of state government; (2) for CJS costs, federal corrections costs were excluded; (3) from all studies, mortality costs and lost productivity costs were excluded, as were estimates of the "statistical value of life;"[50] and (4) all cost estimates are shown in 2021 dollars, adjusted using the Consumer Price Index ("CPI").[51]

6.7 Adjustments

Healthcare, CJS, and SFA attributable cost estimates from the literature were generally intended to reflect national costs or, more generally, a wider scope of costs than featured in the opioid MDL. Thus, to reflect state and local costs more accurately, the attributable cost ceiling approach necessitates some important adjustments. These are as follows: (1) adjustments to healthcare and SFA cost estimates to account for shared state and federal co-funding of Medicaid programs and federal grants supporting a relatively high proportion of state and local SFA programs; (2) adjustments to healthcare, CJS, and SFA costs to account for opioids sourced from the health care system, given that the focus of the opioid MDL cases has been exclusively on prescription opioids; and (3) adjustments to CJS and SFA costs to account for fixed versus variable operating costs, which are accounting and economic concepts that figure prominently in the calculation of attributable costs and abatement cost in any setting.

[50] Mortality and productivity costs are excluded because those costs are typically not included in damages and abatement cost calculations.

[51] CPI adjustment factors applied were as follows (each with respect to trending up to 2021 values): 14.33% (2015); 12.90% (2016); 10.55% (2017); 7.91% (2018); 5.99% (2019); 4.70% (2020).

6.7.1 *State and Federal Cost Sharing*

For most of the services typically identified as allegedly being "affected by" OUD externalities in some way, there is significant operational cost sharing between counties, states, and the federal government. This is a very important consideration regarding abatement, as such cost-sharing arrangements are especially common among health and social services.[52] For healthcare costs, the Centers for Medicare and Medicaid Services ("CMS") administers the Medicaid program as a "co-funded" program, whereby approximately 30–50% of incurred costs are funded by state Medicaid programs, and approximately 50–70% are funded by the federal government.[53] The exact split varies by state; for example, in Ohio, where the opioid MDL is based, the federal government funds 64% of the Medicaid program and the state of Ohio funds the remaining 36%.[54] Across all states, the average Medicaid funding split between state and federal governments is about 31% state and 69% federal.[55] Note that the federal government does not act as an indemnity insurer in this capacity; rather, the total program budget is shared between the two entities to "co-fund" the programs. Similar cost sharing arrangements exist for SFA. In general, the federal government funds about 65% of all public welfare expenditures, mainly through intergovernmental federal grants made directly to state and local governments.[56] Operating costs of state and local CJS is minimally co-funded by federal sources, mostly limited to *ad hoc* grants. Thus, it is reasonable to assume that states incur about 95% of CJS costs.[57]

6.7.2 *Opioid Sources*

The opioid MDL has thus far focused mainly on prescription opioids, with some of the entities in the prescription opioid supply chain alleged to have

[52] See generally R. D. Lee, R. W. Johnson, and P. G. Joyce, *Public Budgeting Systems (10th Edition)* (Burlington, MA: Jones & Bartlett Learning, 2021).

[53] See generally Commonwealth Fund, "What Is Medicaid's Value?," (New York, NY 2019).

[54] KFF, "Medicaid in Ohio," (Washinton, D.C.: Kaiser Family Foundation, 2022).

[55] E. Williams, R. Rudowitz, and A. Burns, "Medicaid Financing: The Basics," (Washington, D.C.: Kaiser Family Foundation, 2023).

[56] Urban Institute, "Public Welfare Expenditures," in *State and Local Backgrounders* (Washington, DC: The Urban Institute, 2022).

[57] See generally "Criminal Justice Expenditures: Police, Corrections, and Courts," (Washington, D.C.: The Urban Institute, 2022).

contributed to an increase in the volume of opioids. Consequently, in the attributable cost ceiling model, the relevant supply of opioids should be limited to those obtained *directly from the health system* (i.e., via a valid prescription from a provider. As discussed in Chap. 3, an important source of misused prescription opioids is opioids that are diverted from medical use to non-medical use, and those sourced illegally from black markets. Again, Park and Wu found that 36.6% of individuals who reported opioid misuse during the past year obtained the opioids directly from the health system, with another 40% or misusers sourcing opioids from family and friends and about 23% sourcing from drug dealers and other illegal means.[58] These results are broadly consistent with other studies.[59] Based on these studies, abatement costs are adjusted to include only those costs that are plausibly attributable to healthcare sources. The overall estimate from Park and Wu (36.6%) is used because of its consistency with other sources and the rigor of the study design. The results of Hulme et al., who find a rate of only 29% of misused opioids sourced from the health care system, suggest that the Park and Wu study represents a cautious estimate. As noted above, this adjustment applies to all the cost categories.

6.7.3 Fixed and Variable Costs

Claimants in the opioid MDL argue generally that OUD results in higher operating costs incurred by state and local departments and programs impacted by OUD.[60] It is true that, in general, public agencies are likely to incur operating costs attributable to an exogenous effect, such as a weather event or a public nuisance. However, not all operating costs are the same. Operating costs can be parsed into *fixed* costs and *variable*

[58] J. Y. Park and L. T. Wu, "Sources of Misused Prescription Opioids and Their Association with Prescription Opioid Use Disorder in the United States: Sex and Age Differences," *Subst Use Misuse* 55, no. 6 (2020).

[59] See generally T. S. Schepis, S. E. McCabe, and C. J. Teter, "Sources of opioid medication for misuse in older adults: results from a nationally representative survey," *Pain* 159, no. 8 (2018); T. S. Schepis, T. E. Wilens, and S. E. McCabe, "Prescription Drug Misuse: Sources of Controlled Medications in Adolescents," *J Am Acad Child Adolesc Psychiatry* 58, no. 7 (2019). Also refer to S. Hulme, D. Bright, and S. Nielsen, "The source and diversion of pharmaceutical drugs for non-medical use: A systematic review and meta-analysis," *Drug Alcohol Depend* 186 (2018).

[60] Weeks and Sanford, "Financial Impact of the Opioid Crisis on Local Government: Quantifying Costs for Litigation and Policymaking."

costs. Fixed costs refer to costs that are necessary before the first client or customer can be served. That is, in many industries and markets, significant investments in fixed assets must be undertaken before the first customer purchases a coffee at Starbucks, before the first patient can be treated at a hospital, or before the first OUD-affected individual can be treated in a healthcare setting, processed in a CJS setting, or assisted in an SFA setting. Fixed costs typically include physical buildings, capital-intensive durable equipment (e.g., commercial kitchen appliances, vehicles, imaging equipment, etc., depending on the industry), and, in some cases, other types of supplies and equipment that have minimal variation with the level of output.

As a general illustration of fixed versus variable costs, consider a sandwich shop with one building and five employees. Assume that the shop typically serves 100 customers per day. Further assume that the same building and the same five employees might also be able to serve double the number of customers each day. This suggests that the production inputs (capital and labor) were not fully utilized at 100 customers per day. In both instances, the same fixed costs of the building are incurred, and the total wage costs do not change, even after a 100% increase in demand. Thus, the shop in this example was able to "scale up" at minimal additional costs, with perhaps some added variable costs in the form of materials and supplies (e.g., bread, sandwich fillings, etc.). There is likely a maximum number of daily customers who could be handled by the shop with its five employees, perhaps 300, after which it might be necessary to hire another employee to handle the increasing volume. But the main point is that costs would not rise proportionally with demand; even after a tripling in volume, the building remained the same size, and the number of employees increased by only 20%. This is of course a hypothetical example, but these types of relationships between costs and output are common throughout the economy, including in the provision of public health services and in the operations of a variety of healthcare institutions.[61]

The concepts of fixed and variable costs are closely related to the economic concepts of "economies of scale" and "economies of scope." Economies of scale occur when the average cost of the production of one

[61] P. M. Bernet and S. Singh, "Economies of scale in the production of public health services: an analysis of local health districts in Florida," *Am J Public Health* 105 Suppl 2, no. Suppl 2 (2015). Also see H. T. Gold et al., "Cost data in implementation science: categories and approaches to costing," *Implement Sci* 17, no. 1 (2022).

additional unit is less than the average costs of previously produced units. This typically occurs in production processes with relatively high fixed costs, as the fixed cost share of the total costs of each subsequent unit produced declines as production volume increases. For operations that are already established (i.e., buildings and equipment leased or purchased and set up), when economies of scale are present the unit costs of subsequent production will decline as production volume grows. In some cases, there may be short-term or temporary discontinuities in economies of scale, whereby current capacity becomes maximized or otherwise constrained, requiring a new investment in fixed costs to increase capacity for future production. In contrast, economies of scope refer to components of production processes that are less costly to perform together rather than separately. For example, it is probably less expensive to combine needle exchange programs, naloxone distribution, and fentanyl test strip distribution, rather than establish three separate programs to distribute each product individually. Providing the services together may enable the use of fewer staff, allow for higher levels of staff productivity (i.e., output per hour), and allow for lower combined capital costs (e.g., the purchase or rental of a single facility to support all three functions). In addition to economies of scale and scope, as mentioned above, it is also common for states and municipalities to receive significant volume discounts, favorable financing terms, and low lease costs on the purchasing of equipment, such as vehicles.[62]

These concepts are very important to the estimation of OUD-attributable costs and abatement costs because a large proportion of the average costs (i.e., total operating costs divided by total quantity of output) for police, courts, corrections, and social programs are expected to be relatively fixed in the short run. This is compounded by the fact that budgets for these types of programs are publicly funded from general tax revenue and federal grants and are generally determined in advance of when the services are utilized. In the short run, states and municipalities cannot easily add physical capacity (e.g., expanded/additional buildings, police stations, court houses, and prisons); likewise, with relatively fixed resources in the short run, state and local governments are also in some cases limited in their ability to add variable costs (e.g., personnel; supplies). It is also likely that both economies of scale and scope are prominently featured in the

[62] See generally Crow, "Patrol Fleet Leasing Equals Efficient Spending."

provision of state and local services.[63] The healthcare system and the CJS system are known for having high fixed costs, and it is common in public health delivery systems to look for ways to combine delivery of services to capture economies of scope.[64]

In the CJS setting, Wilson and Lemoine conducted a comprehensive literature review of the role of marginal, variable, and fixed costs in the corrections sector of CJS.[65] The authors focused on "marginal costs," which is a common concept in the field of economics. Marginal cost refers to the additional costs needed to produce one additional unit of output. In the case of law enforcement, marginal costs may refer to the added costs associated with one additional arrest or one additional preventative effort. In the instance of courts, it might be the costs associated with one additional court case added to the docket. In the example of prisons, it might be the costs associated with housing one additional inmate. It follows that marginal costs pertain primarily to variable costs, which can be adjusted in the short run. Marginal costs are less affected by fixed costs, which are more difficult to adjust in the short run and are not sensitive to changes in variable costs and output. Wilson and Lemoine found that in the short run about 80% of average CJS costs are fixed; that is, these costs do not change with fluctuations in the number of individuals entering the CJS. In the longer run, however, this amount falls to about 30–40%. In the healthcare sector, the proportions are roughly similar, with about 84% of total operating costs considered fixed in the short run.[66]

The economic concepts of short-run and long-run do not necessarily pertain to specific lengths of time, as the length of time would vary considerably by industry and by the ratio of fixed versus variable costs required to

[63] For example, a recent report from the U.S. Government Accountability Office provides many examples of programs that feature relatively high fixed costs and reviews the methods for estimating total operating costs for such programs. See GAO, "Cost Estimating and Assessment Guide: Best Practices for Developing and Managing Program Costs," in *GAO Best Practices* (Washington, D.C.: U.S. Government Accountability Office, 2020).

[64] G. P. Mays et al., "Understanding the organization of public health delivery systems: an empirical typology," *Milbank Q* 88, no. 1 (2010).

[65] Wilson and Lemoine, "Methods of Calculating the Marginal Cost of Incarceration: A Scoping Review."

[66] R. R. Roberts et al., "Distribution of variable vs fixed costs of hospital care," *Jama* 281, no. 7 (1999).

operate.[67] In the case of CJS and SFA, if 80% of costs are estimated to be fixed in the short run and 30–40% are estimated to be fixed in the long run, it is reasonable to assume that, for some arbitrarily "moderate" length of time, about 50% of costs would be fixed and 50% variable. Thus, a reasonable and cautious assumption would be that 50% of CJS and SFA costs are fixed over some moderate length of time and not influenced by variable OUD-attributable effects. This is likely a conservative estimate in that it could be argued that a higher proportion of costs (60–70%) remains fixed for a relatively long period of time, given the nature of operations characterized by high fixed costs and rigid tax-based budgets determined several years prior. For example, a study by the U.S. Department of Justice found that prison costs are 86% fixed in the short run and 56% fixed in the long run, with an average of which is 71% fixed costs.[68]

6.8 Extrapolations

Calculations of attributable costs and abatement costs can be based on operational data from the past or estimates of future costs, or some combination of both. The opioid MDL has generally focused on extrapolated abatement costs going forward, with variable extrapolation periods depending on jurisdiction. The general approach has been to estimate the total costs of all abatement programs and extrapolate those costs forward. Some stakeholders in the national opioid litigation have suggested that abatement cost time horizons should be at least 15–20 years into the future to bring OUD-attributable state and local costs and OUD mortality rates back to "pre-epidemic" levels.[69] However, it is again important to emphasize that the focus of the opioid MDL and this analysis is the role of

[67] See generally W. Nicholson and C. Snyder, *Microeconomic Theory: Basic Principles and Extensions, 12th Edition* (Cengage Learning, 2016).

[68] C. Henrichson and S. Galgano, "A Guide to Calculating Justice-System Marginal Costs," (Washington, D.C.: U.S. Department of Justice: Bureau of Justice Assistance, 2013).

[69] The goal of returning OUD rates to "pre-epidemic" levels has been featured by plaintiffs in the opioid MDL, with estimates of abatement windows generally between 10–20 years. See generally Weeks and Sanford, "Financial Impact of the Opioid Crisis on Local Government: Quantifying Costs for Litigation and Policymaking."; CRS, "Overview of the Opioid Litigation and Related Settlements and Settlement Proposals," in *Legal Sidebar* (U.S. Congressional Research Service, 2019); Opioid MDL, "MDL 2804 Case No. 1:17-md-2804 Judge Dan Aaron Polster: Abatement Order," in *Re: National Opioid Litigation* (Ohio: United States District Court Northern District of Ohio, Eastern Division, 2022).

prescription opioids; thus, from this perspective, it seems much more appropriate to consider instead when opioid prescription rates will return to pre-crisis prescription rates. Clearly, as discussed briefly in Chap. 3, the volume of prescription opioid sales per capita began to decline in 2012–2013 and has fallen consistently every year since. Again, this is largely due to changes in prescribing guidelines, changes in federal and state policies, changes in monitoring practices on the part of physicians and other health care organizations, and the implementation of PDMPs and other abatement-oriented programs. Moreover, it is unlikely that any of these changes will be "rolled back" in the upcoming years; if any changes occur, it will be to further emphasize due diligence in prescribing opioids, improving monitoring, and further restricting the supply of diverted opioids. This will have the effect of continuing to restrict the supply of prescription opioids. As these prescription supply restrictions occur, the prices of illicit opioids will likely increase, which in turn will reduce demand for illicit opioids.

The opioid prescription data from the CDC presented in Chap. 3 dates back as far as 2006. However, Kenan et al. reported U.S. opioid prescription rates of 61.88 per 100 in 2000,[70] which is only five years after the FDA approval of OxyContin. After peaking in 2012, according to the CDC data, rates declined to pre-2000 levels by 2017, where the national rates were 59 prescriptions per 100. Thus, nationally, starting in 2000, opioid prescription rates took 12 years to peak, but less than half that time (5 years) to return (by 2017) to the 2000 levels. Given this precipitous decline, it seems unreasonable to assume that it would take more than 15–20 years to return to "pre-epidemic" levels, which is the approximate length of time MDL settlements are expected to be paid out.[71] These same trends can be seen for all opioid drugs, regardless of the volume measure.[72] This logic forms the basis for employing a much more realistic 10-year abatement window in the cost ceiling models, with 2021 as the

[70] K. Kenan, K. Mack, and L. Paulozzi, "Trends in prescriptions for oxycodone and other commonly used opioids in the United States, 2000–2010," *Open Med* 6, no. 2 (2012).

[71] See generally S. Mermin, R. Falkner, and K. Greene, "Understanding Opioid Settlement Spending Plans Across States: Key Components and Approaches," (Washington, D.C.: National Academy for State Health Policy, 2022).

[72] See, for example, J.H. Duff et al., "Consumption of Prescription Opioids for Pain: A Comparison of Opioid Use in the United States and Other Countries," (Washington, D.C.: Congressional Research Service (CRS), 2021).

base year and 2030 as the extrapolation endpoint. Figure 6.1 shows the CDC opioid prescription data extrapolated forward based on the average annual rate of change in prescription opioids per capita from 2015 to 2020 in the U.S., which was – 10.0%. This 6-year average annual decline was applied to 2021 data and extrapolated forward to 2030 based on the rationale discussed above.

A logarithmic function trend line (dashed line in red) is also included in Fig. 6.1, which depicts gradual flattening of rates over time.[73] In practice, insofar as regulations and monitoring ultimately result in the issuing of prescriptions solely for patients for whom there is unequivocal medical need and all non-opioid options have been exhausted, this trend line will likely flatten at some point, but that point could be relatively low, as the trend line suggests (perhaps roughly 0.15 prescriptions per capita). Again, the flattening of the curve will generally align with clinical utility and

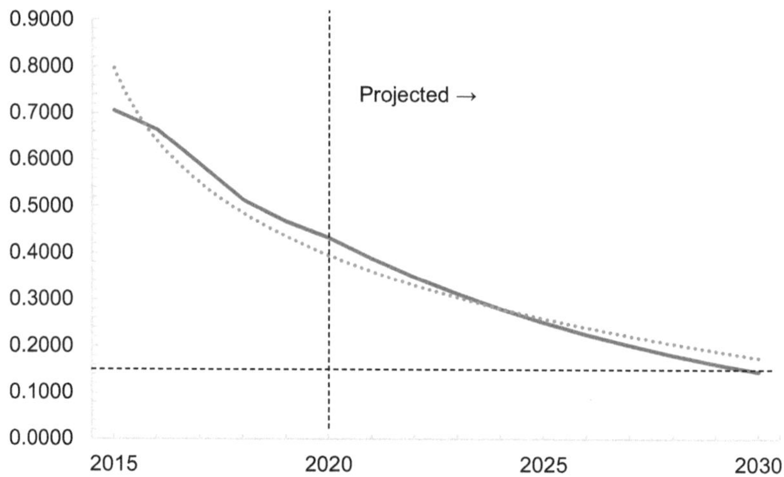

Fig. 6.1 Opioid prescription rate per capita, U.S., 2010–2020 and Projections to 2030

[73] A logarithmic trend line was added because it is presumed that, insofar as some degree of legal medical use of opioids remains possible, this number will decline initially at a constant rate and then after some period it will begin to decline at an increasingly slower rate as it approaches a "floor" that represents medical need.

medical need; that is, a level reflective of those patients for whom opioids are considered a clinically appropriate treatment. Regardless of the exact point at which the trend line will flatten, the main implications of this are twofold. First, it would be unreasonable to assume that prescription opioid rates will continue anywhere near the levels that they have been at in the past, including recent years. Second, it would be unreasonable to assume that OUD rates attributable to prescription opioids, or attributable to the health system more generally, will continue to increase or even stay the same, given the changes in prescribing guidelines and modified regulations that are now in place. Moreover, illicit trafficked opioids continue to infiltrate markets throughout the U.S., and the incursion of illicit opioids is expected to further displace opioids sourced from the healthcare system.[74]

6.9 Inflation and Net Present Value

The final adjustments are to account for future economy-wide inflation and the present value of future attributable costs and future abatement costs. It is necessary to adjust future expenditures for net present value ("NPV") to account for the "time value" of money; that is, a dollar now is not worth as much as a dollar in the future. These types of adjustments are very important in any case where future costs or income streams are expected.[75] NPV adjustments require the use of an appropriate discount rate, which represents the typical time value of money, or the value of "a dollar now versus a dollar in the future." In the health care industry, there are several options for measures of inflation, but the most straightforward recommended approach is to use the Consumer Price Index ("CPI"). The primary reasons for the effectiveness of the CPI in capturing healthcare inflation are: (1) healthcare in the U.S. is mainly purchased in "bundles" of services and supplies, rather than specific healthcare inputs; and (2) there is

[74] Supporting both points, and consistent with national trends, about 90% of opioid-related arrests in Pennsylvania in 2021 were for heroin and fentanyl (calculated using data from the Pennsylvania State Police).

[75] See generally M. Haacker, T. B. Hallett, and R. Atun, "On discount rates for economic evaluations in global health," *Health Policy Plan* 35, no. 1 (2020); L. Hultkrantz, "Discounting in economic evaluation of healthcare interventions: what about the risk term?," *Eur J Health Econ* 22, no. 3 (2021); M. Krahn and A. Gafni, "Discounting in the economic evaluation of health care interventions," *Med Care* 31, no. 5 (1993).

rapid technological change in healthcare that is constantly altering the relative costs of services (i.e., improvements in processes and outcomes, prescription drugs coming off patent, etc.).[76] Accordingly, to adjust for inflation in future cost projections, I use the average annual change in CPI from 2000 to present (i.e., an approximately 25-year period), which is equal to 2.5%.[77]

In addition to accounting for inflation, NPV adjustments require the use of an appropriate discount rate, which represents the typical time value of money. The standard economic approach to deriving appropriate discount rates is to consider the average returns on low to moderate-risk investments. Economists will typically base discount rates on long-term U.S. Treasury bonds (e.g., 30-year) and other types of relatively low-risk investments, such as highly rated municipal bonds, asset-backed securities, and corporate bonds. The average return on U.S. 30-year treasury bonds from 2000 to present is 3.9%, with rates climbing in recent years. However, Treasury bills are not the only low-risk investment options, which include investment-grade municipal bonds (6.6%),[78] asset-backed securities (5.2%),[79] and corporate bonds (6.4%).[80] Averaging the rates of all four of these low-risk investment options results in a discount rate of 5.5%. To be cautious, a discount rate of 5.0% is assumed. This rate is broadly consistent with those used in a variety of economics studies,[81] and is also broadly consistent with U.S. Federal Reserve's propensity to raise interest rates in response to rising inflation.[82] Note also that, for relatively long-term projections, economists typically assume that interest rates are

[76] See generally D. M. Cutler and E. R. Berndt, *Medical Care Output and Productivity (Volume 62), 1st Edition*, National Bureau of Economic Research Studies in Income and Wealth (Chicago, IL: University of Chicago Press, 2001); A. Dunn, A. Hall, and S. Dauda, "Are Medical Care Prices Still Declining? A Re-Examination Based on Cost-Effectiveness Studies," *Econometrica* 90, no. 2 (2022).

[77] See generally U.S. Bureau of Labor Statistics (BLS), Consumer Prices Indices.

[78] Fifteen-year average of the Bloomberg US Mortgage-Based Securities ("MBS") Index

[79] Fifteen-year average of the Bloomberg US Municipal Long Bond ("MLB") Index (factoring in tax benefits)

[80] Ten-year average of Moody's Seasoned Corporate Bond Yield

[81] See generally CBO, "How CBO Uses Discount Rates to Estimate the Present Value of Future Costs or Savings," (Washington, D.C.: U.S. Congressional Budget Office, 2024).

[82] J. Cox, "Fed approves hike that takes interest rates to highest level in more than 22 years," (New York City, NY: CNBC, 2023).

higher than inflation rates, as over the long run a rational investor would only undertake investments that were expected to "outperform" general inflation.[83]

Adjusting for NPV is particularly important when damages and abatement costs include long periods of time and depreciable assets. When assets with comparatively high sunk costs or fixed costs are purchased, costs to the purchaser are typically assigned annually based on depreciation, whereby the cost of the asset is allocated annually among the remaining years of the asset's useful or expected life. For example, a police vehicle with a total cost of $50,000 may have an expected useful life of five years, from t_1 to t_5, and a salvage value of $10,000. In this case, the initial costs in the purchase year (t_1) may be recorded as the net asset value ($40,000) divided by five, or $8000. However, in year t_1, expected future year cost allocations will be valued at less than $8000 due to the time value of money (i.e., considering the NPV). Depending on assumptions regarding salvage value and discounts rates, the accounting costs of the vehicle in t_1, which may be the year in which a product liability damages decision is made, could be considerably less than the $50,000 acquisition cost. Moreover, the police vehicle will likely serve many uses, of which opioid-related crimes would be one of many. In extrapolations to future time periods, costs in future years would need to be similarly adjusted for NPV and other factors associated with cost attribution.

6.10 Model Results

These three adjustments were applied directly to the study averages for each of the three attributable cost categories and then extrapolated forward based on the average annual rate of decline in prescription opioids of – 10% and average annual inflation rate of 2.5%. These results are shown in Table 6.3. Adjusted study averages resulted in 2021 costs of $526.69 million for healthcare, $1,776.90 million for the criminal justice system costs of, and $545.83 million for social and family assistance. Given that the studies included in these averages were focused on annual costs, the study averages can be thought of as average annual costs, which are then adjusted for state and local share, sourced from the healthcare system, and fixed costs. Adjusted for inflation and NPV, the 10-year totals are $3027.27 million

[83] See, for example, S. Boocker, M. Ng, and D. Wessel, "What is the Neutral Rate of Interest?," in *Commentary* (Washington, D.C.: Brookings Institution, 2023).

Table 6.3 Attributable cost ceiling model results based on study averages (2021), adjusted total costs based on study averages (2021), and total ten-year extrapolated costs based on study averages, 2021–2030

	Study annualaverages (2021) (a)	*State & local share (b) (%)*	*Sourced from health system (b) (%)*	*Fixed costs (b) (%)*	*Adjustedstudy annualaverages (2021)*	*Total 10-year extrapolated costs (2021–2030)(c, d)*
HC	$9,284,094,846	31.0	36.6	50.0	$526,686,701	$3,027,269,689
CJS	$10,220,898,342	95.0	36.6	50.0	$1,776,903,177	$10,213,216,170
SFA	$8,522,000,000	35.0	36.6	50.0	$545,834,100	$3,137,324,379
Total	$28,026,993,188				$2,849,423,977	$16,377,810,238

Notes HC = healthcare costs; CJS = criminal justice system costs, and SFA = social and family assistance costs; (a) based on averages of studies reviewed (see text); (b) adjustments based on literature (see text); and (c) sum of annual costs, 2021–2030, with projected costs based on average annual inflation rate (2.5%) and average annual decline in rate of prescription opioid utilization (– 10%); (d) adjusted for net present value (see text)

for healthcare, $10,213.22 million for the criminal justice system, and $3137.32 million for social and family assistance, summing to a 10-year total national attributable cost of $16,377.81 million.

The interpretation of this finding is that, considering the published results of the quantitative cost studies most cited regarding opioid-attributable costs, the most that could be apportioned to state and local governments and attributed to prescription opioids over an extrapolated 10-year period would be $16,377.81 million. To see how this amount compares to some of the plaintiff claims in the opioid MDL, we can apportion the amount to specific counties based on opioid dispensing rates. Returning to the two Ohio counties featured in the court's abatement order regarding large retail pharmacies, Lake County costs were estimated to be $1481 million, and Trumbull County costs were estimated to be $1848 million. As of 2020, based on the CDC data referenced earlier, these counties had 0.0625% and 0.0563% shares of national opioid prescriptions, respectively. Applying these shares to the total amount from the cost ceiling model results in estimated attributable costs for Lake County and Trumbull County of $10.24 million and $9.22 million, respectively. In other words, based on the cost ceiling model, attributable costs in the two counties would be less than 1% of the plaintiff abatement cost estimates, which for the two counties totaled more than $3329 million. Again, it is important to note that the cost ceiling model results in an estimate of the total attributable costs or damages associated with OUD and does not directly provide an estimate of future abatement costs; as such, we would not necessarily expect the model amounts to equal the claimed amounts. In the next chapter, abatement costs are estimated and similarly apportioned to the two Ohio counties for comparison purposes.

6.11 Chapter Summary

The attributable costs and damages approach was estimated using a literature-based attributable cost ceiling model. The approach is a typical attributable cost or damages approach, with necessary adjustments for state and local share of attributable costs, opioids sourced from the healthcare system and fixed versus variable costs. The total ten-year extrapolated NPV-adjusted attributable costs across all three categories would be $16,377.81 million nationally. When apportioned to the two Ohio counties featured in an opioid MDL abatement order, the amounts derived from the cost ceiling model are less than 1% of those claimed by plaintiffs in the two Ohio counties. The plaintiff amounts are based on estimated abatement costs, rather than attributable costs, and that difference may explain part of the difference. This will be explored in the next chapter, where an abatement cost model is developed, more broadly consistent with the general approach taken by plaintiffs in the MDL. The abatement model approach is focused on the "ground up" aggregation of operational costs of programs designed primarily to abate or mitigate the externality, with similar adjustments for state and local share of attributable costs and for opioids sourced from the healthcare system.

References

Adi, Y., Juarez-Garcia, A., Wang, D., Jowett, S., Frew, E., Day, E., Bayliss, S., Roberts, T., & Burls, A. (2007, February). Oral naltrexone as a treatment for relapse prevention in formerly opioid-dependent drug users: A systematic review and economic evaluation. *Health Technology Assessment, 11*(6), iii–iv, 1–85.

Arora, V., Moriates, C., & Shah, N. (2015, November 1). The challenge of understanding health care costs and charges. *AMA Journal of Ethics, 17*(11), 1046–1052.

Bai, G., & Anderson, G. F. (2015, June). Extreme markup: The fifty US hospitals with the highest charge-to-cost ratios. *Health Affairs (Millwood), 34*(6), 922–928.

Bernet, P. M., & Singh, S. (2015, April). Economies of scale in the production of public health services: An analysis of local health districts in Florida. *American Journal of Public Health, 105*(Suppl 2), S260–7.

Birnbaum, H. G., White, A. G., Schiller, M., Waldman, T., Cleveland, J. M., & Roland, C. L. (2011, April). Societal costs of prescription opioid abuse, dependence, and misuse in the United States. *Pain Medicine, 12*(4), 657–667.

BJS. (2023). *Correctional populations in the United States, 2021 – Statistical tables.* U.S. Bureau of Justice Statistics.

Blanco, C., Wiley, T. R. A., Lloyd, J. J., Lopez, M. F., & Volkow, N. D. (2020, May 28). America's opioid crisis: The need for an integrated public health approach. *Translational Psychiatry, 10*(1), 167.

Boocker, S., Ng, M., & Wessel, D. (2023). What is the neutral rate of interest? In *Commentary*. Brookings Institution.

Caulkins, J. P., Gould, A., Pardo, B., Reuter, P., & Stein, B. D. (2021). Opioids and the criminal justice system: New challenges posed by the modern opioid epidemic. *Annual Review of Criminology, 4*(1), 353–375.

CBO. (2024). *How CBO uses discount rates to estimate the present value of future costs or savings.* U.S. Congressional Budget Office.

Commonwealth Fund. (2019). *What is medicaid's value?*.

Cox, J. (2023). *Fed approves hike that takes interest rates to highest level in more than 22 years.* CNBC.

Crow, T. L. (2006). Patrol fleet leasing equals efficient spending. *The Bill Blackwood Law Enforcement Management Institute of Texas.*

CRS. (2019). Overview of the opioid litigation and related settlements and settlement proposals. In *Legal Sidebar*: U.S. Congressional Research Service.

Cunningham, P., Rudowitz, R., Young, K., Garfield, R., & Foutz, J. (2016). *Understanding medicaid hospital payments and the impact of recent policy changes.* Kaiser Family Foundation (KFF).

Cutler, D. M., & Berndt, E. R. (2001). *Medical care output and productivity* (Vol. 62, 1st ed.). National Bureau of Economic Research Studies in Income and Wealth. University of Chicago Press.

Davenport, S., Weaver, A., & Caverly, M. (2019). *Economic impact of non-medical opioid use in the United States: Annual estimates and projections for 2015 through 2019.* Society of Actuaries.

Donaher, P. A., & Welsh, C. (2006, May 1). Managing opioid addiction with buprenorphine. *American Family Physician*, *73*(9), 1573–1578.

Duff, J. H., Tharakan, S. M., Davis-Castro, C. Y., & Romero, P. D. (2021). *Consumption of prescription opioids for pain: A comparison of opioid use in the United States and other countries.* Congressional Research Service (CRS).

Dunn, A., Hall, A., & Dauda, S. (2022). Are medical care prices still declining? A re-examination based on cost-effectiveness studies. *Econometrica*, *90*(2), 859–886.

Etzioni, R., Mandel, M., & Gulati, R. (2020). Causal inference. In *Statistics for health data science* (Chap. 8). Springer.

FDCF. (2020). *Florida's state opioid response project: Annual report, 2019 (Updated January 2020).* Florida Department of Children and Families (FDCF).

Finkler, S. A. (1994). *Issues in cost accounting for health care organizations.* Aspen Publishers, Inc.

Florence, C., Luo, F., & Rice, K. (2021, January 1). The economic burden of opioid use disorder and fatal opioid overdose in the United States, 2017. *Drug and Alcohol Dependence*, *218*, 108350.

Florence, C. S., Zhou, C., Luo, F., & Xu, L. (2016, October). The economic burden of prescription opioid overdose, abuse, and dependence in the United States, 2013. *Medical Care*, *54*(10), 901–906.

GAO. (2020). *Cost estimating and assessment guide: Best practices for developing and managing program costs.* GAO Best Practices. U.S. Government Accountability Office.

Gold, H. T., McDermott, C., Hoomans, T., & Wagner, T. H. (2022, January 28). Cost data in implementation science: Categories and approaches to costing. *Implementation Science*, *17*(1), 11.

Grella, C. E., Karno, M. P., Warda, U. S., Niv, N., & Moore, A. A. (2009, June–July). Gender and comorbidity among individuals with opioid use disorders in the NESARC study. *Addictive Behaviors*, *34*(6–7), 498–504.

Griffith, G. J., Morris, T. T., Tudball, M. J., Herbert, A., Mancano, G., Pike, L., Sharp, G. C., et al. (2020, November 12). Collider bias undermines our understanding of COVID-19 disease risk and severity. *Nature Communications*, *11*(1), 5749.

Haacker, M., Hallett, T. B., & Atun, R. (2020, February 1). On discount rates for economic evaluations in global health. *Health Policy and Planning*, *35*(1), 107–114.

Haegerich, T. M., Jones, C. M., Cote, P. O., Robinson, A., & Ross, L. (2019, November 1). Evidence for state, community and systems-level prevention strategies to address the opioid crisis. *Drug and Alcohol Dependence*, *204*, 107563.

Hansen, R. N., Oster, G., Edelsberg, J., Woody, G. E., & Sullivan, S. D. (2011, March–April). Economic costs of nonmedical use of prescription opioids. *Clinical Journal of Pain*, *27*(3), 194–202.

Hargett, J., Criswell, A., & Palokas, M. (2022, November 1). Nonpharmacological interventions for acute pain management in patients with opioid abuse or opioid tolerance: A scoping review. *JBI Evidence Synthesis*, *20*(11), 2697–2720.

Henrichson, C., & Galgano, S. (2013). *A guide to calculating justice-system marginal costs.* U.S. Department of Justice: Bureau of Justice Assistance.

Hsia, R. Y., Antwi, Y. A., & Weber, E. (2014). Analysis of variation in charges and prices paid for vaginal and caesarean section births: A cross-sectional study. *BMJ Open*, *4*(1), e004017.

Hulme, S., Bright, D., & Nielsen, S. (2018, May 1). The source and diversion of pharmaceutical drugs for non-medical use: A systematic review and meta-analysis. *Drug and Alcohol Dependence*, *186*, 242–256.

Hultkrantz, L. (2021, April). Discounting in economic evaluation of healthcare interventions: What about the risk term?. *European Journal of Health Economics*, *22*(3), 357–363.

Kenan, K., Mack, K., & Paulozzi, L. (2012). Trends in prescriptions for oxycodone and other commonly used opioids in the United States, 2000–2010. *Open Medicine*, *62*, e41–7.

KFF. (2022). *Medicaid in Ohio.* Kaiser Family Foundation.

King, J. B., Sainski-Nguyen, A. M., & Bellows, B. K. (2016). Office-based buprenorphine versus clinic-based methadone: A cost-effectiveness analysis. *Journal of Pain & Palliative Care Pharmacotherapy*, *30*(1), 55–65.

Krahn, M., & Gafni, A. (1993, May). Discounting in the economic evaluation of health care interventions. *Medical Care*, *31*(5), 403–418.

Langabeer, J. R., Stotts, A. L., Bobrow, B. J., Wang, H. E., Chambers, K. A., Yatsco, A. J., Cardenas-Turanzas, M., & Champagne-Langabeer, T. (2021, April 1). Prevalence and charges of opioid-related visits to U.S. emergency departments. *Drug and Alcohol Dependence*, *221*, 108568.

Lee, B., Zhao, W., Yang, K. C., Ahn, Y. Y., & Perry, B. L. (2021, February 1). Systematic evaluation of state policy interventions targeting the US opioid epidemic, 2007–2018. *JAMA Network Open*, *4*(2), e2036687.

Lee, R. D., Johnson, R. W., & Joyce, P. G. (2021). *Public budgeting systems* (10th ed.). Jones & Bartlett Learning.

Leslie, D. L., Ba, D. M., Agbese, E., Xing, X., & Liu, G. (2019, July). The economic burden of the opioid epidemic on states: The case of Medicaid. *American Journal of Managed Care*, 25(13 Suppl), S243–S249.

Li, M., Peterson, C., Xu, L., Mikosz, C. A., & Luo, F. (2023, January 3). Medical costs of substance use disorders in the US employer-sponsored insurance population. *JAMA Network Open*, *6*(1), e2252378.

Li, Y., Zhu, Y., Chen, C., Wang, X., Choi, Y., Henriksen, C., & Winterstein, A. G. (2018, October). Internal validation of Medicaid Analytic eXtract (MAX) data capture for comprehensive managed care plan enrollees from 2007 to 2010. *Pharmacoepidemiology and Drug Safety*, *27*(10), 1067–1076.

Luo, F., Li, M., & Florence, C. (2021, April 16). State-level economic costs of opioid use disorder and fatal opioid overdose—United States, 2017. *MMWR Morbidity and Mortality Weekly Report*, *70*(15) 541–546.

Mays, G. P., Scutchfield, F. D., Bhandari, M. W., & Smith, S. A. (2010, March). Understanding the organization of public health delivery systems: An empirical typology. *Milbank Quarterly*, *88*(1), 81–111.

McAdam-Marx, C., Roland, C. L., Cleveland, J., & Oderda, G. M. (2010, March). Costs of opioid abuse and misuse determined from a Medicaid database. *Journal of Pain & Palliative Care Pharmacotherapy*, *24*(1), 5–18.

Mermin, S., Falkner, R., & Greene, K. (2022). *Understanding opioid settlement spending plans across states: Key components and approaches*. National Academy for State Health Policy.

Murphy, S. M., McCollister, K. E., Leff, J. A., Yang, X., Jeng, P. J., Lee, J. D., Nunes, E. V., et al. (2019, January 15). Cost-effectiveness of buprenorphine-naloxone versus extended-release naltrexone to prevent opioid relapse. *Annals of Internal Medicine*, *170*(2), 90–98.

Nguyen, J. K., & Sanghavi, P. (2022, August). A national assessment of legacy versus new generation Medicaid data. *Health Services Research*, *57*(4), 944–956.

Nicholson, W., & Snyder, C. (2016). *Microeconomic theory: Basic principles and extensions* (12th ed.). Cengage Learning.

Niven, D. J., Berthiaume, L. R., Fick, G. H., & Laupland, K. B. (2012). Matched case-control studies: A review of reported statistical methodology. *Clinical Epidemiology*, *4*, 99–110.

OECD. (2008). Monopsony and buyer power. In *Series Roundtables on Competition Policy (Competition Committee)*. Organization for Economic Cooperation and Development.

Opioid, M. D. L. (2022). MDL 2804 Case No. 1:17-md-2804 judge Dan Aaron Polster: Abatement order. In *Re: National Opioid Litigation*. United States District Court Northern District of Ohio, Eastern Division.

Pan, Y., & Xu, R. (2022, June 16). Mining comorbidities of opioid use disorder from FDA adverse event reporting system and patient electronic health records. *BMC Medical Informatics and Decision Making*, *22*(Suppl 2), 155.

Park, J. Y., & Wu, L. T. (2020). Sources of misused prescription opioids and their association with prescription opioid use disorder in the United States: Sex and age differences. *Substance Use & Misuse*, *55*(6), 928–936.

Pearce, N. (2016, February 25). Analysis of matched case-control studies. *Bmj*, *352*, i969.

Peterson, C., Li, M., Xu, L., Mikosz, C. A., & Luo, F. (2021, March 1). Assessment of annual cost of substance use disorder in US hospitals. *JAMA Network Open*, *4*(3), e210242.

Qeadan, F., Nicolson, A., Tingey, B., Moffett, M. L., & Azagba, S. (2025, July 4). Healthcare utilization trends among patients with opioid use disorder in U.S. hospitals: An analysis of length of stay, total charges, and costs, 2005–2020. *BMC Health Services Research*, *25*(1), 927.

Redelmeier, D. A., Bell, C. M., Detsky, A. S., & Pansegrau, G. K. (2000, May 22). Charges for medical care at different hospitals. *Archives of Internal Medicine*, *160*(10), 1417–1422.

Rhubart, D., Chen, Q., Sterner, G., Newton, R., Shaw, B., & Scanlon, D. (2022, December). Conceptualizing and measuring abatement from the opioid epidemic: A case study from Pennsylvania. *Milbank Quarterly*, *100*(4), 991–1005.

Roberts, R. R., Frutos, P. W., Ciavarella, G. G., Gussow, L. M., Mensah, E. K., Kampe, L. M., Straus, H. E., Joseph, G., & Rydman, R. J. (1999, February 17). Distribution of variable vs fixed costs of hospital care. *Jama*, *281*(7), 644–649.

Rose, S., & van der Laan, M. J. (2009). Why match? Investigating matched case control study designs with causal effect estimation. *The International Journal of Biostatistics*, *5*.

Scarpati, L. M., Kirson, N. Y., Zichlin, M. L., Jia, Z. B., Birnbaum, H. G., & Howard, J. C. (2017, May). Drivers of excess costs of opioid abuse among a commercially insured population. *American Journal of Managed Care*, *23*(5), 276–282.

Schepis, T. S., McCabe, S. E., & Teter, C. J. (2018, August). Sources of opioid medication for misuse in older adults: Results from a nationally representative survey. *Pain*, *159*(8), 1543–1549.

Schepis, T. S., Wilens, T. E., & McCabe, S. E. (2019, July). Prescription drug misuse: Sources of controlled medications in adolescents. *Journal of the American Academy of Child and Adolescent Psychiatry* 58(7), 670–80.e4.

Schuckit, M. A. (2016). Treatment of opioid-use disorders. *New England Journal of Medicine, 375*(4), 357–368.

Scott, C. K., Dennis, M. L., Grella, C. E., Mischel, A. F., & Carnevale, J. (2021, July 24). The impact of the opioid crisis on U.S. state prison systems. *Health Justice, 9*(1), 17.

Shah, A., Duncan, M., Atreja, N., Tai, K. S., & Gore, M. (2018, April). Healthcare utilization and costs associated with treatment for opioid dependence. *Journal of Medical Economics, 21*(4), 406–415.

Shahar, E., & Shahar, D. J. (2012). Causal diagrams and the logic of matched case-control studies. *Clinical Epidemiology, 4*, 137–144.

Shei, A., Rice, J. B., Kirson, N. Y., Bodnar, K., Enloe, C. J., Birnbaum, H. G., Holly, P., & Ben-Joseph, R. (2015, October). Characteristics of high-cost patients diagnosed with opioid abuse. *Journal of Managed Care & Specialty Pharmacy, 21*(10), 902–912.

Strain, E. C. (2002, July–August). Assessment and treatment of comorbid psychiatric disorders in opioid-dependent patients. *Clinical Journal of Pain, 18*(4 Suppl), S14–27.

Tanz, L. J., Dinwiddie, A. T., Mattson, C. L., O'Donnell, J., & Davis, N. L. (2022, December 16). Drug overdose deaths among persons aged 10–19 years - United States, July 2019–December 2021. *MMWR Morbidity and Mortality Weekly Report, 71*(50), 1576–1582.

Tenny, S., Kerndt, C. C., & Hoffman, M. R. (2022). Case control studies. In *StatPearls*. StatPearls Publishing Copyright © 2022, StatPearls Publishing LLC.

U.S. House of Representatives. (2005). Pricing practices of hospitals. Committee on Ways and Means, Subcommittee on Oversight, 108th Congress.

Urban Institute. (2022). *Criminal justice expenditures: Police, corrections, and courts*. The Urban Institute.

Urban Institute. (2022). Public welfare expenditures. In *State and local backgrounders*. The Urban Institute.

USSC. (2015). Report to the Congress: Impact of the Fair Sentencing Act of 2010. United States Sentencing Commission.

van Oostrom, S. H., Picavet, H. S., de Bruin, S. R., Stirbu, I., Korevaar, J. C., Schellevis, F. G., & Baan, C. A. (2014, April 7). Multimorbidity of chronic diseases and health care utilization in general practice. *BMC Family Practice, 15*, 61.

Wakeman, S. E., Larochelle, M. R., Ameli, O., Chaisson, C. E., McPheeters, J. T., Crown, W. H., Azocar, F., & Sanghavi, D. M. (2020, February 5). Comparative effectiveness of different treatment pathways for opioid use disorder. *JAMA Network Open, 3*(2), e1920622.

Ward, M. C., Lally, C., & Druss, B. G. (2017, January). Medicaid expenditures for fee-for-service enrollees with behavioral diagnoses: Findings from a 50 state claims analysis. *Community Mental Health Journal*, *53*(1), 1–7.

Weeks, E., & Sanford, P. (2019). Financial impact of the opioid crisis on local government: Quantifying costs for litigation and policymaking. *Kansas Law Review*, *67*.

Weiss, A. J., Elixhauser, A., Barrett, M. L., Steiner, C. A., Bailey, M. K., & O'Malley, L. (2006). Opioid-related inpatient stays and emergency department visits by state, 2009–2014. In *Healthcare Cost and Utilization Project (HCUP) Statistical Briefs*. Agency for Healthcare Research and Quality (US).

Welch, W. P., Miller, M. E., Welch, H. G., Fisher, E. S., & Wennberg, J. E. (1993, March 4). Geographic variation in expenditures for physicians' services in the United States. *New England Journal of Medicine*, *328*(9), 621–627.

Williams, E., Rudowitz, R., & Burns, A. (2023). *Medicaid financing: The basics.* Kaiser Family Foundation.

Wilson, S. J., & Lemoine, J. (2021). Methods of calculating the marginal cost of incarceration: A scoping review. *Criminal Justice Policy Review*.

Winkelman, T. N. A., & Silva, R. S. (2021, September 1). opioid use disorder treatment for people involved in the US criminal justice system-Promising advances and critical implementation challenges. *JAMA Network Open*, *4*(9), e2125120.

Yuan, W., Beaulieu-Jones, B. K., Yu, K. H., Lipnick, S. L., Palmer, N., Loscalzo, J., Cai, T., & Kohane, I. S. (2021, February 17). Temporal bias in case-control design: Preventing reliable predictions of the future. *Nature Communications*, *12*(1), 1107.

Zajac, G., Nur, S. A., Kreager, D. A., & Sterner, G. (2019, July). Estimated costs to the Pennsylvania criminal justice system resulting from the opioid crisis. *American Journal of Managed Care*, *25*(13 Suppl), S250–S255.

Zullo, A. R., Danko, K. J., Moyo, P., Adam, G. P., Riester, M., Kimmel, H. J., Panagiotou, O. A. et al. (2020). AHRQ comparative effectiveness technical briefs. In *Prevention, diagnosis, and management of opioids, opioid misuse, and opioid use disorder in older adults*. Agency for Healthcare Research and Quality (US).

CHAPTER 7

Abatement Costs

In addition to the cost ceiling model based on attributable costs, an alternative approach is to estimate a cost ceiling model based on *abatement* costs. The abatement cost ceiling model uses the same approach as the attributable cost model but instead relies on published literature and reports on the implementation and operational costs associated with the most frequently adopted OUD abatement programs at the state or county level, employing the same adjustments as the attributable cost model. In the Ohio retail pharmacy matter, in the abatement order the court made clear the distinction between damages and abatement costs, citing language from an earlier MDL decision: "The goal is not to compensate the harmed party for harms already caused by the nuisance. This would be an award of damages. Instead, an abatement remedy is intended to compensate the plaintiff for the *costs of rectifying the nuisance*, going forward" (emphasis added). A reasonable hypothesis would be that the "costs of rectifying the nuisance" should be less than the total costs attributed to the nuisance, because the latter would presumably be a subset of the former. Attributable costs are typically based on statistical models of *ex post* cost differentials between impacted and non-impacted entities or individuals, whereas abatement costs reflect *ex ante* expected costs of prevention and abatement. The remainder of this chapter describes the methods and results of a literature-based abatement cost ceiling model.

J. E. Schneider, *The Economics of Pain*, Global Perspectives on Wealth and Distribution,
https://doi.org/10.1007/978-3-032-20355-7_7

7.1 Abatement Cost Ceiling

Like the attributable cost ceiling model, the abatement cost ceiling model is based on published literature and reports. A comprehensive review of the literature and reports on state and local opioid abatement programs was undertaken, the results of which were used to parametrize the model. The objective of the search was to identify sources that identified types of programs implemented and the operational costs of those programs. To effectively mitigate OUD-related harms, public health experts generally agree that abatement programs should be focused on one or more of three broad areas: prevention, treatment, and management.[1] In terms of supply and demand, abatement programs should generally address controls on the supply of opioids, reduction of the demand for opioids, and reduction of the likelihood that use of opioids will result in harm or excess costs.[2] Thus, the focus of the search was on "evidence based" programs aimed at either prevention, treatment, or general mitigation; that is, programs and initiatives that have been studied empirically and have been determined to be effective in reducing the prevalence and effects of OUD. Some programs, such as vocational assistance, may be desirable from a social policy perspective, but do not *per se* reduce direct harms associated with OUD. The search revealed a wide variety of programs, representing a mix of existing implemented approaches and planned approaches.[3] However, not all sources provided sufficient information on program structure and operational costs, so an additional selection criterion was adequacy of reported program data, especially operating costs. Based on the search criteria, the following eight evidence-based abatement programs were

[1] J. J. Carroll, T. C. Green, and R. K. Noonan, "Evidence-Based Strategies for Preventing Opioid Overdose: What's Working in the United States," (Washington, D.C.: National Center for Injury Prevention and Control, Centers for Disease Control and Prevention, U.S. Department of Health and Human Services, 2018).

[2] See generally NASEM, *Pain Management and the Opioid Epidemic: Balancing Societal and Indidivual Benefits and Risks of Prescription Opioid Use*, ed. R. J. Bonnie, M. A. Ford, and J. K. Phillips, Consensus Study Report of National Academies of Sciences, Engineering and Medicine (NASEM) (Washington, D.C.: National Academies Press, 2017).

[3] A comprehensive list, for example, is provided in ASPPH, "Brining Science to Bear on Opioids: Report and Recommendations from the ASPPH Task Force on Public Health Initiatives to Address the Opioid Crisis," (Association of Schools and Programs of Public Health (ASPPH), 2019). Also see Carroll, Green, and Noonan, "Evidence-Based Strategies for Preventing Opioid Overdose: What's Working in the United States."

identified and reviewed, each with sufficient data to estimate average annual operational costs: (1) targeted naloxone distribution; (2) medication-assisted treatment; (3) prescription drug monitoring programs, or PDMPs, which were briefly mentioned in Chap. 2; (4) education, including training programs and public awareness campaigns; (5) prescription drug disposal; (6) fentanyl testing, including test strips and screening; (7) syringe exchanges; and (8) various smaller-scale programs that vary by state and county. In addition, these eight groupings are the ones most identified in accounts of how states are currently spending or planning to spend settlement funds.[4] Though the following sections discuss the efficacy and costs of each of these programs individually, there is additional evidence suggesting that the programs to some extent function synergistically with each other, resulting in higher overall efficacy.[5] This is most likely due to the "ecosystem" aspects of the opioid crisis, driven by the interconnectedness among medical need, mental health, substance abuse, and socioeconomic factors.[6]

The subsections that follow describe each abatement program, the evidence supporting them, and the estimated cumulative ten-year national costs of the programs. For each program, consistent with the attributable cost ceiling model, extrapolations relied on an adjustment for average annual declining rates of prescription opioids (−10%), inflation (2.5%), and NPV discount rate (5%). In addition, adjustments are made for the same factors used to adjust attributable cost estimates, including adjustments for state and local government shares and opioids sourced from the healthcare system. However, after reviewing the literature on abatement programs, most available estimates of program costs are focused on variable costs, rather than fixed costs. Accordingly, to be cautious, the fixed cost adjustment was not applied in the abatement cost model. Without the fixed cost adjustment, the abatement cost ceiling model likely represents an overestimation of abatement costs, because some non-zero proportion of the reported operating cost estimates are likely to represent costs that are relatively fixed through all or most of the extrapolation period.

[4] See generally NASHP, "An Early Look at State Opioid Settlement Spending Decisions," (Washington, D.C.: National Academy for State Health Policy, 2023).

[5] NASEM, *Pain Management and the Opioid Epidemic: Balancing Societal and Indidivual Benefits and Risks of Prescription Opioid Use.*

[6] For example, see B. D. Stein et al., "America's Opioid Ecosystem," (Santa Monica, CA: RAND Corporation, 2023).

7.2 Naloxone Distribution

Targeted distribution of naloxone to first responders, emergency departments, urgent care centers, and drug treatment centers can "safely reverse the potentially fatal effects of an opioid overdose" and has been consistently shown to reduce mortality associated with overdose.[7] Naloxone was approved for use in 1971 and has, for the past several decades, been stocked in most EDs, hospitals, and urgent care settings. The recent opioid-related initiatives surrounding naloxone have been focused on *targeted* distribution, including stocking naloxone in additional locations, in closer proximity to where overdoses are likely to occur, such as homes, schools, jails, correctional facilities, and other community-based settings.[8] Targeted naloxone distribution is based on facilitating more rapid access to naloxone by positioning naloxone closer to where it is needed so that it can be administered more expeditiously, as timing of naloxone administration is critical.[9] There is ample evidence showing that targeted distribution is very effective at reducing overdose deaths and has also been shown to be cost-effective compared to other preventative alternatives.[10]

[7] Carroll, Green, and Noonan, "Evidence-Based Strategies for Preventing Opioid Overdose: What's Working in the United States."

[8] See generally S. M. Bagley et al., "Expanding access to naloxone for family members: The Massachusetts experience," *Drug Alcohol Rev* 37, no. 4 (2018); E. M. Oliva et al., "Saving Lives: The Veterans Health Administration (VHA) Rapid Naloxone Initiative," *Jt Comm J Qual Patient Saf* 47, no. 8 (2021); A. L. Spector et al., "A qualitative examination of naloxone access in three states: Connecticut, Kentucky, and Wisconsin," *BMC Public Health* 22, no. 1 (2022); C. G. Wilson et al., "Development of a targeted naloxone coprescribing program in a primary care practice," *J Am Pharm Assoc (2003)* 57, no. 2s (2017); X. Zang et al., "Targeting community-based naloxone distribution using opioid overdose death rates: A descriptive analysis of naloxone rescue kits and opioid overdose deaths in Massachusetts and Rhode Island," *Int J Drug Policy* 98 (2021).

[9] See generally R. Rzasa Lynn and J. L. Galinkin, "Naloxone dosage for opioid reversal: current evidence and clinical implications," *Ther Adv Drug Saf* 9, no. 1 (2018).

[10] See generally J. Weiner, S. M. Murphy, and C. Behrends, "Expanding Access to Naloxone: A Review of Distribution Strategies," in *Issue Brief* (Philadelphia, PA: Leonard Davis Institute of Health Economics; Center for Health Economics of Treatment Interventions for Substance Use Disorder, HCV, and HIV; University of Pennsylvania, 2019); C. N. Behrends et al., "Costs of opioid overdose education and naloxone distribution in New York City," *Subst Abus* 43, no. 1 (2022); N. Cherrier et al., "Community Distribution of Naloxone: A Systematic Review of Economic Evaluations," *Pharmacoecon Open* 6, no. 3 (2022); J. Devries, S. Rafie, and G. Polston, "Implementing an overdose education and naloxone distribution program in a health system," *J Am Pharm Assoc (2003)*

The state and local annual operational costs of targeted naloxone distribution can be estimated by multiplying the expected need or demand (above what is already stocked by facilities) by the average price per kit, which as of 2023 was about $31. There would be an administrative expense associated with managing programs and transporting products; consequently, adding a 50% administrative overhead rate results in an average cost of $46.50 per kit. According to Irvine et al., based on a study of 11 states, the high end of the range to "achieve a target of naloxone use in 80% of witnessed overdoses" was an additional 1270 kits per 100,000 population.[11] Cautiously assuming that every state is as "understocked" as the least stocked state in the Irvine et al. study, extrapolating this demand to the U.S. population results in demand for an additional 4,232,752 kits at a total annual cost (in 2021 dollars) of $196.82 million. Extrapolating forward this amount using the same approach described in the previous chapter in the context of the attributable cost ceiling model results in a total ten-year operational cost of $1,131.29 million. This amount then needs to be adjusted for what would be the state and local share of this amount, given that, as discussed in the previous chapter, the federal government provides grant and matching funding for many state and local health and social services. As discussed earlier, health care costs are typically funded 42.5% by state and local governments, with the remainder funded by the federal government. This estimated "weight" is based on an average of Medicaid funding (which is about 31% state and local)[12] and other health care

57, no. 2s (2017); A. Moustaqim-Barrette et al., "Take-home naloxone programs for suspected opioid overdose in community settings: a scoping umbrella review," *BMC Public Health* 21, no. 1 (2021); S. Nielsen et al., "The cost and impact of distributing naloxone to people who are prescribed opioids to prevent opioid-related deaths: findings from a modelling study," *Addiction* 117, no. 4 (2022); M. Sohn et al., "Association of Naloxone Coprescription Laws With Naloxone Prescription Dispensing in the United States," *JAMA Netw Open* 2, no. 6 (2019); T. Townsend et al., "Cost-effectiveness analysis of alternative naloxone distribution strategies: First responder and lay distribution in the United States," *Int J Drug Policy* 75 (2020); Weiner, Murphy, and Behrends, "Expanding Access to Naloxone: A Review of Distribution Strategies."

[11] M. A. Irvine et al., "Estimating naloxone need in the USA across fentanyl, heroin, and prescription opioid epidemics: a modelling study," *Lancet Public Health* 7, no. 3 (2022).

[12] E. Williams, R. Rudowitz, and A. Burns, "Medicaid Financing: The Basics," (Washington, D.C.: Kaiser Family Foundation, 2023).

expenditures (which are about 54% state and local).[13] Applying the 42.5% weight, plus an additional "sourced from the healthcare system" adjustment (36.6%, as described earlier), the ten-year total national NPV-adjusted estimated operational costs associated with increasing targeted naloxone distribution to sufficient levels are $175.97 million.

7.3 Medical Treatment

Like other forms of SUD, medication-assisted treatment for OUD typically consists of some combination of pharmacotherapy (usually a combination of buprenorphine, methadone, or naltrexone), inpatient detoxification, intensive behavioral health, and non-intensive behavioral health, each of which has been shown to be clinically effective in treating SUD, including OUD.[14] According to the CDC, "Numerous studies have shown that MAT [medication-assisted treatment] contributes to significant reductions in opioid use, criminal activity, overdose, and other risky behaviors. MAT quells cravings and allows patients receiving it to stabilize their physical dependency. This stability allows MAT patients to achieve healthy social, psychological, and lifestyle changes."[15] The most cost-effective treatments have generally been shown to be pharmacotherapy with some combination of methadone, buprenorphine, or naltrexone.[16]

[13] Urban Institute, "Health and Hospital Expenditures," in *State and Local Backgrounders* (Washington, D.C.: The Urban Institute, 2023).

[14] See generally J. M. Leyrer-Jackson, A. M. Acuña, and M. F. Olive, "Current and emerging pharmacotherapies for opioid dependence treatments in adults: a comprehensive update," *Expert Opin Pharmacother* 23, no. 16 (2022); D. Polsky et al., "Cost-effectiveness of extended buprenorphine-naloxone treatment for opioid-dependent youth: data from a randomized trial," *Addiction* 105, no. 9 (2010); S. E. Wakeman et al., "Comparative Effectiveness of Different Treatment Pathways for Opioid Use Disorder," *JAMA Netw Open* 3, no. 2 (2020); Paul J Whelan and Kimberly Remski, "Buprenorphine vs methadone treatment: A review of evidence in both developed and developing worlds," *Journal of neurosciences in rural practice* 3, no. 01 (2012); J. Ma et al., "Effects of medication-assisted treatment on mortality among opioids users: a systematic review and meta-analysis, " *Mol Psychiatry* 24, no. 12 (2019); NIDA, "Medications to Treat Opioid Use Disorder," in *Research Report* (Washington, D.C.: U.S. National Institute on Drug Abuse (NIDA), 2021).

[15] Carroll, Green, and Noonan, "Evidence-Based Strategies for Preventing Opioid Overdose: What's Working in the United States."

[16] See generally P. G. Barnett and S. S. Hui, "The cost-effectiveness of methadone maintenance," *Mt Sinai J Med* 67, no. 5–6 (2000); M. Fairley et al., "Cost-effectiveness of Treatments for Opioid Use Disorder," *JAMA Psychiatry* 78, no. 7 (2021); A. H. Harris, E. Gospodarevskaya, and

The costs of SUD treatment attributable to OUD can be calculated in several different ways using data from the studies reviewed in the preceding chapter. A study by a CDC research team led by Lou et al., which was briefly discussed in the previous chapter, calculated OUD-attributable healthcare costs for 38 states and the District of Columbia, with SUD treatment, consisting primarily of MAT, reported as a separate category.[17] For these states, the average OUD-attributable healthcare cost related to SUD treatment per individual was $1660. The NSDUH estimates a total OUD prevalence of about 6 million in the U.S. in 2021.[18] Adjusting the prevalence estimate for an estimate of "cost-incurring OUD," which was estimated to be about 1.13% (or about 50% of the overall OUD prevalence of 2.2%; refer to Chap. 3), results in total annual national OUD-attributable MAT costs of $5504.62 million in 2021 dollars.[19] Extrapolating the national estimate forward for the ten-year period using the prescription opioid decline rate and adjusting for NPV and inflation, sums to $31,639.25 million. Applying the same state and local funding weight as above (42.5%), plus an additional "sourced from the healthcare system" adjustment (36.6%, as described earlier), the ten-year total national estimated operational abatement costs associated with OUD-attributable SUD treatment are $4921.49 million.

A. J. Ritter, "A randomised trial of the cost effectiveness of buprenorphine as an alternative to methadone maintenance treatment for heroin dependence in a primary care setting," *Pharmacoeconomics* 23, no. 1 (2005); J. B. King, A. M. Sainski-Nguyen, and B. K. Bellows, "Office-Based Buprenorphine Versus Clinic-Based Methadone: A Cost-Effectiveness Analysis," *J Pain Palliat Care Pharmacother* 30, no. 1 (2016); C. L. Masson et al., "Cost and cost-effectiveness of standard methadone maintenance treatment compared to enriched 180-day methadone detoxification," *Addiction* 99, no. 6 (2004); S. M. Murphy et al., "Cost-Effectiveness of Buprenorphine-Naloxone Versus Extended-Release Naltrexone to Prevent Opioid Relapse," *Ann Intern Med* 170, no. 2 (2019); Polsky et al., "Cost-effectiveness of extended buprenorphine-naloxone treatment for opioid-dependent youth: data from a randomized trial."; Fairley et al., "Cost-effectiveness of Treatments for Opioid Use Disorder."

[17] F. Luo, M. Li, and C. Florence, "State-Level Economic Costs of Opioid Use Disorder and Fatal Opioid Overdose—United States, 2017," *MMWR Morb Mortal Wkly Rep* 70, no. 15 (2021).

[18] SAMHSA, "Key Substance Use and Mental Health Indicators in the United States: Results from the 2021 National Survey on Drug Use and Health," in *HHS Publication No. PEP22-07-01-005, NSDUH Series H-57* (Washington, D.C.: U.S. Substance Abuse and Mental Health Services Administration, 2022).

[19] Note that in Lou et al. this amount pertains only to costs related to associated SUD treatment, as opposed to total healthcare costs attributable to OUD (which was the main studies discussed in Chap. 5).

7.4 Drug Monitoring

Prescription drug monitoring programs, or PDMPs, are electronic databases that compile and track prescriptions of controlled drugs, such as opioids, but in some states include additional drugs with a high likelihood of diversion, such as anabolic steroids, depressants, tranquilizers, hallucinogens, narcotics, and stimulants. The programs are administered at the state level and have been in existence since 1940. As of 2002, only 15 states maintained PDMP programs, but by 2022 all states had implemented programs.[20] The programs are designed to link together prescription data at the person level, which then allows health systems, physicians and pharmacists to assist in the identification of suspicious orders, unnecessary prescriptions, and individuals engaging in drug-seeking behavior (e.g., obtaining prescriptions from multiple providers, or "doctor shopping").[21] In addition to physicians and pharmacists, the systems are also queried by licensing authorities, law enforcement, drug control authorities, medical examiners, courts, criminal diversion programs, addiction treatment programs, public and private payers, and other public health and community agencies.[22] Studies have shown that PDMPs have been generally effective at reducing opioid utilization.[23] For example, Florida's PDMP,

[20] GAO, "Prescription Drugs: State Monitoring Programs Provide Useful Tool to Reduce Diversion" in *Report to the Subcommittee on Oversight and Investigations, Committee on Energy and Commerce, House of Representatives* (Washington, D.C.: U.S. General Accounting Office (now U.S. Government Accountability Office), 2002).

[21] F. Alogaili, N. Abdul Ghani, and N. Ahmad Kharman Shah, "Prescription drug monitoring programs in the US: A systematic literature review on its strength and weakness," *J Infect Public Health* 13, no. 10 (2020); T. Clark et al., "Prescription Drug Monitoring Programs: An Assessment of the Evidence for Best Practices," (Boston, MA: Pew Charitable Trusts / Heller School for Social Policy and Management, Brandeis University, 2012); D. Hoppe, L. Karimi, and H. Khalil, "Mapping the research addressing prescription drug monitoring programs: A scoping review," *Drug Alcohol Rev* 41, no. 4 (2022); E. Tay et al., "Prescription drug monitoring programs evaluation: A systematic review of reviews," *Drug Alcohol Depend* 247 (2023); C. S. Kruse et al., "Health Information Technology and Doctor Shopping: A Systematic Review," *Healthcare (Basel)* 8, no. 3 (2020).

[22] Clark et al., "Prescription Drug Monitoring Programs: An Assessment of the Evidence for Best Practices."

[23] See generally P. Moyo et al., "Impact of prescription drug monitoring programs (PDMPs) on opioid utilization among Medicare beneficiaries in 10 US States," *Addiction* 112, no. 10 (2017); L. Rutkow et al., "Effect of Florida's Prescription Drug Monitoring Program and Pill Mill Laws on Opioid Prescribing and Use," *JAMA Intern Med* 175, no. 10

12 months post-implementation, was associated with a 1.4% decrease in opioid prescriptions, a 2.5% decrease in opioid volume, and a 5.6% decrease in MME per transaction.[24] Some studies have shown that PDMPs achieve their effectiveness in part by increasing the "hassle factor" associated with the prescribing of scheduled drugs, showing that in some cases the time and effort necessary to query the systems discourages physicians from prescribing opioids.[25]

The average annual operating costs of PDMPs have been reported to be between $0.5 million and $1 million per state program.[26] Taking the midpoint of this range and expressing it in 2021 dollars, average annual per-program operating costs are estimated to be about $1.13 million per program per state, or roughly $56.48 million nationally. The seemingly low operational costs of these data-driven programs are because total costs consist mostly of fixed costs (computing equipment, telecommunications, cloud storage, etc.), and given that many of these programs have been in existence for some time, operating costs are primarily variable rather than fixed. The result is a national NPV-adjusted ten-year cost of $324.65 million. However, federal grants fund about 20% of PDMPs, and about 20% of PDMP system queries are non-opioid related.[27] Thus, an additional 64% weight was applied to the total, resulting in a national 10-year

(2015); Tay et al., "Prescription drug monitoring programs evaluation: A systematic review of reviews."; R. L. Haffajee et al., "Four States With Robust Prescription Drug Monitoring Programs Reduced Opioid Dosages," *Health Aff (Millwood)* 37, no. 6 (2018); V. Puac-Polanco et al., "Prescription Drug Monitoring Programs and Prescription Opioid-Related Outcomes in the United States," *Epidemiol Rev* 42, no. 1 (2020).

[24] Rutkow et al., "Effect of Florida's Prescription Drug Monitoring Program and Pill Mill Laws on Opioid Prescribing and Use."

[25] A. Alpert, S. Dykstra, and M. Jacobson, "Hassle Costs versus Information: How Do Prescription Drug Monitoring Programs Reduce Opioid Prescribing?," *American Economic Journal: Economic Policy* 16, no. 1 (2024). Also refer to M. A. Bachhuber et al., "Physician Time Burden Associated with Querying Prescription Drug Monitoring Programs," *Pain Med* 19, no. 10 (2018).

[26] See generally Clark et al., "Prescription Drug Monitoring Programs: An Assessment of the Evidence for Best Practices."; CRS, "Prescription Drug Monitoring Programs," (Washington, D.C.: U.S. Congressional Research Service, 2018); GAO, "Prescription Drugs: State Monitoring Programs Provide Useful Tool to Reduce Diversion "; Tay et al., "Prescription drug monitoring programs evaluation: A systematic review of reviews."

[27] CRS, "Prescription Drug Monitoring Programs."; GAO, "Prescription Drugs: State Monitoring Programs Provide Useful Tool to Reduce Diversion".

NPV-adjusted PDMP added operational cost of $207.78 million. Note that an additional adjustment for "sourced from the healthcare system" is not necessary for PDMPs, as they are (by definition) only applicable to legally prescribed drugs.

7.5 Education

Most health-related preventative efforts include an education component aimed at educating and training healthcare providers and a "public awareness" component designed to improve "health literacy" and communicate highly summarized information to the public regarding risks, resources, and treatments.[28] Knowledge of opioid risks and OUD treatment best practices among healthcare providers has been uneven throughout the opioid crisis.[29] Ongoing education and training of providers has been shown to be a critical element in reducing opioid utilization. Part of that effort has been the implementation of "academic detailing," which is a process through which current scientific information is summarized and communicated to providers. The CDC describes the role of academic detailing as follows: "researchers who produce and seek to disseminate scientific medical knowledge are rarely trained in effective communication strategies. Academic detailing corrects this disparity by 'marketing' new science to healthcare providers in a compelling and efficacious manner."[30] Providers have also received opioid-related training through their institutions, including a mix of specific training sessions and organizational adoption of opioid-specific prescribing and treatment clinical practice guidelines.[31] Provider-focused educational and

[28] C. Stock, "Grand Challenges for Public Health Education and Promotion," *Front Public Health* 10 (2022).

[29] B. Prempreet et al., "Opioid Knowledge and Prescribing Habits at a Large Tertiary Care Academic Center," *Cureus* 14, no. 8 (2022); E. Gugala et al., "Opioid harm reduction: A scoping review of physician and system-level gaps in knowledge, education, and practice," *Subst Abus* 43, no. 1 (2022).

[30] Carroll, Green, and Noonan, "Evidence-Based Strategies for Preventing Opioid Overdose: What's Working in the United States."

[31] Refer to, for example, T. Bongiovanni et al., "Adopting best practices in post-operative analgesia prescribing in a safety-net hospital: Residents as a conduit to change," *Am J Surg* 219, no. 2 (2020); J. Perrone, S. G. Weiner, and L. S. Nelson, "Stewarding Recovery from the Opioid Crisis Through Health System Initiatives," *West J Emerg Med* 20, no. 2 (2019); A. Quanbeck et al., "The Balanced Opioid Initiative: protocol for a clustered, sequential, multiple-assignment randomized trial to construct an adaptive

training programs have been shown to be effective in reducing the number of opioid prescriptions.[32] There have also been numerous education and health promotion campaigns aimed at patients and the general public, and these have also generally been shown to be effective at increasing general knowledge of risks and available treatments and resources.[33]

Programs aimed at education, training, and public awareness are heterogenous in design, breadth, and implementation, leading to considerable variation in scale and scope and costs. A detailed report from the Utah legislature provides some useful insights into how states and local governments have been approaching education and awareness regarding opioids.[34] As of 2018, Utah had established an opioid education and awareness campaign with total operating costs of about $4.4 million annually. The program includes specific initiatives designed to, for example, "Promote public awareness of the signs, symptoms, and risks of opioid misuse and overdose" and "Increase the availability of educational materials and other resources

implementation strategy to improve guideline-concordant opioid prescribing in primary care," *Implement Sci* 15, no. 1 (2020).

[32] Refer to, for example, M. V. Hill et al., "An Educational Intervention Decreases Opioid Prescribing After General Surgical Operations," *Ann Surg* 267, no. 3 (2018); Z. Malik et al., "A Systematic Review of Pain Management Education in Graduate Medical Education," *J Grad Med Educ* 14, no. 2 (2022); B. J. Slater et al., "Provider education leads to sustained reduction in pediatric opioid prescribing after surgery," *J Pediatr Surg* (2021); A. Sud, G. R. Molska, and F. Salamanca-Buentello, "Evaluations of Continuing Health Provider Education Focused on Opioid Prescribing: A Scoping Review," *Acad Med* 97, no. 2 (2022); D. Wood et al., "Impact of a prescriber and patient educational intervention on discharge analgesia prescribing and hospital readmission rates following elective unilateral total hip and knee arthroplasty," *BMJ Open Qual* 11, no. 3 (2022).

[33] See generally J. M. Rath et al., "Educating Young Adults about Opioid Misuse: Evidence from a Mass Media Intervention," *Int J Environ Res Public Health* 19, no. 1 (2021); J. Yang and M. Mackert, "The Effectiveness of CDC's Rx Awareness Campaigns on Reducing Opioid Stigma: Implications for Health Communication," *Health Commun* 38, no. 5 (2023); Behrends et al., "Costs of opioid overdose education and naloxone distribution in New York City."; M. Enich et al., "Overdose education and naloxone distribution program design informed by people who use drugs and naloxone distributors," *Prev Med Rep* 35 (2023); K. L. Hines et al., "Impact of naloxone education for patients receiving buprenorphine-containing prescriptions indicated for opioid use disorder at an independent community pharmacy," *J Am Pharm Assoc (2003)* 60, no. 6 (2020); N. N. Kadakia et al., "Patient education interventions for prescription opioids: A systematic review," ibid., no. 4.

[34] R. Frandsen, "Budget Deep-Dive: Opioid Outreach Efforts," in *Legislative Fiscal Analyst Issue Brief* (Salt Lake City, UT: Office of the Legislative Fiscal Analyst; Social Services Appropriations Subcommittee, 2017).

designed to assist individuals at increased risk of opioid overdose, their families, and others in a position to help prevent or respond to an overdose event." The Utah program is funded by approximately 15% state general funds and 85% federal and private sector funding. To generate a national cost estimate, the Utah amount was increased by approximately 50% from $4.4 million to $6.5 million to allow for a broader scope of services and to account for Utah's population relative to other, larger states. The estimate was then adjusted to 2021 dollars ($7.19 million) and then multiplied by 50 to generate a national estimate. Extrapolation forward was based on the average annual decline in the volume of prescription opioids, resulting in a ten-year NPV-adjusted national total of $2065.02 million. This amount was then adjusted for state and local share (estimated to be an average of 50%)[35] and sourced from the healthcare system (36.6%), resulting in a total NPV-adjusted ten-year national operating cost of $377.90 million.

7.6 Drug Disposal

Diversion of prescription medications is exacerbated by unsecured storage of unused portions of dispensed prescriptions, which, as discussed in Chap. 3 can range from 50% to 75% of the volume of filled prescriptions. Drug disposal and drug "take back" programs are means to facilitate and encourage disposal of unused pills, serving the dual purpose of reducing the supply of "divertible" drugs but also reducing the environmental hazards associated with the accumulation of unused prescription medications in landfills and water treatment facilities.[36] Drug disposal and

[35] This is cautious estimate, given the distribution of funding for the Utah program, which is only about 15% state and local funding, and 85% federal funding. However, the 50% estimate is likely to be more reflective of the average funding distribution nationally. See generally Urban Institute, "Public Welfare Expenditures," in *State and Local Backgrounders* (Washington, DC: The Urban Institute, 2022). Also note that in addition to co-funding state programs, the federal government has launched and will likely continue to operate public messaging campaigns on the part of the FDA, CDC, DHHS, and DEA. See, for example, CDC, "Addressing the Prescription Opioid Crisis: CDC Rx Awareness Campaign Overview," (Washington, D.C.: U.S. Centers for Disease Control and Prevention, 2017).

[36] S. Lystlund et al., "Patient participation in a clinic-based community pharmacy medication take-back program," *J Am Pharm Assoc (2003)* 54, no. 3 (2014); R. Guerrero-Preston and P. Brandt-Rauf, "Pharmaceutical residues in the drinking water supply: modeling residue concentrations in surface waters of drugs prescribed in the United States," *P R Health Sci J* 27, no. 3 (2008).

take-back programs are viewed favorably by the public,[37] and have also been shown to be effective in reducing the supply of unused pills.[38] The CDC and the Stanford-Lancet Commission both identified drug disposal as a critical part of reducing diversion.[39] Improved drug disposal was also one of the abatement recommendations put forward in the National Academies of Science *Consensus Study Report*.[40] These programs are variable in design and scope, consisting of pharmacy-based initiatives, hospital and outpatient-based initiatives, and state and federal initiatives, like the DEA's "National Prescription Drug Take Back Day."[41]

Operational costs of drug disposal programs have been estimated to be between $300,000 and $1 million annually, depending on the scale and scope of the program.[42] Taking the midpoint of this range and adjusting to 2021 dollars, the expected cost per program would be about $733,853 annually. Many pharmacies currently provide means through which to return unused medications, and state and federal programs provide additional disposal

[37] See generally Lystlund et al., "Patient participation in a clinic-based community pharmacy medication take-back program."; A. V. Thach, C. M. Brown, and N. Pope, "Consumer perceptions about a community pharmacy-based medication take back program," *J Environ Manage* 127 (2013); I. Yanovitzky, "A Multiyear Assessment of Public Response to a Statewide Drug Take-Back and Disposal Campaign, 2010 to 2012," *Health Educ Behav* 44, no. 4 (2017).

[38] D. E. Buffington et al., "Understanding factors that contribute to the disposal of unused opioid medication," *J Pain Res* 12 (2019); GAO, "Prescription Opioids: Patient Options for Safe and Effective Disposal of Unused Opioids," (Washington, D.C.: U.S. Government Accountability Office, 2019); J. D. Lamplot et al., "Postoperative Disposal of Unused Opioids: A Systematic Review," *Hss j* 17, no. 2 (2021); W. L. A. Schäfer et al., "Primary prevention of prescription opioid diversion: a systematic review of medication disposal interventions," *Am J Drug Alcohol Abuse* 47, no. 5 (2021).

[39] K. Humphreys et al., "Responding to the opioid crisis in North America and beyond: recommendations of the Stanford-Lancet Commission," *Lancet* 399, no. 10324 (2022).

[40] NASEM, *Pain Management and the Opioid Epidemic: Balancing Societal and Indidivual Benefits and Risks of Prescription Opioid Use.*

[41] P. R. Lewis et al., "Bringing Opiates Off the Streets and Undertaking Excess Scripts: A novel opiate reclamation and prescription reduction program," *Surgery* 174, no. 3 (2023); M. N. Robertson et al., "Increasing Uptake of Prescription Drug Take-Back Boxes: Eliciting Preferences and Applying the Theory of Planned Behavior to Predict Use," *Health Educ Behav* (2022); FDA, "Drug Disposal: Drug Take Back Locations," (Washington, D.C.: U.S. Food and Drug Administration & U.S. Drug Enforcement Administration, 2022).

[42] S. Dangi-Garimella, "Safe disposal of prescription medication faces a cost barrier," *American Journal of Managed Care* May 4 (2016).

options. Thus, this analysis assumes that another 20 programs per state are needed, with the average scale and scope of those programs reflected in the estimated per-program cost. That is, added programs may consist of a mix of recurring statewide or county programs combined with expanded pharmacy-based programs. Based on an average of 20 programs per state (i.e., 1000 total programs nationwide), the total costs of drug disposal programs are estimated to be $733.85 million per year. Extrapolating forward results in a ten-year total cost of $4218.01 million. Two additional adjustments are necessary. First, like other state and local programs, it is expected that the federal government would fund at least 20% of the costs of these programs through grants and other forms of co-funding.[43] Second, these programs are designed to encourage the return of all unused drugs, not just opioids or other controlled substances. A 2015 study by Yang et al., for example, found that only 4.4% of returned drugs were classified as opioids.[44] Although the study was conducted close to the peak of prescription opioid supply in the U.S. (which was around 2012), at that time, there was presumably somewhat less public awareness of the harms of opioids, specifically the harms of diverted opioids, compared to later years. Thus, a more realistic assumption post-2012 might be about 30% of returned drugs consisting of opioids. Applying these adjustments, the ten-year NPV-adjusted national operational costs would be $1012.32 million.

7.7 Fentanyl Detection

In recent years the abuse of illicit fentanyl, typically sourced by dealers and online sellers, has intensified, and has emerged as one of the main sources of OUD.[45] Apart from law enforcement activities directed at interrupting the supply of illicit opioids, two fentanyl-related abatement programs have been featured: (1) screening for fentanyl in routine clinical toxicology testing; and (2) distribution of fentanyl test strips. Regarding screening, according to the CDC, "The addition of fentanyl testing in routine clinical

[43] This is a cautious estimate, as there are a large variety of grants available to support these types of programs. See, for example, NACO, "Where to Find Funding to Help Make Every Day Take Back Day," (Washington, D.C.: National Association of Counties, 2022).

[44] C. H. J. Yang, M. Doshi, and N. A. Mason, "Analysis of Medications Returned During a Medication Take-Back Event," *Pharmacy (Basel)* 3, no. 3 (2015).

[45] M. M. Jeffery et al., "Fentanyl-Associated Overdose Deaths Outside the Hospital," *N Engl J Med* 389, no. 1 (2023).

toxicology tests allows for early warnings of supply contamination and provides one of the best sources of routine surveillance for fentanyl in the local drug supply. The results of fentanyl screens may also have implications for the clinical management…"[46] Another fentanyl-related abatement program that has shown efficacy is the distribution of fentanyl test strips ("FTS"). Test strips, which are compact and low cost, allow users to rapidly test drugs prior to consumption and identify whether there is a significant level of fentanyl present. In surveys, users have indicated a relatively high acceptance of FTS and have indicated that they would use FTSs if they were readily available.[47]

Fentanyl test strips are relatively inexpensive, costing about $1.00 per strip.[48] Adding a generous 50% for administration, distribution, and program management, the actual cost of a fentanyl strip to state and local governments could be about $1.50 per strip.[49] As a volume estimate, it seems sensible to associate the needed volume of FTS with the needed volume of naloxone, given the economies of scope in providing both; that is, earlier we identified the need for another 4,232,752 naloxone kits and could expect the same need for fentanyl kits, as these products are often distributed together.[50] Fentanyl test kits contain 10 test strips, so the expected need for fentanyl test strips would be 42,327,520 strips. At $1.50 per strip, total national annual costs in 2021 dollars would be $63.49 million. Extrapolating forward, again applying the rate of decline in prescription opioid utilization and adjusting for inflation and NPV, results in a ten-year total national cost of $364.93 million. Two other adjustments

[46] Carroll, Green, and Noonan, "Evidence-Based Strategies for Preventing Opioid Overdose: What's Working in the United States."

[47] J. E. Goldman et al., "Perspectives on rapid fentanyl test strips as a harm reduction practice among young adults who use drugs: a qualitative study," *Harm Reduct J* 16, no. 1 (2019); M. S. Krieger et al., "High willingness to use rapid fentanyl test strips among young adults who use drugs," ibid.15 (2018).

[48] G. Appel, B. Farmer, and J. Avery, "Fentanyl Test Strips Empower People And Save Lives—So Why Aren't They More Widespread?," *Health Affairs*, no. Blog, June 2 (2021).

[49] Data on state and local "overhead" expenses are highly variable, due mostly to differences in how expenses are categorized and allocated to overhead. At the national level, administrative expenses in the health sector of the economy are roughly 15–25% of total costs. See generally M. Chernew and H. Mintz, "Administrative Expenses in the US Health Care System: Why So High?," *Jama* 326, no. 17 (2021).

[50] For example, see Division of Public Health, "Delaware Division of Public Health Launches New Fentanyl Test Strip Distribution," (State of Delaware, 2022).

are necessary. First, like drug disposal programs, state and local governments can expect to fund at least 20% of the costs of the programs with federal grants.[51] Second, these costs need to be adjusted by 36.6% to reflect the proportion of opioids sourced from the health system. This results in a total ten-year NPV-adjusted national cost of $106.85 million.

7.8 Syringe Exchanges

Syringe exchange programs ("SEPs")[52] and syringe service programs ("SSPs") provide opportunities for illicit drug users to exchange used and contaminated syringes for new, sterile needles and clean injection equipment. There are two distinct benefits associated with these types of programs: (1) provision of sterile needles reduces the likelihood of transmission of infectious diseases such as HIV and hepatitis C, which impose added burdens on public health systems;[53] and (2) provision of sterile needles creates an "access point" to the public health support system, whereby at-risk individuals can obtain related materials (e.g., naloxone and FTS) and referrals can be made to other public health support services, such as SUD treatment, screening and treatment for HIV, immunizations and vaccinations, additional naloxone access, and other programs.[54] Syringe programs have proven efficacy in both domains.[55] The programs

[51] CDC, "Federal Grantees May Now Use Funds to Purchase Fentanyl Test Strips," (Washington, D.C.: Centers for Disease Control and Prevention (CDC) & Substance Abuse and Mental Health Services Administration (SAMHSA) 2021).

[52] Also referred to as needle exchange programs ("NEPs").

[53] See, for example, E. J. Aspinall et al., "Are needle and syringe programmes associated with a reduction in HIV transmission among people who inject drugs: a systematic review and meta-analysis," *Int J Epidemiol* 43, no. 1 (2014).

[54] See, for example, R. M. Fernandes et al., "Effectiveness of needle and syringe Programmes in people who inject drugs—An overview of systematic reviews," *BMC Public Health* 17, no. 1 (2017); L. Platt et al., "Needle syringe programmes and opioid substitution therapy for preventing hepatitis C transmission in people who inject drugs," *Cochrane Database Syst Rev* 9, no. 9 (2017).

[55] See generally Carroll, Green, and Noonan, "Evidence-Based Strategies for Preventing Opioid Overdose: What's Working in the United States."; R. Heimer, "Syringe exchange programs: lowering the transmission of syringe-borne diseases and beyond," *Public Health Rep* 113 Suppl 1, no. Suppl 1 (1998); M. Kidorf et al., "Benefits of concurrent syringe exchange and substance abuse treatment participation," *J Subst Abuse Treat* 40, no. 3 (2011); S. Saab et al., "Toward the elimination of hepatitis C in the United States," *Hepatology* 67, no. 6 (2018).

are also associated with relatively high rates of return on investment ("ROI"); for example, Nguyen et al. found the programs are cost-saving due to infectious diseases averted and are associated with high ROIs.[56]

The operational costs of syringe exchange programs vary by the size and type of program, which in turn depends on whether the program is in a large urban setting or a smaller urban or suburban setting. Based on budget and survey data from SSPs in Maine, California, Kentucky, and Atlanta, Teshale et al. determined that SSP operational costs (including one-time start-up costs) ranged from $0.45 million for a small rural program to $1.86 million for a large urban SSP.[57] Another study found that the implementation costs within one large health system was $0.41 million per year, consistent with the low end of the Teshale et al. range.[58] Taking the high end of the Teshale et al. range and adjusting to 2021 dollars results in average SSP operating costs of $2.1 million per program per year. Using the same count estimate as drug disposal programs (20 added programs per state and 1000 nationally) results in a total national cost of $2094.30 million. Extrapolating forward 10 years based on the decline in the rate of prescription opioids results in an inflation and NPV-adjusted total ten-year national cost of $12,037.55 million. Three other adjustments are necessary. First, although federal funding of syringe exchange programs is limited by statute, there are several exceptions and some alternative funding streams, leaving state and local governments to fund about 87% of program costs.[59] Second, needle exchange programs are not targeted exclusively at opioids; for example, a recent systematic review found that 83.4% of intravenous drug users primarily inject opioid-based drugs, such as heroin.[60] Third, these costs need to be adjusted by

[56] T. Q. Nguyen et al., "Syringe exchange in the United States: a national level economic evaluation of hypothetical increases in investment," *AIDS Behav* 18, no. 11 (2014).

[57] E. H. Teshale et al., "Estimated cost of comprehensive syringe service program in the United States," *PLoS One* 14, no. 4 (2019).

[58] T. S. Bartholomew et al., "Implementation and first-year operating costs of an academic medical center-based syringe services program," *Harm Reduct J* 18, no. 1 (2021).

[59] D. C. Des Jarlais, C. McKnight, and J. Milliken, "Public funding of US syringe exchange programs," *J Urban Health* 81, no. 1 (2004).

[60] L. Degenhardt et al., "Global prevalence of injecting drug use and sociodemographic characteristics and prevalence of HIV, HBV, and HCV in people who inject drugs: a multistage systematic review," *Lancet Glob Health* 5, no. 12 (2017).

36.6% to reflect the proportion of opioids sourced from the healthcare system. This results in a total ten-year national cost of $3196.72 million.

7.9 Other Programs

The programs described above represent the most common OUD mitigation programs implemented by states and counties nationally. However, there are additional programs, typically smaller and more innovative, implemented by many states, in some cases tailored to the specific needs of the state and county. Examples include data management systems, web-based tools, digital and application-based tools, peer mentoring and leadership development, modifications of "Good Samaritan" laws, and efforts to enhance coordination across programs.[61] For example, some of these programs may qualify for federal grant funding from the CDC as part of the Overdose Data to Action ("OD2A") cooperative agreement, which includes partial funding of programs aimed at "timelier tracking of nonfatal and fatal drug overdoses, improving toxicology to better track polysubstance-involved deaths, enhancing linkage to care for people with opioid use disorder and risk for opioid overdose" and "implementing other innovative surveillance and prevention activities."[62] An example of a program designed to encourage innovative approaches to OUD in the criminal justice system is the Justice Community Opioid Innovation Network ("JCOIN") program, which is part of the broader NIH "HEAL Initiative."[63] The JCOIN program supports research and program development designed to "increase high-quality care for people in justice settings with opioid misuse or opioid use disorder," with the overarching objective to identify and test "strategies

[61] See generally G. C. Alexander and O. Mansour, "Distribution of Abatement Funds Arising From US Opioid Litigation," *Jama* 328, no. 19 (2022); S. Whaley and J. Sharfstein, "The Opioid Settlements-Will the First Steps Be in the Right Direction?," *JAMA Health Forum* 4, no. 9 (2023); Alexander and Mansour, "Distribution of Abatement Funds Arising From US Opioid Litigation."; Carroll, Green, and Noonan, "Evidence-Based Strategies for Preventing Opioid Overdose: What's Working in the United States."; Whaley and Sharfstein, "The Opioid Settlements-Will the First Steps Be in the Right Direction?."

[62] CDC, "Understanding the Opioid Overdose Epidemic," (Washington, D.C.: U.S. Centers for Disease Control and Prevention, 2022).

[63] The NIH program is entitled Helping to End Addiction Long-term, or more commonly referred to as the "HEAL Initiative." The program offers grants to explore novel approaches to addressing OUD, including novel medical treatments and interventions and identifying best-practices in pain management.

to expand effective treatment and care in partnership with local and state justice systems and community-based treatment providers."[64] In addition to JCOIN, other programs include the HEALing Communities Study, Recovery Research Networks, and Improving Delivery of Healthcare Services for Polysubstance Use. These programs are funded by the federal government, but to some extent represent "research and development" efforts to encourage states, local governments, and local health systems to design and implement sustainable mitigation and abatement programs.

The heterogeneous nature of the programs resulting from these initiatives, and others like them, complicates the derivation of precise cost estimates. For example, the NIH HEAL Initiative, which includes programs like JCOIN, has awarded about $1500 million in funding,[65] or roughly $30 million per state. Assuming that about one third of these grants will result in the implementation of sustained public health programs,[66] with annual program costs roughly equal to the grant amounts, the resulting operating costs would be approximately $10 million per state and $500 million nationally. The national ten-year sum, after adjusting for inflation and NPV, is $2873.88 million. After adjusting for state and local share (50%) and sourced from the healthcare system, the adjusted ten-year cost estimate is $525.92 million.

7.10 Total Abatement Costs

The results of the preceding cost analyses are summarized in Table 7.1. The costs of all seven programs, adjusted for NPV and extrapolated to the national level and forward to 2030, total $10,524.95 million. Again, this estimate of total abatement costs is based on summing the expected state and local costs of the seven most effective abatement programs, plus an allowance for smaller innovative programs. This amount is about

[64] NIH, "Justice Community Opioid Innovation Network (JCOIN)," (Washington, DC: National Institutes for Health, HEAL Initiative, 2024a).

[65] See generally "NIH HEAL Initiative: Funded Projects," (Washington, DC: HEAL Initiative, National Institutes of Health, 2023); "NIH HEAL Initiative: 2024 Annual Report," (Washington, D.C.: National Institutes for Health, 2024b).

[66] For a general discussion of the conversion rates for public health demonstration-type projects, see generally P. Rocco and A.S. Kelly, "An Engine of Change? The Affordable Care Act and the Shifting Politics of Demonstration Projects," *RSF: The Russell Sage Foundation Journal of the Social Sciences* 6, no. 2 (2020).

Table 7.1 Opioid abatement cost estimates based on reported program operational costs: Extrapolated to national 10-year estimated ($2021)

Abatement program	*Estimated total annual cost ($2021) (a)*	*Estimated extrapolated 10-year cost($2021) (b, d)*	*Total weight (c) (%)*	*Estimated total 10-year abatement cost ($2021)(d)*
Naloxone distribution	$196,822,967	$1,131,291,526	15.56%	$175,972,397
Medication-assisted treatment	$5,504,620,679	$31,639,248,364	15.56%	$4,921,485,083
Prescription drug monitoring	$56,483,359	$324,652,891	64.00%	$207,777,850
Education & training	$359,274,099	$2,065,021,935	18.30%	$377,899,014
Prescription drug disposal	$733,852,796	$4,218,011,056	24.00%	$1,012,322,653
Fentanyl testing	$63,491,280	$364,932,750	29.28%	$106,852,309
Syringe exchanges	$2,094,302,980	$12,037,554,629	26.56%	$3,196,720,453
Other programs	$500,000,000	$2,873,880,891	18.30%	$525,920,203
TOTAL	$9,008,848,160	$54,654,594,044		$10,524,949,963

Sources See text. *Notes* (a) study data is from various years, trended forward to 2021 dollars using the Consumer Price Index (CPI); (b) extrapolations rely on either the decline in prescription opioid volume or average inflation over past 10 years (see text); (c) weights are a composite value based on a variety of adjustments, including state and local funding (versus federal), share of activities associated with opioids, and percent of opioids sourced from the healthcare system (see text).; (d) adjusted for net present value (see text in previous chapter)

64%, or roughly two thirds, of the attributable cost ceiling amount of $16,377.81 million. The difference in the two approaches is likely driven by the different methodological approaches. The attributable cost ceiling approach is based on published cost estimates that are largely derived from the apportionment of *incurred* costs to opioid-related tasks or harms. Thus, it is not surprising that the attributable cost ceiling approach results in a higher estimate, as the attributable cost approach is not strictly limited to abatement-related activities and instead includes a mix of abatement activities and what economists would generally refer to as "damages." The attributable cost ceiling approach is therefore more reflective of what would normally be considered economic damages, whereas the abatement program cost ceiling approach is more reflective of what would normally be considered the total estimated costs of mitigation.

Both the attributable cost approach and the abatement cost approach rely on reasonable and necessary adjustments to reflect costs covered by state and local governments and costs associated with opioids sourced from the health care system, both of which constitute the primary focus of the legal disputes. Together, these estimates can also be thought of as a *range* of plausible total abatement costs, meaning that the "true" abatement cost nationally should fall between the direct abatement cost estimate ($10,524.95 million) and the attributable cost ceiling ($16,377.81million). Again, returning to the two Ohio counties featured in the court's abatement order regarding large retail pharmacies, as discussed in the previous chapter, Lake County and Trumbull County had 0.0625% and 0.0563% shares of national opioid prescriptions, respectively. Applying these shares to the total amount from the abatement cost ceiling model results in estimated abatement costs for Lake County and Trumbull County of $6.58 million and $5.93 million, respectively. In other words, based on the abatement cost ceiling model, estimated abatement costs in the two counties ($12.51 million) would be less than 0.5% of the plaintiff's estimated abatement cost estimates, which for the two counties totaled more than $3329 million.

7.11 Acceptable Risk and Optimal Abatement

The discussion thus far regarding abatement costs has set aside the issue of what might be considered "optimal" levels of abatement; that is, the levels of abatement expected to be achieved in the wake of full implementation of the most effective abatement programs. For example, in environmental cases, there are typically thresholds of contamination that must be met to satisfy regulators, but contaminants do not necessarily require *full* eradication to meet safe, acceptable, or tolerable levels. In some cases, these thresholds represent natural inflection points, whereby the resources required for further mitigation become prohibitively costly, consistent with what economists describe as diminishing marginal returns. One researcher described it this way: "... it costs a certain amount of money to get to one level of clean-up, but to get the last few molecules, if that is where we set the [acceptable] level of risk, is very expensive."[67] Referring back to the earlier discussion of marginal costs, the inflection point could be considered the level of abatement whereby the marginal costs of an additional OUD case prevented exceed the expected costs associated with that added OUD case.

In most countries there are public health analogs to these threshold problems, whereby at a societal level we have implicitly determined "acceptable" or "tolerable" levels of harms from factors that are, at least theoretically, either preventable or mostly "mitigatable;" for example, illness and mortality related to tobacco use and alcohol abuse and injuries and mortality resulting from motor vehicle accidents and gun violence. In the case of alcohol misuse, we know that about 10% of individuals who regularly consume alcohol will develop an alcohol use disorder ("AUD").[68] We also know that in the U.S., alcohol-related deaths number about 180,000 per year, which is substantially higher than the average annual number of OUD-attributable deaths.[69] The World Health Organization ("WHO") has identified numerous evidence-based areas in which governments should channel additional resources toward mitigation of alcohol abuse.[70] However, despite having some ability to reduce the harms associated with alcohol abuse, as the WHO suggests, the prevalence of AUD in the U.S. averages around 10–11%. Similarly, stricter gun laws have been shown to reduce rates of gun violence,

[67] M.L. Manewitz, "Potentially Responsible Parties: Liability Issues," *Fordham Environmental Law Review* 5, no. 2 (2011).

[68] CDC, "Most people who drink excessively are not alcohol dependent," *Preventing Chronic Disease* (2014).

[69] M. B. Esser et al., "Deaths from Excessive Alcohol Use—United States, 2016–2021," *MMWR Morb Mortal Wkly Rep* 73, no. 8 (2024).

[70] WHO, "10 areas governments could work with to reduce the harmful use of alcohol," (Geneva, Switzerland: World Health Organization, 2019).

with significant differences observed at the state level within the U.S.[71] and even more dramatic differences observed globally between countries with and without strict controls.[72] However, most states in the U.S. have opted for minimal controls.[73] The implication is that, as a society, relatively high levels of substance use disorders and gun violence are implicitly accepted despite having evidence-based tools available to lower the rates of both. Likely explanations are that (1) the harms or externalities of both are considered within the range of acceptable or tolerable, and (2) the marginal costs of higher levels of abatement would be prohibitively high.[74]

Adverse events from approved medical treatment are an example of the acceptable risk standard. According to the FDA's *Guidance for Industry* regarding risk management, "Because all drugs can have adverse effects, the demonstration of safety requires showing that the benefits of the drug outweigh its risks."[75] The report further notes that: "... benefit-risk assessment becomes more challenging in cases where the potential for serious safety risks is identified or expected to exist, e.g., risks that are life-threatening or associated with significant morbidity." The FDA report also states that "making an informed judgment that a drug has a favorable benefit-risk profile requires determining that the drug's benefits and risks are sufficiently characterized and that the benefits to the indicated population will outweigh the safety risks if the product is approved."[76]

[71] See generally F. Jehan et al., "The burden of firearm violence in the United States: stricter laws result in safer states," *J Inj Violence Res* 10, no. 1 (2018); J. Tseng et al., "Firearm legislation, gun violence, and mortality in children and young adults: A retrospective cohort study of 27,566 children in the USA," *Int J Surg* 57 (2018).

[72] See, for example, C. Gilligan, "U.S. Remains an Outlier in Firearm Possession, Gun-Related Deaths," *U.S. News and World Report* January 30 (2023).

[73] See generally P. J. Cook, J. Ludwig, and A. Samaha, "Gun Control after Heller: Litigating against Regulation," in *Regulation versus Litigation: Perspectives from Economics and Law*, ed. D. P. Kessler (Chicago, IL: National Bureau of Economic Research | The University of Chicago Press, 2011).

[74] A third possible explanation is that the "political costs" are too high further abate these types of harms, due to some combination of transaction costs (e.g., information asymmetries) and the influence of private interests. See generally A.K. Dixit, *The Making of Economic Policy: A Transaction-Cost Politics Perspective*, Munich Lectures in Economics (Cambridge, MA: The MIT Press, 1996).

[75] FDA, "Benefit-Risk Assessment for New Drug and Biological Products: Guidance for Industry," (Washington, D.C.: U.S. Food & Drug Administration, 2021a).

[76] Ibid.

Individuals tend to make the same implicit tradeoffs. For example, in a survey of risk acceptance among patients with rheumatic disease, O'Brien et al. found that "... the average individual is prepared to accept a 1 in 5 [20%] chance of immediate death from a drug which offers a complete cure from the disease."[77] Interestingly, the study also found that the same patients will accept a 15% chance of death from a prescription drug offering complete relief of pain.

Like other approved drugs with known probabilities of adverse events, opioids and OUD-related harms can be viewed through the lens of acceptable risk. Specifically, analogous to other drug adverse events, there will be a level of OUD that represents an acceptable risk associated with opioid-based pain treatment, a risk that would have been considered by regulators[78] and would have been anticipated by actuaries and subsequently incorporated into risk-adjusted cost projections and insurance premiums by public and private payers. Likewise, similar to alcohol and tobacco, there will be some explicit or implicit level of harm from OUD that will be considered acceptable by state and local governments. It is unrealistic for that number to be 0%, especially given that a substantial proportion of OUD is attributable to illicit opioids, the control over which is outside the purview of the healthcare system. Indeed, in the preceding discussion of the abatement cost model, there is an implicit level of acceptable risk incorporated into the operating cost estimates associated with each abatement program; in other words, we know that no single program, even if implemented optimally, will result in "full" mitigation. However, together these programs can be expected to lead to declines in

[77] B. J. O'Brien, J. Elswood, and A. Calin, "Willingness to accept risk in the treatment of rheumatic disease," *J Epidemiol Community Health* 44, no. 3 (1990).

[78] The FDA approval of opioids will be considered further in this chapter. However, at this point it is important to note that the FDA did indeed consider risk of addiction in their approval of all prescription opioid drugs. Thus, discussions regarding the role of the FDA in the opioid crisis generally focus on *how* the FDA evaluated addiction risk, not whether they evaluated addiction risk. For example, regarding the approval of OxyContin, the FDA remarked that "At the time of approval, FDA believed the controlled-release formulation of OxyContin would result in *less* abuse potential, since the drug would be absorbed slowly and there would not be an immediate 'rush' or high that would promote abuse. In part, FDA based its judgment on the prior marketing history of a similar product, MS Contin, a controlled-release formulation of morphine approved by FDA and used in the medical community since 1987 without significant reports of abuse and misuse." See FDA, "Timeline of Selected FDA Activities and Significant Events Addressing Opioid Misuse and Abuse," (U.S. Food and Drug Administration, 2021b).

risks and harms such that "acceptable" levels can be obtained. Abatement goals should be adjusted accordingly. In other words, if these programs, implemented at the levels suggested above, can reduce some or even most of the "excess" OUD cases (and leaving mainly those adverse events that would be considered actuarially expected), such an outcome should be considered a desirable outcome from a public health policy perspective.

7.12 Cost Allocations

Attributable cost and abatement cost estimates were derived directly from the most frequently cited studies of the attributable costs of the opioid crisis, as described in detail in the preceding sections. Reasonable adjustments were then applied to the published estimates to make them more comparable to the types of attributable costs and abatement costs at issue in the opioid MDL. For the damages and attributable cost estimates, these included adjustments for state and local shares, opioids sourced from the healthcare system, and fixed versus variable operating costs. Similar adjustments were made to some of the abatement estimates. The result was a total national ten-year NPV-adjusted attributable cost ceiling estimate of $16,377.81 million and abatement cost ceiling estimate of $10,524.95 million. From an economics (rather than legal) perspective it can be argued that these amounts are the amounts that should be allocated among PRP groups, but this simple allocation method could of course be applied to any set of cost ceiling estimates. Again, the proportional allocation approach simply assigns equal shares to each PRP group, while the weighted allocation method distinguishes between PRPs that are more causative versus less causative or participatory. Table 7.2 shows how the two allocation models distribute each respective type of cost across the PRPs.

For attributable costs and damages, the proportional allocation method results in $1091.91 million assigned to each PRP group, and the weighted allocation method results in a range of $545.95 million to $1290.57 million assigned to each PRP group, depending on assumed causative status. For abatement costs, the proportional allocation method results in $701.70 million assigned to each PRP group, and the weighted allocation method results in a range of $350.85 million to $829.37 million assigned to each PRP group, depending on assumed causative status. For example, the national share assigned to physicians ranges from $701.70 million to $1290.57 million,

Table 7.2 Proportional and weighted allocation methods and resulting share of NPV-adjusted total ten-year U.S. state and local cumulative attributable costs and abatement cost estimates (in millions), 2021–2030

	PRP group	*Attributable costs*		*Abatement costs*	
		Proportional allocation $\Phi = 0.067$ (c) (millions)	*Weighted allocation $\Phi_c = 0.033$ $\Phi_p = 0.079$ (d) (millions)*	*Proportional allocation $\Phi = 0.067$ (c) (millions)*	*Weighted allocation $\Phi_c = 0.033$ $\Phi_p = 0.079$ (d) (millions)*
1	FDA (a, b)	$1091.91	$1290.57	$701.70	$829.37
2	DEA (a, b)	$1,091.91	$1290.57	$701.70	$829.37
3	CDC (a)	$1091.91	$545.95	$701.70	$350.85
4	Physicians (b)	$1091.91	$1290.57	$701.70	$829.37
5	Health Systems (b)	$1091.91	$1290.57	$701.70	$829.37
6	Patients (a)	$1091.91	$545.95	$701.70	$350.85
7	Federal government (a, b)	$1091.91	$1290.57	$701.70	$829.37
8	State governments (a, b)	$1091.91	$1290.57	$701.70	$829.37
9	Accreditation agencies (b)	$1091.91	$1290.57	$701.70	$829.37
10	Private payers (b)	$1091.91	$1290.57	$701.70	$829.37
11	Manufacturers (b)	$1091.91	$1290.57	$701.70	$829.37
12	Distributors (b)	$1091.91	$1290.57	$701.70	$829.37
13	Consultants	$1091.91	$545.95	$701.70	$350.85
14	Retail Pharmacies	$1091.91	$545.95	$701.70	$350.85
15	Drug traffickers (a, b)	$1091.91	$1290.57	$701.70	$829.37
	U.S. 10-Year Total	$16,377.81	$16,377.81	$10,524.95	$10,524.95

Notes See text. NPV = net present value; (a) expected to be considered an "orphan" share; (b) considered in literature and by design to have been comparatively ***more*** "causative" compared to other potentially responsible parties; (c) allocation based on uniform $\phi = 6.67\%$ per PRP; (d) allocation based on estimation of causative role, where lower rate is 50% of the proportional rate ($\phi_p = 3.33\%$) and the higher rate is the pro-rated to $\phi_c = 7.88\%$ so that all PRP group shares sum to 100%

depending on cost method and assumptions regarding causation. These allocated attributable cost and abatement cost amounts are clearly considerably lower than what has been put forward by plaintiffs or awarded by courts thus far in the opioid legal proceedings. For example, in the Ohio abatement decision, after some adjustments, the court determined that retail pharmacies were responsible for $306.2 million and $344.4 million in Lake and Trumbull counties, respectively. The total awarded for the two counties, $650.6 million, is more than 60% of the national total attributable cost ceiling for retail pharmacies, and nearly *double* the weighted abatement cost ceiling estimate for retail pharmacies for the entire U.S.

The attributable cost ceiling and abatement cost ceiling amounts can also be compared to some of the settlements reached thus far in the opioid MDL, though such amounts at the time of this writing are considered preliminary, and it may take some considerable additional time for the majority of cases to resolve. As of the beginning of 2024, settlement amounts have totaled about $56,643 million,[79] which is more than 3.5 times greater than the ten-year national attributable cost ceiling estimate and nearly six times greater than the ten-year national abatement cost ceiling estimate. Settlements thus far have included roughly $19,770 million from manufacturers, $21,000 million from distributors, $15,200 million from retail pharmacies, and $573 million from consultants. Compared to the results of the attributable cost ceiling model and the abatement cost ceilings model, regardless of whether a proportional or weighted apportionment is applied, these settlement amounts suggest that manufacturers, distributors, and retail pharmacies may have "overpaid" by at least $40 billion. Again, these are very rough estimates of overpayment, as total settlement amounts are likely to change because many of the cases are not fully resolved. However, if the settlement amounts do change, they are likely to increase,[80] making the incongruence between apportioned cost ceiling estimates and settlement amounts even larger.

[79] Settlement amounts were gathered from a variety of online news sources, mainly websites that track settlements (e.g., http://www.opioidsettlementtracker.com). Note also that settlement amounts have not been finalized at the time of this writing and are likely to increase in the 2023–2025 period as more cases reach settlements.

[80] See generally Whaley and Sharfstein, "The Opioid Settlements-Will the First Steps Be in the Right Direction?."

7.13 Chapter Summary

As expected, the two cost calculation approaches result in two markedly different estimates, but the rank order is as expected; that is, it makes sense that the *ex-post* attribution method would result in a larger estimate, capturing some costs that are not directly related to the externality. The difference could be due in part to some of the methodological challenges described earlier, the net effect of which was hypothesized to "over attribute" costs to OUD. However, most of the difference is likely due to the "damages versus abatement" approach. The attributable cost method (i.e., the traditional damages approach), while mostly capturing the costs of mitigating an externality, will in some cases also capture incurred costs, due to the way that costs and expenditures are typically logged in databases. Consider the example of healthcare costs. State Medicaid data, which was used in most of the extant opioid cost studies, includes costs attributable to opioid-related management of SUDs, which reasonably could be considered an abatement cost, but also includes other related healthcare costs for patients with an OUD diagnosis (e.g., an OUD patient who has an inpatient stay for an infection, or an OUD patient with mental health and SUD comorbidities). The expenses associated with the latter example are likely to include costs attributable to abatement and other costs that are generally attributable to the OUD diagnosis.

The implications of the cost analysis presented in this chapter can be summarized as follows. First and foremost, the two methods together provide a range of what could be considered reasonable, with the low end of the range being national ten-year abatement-related costs of $10,524.95 million and the high end of the range being $16,377.81 million, reflective of what could be considered an attributable cost ceiling. The second implication is that studies of the attributable costs of opioids reach remarkably consistent findings, even across different methodological approaches. Although there are some common methodological challenges to the design and conduct of studies of attributable costs, the fact that these studies reached such similar conclusions suggests that these limitations probably did not result in substantial biases. If there is a consistent bias, it is likely in the direction of overestimation of costs due to the methodological issues discussed earlier in the chapter. The third important implication is that several adjustments are required to bring national estimates in line with attributable costs faced by state and local governments. For healthcare, the adjustment is substantial due to the cost-sharing arrangements between

Medicaid and the federal government. The other adjustments are equally important. Adjusting for the share of opioids sourced from the health care system is necessary to keep the focus on *prescription* opioids, especially in recent years and going forward, as the share of prescription opioids continues to decline and the share of illicit opioids grows.

Finally, calculating attributable cost and abatement cost ceilings has intuitive appeal because the approaches employed by plaintiffs in abatement calculations are likely to represent unreasonably high estimates, and the cost ceiling approaches are a means by which to check for face validity. In just *two* Ohio counties, *excluding* Medicaid-covered healthcare costs, plaintiff demands reached more than $3 billion, which represents about 20% of the cost attributable ceiling total derived from published cost estimates for the entire U.S., even with healthcare costs included in the published estimates, and about 30% of the total national estimated ten-year abatement cost ceiling. Again, as of 2020, based on the CDC data referenced earlier, these counties had 0.0625% and 0.0563% shares of national opioid prescriptions, respectively. Hence, based on the national abatement cost ceiling and applying these opioid prescription volume weights, abatement costs would be $6.6 million and $5.9 million for the two counties, respectively. Like the findings from the attributable cost model, these amounts are less than 1% of the plaintiff's estimated abatement costs.

References

Alexander, G. C., & Mansour, O. (2022, November 15). Distribution of abatement funds arising from US opioid litigation. *JAMA*, 328(19), 1901–1902.

Alogaili, F., Ghani, N. A., & Ahmad Kharman Shah, N. (2020, October). Prescription drug monitoring programs in the US: A systematic literature review on its strength and weakness. *Journal of Infection and Public Health*, *13*(10), 1456–1461.

Alpert, A., Dykstra, S., & Jacobson, M. (2024). Hassle costs versus information: How do prescription drug monitoring programs reduce opioid prescribing? *American Economic Journal: Economic Policy*, *16*(1), 87–123.

Appel, G., Farmer, B., & Avery, J. (2021, June 2). Fentanyl test strips empower people and save lives—so why aren't they more widespread?. *Health Affairs*.

Aspinall, E. J., Nambiar, D., Goldberg, D. J., Hickman, M., Weir, A., Van Velzen, E., Palmateer, N., et al. (2014, February). Are needle and syringe programmes associated with a reduction in HIV transmission among people who inject drugs: A systematic review and meta-analysis. *International Journal of Epidemiology*, *43*(1), 235–248.

ASPPH. (2019). Brining science to bear on opioids: Report and recommendations from the ASPPH task force on public health initiatives to address the opioid crisis. Association of Schools and Programs of Public Health (ASPPH).

Bachhuber, M. A., Saloner, B., LaRochelle, M., Merlin, J. S., Maughan, B. C., Polsky, D., Shaparin, N., & Murphy, S. M. (2018, October 1). Physician time burden associated with querying prescription drug monitoring programs. *Pain Medicine, 19*(10), 1952–1960.

Bagley, S. M., Forman, L. S., Ruiz, S., Cranston, K., & Walley, A. Y. (2018, May). Expanding access to naloxone for family members: The Massachusetts experience. *Drug and Alcohol Review, 37*(4), 480–486.

Barnett, P. G., & Hui, S. S. (2000, October–November). The cost-effectiveness of methadone maintenance. *Mount Sinai Journal of Medicine, 67*(5–6), 365–374.

Bartholomew, T. S., Patel, H., McCollister, K., Feaster, D. J., & Tookes, H. E. (2021, November 19). Implementation and first-year operating costs of an academic medical center-based syringe services program. *Harm Reduction Journal, 18*(1), 116.

Behrends, C. N., Gutkind, S., Winkelstein, E., Wright, M., Dolatshahi, J., Welch, A., Paone, D., Kunins, H. V., & Schackman, B. R. (2022). Costs of opioid overdose education and naloxone distribution in New York City. *Substance Abuse, 43*(1), 692–698.

Bongiovanni, T., Hansen, K., Lancaster, E., O'Sullivan, P., Hirose, K., & Wick, E. (2020, February). Adopting best practices in post-operative analgesia prescribing in a safety-net hospital: Residents as a conduit to change. *American Journal of Surgery, 219*(2) 299–303.

Buffington, D. E., Lozicki, A., Alfieri, T., & Bond, T. C. (2019). Understanding factors that contribute to the disposal of unused opioid medication. *Journal of Pain Research, 12*, 725–732.

Carroll, J. J., Green, T. C., & Noonan, R. K. (2018). *Evidence-based strategies for preventing opioid overdose: what's working in the United States.* National Center for Injury Prevention and Control, Centers for Disease Control and Prevention, U.S. Department of Health and Human Services.

CDC. (2017). *Addressing the prescription opioid crisis: CDC Rx awareness campaign overview.* U.S. Centers for Disease Control and Prevention.

CDC. (2021). Federal grantees may now use funds to purchase fentanyl test strips. Centers for Disease Control and Prevention (CDC) & Substance Abuse and Mental Health Services Administration (SAMHSA).

CDC. (2014). Most people who drink excessively are not alcohol dependent. *Preventing Chronic Disease.*

CDC. (2022). Understanding the opioid overdose epidemic. U.S. Centers for Disease Control and Prevention.

Chernew, M., & Mintz, H. (2021, November 2). Administrative expenses in the US health care system: Why so high? *Jama 326*(17), 1679–1680.

Cherrier, N., Kearon, J., Tetreault, R., Garasia, S., & Guindon, E. (2022, May). Community distribution of naloxone: A systematic review of economic evaluations. *Pharmacoeconomics Open*, *6*(3), 329–342.

Clark, T., Eadie, J., Kreiner, P., & Strickler, G. (2012). *Prescription drug monitoring programs: An assessment of the evidence for best practices*. Pew Charitable Trusts/Heller School for Social Policy and Management, Brandeis University.

Cook, P. J., Ludwig, J., & Samaha, A. (2011). Gun control after Heller: Litigating against regulation. In D. P. Kessler (Ed.), *Regulation versus litigation: Perspectives from economics and law*. National Bureau of Economic Research | The University of Chicago Press.

CRS. (2018). Prescription drug monitoring programs. U.S. Congressional Research Service.

Dangi-Garimella, S. (2016, May 4). Safe disposal of prescription medication faces a cost barrier. *American Journal of Managed Care*.

Degenhardt, L., Peacock, A., Colledge, S., Leung, J., Grebely, J., Vickerman, P., Stone, J., et al. (2017, December). Global prevalence of injecting drug use and sociodemographic characteristics and prevalence of HIV, HBV, and HCV in people who inject drugs: A multistage systematic review. *The Lancet Global Health*, *5*(12), e1192–e1207.

Des Jarlais, D. C., McKnight, C., & Milliken, J. (2004, March). Public funding of US syringe exchange programs. *Journal of Urban Health*, *81*(1), 118–121.

Devries, J., Rafie, S., & Polston, G. (2017, March–April). Implementing an overdose education and naloxone distribution program in a health system. *Journal of the American Pharmacists Association (2003)*, *57*(2s), S154–S160.

Division of Public Health. (2022). *Delaware division of public health launches new fentanyl test strip distribution*. State of Delaware.

Dixit, A. K. (1996). *The making of economic policy: A transaction-cost politics perspective. Munich lectures in economics*. The MIT Press.

Enich, M., Flumo, R., Campos, S., Flores, N., Sullivan, N., Mellor, J., O'Neill, C., & Nyaku, A. N. (2023, October). Overdose education and naloxone distribution program design informed by people who use drugs and naloxone distributors. *Preventive Medicine Reports*, *35*, 102374.

Esser, M. B., Sherk, A., Liu, Y., & Naimi, T. S. (2024, February 29). Deaths from excessive alcohol use—United States, 2016–2021. *Morbidity and Mortality Weekly Report*, *73*(8), 154–161.

Fairley, M., Humphreys, K., Joyce, V. R., Bounthavong, M., Trafton, J., Combs, A., Oliva, E. M., et al. (2021, July 1). Cost-effectiveness of treatments for opioid use disorder. *JAMA Psychiatry*, *78*(7), 767–777.

FDA. (2021a). *Benefit-risk assessment for new drug and biological products: Guidance for industry*. U.S. Food & Drug Administration.

FDA. (2022). Drug disposal: Drug take back locations. U.S. Food and Drug Administration & U.S. Drug Enforcement Administration.

FDA. (2021b). Timeline of selected FDA activities and significant events addressing opioid misuse and abuse. U.S. Food and Drug Administration.

Fernandes, R. M., Cary, M., Duarte, G., Jesus, G., Alarcão, J., Torre, C., Costa, S., Costa, J., & Carneiro, A. V. (2017, April 11). Effectiveness of needle and syringe programmes in people who inject drugs—an overview of systematic reviews. *BMC Public Health*, *17*(1), 309.

Frandsen, R. (2017). *Budget deep-dive: Opioid outreach efforts*. Legislative Fiscal Analyst Issue Brief. Office of the Legislative Fiscal Analyst; Social Services Appropriations Subcommittee.

GAO. (2002). Prescription drugs: State monitoring programs provide useful tool to reduce diversion. In *Report to the Subcommittee on Oversight and Investigations, Committee on Energy and Commerce, House of Representatives*. U.S. General Accounting Office (now U.S. Government Accountability Office).

GAO. (2019). *Prescription opioids: Patient options for safe and effective disposal of unused opioids*. U.S. Government Accountability Office.

Gilligan, C. (2023, January 30). U.S. remains an outlier in firearm possession, gun-related deaths. *U.S. News and World Report*.

Goldman, J. E., Waye, K. M., Periera, K. A., Krieger, M. S., Yedinak, J. L., & Marshall, B. D. L. (2019, January 8). Perspectives on rapid fentanyl test strips as a harm reduction practice among young adults who use drugs: A qualitative study. *Harm Reduction Journal*, *16*(1), 3.

Guerrero-Preston, R., & Brandt-Rauf, P. (2008, September). Pharmaceutical residues in the drinking water supply: Modeling residue concentrations in surface waters of drugs prescribed in the United States. *Puerto Rico Health Sciences Journall*, *27*(3), 236–240.

Gugala, E., Briggs, O., Moczygemba, L. R., Brown, C. M., & Hill, L. G. (2022). Opioid harm reduction: A scoping review of physician and system-level gaps in knowledge, education, and practice. *Substance Abuse*, *43*(1), 972–987.

Haffajee, R. L., Mello, M. M., Zhang, F., Zaslavsky, A. M., Larochelle, M. R., & Wharam, J. F. (2018, June). Four states with robust prescription drug monitoring programs reduced opioid dosages. *Health Affairs (Millwood)*, *37*(6), 964–974.

Harris, A. H., Gospodarevskaya, E., & Ritter, A. J. (2005). A randomised trial of the cost effectiveness of buprenorphine as an alternative to methadone maintenance treatment for heroin dependence in a primary care setting. *Pharmacoeconomics*, *23*(1), 77–91.

Heimer, R. (1998, June). Syringe exchange programs: Lowering the transmission of syringe-borne diseases and beyond. *Public Health Reports*, 113(Suppl 1), 67–74.

Hill, M. V., Stucke, R. S., McMahon, M. L., Beeman, J. L., & Barth, R. J., Jr. (2018, March). An educational intervention decreases opioid prescribing after general surgical operations. *Annals of Surgery*, *267*(3), 468–472.

Hines, K. L., Garofoli, G. K., Garofoli, M. P., Elswick, B. M., & Winstanley, E. L. (2020, November–December). Impact of naloxone education for patients receiving buprenorphine-containing prescriptions indicated for opioid use disorder at an independent community pharmacy. *Journal of the American Pharmacists Association (2003)*, *60*(6), e205–e214.

Hoppe, D., Karimi, L., & Khalil, H. (2022, May). Mapping the research addressing prescription drug monitoring programs: A scoping review. *Drug and Alcohol Review*, *41*(4), 803–817.

Humphreys, K., Shover, C. L., Andrews, C. M., Bohnert, A. S. B., Brandeau, M. L., Caulkins, J. P., Chen, J. H., et al. (2022, February 5). Responding to the opioid crisis in North America and beyond: Recommendations of the Stanford-Lancet Commission. *Lancet*, *399*(10324), 555–604.

Irvine, M. A., Oller, D., Boggis, J., Bishop, B., Coombs, D., Wheeler, E., Doe-Simkins, M., et al. (2022, March). Estimating naloxone need in the USA across fentanyl, heroin, and prescription opioid epidemics: A modelling study. *The Lancet Public Health*, *7*(3), e210–e218.

Jeffery, M. M., Stevens, M., D'Onofrio, G., & Melnick, E. R. (2023, July 6). Fentanyl-associated overdose deaths outside the hospital. *New England Journal of Medicine*, *389*(1), 87–88.

Jehan, F., Pandit, V., O'Keeffe, T., Azim, A., Jain, A., Tai, S. A., Tang, A., et al. (2018, January). The burden of firearm violence in the United States: Stricter laws result in safer states. *Journal of Injury and Violence Research*, *10*(1), 11–16.

Kadakia, N. N., Rogers, R. L., Reed, J. B., Dark, E. R., & Plake, K. I. (2020, July–August). Patient education interventions for prescription opioids: A systematic review. *Journal of the American Pharmacists Association (2003)*, *60*(4), e31–e42.

Kidorf, M., King, V. L., Peirce, J., Kolodner, K., & Brooner, R. K. (2011, April). Benefits of concurrent syringe exchange and substance abuse treatment participation. *Journal of Substance Abuse Treatment*, *40*(3), 265–271.

King, J. B., Sainski-Nguyen, A. M., & Bellows, B. K. (2016). Office-based buprenorphine versus clinic-based methadone: A cost-effectiveness analysis. *Journal of Pain & Palliative Care Pharmacotherapy*, *30*(1), 55–65.

Krieger, M. S., Yedinak, J. L., Buxton, J. A., Lysyshyn, M., Bernstein, E., Rich, J. D., Green, T. C., Hadland, S. E., & Marshall, B. D. L. (2018, February 8). High willingness to use rapid fentanyl test strips among young adults who use drugs. *Harm Reduction Journal*, *15*(1), 7.

Kruse, C. S., Kindred, B., Brar, S., Gutierrez, G., & Cormier, K. (2020, August 28). Health information technology and doctor shopping: A systematic review. *Healthcare (Basel)*, *8*(3).

Lamplot, J. D., Premkumar, A., James, E. W., Lawton, C. D., & Pearle, A. D. (2021 July). Postoperative disposal of unused opioids: A systematic review. *HSS Journal, 17*(2), 235–243.

Lewis, P. R., Pelzl, C., Benzer, E., Szad, S., Judge, C., Wang, A., & Van Gent, M. (2023, September). Bringing opiates off the streets and undertaking excess scripts: A novel opiate reclamation and prescription reduction program. *Surgery, 174*(3), 574–580.

Leyrer-Jackson, J. M., Acuña, A. M., & Olive, M. F. (2022, November). Current and emerging pharmacotherapies for opioid dependence treatments in adults: A comprehensive update. *Expert Opinion on Pharmacotherapy, 23*(16), 1819–1830.

Luo, F., Li, M., & Florence, C. (2021, April 16). State-level economic costs of opioid use disorder and fatal opioid overdose—United States, 2017. *Morbidity and Mortality Weekly Report, 70*(15), 541–546.

Lystlund, S., Stevens, E., Planas, L. G., & Marcy, T. R. (2014, May–June). Patient participation in a clinic-based community pharmacy medication take-back program. *Journal of the American Pharmacists Association (2003), 54*(3), 280–284.

Ma, J., Bao, Y. P., Wang, R. J., Su, M. F., Liu, M. X., Li, J. Q., Degenhardt, L., et al. (2019, December). Effects of medication-assisted treatment on mortality among opioids users: A systematic review and meta-analysis. *Molecular Psychiatry, 24*(12), 1868–1883.

Malik, Z., Ahn, J., Thompson, K., & Palma, A. (2022, April). A systematic review of pain management education in graduate medical education. *Journal of Graduate Medical Education, 14*(2), 178–190.

Manewitz, M. L. (2011). Potentially responsible parties: Liability issues. *Fordham Environmental Law Review, 5*(2), Article 6.

Masson, C. L., Barnett, P. G., Sees, K. L., Delucchi, K. L., Rosen, A., Wong, W., & Hall, S. M. (2004, June). Cost and cost-effectiveness of standard methadone maintenance treatment compared to enriched 180-day methadone detoxification. *Addiction, 99*(6), 718–726.

Moustaqim-Barrette, A., Dhillon, D., Ng, J., Sundvick, K., Ali, F., Elton-Marshall, T., Leece, P., et al. (2021, March 26). Take-home naloxone programs for suspected opioid overdose in community settings: A scoping umbrella review. *BMC Public Health, 21*(1), 597.

Moyo, P., Simoni-Wastila, L., Griffin, B. A., Onukwugha, E., Harrington, D., Alexander, G. C., & Palumbo, F. (2017, October). Impact of prescription drug monitoring programs (PDMPs) on opioid utilization among Medicare beneficiaries in 10 US states. *Addiction, 112*(10), 1784–1796.

Murphy, S. M., McCollister, K. E., Leff, J. A., Yang, X., Jeng, P. J., Lee, J. D., Nunes, E. V., et al. (2019, January 15). Cost-effectiveness of buprenorphine-naloxone versus extended-release naltrexone to prevent opioid relapse. *Annals of Internal Medicine, 170*(2), 90–98.

NACO. (2022). *Where to find funding to help make every day take back day.* National Association of Counties.

NASEM. (2017). *Pain management and the opioid epidemic: Balancing societal and indidivual benefits and risks of prescription opioid use.* Consensus study report of National Academies of Sciences, Engineering and Medicine (NASEM). R. J. Bonnie, M. A. Ford, & J. K. Phillips. (Eds.), National Academies Press.

NASHP. (2023). *An early look at state opioid settlement spending decisions.* National Academy for State Health Policy.

Nguyen, T. Q., Weir, B. W., Des Jarlais, D. C., Pinkerton, S. D., & Holtgrave, D. R. (2014, November). Syringe exchange in the United States: A national level economic evaluation of hypothetical increases in investment. *AIDS and Behavior,18*(11), 2144–2155.

NIDA. (2021). Medications to treat opioid use disorder. In *Research Report.* U.S. National Institute on Drug Abuse (NIDA).

Nielsen, S., Scott, N., Tidhar, T., Quiroga, M. D. M., Lenton, S., & Dietze, P. (2022, April). The cost and impact of distributing naloxone to people who are prescribed opioids to prevent opioid-related deaths: Findings from a modelling study. *Addiction, 117*(4), 1009–1019

NIH. (2024a). *Justice community opioid innovation network (JCOIN).* National Institutes for Health, HEAL Initiative.

NIH. (2024b). *NIH HEAL initiative: 2024 Annual report.* National Institutes for Health.

NIH. (2023). *NIH HEAL initiative: Funded projects.* HEAL Initiative, National Institutes of Health.

O'Brien, B. J., Elswood, J., & Calin, A. (1990, September). Willingness to accept risk in the treatment of rheumatic disease. *Journal of Epidemiology and Community Health, 44*(3), 249–252.

Oliva, E. M., Richardson, J., Harvey, M. A., & Bellino, P. (2021, August). Saving lives: The Veterans Health Administration (VHA) rapid naloxone initiative. *Joint Commission Journal on Quality and Patient Safety, 47*(8), 469–480.

Perrone, J., Weiner, S. G., & Nelson, L. S. (2019, March). Stewarding recovery from the opioid crisis through health system initiatives. *Western Journal of Emergency Medicine, 20*(2), 198–202.

Platt, L., Minozzi, S., Reed, J., Vickerman, P., Hagan, H., French, C., Jordan, A., et al. (2017, September 18). Needle syringe programmes and opioid substitution therapy for preventing Hepatitis C transmission in people who inject drugs. *Cochrane Database of Systematic Reviews, 9*(9), Cd012021.

Polsky, D., Glick, H. A., Yang, J., Subramaniam, G. A., Poole, S. A., & Woody, G. E. (2010, September). Cost-effectiveness of extended buprenorphine-naloxone treatment for opioid-dependent youth: Data from a randomized trial. *Addiction, 105*(9), 1616–1624.

Prempreet, B., Brennan, M., Grigoropoulos, G., Hintz, A., Parikh, S., Shah, N., & Wozniak, A. (2022, August). Opioid knowledge and prescribing habits at a large tertiary care academic center. *Cureus*, *14*(8), e27843.

Puac-Polanco, V., Chihuri, S., Fink, D. S., Cerdá, M., Keyes, K. M., & Li, G. (2020, January 31). Prescription drug monitoring programs and prescription opioid-related outcomes in the United States. *Epidemiologic Reviews*, *42*(1), 134–153.

Quanbeck, A., Almirall, D., Jacobson, N., Brown, R. T., Landeck, J. K., Madden, L., Cohen, A. et al. (2020, April 25). The balanced opioid initiative: Protocol for a clustered, sequential, multiple-assignment randomized trial to construct an adaptive implementation strategy to improve guideline-concordant opioid prescribing in primary care. *Implementation Science*, *15*(1), 26.

Rath, J. M., Perks, S. N., Vallone, D. M., Barton, A. A., Stephens, D. K., Simard, B., & Hair, E. C. (2021, December 21). Educating young adults about opioid misuse: Evidence from a mass media intervention. *International Journal of Environmental Research and Public Health*, *19*(1).

Robertson, M. N., Seitz, H. H., Downey, L. H., Hardman, A. M., Steen, J. S., & Buys, D. R. (2022, September 20). Increasing uptake of prescription drug take-back boxes: Eliciting preferences and applying the theory of planned behavior to predict use. *Health Education & Behavior*, 10901981221116778.

Rocco, P., & Kelly, A. S. (2020). An engine of change? The Affordable Care Act and the shifting politics of demonstration projects. *RSF: The Russell Sage Foundation Journal of the Social Sciences*, *6*(2), 67–84.

Rutkow, L., Chang, H. Y., Daubresse, M., Webster, D. W., Stuart, E. A., & Alexander, G. C. (2015, October). Effect of Florida's prescription drug monitoring program and pill mill laws on opioid prescribing and use. *JAMA Internal Medicine*, *175*(10), 1642–1649.

Rzasa Lynn, R., & Galinkin, J. L. (2018, January). Naloxone dosage for opioid reversal: Current evidence and clinical implications. *Therapeutic Advances in Drug Safety*, *9*(1), 63–88.

Saab, S., Le, L., Saggi, S., Sundaram, V., & Tong, M. J. (2018, June). Toward the elimination of Hepatitis C in the United States. *Hepatology*, *67*(6), 2449–2459.

SAMHSA. (2022). *Key substance use and mental health indicators in the United States: Results from the 2021 National Survey on Drug Use and Health*. In HHS Publication No. PEP22-07-01-005, NSDUH Series H-57. U.S. Substance Abuse and Mental Health Services Administration.

Schäfer, W. L. A., Johnson, J. K., Wafford, Q. E., Plummer, S. G., & Stulberg, J. J. (2021, September 3). Primary prevention of prescription opioid diversion: A systematic review of medication disposal interventions. *American Journal of Drug and Alcohol Abuse*, *47*(5), 548–558.

Slater, B. J., Corvin, C. G., Heiss, K., Vandewalle, R., Shah, S. R., Cunningham, M., Huang, E. et al. (2021, August 8). Provider education leads to sustained reduction in pediatric opioid prescribing after surgery. *Journal of Pediatric Surgery*.

Sohn, M., Talbert, J. C., Huang, Z., Lofwall, M. R., & Freeman, P. R. (2019, June 5). Association of naloxone coprescription laws with naloxone prescription dispensing in the United States. *JAMA Network Open*, *2*(6), e196215.

Spector, A. L., Galletly, C. L., Christenson, E. A., Montaque, H. D. G., & Dickson-Gomez, J. (2022, July 19). A qualitative examination of naloxone access in three states: Connecticut, Kentucky, and Wisconsin. *BMC Public Health*, *22*(1), 1387.

Stein, B. D., Kilmer, B., Taylor, J., & Vaiana, M. E. (2023). *America's opioid ecosystem*. RAND Corporation.

Stock, C. (2022). Grand challenges for public health education and promotion. *Frontiers in Public Health*, *10*, 917685.

Sud, A., Molska, G. R., & Salamanca-Buentello, F. (2022, February 1). Evaluations of continuing health provider education focused on opioid prescribing: A scoping review. *Academic Medicine*, *97*(2), 286–299.

Tay, E., Makeham, M., Laba, T. L., & Baysari, M. (2023, June 1). Prescription drug monitoring programs evaluation: A systematic review of reviews. *Drug and Alcohol Dependence*, *247* 109887.

Teshale, E. H., Asher, A., Aslam, M. V., Augustine, R., Duncan, E., Rose-Wood, A., Ward, J. et al. (2019). Estimated cost of comprehensive syringe service program in the United States. *PLoS One*, *14*(4), e0216205.

Thach, A. V., Brown, C. M., & Pope, N. (2013, September 30). Consumer perceptions about a community pharmacy-based medication take back program. *Journal of Environmental Management*, *127* 23–27.

Townsend, T., Blostein, F., Doan, T., Madson-Olson, S., Galecki, P., & Hutton, D. W. (2020), January). Cost-effectiveness analysis of alternative naloxone distribution strategies: First responder and lay distribution in the United States. *International Journal of Drug Policy*, *75*, 102536.

Tseng, J., Nuño, M., Lewis, A. V., Srour, M., Margulies, D. R., & Alban, R. F. (2018, September). Firearm legislation, gun violence, and mortality in children and young adults: A retrospective cohort study of 27,566 children in the USA. *International Journal of Surgery*, *57*, 30–34.

Urban Institute. (2023). Health and hospital expenditures. In *State and Local Backgrounders*. The Urban Institute.

Urban Institute. (2022). Public welfare expenditures. In *State and Local Backgrounders*. The Urban Institute.

Wakeman, S. E., Larochelle, M. R., Ameli, O., Chaisson, C. E., McPheeters, J. T., Crown, W. H., Azocar, F., & Sanghavi, D. M. (2020, February 5). Comparative effectiveness of different treatment pathways for opioid use disorder. *JAMA Network Open*, *3*(2), e1920622.

Weiner, J., Murphy, S. M., & Behrends, C. (2019). Expanding access to naloxone: A review of distribution strategies. In *Issue Brief*. Leonard Davis Institute of Health Economics; Center for Health Economics of Treatment Interventions for Substance Use Disorder, HCV, and HIV; University of Pennsylvania.

Whaley, S., & Sharfstein, J. (2023, September 1). The opioid settlements—will the first steps be in the right direction?. *JAMA Health Forum* *4*(9), e234017.

Whelan, P. J., & Remski, K. (2012). Buprenorphine vs methadone treatment: A review of evidence in both developed and developing worlds. *Journal of Neurosciences in Rural Practice*, *3*(1), 45–50.

WHO. (2019). *10 areas governments could work with to reduce the harmful use of alcohol*. World Health Organization.

Williams, E., Rudowitz, R., & Burns, A. (2023). *Medicaid financing: The basics*. Kaiser Family Foundation.

Wilson, C. G., Rodriguez, F., Carrington, A. C., & Fagan, E. B. (2017, March–April). Development of a targeted naloxone coprescribing program in a primary care practice. *Journal of the American Pharmacists Association (2003)*, *57*(2s), S130–S134.

Wood, D., Moy, S. F., Zhang, S., & Lightfoot, N. (2022, August). Impact of a prescriber and patient educational intervention on discharge analgesia prescribing and hospital readmission rates following elective unilateral total hip and knee arthroplasty. *BMJ Open Quality*, *11*(3).

Yang, C. H. J., Doshi, M., & Mason, N. A. (2015, July 27). Analysis of medications returned during a medication take-back event. *Pharmacy (Basel)*, *3*(3), 79–88.

Yang, J., & Mackert, M. (2023, May). The effectiveness of CDC's Rx awareness campaigns on reducing opioid stigma: Implications for health communication. *Health Communication*, *38*(5), 925–934.

Yanovitzky, I. (2017, August). A multiyear assessment of public response to a statewide drug take-back and disposal campaign, 2010 to 2012. *Health Education & Behavior*, *44*(4), 590–597.

Zang, X., Macmadu, A., Krieger, M. S., Behrends, C. N., Green, T. C., Morgan, J. R., Murphy, S. M. et al. (2021, December). Targeting community-based naloxone distribution using opioid overdose death rates: A descriptive analysis of naloxone rescue kits and opioid overdose deaths in Massachusetts and Rhode Island. *International Journal of Drug Policy*, *98*, 103435.

CHAPTER 8

Remedies

Having dissected the main components of the opioid litigation, including the underlying epidemiology, causal factors, and costs, a recurring theme has been that courts, to some extent, have taken up where regulatory institutions struggled, setting up a tension between regulation and litigation as different means of addressing the problems associated with certain harms and negative externalities. The genesis of regulation in the U.S. centered on the concept of the "public interest," and the importance of protecting the public from either the "excesses of capitalism" or the abundant risks of certain kinds of transactions (e.g., transportation, power, food, and healthcare) and the quality of public goods, such as air and water.[1] The consideration of regulation and litigation, or "court ordering," as alternative forms of governance for certain kinds of transactions (or problems) is of course not new, and has in the past fallen under the larger umbrella of institutional economics and specifically transaction cost economics, wherein the central line of inquiry is the optimal alignment of transactions, which differ in their attributes, with governance structures,

[1] See, for example, R. C. Leone, "Public Interest Advocacy and the Regulatory Process," *Annals of the American Academy of Political and Social Science* 400, no. March (1972); A. Ogus, *Regulation: Legal Form and Economic Theory*, Clarendon Law Series (New York, NY: Oxford Univeristy Press, 1994).

J. E. Schneider, *The Economics of Pain*, Global Perspectives on Wealth and Distribution,
https://doi.org/10.1007/978-3-032-20355-7_8

which differ in their costs and competencies.[2] In more recent years, specific issues of "regulation versus litigation" have been addressed in greater detail, particularly within the law and economics field.[3]

In this chapter, remedies to the opioid crisis are explored within the context of *ex ante* regulation versus *ex post* litigation; specifically, the focus is on how a "regulation versus litigation" conceptual framework may help inform stakeholders on how to optimally manage similar problems in the future. The opioid crisis is a fitting issue through which to view the regulation versus litigation debate. In the case of opioids, the regulatory apparatus serving as the gatekeeper of prescription drugs largely failed to execute its main approval and monitoring functions, essentially leaving the courts to sort out questions regarding causation, responsibility, and abatement.[4] An important question is whether this outcome was more or less inevitable, given the design of regulatory institutions, or could it have been managed more effectively, perhaps with better (or different) regulatory mechanisms and more parsimonious use of the judicial system to fill regulatory gaps. In the following sections, these issues are explored as potential organizational or governance remedies. Here, the term remedies is to be distinguished from specific abatement type programs (e.g., like those reviewed in the previous chapter), which are targeted "programmatic solutions" as opposed to broader organizational remedies.

[2] See generally R. H. Coase, "The Nature of the Firm," *Economica* 4, no. November (1937); O. E. Williamson, "Transaction-Cost Economics: The Governance of Contractual Relations," *Journal of Law and Economics* 22, no. 2 (1979); *The Mechanisms of Governance* (New York, NY: Oxford Univeristy Press, 1996).

[3] See, for example, D. P. Kessler, *Regulation versus Litigation: Perspectives from Law and Economics* (Chicago: The University of Chicago Press, 2011); E. Helland and J. Klick, "The Tradeoffs between Regulation and Litigation: Evidence from Insurance Class Actions," *Journal of Tort Law* 1, no. 3 (2006); T. Buchholz et al., "Litigation or Government Regulation?," in *Conference Series: Litigation through Regulation: Assessing the Role of Bounty Hunters and Bureaucrats in the American Regulatory Regime*, ed. CLP (New York, NY: Manhattan Institute, Center for Legal Policy, 2000); W. K. Viscusi and J. Hersch, "Tobacco Regulation through Litigation," in *Regulation versus Litigation: Perspectives from Economics and Law*, ed. D. P. Kessler (Chicago, IL: National Bureau of Economic Research & The University of Chicago Press, 2011).

[4] Note that, in the case of opioids (and other prescription drug cases preceding opioids), regulatory approval did not in any way "preempt" post-market litigation, though overall the FDA approval figured quite prominently in defense arguments and in the research on root causes. See generally T. J. Philipson, E. Sun, and D. Goldman, "The Effects of Product Liability Exemption in the Presence of the FDA," ibid. (National Bureau of Economic Research | The University of Chicago Press).

8.1 Externalities

The economic theory of externalities provides a framework through which to consider potential policy and governance solutions to problems like the opioid crisis. The concept of externalities was briefly introduced in Chap. 3, but it is worth revising it here in the context of remedies and solutions. Economic theory typically portrays the production process in the form of what is called a production function, which generally takes the form $y = f(x)$, where y denotes production volume and x is a set of variables describing production inputs, such as labor, supplies, and capital. The function describes the "technology" of production in that it portrays the technical relationship between inputs (x) and outputs (y), which can support inferences regarding productive efficiency and productivity; for example, "how much x is required to produce one unit of y?" Externalities are said to exist in certain cases where an external factor (z) imposes a cost that must be incorporated into production, such that $y = f(x, z)$. The usual example of this is that a factory pollutes a river or stream that a downstream farmer requires for crop irrigation. In this example, the farmer's production function would normally be $y = f(x)$. However, due to the polluted water (which he now must filter at an added cost) his production function now becomes $y = f(x, z)$. In other words, the farmer must now incur an added production cost (z), one that is external to his own production function. In contrast, the factory would be disposing of waste at a lower cost than it might have otherwise incurred. If laws required that the factory properly filter its waste prior to discharge, the cost (z) would be "restored" to the factory production function.

Much of the economic literature on externalities has focused on remedies to these types of problems. The usual remedies, in the context of the factory-farmer example above, are to tax the factory based on its volume of production and its corresponding level of pollution, tax consumers purchasing the product, or regulate the factory to constrain its ability to pollute the river.[5] Taxing the factory has the potential to accomplish two goals: (1) raising the production costs of the factory, which in turn would likely result in the factory raising its prices and producing less of the polluting product; and (2) generating tax revenue, which could be reallocated by the government to mitigate the pollution. A consumer tax on the products produced by the factory would essentially have the same effects, as raising consumer prices would result in less consumption of the

[5] A. A. Papandreou, *Externality and Institutions* (Oxford, UK: Clarendon Press, 1994).

product. However, product-specific taxes present administrative burdens, and have been implemented sparingly in most developed countries. An alternative to taxes is government regulation. Government could impose regulations on the factory, perhaps designed to limit the allowable volume or content of discharge. The factory would incur added costs (z) to comply with the regulations, thereby increasing its production costs. This is analogous to the approach to externalities associated with drug adverse events in the U.S., where the FDA imposes regulations on manufacturers in the form of the approval process and, in some cases, additional post-market studies and surveillance, both of which result in significant added development costs to manufacturers. In the example of the polluting factory, another option is to use the courts to require the factory, if deemed responsible, to pay for damages (z) incurred by the farmer. Note that in these simple examples, all solutions shift the full cost of the externality to the factory's production function.

In some cases, however, taxes, regulation, and litigation may not represent socially optimal organizational choices, as these options can in some cases shift full responsibility for the attributable costs (z) to the factory (and perhaps other members of the supply chain), as the farmer continues to benefit from the low (or zero) cost associated with the use of clean water for irrigation. Nobel laureate Ronald Coase, in *The Problem of Social Cost*,[6] argued that in many cases, depending on transaction costs and organizational costs, a better outcome may be achieved through private bargaining between the factory and farmer, as both would presumably benefit from their respective ongoing uses of the river. Such bargaining could be in the form of private negotiations or alternative dispute resolution ("ADR"), such as mediation.[7] The outcome of such bargaining could be, for example, some cost-sharing arrangement whereby each party agrees to pay a portion of z, and neither pays the full amount. An *a priori* assumption that the factory is liable for the entire cost of the externality is, Coase would argue, mostly arbitrary. The bargaining approach would effectively raise costs (and prices) for both, but in most cases by amounts less than having either one of them bear the full burden. In cases where private bargaining is prohibitively complex or costly, other

[6] R. H. Coase, "The Problem of Social Cost," *Journal of Law and Economics* 3 (1960).

[7] See generally M. A. Landrum, "Through the Mists: ADR and Product Liability Claims in the Twenty-first Century," *William Mitchell Law Review* 27, no. 1 (2000).

organizational alternatives may represent better solutions. Should any of those fail, litigation is typically considered the last resort.

8.2 Transaction Cost Economics

Coase's view of private ordering (via bargaining) and regulation (via administrative controls) as remedies to the externality problem is part of the larger body of work in institutional economics and, specifically, transaction cost economics ("TCE"), which focuses generally on the alignment of transaction attributes with optimal forms of governance.[8] In the case of externalities, the most efficient organizational solution to the externality problem depends on the specific attributes of the externality and the transactions associated therewith, and may take the form of markets, markets with specific taxes and fees, private bargaining, government regulation, court ordering, etc. The critical unit of analysis within the TCE framework is the transaction. Simple transactions are normally organized most efficiently in standard markets, where prices serve as a sufficient conveyor of information and market demand and supply are (more or less) free to adjust to exogenous changes in market conditions. Conversely, more complex transactions are normally more efficiently organized in settings that feature administrative controls. In the case of private ordering, governance of more complex transactions can be achieved, for example, through vertical integration (i.e., "make or buy").[9] In the case of complex transactions associated with externalities, optimal organizational forms can include market governance (e.g., bargaining and third-party mediation) and non-market governance (e.g., taxes, regulation, and litigation).

Transaction complexity is typically defined as transactions with one or more of the following attributes: (1) asset specificity; (2) frequency; and (3) uncertainty.[10] All three of these attributes can be associated with elevated risk to consumers or suppliers (or to contracting parties more generally), thereby increasing the costs of reliance on standard markets. Asset specificity

[8] See generally Williamson, *The Mechanisms of Governance*; C. Menard and M. M. Shirley, eds., *Handbook of the New Institutional Economics* (Berlin: Springer, 2008); Williamson, "Transaction-Cost Economics: The Governance of Contractual Relations."

[9] See, for example, S. E. Masten, J. W. Meehan, and E. A. Snyder, "Vertical integration in the U.S. auto industry: A note on the influence of transaction specific assets," *Journal of Economic Behavior & Organization* 12, no. 2 (1989).

[10] See generally Williamson, *The Mechanisms of Governance.*

refers to the degree to which a transaction requires a "relationship specific" investment; for example, a supplier having to invest is specialized and dedicated machinery to produce a specific part for an automobile manufacturer, with the machinery being non-redeployable to alternative uses. Typically, these relationships arise in long-term contracts where switching suppliers in the short run is not feasible without significant added costs.[11] The investment by the supplier is essentially a "sunk cost" because the machinery is non-redeployable to alternative uses. A contract hold-up or contract breach between the manufacturer and supplier renders the relationship-specific investment a loss. Transactions that occur with relatively high frequency are also associated with elevated risk; for example, when printed media like newspapers were a ubiquitous mode of communication, a newspaper publisher required exceptionally reliable daily supplies of ink and paper, and disruptions in the supply of either input could halt production of the newspaper. Finally, uncertainty is somewhat of a catch-all attribute that is rooted in the complexity and accessibility of some types of information. The presence of high levels of uncertainty can result in asymmetrically distributed information among stakeholders, coupled with high search costs and evaluation costs.[12] Uncertainty and information costs are of particular importance given what March and Simon referred to as "cognitive limits on rationality" (i.e., "bounded rationality") which posits that economic actors are intendedly rational but for the inherent cognitive limits on the human capacity to obtain and interpret complex information.[13] Uncertainty also underlies moral hazard and adverse selection, which are common features of complex transactions. Note that uncertainty typically has two parts, one associated with the level of uncertainty and another associated with the consequences of that uncertainty.[14]

[11] See, for example, P. L. Joskow, "Contract Duration of Relationship-Specific Investments: Empirical Evidence from Coal Markets," *American Economic Review* 77, no. 1; March (1987); S. E. Masten and K. J. Crocker, "Efficient Adaptation in Long-Term Contracts: Take-or-Pay Provisions for Natural Gas," ibid.75, no. 5; December (1985).

[12] See, for example, G. E. Smith, M. P. Venkatraman, and R. R. Dholakia, "Diagnosing the search cost effect: Waiting time and the moderating impact of prior category knowledge," *Journal of Economic Psychology* 20, no. 3 (1999).

[13] J. G. March and H. A. Simon, *Organizations* (New York, NY: John Wiley & Sons, Inc., 1958).

[14] A useful discussion of the role of uncertainty in O. E. Williamson, "Comparative Economic Organization: The Analysis of Discrete Structural Alternatives," *Administrative Science Quarterly* 36, no. June (1991).

8.3 Prescription Drug Transactions

Transactions involving medical products and services, including pharmaceuticals and medical devices, are arguably some of the most complex transactions in the economy. Although asset specificity may be important in certain issues relating to the boundaries of healthcare firms (e.g., the purchase of imaging equipment by an orthopedic office),[15] frequency and uncertainty are typically important considerations in a wide variety of healthcare transactions. The importance of frequency is straightforward in healthcare transactions, as supply chain disruptions can have enormous consequences on the health and well-being of consumers and patients. Healthcare providers require ready and frequent access to a multitude of equipment and supplies, and pharmaceutical and medical device makers depend heavily on the reliability and quality of materials used in the production of their products. Disruptions in production can have direct consequences on health, particularly those with chronic and ongoing needs. For example, the global supply shortages experienced during the COVID-19 pandemic highlighted the critical importance of reliability in the healthcare supply chain.[16] Also, though medical supply markets are at least somewhat competitive, featuring more than one seller, for some equipment and supplies, there is only a single supplier, thereby increasing the risk of hold-up.[17]

As important as transaction frequency may be in healthcare, uncertainty is the most pervasive transaction attribute.[18] In his landmark 1963 essay on the role of uncertainty in healthcare markets, Kenneth Arrow emphasized the importance of uncertainty in two dimensions in particular: (1) uncertainty in the probability of contracting disease, and (2) uncertainty in the effectiveness of treatments.[19] The first of these gives rise to insurance and third-party

[15] See, for example, R. L. Ohsfeldt, P. Li, and J. E. Schneider, "In-office magnetic resonance imaging (MRI) equipment ownership and MRI volume among medicare patients in orthopedic practices," *Health Econ Rev* 5, no. 1 (2015); T. S. Snail and J. C. Robinson, "Organizational diversification in the American hospital," *Annu Rev Public Health* 19 (1998).

[16] See, for example, C. P. Bown, "How COVID-19 Medical Supply Shortages Led to Extraordinary Trade and Industrial Policy," 17, no. 1 (2022).

[17] See generally L. Dafny, "Addressing Consolidation in Health Care Markets," *JAMA* 325, no. 10 (2021).

[18] For a review, see P. J. Hammer et al., *Uncertain Times: Kenneth Arrow and the Changing Economics of Health Care* (Durham, N.C.: Duke University Press, 2003).

[19] K. J. Arrow, "Uncertainty and the Welfare Economics of Medical Care," *The American Economic Review* 53, no. 5; December (1963).

payers, as insurance is a means to manage the risks associated with the unpredictability of illness. However, health insurance is further complicated by the risks of moral hazard, discussed earlier, and adverse selection,[20] both of which are more likely to occur in the presence of uncertainty and can also in some cases hinder the effectiveness of insurance as a risk management tool. The second type of uncertainty forms the basis for many types of healthcare regulation, such as the FDA control over which medical devices can be marketed to providers and which prescription drugs are permitted to reach consumers.[21] Prescription drugs and medical devices, like many medical treatments, are scientifically complex and difficult for the layperson to assess, thereby creating asymmetrically distributed information among sellers (manufacturers) and consumers (providers and patients). Moreover, there are additional layers of uncertainty regarding the prevalence and magnitude of adverse events and side effects, even when the drug or device otherwise performs its primary intended functions as expected. Thus, there are relatively high levels of uncertainty regarding whether a drug or device will work and added layers of uncertainty regarding the benefit-cost properties, which include acquisition costs and the costs associated with adverse events and side effects, particularly those that come to light post-approval. This is not to say that the impact of uncertainty is unidirectional; rather, the same uncertainty regarding treatment effectiveness affects manufacturers in the form of exceptionally high research and development ("R&D") risks and costs, where the vast majority of promising treatments fail during the R&D process.[22] Finally, as with any medical product or service wherein uncertainty

[20] Adverse selection refers to the cyclical process whereby the cost-benefit assessment of purchasing insurance is driven by risk and expected costs, which (in the case of health insurance) are lower for healthier individuals. As healthier enrollees drop coverage, the total costs of the remaining enrollee pool increases, thereby resulting in the next tier of low-risk enrollees dropping coverage. The process converges on progressively higher rates charged to a continuously shrinking pool of enrollees. In the absence of additional mechanisms, such a group coverage (e.g., employer-based coverage) or universal coverage (e.g., Medicare or Medicaid), health insurers are at risk for offering coverage policies that are unaffordable to those who would benefit the most. See generally D. M. Cutler and R. J. Zeckhauser, "Adverse Selection in Health Insurance," in *Frontiers in Health Policy Research*, ed. A. M. Garber (Cambridge, MA: MIT Press, 1998).

[21] See generally U. E. Reinhardt, "The Pharmaceutical Sector in Health Care," in *Pharmaceutical Innovation: Incentives, Compeitition, and Cost-Benefit Analysis in International Perspective*, ed. F. A. Sloan and C. R. Hsieh (New York, NY: Cambridge University Press, 2007).

[22] See generally ibid. Also see P.M. Danzon and S. Nicholson, *The Oxford Handbook of The Economics of the Biopharmaceutical Industry* (New York, NY: Oxford University Press, 2012).

and information asymmetry is featured, there is also the risk of opportunistic behavior on the part of suppliers, sellers, and other stakeholders. Difficulty in evaluating the risks and benefits of a medical intervention can create opportunities for manufacturers, distributors, and providers to increase the volume and intensity of services, as consumers and regulators face higher search costs in assessing medical need, quality of care, and other product and service attributes. Conditions associated with more subjective diagnoses, such as pain, are particularly susceptible to overconsumption of treatment; however, in some circumstances, uncertainty and subjectivity in diagnosis can also lead to underconsumption of treatment.[23]

The complex attributes of healthcare transactions are relevant to the opioid crisis in at least four ways, some of which have been at least partly discussed in earlier chapters. First, shortly after introduction to the market, uncertainty in treatment effectiveness led to widespread misunderstandings among providers and patients as to the risks of dependency, addiction, and serious adverse events such as dependency and OUD. The importance of this uncertainty was not only featured prominently in the regulatory approval process but was also observed throughout the medical community.[24] Second, the existing medical products regulatory apparatus in the U.S. was born out of the need to control product quality, and more broadly to address uncertainty and the information imbalance between suppliers, providers, and consumers.[25] That is, the existence of medical products regulation was largely driven by the complexity of some types of healthcare transactions, particularly with regard to uncertainty. Third, from a"regulatory failure" perspective, were the medical regulatory apparatus to have functioned as intended, it could be argued that the opioid crisis would not have happened or might have played out with considerably smaller scale and scope,

[23] See, for example, P. L. Pentin, "Drug seeking or pain crisis? Responsible prescribing of opioids in the emergency department," *Virtual Mentor* 15, no. 5 (2013); J.C. Hackworth et al., "The burden of acute pain in the U.S. in the wake of the opioid crisis," *Frontiers in Pain Research* Volume 6 (2025).

[24] See, for example, C. S. Hwang et al., "Primary Care Physicians' Knowledge And Attitudes Regarding Prescription Opioid Abuse and Diversion," *The Clinical Journal of Pain* 32, no. 4 (2016).

[25] See generally A. Malani and T. Philipson, "The Regulation of Medical Products," in *The Economics of the Biopharmaceutical Industry*, ed. P. M. Danzon and S. Nicholson (New York, NY: Oxford University Press, 2012). For historical context, see J. M. Spivak, "Regulation of Medical Devices," *Annals of the American Academy of Political and Social Science* 400, no. March (1972).

ameliorated before any extensive corrective actions were necessary. Fourth, the complexity of healthcare transactions and nuances associated with resulting externalities hindered the identification and implementation of effective solutions to the crisis, as evidenced in part by the lengthy delay between the widespread acknowledgement of the crisis and the targeted implementation of programs aimed at mitigation and abatement.[26] Moreover, as discussed at the onset of this chapter, transaction complexity muddied the waters regarding the relative merits of regulation versus courts in the various deliberations over feasible solutions to the crisis.[27]

8.4 Regulatory Governance

From the transaction cost economics TCE perspective, Coase recognized that in some cases "the administrative costs might well be so high as to make any attempt to deal with the problem within the confines of a single firm impossible. An alternative solution is direct government regulation."[28] Regulatory governance can be defined in various ways, but generally it refers to a nexus of laws, measurement tools, enforcement tools, and, in some cases, organizational structures (such as agencies and bureaus) that are intended to govern and monitor certain aspects of private industry.[29] Victor Goldberg described regulation in the context of "administered contracts,"

[26] An interesting discussion of this issue can be found in T. Rhodes and K. Lancaster, "Early warnings and slow deaths: A sociology of outbreak and overdose," *International Journal of Drug Policy* 117 (2023).

[27] See generally NASEM, *Pain Management and the Opioid Epidemic: Balancing Societal and Indidivual Benefits and Risks of Prescription Opioid Use*, ed. R. J. Bonnie, M. A. Ford, and J. K. Phillips, Consensus Study Report of National Academies of Sciences, Engineering and Medicine (NASEM) (Washington, D.C.: National Academies Press, 2017).

[28] Coase, "The Problem of Social Cost." (p. 22).

[29] See generally A. E. Kahn, *The Economics of Regulation: Principles and Institutions* (Cambridge, MA: The MIT Press, 1988). Hereafter, I refer to "regulation" to refer to the general concept of government regulation, and the term "regulatory agency" to generically refer to any governmental regulatory body, including the large long-standing U.S. regulatory agencies such as the FDA, DEA, EPA, the Federal Communications Commission ("FCC"), the Federal Aviation Administration ("FAA"), and the Securities and Exchange Commission ("SEC"). For the purposes of this book, I have considered the CDC a regulatory agency in a very broad sense though it is not typically considered as such given its extensive support and surveillance functions. Also, note that "self-regulation" of the medical profession is an important feature of the opioid crisis (as discussed in Chap. 4), but such forms of regulation bear little resemblance to the traditional agency approach to regulation.

based on the supposition that regulatory mechanisms in some cases may represent the most efficient means of organizing certain kinds of transactions, observing that "failure to appreciate the complexity of contractual arrangements in the private sector is apt to leave the analyst unduly sanguine as to the efficacy of private market solutions to problems in the regulatory sector" (p. 427).[30] Goldberg further posited that regulation could also be viewed in the context of "the implicit contract between the regulated firm(s) and the regulatory agency serving as the collective contract. [...] Conceptually, we can treat judges and legislators as agents enforcing and revising the rules under which individual transactions take place." (p. 429). In this sense, regulatory governance can be thought of as an *ex ante* approach to governing complex transactions, with legislators and courts designing mechanisms to address problems and harms for which there is a non-trivial probability of occurrence (e.g., a severe adverse event associated with a prescription drug).

The core capabilities of regulatory agencies vary along with the laws that establish them, but most share a set of common attributes.[31] First, regulatory agencies typically employ a variety of administrative rules and controls to which regulated entities are obligated by law to comply. These controls can take the form of, for example, licensure (i.e., permission to serve the market), allowable limits on output, minimum quality and safety standards, mandatory disclosures and reporting, and price controls. Compliance can be incentivized through the use of monetary penalties for non-adherence and, if necessary, legal remedies, including market exclusion. Second, regulatory agencies can develop and maintain specialized industry knowledge and skills, and such knowledge can in turn support more efficient problem solving and support coordinated adaptation to exogenous changes in industry features (i.e., technological change) and market conditions. Third, regulatory agencies provide a means through which to equitably and fairly enforce regulations across all industry entities, and to do so transparently and consistently over time. Note that a related benefit of this feature is that it reduces some of the

[30] V. P. Goldberg, "Regulation and Administered Contracts," *Bell Journal of Economics* 7, no. 2; Autumn (1976).

[31] See generally S. Breyer, *Regulation and Its Reform* (Cambridge, MA: Harvard University Press, 1982); R.G. Noll, "Government Regulatory Behavior: A Multidisciplinary Survey and Synthesis," in *Regulatory Policy and the Social Sciences*, ed. R. G. Noll (Berkeley, CA: University of California Press, 1985).

uncertainty faced by regulated entities, relative to their unregulated counterparts. Finally, regulation in some cases serves as a barrier to entry for potential market entrants, potentially resulting in higher prices and profits for established firms. While barriers to entry do not necessarily benefit consumers, there may be instances where unrestricted market entry can result in negative externalities, the costs of which can fall on both suppliers and consumers. These scenarios are often referred to "destructive competition" or "cut-throat competition," examples of which can include public utilities, shipping, natural resource extraction, agriculture and fishing, transportation, and healthcare.[32]

The long history of regulation in the U.S. has produced a large body of research on the drawbacks and limitations associated with regulatory agencies and mechanisms, as well as the factors leading to regulatory failure, many of which were featured in the deregulatory movements of the 1970s and 1980s. Some of these issues were briefly introduced earlier (Chap. 4) in the context of contributing factors in the opioid crisis. First, regulatory agencies share some of the attributes of hierarchical enterprise and public bureaucracies in that they are good at coordinated adaptation (i.e., having all the subcomponents take coordinated actions in response to a single directive),[33] but generally lack the ability to respond rapidly and autonomously to changes in industry and market conditions (i.e., autonomous adaptation). Bureaucratic inertia is largely attributed to low-powered incentives on the part of agency leaders and the necessary legislative action required to implement major changes in regulatory structures and mechanisms.[34]

[32] See, for example, Breyer, *Regulation and Its Reform*; P. L. Joskow and R. C. Noll, "Regulation in Theory and Practice: An Overview," in *Studies in Public Regulation*, ed. G. Fromm (Cambridge, MA: The MIT Press, 1981); Kahn, *The Economics of Regulation: Principles and Institutions*; J. E. Schneider, "Changes in the Effects of Mandatory Rate Regulation On Growth in Hospital Operating Costs, 1980–1996," *Review of Industrial Organization* 22, no. 4 (2003); W. K. Viscusi, J. M. Vernon, and J. E. Harrington, *Economics of Regulation and Antitrust (Second Edition)* (Cambridge (MA): The MIT Press, 1995).

[33] See generally Williamson, "Comparative Economic Organization: The Analysis of Discrete Structural Alternatives."

[34] See, for example, M.H. Bernstein, "Independent Regulatory Agencies: A Perspective on Their Reform," *Annals of the American Academy of Political and Social Science* 400, no. March (1972); Breyer, *Regulation and Its Reform*; R. H. K. Vietor, *Contrived Competition: Regulation and Deregulation in America* (Cambridge, MA: The Belknap Press of Harvard University Press, 1994).

Second, regulatory mechanisms typically represent a mix of responses to *ex post* experiences and *ex ante* anticipations. The limitations of mechanisms designed based on past experiences is rooted in the aforementioned adaptation challenges; that is, the inherent difficulty in adaptation to unforeseen changes in exogenous factors. Even when regulators are aware of the limitations of past experiences, the alternative—the disproportionate weighting of future anticipations—is equally limited by the presence of uncertainty, which is expected to be higher in regulated markets in which industry and market uncertainty were among the primary bases for government regulation. Another important adaptive issue is the propensity for performance-based rules to become levels targeted by industry; for example, the setting of a maximum allowable concentration of a pollutant is at risk of being viewed as an optimal level by industry, assuming that there are non-trivial costs associated with maintaining levels below the ceiling. In so doing, incentives to improve processes to reduce emissions below the regulatory ceilings are attenuated.[35]

Third, regulatory agencies, like most political institutions, are susceptible to industry influence. Industry influence is the inevitable result of several factors, including a political system that allows for a prominent role for lobbying and campaign contributions by regulated industries, low-powered incentives on the part of regulatory agency leaders, and the employment of former industry executives in leadership roles at regulatory agencies.[36] Opportunistic influencing by industry and other special interests has the potential to result in the disproportionate weighting of industry welfare over consumer welfare and, at its extreme, can effectively neuter some of the key functions of regulatory agencies. Finally, controls on market entry, as alluded to in the context of the advantages of government regulation, can negatively impact consumer welfare by sustaining monopoly or oligopoly pricing and limiting consumer choice. However, the effects of controls on market entry must be weighed against the effects

[35] See, for example, the discussion by C. Coglianese, "The Limits of Performance-Based Regulation," *University of Michigan Journal of Law Reform* 50, no. 3 (2017).

[36] See, for example, Bernstein, "Independent Regulatory Agencies: A Perspective on Their Reform."; Leone, "Public Interest Advocacy and the Regulatory Process."; P. J. Quirk, *Industry Influence in Federal Regulatory Agencies* (Princeton, NJ: Princeton University Press, 2016); G. M. Grossman and E. Helpman, *Special Interest Politics* (Cambridge, MA: The MIT Press, 2001); S. Krislov and L. D. Musolf, *The Politics of Regulation* (Boston: Houghton Mifflin Company, 1964).

of unrestricted entry, which in some industries (particularly those with complex transactions) may not represent the most efficient form of governance.

8.5 Court Ordering

Reliance on courts to govern industries with complex transactions and externalities is often dismissed as a viable *ex ante* governance structure, largely due to the comparatively high costs of using the courts, but also due to the inefficiencies associated with unpredictable timelines and the potential for arbitrary awards by juries. However, there are some advantages to court ordering that should be considered alongside market and regulatory approaches. First, courts offer a framework of support for "relational contracting," whereby parties "agree to agree" in the event of unforeseen exogenous factors that can impact the applicability and relevance of *ex ante* contract terms.[37] From an adaptation perspective, alternative dispute resolution mechanisms like arbitration and mediation offer relatively straightforward means through which to accommodate necessary adaptation, with the credible threat of jury trials serving as sufficient incentives for cooperation on behalf of interested parties. In addition, it is not necessary to precisely define all terms *ex ante*, as a long-term relational contract framework allows terms to be modified as needed.[38] Second, courts are generally less susceptible to industry influence.[39] This is in part due to the intentional impartiality of mediators and judges, but also to the *ad hoc* nature of the whole process, whereby both sides of a dispute conduct discovery and assemble experts during a delimited time period, as opposed to sole reliance on existing and entrenched regulatory agency leadership and staff. Finally, courts are not aligned with a particular scientific or industry ideology, which allows for the possibility of novel

[37] See, for example, V. P. Goldberg, "Relational Contract," in *The New Palgrave Dictionary of Economics and the Law: Volume 1–3: A-Z*, ed. P. Newman (London: Palgrave Macmillan UK, 2002); "Relational Exchange: Economics and Complex Contracts," in *Readings in the Economics of Contract Law*, ed. V. P. Goldberg (New York, NY: Cambridge University Press, 1989).

[38] "Relational Exchange: Economics and Complex Contracts."

[39] See generally R. A. Posner, "Regulation (Agencies) versus Litigation (Courts)," in *Regulation versus Litigation: Perspectives from Economics and Law*, ed. D. P. Kessler (Chicago, IL: The University of Chicago Press, 2011).

solutions, free from the confines of a particular discipline.[40] For example, a court ruling in an environmental contamination case is not required to be chosen from a menu of options presented by the field of environmental science, though in many cases such an outcome may be obtained.

Alongside these strengths, there are some important disadvantages to court ordering. First, reliance on courts, particularly for large-scale issues such as mass torts, can be very costly.[41] For example, the ongoing asbestos litigation is expected to cost about $265 billion. Parties assemble teams *ad hoc*, with judges, attorneys, and experts having to acquire specialized knowledge for the sole purposes of the litigation. Attorneys and experts have comparatively high opportunity costs,[42] and complex cases such as mass torts can require significant time commitments for discovery and trial and can continue for several years. Moreover, as demonstrated in the preceding chapters, courts provide few constraints to ensure that settlements and awards are reasonable reflections of "real world" attributable costs or abatement costs, and jury awards with punitive components add considerable uncertainty to the total expected costs of litigation.[43] Second, courts are mostly limited to working within the confines of existing policy, established case law, and other legal precedents to decide on critical parameters. These parameters can include the admissibility and interpretation of technical and scientific evidence, the qualifications of experts, and the appropriateness and effectiveness of proposed remedies. Past legal precedent is likely to be applied even if the appropriateness of the application to contemporary issues may be limited.[44] Venturing too far beyond these confines increases the likelihood of appeals, which in turn generates additional costs and uncertainty. Finally, in some cases courts can magnify issues of information asymmetry and increase search costs as parties

[40] Ibid.

[41] See generally D. R. Hensler and M. A. Peterson, "Understanding Mass Personal Injury Litigation," in *Research Summary* (Santa Monica, CA: RAND Corporation, 1995).

[42] Opportunity costs refer to the value of the "next best" alternative use of an input, such as time. Retained content experts are often employed full-time in activities that utilize the same expertise required by courts; thus, in many cases they must be paid more than their normal compensation in order to offset the disruption of serving as an expert.

[43] See generally C. R. Sunstein et al., *Punitive Damages: How Juries Decide* (Chicago, IL: University of Chicago Press, 2002).

[44] See generally F. Schauer and R. J. Zeckhauser, "The Trouble with Cases," in *Regulation versus Litigation: Perspectives from Economics and Law*, ed. D. P. Kessler (Chicago, IL: The University of Chicago Press, 2011).

leverage the rules regarding discovery as a means to influence and control the volume and types of evidence that are allowed to be presented to juries.[45]

8.6 The Case of Opioids

There has been little debate as to whether regulatory governance, compared to markets, has been an appropriate organizational solution to the inherent risks associated with prescription drugs. Although champions of free-market capitalism and libertarianism have mused philosophically about relying less on regulation and more heavily on markets to punish rogue pharmaceutical makers and low-quality doctors,[46] pre-regulatory experiences globally highlight the exceedingly high risks of the "hands off" approach applied to markets for medical products and services.[47] There are a number of specific features of pharmaceutical and device markets that point to the need for added controls, including the comparatively high risks associated with the intrusion of low-quality and counterfeit drugs and devices, the prevalence of serious adverse events, and the risks of serious harm to consumers. Moreover, as discussed earlier, there is considerable uncertainty regarding health and safety risks and high search costs associated with the assessment of medical product quality and effectiveness.[48] These market complexities ultimately led to the establishment of the FDA as part of the 1906 Food and Drug Act. Initially, regulations were mainly post-market and aimed principally at mislabeled or adulterated drugs, but in 1938, the Federal Food, Drug, and Cosmetic Act added additional regulatory rules requiring evidence of drug and medical device safety.[49] In 1962, the Act was amended to require manufacturers to also

[45] See, for example, D. A. Elwell, "Industry-Influenced Evidence: Bias, Conflict, and Manipulation in Scientific Evidence," *Boston College Law Review* 61, no. 6 (2020).

[46] See, for example, G. P. O'Driscoll and L. Hoskins, "The Case for Market-Based Regulation," *Cato Journal* 26, no. 3 (2006).

[47] See, for example, the discussion in Reinhardt, "The Pharmaceutical Sector in Health Care."

[48] See generally J. Avorn, "The marketplace can't give us the drug safety data we need," *MedGenMed* 9, no. 1 (2007).

[49] See generally Malani and Philipson, "The Regulation of Medical Products."; S. S. Mehta, *Commercializing Successful Biomedical Technologies: Basic Principles for the Development of Drugs, Diagnostics and Devices* (Cambridge, UK: Cambridge University Press, 2008); A. A. Ciociola, L. B. Cohen, and P. Kulkarni, "How drugs are developed and approved by the FDA: current process and future directions," *Am J Gastroenterol* 109, no. 5 (2014); A. T. Borchers et al., "The history and contemporary challenges of the US Food and Drug Administration," *Clin Ther* 29, no. 1 (2007).

submit detailed evidence of product effectiveness as a condition for entry into U.S. markets. Currently, as a condition of FDA approval (which is necessary for market entry and insurance payment), drugs sold in the U.S. must successfully complete numerous phases of vetting, including animal testing, toxicology, basic effectiveness, rigorous clinical studies, and post-market studies, event reporting, and monitoring.[50] Similar procedures aimed at medical devices were added in 1976. Throughout its drug and device review processes, specific rules and guidelines govern the interactions between the FDA and industry, with the nominal objective being the maintenance of FDA's impartiality and independence.[51]

8.6.1 Opioid Regulation

The failures of the regulatory approach in the case of opioids were briefly discussed earlier in the context of causal factors associated with the growth in opioid supply (refer to Chap. 4). However, it is worth revisiting these issues in the context of optimal governance and the "regulation versus litigation" question. Broadly, the FDA clearly underestimated the risks of opioids in its initial approval process and failed in its subsequent monitoring role to fully understand how those risks were impacting patients. Specifically, three factors appeared to be critical to the FDA's mishandling of the emerging opioid crisis: (1) uncertainty surrounding the clinical effects of opioids and asymmetrically distributed information and comparatively high search costs likely present barriers to addressing uncertainty; (2) the role of special interests and industry influence; and (3) general bureaucratic inertia common to large vertically structured organizations. Given the critical role of regulatory mechanisms in the opioid crisis, each of these warrants some additional discussion.

Uncertainty surrounding the clinical effects of opioids was poorly understood by the FDA, particularly with regard to post-market monitoring and surveillance, as overdose data began to be compiled and narrative accounts

[50] For example, see E. R. Brill et al., "Postmarket Surveillance of Mesh Performance After Inguinal Hernia Repair," *JAMA Surg* (2025); R. Mehran et al., "Post-market approval surveillance: a call for a more integrated and comprehensive approach," *Circulation* 109, no. 25 (2004); R. J. Meyer, "Regulatory considerations for determining postmarketing study commitments," *Clin Pharmacol Ther* 82, no. 2 (2007).

[51] See generally J.T. Mitchel, "FDA relations during drug development," *Dialogues Clin Neurosci* 2, no. 3 (2000).

increasingly reported elevated risks of misuse, dependency, and OUD.[52] For example, an OIG report on the effectiveness of the FDA's post-market surveillance of opioids concluded that "While the severity of the opioid crisis became more apparent over time and the Federal Government and States launched initiatives to combat opioid abuse, FDA struggled to measure the effectiveness of the REMS for TIRF drugs and for ER/LA opioids in mitigating the misuse of opioids."[53] Though the agency was staffed with experts who possessed the training, skills, and knowledge to make informed decisions in the presence of such uncertainty, several years past before an accurate assessment of opioid risks took place. One explanation for this lag is the unintended consequences of the Prescription Drug User Fee Act ("PDUFA of 1992, which allowed the FDA to collect processing fees for new drug approvals in exchange for more expeditious reviews of applications. It has been argued that PDUFA shifted the FDA's focus away from post-market surveillance and toward new drug approval, in part to meet the goals of shorter review times but also due in part to the increasing interaction between FDA officials and manufacturers in the revised review processes.[54] Wang et al. summarized the problem this way: "The imbalance of FDA's new drug review and post-market safety review has become reliant on industry to detect risks only after its drug is on the market. The FDA had to prioritize speed over safety, thus aligning its goal with the pharmaceutical industry."[55] At the same time, misaligned incentives and asymmetrically distributed information among key stakeholders (mainly manufacturers, FDA, and physicians) likely exacerbated problems stemming from uncertainty.[56]

[52] The failure of the FDA in the initial approval process has in part been attributed to the design of the key clinical studies, which have been argued to have biased the results in favor of opioids, and continued to do so in subsequent post-market studies. See generally A. Kolodny, "How FDA Failures Contributed to the Opioid Crisis," *AMA J Ethics* 22, no. 1 (2020).

[53] OIG, "FDA's Risk Evaluation and Mitigation Strategies: Uncertain Effectiveness in Addressing the Opioid Crisis," (Washington, DC: U.S. Department of Health and Human Services, Office of Inspector General, 2020). The acronyms referenced in the quote are defined as follows: Risk Evaluation and Mitigation Strategy ("REMS"); Transmucosal immediate-release fentanyl ("TIRF"); and extended release/long-acting ("ER/LA").

[54] See, for example, W. Wang and A. I. Wertheimer, "History, status, and politicization of the FDA," *Research in Social and Administrative Pharmacy* 18, no. 5 (2022).

[55] Ibid.

[56] See generally A. Boloori et al., "Misalignment of Stakeholder Incentives in the Opioid Crisis," *Int J Environ Res Public Health* 17, no. 20 (2020).

Analogous to broader discussions of regulatory failure, the second explanation for FDA failure is that the agency poorly managed conflicts of interest and was believed to have been unduly influenced by special interests, including politicians, industry representatives, and professional medical societies. Evidence of influence has generally focused on two factors: (1) the changes initiated by PDUFA, which significantly increased industry's role in the drug approval process, and (2) the "revolving door" between the FDA and industry, which can create incentives for regulatory officials to accommodate industry needs to keep open the possibility of future employment in industry. Regarding the first influence factor, there is evidence that PDUFA encouraged greater industry collaboration, and some have argued that this alliance may have resulted in greater deference to industry input in the decision-making during the approval and post-market surveillance stages.[57] For example, according to Mitchell et al., "The majority of policy changes enacted through PDUFA legislation have favored industry through decreasing regulatory standards, shortening approval times, and increasing industry involvement in FDA decision-making. FDA's budgetary dependence on the industry, the urgency of each PDUFA reauthorization's passage to maintain uninterrupted funding, and the industry's required participation in PDUFA negotiations may advantage the industry."[58]

The second influence factor, the so-called "revolving door" effects, has also been discussed extensively in the literature.[59] For example, Doshi opined that "The revolving door between the FDA and industry surprises few anymore, despite the widely acknowledged potential it has for undermining public trust in government. And stories about FDA commissioners' heavy ties to industry have become commonplace: nine of the

[57] See generally A. P. Mitchell, N. U. Trivedi, and P. B. Bach, "The Prescription Drug User Fee Act: Much More Than User Fees," *Med Care* 60, no. 4 (2022); M. K. Olson, "Explaining reductions in FDA drug review times: PDUFA matters," *Health Aff (Millwood)* Suppl Web Exclusives (2003); Wang and Wertheimer, "History, status, and politicization of the FDA."

[58] Mitchell, Trivedi, and Bach, "The Prescription Drug User Fee Act: Much More Than User Fees."

[59] See, for example, P. Doshi, "Revolving doors: board memberships, hedge funds, and the FDA chiefs responsible for regulating industry," *BMJ* 385 (2024); S. Lupkin, "When Drug Reviewers Leave The FDA, They Often Work For Pharma," in *KFF Health News* (Washington, D.C.: Kaiser Family Foundation, 2016); Wang and Wertheimer, "History, status, and politicization of the FDA."

FDA's past 10 commissioners went on to work for the drug industry or serve on the board of directors of a drug company."[60] These reports were also made by Andrew Kolodny in his essay on FDA responsibility for the opioid crisis, arguing that "the 2 principal FDA reviewers who originally approved Purdue's oxycodone application both took positions at Purdue after leaving the agency. Over the past 20 years, several other FDA staff involved in opioid approvals also left the FDA to work for opioid makers."[61] More generally, as discussed in Chap. 4, there were a multitude of organizations clamoring for means to address the calls for more aggressive treatment of pain, and the lobbying efforts of these various organizations appeared to have spilled over to FDA functions through multiple pathways.[62]

Finally, it is likely that the delay by the FDA was in part the result of the adaptive features of bureaucracies, which lack design features and incentive structures to enable autonomous adaptation to exogenous factors. Perceived "disfunction" at the FDA has been identified as the cause of a number of problems, most of which fall into the two categories of (1) approving treatments in the absence of sufficient quality and safety data, or (2) improperly or unnecessarily delaying or withholding effective treatments from the market. In his critical assessment of the FDA, Miller likened these problems to the statistical concepts of Type 1 and Type 2 error, noting that "A regulator can err by permitting something bad to happen (e.g., approving a harmful product, a Type I error) or by preventing something salubrious from becoming available (e.g., not approving a beneficial product, a Type II error)."[63] These two types of errors are the result of very different incentives, but are both impacted by bureaucratic dysfunction. For example, during the COVID-19 pandemic, *Forbes* wrote that "The FDA's perpetual tardiness is a product of its culture—and the incentives its employees face. Agency officials don't get in trouble if a drug or medical device that could save lives never makes it to market. But if an

[60] Doshi, "Revolving doors: board memberships, hedge funds, and the FDA chiefs responsible for regulating industry."

[61] Kolodny, "How FDA Failures Contributed to the Opioid Crisis."

[62] See generally H. Fernandez Lynch, S. Joffe, and M. S. McCoy, "The limits of acceptable political influence over the FDA," *Nature Medicine* 27, no. 2 (2021); Wang and Wertheimer, "History, status, and politicization of the FDA."

[63] H. I. Miller, "The FDA: Challenges for a New Century, a Rough Road Ahead for Would-Be Reformers," *New York University Journal of Law & Liberty* 11 (2017).

FDA-approved product injures or kills someone, then the agency could take some serious blows from Congress and the public."[64] The "perpetual tardiness" has been echoed by other observers, with an in-depth analysis of FDA procedures published in *Science* observing that "FDA's enforcement of clinical research regulations is often light-handed, slow-moving, and secretive."[65]

The challenges faced by the FDA appeared to have been shared at least in part by the DEA. In world of hypothetical ideals, the opioid crisis would have been averted by the creation of a department or agency charged specifically with establishing production and distribution limits, particularly for prescription drugs with higher risks for serious adverse events and elevated risks for diversion. In a perfect world, such quotas would be based on rigorous statistical models of medical need. If that sounds too good to be true, it is not; these are exactly the roles assigned to the DEA in 1973. The failure of the DEA in preventing and mitigating the opioid crisis is also one attributable in large part to uncertainty and the relative costs of complex health information. This is evident in its struggles to accurately assess medical need for opioids. As argued in earlier chapters, there were a multitude of factors driving demand for opioids, and even the most advanced statistical models could only explain about 33% of the observed variation in opioid utilization. Thus, even under the best of circumstances, the derivation of production and manufacturer quotas delimited by objective measures of medical need is an ambitious undertaking. That is likely among the reasons why DEA quotas are based partly on past-year sales.[66] However, basing quotas on past year sales risks the propagation of estimation errors from one time period to the next. By most accounts, neither the FDA nor the DEA proved capable of evaluating the accuracy or appropriateness of the demand model results, nor the ramifications of *ad hoc* modifications of model results for the purpose of setting production and distribution quotas.[67] Thus, the inability of the DEA to accurately estimate medical need was due in part to the uncertainty associated with such modelling tasks and also in part to the inherent adaptability challenges of

[64] S. Pipes, "The FDA's Dysfunction Is a Public Health Crisis of Its Own," *Forbes* April 21 (2022).

[65] C. Piller, "Official Inaction," *Science* October 1 (2020).

[66] See, for example, GAO, "Controlled Substance Quotas," in *GAO/GGD-95-52 R* (Washington, D.C.: U.S. General Accounting Office, 1995).

[67] See generally NASEM, *Pain Management and the Opioid Epidemic: Balancing Societal and Indidivual Benefits and Risks of Prescription Opioid Use.*

bureaucracies. Not surprisingly, like the FDA, the DEA also appears to have been unduly influenced by special interests. The DEA's version of a revolving door was described in detail by investigative journalists Highman and Horwitz, who chronicled the inconsistent operations of the DEA during the opioid crisis, and the probable conflicts of interest among officers cycling between the DEA and manufacturers and distributors.[68]

Finally, the story of the CDC's ineffectiveness in managing the opioid crisis may simply be one of broad bureaucratic inertia, but it also appears to have been hampered by uncertainty regarding the scope of its functions. Having initially called upon the medical community, including insurers, to utilize their data in a monitoring and surveillance capacity to track opioid misuse and overdose, the CDC was relatively quiet on the topic for several years, even as some public health experts began using the term "epidemic" to describe the opioid crisis. It is unclear why the agency did not elevate its role as worrisome adverse event reports began to surface, but it seems plausible that CDC officials may have believed that FDA and DEA oversight would suffice. The only noteworthy action taken by the CDC was its issuance of opioid prescribing guidelines in 2016, but as discussed in Chap. 4, apart from the lagged response and potential conflicts of interest in the development process,[69] the guidelines caused considerable confusion among providers and are believed to have contributed to the undertreatment of pain.[70]

8.6.2 Opioid Litigation

The involvement of courts in the opioid crisis has highlighted many of the advantages and disadvantages of court ordering in resolving problems associated with medical products, particularly those preceded by regulatory

[68] S. Higham and S. Horwitz, *American Cartel: Inside the Battle to Bring Down the Opioid Industry* (New York, NY: Twelve / Hachette Book Group, 2022).

[69] D. H. Lin et al., "Financial Conflicts of Interest and the Centers for Disease Control and Prevention's 2016 Guideline for Prescribing Opioids for Chronic Pain," *JAMA Internal Medicine* 177, no. 3 (2017).

[70] See generally K. Humphreys et al., "Responding to the opioid crisis in North America and beyond: recommendations of the Stanford-Lancet Commission," *Lancet* 399, no. 10324 (2022); J. V. Pergolizzi, Jr., M. Rosenblatt, and J. A. LeQuang, "Three Years Down the Road: The Aftermath of the CDC Guideline for Prescribing Opioids for Chronic Pain," *Adv Ther* 36, no. 6 (2019); J. F. Scherrer et al., "Comparison of Opioids Prescribed for Patients at Risk for Opioid Misuse Before and After Publication of the Centers for Disease Control and Prevention's Opioid Prescribing Guidelines," *JAMA Netw Open* 3, no. 12 (2020).

failure. Starting with the positive features, litigation appears to have accomplished at least three objectives. First, the adaptive features of litigation were advantageous given the bureaucratic inertia on behalf of the regulatory agencies. Cases were filed in three waves, but the first and second iterations were filed in early 2000s,[71] shortly after the first round of reports of elevated risk of dependency and overdose, and at least a decade before any meaningful corrective action was taken by any of the three regulatory agencies.[72] The second advantage of courts was in deterrence. Even as most of the initial individual cases of the early 2000s were dismissed on summary judgment, the second wave of state and local cases gained traction, and the publicity surrounding the initial round of settlements prompted the DEA to pursue legal action against pill mills and other high-volume prescribers.[73] The aggregate impact of these developments served to a create a "chilling effect" on opioid prescribers, which contributed to the precipitous decline in opioid prescribing that started around 2012.[74] Once the litigation was consolidated in the MDL, and broadened to include distributors, pharmacies, and some other components of the supply chain, the deterrence factor intensified, and likely contributed at least in part to the wave of settlements in the mid-2020s, as well as encouraging the proliferation of some policy solutions to the crisis, such as the CDC's opioid prescribing guidelines.[75]

[71] See generally R. L. Haffajee, "The Public Health Value of Opioid Litigation," *J Law Med Ethics* 48, no. 2 (2020).

[72] See generally M. R. Jones et al., "A Brief History of the Opioid Epidemic and Strategies for Pain Medicine," *Pain Ther* 7, no. 1 (2018); G. K. Singh et al., "Opioid Epidemic in the United States: Empirical Trends, and A Literature Review of Social Determinants and Epidemiological, Pain Management, and Treatment Patterns," *Int J MCH AIDS* 8, no. 2 (2019).

[73] See generally Haffajee, "The Public Health Value of Opioid Litigation."; A. B. Lemann, "The Opioid Litigation's Challenge for Tort Theory," *Brooklyn Law Review* 90, no. 4 (2025).

[74] See, for example, C. L. Sedney et al., ""The DEA would come in and destroy you": a qualitative study of fear and unintended consequences among opioid prescribers in WV," *Subst Abuse Treat Prev Policy* 17, no. 1 (2022); Haffajee, "The Public Health Value of Opioid Litigation."; C. Schmidt, "Experts Worry About Chilling Effect of Federal Regulations on Treating Pain," *JNCI: Journal of the National Cancer Institute* 97, no. 8 (2005); L.R. Webster, "The Chilling Effect: Opioids and Law Enforcement," in *The Painful Truth: What Chronic Pain Is Really Like and Why It Matters to Each of Us*, ed. L. R. Webster (New York, NY: Oxford University Press, 2016).

[75] See, for example, I. J. Rao, K. Humphreys, and M. L. Brandeau, "Effectiveness of Policies for Addressing the US Opioid Epidemic: A Model-Based Analysis from the Stanford-Lancet Commission on the North American Opioid Crisis," *The Lancet Regional Health—Americas* 3 (2021).

The positive aspects of the litigation were offset by a number of important drawbacks, some of which were discussed earlier. First, in terms of administrative costs, it is likely that the total costs of opioid litigation, after the final cases are resolved, will have far exceeded the costs of organizational modifications to the regulatory mechanisms and processes employed by the FDA, DEA, and CDC. Insurance industry estimates indicate that the total costs of opioid litigation, which are believed to be at least $230 billion as of 2025, are rapidly approaching the aggregate costs of the ongoing asbestos litigation.[76] Second, the same "chilling effect" that curtailed utilization of prescription opioids is also believed to have contributed to the undertreatment of pain, likely due to the "blunt instrument" aspects of litigation, which can result in spillover effects beyond the scope considered by the courts.[77] Third, the migration of the opioid crisis into the realm of the courts resulted in the perpetuation of a relatively narrow view of causation, beginning with manufacturers in the individual cases but expanding only marginally thereafter, even after more than a decade of reports identifying other critical causal factors. To be sure, it would not normally be the responsibility of the courts to identify all causal factors, but in the case of opioids, it could be argued that the decades-long focus on manufacturers, distributors, and pharmacies served as a distraction from the identification of root causes and the subsequent implementation of targeted solutions aimed at those root causes. This is especially important because there were two channels through which opioids were getting into the hands of misusers—prescription opioids via the health system and illicit opioids via drug traffickers and dealers—only one of which was addressed as part of the opioid MDL. This raises a related limitation of court ordering brought to light by the opioid litigation, which is that mass tort litigation tends to default to readily identifiable defendants and causal factors, and is largely indifferent as to whether the final pool of identified defendants are responsible for 90% of the total harm or 5% of the total harm. From an abatement and mitigation perspective, this is clearly one of the drawbacks of reliance on court ordering.

[76] E. Bragg and V. Despotaki, "How Much Will Opioid Litigation Cost Insurers?," in *Emerging Issues Weekly Newsletter* (Jersey City, NJ: Verisk Analytics, 2023).

[77] See generally Hackworth et al., "Burden of Acute Pain."; Schmidt, "Experts Worry About Chilling Effect of Federal Regulations on Treating Pain."; Webster, "The Chilling Effect: Opioids and Law Enforcement."

The fourth limitation of the courts in addressing the opioid crisis is their inability to cultivate an accurate portrayal of damages from either side. Given the cost ceiling analyses presented earlier, it is clear that the courts were, at best, a blunt instrument in terms of fostering the identification of true and accurate attributable costs and abatement costs. In addition to the usual uncertainty associated with calculating future costs, especially healthcare costs, claimants faced powerful incentives to overstate costs.[78] This was evident in the "kitchen sink" approach put forward in the Ohio county pharmacy cases, coupled with the lack of basic adjustments for intuitive issues like the proportion of opioids sourced from the healthcare system, fixed versus variable costs of abatement programs, and federal cost sharing. Again, in the Ohio county cases, the judge himself commented on the excesses of claimants' abatement cost estimations.[79] Similarly, defendants were reluctant to conduct their own calculations of abatement costs, likely due to concerns that such calculations would establish a cost floor.[80] Thus, what was really needed—an accurate assessment of abatement costs—never materialized in the course of the proceedings. Of course, it is expected that claimants and defendants will bring differing damages and abatement amounts to trial, but a potentially larger problem is that juries have also been shown to struggle in the determination of damages, let alone those based on complex, multifaceted, and long-term abatement cost estimations.[81]

[78] Incentives for claimants to overstate damages have been discussed generally. See, for example, E. Zervogianni, "Remedies for damage to property: money damages or restitution in natura?," *International Review of Law and Economics* 24, no. 4 (2004). Regarding claimants in the opioid litigation, see generally C. J. Masterman, "Opioid Settlements and Profitable Public Nuisances," *Touro L. Rev.* 40, no. 393 (2025).

[79] Opioid MDL, "MDL 2804 Case No. 1:17-md-2804 Judge Dan Aaron Polster: Abatement Order," in *Re: National Opioid Litigation* (Ohio: United States District Court Northern District of Ohio, Eastern Division, 2022). The relevant quote was "... the Plaintiffs' plan is unrealistic because it asks for the sun and the moon: over $3.0 Billion from these three Defendants alone, jointly and severally." (§I.)

[80] Ibid. The relevant quote was "Defendants also largely ignored the Court's directives to submit their own proposed abatement plan, and not to merely attack and criticize Plaintiffs' proposed abatement plan. Despite the Court's order that the parties each propose a detailed plan for abatement, initially only the Plaintiffs proposed one. Upon further Court order compelling them to submit a plan, Defendants eventually submitted three paragraphs suggesting a proper abatement remedy would be comprised of drug takeback programs to facilitate disposal of diverted opioids-and nothing more." (§I.)

[81] See, for example, W. K. Viscusi, "Corporate Risk Analysis: A Reckless Act?," *Stanford Law Review* 52, no. 3 (2000).

8.7 Regulation or Litigation?

This brings us to the question regarding which of the governance options, regulation or litigation, represents the "better" approach to managing the risks associated with pharmaceutical drugs? Globally, there is a general consensus that the inherent risks of pharmaceutical transactions imply that some form of government regulation is the preferred form of governance.[82] Consequently, the question of whether transactions for pharmaceuticals are better suited to *ex ante* regulatory governance versus *ex post* court ordering reduces to two pivotal governance issues: (1) the identification of specific components and mechanisms of the pharmaceutical regulatory process that either failed or are otherwise in need of reform; and (2) the specific elements of the regulatory apparatus, regardless of success or failure, that are more efficiently left for the courts to administer. If regulatory functions can be improved such that the drug approval and subsequent monitoring processes are sufficient to prevent another crisis similar to opioids, recourse to product liability litigation would be needed much less frequently and perhaps invoked before problems accelerate and harms accumulate. However, it may also be the case that, irrespective of the functionality of some regulatory processes, some components may be most efficiently delegated to the courts.

The first governance issue is a standard "regulatory reform" story, of which there were many during the era of deregulation in the 1970s and 1980s.[83] These reforms were radical and mostly eliminated various types of economic controls, such as administered pricing, in favor of mechanisms aimed at promoting market incentives while continuing to enforce quality and safety standards.[84] The focus of this first wave of regulatory reform was the large government agencies that emerged from the era of controls on economic activity "affected by the public interest," such as transportation, telecommunications, and public utilities. Though some other agencies were swept up in the reform movement, the ones not employing economic mechanisms were largely left alone. Among these

[82] See generally Reinhardt, "The Pharmaceutical Sector in Health Care."

[83] See, for example, P. W. MacAvoy, ed. *The Crisis of the Regulatory Commissions* Problems of the Modern Economy (New York: W.W. Norton & Company, Inc., 1970).

[84] There are several comprehensive discussions of the causes and effects of deregulation; see, for example, M. Derthick and P. J. Quirk, "Why the Regulators Chose to Deregulate," in *Regulatory Policy and the Social Sciences*, ed. R. C. Noll (Berkeley, CA: University of California Press, 1985); Vietor, *Contrived Competition: Regulation and Deregulation in America*.

were the FDA, DEA, and CDC. While the FDA is often a target of calls for reforms, changes have been incremental and mainly aimed at ways in which to scale up its capacity to evaluate new drugs. The litany of proposed FDA reforms in the recent past would warrant an entire separate chapter, but to briefly summarize, reform proposals on the medical products side of the FDA have generally included some version of the following: (1) strengthening standards and controls aimed at conflicts of interest, particularly those surrounding the "revolving door" problem;[85] (2) rebalancing the priorities for the agency such that post-market surveillance and monitoring processes can be provided more resources and support;[86] (3) streamlining the drug and device approval process, without compromising health and safety, to assure that novel high-value products reach the market faster;[87] (4) improvements in the quality standards for clinical studies, including conflicts of interest on the part of study investigators, the appropriateness of study design, and the integrity of the research process;[88] and (5) various reorganization schemes, nominally intended to reduce bureaucratic layers and better capture economies of scale and scope among the broad spectrum of agency functions.[89] Specific to opioids, among these efforts it is the first, second, and fourth groups of reform efforts that could have potentially, if implemented effectively, impacted the trajectory of the opioid crisis.

The second governance issue, which is identifying the functions of the regulatory apparatus that may be more efficiently delivered by the courts, is conceptually similar to organizational issues routinely arising in private enterprise in the presence of complex transactions and externalities, where firms face incentives to seek the most efficient "boundaries of the firm" to accomplish organizational goals, engaging in what Williamson refers to as

[85] For a detailed discussion of this issue, see L. Karas, "FDA's Revolving Door: Reckoning and Reform," *Stanford Law & Policy Review* 34, no. 1 (2023).

[86] See generally OIG, "FDA's Risk Evaluation and Mitigation Strategies: Uncertain Effectiveness in Addressing the Opioid Crisis."; Olson, "Explaining reductions in FDA drug review times: PDUFA matters."; Mitchell, Trivedi, and Bach, "The Prescription Drug User Fee Act: Much More Than User Fees."

[87] See, for example, Miller, "The FDA: Challenges for a New Century, a Rough Road Ahead for Would-Be Reformers."

[88] See generally Piller, "Official Inaction."

[89] See, for example, S. Gottlieb and M. B. McClellan, "Why a Planned Reorganization of the FDA Creates Major Challenges," *JAMA Health Forum* 6, no. 5 (2025).

"first-order economizing."[90] Given the potential harms associated with prescription drugs with significant probabilities of serious adverse events, it is unlikely that any of the FDA's prescription drug regulatory functions could intentionally be relegated to the courts. Moreover, there are some important practical considerations. The FDA approves on average more than 50 new pharmaceutical drugs each year.[91] Accordingly, any sort of systematic reliance on *ex post* litigation to govern product quality would likely be associated with excessively high costs and avoidable harms, which in turn would make such an approach less efficient than alternatives.

Instead, a more efficient approach might be to identify a subset of medical products whose risk profile might justify explicit acknowledgement of an elevated likelihood of post-market litigation. Such products would receive a higher level of pre-market and post-market vetting, but in addition, the expected costs of post-market harms and litigation costs could be factored into FDA risk-benefit analyses. Revisiting the discussion of acceptable risk (Chap. 7), the drug approval process and the post-market surveillance process are both substantially impacted by uncertainty and are both candidates for the same type of acceptable risk modelling that was alluded to earlier. In other words, there is a risk level whereby the FDA faces a critical decision: (1) they could either *ex ante* deny approval, or (2) they could approve, but with significant *ex post* risk management. The latter satisfies the organizational objective of getting potentially high-value drugs to market sooner, but with added risk. For some drugs and devices, post-market risks are known to be considerably high. For these types of products, there is likely some level of added risk such that the optimal solution may be the empirical incorporatiodn of the expected costs and expected benefits of post-market litigation into formal cost-benefit and risk-benefit models. In other words, regulators would recognize situations featuring high uncertainty and elevated probability of the occurrence of serious adverse events and would approach the risk-benefit assessment with the understanding that courts may necessarily be relied upon to fill potential (and presumably unavoidable) obstacles to optimal oversight. Given that one of the benefits of court ordering is its ability to

[90] Williamson, "Comparative Economic Organization: The Analysis of Discrete Structural Alternatives."; J. Roberts, *The Modern Firm: Organizational Design for Performance and Growth* (Oxford, UK: Oxford University Press, 2004).

[91] B. G. de la Torre and F. Albericio, "The Pharmaceutical Industry in 2023: An Analysis of FDA Drug Approvals from the Perspective of Molecules," *Molecules* 29, no. 3 (2024).

act relatively quickly, such explicit reliance could be considered a reasonable governance alternative.

Conceptually, this "make or buy" approach to government regulation is akin to what Posner describes as a "mixed" or "hybrid" approach, which Posner submits has the potential to "exploit the complementarities between agencies and courts."[92] Similarly, Helland and Klick observe that insofar as litigation and regulation substitute for each other in the deterrence of harmful activities, then we can best view class actions not as a procedural device designed to facilitate individual litigation but as one part of the larger structure of administrative regulation."[93] The authors further posit that "As a second best solution, in cases where regulators lack information or enforcement resources, class actions have the potential to play a role in an optimal regulatory design."[94] Helland and Klick's own empirical analysis of claims against insurance companies found no evidence that regulation and litigation substitute for each other; instead, their findings suggest that regulation and litigation tend to "piggyback on each other." It makes sense that the roles of regulators and courts would be complementary, but it is important to emphasize that the interplay between regulators and courts could be part of a designed process, one intended to identify high-risk products *ex ante* with consideration of *ex post* litigation in the overall cost-benefit calculus. Such intentionality in the design of regulatory mechanisms would also de facto encourage the courts to improve standards and processes regarding product liability.

8.8 Chapter Summary

The U.S. opioid crisis has been defined by its pushing of regulatory agencies to their limits, and filling regulatory gaps with product liability litigation that, in the end, also struggled to deal with the myriad challenges posed by opioids. Accordingly, this chapter explored the fundamental tension between *ex ante* regulation and *ex post* litigation in the handling of the opioid crisis, adopting a comparative governance approach that highlighted the pros and cons of regulation versus litigation in governing

[92] Posner, "Regulation (Agencies) versus Litigation (Courts)."

[93] Helland and Klick, "The Tradeoffs between Regulation and Litigation: Evidence from Insurance Class Actions."

[94] Ibid.

complex externalities and transactions, such as those associated with high-risk medical products generally and opioids specifically. The opioid crisis has highlighted some important limitations of the existing prescription drug regulatory apparatus, including excessive bureaucracy and disproportionate attention on pre-market approval versus post-market surveillance. Given the importance of the laboratory of the "real world" in improving the understanding of the effectiveness and risks of medical products, it makes sense that the strengthening of post-market surveillance should be part of any FDA and DEA reform efforts. However, as the discussion in this chapter implied, there may be good reasons to assume that, for products with particularly high risks, the probability of post-market litigation should be considered in risk-benefit and cost-benefit analyses or at least acknowledged so that efforts can also be directed to improving how courts deal with medical products liability matters.

References

Arrow, K. J. (1963, December). Uncertainty and the welfare economics of medical care. *The American Economic Review*, *53*(5), 941–973.

Avorn, J. (2007, Febuary 9). The marketplace can't give us the drug safety data we need. *MedGenMed*, *9*(1), 29.

Bernstein, M. H. (1972). Independent regulatory agencies: A perspective on their reform. *Annals of the American Academy of Political and Social Science*, *400* (March).

Boloori, A., Arnetz, B. B., Viens, F., Maiti, T., & Arnetz, J. E. (2020, October 16). Misalignment of stakeholder incentives in the opioid crisis. *International Journal of Environmental Research and Public Health*, *17*(20).

Borchers, A. T., Hagie, F., Keen, C. L., & Gershwin, M. E. (2007, January). The history and contemporary challenges of the US food and drug administration. *Clinical Therapeutics*, *29*(1), 1–16.

Bown, C. P. (2022, January). How COVID-19 medical supply shortages led to extraordinary trade and industrial policy. *17*(1), 114–135.

Bragg, E., & Despotaki, V. (2023). How much will opioid litigation cost insurers? In *Emerging Issues Weekly Newsletter*. Verisk Analytics.

Breyer, S. (1982). *Regulation and its reform*. Harvard University Press.

Brill, E. R., Chan, P. H., Chang, R. N., Prentice, H. A., Sucher, K., Bell, R. L., Mostaedi, R., & Paxton, E. W. (2025, October 29). Postmarket surveillance of mesh performance after inguinal hernia repair. *JAMA Surg*.

Buchholz, T., Calabresi, G., Kessler, D., Viscusi, W. K., & Warren, E. (2000). Litigation or government regulation? In CLP (Ed.), *Conference series: Litigation through regulation: Assessing the role of bounty hunters and bureaucrats in the American regulatory regime*. Manhattan Institute, Center for Legal Policy.

Ciociola, A. A., Cohen, L. B., & Kulkarni, P. (2014, May). How drugs are developed and approved by the FDA: Current process and future directions. *American Journal of Gastroenterology, 109*(5) 620–623.

Coase, R. H. (1937, November). The nature of the firm. *Economica, 4*.

Coase, R. H. (1960). The problem of social cost. *Journal of Law and Economics, 3*, 1–44.

Coglianese, C. (2017). The limits of performance-based regulation. *University of Michigan Journal of Law Reform, 50*(3).

Cutler, D. M., & Zeckhauser, R. J. (1998). Adverse selection in health insurance. In A. M. Garber (Ed.), *Frontiers in health policy research*. MIT Press.

Dafny, L. (2021). Addressing Consolidation in health care markets. *JAMA, 325* (10), 927–928.

Danzon, P. M., & Nicholson, S. (2012). *The oxford handbook of the economics of the biopharmaceutical industry*. Oxford University Press.

de la Torre, B. G., & Albericio, F. (2024, January 25). The pharmaceutical industry in 2023: An analysis of FDA drug approvals from the perspective of molecules. *Molecules, 29*(3).

Derthick, M., & Quirk, P. J. (1985). Why the regulators chose to deregulate. In R. C. Noll (Ed.), *Regulatory policy and the social sciences*. University of California Press.

Doshi, P. (2024). Revolving doors: Board memberships, hedge funds, and the FDA chiefs responsible for regulating industry. *BMJ, 385*, q975.

Elwell, D. A. (2020). Industry-Influenced evidence: Bias, conflict, and manipulation in scientific evidence. *Boston College Law Review, 61*(6).

Fernandez Lynch, H., Joffe, S., & McCoy, M. S. (2021, January 2). The limits of acceptable political influence over the FDA. *Nature Medicine, 27*(2), 188–190.

GAO. (1995). *Controlled substance quotas*. In GAO/GGD-95-52R. U.S. General Accounting Office.

Goldberg, V. P. (1976). Regulation and administered contracts. *Bell Journal of Economics, 7*(2), 426–448. Autumn.

Goldberg, V. P. (1989). Relational Exchange: Economics and Complex Contracts. In V. P. Goldberg (Ed.), *Readings in the economics of contract law*. Cambridge University Press.

Goldberg, V. P. (2002). Relational Contract. In P. Newman (Ed.), *The new palgrave dictionary of economics and the law: Volume 1–3: A–Z* (pp. 1689–1694). Palgrave Macmillan UK.

Gottlieb, S., & McClellan, M. B. (2025). Why a planned reorganization of the FDA creates major challenges. *JAMA Health Forum, 6*(5), e252326.

Grossman, G. M., & Helpman, E. (2001). *Special interest politics*. The MIT Press.

Hackworth, J. C., Schneider, J. E., Valle, M. D., Fam, D., Argoff, C., Offidani, E., & Potenziano, J. (2025, October 7). The burden of acute pain in the U.S. in the wake of the opioid crisis. *Frontiers in Pain Research, 6.*

Haffajee, R. L. (2020, June). The public health value of opioid litigation. *Journal of Law, Medicine & Ethics, 48*(2), 279–292.

Hammer, P. J., Haas-wilson, D., Peterson, M. A., & Sage, W. M. (2003). *Uncertain times: Kenneth arrow and the changing economics of health care.* Duke University Press.

Helland, E., & Klick, J. (2006). The tradeoffs between regulation and litigation: Evidence from insurance class actions. *Journal of Tort Law, 1*(3).

Hensler, D. R., & Peterson, M. A. (1995). Understanding mass personal injury litigation. In *Research summary.* RAND Corporation.

Higham, S., & Horwitz, S. (2022). *American cartel: Inside the battle to bring down the opioid industry.* Twelve/Hachette Book Group.

Humphreys, K., Shover, C. L., Andrews, C. M., Bohnert, A. S. B., Brandeau, M. L., Caulkins, J. P., Chen, J. H., et al. (2022, Febuary 5). Responding to the opioid crisis in North America and beyond: Recommendations of the Stanford-Lancet Commission. *Lancet, 399*(10324), 555–604.

Hwang, C. S., Turner, L. W., Kruszewski, S. P., Kolodny, A., & Alexander, G. C. (2016). Primary care physicians' knowledge and attitudes regarding prescription opioid abuse and diversion. *The Clinical Journal of Pain, 32*(4).

Jones, M. R., Viswanath, O., Peck, J., Kaye, A. D., Gill, J. S., & Simopoulos, T. T. (2018, June). A brief history of the opioid epidemic and strategies for pain medicine. *Pain and Therapy, 7*(1) 13–21.

Joskow, P. L. (1987, March). Contract duration of relationship-specific investments: Empirical evidence from coal markets. *American Economic Review, 77* (1), 168–185.

Joskow, P. L., & Noll, R. C. (1981). Regulation in theory and practice: An overview. In G. Fromm (Ed.), *Studies in public regulation.* The MIT Press.

Kahn, A. E. (1988). *The economics of regulation: Principles and institutions.* The MIT Press.

Karas, L. (2023). FDA's revolving door: Reckoning and reform. *Stanford Law & Policy Review, 34*(1).

Kessler, D. P. (2011). *Regulation versus litigation: Perspectives from law and economics.* The University of Chicago Press.

Kolodny, A. (2020, August 1). How FDA failures contributed to the opioid crisis. *AMA Journal of Ethics, 22*(1), E743–E750.

Krislov, S., & Musolf, L. D. (1964). *The politics of regulation.* Houghton Mifflin Company.

Landrum, M. A. (2000). Through the mists: ADR and product liability claims in the Twenty-first Century. *William Mitchell Law Review, 27*(1).

Lemann, A. B. (2025). The opioid litigation's challenge for tort theory. *Brooklyn Law Review*, *90*(4).
Leone, R. C. (1972). Public interest advocacy and the regulatory process. *Annals of the American Academy of Political and Social Science*, *400*(March).
Lin, D. H., Lucas, E., Murimi, I. B., Kolodny, A., & Alexander, G. C. (2017). Financial conflicts of interest and the centers for disease control and prevention's 2016 guideline for prescribing opioids for chronic pain. *JAMA Internal Medicine*, *177*(3), 427–428.
Lupkin, S. (2016). When drug reviewers leave the fda, they often work for pharma. In *KFF Health News*. Kaiser Family Foundation.
MacAvoy, P. W., (Ed.). (1970). The crisis of the regulatory commissions. Edited by E.S. Phelps, *Problems of the modern economy*. W.W. Norton & Company, Inc.
Malani, A., & Philipson, T. (2012). The regulation of medical products. Edited by P. M. Danzon & S. Nicholson, *Chap. 5 In the economics of the biopharmaceutical industry*. Oxford University Press.
March, J. G., & Simon, H. A. (1958). *Organizations*. John Wiley & Sons, Inc.
Masten, S. E., & Crocker, K. J. (1985, December). Efficient adaptation in long-term contracts: Take-or-Pay provisions for natural gas. *American Economic Review*, *75*(5), 1083–1093.
Masten, S. E., Meehan, J. W., & Snyder, E. A. (1989, January 10). Vertical integration in the U.S. auto industry: A note on the influence of transaction specific assets. *Journal of Economic Behavior & Organization*, *12*(2), 265–273.
Masterman, C. J. (2025). Opioid settlements and profitable public nuisances. *Touro Law Review*, *40*(393).
Mehran, R., Leon, M. B., Feigal, D. A., Jefferys, D., Simons, M., Chronos, N., Fogarty, T. J., et al. (2004, June 29). Post-market approval surveillance: A call for a more integrated and comprehensive approach. *Circulation*, *109*(25), 3073–3077.
Mehta, S. S. (2008). *Commercializing successful biomedical technologies: Basic principles for the development of drugs, diagnostics and devices*. Cambridge University Press.
Menard, C., & Shirley, M. M. (Eds.). (2008). *Handbook of the new institutional economics*. Springer.
Meyer, R. J. (2007, August). Regulatory considerations for determining postmarketing study commitments. *Clinical Pharmacology & Therapeutics*, *82*(2), 228–230.
Miller, H. I. (2017). The FDA: Challenges for a new century, a rough road ahead for would-be reformers. *New York University Journal of Law & Liberty*, *11*, 803–837.
Mitchel, J. T. (2000, September). FDA relations during drug development. *Dialogues in Clinical Neuroscience*, *2*(3), 213–217.
Mitchell, A. P., Trivedi, N. U., & Bach, P. B. (2022, April 1). The prescription drug user fee act: Much more than user fees. *Medical Care*, *60*(4), 287–293.

NASEM. (2017). *Pain management and the opioid epidemic: Balancing societal and indidivual benefits and risks of prescription opioid use. Consensus study report of national academies of sciences, engineering and medicine (NASEM)*. Edited by R. J. Bonnie, M. A. Ford, & J. K. Phillips. National Academies Press.
Noll, R. G. (1985). Government regulatory behavior: A multidisciplinary survey and synthesis. In R. G. Noll (Ed.), *Regulatory policy and the social sciences.* University of California Press.
O'Driscoll, G. P., & Hoskins, L. (2006). The case for market-based regulation. *Cato Journal, 26*(3).
Ogus, A. (1994). *Regulation: Legal form and economic theory. Clarendon law series.* Oxford Univeristy Press.
Ohsfeldt, R. L., Li, P., & Schneider, J. E. (2015, December). In-office magnetic resonance imaging (MRI) equipment ownership and MRI volume among medicare patients in orthopedic practices. *Health Economics Review, 5*(1), 31.
OIG. (2020). *FDA's risk evaluation and mitigation strategies: Uncertain effectiveness in addressing the opioid crisis.* U.S. Department of Health and Human Services, Office of Inspector General.
Olson, M. K. (2003, July-December). Explaining reductions in FDA drug review times: PDUFA matters. *Health Affairs (Millwood) Supplement Web Exclusives*, W4–s1–w4–s2.
Opioid, M. D. L. (2022). MDL 2804 Case No. 1:17-md-2804 Judge Dan Aaron Polster: Abatement Order. *Re: National Opioid Litigation.* United States District Court Northern District of Ohio, Eastern Division.
Papandreou, A. A. (1994). *Externality and Institutions.* Clarendon Press.
Pentin, P. L. (2013, May 1). Drug seeking or pain crisis? Responsible prescribing of opioids in the emergency department. *Virtual Mentor, 15*(5), 410–415.
Pergolizzi Jr, J. V., Rosenblatt, M., & LeQuang, J. A. (2019, June). Three years down the road: The aftermath of the cdc guideline for prescribing opioids for chronic pain. *Advances in Therapy, 36*(6) 1235–1240.
Philipson, T. J., Sun, E., & Goldman, D. (2011). The effects of product liability exemption in the presence of the FDA. In D. P. Kessler (Ed.), *Regulation versus litigation: Perspectives from economics and law.* National Bureau of Economic Research | The University of Chicago Press.
Piller, C. (2020, October 1). Official Inaction. *Science.*
Pipes, S. (2022, April 21). The FDA's dysfunction is a public health crisis of its own. *Forbes.*
Posner, R. A. (2011). Regulation (Agencies) versus Litigation (Courts). In D. P. Kessler (Ed.), *Regulation versus litigation: Perspectives from economics and law.* The University of Chicago Press.
Quirk, P. J. (2016). *Industry influence in federal regulatory agencies.* Princeton University Press.

Rao, I. J., Humphreys, K., & Brandeau, M. L. (2021). Effectiveness of policies for addressing the us opioid epidemic: A Model-based analysis from the stanford-lancet commission on the north american opioid crisis. *The Lancet Regional Health – Americas, 3.*

Reinhardt, U. E. (2007). The pharmaceutical sector in health care. In F. A. Sloan & C. R. Hsieh (Eds.), *Pharmaceutical innovation: Incentives, competition, and cost-benefit analysis in international perspective.* Cambridge University Press.

Rhodes, T., & Lancaster, K. (2023, January 7). Early warnings and slow deaths: A sociology of outbreak and overdose *International Journal of Drug Policy, 117*, 104065.

Roberts, J. (2004). *The modern firm: Organizational design for performance and growth.* Oxford University Press.

Schauer, F., & Zeckhauser, R. J. (2011). The trouble with cases. In D. P. Kessler (Ed.), *Regulation versus litigation: Perspectives from economics and law.* The University of Chicago Press.

Scherrer, J. F., Tucker, J., Salas, J., Zhang, Z., & Grucza, R. (2020, December 1) Comparison of opioids prescribed for patients at risk for opioid misuse before and after publication of the centers for disease control and prevention's opioid prescribing guidelines. *JAMA Network Open, 3*(12) e2027481.

Schmidt, C. (2005). Experts worry about chilling effect of federal regulations on treating pain. *JNCI: Journal of the National Cancer Institute, 97*(8), 554–555.

Schneider, J. E. (2003, January 6). Changes in the effects of mandatory rate regulation on growth in hospital operating costs, 1980–1996. *Review of Industrial Organization, 22*(4), 297–312.

Sedney, C. L., Haggerty, T., Dekeseredy, P., Nwafor, D., Caretta, M. A., Brownstein, H. H., & Pollini, R. A. (2022, March 10). The DEA would come in and destroy you: A qualitative study of fear and unintended consequences among opioid prescribers in WV. *Substance Abuse Treatment, Prevention, and Policy, 17*(1), 19.

Singh, G. K., Kim, I. E., Girmay, M., Perry, C., Daus, G. P., Vedamuthu, I. P., Reyes, A. A. D. L., et al. (2019). Opioid epidemic in the united states: Empirical trends, and a literature review of social determinants and epidemiological, pain management, and treatment patterns. *International Journal of Maternal and Child Health and AIDS, 8*(2), 89–100.

Smith, G. E., Venkatraman, M. P., & Dholakia, R. R. (1999, January 6). Diagnosing the search cost effect: Waiting time and the moderating impact of prior category knowledge. *Journal of Economic Psychology, 20*(3), 285–314.

Snail, T. S., & Robinson, J. C. (1998). Organizational diversification in the American hospital. *Annual Review of Public Health, 19*, 417–453.

Spivak, J. M. (1972). Regulation of medical devices. *Annals of the American Academy of Political and Social Science, 400*(March), 82–94.

Sunstein, C. R., Hastie, R., Payne, J. W., Schkade, D. A., & Viscusi, W. K. (2002). *Punitive Damages: How Juries Decide*. University of Chicago Press.
Vietor, R. H. K. (1994). *Contrived competition: Regulation and deregulation in America*. The Belknap Press of Harvard University Press.
Viscusi, W. K. (2000). Corporate risk analysis: A reckless act? *Stanford Law Review*, *52*(3), 547–597.
Viscusi, W. K., & Hersch, J. (2011). Tobacco regulation through litigation. In D. P. Kessler (Ed.), *Regulation versus litigation: Perspectives from economics and law*. National Bureau of Economic Research & The University of Chicago Press.
Viscusi, W. K., Vernon, J. M., & Harrington, J. E. (1995). *Economics of regulation and antitrust* (2nd ed.). The MIT Press.
Wang, W., & Wertheimer, A. I. (2022, January 5). History, status, and politicization of the FDA. *Research in Social and Administrative Pharmacy*, *18*(5), 2811–2816.
Webster, L. R. (2016). The chilling effect: Opioids and law enforcement. In L. R. Webster (Ed.), *The painful truth: What chronic pain is really like and why it matters to each of us*. Oxford University Press.
Williamson, O. E. (1979). Transaction-cost economics: The governance of contractual relations. *Journal of Law and Economics*, *22*(2), 233–261.
Williamson, O. E. (1991). Comparative economic organization: The analysis of discrete structural alternatives. *Administrative Science Quarterly*, *36*(June), 269–296.
Williamson, O. E. (1996). *The mechanisms of governance*. Oxford Univeristy Press.
Zervogianni, E. (2004, January 12). Remedies for damage to property: Money damages or restitution in natura? *International Review of Law and Economics*, *24*(4), 525–541.

CHAPTER 9

Conclusions and Recommendations

The principal aim of this book has been to determine the causal factors underlying the U.S. opioid crisis, develop accurate estimates of the attributable costs and abatement costs associated with harms attributable to the increase in opioid supply, and to explore some of the regulatory issues that contributed to the crisis. In addition, the discussion throughout the book has highlighted how the analysis of product liability and externalities can become very challenging in the presence of complicated epidemiological factors, multifaceted supply chain dynamics, and uncertainty in the magnitude and prevalence of serious adverse events. Moreover, the externality in question, harm-incurring OUD, is not the result of a product defect and in most instances does not result from product misuse or manufacturer failure to warn. Although healthcare companies have been the primary defendants in the litigation, there is an illicit version of the product that is significantly more dangerous, more likely to be misused by those with existing substance use disorders, and more likely to result in negative externalities. Illicit drugs are not sourced from the health system and therefore are unaffected by health system change or litigation aimed at health sector components. Thus, mitigation policies aimed solely at specific pieces of the healthcare system are likely to have limited value as trends toward utilization of illicit opioids continues. The principal defendants in the opioid litigation represent only one fifth of the supply chain components, despite the incontrovertible fact that not a single prescription opioid could have reached the U.S. market

J. E. Schneider, *The Economics of Pain*, Global Perspectives on Wealth and Distribution,
https://doi.org/10.1007/978-3-032-20355-7_9

without the explicit and purposeful actions of numerous levels of the prescription drug supply chain. These members of the supply chain, which included an array of public and private regulators and health care providers, continued to supply opioids to the market for more than a decade after it became known that the drugs were associated with overuse and substance use disorder among certain subgroups of the population. Finally, claimants in the opioid matter have largely missed the opportunity for accuracy in the calculation of abatement costs, instead putting forward abatement amounts that, if extrapolated to the national level, would far exceed the total gross domestic product of most mid-sized countries.

9.1 Product Liability

The opioid MDL is not a product defect liability case, mainly because opioids continue to be prescribed for clinical use, in most cases in the exact same formulations and packaging as the products generally associated with the origins of the crisis. Another reason that prescription opioids are not considered defective or extraordinarily dangerous is because they were explicitly approved by regulators *ex ante*, in the exact same formulations found in past and current supplies and, despite the opioid crisis, have not been limited or banned by those same regulators. Instead, the opioid MDL fits into the broader product liability area of "failure to warn," combined with opportunistic behavior on the part of some entities to exploit information symmetries existing throughout most levels of the pharmaceutical supply chain. The opioid crisis is also an unusual product liability application in that it has played out in one of the most heavily regulated industries in the U.S., under the watchful eye of not one regulator but three federal regulators, 50 state medical boards, numerous specialty medical societies, and an influential accreditation authority. Perhaps most importantly, the opioid crisis is multifactorial, an issue that was explored in greater detail in Chap. 4, the result of a "perfect storm" of concurrent demand and supply factors. Unlike asbestos or tobacco, the causes of changes in opioid supply are numerous and complex, involving a pharmaceutical supply chain with numerous regulators and rule makers and numerous points at which the opioid supply could have been moderated. In the absence of some form of explicit or implicit action or consent from all the entities in the opioid supply chain, not a single opioid would be able to reach the U.S. market or stay on the U.S. market for any appreciable amount of time.

9.2 Main Findings

The specific aims of this book have been to address four important questions regarding the opioid crisis: (1) What was the true scale of the opioid crisis, in terms of epidemiology and costs? (2) What were the main root-cause factors that contributed to the opioid crisis? (3) How might responsibility for the crisis be reasonably and fairly allocated across the myriad contributing factors? (4) Given that the opioid crisis played out in one of the country's most regulated industries, how did that happen, and what are the implications for the future interplay between regulators and litigators? The first question focuses on the true scale of the crisis. Given the extensive media attention directed at the opioid crisis, it is unclear to the casual observer how the crisis ranks in terms of social and public health programs in the U.S. and abroad. From an epidemiology perspective, the crisis ranks significantly less prevalent than tobacco use and alcohol use disorder, and use of prescription opioids results in adverse event rates similar to those of many other prescription drugs but well below the adverse event rates associated with other substance use disorders, such as alcohol use disorder. This is not to say that the crisis has not caused harm and generated substantial costs; as discussed in several of the preceding chapters, opioid-related harms and costs are substantial, regardless of the approach to measurement. However, attributable costs and abatement costs are not as high as claimants have asserted, and the opioid MDL has proceeded based on inaccurate assessments of attributable costs and abatement costs.

9.2.1 Epidemiology

The burden of pain remains a global medical and public health concern. Opioids have established clinical efficacy in several treatment domains and have generally been viewed by the clinical community as an important tool in efforts to reduce the global burden of pain. However, the experience of pain is exceedingly personal and subjective, which increases information asymmetry between patients and physicians and creates fertile ground for opportunistic behavior on the part of patients seeking opioids and physicians seeking expedient means of appeasing patients who may or may not be experiencing treatable levels of pain. These dynamics make it more challenging for physicians to make decisions regarding medical need with any level of precision, which in turn results in high levels of geographic variability in prescribing patterns.

The prevalence of NPOU (4–10%), opioid misuse (3–4%), and OUD (2–3%), while concerning from a public health perspective, are broadly aligned with adverse event rates for many prescription drugs. About 40% of misused opioids are sourced from diversion, obtained illegally from family, friends, or others. A little more than a third (37%) are sourced directly from the health care system. Another 23% are sourced from illicit channels, such as drug dealers. While misuse rates have remained relatively stable in recent years, rates of prescription opioid utilization have fallen precipitously, suggesting that OUD rates have been buoyed by the incursion of illicit opioids. Rapidly declining rates of prescription opioid utilization over the past decade are due mainly to changes in clinical practice guidelines, increased oversight on the part of state and federal regulators, and other programs, such as public awareness campaigns and drug take-back programs. They have also been the result of greater incursion of illicit opioids, spurred by changes in drug cartel behavior. The subgroup of opioid misusers (about 3.4%) can be further divided evenly into three groups, based on severity: non-OUD, non-cost-incurring OUD, and cost-incurring OUD. Only one of those groups, cost-incurring OUD, is likely to result in measurable harm and constitute a public nuisance, and this group represents only about a third of the group who misuse opioids (or about 1.1%). Moreover, the public nuisance aspects of cost-incurring OUD in the community are very difficult to disentangle in terms of source, though we know an increasing proportion of the nuisance is caused by illicit opioids rather than prescription opioids. The main implication of this is that the harm is unusually remote from the source, and such distance greatly complicates the ability to attribute the costs of the harm and abatement to the source of the externality.

9.2.2 Causation

One of the primary objectives of this book has been to identify and categorize the root causes of the opioid crisis. Normally, the determination of root causes is of paramount importance in the public health community.[1] According to Glass et al., for example, "The history of public

[1] See generally T. A. Glass et al., "Causal inference in public health," *Annu Rev Public Health* 34 (2013).

health and of its quantitative disciplines, epidemiology and biostatistics, can be seen as one long discourse on disease causation, the ultimate targets of which are to find and to mitigate reversible causes."[2] However, unpacking the complex web of causation underlying the growth in opioid supply appears to not have been an objective of state and local counties involved in the opioid MDL, and was of relatively little concern to policy makers until more than a decade after FDA approval of the first long-acting opioids. The third question concerns lessons learned. While states and counties still have some abatement work ahead of them, the intensity of involvement from the public health and academic communities has resulted in a body of evidence from which some potentially useful lessons can be learned, and these lessons extend beyond public health and into economics, law, and policy. These lessons are embedded throughout the preceding chapters, but will be further explored in this chapter, along with some additional review.

One of the pillars of epidemiological analysis is the identification of causal pathways. The causal pathway from opioid supply to public nuisance-causing OUD, however, is considerably more complex than the standard epidemiological causal model. To begin, opioid misuse has been shown to be caused by a variety of patient-level characteristics, including past drug misuse, mental health status, and socioeconomic status. And again, for an opioid to get into the hands of a consumer, it travels through a labyrinth of regulatory oversight by federal and state governing bodies and accreditation agencies, followed by organizational control by payers, health systems, and physicians, who establish clinical norms and standards regarding medical appropriateness and, in the case of treating physicians, make the ultimate decisions regarding medical need. To say that one segment of the supply chain failed is to say that the entire system failed.

One of the key conclusions from the previous chapters is that the causes of the opioid crisis are much more nuanced and complicated than is commonly reported. The opioid crisis clearly grew out of the confluence of several important contributing factors, with each contributing to a part of the "perfect storm" that led to growth in the rates of prescription opioids. Literature, reports, and commentary from experts consistently point to nine factors consisting of a mix of supply push and demand-pull

[2] Ibid.

factors that can also be thought of as enabling or causative factors, the influence of which combined in synergistic and additive ways to increase the volume of opioids on the market, including regulatory failure, medical need, public policy, medical advocacy, ratings and accreditation, manufacturer marketing, socioeconomic factors, and advisor advocacy. The overall supply of opioids in the U.S. has also been driven by an increase in illegally trafficked *illicit* opioids; accordingly, drug trafficking is identified as the tenth contributing factor. Regarding medical need, about a third of the differences in physician prescribing patterns is attributed to normal variation in practice patterns. Another third has been shown to vary based on medical need, patient characteristics, and socioeconomic factors. The West Virginia case study illustrates, in a descriptive and conceptual way, how these myriad causal factors have been featured in a state broadly impacted by the opioid crisis.

9.2.3 Gateway Hypotheses

One conjecture frequently voiced during the opioid crisis is that differentiation between prescription opioids and illicit opioids is not of great importance because, in the absence of prescription opioids, there would not have been any meaningful increase in the supply of illicit opioids. Often referred to as the "gateway hypothesis," the argument generally posits that, for most illicit drug users and persons with OUD attributed to illicit drug use, prescription opioids at some time in the past served as a "gateway" to illicit opioid use. The nominal basis for this hypothesis is that some studies have shown an association between illicit opioid use and prior misuse of prescription opioids.[3] However, the gateway hypothesis is undermined by three important facts. First, illicit markets for opioids long predate the approval of prescription opioids by the FDA. Some of this history has been discussed earlier. Second, the gateway hypothesis has been explored generally (for example, in adolescents progressing from alcohol or marijuana), but the supporting evidence of the relative

[3] See, for example, S. E. Lankenau et al., "Misuse of prescription and illicit drugs among high-risk young adults in Los Angeles and New York," *J Public Health Res* 1, no. 1 (2012); P. Mateu-Gelabert et al., "Injection and sexual HIV/HCV risk behaviors associated with nonmedical use of prescription opioids among young adults in New York City," *J Subst Abuse Treat* 48, no. 1 (2015); R. A. Pollini et al., "Problematic use of prescription-type opioids prior to heroin use among young heroin injectors," *Subst Abuse Rehabil* 2, no. 1 (2011).

importance of gateway substances has been mixed.[4] Third, empirical investigations of the gateway hypothesis in illicit drug use have been based on survey respondents identified either by observed drug abuse behavior or voluntary response to surveys conducted among populations known for high prevalence of illicit drug use. Consequently, this approach generally results in substantial potential for bias.[5]

9.2.4 *Responsibility*

Pharmaceutical supply chains are complex systems that require explicit actions on the part of developers, manufacturers, regulators, distributors, physicians, provider groups, accreditation agencies, payers, and pharmacies before a single drug can get into the hands of a consumer. The seven contributing factors identified in Chap. 4 map to 15 PRP groups. This is not to argue that these 15 PRP groups are liable; that is for the courts to decide. The main point is that this number of PRP groups is considerably higher than the tripartite identified in the 1970 CSA, which formed the basis of liability allocation in the Ohio abatement order.[6] However, there is ample evidence supporting the identification of each one of the 15 PRP groups as having an important and, in some cases, pivotal role in the opioid crisis, with several of the entities arguably having a causative or enabling role. Moreover, several of the PRPs could be considered "orphan" PRP groups, deserving of a share of the responsibility if only to not unfairly burden the more readily available non-orphan PRP groups. While it may be conceptually convenient to fall back on the three traditional members of the pharmaceutical supply chain, the U.S. opioid crisis provides a compelling example of why the three entities constitute a relatively narrow portrayal of the modern-day pharmaceutical supply chain. As many experts have argued, it is difficult to conceive of the growth in prescription opioid supply beginning in the early 2000s as being possible without the

[4] See generally M. L. Miller and Y. L. Hurd, "Testing the Gateway Hypothesis," *Neuropsychopharmacology* 42, no. 5 (2017).

[5] For a discussion of these issues, see for example T. Lines et al., "Nature and extent of selection bias resulting from convenience sampling in the emergency department," *Emerg Med J* 39, no. 4 (2022).

[6] Opioid MDL, "MDL 2804 Case No. 1:17-md-2804 Judge Dan Aaron Polster: Abatement Order," in *Re: National Opioid Litigation* (Ohio: United States District Court Northern District of Ohio, Eastern Division, 2022).

"perfect storm" of actions and inactions on the part of these PRP groups. As noted throughout the earlier discussion of responsibility, conceptualizing the problem in the context of PRPs does not imply a legal framework based on case law or other precedents; rather, it is based on epidemiology and its quest for understanding causation and economics and the importance of identifying factors contributing to externalities.

The problem of externalities is itself an allocation problem, where the costs of the externality are not allocated efficiently because they are external to the market transaction. Accordingly, any solution to an externality problem should be aimed at determining allocation mechanisms that improve the allocation of externality costs, rather than further distorting it. In externality cases with multiple causal pathways and multiple PRP groups, it is necessary to develop models designed to fairly and equitably allocate attributable costs and abatement costs. In environmental cases, such allocation approaches have relied primarily on volumetric measures, such as the amount of product produced by the past users of a particular production site. In cases where volumetric approaches are not practical, allocation approaches have been somewhat more arbitrary, based on approximations of what might be considered fair and reasonable. The latter approach was taken in the Ohio decision regarding retail pharmacies, where 33.3% of responsibility for the adjusted abatement costs in two counties was allocated to retail pharmacies simply because they constituted one of the three members of the CSA tripartite. The arbitrariness of assigning 33.3% to retail pharmacies suggests that other allocation methods may have also been appropriate, assuming reasonable arguments can be made to support such allocation approaches and that the underlying methods are deemed fair and reasonable. The preceding analysis considered two different simple allocation approaches: one like the Ohio decision, where costs are allocated evenly among PRP groups, and one with some simple adjustments for assumptions regarding the degree of causality associated with the PRP group, based on the literature and reports on multi-factor causation in changes in opioid supply. Both allocation approaches, regardless of type of cost calculation, result in amounts that are substantially less than some of the settlements that have already been reached.

In the case of multiple responsible parties, each responsible party is apportioned a share of responsibility (ϕ) such that $\Sigma\phi \leq 1$ across all responsible parties. Also recall from Chap. 2 the discussion of the degree of liability or negligence, which is expressed as λ where $0 \leq \lambda \leq 1$, with liability apportioned λ to responsible parties and 1-λ to claimants. Accordingly, for defendant i in a case involving multiple defendants, the level of responsibility "r" can be expressed as $r_i = \lambda_i \phi_i$. Given the fifteen PRPs identified in Chap. 5, this allocation approach would result in $\phi = 6.67\%$ for each of the PRP groups. This assumes that most of the twelve PRP groups outside of the traditional tripartite are allocated "orphan" shares. Again, this aspect of allocation is ultimately a legal debate left to the courts to decide, but from an economic perspective, it accomplishes the goal of reasonably distributing responsibility for the harm or negative externality. However, as we discussed, one could reasonably consider the CDC, consultants, pharmacies, and patients as lower-share PRP groups, while assigning higher shares to the other PRP groups. In this "weighted" approach, the derivation of weights could be calculated by assigning the participatory PRP groups a share equal to 50% of the proportional rate [i.e., ϕ (0.50), or $\phi_P = 50\%$ x $6.67\% = 3.33\%$] and pro-rate the higher causative PRP share to $\phi_c =$ 7.88% such that the shares for the 15 PRP groups sum to 100% (i.e., $\Sigma\phi_{P,c} = 1$). These estimated shares can then be applied to the attributable cost ceiling and the abatement cost ceiling, or some other amount determined by the courts.

9.2.5 Costs

In litigation, the concept of damages aligns with what health researchers and health economists typically refer to as attributable costs. The cost analyses presented in this book started with this traditional approach to damages. The methodological approach was to make use of the peer-reviewed literature on opioid attributable costs, adjusting those data to reflect the costs at issue in the opioid MDL, which is focused on prescription opioids and costs incurred by state and local governments. The goal was to calculate an attributable cost ceiling, which is the most likely attributable amount faced by state and local governments. A meta-analysis was conducted of peer-reviewed published studies that estimated costs associated with healthcare, the criminal justice system, and social and family assistance programs. Studies of the attributable costs of opioids reach remarkably consistent findings, even across different methodological approaches. Although there are some common methodological challenges to the design and conduct of studies of attributable costs, the fact that these studies reached such similar conclusions suggests that these limitations probably did not result in substantial biases, or at least that each is biased similarly. If there is a consistent bias, it is likely in the direction of overestimation of costs due to the methodological issues associated with the matched case control studies featured in studies of attributable costs. These costs were then adjusted for the proportion paid for by state and local funds (as opposed to federal), the proportion sourced from the healthcare system (again, due to the focus on prescription opioids), and an adjustment for fixed versus variable operating costs. This resulted in a total U.S. ten-year attributable cost ceiling of $16,377.81 million.

In some cases, the relevant costs in product liability matters are the costs required to mitigate the externality, as opposed to the attributable costs of the externality. The attributable costs of alcohol use disorder, for example, include its direct effects on health in the form of a variety of acute and chronic conditions.[7] However, abatement costs associated with alcohol misuse might include the costs of efforts such as public health education, stricter enforcement of alcohol-related laws, reduced access (i.e., age restrictions; stricter controls on retail sales outlet density), and other preventative measures. Several types of programs have been shown to mitigate and reduce opioid supply, opioid misuse, or OUD. The abatement-oriented programs associated with consistent empirical evidence of effectiveness include the following: targeted naloxone distribution; access to medication-assisted treatment; use of prescription drug monitoring programs; programs aimed at education, training, and public awareness; prescription drug disposal programs; access to fentanyl testing, including test strips and screening; syringe exchanges; and other customized programs that vary by state and county.

Compiling published cost estimates on the operating costs of each abatement program and applying the same adjustments made to attributable costs results in a total U.S. ten-year abatement cost ceiling of $10,524.95 million. As expected, the two cost ceiling derivation approaches result in two different estimates, but the rank order is as expected; that is, it makes sense that the *ex-post* attribution method would result in a larger estimate, capturing some costs that are not directly related to the mitigation of the externality.[8] Together, the two cost ceiling methods provide a range of national ten-year externality-related costs that could be considered

[7] K. D. Shield, C. Parry, and J. Rehm, "Chronic diseases and conditions related to alcohol use," *Alcohol Res* 35, no. 2 (2013).

[8] See, for example, E. Zervogianni, "Remedies for damage to property: money damages or restitution in natura?," *International Review of Law and Economics* 24, no. 4 (2004).

reasonable ($10,524.95 million to $16,377.81 million). Some of the abatement cost estimates featured in the opioid MDL lie far outside of this range. In the Ohio abatement decision regarding Lake County and Trumbull County, total 15-year abatement costs were estimated by the counties to be $1.481 billion and $1.848 billion, respectively, summing to more than $3.3 billion. This amount represents nearly 20% of the high end of the 10-year abatement cost ceiling for the entire U.S., though the populations of these counties represent only 0.13% of the U.S. population. Allocating abatement costs in ways that are not fair and reasonable with regard to responsible parties and not accurate in terms of costs can result in inefficient outcomes, such as suppressed innovation, increased costs, skepticism regarding the extent of the problem, and, perhaps more importantly, an increased likelihood of the same problems emerging in the future.[9]

9.3 Some Recommendations

The analyses presented in this book have numerous implications for public policy, particularly around the regulation of prescription drugs. Specifically, four policy recommendations emerge from the discussions. First, there is a comparative governance question that should be addressed in a proactive rather than reactive manner, with the intent of allocating responsibility based on core competencies. Second, the opioid crisis acted as a pressure test of current regulatory mechanisms and institutions, and the preponderance of evidence suggests that the regulatory system failed in several ways. Efforts should focus on regulatory reforms aimed at more rigorous and timely post-market monitoring, and the streamlining of pathways to implement post-market restrictions if deemed necessary. Third, in matters related to health and safety, the correct determination of causation is especially important because of its critical role in abatement. Fourth, the measurement of attributable costs and abatement costs is complex and warrants careful consideration, with the use of multiple sources for verification.

[9] See generally A. Andersson, M. V. Brady, and J. Pohjola, "How unnecessarily high abatement costs and unresolved distributional issues undermine nutrient reductions to the Baltic Sea," *Ambio* 51, no. 1 (2022); C. Fischer and R.D. Morgenstern, "Carbon Abatement Costs: Why the Wide Range of Estimates? (Discussion Paper 03–42)," (Washington, D.C.: Resources for the Future, 2003); D.P. Kessler, "The Economic Effects of the Liability System," (Palo Alto, CA: Hoover Institution, 1999).

9.3.1 Comparative Governance

As discussed in Chap. 8, the U.S. opioid crisis has been defined in part by the failure of regulatory agencies, and the filling of gaps vacated by regulators with product liability litigation that, in the end, was associated with its own struggles and limitations. The opioid crisis has highlighted some important limitations of the existing prescription drug regulatory apparatus, including excessive bureaucracy and disproportionate attention on pre-market approval versus post-market surveillance. However, as the discussion in Chap. 8 implied, there may be good reasons to assume that, for products with particularly high risks, the probability of post-market litigation should be considered in cost-benefit analysis or at least acknowledged so that efforts can also be directed to improving how courts deal with medical products liability matters. Whereas there is a large volume of scholarly research on the pros and cons of regulation and the minutiae associated with "good" versus "bad" regulatory policy, any shift to reliance on courts to manage complex transactions and externalities would need to undergo the same level of scrutiny. Is *ex post* litigation a more effective solution than *ex ante* regulation? Are courts more effective at reaching socially optimal outcomes (e.g., reducing pollution) compared to regulation? In the case of opioids, courts became involved when regulators failed, but that does not necessarily imply that regulation is not a suitable mechanism of control for drugs associated with serious adverse events. Instead, it seems to suggest, as many on all sides of the debate have argued, that the opioid crisis "pressure tested" the prescription drug regulatory apparatus and in that process identified numerous areas for improvement, including improvements in the approval and post-market surveillance processes led by the FDA, the establishing and monitoring of production quotas by the DEA, the effectiveness of the CDC in the early identification of concerning trends (e.g., the rise in prevalence of opioid-related overdoes), and the reliance on self-regulation of the medical profession.

Insofar as the reliance on courts to resolve aspects of cases involving high-risk medical products will persist, it is imperative to improve the way that courts analyze, assess, and understand complicated clinical, economic, and public health information. The legal systems in the U.S. and abroad are not generally known for their innovation and forward thinking; rather, the system is inherently backward-looking and, in most cases, adapts slowly to societal change, industrial change, organizational evolution, and methods of scientific inquiry.[10] As such, the courts are somewhat limited in their ability to help solve contemporary economic and public health problems. However, there may be some areas in which courts adapt quickly, such as allowing cases and basic facts to be quickly established. This feature can have an important role in managing high-risk medical products, wherein regulators face unusually high uncertainty and information costs coupled with bureaucratic inertia.

9.3.2 *Regulation and Regulatory Failure*

A second and related recommendation is that regulatory failure can occur in even the most heavily regulated industries, and it cannot be assumed that the presence of established regulators will prevent or even correct problems when they surface. The FDA has been in existence since 1906, with 117 years to adjust and hone its oversight of food and drugs in the U.S. If we consider the typical adult lifespan to be ages 18 to 80, or about 62 years, the FDA has had nearly two adult lifetimes to figure out how to prevent crises associated with the drugs that they are charged with overseeing. While the DEA is somewhat "newer," having been around since 1973, it is difficult to argue that the agency continues to experience growing pains. One of the most consistent themes of this book is that the opioid crisis unfolded within an industry that is regulated by the FDA, DEA, and CDC, as well as private sector oversight from the Joint Commission and self-regulation on the part of the medical profession. While all three federal entities appeared to possess some general awareness of the problems associated with opioids, they were mostly powerless in preventing the growth in opioid supply and the increasing prevalence of OUD. Similarly, the Joint Commission and the medical profession also appeared to be ineffective in the face of the crisis. The reasons for this regulatory failure remain an important topic of discussion and probably will not be fully understood for some time. Courts became involved largely due to this regulatory failure, but the importance of regulatory failure as a key causal factor has largely been absent from legal proceedings. In the absence of an admission that the regulatory system failed in the case

[10] See generally L. Anderlini, L. Felli, and A. Riboni, "Legal efficiency and consistency," *European Economic Review* 121 (2020); R.K. Craig et al., "Balancing stability and flexibility in adaptive governance: an analysis of tools available in U.S. environmental law," *Ecology and Society* 22, no. 2 (2017).

of opioids, and in the absence of regulatory reforms aimed at high-risk medical products, the door is open for the crisis to repeat itself, with the incentives faced by regulators remaining largely unchanged.

9.3.3 *Courts and Causation*

The third recommendation flows from the first two. In large-scale externality and product liability cases with complexity in industry structure, non-standard transaction attributes, and multifaceted epidemiologic factors at play, courts should be more exhaustive in their consideration of causation. In other words, courts should resist the temptation to identify easy targets, even if legal precedent provides cover to do so. If courts are relied upon to at least partly serve roles vacated by regulators, in some instances, they may be required to adopt a regulator-type approach to the identification of root causes, rather than a strictly precedent-driven and relatively narrow legal approach. This would help identify and mitigate root causes, which serves more of a welfare-enhancing preventative role rather than one focused myopically on liability and damages. If a community is being poisoned by contaminated drinking water, even laypersons would correctly guess that the first order of business would be to identify the sources of the contamination. Public health experts would further suggest that the process not end after the identification of a single source and should continue until all, or at least most relevant causes, have been identified and eventually mitigated. This logic makes sense in classic public health examples like water contamination, but has been largely absent from the opioid litigation, where impacted parties and courts appear to be content with relatively narrow perspectives on causation. During the opioid crisis, several stakeholders strayed from the epidemiological principles emphasizing the importance of thorough identification of root causes; indeed, the founders of epidemiology, pioneers like John Snow, were obsessed with the determination of causation, and with good reason, given that eliminating or lessening the cause is almost always easier than treating the harms.

9.3.4 *Cost Measurement*

A fourth recommendation is that the costs of an externality or public nuisance should be carefully considered, and time and resources should be devoted to the accurate calculation of attributable costs or abatement costs. In the case of opioids, cases brought by states and counties included massive budgets, with two counties in Ohio arguing that abatement costs in the counties should be more than $3 billion. This amounts to more than 20% of the high end of the cost ceiling estimate for the entire country, despite the two Ohio counties accounting for only 0.13% of the U.S. population. Extrapolated to the national level, such costs would far exceed the entire GDP of most countries and far exceed the size of many of America's largest industries, including the entire automobile industry. While the opioid crisis clearly resulted in tangible attributable costs and abatement costs, the actual amounts are likely significantly lower than what claimants have argued. Published studies of attributable costs offer a good starting point, but the data from those studies require some important adjustments to align with the objectives of the case. Specifically, the only relevant abatement costs are the ones incurred by states and counties, which are the principal plaintiffs in the MDL, and the ones that pertain to opioids sourced from the healthcare system, since defendants in the MDL have no discernible connection to or responsibility for the influx of illicit opioids. Perhaps more importantly, claimant cost estimates do not appear to consider issues relating to fixed versus variable costs and assume instead that all costs are variable and that economies of scale and scope are not important. In these instances, it should be the responsibility of the courts to raise this issue and require that cost estimates include these rudimentary adjustments. The court indeed opined that plaintiffs were "asking for the sun and the moon,"[11] but this appears to have been based on the fact that some portion of the plaintiff's abatement cost requests were not directly related to abatement, rather than the type of logic and data put forth in the attributable cost and abatement cost models in the preceding chapters.

References

Anderlini, L., Felli, L., & Riboni, A. (2020, January 1). Legal efficiency and consistency. *European Economic Review*, *121*, 103323.

Andersson, A., Brady, M. V., & Pohjola, J. (2022, January). How unnecessarily high abatement costs and unresolved distributional issues undermine nutrient reductions to the Baltic Sea. *Ambio*, *51*(1), 51–68.

Craig, R. K., Garmestani, A. S., Allen, C. R., Arnold, C. A., Birgé, H., DeCaro, D. A., Fremier, A. K., Gosnell, H., & Schlager, E. (2017). Balancing stability

[11] Opioid MDL, "MDL 2804 Case No. 1:17-md-2804 Judge Dan Aaron Polster: Abatement Order." (§I.)

and flexibility in adaptive governance: An analysis of tools available in U.S. environmental law. *Ecology and Society*, *22*(2).

Fischer, C., & Morgenstern, R. D. (2003). Carbon abatement costs: Why the wide range of estimates? (Discussion Paper 03–42). Resources for the Future.

Glass, T. A., Goodman, S. N., Hernán, M. A., & Samet, J. M. (2013). Causal inference in public health. *Annual Review of Public Health*, *34*, 61–75.

Kessler, D. P. (1999). *The economic effects of the liability system*. Hoover Institution.

Lankenau, S. E., Schrager, S. M., Silva, K., Kecojevic, A., Bloom, J. J., Wong, C., & Iverson, E. (2012, February 14). Misuse of prescription and illicit drugs among high-risk young adults in Los Angeles and New York. *Journal of Public Health Research*, *1*(1), 22–30.

Lines, T., Burdick, C., Dewez, X., Aldridge, E., Neal-Williams, T., Walker, K., Akhlaghi, H., Paul, B., & Taylor, D. M. (2022, April). Nature and extent of selection bias resulting from convenience sampling in the emergency department. *Emergency Medicine Journal*, *39*(4) 325–330.

Mateu-Gelabert, P., Guarino, H., Jessell, L., & Teper, A. (2015, January). Injection and sexual HIV/HCV risk behaviors associated with nonmedical use of prescription opioids among young adults in New York City. *Journal of Substance Abuse Treatment*, *48*(1), 13–20.

Miller, M. L., & Hurd, Y. L. (2017). Testing the gateway hypothesis. *Neuropsychopharmacology*, *42*(5), 985–986.

Opioid, M. D. L. (2022). MDL 2804 case no. 1:17-md-2804 judge Dan Aaron Polster: Abatement order. In *Re: National Opioid Litigation*. United States District Court Northern District of Ohio, Eastern Division.

Pollini, R. A., Banta-Green, C. J., Cuevas-Mota, J., Metzner, M., Teshale, E., & Garfein, R. S. (2011, October). Problematic use of prescription-type opioids prior to heroin use among young heroin injectors. *Substance Abuse and Rehabilitation*, *2*(1), 173–180.

Shield, K. D., Parry, C., & Rehm, J. (2013). Chronic diseases and conditions related to alcohol use. *Alcohol Research*, *35*(2), 155–173.

Zervogianni, E. (2004, January 12). Remedies for damage to property: Money damages or restitution in natura? *International Review of Law and Economics*, *24*(4), 525–541.

Index

J. E. Schneider, *The Economics of Pain*, Global Perspectives on Wealth and Distribution,
https://doi.org/10.1007/978-3-032-20355-7

W

Kolibri 360 GmbH
Ferdinand-Jühlke-Straße 7
99095 Erfurt, Deutschland
produktsicherheit@kolibri360.de